BUILDING JERUSALEM

BUILDING JERUSALEM

The Rise and Fall of the Victorian City

———

TRISTRAM HUNT

METROPOLITAN BOOKS

HENRY HOLT AND COMPANY | NEW YORK

Metropolitan Books
Henry Holt and Company, LLC
Publishers since 1866
175 Fifth Avenue
New York, New York 10010
www.henryholt.com

Metropolitan Books® and 𝕞® are registered trademarks of
Henry Holt and Company, LLC.

Library of Congress Cataloging-in-Publication Data
Hunt, Tristram, 1974–
  Building Jerusalem : the rise and fall of the Victorian city / Tristram Hunt.
    p. cm.
  Includes bibliographical references.
  ISBN-13: 978-0-8050-8026-1
  ISBN-10: 0-8050-8026-0
    1. Cities and towns—Great Britain—History—19th century.   I. Title.
HT133.H86   2005
307.76'0941'09034—dc22   2005053116

Henry Holt books are available for special promotions and
premiums. For details contact: Director, Special Markets.

Originally published in the United Kingdom
by Weidenfeld & Nicolson in 2004

Printed in the United States of America

1 3 5 7 9 10 8 6 4 2

To my parents

And did those feet in ancient time
Walk upon England's mountains green?
    And was the holy Lamb of God
On England's pleasant pastures seen?
    And did the Countenance Divine
Shine forth upon our clouded hills?
    And was Jerusalem builded here
Among these dark Satanic mills?

—WILLIAM BLAKE, 'JERUSALEM'

CONTENTS

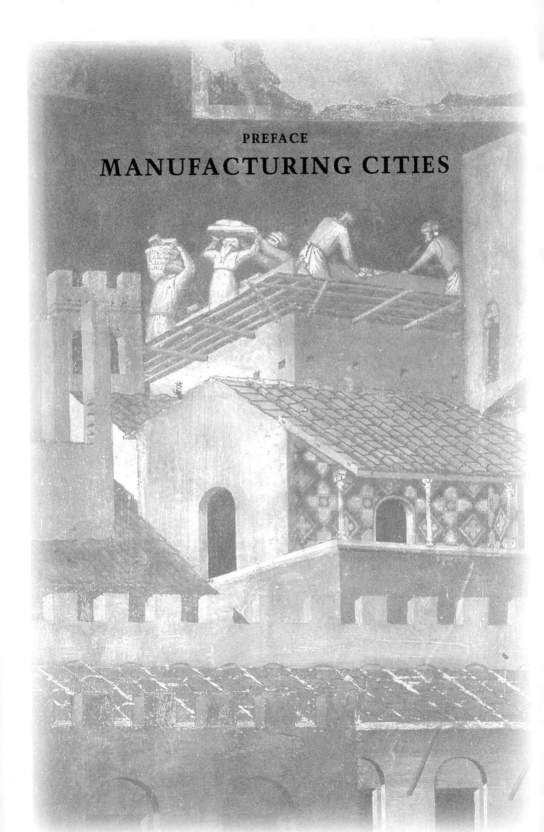

PREFACE

MANUFACTURING CITIES

Long before the thunder of Stephenson's Rocket, before the steam-powered factory and the northern mill town, a passenger seated on the box of a horse-drawn mail coach might witness the rhythms of another country. Suppose only that his travels took him through England's central plain, 'watered at one extremity by the Avon, and at the other by the Trent', the journey would glide through 'long lines of bushy willows marking the watercourses . . . the golden corn-ricks clustered near the roofs of some midland homestead'. Passing through the 'trim cheerful villages, with a neat or handsome parsonage and grey churches in their midst, there was the pleasant tinkle of the blacksmith's anvil, the patient cart-horses waiting at his door; the basket-maker peeling his willow wands in the sunshine; the wheelwright putting the last touch to a blue cart with red wheels; here and there a cottage with bright transparent windows showing pots full of blooming balsams or geraniums, and little gardens in front all double daisies or dark wallflowers'. The inhabitants here readied themselves about their own affairs, untroubled by that 'mysterious distant system of things called "Gover'ment"'.

But as the day wore on, the scene would darken, the traveler passing from one era of English life to another. 'The land would begin to be blackened with coal-pits, the rattle of hand-looms to be heard in hamlets and villages. Here were powerful men walking queerly with knees bent outward from squatting in the mine, going home to throw themselves down

in their blackened flannel and sleep through the daylight . . .
here the pale eager faces of handloom-weavers, men and
women, haggard from sitting up late at night to finish the
week's work.'

And there on the horizon glowed 'the breath of the manufacturing town, which made a cloudy day and a red gloom by
night . . . filling the air with eager unrest'. 'The busy scene of
the shuttle and the wheel, of the roaring furnace, of the shaft
and the pulley, seemed to make but crowded nests in the
midst of the large-spaced, slow-moving life of homesteads and
faraway cottages.' For here was a population not convinced
that old England was as good as possible. Here was the city.[1]

When George Eliot recounted this transition from country
to city, agriculture to industry, the revolution she described
had long since calcified. Eliot composed her historical novel,
Felix Holt: The Radical, after the 1851 census had christened
England the first industrialised, urban nation with over fifty
per cent of its population resident in towns or cities. The bald
statistic merely confirmed what had been apparent for
decades: the progressive decline of rural life, of traditions of
ancient husbandry and village custom. Within Queen
Victoria's reign, William Blake's green and pleasant land
became a nation of cities; the British an urban people.
Industrialisation and urbanisation went hand in hand to shat-
ter practices centuries-old and to crown Britain the 'workshop
of the world' decades before her commercial and military
rivals in continental Europe or North America. Britain was
the first. The horrors, the wonders; the isolation, the excitement; the inequality, the opportunity of the city all appeared
in their modern guise for the first time in nineteenth-century
Britain.

The emergence of the modern city did not occur overnight.
The movement from the land to the city was the achievement
of generations. In the early 1720s, one hundred years before
the events depicted in *Felix Holt*, the novelist Daniel Defoe
had set off on *A Tour Through the Whole Island of Great*

Britain to discover a nation girding itself for change. In Liverpool, Defoe witnessed 'an increasing flourishing town, and if they go on in trade, as they have done for some time, 'tis probable it will in a little time be as big as the city of Dublin'. Sheffield he thought 'very populous and large, the streets narrow, and the houses dark and black, occasioned by the continued smoke of the forges, which are always at work. Here they make all sorts of cutlery-ware, but especially that of edged-tools, knives, razors, axes, etc. and nails.' He noted that 'the manufacture of hard ware, which has been so ancient in this town, is not only continued, but much increased'.

Meanwhile, in the north-east the smoke of Newcastle's coals 'makes it not the pleasantest place in the world to live in'.[2] As would so often prove the case in future Victorian accounts, it was Manchester, 'the greatest mere village in England', which mesmerised the journeying novelist. He stood in wonder at the city's fast-expanding cotton industry, the 'trade we all know', and predicted that 'as the manufacture is increased, the people must be increased in course'. Manchester, the ancient Roman settlement of Mamecestre, was beginning its transition toward 'Cottonopolis', the celebrated 'shock city' of the nineteenth century. 'Yet', Defoe warned, 'as the town and parish of Manchester is the centre of the manufacture, the increase of that manufacture would certainly increase there first, and then the people there not being sufficient, it might spread itself further.'[3]

Spread itself it did. 'Every rural sound is sunk in the clamours of cotton works,' complained the reactionary aristocrat John Byng in his private diary, 'and the simple peasant is changed into the impudent mechanic.' Riding through 1790s Britain, the romantic patriot Byng, an officer wedded to the old order of land and rank, depicted a society undergoing a dishonourable revolution he felt powerless to halt. 'I dread trade, I hate its clamour.' '"But see you not the great increase of Manchester?" Yes; I see the hearty husbandman suck'd into

the gulf of sickly traffic; and whilst some towns swell into
unnatural numbers, lost is the sturdy yeoman and honest cot-
tager!' The countryside was being defiled, villages pulled
down, farms emptied, and fields left unsown. And all the
while, 'Birmingham, Manchester and Sheffield swarm with
inhabitants; but look at them, what a set of mean, drunken
wretches!' Indeed, 'there are no two towns in England I wish
so much to avoid as Birmingham and Manchester; and yet
how often I do get into them: just like certain vices that one
must commit.'[4]

The coming of the city, like the arrival of steam, for all its
gradual ascent remained nonetheless a volcanic, bewildering
process. The modern city – its traffic, its industry, its commerce, its people, its chaos – had never been experienced by
mankind before. The Tory politician Sir Robert Peel spoke in
the 1830s of 'the rapidity with which places, which at no
remote period were inconsiderable villages, have through
manufacturing industry, started into life and into great
wealth and importance'.[5]

This book is a history of those who first faced the changes.
The pioneers of urban society: the men and women, associations and movements, that opposed, celebrated and eventually marshalled the emergent social and economic forces into
creating the Victorian city. William Blake's vision of
Jerusalem, first evoked in a celebrated verse at the front of his
epic homily *Milton*, was primarily an emotional rather than a
physical edifice. His city on the hill was lifted up by
Countenance Divine from the 'dark Satanics mills', the bleak
symbols of industrial production and mental confinement
erected by mechanical, Enlightenment modes of thought. But
others, who read Blake's lines more literally, were determined
to build their own bricks-and-mortar Jerusalems, their own
cities on the hill, in *celebration* of the mills of the Industrial
Revolution.[6]

Manchester, Glasgow, Liverpool, London – as well as nineteenth-century Berlin, Paris and Chicago – constituted the

vanguard of the modern city. Notions of urban life and debates about the meaning of the city which were first developed in these conurbations – the sociology of the city, the politics of the city, the culture of the city, sex and the city – continue to dominate modern approaches to city life some two hundred years on. For each time we step into the streets of our historic cities, we re-enter the Victorian urban world. From the Gothic spires of London's Houses of Parliament to the neo-classicism of Liverpool's St. George's Hall; from the tenements of New York City to the warehouses of Boston; from the boulevards of Paris to the delicate gardens of Vienna, the Victorian city is with us. The visions and prejudices those buildings, parks and monuments embody continue subtly to determine our own conception of the city. They remain our civic landmarks.

This work explores the people and principles who attempted to define the modern city, to shape the emergent terrain of industry, urbanisation and immigration on their own terms. As such it investigates the array of ideologies and fashions which gripped the nineteenth-century imagination: the vogue for medievalism; the beginnings of municipal socialism; the Victorian ardour for Renaissance Italy; social Darwinism and the growth of eugenic thinking; and the cultural triumph of the middle classes. Many of these political philosophies and social movements, which played such a part in shaping Victorian thought, are themselves most provocatively developed through a history of cities.

For the relationship between urban growth and intellectual change was symbiotic. Ideas influenced the city as much as fears and hopes surrounding city life moulded public debate. As Ferdinand Braudel famously put it, 'Towns are like electrical transformers. They increase tension, accelerate the rhythm of exchange and ceaselessly stir up men's lives.'[7] Consequently, this book is also an account of the power of the Victorian city; how it inevitably came to dominate Victorian literature, culture and politics from the novels of Charles

Dickens, to the architecture of Charles Barry, to the philosophy of John Ruskin, to the political thought of Joseph
Chamberlain. Coursing through the writings and speeches of
the Victorian cultural titans, as well as in the discussions and
lectures within the burgeoning Mechanics' Institutes and
debating societies, the spectre of the city was all-consuming.

Part of the ambition of this work is to re-engage some of
those political, religious and cultural debates with what we
now understand about the concrete development of city life.
For this is primarily an intellectual history which seeks to
show how ideas matter and influence events. Too much recent
urban history has retreated into a tale of bureaucratic development – of planning, transport, housing – without discussing
the ideas which provided the context in which attitudes were
formulated and decisions taken. Alternatively, it has fallen
into the quagmire of postmodernism with works on civic history actively designed to prevent a coherent understanding of
the past. Amidst discourses of 'heterotopia', 'parasexuality'
and 'spatial aneurism,' the intelligent general reader is left
unsurprisingly bewildered.[8] Consequently, the compelling
public conversation that accompanied the development of the
Victorian city has fallen from popular historical view.

Today, that conversation is more urgent than ever. As
European and American cities continue to sprawl from suburbia to exurbia, we have lost sight of the virtue of the city. The
vibrant inner cities of London and Paris, Philadelphia and
Chicago are increasingly represented by the modern media as
subversive ghettoes rather than templates of healthy civic
life. The model citizen avoids the energy and edge of the
metropolis to divide his time between sanitised office park
and out of town boomburb. Private life has all but killed off
the public realm. Meanwhile, where urban regeneration is
occurring (in select 'boho' downtowns), it is marketed as an
economic tool rather than social and cultural good.

The characters, buildings and debates recounted in these
pages aim to revive a lost spirit of intellectual excitement

about the city. This history illustrates what can happen when
urban life stands at the heart of public debate: when radical
philosophies such as Gothicism, romanticism and socialism
competed to carve out the perimeters of a new civic vision.
This was the age when Charles Dickens, Benjamin Disraeli,
Thomas Macaulay and Elizabeth Gaskell sought to mould the
Victorian city from the welter of ideas which lit up the century. It was, above all, the age which confirmed the historic
truth that vibrant civic life has always been fundamental to
an intellectually adventurous society.

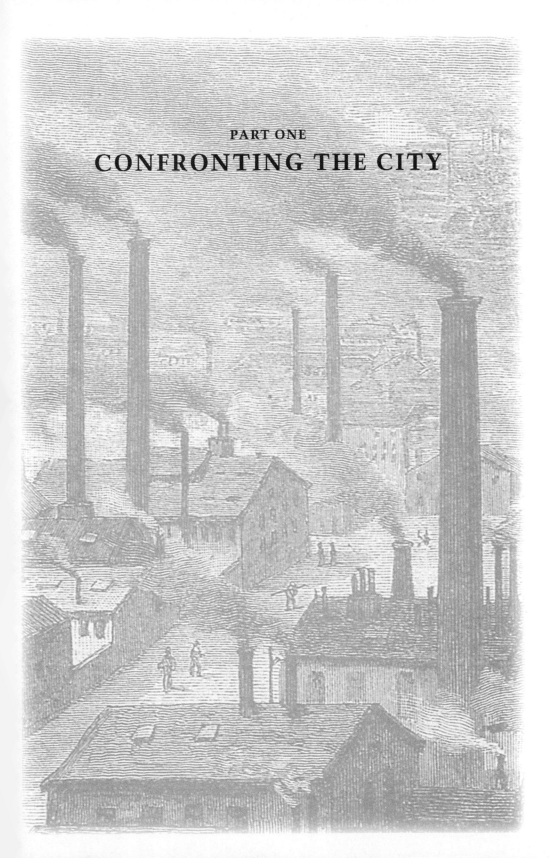

PART ONE

CONFRONTING THE CITY

[1]
THE NEW HADES

In 1827 James Phillips Kay, the younger son of a Non-conformist cotton manufacturer, left Edinburgh for Manchester. With his medical doctorate in hand, he said goodbye to 'the Athens of the North', the Scottish capital of sweeping Georgian terraces and sumptuous classical architecture replete with its bustling social scene of dons, lawyers and natural philosophers. Edinburgh was the city that had played host to the eighteenth-century Scottish Enlightenment, providing inspiration for David Hume, Adam Ferguson, James Mill and a host of avant-garde thinkers; and, as late as the 1830s, a city that remained a byword for civilised, urbane living. But Kay, the earnest, socially committed man of medicine, had decided to swap the pleasant existence of Princes Street for one of the most thankless jobs in Britain's most infectious, most filthy conurbation: he was to become physician to the Ardwick and Ancoats Dispensary, Manchester.

As a student, Kay had excelled in the study of typhus and asphyxia. He was acknowledged by his medical peers, not least by fellow student Charles Darwin, as the brightest of their generation with his 'earnest never-swerving attention to lectures' and 'massive forehead'.[1] Unlike many colleagues, Kay's keen Christian conscience had also spurred him to take his medical learning outside the laboratory and put it at the disposal of Edinburgh's burgeoning poor. For on the other side of the city, away from the prosperous New Town, there existed a very different world of rookeries and dank cellars. In the wynds and closes of Edinburgh's Cowgate and Canongate districts, where chichi shops and Irish theme pubs now line the steep streets, Kay witnessed the startling battery of diseases which bedevilled the Irish and Scottish labouring classes. In the Old Town could be visited 'dens inhabited by outdoor paupers, beggars, vagrants, the parents of ragged schoolchildren ... hidden among the masses of rotten, rat-haunted buildings behind the Grassmarket, Cowgate, West Port etc. They are as repulsive as the class which inhabits them ... No description can convey an adequate idea of the horrors of these places.'[2]

Yet it was only when the fresh-faced doctor reached Manchester that he was confronted with the full awful connection between poverty, poor housing and high mortality. As he arrived in Lancashire, Manchester stood on the precipice of a public health catastrophe. During the early 1830s, a particularly virulent strand of Asiatic cholera had swept through Europe depositing death in its wake. In 1832 the trade routes carried it to Britain's north-eastern ports (landing most likely at Sunderland) from where it rapidly spread across the country. Kay knew that Manchester's combination of hapless sanitation, damp cellars and relentless poverty made the city a natural breeding ground for the disease. And by June it had hit. Cholera engulfed the low-lying slums and Dr Kay worked his salutary way through the afflicted population. Though expecting worse than the Edinburgh wynds, he was still astounded by the misery he confronted:

He whose duty it is to follow the steps of this messenger of death [cholera], must descend to the abodes of poverty, must frequent the close alleys, the crowded courts, the overpopulated habitations of wretchedness, where pauperism and disease congregate round the source of social discontent and political disorder in the centre of our large towns, and behold with alarm, in the hot-bed of pestilence, ills that fester in secret, at the very heart of society.[3]

For the godly Kay the presence of such states of life was

nothing short of sinful. While evangelical politicians in Westminster called for national days of fasting and 'humiliation'
in the face of God's plague, Kay pursued a decidedly more
scientific approach. It was essential to strike at the social
conditions of the city – the housing, sanitation and employment opportunities which meant residents had 'neither moral
dignity nor intellectual nor organic strength to resist the
seductions of appetite'. To understand the city, it was vital to
study and expose the misery of modern, urban existence.

In 1832 Kay did just that with an eloquent testimony to the
terrible conditions he had uncovered, *The Moral and Physical
Condition of the Working Classes Employed in the Cotton
Manufacture in Manchester*. With its disturbing description
of unnecessary suffering amidst commercial prosperity, 'a
slumbering giant ... in the midst of so much opulence', the
book became a best-seller. The poverty and disarray which Kay
systematically unearthed in Manchester irreversibly fractured
the old, Regency vision of urban civility.

Instead of Jane Austen's sunny world of Bath and Cheltenham with their assembly dances and polite society, instead
of the witticisms of Pope's and Swift's Georgian London or
Ferguson's Edinburgh, there now stood the horror of Manchester's Ancoats and Liverpool's Leeds Street. The previous
century had seen the rapid expansion of London – what
William Cobbett called the 'Great Wen' – and with it the
misery of Hogarth's 'Gin Lane', but the spiralling conurbations
of Manchester, Liverpool, Leeds, Bradford and Birmingham
presented the problems of urbanisation in a far more immediate, more threatening light. The civic theatre of the 1800s
metropolis, the elegant world of Nash and Soane with its
planned parades and delicate urban aesthetic, its Regent Street
and Trafalgar Square, was now facing a chaotic array of forces.
Kay's ground-breaking book hurtled attention northward to
the industrialising cities and set out the dilemmas which
dominated discussion of city life at the start of Victoria's reign:
the presence of a working class, the problems of housing, the
desperate need for proper sanitation and civic governance,

the mass influx of Irish immigrants, and the coming of the factory.

i 'IT'S THIS STEAM'

Britain was the first modern nation to industrialise and to urbanise. But it was the French who first pointed it out. The unprecedented economic turmoil of the late eighteenth and early nineteenth century inspired the French economist Jean-Baptiste Say to introduce the concept of 'la révolution industrielle' to be understood in the same historical league as their very own French Revolution. Britain had to wait until 1884 (by which time it was all over) until the Oxford don Arnold Toynbee reproduced the term 'Industrial Revolution' in a series of lectures on the topic. For Toynbee, looking back from the eirenic calm of late-Victorian Oxford, the process of industrialisation had ushered in 'a period as disastrous and as terrible as any through which any nation has passed'. The influence of Adam Smith's paean to economic liberalism, *The Wealth of Nations*, combined with the steam engine, 'destroyed the old world and built a new one'. The old system of medieval regulation and an equitable moral economy was overthrown by aggressive competition while 'a "cash-nexus" was substituted for the human tie'. Britain changed for ever as villages became towns and towns became cities, 'where men came together not for the purposes of social life, but to make calicoes or hardware, or broad cloths – in the new cities, the old warm attachments, born of ancient, local contiguity and personal intercourse, vanished in the fierce contest for wealth among thousands who had never seen each other's faces before'.[4]

Contrary to Toynbee's schema, industrialisation was not initially an urban phenomenon. The majority of factories (or 'manufactories', as they were christened) were located in rural locations, such as the Derwent Valley in Derbyshire, because of the need for access to water and it was only from the 1800s that mechanisation started substantially to affect the cities. It was the cotton industry which fired the Industrial Revolution. For generations spun yarn had been twisted by human fingers and then woven manually on a handloom. That all changed with the invention of the spinning-jenny by James Hargreaves in 1764 – which fortuitously occurred just as James Watt was discovering the potential of steam-power. But it was Richard Arkwright's water-frame and the establishment of the first cotton-spinning factory in Manchester, which used a steam engine to recirculate the water to power its waterwheel, that started to kill off the domestic workplace. When this was augmented by Crompton's mule, which spun even finer yarn, the fate of the handloom weavers – one of the wealthiest and most articulate artisan communities of the eighteenth century – was sealed. In their place came steam-powered mills and manufactories for the cotton, woollen, silk and lace industries. Now on one site could be housed hundreds and later thousands of workers who had previously worked at their own pace and for their own wage in a domestic, familial environment.

As the handloom weavers were drawn towards factory life or lost to penury, the steam engine's demand for coal opened up England and Scotland's coalfields. Meanwhile Abraham Darby's advances in iron production, through the use of coke-smelting rather than charcoal, shunted Britain into the age of the Iron Bridge. The revolution in the cotton industry, in iron manufacture, and the development of energy sources ripped apart old economic practices from ship-building to pottery to glass-making to woollens. Not every sector was affected by industrialisation and it is currently fashionable in historical circles to belittle the significance of the Industrial Revolution as a coherent economic event. But those living through the times knew something terrible, something almost unfathomable was occurring to their society. As Mr Deane put it in George Eliot's *The Mill on the Floss*, 'You see, Tom ... the world goes on at a smarter pace now than it did when I was a young fellow... It's this steam, you see.'

Despite the revisions by economic historians, what is not

open to doubt is the impact of industrialisation on the Victorian city. The 1841 census gives a clear tally of urbanisation in the first half of the nineteenth century. With an overall English population of nearly fifteen million, London remained the pre-eminent city with almost two million inhabitants. But its growth rate of two and a half per cent a year was effortlessly outstripped by the cities of the fast-expanding north. Between 1800 and 1841, Sheffield more than doubled its population from 45,000 to 111,000 on the back of the manufacture of cutlery and then iron and steel production. During the same period, Bradford's successful woollen and worsted industries saw it grow by ten per cent a year from a population of 13,000 to over 104,000. Leeds's combination of woollen industry and commercial and legal work saw the city inhabitants triple from 50,000 at the start of the century to over 150,000 by 1841. Meanwhile, Liverpool's population mushroomed from 80,000 to over 280,000 as the port cemented its dominance over Bristol, handling some four million tons of shipping by the mid-century. The city's new rival, Manchester, 'Cottonopolis' itself, expanded from 95,000 to 310,000. In Scotland, the city of Glasgow outdid them all. Its successful transition from transatlantic commercial hub in the eighteenth century to manufacturing and cotton base meant that for the first third of the nineteenth century it grew more rapidly than any other European city of its size. By 1841 its population stood at over 260,000, making it the fourth largest British city behind London, Manchester and Liverpool.[5]

What drove much of this growth was not simply higher birth rates, thanks to a demographically young population, but migration. Forced out of the countryside by the enclosures and the decline of labour-intensive agriculture, and lured by the higher wages offered by mill-work and manufacturing, tens of thousands of rural migrants flooded to the industrialising cities. According to the most recent estimate, at least forty per cent of the demographic growth of urban Britain in the nineteenth century can be attributed to arrivals from rural areas.[6] In almost all the fast-expanding towns of Victorian

Britain, the migrant communities outnumbered the indigenous. By the mid-century, in cities like Bradford and Glasgow more than seventy-five per cent of the population aged over twenty years old had been born elsewhere. Glasgow's migrants were drawn to the city's mills, mines and workshops from the depressed border Lowlands as well as the cleared lands of the West Highlands. Liverpool attracted the poor and the ambitious from Lancashire and Cheshire, but also a substantial number of Scottish and Welsh immigrants. London meanwhile sucked in unemployed farmhands from the hamlets and towns of the Home Counties, earning its reputation as the 'Great Wen': a corrupt tumescence unable to sustain itself by natural growth and instead dependent upon consuming the healthy offspring of rural England.

Interestingly, amongst the largest group of rural-urban migrants were not in fact millhands but young country girls who went into domestic service for the newly prosperous urban middle class. For although industrialisation touched every aspect of the city, very few places became the simple mill towns of Coketown lore. Excepting maybe Oldham and Ashton, most industrial cities had a heterogeneous economic base which encompassed the commerce, financial, retail, service, as well as industrial sectors. Manchester was as much dependent upon its mercantile base, construction industry and retail sector as its cotton mills. The 1841 census revealed that some 41,000 were employed in textiles in Manchester while domestic service gave jobs to 14,000 and the building and retail trades provided work for another 7,000 each. The city's wealthiest citizens were more likely to be bankers, brewers or merchants than the mill-owner of popular myth.[7]

Aside from the rural influx, the second major tranche of migrants came from Ireland. Already attracted by new employment opportunities in the cotton and construction industries of the north-west, their numbers swelled as they crossed the Irish Sea fleeing the poverty and starvation which culminated in the 1846 Potato Famine. One contemporary described their arrival as 'an evil of the very greatest magnitude' and put the annual intake at 50,000, with the number of Irish immigrants reaching 120,000 in London; 40,000 apiece in Manchester and Glasgow; and 34,000 in Liverpool.[8] The 1851 census revealed the percentage of Irish-born as accounting for 4.6 per cent of the population in London, thirteen per cent of Manchester and Salford, eighteen per cent of Glasgow and an unsurprisingly substantial twenty-two per cent of Liverpool.[9] By the early 1860s the Irish in England and Wales were approaching a community of 800,000. And, as we shall see, their presence did not go unnoticed.

ii SIGHT AND SOUND OF THE CITY

The influx of migrants, combined with the extraordinary growth in industrial production, produced a wholly novel urban landscape. Never before had such a foul conglomeration of people, commerce, traffic and squalor been witnessed in Britain. It is hard to over-emphasise the diabolic misery of the early Victorian city. Though today we are used to images of the slums of São Paulo, the street children of Bogotá, or the scavengers of Manila, eye-witness accounts of the newly industrialising towns of northern England remain startling.

The first sensation to hit contemporary observers was the sheer ugliness of the city. The republican-turned-Tory Poet Laureate, Robert Southey, was struck by the hideousness of industrialisation as early as 1808. Under the exotic Spanish *nom de plume* 'Don Manuel Alvarez Espriella', Southey recorded his travels around England as steam-power, immigration and early manufactories began to transform the civic fabric. While his favoured provincial centres of Exeter and Salisbury had successfully avoided the ravages of growth, he discovered that the old Midlands town of Birmingham had been far less fortunate. Espriella found it in a disgusting state – in particular, the ubiquitous filth. Dirt seemed to smother the entire town, 'here it is active and moving, a living principle of mischief, which fills the whole atmosphere and penetrates everywhere'.[10] The noxious plumes emitted from

Birmingham's workshops were a source of both wonder and incredulity. A heavy cloud of smoke, fed by black columns sent up from steam engines, dominated the city's skyline. But through it still peered 'the tower of some manufactory ... vomiting up flames and smoke, and blasting every thing around with its metallic vapours'.[11]

In early nineteenth-century accounts, the chimneys did always seem to 'vomit'. The language of vomiting, the rejection by the body of unclean or harmful elements, was taken up by Kay in his account of Manchester. He described the city's Irish quarter along Oxford Road as surrounded 'by some of the largest factories of the town, whose chimneys vomit forth dense clouds of smoke, which hang heavily over this insalubrious region'.[12] A Prussian visitor to the city, the bureaucrat and industrial spy John Georg May, described how 'there are hundreds of factories in Manchester which tower up to five and six storeys in height. The huge chimneys at the side of these buildings belch forth black coal vapours and this tells us that powerful steam engines are used here... The houses are blackened by it.'[13] Some years later a Parisian visitor to Manchester, the liberal journalist Leon Faucher, was similarly appalled by 'the fogs which exhale from this marshy district, and the clouds of smoke vomited forth from the numberless chimneys'.[14] The vomiting metaphor only added to the impression of the industrial city as an unnatural, grotesque outgrowth from the nation's otherwise healthy corpus.

And the chimneys were certainly producing unnatural consequences. The 1843 Select Committee on Smoke Prevention described how Manchester's 'nearly 500 chimneys discharging masses of the densest smoke' rendered the air 'visibly impure, and no doubt unhealthy, abounding in soot, soiling the clothing and furniture of the inhabitants'.[15] In Leeds, washing hung out to dry would become filthy with soot, grime and dirt within hours. London was, of course, notorious for its thick fogs, or 'pea-soupers', which were predominantly the result of domestic coal fires rather than heavy industry. Thomas

Carlyle described precisely such a *'London* fog' in February
1853 as 'the *blackest* I ever saw... you could *not* see one street-
lamp from another ... various persons asking us, "Have the
goodness to tell me *where I am!"* My new shirt was quite
black in the inside of the collar when I took it up the next
morning.'[16]

After the appalling sight of the city, came the smell. Rivers
were a particular problem. The Irwell was described by the
Scottish novelist Hugh Miller as 'a flood of liquid manure, in
which all life dies, whether animal or vegetable, and which
resembles nothing in nature, except perhaps the stream
thrown out in eruption by some mud-volcano'.[17] Similarly,
the Tame in Birmingham, the Mersey in Liverpool and the
Beck Canal in Bradford all quickly became clogged with industrial and human excrement. Dealing with the enormous quan-
tities of excrement produced by the expanding populations
was a major problem for the ramshackle system of urban
administration. By the 1840s Manchester was emitting over
70,000 tons of human faeces a year – large amounts of which
were simply thrown into the street, festered in cesspools or
pushed into rivers. Where once there was fishing and fresh
water, there now gurgled vast latrines. The Aire in Leeds
seemed to have been composed of as much filth as water. It
was described as 'full of refuse' from 'water closets, cesspools,
privies, common drains, dung-hill drainings' as well as 'wastes
from slaughter houses, chemical soap, gas, dye-houses, old
urine wash'. Finally, there were 'dead animals, vegetable sub-
stances and occasionally a decomposed human body'.[18]

Adding their contribution to the stench of human waste was
the extraordinary profusion of animals and slaughterhouses in
the midst of the city. Rural migrants brought their animal
ways with them and refused to be parted from beasts which
often constituted a major source of income. Pigs, cows and
horses were to be found in the middle of Manchester and
London up until the mid-1850s. In 1850 it was estimated that
a massive 20,000 tons of animal manure were deposited on
the streets of London every year. In the East End, the social

reformer Henrietta Barnett remembered with horror the sight of

> herds of cattle driven through the Whitechapel streets ...
> Sometimes the poor creatures would entangle their great
> horns in the spokes of moving wheels ... Sometimes in
> their fear they would rush on to the pavement, scattering the
> pedestrians whether they were hale and young, or pregnant
> women and frail folk. Around the slaughter-houses, where
> the sheep were dragged in backwards by their legs, the
> bullocks hounded in by dogs and blows, the children would
> stand eager for fresh sights of blood, excited by the horror
> and danger of the scenes.[19]

Pig-owners were a particularly vociferous lobby group, resisting any attempts to limit the number of pigsties in the city. Kay himself visited an Irish family in Edinburgh which lived with a pig. While in Manchester, it was suggested by one social investigator that 'the Irishman loves his pig as the Arab loves his horse ... he eats and sleeps with it, his children play with it, ride upon it, roll in the dirt with it, as any one may see a thousand times repeated in all the great towns of England'.[20] Another remarked how 'Pigs move about in complete freedom just as in Naples or the Orient. In these streets they have as much dignity as the human inhabitants.'[21]

The presence of this domestic farm combined with an active, inner-city tanning industry, with its refuse of blood, bones and hide, added to the noxious stench of the Victorian city. The doctor William Strange described the resultant atmosphere of cities as 'charged with the exhalations from the persons and dwellings of the crowded population, and ... rendered still more infectious by the effluvia from the cesspools, dungheaps, pigsties etc., which abound therein'. In addition to the smells from human and animal habitation there was industrial pollution. The tar works, chemical works, glue factories, knackers' yards – all situated in the heart of the city – produced a lethal cocktail of fumes, the consequence of inhaling which was often fatal. 'Habitual residence in such localities gradually depresses the nervous energies ... The whole system sinks below the natural standard of vitality, the body becomes debilitated, and the mental powers and moral feelings are blunted, or almost wholly obscured.'[22] George Buchanan, a reforming bureaucrat from the Local Government Board, attributed to the stink of the city more obvious side effects. Most notably, 'loss of appetite, nausea, sometimes actual vomiting, sometimes diarrhoea, headache, giddiness, faintness, a general sense of depression and malaise'.[23]

After the smell, came the noise of the city. It is noteworthy to remember just how quiet the pre-industrial world must have been. A rural civilisation based around an agricultural and domestic economy was used to the familiar sound of the farm, the handloom and the market town; not the roar of the furnace, the mill, or high street. In his *Lectures on the Industrial Revolution*, Arnold Toynbee described how industrialisation exchanged the contented hum of provincial proto-industry for the sinister din of manufacturing: 'The spinning-wheel and the hand-loom were silenced, and manufactures were transferred from scattered villages and quiet homesteads to factories and cities filled with noise.'[24] In *Das Kapital*, Karl Marx declared how the working class were 'stunned at first by the noise and turmoil' of the industrial city. And anyone who has heard the noise of a beating loom can certainly imagine an entire workforce becoming progressively deafened by the crash of mechanised industry.

When Robert Southey or 'Don Espriella' visited Birmingham, he was bewildered by the clamour. 'I am still giddy, dizzied with the hammering of presses, the clatter of engines, and the whirling of wheels: my head aches with the multiplicity of infernal noises'. The city's hammers 'seem never to be at rest'.[25] Another visitor to Birmingham described how 'One hears nothing but the sound of hammers and the whistle of steam escaping from boilers.' Jane Austen went further and decried the very name Birmingham. In *Emma*, the snobbish Mrs Elton announces that Birmingham 'is not a place to promise much, you know, Mr Weston. One has no great hopes from Birmingham. I always say there is something direful in the sound.' In Manchester, it was even worse. 'Hast thou heard, with sound ears', asked Thomas Carlyle, 'the awakening of a Manchester, on Monday morning, at half-past five by the clock; the rushing-off of its thousand mills, like the boom of an Atlantic tide, ten thousand times ten-thousand spools and spindles all set humming there, – it is perhaps if thou knew it well, sublime as a Niagra, or more so.'[26]

In Manchester, it was always worse. With its flourishing cotton industry – supported by an ideally damp climate, soft water and ready coal supplies – and concentration of steam-powered mills, the city was the *ne plus ultra* of the Industrial Revolution. And like Paris in the 1900s, London in the 1960s, or Tokyo in the 1980s, sociologists, journalists, politicians and novelists were unable to resist its charms. In 1833, as James Kay was dispensing assistance to cholera victims, the city received one of its most gifted chroniclers, the young French aristocrat, one-time magistrate and aspiring political scientist, Alexis de Tocqueville (who would later meet with Kay at the Manchester Statistical Society). Like May, Faucher and so many other Continental visitors before him, de Tocqueville was drawn irresistibly to Manchester – an entirely new city which could, unlike Rome, Paris or Venice, be charted afresh without any historical or literary preconceptions. There de Tocqueville intended to investigate, in that classic French manner, the *mores* of the first industrial nation.

As de Tocqueville approached the city, he spotted 'thirty or forty factories rise on the top of hills' belching out their foul waste. In fact, he heard Manchester before he entered, for it seemed its inhabitants could never escape from the 'crunching wheels of machinery', 'the noise of the furnaces', 'the shriek of steam from boilers' or the incessant, 'regular beat of the looms'.[27] Inside the rambling, rumbling city he found 'fetid, muddy waters, stained with a thousand colours by the factories they pass'. Streams ran as they saw fit while 'houses are built haphazard on their banks'. 'Often from the top of their steep bank one sees an attempt at a road opening through the debris of the earth, and the foundations of some houses or the recent ruins of others. It is the Styx of this new Hades.' With no controls on pollution emissions, the city was daily enveloped in a blanket of black smoke. 'The sun seen through it is a disc without rays.'[28] The cloak of smog and absence of sunlight, combined with the resulting vitamin deficiency, led to shocking levels of rickets and related physical deformities amongst the industrial populace.

This situation was only exacerbated by the working conditions. The noise and pollution, the danger from the machines, and the physical disfigurement from long hours of repetitive manual work were all blamed for the high mortality plaguing the working classes. A pioneering surgeon in Leeds, C. Turner Thackrah, was shocked to discover the death of 450 people a year as a result of machine accidents alone. He branched out his research into a more general inquiry into the human cost of manufacturing and exposed the scandal of mental and physical decay, impaired health and the premature death prevalent amongst the industrial working class. The combination of a terrible diet devoid of protein, damp and unhealthy housing conditions, and the long hours and industrial poisoning of the factory was producing a 'small, sickly, pallid, thin ... degenerate race – human beings stunted, enfeebled, and depraved'. He concluded that the manufacturing industries in Manchester, Sheffield, Birmingham and Leeds were in fact mass killers. 'If we should suppose that 50,000 persons die annually in Great Britain from the effects of manufactures, civic states, and the intemperance connected with these states and occupations, our estimate I am convinced would be considerably below the truth.' Can we view with apathy, he asked, 'such a superfluous mortality, such a waste of human life?'[29]

Even the satirical chronicler of industrial life, Wilmot Henry Jones, could find little to laugh about in the terrible human cost of industrialisation. Writing under the name Geoffrey Gimcrack, he wrote a poem entitled 'One O'Clock', in which he falls asleep and awakes in the middle of Manchester's industrial quarter:

Wherein pale thousands labour'd day and night
For filthy lucre, or for bare subsistence; –
Not only men, but women I saw there,
And poor ragg'd children, stinted in their growth
By early toil, and heat, bad food, and filth.[30]

Another prying French intellectual, the philosopher Hippolyte Taine, was equally disturbed by the mills and factories which spread along the waterways of Manchester and Salford. He looked in awe at a factory six storeys high with forty windows a storey, each lit by gaslight and each roaring with machines. But for him the city resembled nothing more than 'a great jerry-built barracks, a "work-house" for 400,000 people, a hard-labour penal establishment'. The penning together of thousands of workmen, carrying out mindless, regimented tasks, 'hands active, feet motionless, all day and every day' was simply improper. 'Could there be any kind of life more outraged, more opposed to man's natural instincts?'[31] Aside from the industrial accidents and contorted limbs, one of the nastier diseases which factory workers were exposed to was anthrax. From the 1840s, those working in the woollen mills of Bradford, in particular the sorters of imported wool, were at risk from this seemingly innocuous yet deadly disease. It came to be called 'woolsorters' disease' and rapidly disposed of its victims after a few days of painful coughing and fever. So distinctive was anthrax to the Bradford wool industry that French doctors named it the 'maladie de Bradford'.[32]

With the factory came a new working life. Although those employed in the great mills of Manchester and Bradford constituted a minority, their lifestyles heralded a distinct break from the past. Famously, the historian E.P. Thompson marked this shift as a rupture from a pre-industrial pastoral world where leisure and labour were inseparable, where time was based around tasks (e.g., a day's harvesting), and where rhythms of work and play were conducted on the labourers' terms. An idyllic world eliminated by industrial capitalism. The clock now dominated the day and a new culture of time-discipline created a proletariat subject to the capitalist's whim, with each side engaged in a daily battle over 'wasting-time'.[33] When Southey visited one Manchester factory he was proudly informed by the owner, 'There is no idleness among us.' The child workers came in at five a.m., had half an hour for breakfast, half an hour for dinner and left again at six p.m. – at which point they were replaced by the next shift of children. 'The wheel never stands still.'[34] The culture symbolised by the handloom weaver, of the independent, highly skilled domestic worker, was being progressively eliminated by the industrial capitalism of the city. And it was producing, as the German travel writer Johann George Kohl noted, a new race of people.

> In long rows on every side, and in every direction hurried forward thousands of men, women and children. They spoke not a word, but huddling up their frozen hands in their cotton clothes, they hastened on, clap, clap, along the pavement, to their dreary and monotonous occupation... When hundreds of clocks struck out the hour of six, the streets were again silent and deserted, and the giant factories had swallowed the busy population. All at once, almost in a moment, arose on every side a low, rushing and surging sound, like the sighing of wind among trees. It was the chorus raised by hundreds of thousands of wheels and shuttles, large and small, and by the panting and rushing from hundreds of thousands of steam engines.[35]

At the end of the working day (for those in work), there was little relief to be found at home. The Victorian reverence for hearth and home did not extend to the pauper quarters of the nineteenth-century city. As ever larger numbers poured into the towns, houses were divided up, abandoned alleys and courts brought back into use, and flats cohabited to contain the influx. Church Lane, in the notorious St Giles' district of

London (now fashionable Bloomsbury), housed 655 people in twenty-seven houses in 1841. By 1847 the number of inhabitants in precisely the same number of houses had nearly doubled to 1,095.[36] In Blackfriars parish, Glasgow the population increased by forty per cent between 1831 and 1841 but the amount of accommodation remained unchanged. The 1841 census showed 33,000 additional people living in the city over ten years, but only 3,551 more inhabited dwellings. The inevitable result was systematic overcrowding. 'In the lower lodging-houses, then, twelve and sometimes twenty persons of both sexes and all ages sleep promiscuously on the floor in different degrees of nakedness,' reported a Hand-Loom Weavers Commission. 'These places are, generally as regards dirt, damp and decay, such as no person of common humanity to animals would stable his horse in ... It is my firm belief that penury, dirt, misery, drunkenness, disease and crime culminate in Glasgow to a pitch unparalleled in Great Britain.' [37]

With no legislative prevention, developers responded to demand by subdividing existing tenements or building substandard back-to-back housing which blocked out sunlight, obstructed ventilation and embedded insanitary conditions. The alleys leading to the back-houses turned into open latrines. Liverpool's courts were notorious for their lack of ventilation, with most soon descending into festering culs-de-sac. In Manchester the doctor John Shaw, on one of his rambles with city missionaries, 'found a young woman in the cellar, rather good-looking, with a baby on her knee. The cellar was very damp, without fire in the grate. "You find me," she said, "in a sad mess this morning." She uncovered the bedstead – there was no bed, no blanket or sheet – saying, "That is where we live, with only the clothes we wear to cover us; there is not a crust of bread in the house. I can bear hunger, but I cannot bear the cold, and my poor child is tugging at my empty breast."'[38]

Within these damp cellars also lurked the residuum of the early Victorian city. From the 1820s Irish immigrants began to enter British cities in substantial numbers, taking the boat to Liverpool (from where many left straight away for America), some to south Wales, or even round Land's End all the way to London. Others headed to the Scottish west coast and on to Glasgow. Their numbers began to soar from the late 1830s as agriculture collapsed and the potato blight spread. In Edinburgh, George Bell found one such set of migrants:

> One of the adults, a very aged Irishwoman, who could not speak a word of English, had arrived a short time ago to see two of her sons who have got employment in Edinburgh ... The other inhabitants of this chamber were Irish, and could not explain how they live. Among the number was a man with his wife and family, recently arrived from Sligo. He had occupied a small farm of nine acres, which yielded enough to keep him. The potato disease came; he was starved out of his holding; and the acres he once tilled are now grazed by cattle. If this fellow does not get work soon, he will take up some small trade, and his children will be added to the long list of Edinburgh beggars.[39]

In the cities they faced uniform prejudice and discrimination. As a result, the Irish male immigrant was three times as likely as his British counterpart to find himself in unskilled employment. Their miserable state prompted a Royal Commission on the State of the Irish Poor in Britain in 1836. The Commission's leading light, Sir George Cornewell Lewis, defined his basic premise: 'The Irish emigration into Britain is an example of a less civilised population spreading themselves, as a kind of substratum, beneath a more civilised community, and, without excelling in any branch of industry, obtaining possession of all the lowest departments of manual labour'.[40] The Irish remained stuck in low-wage, low-skill work as navvies, strike-breakers or casual labourers. To many British employers, the Irish were constitutionally unfit for more skilled work. Samuel Hoare, a Liverpool builder, told the Commission of their psychological defects: 'They scarcely ever make good mechanics; they don't look deep into subjects

... they don't make good millwrights or engineers, or anything which requires thought.'[41]

Living together in typically the most unsanitary areas of the city, the Irish gained a reputation not only for having disease but actively spreading infection. The same inquiry was told that their filthy bedding, their lack of furniture, their unclean habits and their crowding together in tenements meant the Irish were frequently the vehicles for communicating infectious diseases. But it was their moral condition, not least their Roman Catholicism, which so appalled the Victorian Englishman. According to even the usually enlightened Kay, 'I should say that the house of an Irishman is that of a person in a lower state of civilisation ... not only as regards his domestic conveniences, but those moral relations which subsist between himself and the members of his family.'[42]

Their living conditions and apparent contentment simply to work, procreate and sleep earned the Irish the common appellation of savages hopelessly enslaved to their passions without any thought of rational endeavour. It was regarded as a reflection of the parlous state of urban life that such people, such a savage race found a home in the industrial city. Kay described the Irish district in Manchester as 'the haunt of hordes, of thieves and desperadoes who defied the law, and is always inhabited by a class resembling savages in their appetites and habits'.[43] De Tocqueville thought of Manchester's Irish community in similar terms. The economic competitiveness of the city was, he rightly argued, partly built on the labour of those who come 'from a country where the needs of men are reduced almost to those of savages and who can work for a very low wage'. As a result, the poor old Anglo-Saxon worker was similarly forced to depress his wage level while the factory owners creamed the profits. The consequence was a paradoxical mix of 'civilization and barbarism'.[44]

Like his contemporaries, Thomas Carlyle was horrified by the condition of the unfortunate Irish. But with less compunction than some of his peers, he depicted the Irish as a subhuman, Celtic race whose presence in the cities was a sign of social disintegration. In 'Chartism' (1839), he described how they 'darken all our towns' before recounting how the depravity of the Irish or 'Milesian' allowed him to take on any work whatever the wage so long as it would buy him his potatoes. The Irish 'Paddy' was a Celtic savage who lodged in a pigsty or dog-kennel and drove out the honest Anglo-Saxon. 'There abides he, in his squalor and unreason, in his falsity and drunken violence, as the ready-made nucleus of degradation and disorder. Whosoever struggles, swimming with difficulty, may now find an example of how the human being can exist not swimming but sunk.'[45] And the Irish were taking down with them the English labourer. In Britain's cities, the 'condition of the lower multitude of English labourers' was dangerously approximating more and more that of the Irish.

iii Life and Death in the City

There were, however, equally pressing dangers in the city as this threat to Anglo-Saxon morality. The open latrines and overflowing cesspools of Liverpool's slums were indicators of a public health system in collapse. Hundreds of thousands were now packed into cities which typically had the sanitary infrastructure for barely one-tenth of their population. And thanks to the work of doctors like James Kay, the state of the urban poor was at last beginning to be publicised. Kay's work spawned a genre of investigative work as writers, doctors and journalists began to expose the terrible putrescence of urban under-life. More importantly, he inspired a rush of societies committed to serious sociological analysis of industrial living conditions. Statistical Societies were established in London and Manchester to enquire further into the life chances of the manufacturing poor and promote enlightened reform. During the 1830s, the deteriorating condition of the nation's cities also produced a new breed of career civil servants determined to improve public health provision.

The boom in social research was officially led by the General

Register Office which, established in 1837, monitored in great statistical detail the collapse in sanitary health and life expectancy. The annual report of the Registrar General, the Chief Medical Officer of his day, typically concluded with a damning indictment of the state of urban sanitation. Sir William Farr, the third holder of the office, was a master at marshalling public opinion through an artful mixture of rhetoric and statistic. His account of lurking death in 1840s London is testimony both to his misguided adherence to a 'miasmatic' cause of mortality (a belief that smells and 'miasmas' spread infection) as well as his almost Dickensian powers of description. Indeed, his report intriguingly predicts Dickens's famous account of the fog encircling London at the start of *Bleak House*. According to Farr,

> the poison which causes death is not a gas, but a sort of atmosphere of organic particles, undergoing incessant transformations; perhaps, like malaria, not odorous, although evolved at the same time as putrid smells; suspended like dust, an aroma, vesicular water in the air, but invisible. If it were for a moment to become visible, and the eye could see it from a central eminence, such as St Paul's, the disease-mist would be found to lie dimly over Eltham, Dulwich, Norwood, Clapham, Battersea, Hampstead and Hackney; growing thicker around Newington, Lambeth, Marylebone, Pancras, Stepney; dark over Westminster, Rotherhithe, Bermondsey, Southwark; and black over Whitechapel and the City of London without the walls.[46]

This vision of London as a bog, as a swamp swarming with infection and sinking in its own (frequently excrementitious) mire would become a favourite motif for Victorian critics of the capital. But of an altogether less literary turn were the Registrar General's statistics. And out they tumbled: neglect of sanitary measures in England and Wales cost the lives of 137 persons per day; annual deaths from typhus fever amounted to 16,000 along with another 150,000 to 200,000 affected by

this wholly preventable disease; between 1838 and 1844 over
100,000 were killed in London by causes peculiar to the environment.

Another civil servant equally appalled by the state of urban
administration was Edwin Chadwick. A junior official in the
Poor Law Commission, the body which charted the impact of
the 1834 New Poor Law on pauperism, Chadwick became a
crusader for public health reform. Though himself a member
of the Church of England, Chadwick like Kay was the son of
a Nonconformist and inherited an equally powerful belief in
the struggle for social amelioration. In his early thirties he was
appointed private secretary to the ageing philosopher Jeremy
Bentham before entering the expanding domain of Victorian
state bureaucracy. A rationalist and man of the Enlightenment,
Chadwick believed in the efficacy of concerted state action –
the benefits of which Frederick the Great had shown in
Prussia – and was convinced of the need for a national public
health policy. To that end, he brought together all the research
carried out by the Poor Law Commission on urban living
conditions and the state of pauperism into one single volume.
His hope, through judicial editing and a bit of spin, was to
shame the political establishment into action.

Chadwick's *Report on the Sanitary Condition of the
Labouring Population of Great Britain* was presented to the
House of Lords in 1842 and became an instant classic, out-
selling every previous government publication. The popularity
of this civil service document can perhaps best be compared
to the runaway success of the *Beveridge Report* in 1942. Even
though the science of Chadwick's report, with its belief that
disease was spread through the 'miasmas' emitted by refuse
in sewers, was wrong the work nonetheless provides a gripping
account of Victorian sanitary conditions. The description of
public health in Glasgow was typical of its shock style:

There were no privies or drains there, and the dungheaps
received all filth which the swarm of wretched inhabitants
could give; and we learned that a considerable part of the

rent of the houses was paid by the produce of the dungheaps. Thus, worse off than wild animals, many of which withdraw to a distance and conceal their ordure, the dwellers in these courts had converted their shame into a kind of money by which their lodging was to be paid...[47]

Manchester didn't fare much better. The city's assistant Poor Law Commissioner, Dr Richard Baron Howard, described how whole streets were 'unpaved and without drains or main-sewers' and were 'so covered with refuse and excrementitious matter as to be almost impassable from depth of mud, and intolerable from stench'. 'In many of these places are to be seen privies in the most disgusting state of filth, open cesspools, obstructed drains, ditches full of stagnant water, dunghills, pigsties etc., from which the most abominable odours are emitted.'

Amidst this squalor, amidst the stench and open latrines, lurked death. Human and animal waste poured into the rivers and streams which supplied domestic drinking water; cesspits and water wells intermingled, spreading typhoid and diar-rhoea. According to Baron Howard, 'Of the 182 patients admit-ted into the temporary fever hospital in Balloon-Street, 135 at least came from unpaved or otherwise filthy streets, or from confined and dirty courts and alleys. Many of the streets in which cases of fever are common are so deep in mire, or so full of hollows and heaps of refuse that the vehicle used for conveying the patients to the House of recovery often cannot be driven along them'.[48]

The commissioners frequently focused on the state of housing. The link between certain diseases and overcrowding was not a difficult connection to make. Badly ventilated houses containing numerous families of the labouring poor were an easy breeding-ground for smallpox, tuberculosis and scarlet fever. The typhus louse happily jumped from body to body spreading its lethal cargo. Still unaware of the water-borne nature of cholera, Kay hazily pinpointed the physical state of Manchester as its cause – 'narrow and loathsome streets, and close courts defiled with refuse'. But it was in the cellars that real misery lurked. Robert Southey regarded the damp and dark cellars as 'so many hot-beds of infection' which meant 'the poor in large towns are rarely or never without infectious fever amongst them'.[49] 'These cellars are, in my opinion, the source of many diseases, particularly catarrh, rheumatic affections, and typhus', according to Chadwick's Liverpool commissioner.[50] The cellars were poorly lit, often a refuse for the upper floors' waste and subject to appalling levels of overcrowding. In one cellar the commissioner found 'upwards of forty people sleeping in the same room'.

Whereas earlier in the nineteenth century municipalities had been able to control and then alleviate outbreaks of infectious disease, by the late 1830s and 1840s this was proving almost impossible.[51] Typhoid, typhus, smallpox, cholera, rickets, scarlet fever, measles, whooping cough, diphtheria, and diarrhoea thrived in the early Victorian city. The most recent research, carried out by the public health historian Simon Szreter, has concluded that forty per cent of all urban deaths in 1840 were the result of infectious diseases. Scarlet fever and typhus (sometimes known as 'Irish fever' or 'ship fever') were spread by the faeces of the body-louse and flourished in overcrowded conditions. In Glasgow, the typhus outbreak of 1836–7 pushed the mortality count sixty per cent above its normal level. With a good eye for the soundbite, Chadwick concluded, 'The annual slaughter in England and Wales from preventable causes of typhus which attacks persons in the vigour of life, appears to be double the amount of what was suffered by the Allied Armies in the battle of Waterloo.'[52]

Another killer, typhoid, was spread by water supplies contaminated with excrement – as was the most feared disease of them all, cholera. During the 1832 outbreak which Kay struggled against, the disease killed 32,000 people across the country. Cholera returned again in 1848 to kill another 62,000 and once more in 1853. It was the brutal rapidity of the disease, and the ease with which it could spread from working-class to middle-class districts, which generated the panic. After a couple of days of stomach cramps, vomiting, and diarrhoea the pulse would collapse and the victim sink into a lethargic death. Kay described one such case of an Irish labourer. 'On my arrival in a two-roomed house, I found an Irishman lying on a bed close to the window. The temperature of his skin was somewhat lower than usual, the pulse was weak and quick. He complained of no pain. The face was rather pale, and the man much dejected.'[53] The pulse gently faded away and within a day the man was dead. Tuberculosis was an equally virulent killer. Thriving amongst overcrowded and poorly ventilated housing, and helped by terrible nutrition, its ubiquitous presence meant that for many urban poor it was simply part of the valley of tears of everyday life. In 1839 the Registrar General estimated that identifiable consumption accounted for almost one-fifth of all deaths.

The result of these sanitary and housing conditions was a total collapse in life chances. Sickly infants living together in cramped, damp cellars made easy pickings. Of the 350,000 deaths in England and Wales in 1842, nearly 80,000 occurred in children under one year old, and nearly 140,000 in children under five years.[54] Those lucky enough to make it beyond the crucial ten-year barrier could not look forward to a much longer existence. In 1841, life expectancy at birth was 26.6 years in Manchester, 28.1 years in Liverpool and twenty-seven years in Glasgow. In the specific case of Glasgow this marked a significant deterioration from the 1820s, when life expectancy stood at thirty-five years – a figure which would not be regained until the 1860s.[55] In London, the situation was equally bleak. Contemporary estimates put life expectancy at thirty-seven years: a relatively healthy average which hid the massive disparities in a capital where the life expectancy of a tradesman was twenty-three and an artisan could expect only twenty-two years of life. The differences were also geographical. In 1839, life expectancy in leafy Camberwell was thirty-four while in the slums of Whitechapel it hovered at twenty-six.[56]

This trend was a devastating reversal of the improvements in life expectancy which had marked the previous hundred years. The extraordinary aspect of industrialisation is that it actually set back improvements in standards of living. For a culture so bewitched by the notion of progress, the social forces and industrial mechanisms which were regarded as the handmaidens of progress brought in fact a massive reversal of previous improvements in life expectancy. Shockingly, the life chances of a slum dweller in early Victorian Glasgow or Liverpool were in fact the lowest since the Black Death.[57]

iv ENGELS'S MANCHESTER

A half-century of analysing the chaos of the industrial city was to climax in one of the angriest and most lucid polemics of the nineteenth century: Friedrich Engels's *The Condition of the Working Class in England* (1845). Written when Engels was only twenty-four, it constituted a mesmerising assault on the entire foundation of the Victorian industrial city.

In 1842 the young Engels was sent by his father from his home in Barmen, Germany to learn the family textiles business in Manchester at the company his father joint-owned, Ermen and Engels. The trip suited both parties. Engels's father was keen to separate his son from the dangerous circle of radical socialists, known as Young Hegelians, with whom he had been associating in Berlin during his military service. And Engels himself was desperate to escape the stifling piety and paternal despotism of his parents' home. But if the aim was for Engels to see the light, forget all that intellectual nonsense and embrace the virtues of industrial capitalism, the trip could not have gone much worse. On the journey to England, he stopped off in Cologne to meet the Young Hegelian philosopher Moses Hess, who excitedly informed him that Britain stood on the verge of revolution. Rushing towards the likeliest site for insurgency, Engels found Manchester awash with rumours of sedition in the wake of the Chartist-inspired Plug Plot riots. But in the face of a military clampdown, nothing

came of it. So Engels settled into his commercial apprenticeship but, unsurprisingly, showed little passion for the business of bleaching and spinning cotton. Instead, he immersed
himself in the politics of the utopian socialist 'halls of science'
run by followers of Robert Owen, before then entering the
world of radical Chartism. In the cauldron of the Industrial
Revolution, Engels hoped to discover some nascent class consciousness – before reporting on his findings for an obscure
Parisian journal run by a certain Karl Marx.

For like de Tocqueville before him, this was precisely what
excited Engels about Manchester: the fact that 'the modern
art of manufacture' had reached its perfection there. 'The
effects of modern manufacture upon the working class must
necessarily develop here most freely and perfectly, and the
manufacturing proletariat present itself in its fullest classic
perfection.'[58] The process of industrialisation had split the city
into two nations of rich and poor. The middling group of
the skilled artisan or lower middle class were an endangered
species. Instead there stood simply the bourgeoisie and the
proletariat engaged in a constant social war: 'the war of all
against all'.[59] It was, for Engels, fertile territory. Already the
city had a history of strikes, machine-breaking and riots, most
memorably at the massacre of 'Peterloo' in 1819 but also more
recently during 1829. The bourgeoisie might not know it, but
revolution was coming their way – 'and the year 1794 will
prove to have been child's play'.[60]

Engels drew upon many of the accounts already discussed
for his treatise on Manchester. He read the work of James Kay
('an excellent book although the author confuses the workers
with the working class in general'), the sociological investigations of Peter Gaskell, Edwin Chadwick's report on sanitary conditions, de Tocqueville's bourgeois ramblings, the
angry broadsides of the Chartist James Leach, and ploughed
through the welter of official statistics from Parliament and
the ceaseless Royal Commissions. Yet, guided round the city
by his Irish lover Mary Burns, Engels also walked the streets
of Manchester and, in an imitation of Kay's visits to the cholera

slums, stepped into the cellars and garrets of the dispossessed working class.

Like others before him, what first struck Engels was the ugliness and pollution of the city. He stood in the Old Town on Dulcie Bridge above the river Irk, the river de Tocqueville had described as the Styx of Manchester's Hades, and saw the 'narrow, coal-black stinking river full of filth and garbage which it deposits on the lower-lying bank. In dry weather, an extended series of the most revolting brackish green pools of slime remain standing on this bank, out of whose depth bubbles of miasmatic gases constantly rise and give forth a stench that is unbearable even on the bridge forty or fifty feet above the level of the water.' The surrounding tanneries, bonemills and gasworks poured their refuse into the Irk, while on the bank lay the filth, offal and debris from the surrounding courts. The river was overlooked by barrack-like factories and crumbling, smoky houses. Above them all loomed 'the Workhouse, the "Poor-Law Bastille" of Manchester, which like a citadel, looks threateningly down from behind its high walls and parapets on the hilltop, upon the working people's quarter below'.[61]

One of the most telling aspects of Manchester life was that the other half, the bourgeoisie, rarely had to come face to face with the horrors of proletariat existence. The divide between the two nations was more than financial. It was physical. The prosperous middle classes made their way to and from the city centre as the demands of their business necessitated. And on their way, according to Engels, 'the members of this money aristocracy' take a route which avoids them having to see 'the grimy misery that lurks to the right and the left'. The thoroughfares leading from the Exchange in all directions out of the city are lined with 'an almost unbroken series of shops' run by the middle and lower bourgeoisie, determined from commercial necessity to keep up appearances. So the wealthy middle classes could swan off to 'the breezy heights of Cheetham Hill, Broughton and Pendleton' to enjoy their 'wholesome country air' and 'fine comfortable houses' without coming into contact with the social consequences of their wealth creation. Engels believed he had never seen 'so systematic a shutting out of the working-class from the thoroughfares, so tender a concealment of everything which might affront the eye and the nerves of the bourgeoisie'.[62]

But Engels was not so stand-offish as his fellow mill-owners. He descended into the slums of Manchester's growing New Town and discovered a way of life difficult to comprehend. It was, he wrote, hard 'to convey a true impression of the filth, ruin, and uninhabitableness, the defiance of all considerations of cleanliness, ventilation, and health' which characterised this district of some 30,000 inhabitants. The sanitation was just as terrible as Chadwick's Poor Law Commissioner, Dr Baron Howard, had found it. In one of the courts he stumbled upon 'a privy without a door' which was so dirty that the inhabitants of the tenement could only leave 'by passing through foul pools of stagnant urine and excrement'.[63] In the houses of Manchester's working class, Engels attested that 'no cleanliness, no convenience, and consequently no comfortable family life is possible ... in such dwellings only a physically degenerate race, robbed of all humanity, degraded, reduced morally and physically to bestiality, could feel comfortable and at home'.[64] Common lodging-houses were singled out as particularly dangerous. They were 'scenes of deeds against which human nature revolts, which would perhaps never have been executed but for this forced centralisation of vice'.

Things were no better in the workplace. Factories were a haven for lust and depravity. But not between classes. For Engels the factory was another arena for the domination of the proletariat by the bourgeoisie. In an interesting take on the stock manufacturer-as-feudal-baron conceit, Engels described how the mill-owner demanded the *jus primae noctis* over his working-class female employees. 'The threat of discharge suffices to overcome all resistance' amongst the factory girls – 'who, in any case, have no strong inducements to chastity'. In short, for the Victorian capitalist, 'the mill is also his harem'.[65] Other than for purposes of sexual gratification, Engels's 'manufacturer' had no concern with the human or moral development of the operative. Their relationship was without sentiment: purely economic, one of purchase and sale. The only nexus between man and man in the industrial city was the cash-nexus. Across the entire spectrum of urban existence, the war of the classes continued.

It was on the other side of Manchester along the river Medlock, one of the Irk's tributaries, that Engels discovered what he needed to find. Down the Oxford Road in the Chorlton district, near where today stands Manchester University and the commercial paraphernalia of student life, was situated Little Ireland. Every writer on Manchester had focused on the city's poverty-stricken and disease-ridden Irish community, but none did so with this degree of polemical opprobrium. Nor with the same political purpose. Engels used a familiar language of savagery, of inhumanity, to describe the community but for ideological rather than 'racist' purposes. 'The race', he declared, 'that lives in these ruinous cottages, behind broken windows, mended with oilskin, sprung doors, and rotten door-posts, or in dark, wet cellars, in measureless filth and stench, in this atmosphere penned in as if with a purpose, this race must really have reached the lowest stage of humanity'.[66] Their homes were pigsties and he referred to the Irish women and children as 'swine'. Their base requirements ('What does such a race want with high wages?') meant they could, as de Tocqueville had pointed out, depress wages and working conditions for the entire city. The Irishman didn't want furniture, decent housing or proper clothing. All he required was drink. 'The southern facile character of the Irishman, his crudity, which places him but little above the savage, his contempt for all humane enjoyments, in which his very crudeness makes him incapable of sharing, his filth and poverty, all favour drunkenness.'[67] Here was the lowest of the low.

Engels's aim was to create the impression that the entire English working class existed in this state of utter dehumanity and he subtly applied this account of the dispossessed Irish to the broader working-class community of Manchester. He ignored differences between the casual labourers of the Irish quarter and the better-off, regularly employed mechanics of Ancoats and elsewhere. The proletariat became the Irish: they were portrayed as a race of subhuman beings reduced to utter pauperisation by the process of urban living and industrial capitalism. As Gareth Stedman Jones has shown, the reason for this sleight of hand had little to do with the condition of the working class in Manchester and everything to do with Engels's developing creed of communism.[68]

For the proletariat to revolt against the bourgeoisie, for them to understand the condition they were in and to organise a class struggle, they needed to understand they had sunk to the lowest point imaginable. The process of absolute pauperisation and dehumanisation, which Engels discovered in the Irish quarter and then applied to his descriptions of the entire working class, was the precondition of proletarian revolt. Without a consciousness of their position in history and the class struggle, the urban proletariat would remain in a politically impotent state of atomisation. That was why in the Engels scheme, the city was a place of hope as much as despair. 'The great cities are the birthplaces of labour movements; in them the workers first began to reflect upon their own condition, and to struggle against it.' Engels's account of Manchester showed that in the industrial city the generation of class consciousness was well under way. The inexorable momentum of industrial capitalism, with wealth in ever fewer hands and an increasingly *lumpen* proletariat, meant that sooner or later 'there comes a stage at which the proletariat perceives how easily the existing power may be overthrown, and then follows a revolution'.[69]

Unfortunately (or perhaps fortunately) for Engels, the Manchester proletariat never did rise up against the industrial bourgeoisie. Which meant that in 1850, after a brief and unhappy return to Germany, the millocrat Engels could settle down in Manchester with his live-in lover Mary Burns. There he remained a partner in Ermen and Engels, albeit a fairly unenthusiastic one, and spent his spare time funding Marx's days in the British Library, fermenting international socialism as well as riding out regularly on his fine stallion with the Cheshire Hunt. After a further twenty years, he was finally bought out of the company and moved down to Regent's Park in London to live as an industrial *rentier* and metropolitan man of letters.

Despite the posthumous success of *The Condition of the Working Class* as a historical source for the social consequences of the Industrial Revolution, it made almost no political impact in nineteenth-century Britain. This might have been because it was originally published in German in 1845, and only received an English translation in the 1880s, appearing first in America and then, finally, in Britain in 1892. The idea of the proletariat as a historical force, the inevitability of the class struggle and triumph of communism were not commonly held interpretations of the Victorian social condition. That did not mean there were not equally sophisticated ideological critiques of the industrial city, but they were ones which were not necessarily reliant upon a Marxist denunciation of industrial capitalism.

Others believed that the physical collapse and social disintegration apparent in the city could not simply be blamed on material causes and new modes of production. Rather, the unprecedented civic disarray was the work of a new ethos in society, an ethic founded upon a novel, self-serving individualism devoid of human emotion. And the Victorian who so successfully identified this deleterious philosophy was not an academic or politician, but a novelist. A novelist moreover who had so far achieved much of his notoriety for his generally affectionate explorations of the Victorian capital. But when Charles Dickens turned his attention northwards, to the industrial mill towns of Lancashire, he was to produce one of the most brutal and evocative denunciations of the industrial city.

CARLYLE AND COKETOWN

It was a town of red brick, or of brick which would have
been red if the smoke and ashes had allowed it; but as
matters stood it was a town of unnatural red and black like
the painted face of a savage. It was a town of machinery and
tall chimneys, out of which interminable serpents of smoke
trailed themselves for ever and ever and never got uncoiled.
It had a black canal in it, and a river that ran purple with
ill-smelling dye, and vast piles of building full of windows
where the piston of the steam-engine worked monotonously
up and down, like the head of an elephant in a state of
melancholy madness.[1]

Since Charles Dickens first recorded the topology of 'Coketown', the name has become a synonym for the Victorian city.
One hundred and fifty years after the publication of *Hard
Times*, if today we think of nineteenth-century city life we
think of the red brick and soot of Coketown. We think of
the pollution, the heavy industry, the struggle between trade
unions and mill-owners and the immiseration of the working
class. Coketown conjures up a nightmare vision of grinding
poverty and moral disintegration that still dominates public,
even specialist understanding of Victorian civic history. When
in 1961 the pioneering urban historian Lewis Mumford wrote
his celebrated work, *The City in History*, he entitled his
chapter on the nineteenth century, 'Paleotechnic Paradise:
Coketown'. Victorian cities were, in a phrase, 'insensate'; they
constituted little more than 'manheaps, machine warrens, not

agents of human association for the promotion of better life'.[2] Today, when the *Daily Telegraph* requires a dismissive short-hand for industrial, northern cities it too reaches for 'Coke-town'.[3]

Despite Dickens's familiar evocation of its urban scenery, Coketown was not designed by him alone. It was, in fact, as much the work of a fellow author who, brick by sooty brick, constructed the ethical foundations which would come to define so many accounts of the Victorian urban past. Brilliantly, Dickens provided a narrative landscape and some dramatic gabling, but the true architect of Coketown was the friend to whom *Hard Times* was inscribed, Thomas Carlyle. For it was Carlyle who identified the bleak moral landscape in which Coketown lay; a mental vista all too readily imagined by the denizens of the early Victorian city.

i The Moral Quagmire

Since the Lord first inveighed against the iniquity of Sodom and Gomorrah, the traditional cry of rustic virtue against urban luxury has echoed down the ages. The Victorian city was no different. For the moral dangers of the industrialising city were assumed to be just as great as the physical. There was no guiding hand of the parson or stern reproach from the landlord in the maelstrom of Manchester or Leeds. Urban life brought to the fore all the fleshly pitfalls of human existence and, with ever increasing fervour, Christian ministers warned of the dangers of the Vanity Fair. Amongst the most portentous was the Paddington curate, James Shergold Boone, who in 1844 delivered a sermon entitled *The Need of Christianity to Cities*:

> Cities are the centres and theatres of human ambition, human cupidity, and human pleasure. On the one side, the appetites, the passions, the carnal corruptions of man are forced, as in a hot-bed, into a rank and foul luxuriance; and countless evils, which would have elsewhere a feeble and difficult existence, are struck out into activity and warmth,

by their mere contact with each other. On the other side, many restraints and safeguards are weakened, or even withdrawn...[4]

Others followed in highlighting the momentous difficulty of living a virtuous life when surrounded by temptation and depravity. As George Bell put it of Edinburgh's pauper netherworld, 'To the physical evils ... a moral ill is appended. The people cannot observe the decencies of life; and the neglect of these debases the mind. A mind thus contaminated, is a soil prepared to receive and quicken the seeds of positive evil.'[5] It was a persistent city trope which Charles Dickens first grappled with in *Oliver Twist, or the Parish Boy's Progress*. Though primarily an attack on the iniquities of the 1834 New Poor Law, the book also dwelt heavily on the damage done to moral judgement by the urban environment. As the Artful Dodger leads the innocent young Oliver through the capital's backstreets of Clerkenwell and Islington, the workhouse escapee is shocked by his new surroundings. 'A dirtier or more wretched place he had never seen. The street was very narrow and muddy, and the air was impregnated with filthy odours ... Covered ways and yards, which here and there diverged from the main street, disclosed little knots of houses, where drunken men and women were positively wallowing in filth.'[6]

In such circumstances, it seemed barely possible for an individual to retain the moral sensibility of a rational human being. And, indeed, ever greater numbers of city dwellers were beginning to behave more akin to animals than men. Later in the book, on a robbery mission with the supremely carnal Bill Sykes, Oliver encounters the monstrous squalor of Smithfield Market. 'The ground was covered, nearly ankle-deep with filth and mire ... tied up to posts by the gutter side were long lines of beasts and oxen, three or four deep. Countrymen, butchers, drovers, hawkers, boys, thieves, idlers, and vagabonds ... were mingled together in a mass ... and the unwashed, unshaven, squalid, and dirty figures constantly running to and fro, and bursting in and out of the throng.'[7] Animal and urban man stand grotesquely fused amidst the unnaturalness of the city. The 'labyrinthine' rookeries of Covent Garden's Seven Dials (now one of London's most fashionable retail and culinary districts) or Jacob's Island were breeding grounds for immorality. Was it any wonder such an environment produced the caricatured criminality of Fagin or the homicidal inclinations of Bill Sykes? It would take all the might of Nancy's Christian goodness, her Mary Magdalene fortitude, for her to remain virtuous in such debilitating circumstances.

In the lurid descriptions of Fagin's lair, *Oliver Twist* also played on the obsession with juvenile crime and the entire subculture of criminal behaviour which blighted the fast-expanding cities. Given the level of immigration and absence of organised policing, along with ever more detailed analyses of social behaviour, it was little wonder that recorded crime mushroomed. Between 1805 and 1848 the numbers committed to trial for indictable offences in England and Wales grew from 4,605 to 30,369, while the numbers convicted multiplied eightfold from 2,783 to 22,900.[8] Most offences were against property, so rose and fell with economic circumstances. And while the risks to wealthy city dwellers were marginal, the literature surrounding the urchins, beggars, thieves, the fences, cracksmen and snakesmen (the job of wriggling through a window for which the tiny Oliver was well suited) was vast. London, in particular, was imagined as a city of incessant crime and vice.

But the capital was also home to a vast tribe which existed just above criminality. Its way of life was illuminated by one of the most gifted of mid-Victorian social chroniclers, Henry Mayhew. A satirist and perpetual bankrupt, Mayhew was a writer with an extraordinary empathy for the listless lives of the casual poor. Through his reports in the *Morning Chronicle*, later compiled into his multi-volume *London Labour and the London Poor*, Mayhew excavated an unknown social archaeology of London's poor.

Mayhew's great skill lay in his understanding of the economic rhythms of the capital's underclass. Contrary to popular perception about Lancashire mills and Yorkshire factories, London during the nineteenth century was the greatest manufacturing centre in the country. The watchmakers of Clerkenwell, the shipbuilders of Millwall, the chemical workers of Stratford, the rubber manufacturers of Hackney, the calico printers of Wandsworth, and the tanners of Southwark comprised a vital industrial hub which underwrote London's financial dominance. However, unlike its northern competitors, London was also the centre of prodigious and conspicuous consumption; it was a port, a capital market and a court society. Its wealthy middle and upper classes constituted a huge demand market for perishable foodstuffs, manufactured goods and an attendant service industry. This economic context affected the entirety of the capital's economy as there did not exist the rigid factory structure, the clear time-demarcations of provincial industrial life. London was a casual, frequently service-oriented economy with small-scale production and strong seasonal variations in employment.

Mayhew realised that the nature of the London economy dictated the lives of the city's poor, producing a different kind of unskilled working class than the factory proletariat of Manchester and Bradford. In a series of sketches he described the irregular, impulsive world of the chimney-sweeper, crossing-sweeper, street entertainer and dustman. Like few before him, Mayhew gave the London poor a voice in their own street dialect which avoided the sentimentality or pious judgement of his peers. He described 'Gander', a crossing-sweep, as 'a big lad of 16, with a face devoid of all expression, until he laughed, when the cheeks, mouth, and forehead instantly became crumpled up with a wonderful quantity of lines and dimples'. In graphic language, Mayhew also dwelt on the dregs of the capital's underclass: the mudlarks, 'certainly about the most deplorable in their appearance of any I have met with in the course of my inquiries', who scavenged the shores of the Thames hunting for bits of old iron, rope, bones and copper nails. Working alongside them were the street-finders, who 'literally "pick up" their living in the public thoroughfares.

They are the "pure" pickers, or those who live by gathering
dogs'-dung; the cigar-end finders, of "hard-ups" as they are
called, who collect the refuse pieces of smoked cigars from
the gutters, and having dried them, sell them as tobacco to
the very poor; the dredgermen or coal-finder ... the bone-
grubbers; and the sewer-hunter.'[9]

Talking to one of the mudlarks, Mayhew elicited a rather
bleak view of the moral state of the metropolis's inhabitants.
'He didn't know what religion his father and mother were, nor
did he know what religion meant. God was God, he said. He
had heard He was good, but didn't know what good He was to
him. He thought he was a Christian, but didn't know what a
Christian was'.[10] The irreligion of the Victorian city was, of
course, a regular theme amongst its critics. James Phillips Kay
described how in Manchester 'The absence of religious feeling,
the neglect of all religious ordinances, affords substantive
evidence of so great a moral degradation of the community, as
to ensure a concomitant civic degradation.'[11] In his travels
across Britain with 'the city and town missionaries', John
Shaw lamented the 'awful mass of humanity' who had never
heard the Word. 'Only 4 per cent of the working-classes attend
a place of worship in London. Need we wonder that profligacy,
drunkenness, thieves and prostitutes, swarm in our streets,
and produce a moral atmosphere such as to endanger the
spiritual life of every man who breathes it for the first time?'
In Liverpool, 'in some few streets well known, there are not
ten families that attend any public place of worship; they plead
want of clothes. A woman, with a dress torn to ribbons, says,
"Would you have me go to worship in this condition?"' The
cities were fermenting a dangerous atheism.[12]

With the collapse in faith came a collapse in sexual morality.
Foreign and domestic visitors alike all remarked on the extraordinary profusion of prostitutes on Britain's streets. 'There
are so many prostitutes in London that one sees them everywhere at any time of day,' remarked the French feminist Flora
Tristan in her London journal, 'all the streets are full of them,
but at certain times they flock in from outlying districts in

which most of them live, and mingle with the crowds in theatres and public places.' It was their effrontery which so appalled onlookers. A German tourist to the capital remarked how strange it was, 'that such spectacles are in no country on earth more shamelessly displayed than in pious and decent England. It goes on to such an extent that often in the theatre one can hardly ward off these repellent priestesses of Venus'.[13] The delicate William Wordsworth, coming into the capital from the innocence of England's 'pastoral hills', recalled his shock at the language of the street.

> I heard, and for the first time in my life
> The voice of woman utter blasphemy –
> Saw woman as she is, to open shame
> Abandoned, and the pride of public vice;
> I shuddered, for a barrier seemed at once
> Thrown in, that from humanity divorced
> Humanity, splitting the race of man
> In twain, yet leaving the same outward form.[14]

Estimating the number of prostitutes plying their trade, from the docks of Liverpool to the wynds of Edinburgh to the clubland of London's Haymarket, became a popular pastime amongst evangelicals. With most unaccompanied women on the city streets classed as prostitutes, estimates ranged up to 80,000 for London, which meant at times almost one in three women of childbearing age (and often under) were assumed to be on the game.

Immorality was not limited to the oldest profession but affected the entirety of urban society. The debilitating physical conditions of the city could only result in harmful moral consequences. Robert Southey feared that the confinement of the labouring class 'in the impure atmosphere of crowded rooms' meant they would inevitably grow up 'without decency, without comfort and without hope'.[15] A House of Commons inquiry into the state of life in industrial cities, the 1840 Select Committee on the Health of Towns, was even

more adamant about the ethical effects of poor housing. 'The
dirt, damp, and discomfort so frequently found in and about
the habitations of the poorer people in these great towns, has
a most pernicious effect on their moral feelings, induces habits
of recklessness and disregard of cleanliness ... and thereby
takes away a strong and useful stimulus to industry and exertion.'[16] Just as promiscuity can increase during the perils of
war, so Edwin Chadwick ascribed the reckless, licentious vice
of cities to this fear of imminent death. 'Seeing the apparent
uncertainty of the morrow, the inhabitants really take no
heed of it, and abandon themselves with the recklessness
and avidity of common soldiers in a war to whatever gross
enjoyment comes within their reach.'

In Liverpool, a Poor Law Commissioner was appalled to
discover a mother and grown-up daughter sleeping on one side
of the room and three burly sailors on the other. In Leeds
things took on a more sinister turn as sexes of all families
slept hugger-mugger in dank garrets 'and consequences occur
which humanity shudders to contemplate'.[17] Amongst the
worst was 'a father and daughter [who] stood at the bar of
Leeds Sessions as criminals, the one in concealing, and the
other in being an accessory to concealing, the birth of an
illegitimate child, born on the body of the daughter by the
father'.[18] Lodging-houses, with rooms full of migrant workers
and transient labourers, were regarded as particular dens of
deprivation with their indiscriminate mix of sexes and ages.
In the workplace, it was no different. The manufacturing
population were liable to succumb to sexual improvidence at
any moment on the factory floor: 'husband and wife sin
equally, and a habitual indifference to sexual rights is generated which adds one other item to the destruction of domestic habits'.[19]

ii A Pageant of Phantoms

The loss of personal control and breakdown of sexual mores
was part of a broader fracturing of society in the industrial

city. As the Revd Boone had warned, the old restraints and safeguards were profoundly weakened in the new urban environment. The 'golden age' of communal solidarity – the product of cottage manufacturing and an arcadian agricultural economy – had been replaced by the divisiveness of industrial capitalism. Factories and workshops, containing hundreds of operatives with distant and brutal employers, now separated the classes. The old social gradation of artisan and apprentice was crassly swallowed up by the demands of mechanisation. And many commentators pre-empted Engels with their depiction of the callous cotton lord. The modern manufacturer was portrayed as having minimal care for his employees; their moral or social well-being had little to do with his business interests.

To be herded together in mills, mindlessly servicing industrial machinery without pride in their labour, could only undermine the self-respect of the British artisan. In the words of Peter Gaskell, a pioneering sociological investigator who paid as much attention to the mental condition of the working classes as Kay had done to the physical, the 'comfort, morality, independence, and loyalty' of the artisan was being replaced by 'misery, demoralization, dependence, and discontent'. The consequence was a total collapse in domestic life and a further reduction of urban man to the state of a savage. 'Recklessness, improvidence, and unnecessary poverty, starvation, drunkenness, parental cruelty and carelessness, filial disobedience, neglect of conjugal rights, absence of maternal love, destruction of brotherly and sisterly affection' – these were all the product of factory work.[20]

The great Romantic novelist Sir Walter Scott was appalled by the harsh new practices of factory life. From his sprawling baronial pile in Scotland, far away from the industrial rhythms of Manchester, Scott lived in a mental world of *noblesse oblige*; an ordered universe built around duty and sacrifice with a clear hierarchy from the castle to the croft. It was the close-knit society conjured up in *Ivanhoe* and the Waverley novels in which the romantic development of individual character stood paramount. So the author was deeply disturbed by the 'unhappy dislocation' between worker and capitalist in the manufacturing industries, blaming it on the 'steam engine' and movement of industry from country to town. And now, 'the manufacturers are transferred to great towns, where a man may assemble five hundred workmen one week and dismiss them the next, without having any further connection with them than to receive a week's work for a week's wages, nor any further solicitude about their future fate than if they were so many old shuttles'. The modern master had no regard for his workforce as 'moral and rational beings'.[21]

A similar critique was put forward by Canon Richard Parkinson, who claimed of Manchester that there was 'no town in the world where the distance between the rich and the poor is so great'. In fact, there was 'far less personal communication between the master cotton spinner and his workmen' than between 'the Duke of Wellington and the humblest labourer on his estate', a contrast that would have appealed to Scott.[22] The industrial tourist and man of letters William Cooke Taylor dwelt on the geographic as well as class separation, contending that Manchester's well-off community of Ardwick knew less about the poverty-stricken Ancoats than it did about China, 'and feels more interested in the condition of New Zealand than of Little Ireland'.[23] Arnold Toynbee, of course, put it most eloquently. 'Between the individual workman and the capitalist who employed hundreds of "hands" a wide gulf opened: the workman ceased to be the cherished dependent, he became the living tool of whom the employer knew less than he did of his steam-engine.'[24]

Benjamin Disraeli, then an out-of-favour young politician and jobbing author, took this urban theme of social division and placed it at the heart of his manifesto-cum-novel, *Sybil, or The Two Nations* (1845). As the political leader of the Tory 'Young England' movement, which argued for a return to the social conservatism and duty of pre-industrial England, Disraeli lambasted the ethos of the great industrial cities. There could now exist, he protested, within one city two

entirely different nations, 'between whom there is no intercourse and no sympathy; who are as ignorant of each other's
habits, thoughts and feelings, as if they were dwellers in different zones, or inhabitants of different planets'. These two
nations were 'formed by different breeding', fed by different
food, and governed by different laws. They were 'THE RICH
AND THE POOR'.[25] In Elizabeth Gaskell's *Mary Barton*, the anti-
hero John Barton was similarly perplexed by the gulf between
'rich and poor'. 'Why are they so separate, so distinct, when
God has made them all? It is not his will that their interests
are so far apart. Whose doing is it?' The contemporary critique
of industrial society was most fluently encapsulated by Marx
and Engels in one beautiful paragraph in the opening pages of
the 1848 *Communist Manifesto*: 'The bourgeoisie, wherever it
has got the upper hand, has put an end to all feudal, patriarchal,
idyllic relations. It has pitilessly torn assunder [sic] the motley
feudal ties that bound man to his "natural superiors", and has
left remaining no other nexus between man and man than
naked self-interest, than callous "cash-payment".'[26]

Other commentators, who were generally enthusiastic in
their approach to urban industrialism, condemned this split
between worker and master as a retrograde step to the sort of
feudal ethos the age of manufacturing should have eliminated.
Manufacturing appeared as the new feudalism, the dungeons
its workshops, and 'the barons are the manufacturers, who, to
gratify their cupidity, condemn those dependent upon them
to the most oppressive and most deplorable slavery'.[27] Leon
Faucher's sightseeing trip around Manchester's factories convinced him of the growing disparities between rich and poor
and the unhealthy dependence of the operative class. 'The
position of the manufacturer in regard to his people, is similar
to that of the feudal baron in regard to his vassals.'[28]

For other critics, the horror of the city did not lie in the two
nations, two opposed classes in a perpetual state of war, but
in the spectre of anomie. The industrial city was a place of
loneliness, of solitariness and often despair. It was a place
without the bonds of religion, apprenticeships, corporations

or community. Given the huge levels of transitory migration, there were few established ties of friendship or obligation. The individual worked in the factory and slept in the lodging-house. Family units dissolved and social responsibility was abrogated. The consequence was a society of utter atomisation – an unwanted liberty of miserable freedoms. This was as true of London as the northern cities. In his tirade against the nation's capital, *London and the Londoners: Or a Second Judgement of Babylon the Great*, Robert Mudie described the solitariness of the Londoner whose habitat was 'desolation, where every street is a crowd; the world around, and yet comfort from no lip, and pity from no eye'.[29]

What modernity welcomes in city living – the self-contained privacy; the empowering lack of hierarchy – was the early Victorian nightmare. Robert Southey expressed the fear most powerfully when he described the inhabitants of industrial cities, 'like the dogs at Lisbon and Constantinople, unowned, unbroken to any useful purpose, subsisting by chance or by prey, living in filth, mischief, wretchedness, a nuisance to the community while they live, and dying miserably at last!'[30] The atomisation of society had left the individual utterly at sea. It was a world which Charles Dickens epitomised in the character of Jo the crossing-sweep in his London epic, *Bleak House* (1852–3). Gently undulating through the text, Jo cuts an anonymous, almost translucent figure sweeping his lonely way through the 'faces never-ending' of a crowded, bustling city. Dickens based the character on an account in *The Examiner* magazine of an interview with a fourteen-year-old crossing-sweep boy called George Ruby. Making his miserable living from sweeping the excrement and filth from the streets of London, Ruby, like Mayhew's mudlarks, knew neither prayers nor God. All he knew was how to sweep a crossing. Like the doomed Jo and the thousands of rural immigrants who charged into the city, Ruby explained he had 'No father, no mother, no friends.'

But unlike Mayhew's cast of characters, Jo the crossing-sweep was a creature without a voice and without a home. For

Thomas Carlyle, such a condition was a terrifying prospect. 'Isolation is the sum-total of wretchedness to man. To be cut off, to be left solitary ... It is the frightfulest enchantment; too truly a work of the Evil One.'[31] The terrible irony was that Jo was part of humanity and ultimately displayed his unalterable connection to society by infecting Esther with fever. In doing so, he replicated the contamination which his habitual doss-house, Tom-All-Alone's, spread through London. 'There is not a drop of Tom's corrupted blood but propagates infection and contagion somewhere... There is not an atom of Tom's slime, not a cubic inch of any pestilential gas in which he lives, not one obscenity or degradation about him, not an ignorance, not a wickedness, not a brutality of his committing, but shall work its retribution, through every order of society, up to the proudest of the proud, and to the highest of the high.'[32] Even as the city denied it, the bonds of humanity remained.

The superficial individualism of the city was reflected in the unnatural frenzy of its inhabitants. Byron referred to London as a 'Babylon': a chaotic labyrinth of the jabbering and jostling. Today we talk admiringly of the 'pace of city life', a theme of personal liberation brought to life by Virginia Woolf in her 1930 essay, 'Street Haunting', in which she spoke of shedding 'the self our friends know us by and becom[ing] part of that vast republican army of anonymous trampers, whose society is so agreeable after the solitude of one's room.'[33] But in the 1830s a predominantly rural mindset was deeply disturbed by the energy of the city. 'How men are hurried here,' wrote Carlyle of the capital, 'how they are hunted and terrifically chased into double-quick speed; so that in self-defence they must not stay to look at one another!'[34] Thomas De Quincey, the self-confessed 'peripatetic, or a walker of the streets', thought the city throng a 'mask of maniacs ... a pageant of phantoms'. And the 'mighty labyrinths of London' meant that a barrier no wider than a street could amount 'in the end to a separation for eternity!'[35]

Typically, Manchester testified to this spirit most startlingly.

The people, like the machines, operated at too dangerous a speed and with the same inanimate indifference. An 1809 pamphlet, *Directions for Walking the Streets of Manchester and the Conduct of Carriages*, warned its readers that 'in walking down Market-street-lane to the Exchange, it is likely that a person will be pushed all ways, at least twenty times, sometimes against the houses, others off the flags, notwithstanding his endeavour to walk regular'.[36] De Tocqueville described how 'crowds are ever hurrying this way and that in the Manchester streets, but their footsteps are brisk, their looks preoccupied and their appearance sombre and harsh'.[37] There was no time for relaxation in the great Cottonopolis. Above all, it was the unfriendliness of the people that struck William Cooke Taylor. 'Every person who passes you in the street has the look of thought and the step of haste.'[38] The conservative journal *Bentley's Miscellany* was appalled at this rudeness: how 'the people hurry through its [Manchester's] streets as if their neighbours had the plague, and the delay of exchanging salutations would expose them to mirth'.[39] Yet one of the peculiarities of Manchester was that as soon as the factory whistle sounded, the bustle and rhythm vanished. 'The very moment when the engines are stopped, and the counting-houses closed, everything which was the thought – the authority – the impulsive force – the moral order of this immense industrial combination, flies from the town, and disappears in an instant.'[40]

iii ROMANCE AND REASON

In 1827, as James Phillips Kay was making his way towards Manchester, a fellow Edinburgh graduate, Thomas Carlyle, was taking his first steps as a published author by submitting a piece to the prestigious *Edinburgh Review*. It was the start of an incredible literary career which is now sadly all too neglected – perhaps unsurprisingly, as ever since it emerged that during his dying days in the Berlin bunker Adolf Hitler sought solace in Carlyle's epic biography of Frederick the

Great the historical standing of this extraordinary Victorian polemicist has been understandably low. Combine this with his defence of the egregious Jamaican butcher Governor Eyre, his vituperative essay on 'The Nigger Question', and his similarly trenchant views on the intelligence of the Irish, and you have a man almost incomprehensible to the twenty-first-century liberal mindset. Yet Carlyle was a figure of immeasurable importance to Victorian public culture: a sophisticated, witty and prophetic writer who pushed ideas to their limits while deepening the very fabric of the English language.

In fact, Carlyle stands at the heart of Victorian intellectual life as perhaps its greatest seer. No serious thinker or politician could afford to ignore his work. In the words of Harriet Martineau, a leading liberal and political opponent of Carlyle, 'Whatever place we assign him, and by whatever name we call him, Thomas Carlyle appears to be the man who has most essentially modified the mind of his time.'[41] George Eliot agreed: 'There is hardly a superior or active mind of this generation that has not been modified by Carlyle's writings.'[42] Sir Robert Peel, W.E. Gladstone, John Ruskin, J.S. Mill, Alfred, Lord Tennyson, Charles Darwin, William Thackeray, Benjamin Disraeli – all were indebted to the legendary 'sage of Chelsea'. In America, Ralph Waldo Emerson became his greatest acolyte and almost full-time salesman; in Italy, the nationalist leader Giuseppe Mazzini remained a loyal, if confused, disciple, more attracted to Carlyle's wife, Jane, than to the man himself. In modern terms, Carlyle (who would certainly disparage the comparison) could be regarded in terms of intellectual stature as the J.M. Keynes of his day. A man whose ideas were disputed and sometimes abhorred but who nonetheless needed to be engaged.

If ever there was a product of his childhood, it was Carlyle.[43] Born in 1795 in Ecclefechan in south-west Scotland, the young Thomas's upbringing was dominated by the raw, unadulterated Calvinism of this small Presbyterian village. His loving father, James Carlyle, combined pious Christianity with a savage temper born of his overriding sense of sin. As Thomas later told friends, his father had 'walked as a man in the full presence of hell and the judgement', believing 'with absolute certitude that the greater number of human beings will suffer in literal fire without any end at all'. Carlyle's mother, Margaret, simply combined pious Christianity with deeper Christianity. In the bleak isolation of their Dumfriesshire existence Margaret was subject to terrible nervous breakdowns – a trait Thomas himself would combine with his own very vivid hypochondria. But Margaret's love for her son was all-consuming and the two enjoyed an extraordinarily intimate letter correspondence right up to her death. This exchange included Thomas being forced to tell his mother the cringing circumstances surrounding his wedding night. Margaret Carlyle and the newly-wed Jane Carlyle never quite saw eye to eye.

Sent to Edinburgh University to train for the clergy, Carlyle quickly marked himself out as a difficult genius. But as his love for mathematics, geometry and logic grew his faith in organised religion began to wane and in 1818 he gave up all hope of joining the ministry on grounds of conscience. His loss of faith was reversed, however, in a famously revelatory stroll along the city's Leith Walk when he rediscovered God by means of a new faith in personal will. Carlyle's new religion was one without theology. Simply by exerting personal will and individual feeling through that essential Victorian activity, work, Carlyle believed one could enjoy spiritual growth. It is no accident that one of the figures standing next to the sweating navvies in Ford Madox Brown's pictorial celebration of the virtue of labour, *Work*, is Carlyle. 'I must work the work of him that sent me for the night cometh, wherein no man can work,' reads the painting's biblical inscription. But Carlyle had discovered that his own work, his own calling, was not to dig ditches but to write.

From the early 1830s, despite his paranoiac fear of failure, Carlyle's reputation as a literary critic, social commentator and public thinker blossomed. After some miserable years divided between Edinburgh and the boondocks of Craigenputtoch, in 1834 Carlyle and Jane moved to 5 Cheyne Row in

Chelsea to embrace London's literary scene. Carlyle immediately wrote to his mother describing what is now one of
London's most desirable addresses as 'a fine, quiet old street
of about twenty houses, with huge old trees opposite us in
front, and then a most silent – brick wall. The river is near,
and very gay.' Today, the house remains as it was thanks to
the National Trust (an institution, I imagine, for which Carlyle
would have had some fairly scathing remarks): the attic he
tried unsuccessfully to convert into a soundproof study; his
drawing room with its leather reading chair and walls laden
with pictures of historical heroes such as Cromwell and
Martin Luther's parents; as well as Jane's (separate) bedroom
complete with surprisingly soppy Valentine's cards. An idiosyncratic collection of visitors from around the world still
pass through the house. Interestingly, the number has more
or less remained the same for the last hundred years at about
fifteen a day.

Carlyle's first piece for the *Edinburgh Review* was a review
of the work of the German Romantic writer Johann Paul
Richter (Jean Paul). Reacting against the artless Pres-
byterianism of his parents, Carlyle had as a boy found solace
in the dreamy visions of Wordsworth, Coleridge, and the Lake
Poets. As a student, he went further and discovered the source
of their inspiration in the German Romantics. And in Goethe
he found a proxy father who understood his unease, his dissatisfaction with the modern world. The 'sage of Weimar' and
future sage of Chelsea communicated regularly and in 1824
Carlyle began to translate Goethe's romantic masterpiece,
Wilhelm Meister, before moving on to the works of Schiller,
Herder and the broader German Romantic *oeuvre*. In their
writings he found a spiritualism and a naturalism which
English philosophy lacked. The German idealists looked to
romance and nature, not to reason or raw logic. It was an
ideology of the heart not the head and it entranced the soulful
Carlyle. From this romantic, idealist base he set about criti-
cising the inadequacies of contemporary Victorian society
through a series of articles, pamphlets and historical accounts.

At the crux of his contempt was the state of the industrial city.

Carlyle defined the nineteenth century as 'the Mechanical Age'. Whereas previous eras were devotional, heroical or moral, the Victorian era was an age of machinery. Mechanisation and the Industrial Revolution were merely signs or symbols of this phenomenon. What Carlyle was concerned with was the moral condition of the Victorian; 'Men are grown mechanical in head and in heart, as well as in hand.' The fault lay not with the social or economic process of industrialisation, but with the harmful moral philosophy which accompanied it. This sensationalist psychology, originally drawn from the writings of John Locke, saw man's physical reaction to pain and pleasure as the root cause of his action. The philosophy of the eighteenth century had advanced a materialist interpretation of what determined man's ambition and it left little room for altruistic notions of duty, obligation or spiritual calling. 'It is no longer the moral, religious, spiritual condition of the people that is our concern, but their physical, practical, economical condition', Carlyle lamented. 'Men are to be guided only by their self-interests.'[44] Or as Edmund Burke more eloquently put it, 'The age of chivalry is gone. That of sophisters, economists, and calculators, has succeeded.' Politics was simply a juggling of this base equation of sensations, enticing the individual to pursue certain avenues through pleasure and repelling him through pain.

The thinker whom Carlyle regarded as most responsible for this alarming moral hiatus was the father of 'utilitarianism', Jeremy Bentham. In Carlyle's eyes, Bentham's complex and arguably ethical philosophical system – which placed the greatest happiness of the greatest number as the lynchpin of public policy – was in fact destroying society. Certainly, Bentham regarded man as a sensationalist being who could be cajoled through a desire for pleasure and a wish to avoid pain.[45] But by understanding man's moral temperament, his progressive hope was to clarify England's arbitrary legal system and unwritten constitution so that each individual had the knowledge and hence power to determine their actions accordingly. It was a democratic and empowering political programme which allowed the individual to make decisions based on a clear knowledge of the potential consequences of their actions. It was, however, an uncompromising philosophy where political options were judged solely by a principle of utility which had little time for tradition, hierarchy, or ties of affection. It proffered an ultra-rationalist science of government.

For Carlyle, this vision of man was cant and quackery. It was also horrifying. The German Romantics had shown man to be a being of enormous emotional complexity whose quest for spiritual growth indicated he was far more than, in Carlyle's words, 'a dead Iron-Balance for weighing Pains and Pleasures'. What Carlyle opposed was the materialism of the utilitarians; the idea that spirit was merely an efflux of the brain. But even if man was little more than a sensationalist calculus, a society oriented around such a principle could never develop individual spirit or promote the true happiness of man. Carlyle was appalled by the growing influence of utilitarian, mechanistic profit-and-loss ideas in Victorian Britain. It seemed to him that 'these men, Liberals, Utilitarians, or whatsoever they are called, will ultimately carry their point, and dissever and destroy most existing Institutions of Society'.

To Carlyle, Bentham's ideas were the reflection of a profound, national crisis of faith – just as Carlyle himself had personally experienced. These materialist, irreligious doctrines, of which utilitarianism was the most blatant, were the product of a religious void within Britain. While talk of a collapse of faith in the context of the confessional state of 1830s Britain might seem peculiar to our truly atheistic society, the early Victorians were terrified by the loss of religion. In his strangely wonderful semi-autobiography, *Sartor Resartus* (1833–4), Carlyle recounted the awfulness of his own spiritual crisis. 'To me the Universe was all void of Life, of Purpose, of Volition, even of Hostility: it was one huge, dead, immeasurable Steam-engine, rolling on, in its dead indifference, to grind me limb from limb.' Yet thankfully, this 'Everlasting No' was followed (because of Leith Walk) by an 'Everlasting Yes' as Carlyle refound faith. 'Love not Pleasure; love God.'[46]

What was more terrifying than individual crises of conscience was when an entire society abjured its religion. In his history of the French Revolution, Carlyle described the ruin of a nation without faith; the guillotine, the *sans-culottes* and the frenzy of the Great Terror were the awful result. Robespierre's Republic of Virtue, with its pagan gods and republican ceremonies, was a warning which cast its shadow across the entire nineteenth century. Carlyle's 1829 jeremiad, 'Signs of the Times', was designed as a wake-up call to a society on the verge of precisely such a disaster. The title of this *Edinburgh Review* essay was aptly taken from Matthew 16:3: 'O ye hypocrites, ye can discern the face of the sky; but can ye not discern the signs of the times'. He told his elite readership of politicians, writers, lawyers and men of culture: 'This is not a Religious age. Only the material, the immediately practical, not the divine and spiritual, is important to us.'[47] As he later warned: 'Ye have forgotten God.' What Carlyle described was a religious and moral crisis of which the predominance of utilitarianism was one of the most symbolic components.

What did all this have to do with the city? The answer is that the consequences of this collective collapse of faith and the predominance of utility played themselves out with gruesome effect in the industrial cities. We tend to think of the Victorian city as a quintessential product of its time, but in the early nineteenth century it was regarded as an awful outgrowth of the materialism and irreligion of the previous century. For Carlyle, it was an eighteenth-century, Age of Reason hangover. In place of faith, duty or affection inspiring man there was merely the pursuit of pleasure. And what gave the individual most pleasure was monetary gain. Mammon, not God, governed industrial society. Carlyle argued, in the phrase which Marx and Engels quietly hijacked, that individual relations in the city had been reduced to the 'cash-nexus'. Just as Sir Walter Scott had condemned the callous hiring and firing mentality of the modern mill-owner, so Carlyle could find few mutual obligations in the city beyond cash payment. 'Free-Trade, Competition, and Devil take the hindmost', this was the Gospel of the day.

Carlyle brought this esoteric critique of utilitarianism shockingly to life by recounting the story of the death of an Irish widow which he had extracted from Dr William Alison's *Observations on the Management of the Poor in Scotland.* Alison, one of the grand old men of the Edinburgh medical profession, had described how a destitute widow living in the mire of the Lanes had traipsed around the city with her three children looking for sustenance and shelter from the local charitable institutions. At each one she was refused. She then turned to her neighbours for help, only to be met with further refusal. In the end she died on the street, exhausted from her travels and chronically ill with typhus. But, in a model for Jo the crossing-sweep's curse on Esther, the widow's typhus infected seventeen others in the Lanes who were also killed. 'She took typhus-fever, and killed 17 of you! – Very curious,' sneered Carlyle. 'The forlorn Irish widow applies to her fellow-creatures, as if saying, "Behold I am sinking, bare of help; ye must help me!" They answer, "No; impossible: thou art no sister of ours." But she proves her sisterhood; her typhus-fever kills them: they actually were her brothers, though denying it! Had man ever to go lower for a proof?'[48] Again, the terribleness of the tale lay in its depiction of the individualist ethic of city life. The anomie, the isolation of modern urban life, 'each man standing separate from the other, having "no business with him" but a cash-account' – this was the most harmful consequence of a faithless, cash-nexus age.

With personal profit and utility as the guiding force, social relations in the city were in a constant state of hostility. '"Laissez-faire", "Supply-and-Demand", "Cash-payment for the sole nexus", and so forth, were not, are not, and will never be, a practicable Law of Union for a Society of Men.' Carlyle depicted an urban nation in a Hobbesian state of war of all against all. There was truly, as Margaret Thatcher once memorably remarked, no such thing as society. 'We call it a Society; and go about professing openly the totalest separation, isolation. Our life is not a mutual helpfulness; but rather, cloaked under due laws-of-war, named "fair competition" and so forth, it is a mutual hostility. We have profoundly forgotten everywhere that *Cash-payment* is not the sole relation of human beings.'[49]

iv BENTHAMITE UTOPIAS

This, then, was Carlyle's charge. Utilitarianism had supplanted the place of religious faith, exchanged social bonds for the cash-nexus and fermented a state of affairs approaching civil war. Bentham and the materialist philosophies of the eighteenth century were to blame for all the ills embodied in the very fabric of the industrial city: the growing divisions between rich and poor, the amorality of the labouring classes, and the poverty and decay. In the years that followed, Carlyle's pinpointing of utilitarianism as the cause of social decay in the city grew into something of a consensus. 'Utilitarianism' slowly morphed into a shorthand for *laissez-faire* politics, personal greed and naked individualism.

Kenelm Digby, the conservative Catholic author, identified utility and Enlightenment philosophy as the curse of the age. In *The Broad Stone of Honour* (1829), he rounded on those men who 'make a separation between the heart and the head', and who 'teach as an axiom in philosophy, that self-love and self-interest are the operative principle of the soul'.[50] James Phillips Kay was not above looking for the psychological roots of Manchester's misery. With gentle Christian reproach, he argued that the 'social body cannot be constructed like a machine, on abstract principles which merely include physical motions, and their numerical results in the production of wealth'.[51] William Cooke Taylor was equally antagonistic towards the ideology of Bentham and Locke. 'Away with that material philosophy', he opined, 'which looks upon man as a mere machine, compounded of thews and sinews.'[52] In Disraeli's *Coningsby, or The New Generation* (1844), the mysterious Sidonia character mournfully explains to the novel's eponymous hero how 'since the peace ... there has been an attempt to reconstruct society on a basis of material motives and calculations'.[53]

But utilitarianism now seemed written into the constitution of the Victorian city, for in 1835, the English local government system, that corrupt mosaic of manorial, parochial, township and borough institutions, was at last reformed. Beginning with the reign of Henry VI, the majority of England's substantial towns had been operated as closed corporations run by so-called 'freemen' in the private interests of the corporation rather than the public interest of the community. The corporations segregated the community between the corporators and the disenfranchised ratepayers who, whilst they counted as citizens or burgesses, enjoyed no political authority. Undemocratic, unaccountable and wholly self-serving, the corporations were uniformly slanted towards the old guard of Tories and Anglicans and wholly unprepared to come to terms with the political requirements of industrialising cities. Instead, they continued just to look after themselves. 'The most active spring of election-bribery and villainy everywhere', *The Times* declared, 'is known to be the Corporation System. The members of Corporations through out England are, for the most part, self-elected and wholly irresponsible... They have used for base purposes the patronage which they usurped, and confiscated to their own benefit the funds of which they were lawfully but trustees.'[54]

In an attempt both to clean out the corruption and establish a stronger Whig presence in the cities, Lord John Russell introduced the Municipal Corporation Bill, creating a uniform civic government for 178 boroughs (but excluding Manchester, Birmingham and Sheffield, none of which was governed by corporations). The private corporations were replaced by public town councils and a recognisably modern system of local government began to take shape. The franchise was opened up beyond the corporation and citizenship extended to the ratepayer community at large. There were annual elections for one-third of councillors, a public audit of accounts, and some form of linkage of the governing body to the wishes of the residency (albeit on a highly limited franchise) rather than a select group of freemen. Crucially, Nonconformists would also be allowed to hold office.

Lord John Russell presented the Bill to Parliament as a logical addendum to the 1832 Reform Act; a simple extension of the reforming principle from national to local politics. Yet critics saw the changes as something altogether more nefarious. Conservatives rightly detected a plan for a liberal takeover of local government, but just as worryingly a surreptitious introduction of utilitarian ideas into municipal life. The corporations were precisely the type of ancient institution which Jeremy Bentham and Adam Smith, who regarded the unelected bodies as part of an arbitrary state apparatus curtailing political and economic liberty, believed needed radical reform. The 'Utilitarian social philosophers', as they were later called by Sidney and Beatrice Webb in their monumental study of English local government, set out to discredit 'local custom and common law'. Their ambition 'was to get back to the individual, the common citizen, the undifferentiated man. Parcelled out into equal electoral districts so that each man should count as one, and for no more than any other man, this mass of identical citizens were to elect their representatives and thereby control their agents, in the dispensable work of government.'[55]

To the Bill's critics, the elevation of the 'undifferentiated man' signalled an assault on the existing bonds of society, pushing England's towns and cities down the road towards utilitarianism and Carlyle's cash-nexus. By introducing democratic representation, the reformers were replacing corporate harmony with atomistic individualism. Rather than seeking the interests of his trade, guild or corporation, the enfranchised ratepayer would now look solely to his own personal benefit.

Blackwood's Magazine led the attack in an article radiating Burkean conservatism: 'The principle on which the ancient burgh government of every European monarchy was founded, was the representation of society by its classes.' The town council came to be the representative of the burgesses, not individually, but by their professions and vocations. 'The only firm and lasting conglomerations of mankind are those which are formed by community of interest or occupation; all other bonds of union are ephemeral in their endurance'.[56] The basis for representation had to be property rather than numbers. Democracy held no ability to unify society and instead stoked up the twin evils of demagoguery and party politics. Similarly, by abolishing the rights of apprentices, the Bill would harm precisely the kind of traditional guild bonds that thickened society. Sir Matthew White Ridley, MP, during the Committee Stage of the Bill, set out the harm which would be inflicted by annulling apprenticeship privileges. 'The master has no tie over the apprentice ... All the ties of civil society which hitherto held these classes together for their mutual benefit, would be torn asunder. All would be confusion and disorder.'[57]

Despite the opposition, the Bill was passed: utilitarianism and individualism were constituted as the statutory governing ethic of industrial society. Even those cities which lacked a corporation were still deemed symbols of utilitarian callousness. By the late 1830s Bentham and his utilitarian disciples were widely cast as whipping boys for all the moral and social defects of the age. John Stuart Mill, despite being the son of the leading utilitarian thinker James Mill, wrote of the 'cold, mechanical and ungenial air which characterizes the popular idea of a Benthamite'.[58] Due in large part to Carlyle's polemics, the utilitarians were comprehensively blamed as the 'guilty men' of the early Victorian city. In Disraeli's *Sybil*, the radical Stephen Morley roundly condemns the 'great cities' where 'men are brought together by the desire of gain'. 'They are not in a state of co-operation, but of isolation, as to making of fortunes; and for all the rest they are careless of neighbours.'[59] The French critic Leon Faucher best summed up the

prevailing view of the manufacturing city. In 1844 he described
Manchester as 'the Utopia of Bentham'. 'Everything is measured in its results by the standard of utility; and if the Beautiful,
the Great, and the Noble, ever take root in Manchester, they
will be developed in accordance with this standard.'[60]

v Facts and Fiction

Charles Dickens was a late arrival to Carlyle's circle. The two
men were brought together by Dickens's journalist friend John
Forster, who was himself a favourite of Jane Carlyle's. Dickens
and Carlyle became good acquaintances if not firm friends.
Mindful of his father's scorn for popular fiction, Carlyle was
contemptuous of Dickens's soppy sentimentalism. He thought
the autobiographical *David Copperfield* the 'innocent water-
iest of twaddle with a suspicion of geniality, – very fit for the
purpose in view', and scorned *Bleak House* as a 'new dud of a
Book'.[61] Carlyle enjoyed *A Tale of Two Cities* slightly more as
Dickens had consulted him extensively, describing his own
history of the French Revolution as a 'wonderful book' in the
preface. Yet Carlyle held Dickens the man in more affection.
He was a regular attendee at his many lectures and, rare
amongst his literary contemporaries, supported Dickens
during the messy separation from his wife.

Dickens on the other hand was an unabashed fan. In later
life he told one of his sons that Carlyle was the man 'who had
influenced him most'.[62] He read *Chartism, Past and Present,
The French Revolution* and pretty much everything that followed. Dickens embraced Carlyle's analysis of industrial
society and the danger of spiritual collapse in a materialist
world. But it was Carlyle's belief that the principle of utility
was responsible for the social disintegration of the industrial
city that really gripped Dickens. And it was that insight which
inspired the creation of Coketown. Indeed, Dickens informed
his great sage that *Hard Times* 'contains nothing in which you
do not think with me, for no man knows your books better
than I'.[63]

Hard Times is one of the few literary moments when Dickens leaves London. His most famous writing on city life centres around the capital: the opening of *Bleak House*, with fog creeping through the Inns; the shattering of Camden Town through railway construction in *Dombey and Son*; the dock-lands world of *Our Mutual Friend*; as well as the descriptions of the infamous gin shops of St Giles in *Sketches by Boz*. Nonetheless, Coketown manages to encapsulate, in a way only Dickens could, the full grisly horror of the industrial city; the horror of everything de Tocqueville, Engels, Faucher, Chadwick and Carlyle struggled to codify. The city is modelled most obviously on Preston, which Dickens visited during the cotton industry lock-outs and strikes of 1852–3. In a letter to John Forster, he described Preston as 'a nasty place ... there is very little in the streets to make the town remarkable'.[64] Yet ultimately, Coketown is a generic construct. In his travels as a journalist for *Household Words*, Dickens had visited Birmingham, Manchester and numerous other industrial cities. Coketown stands as a compendium of urban squalor. The town encompassed all the shock elements of the industrial city.

The first description of Coketown – 'It was a town of red brick, or of brick which would have been red if the smoke and ashes had allowed it; but as matters stood it was a town of unnatural red and black like the painted face of a savage' – is immediately reminiscent of Engels's account of looking onto Manchester's river Irk. The streams were polluted; the sky hidden by smoke (as London was by fog in *Bleak House*); the people buckled by work. Indeed, as Engels saw the process of dehumanisation inherent in the manufacturing process, Dickens describes the mill-workers as '"the Hands" – a race who would have found more favour with some people, if Providence had seen fit to make them only hands, or, like the lower creatures of the seashore, only hands and stomachs'. In his lectures on the Industrial Revolution, Toynbee would re-employ this language of 'the hands'. However, as his hostile depiction of trade unionism indicated, Dickens was only vaguely interested in the class component of industrial society. Rather, it was Carlyle's castigation of the principle of utility which underpinned the work.

Coketown was such an awful, unnatural environment not primarily because of the physical pollution but because of its spirit. It was the embodiment of Carlyle's age of machinery; utility stalked the city. Unusually for him, Dickens had great trouble coming up with the title for the book. Amongst the twelve possible options, he toyed with 'The Grindstone', 'Prove It!' and 'A Matter of Calculation' – all hinting at the utilitarian satire which forms the work's polemical core. 'Now, what I want is, Facts', the book begins. 'Teach these boys and girls nothing but Facts. Facts alone are wanted in life.' There was no room for the individual character or emotional development in the Coketown schema. All that was needed was the basics, as reflected in the style of repetitive, barebones language repeated throughout the book.[65]

To great comic effect, in the character of Gradgrind, the headmaster of the city's McChoakumchild School (the successor to Wackford Squeers's 'DoTheBoys Hall' in *Nicholas Nickleby*), Dickens incorporated all the cold, mechanical and ungenial air of a Benthamite. Dickens's specific target was not actually Jeremy Bentham, but an academic called John Ramsay McCulloch, Professor of Political Economy at the utilitarian-inspired University of London and a militant enthusiast for political economy and the principle of utility. In Gradgrind, Dickens delivered his revenge with a mechanistic caricature who even lived in a utilitarian house. 'A calculated, cast up, balanced, and proved house. Six windows on this side of the door, six on that side.' The necessity for rules extended itself even to the garden. 'A lawn and a garden and an infant avenue, all ruled straight like a botanical account book.'

Coketown's entire civic architecture was designed according to the principle of utility. 'Fact, fact, fact, everywhere in the material aspect of the town; fact, fact, fact, everywhere in the immaterial.' There was no religion, no soul in Coketown. On Sundays the chapels and churches stood empty as 'the Hands' lounged listlessly on the street. What governed relations in the town was the callous cash-nexus. Beyond that no obligations existed. There was no sentiment between man and man. The Gradgrind philosophy was to abolish gratitude, 'and the virtues springing from it were not to be'. 'Every inch of the existence of mankind, from birth to death, was to be a bargain across a counter.'

This was the true pollution of Coketown. Utilitarianism destroyed any sense of emotion or spontaneity. Coketown was an ugly citadel, 'where Nature was as strongly bricked out as killing airs and gases were bricked in'. It produced the unnaturalness (a word which permeates the entire book) of family relations, the absence of the most basic affections, which haunted the Bounderbys and Gradgrinds. When Mr Gradgrind hears of the death of his wife, he briefly interrupts his new duties as a Member of Parliament and then 'buried her in a business-like manner' before quickly returning to work. The collapse of humanity and the chasm between fellow men in Coketown was what cut short the life of the book's pathetic anti-hero, Stephen Blackpool. He was a man isolated and rejected, both by employers and his fellow workers. Caught between the bosses and the trade unions, both products of the cash-nexus ethos, Blackpool was torn apart by the utility of Coketown.

Through his mastery of plot and characterisation, Dickens irrevocably chained the philosophy of utilitarianism to the image of the industrial city. For Gradgrind read Bentham; for Coketown read Manchester. It too was a Benthamite Utopia. And to this day, historians and commentators have accepted the industrial city as a product of utilitarianism. A contributor to Dyos and Wolff's seminal collection, *The Victorian City* (1973), explained how utilitarianism was 'a system of attitudes and values' which affirmed the urban way of life; it 'provided the outline of a philosophy for urban man'. Lewis Mumford, in his chapter on the nineteenth-century city, was adamant that, 'The new conception of human destiny, as the utilitarians projected it, had little place for even sensual delights: it rested on a doctrine of productive exertion, consumptive avarice, and physiological denial.'[66] More recently, the urban historian Sir Peter Hall has described the 'workhouses and model penitentiaries of Victorian London' as 'the built expression of Benthamite utilitarianism'.[67] And only once the Victorian city shed its Benthamite mindset could it mature into a civilised public arena.[68]

The physical grime and soot, if not the philosophical pollution, of Coketown still configures our imagination of the Victorian city. But despite this dominant impression, there thankfully existed far more to nineteenth-century civic identity than class conflict, the cash-nexus, and utility. Before Charles Dickens had even started work on *Hard Times*, an influential body of opinion was already suggesting that a better model of urban living than the anomie and industry of the early Victorian city could be realised. And they looked not to the bleak industrial vista of *Hard Times*, but to an anti-urban utopia: the beguiling lochs, lakes and legends of Sir Walter Scott's *Ivanhoe*.

[3]
PUGIN *VERSUS* THE PANOPTICON

Over three hours late, after endless false starts, the Queen of Beauty at last appeared. Jane Georgina, Lady Seymour, wife of Baron Seymour, the heir to the Duke of Somerset, looked ravishing. With her raven hair and radiant smile shining through draping jewels and a heavily embroidered dress, she seemed the quintessence of Pre-Raphaelite womanhood. One mile from the castle where she stood, the Lists lay ready for the greatest display of chivalry promised since the Middle Ages. A fifty-foot grandstand overlooked a lazy summer meadow where thirteen nobles were soon to display their knightly prowess. Through its centre ran a three-hundred-foot barrier along which each knight would charge – aiming carefully only for his opponent's shield (to avoid the risk of manslaughter charges). By three o'clock in the afternoon one hundred thousand visitors were waiting for the games to begin.

For over a year now, the 13th Earl of Eglinton had been planning this lavish medieval tournament. Affronted by the lack of courtly pomp in Queen Victoria's minimalist 1837 coronation, he had been persuaded by like-minded aristocrats to turn his annual race meeting at Eglinton Park into a day of medieval games and feasting. On 28 August 1839, tens of thousands of invited VIP guests and members of the general public lucky enough to secure tickets gathered together in the glorious parkland of Eglinton's Ayrshire retreat. Society figures had journeyed up by railway from London the previous day, catching the 8.45 a.m. from Euston to Liverpool, and then taking the steamer to Ardrossan on the Scottish west coast to arrive for breakfast. It was then another quick train ride to the village of Irvine, outside which stood Eglinton's mock-Gothic castle complete with turrets, battlements and a moat. Every inn and cottage from coast to castle was booked in anticipation of the country's most talked-about tournament. With representatives from all the major daily and evening papers, the event was sure to enjoy favourable coverage. And, thankfully, it was a clear, sunny day with views straight across the Irish Sea to the Isle of Arran.

Benjamin Disraeli, though not himself at Eglinton, cobbled together an account of the castle scene from contemporary newspaper reports for his novel *Endymion*:

> The grounds round the castle seemed to be filled every day with groups of busy persons in fanciful costume, all practising their duties and rehearsing their parts; swordsmen and bowmen, and seneschals and esquires, and grooms and pages, and heralds in tabards, and pursuivants, and banner-bearers. The splendid pavilions of the knights were now completed, and the gorgeous throne of the Queen of Beauty, surrounded by crimson galleries, tier above tier, for thousands of favoured guests, were receiving only their last stroke of magnificence.[1]

At midday, when the procession from the castle to the Lists was scheduled to begin, the nineteenth-century knights were still trying to mount their charges. 'The Dragon', 'The Burning Tower', 'The Swan', 'The Griffin' and nine other combatants had hopelessly underestimated the time needed for a medieval nobleman to ready himself for the tilt. Lord Eglinton himself had trouble fitting into his specially designed, *haute couture* gold suit of armour and it was a good three hours before they were at last ready to leave the castle. So, finally, Lady Seymour was summoned as the Queen of Beauty to lead the procession of archers, heralds, knights and pages down to the Lists. But as she stepped onto the castle porch and approached her horse, the sky darkened. There was a rumble of thunder, a fork of lightning and then torrential, unbridled rain. The Gulf Stream, which can make the west coast of Scotland so unseasonably warm, had turned nasty and deposited across Irvine a monstrous tropical downpour.

Eglinton valiantly struggled on, leading the sodden train down to the joust. But as the invited guests ascended the specially constructed grandstand, it collapsed beneath them. The royal box was flooded and the Queen of Beauty, the *belle* of the tournament, scampered back to the castle. The herald's attempt to read the terms of combat was suffocated amidst the crashing storm. No challenge was presented, no glove thrown down, and no one had the slightest clue as to the rules of engagement. With rain lashing through their visors and with the Lists sodden, the knights haplessly thundered past each other. And the crowd – at first bored, then angry and wet, and now just amused at the bizarre spectacle – began to laugh. The spell was broken and the games, first imagined as a source of pride and valour, suddenly appeared ridiculous. The mortified Eglinton abandoned the tournament and apologised to the spectators. It was a fiasco, and at £40,000 a painfully expensive one. Years later, the earl recorded the events in his personal diary. 'I gave a tournament at Eglinton', he wrote with disingenuous understatement of 1839.[2]

For years to come the Eglinton tournament was ridiculed as the depth of Victorian folly – the *reductio ad absurdum* of the medieval craze sweeping the country. However, the debacle addresses one of the more intriguing ironies of the early Victorian age: that a society so hungry for progress and modernity was at the same time suffused in medievalism; that a culture of innovation – pioneering extraordinary advances in factory mechanisation, railways, engineering, geographical exploration, psychology, chemistry – prospered within a broader culture of rampant, even aggressive historicism. Extraordinarily, even the Great Exhibition of 1851, a showcase for Britain's industrial and scientific pre-eminence, gave pride of place within its Crystal Palace to a medieval court dripping with Gothic arts and crafts. And when Victoria and Albert were honoured with equestrian statues in the commercial fulcrum of Glasgow's George Square, they were cast by Carlo Marochetti in a decidedly medieval motif.

Nowhere was this tension between strident modernity and historical enthusiasm more evident than in the Victorian city. The booming, industrialising cities were symbols of all that was modern in nineteenth-century Britain: pollution, factories, immigration and the ungenial philosophy of utilitarianism. Yet as the century progressed they became festooned with paeans to the past. Medieval architecture and design dominated the urban skyline. Bradford City Hall; Halifax Town Hall; Glasgow University – these dark Gothic edifices were the symbols of the Victorian city. And the paradox was writ even larger amongst the cities' expanding railway stations. 'Railway termini and hotels are to the nineteenth century what monasteries and cathedrals were to the thirteenth century. They are truly the only real representative buildings we have,' suggested one Victorian architectural journal. But in Bristol, Middlesbrough and at London's St Pancras, the railway stations could easily have been mistaken for cathedrals or monasteries. The 'iron horse', the *agent provocateur* of industrial progress, typically terminated among Gothic spires and vaulted roofs more reminiscent of the fourteenth than the nineteenth century.[3]

This chapter charts the medieval response to the urban world of nineteenth-century Britain: how Victorian architects, designers and civic leaders sought to create a better city than Dickens's 'Coketown'; to build new Jerusalems from the dark Satanic mills in order to show that faith and community did not, as Carlyle had prophesied, need to absolve themselves from urban life. In doing so, they turned the Victorian city into a battleground between competing civic visions. It was a struggle between the utility and class divisions of Coketown and the hope for a more inclusive urban community. In architectural shorthand, it emerged into a struggle between the class war of the factory or the co-operative community of the monastery; the workhouse or the hospital; the Panopticon penitentiary or A.W.N. Pugin's world of Catholic co-operation and social harmony. Aesthetically, the medievalists triumphed. And in doing so, they built a legacy we still see today in the spires of our Gothic churches and the brooding medievalism of our railway stations, town halls and Houses of Parliament.

i THE AGE OF CHIVALRY

Victorian medievalism was a massive cultural movement embracing fashion, architecture, politics, literature and religion. No sooner had Edmund Burke declared the age of chivalry dead, than it resurfaced with unbounded gusto. It was *the* dominant cultural motif of the early Victorian period. Charles Dickens, wonderfully, summed up the facile preoccupation with a past few understood but all acknowledged to be the greatest, most heroic age. '"Don't you dote upon the Middle Ages, Mr Carker?"', Mrs Skewton inquired during a trip around Warwick Castle in *Dombey and Son*. '"Such charming times! ... So full of faith! So vigorous and forcible! So perfectly removed from the commonplace! If they would only leave us a little more of the poetry of existence in these terrible days!"'[4] Benjamin Disraeli's Lady Everingham expressed similar enthusiasm during a trip around a battle-scarred feudal manor in *Coningsby*, '"I always fancy a siege must be so very interesting," said Lady Everingham. "It must be so exciting."'[5]

The medieval passion emerged in the late eighteenth century as an aesthetic and then literary phenomenon as the traditionally negative connotations of Gothick – of Continental superstition, tyranny and deceit – were jettisoned in favour of 'Gothic', a romantic sentiment denoting freedom and naturalism. Picturesque Gothic designs in gardening and domestic architecture began to compete with Enlightenment classicism – most notably, Horace Walpole's over-decorated house, Strawberry Hill, in Twickenham. From Painswick House in Gloucestershire to Esher Place to Alfred's Hall in

Cirencester Park, ruins and rococo were soon the order of the day.

As interest in Gothic design expanded, so it was professionalised, though the phrase 'Gothic' was rarely used, with most preferring to employ 'Christian' or 'Pointed' to describe medieval architecture. In 1814, the author and publisher John Britton initiated a series of guides to England's great Gothic cathedrals, *Cathedral Antiquities of England*.[6] In a less ecclesiastical vein, Britton also churned out *Picturesque Views of the English Cities* which celebrated the secular successes of Gothic design. Along with his French émigré draughtsman Augustus Pugin, Britton started to codify stylistic periods, explain Gothic terminology, and list celebrated examples of Christian architecture. In 1827 he brought together his work in *A Chronological History and Graphic Illustrations of Christian Architecture in England* which, with its elegant steel engravings of great national buildings, sold well to a patriotic audience supportive of what was increasingly regarded as England's 'national' style.

Working alongside Britton, the architect Thomas Rickman tried with slightly greater rigour to classify the different stages of Gothic design. In a series of lectures to Liverpool's Literary and Philosophical Society, later brought together as an *Attempt to Discriminate the Styles of Architecture in England, from the Conquest to the Reformation* (1817), he established a four-part chronology of Gothic. The first period, covering the Norman invasion to the end of the twelfth century, he unsurprisingly entitled the 'Norman style'; the second, covering the thirteenth century, was the 'Early English style'; 'Decorated English' for the 1300s; and finally, 'Perpendicular English' ran from the end of the fourteenth century right through to the mid-1500s. Perpendicular Gothic – with its strong vertical lines and elaborate roof vaulting, its flying buttresses and hammerbeam roofs – quickly triumphed as the most popular historical style, as seen to greatest effect in London's Westminster Hall or King's College Chapel in Cambridge. Rickman's classifications codified Victorian discussions of Gothic architecture for the next hundred years. And, as with Britton, what particularly appealed to a general public increasingly attuned to questions of national identity was the contention that, despite its northern European heritage and even the appellation 'Norman', the genre was determinedly and unquestionably English. This view was endorsed by the architect George Gilbert Scott when he later urged his fellow designers to 'adapt a style of art which accidentally was medieval, but is *essentially national*, to the wants and requirements of our own day'. Indeed, it was the Gothic association with the national past which meant that 'above all others [it] is calculated to enlist our love and sympathy'.[7]

While Britton, Rickman and their numerous disciples adeptly nurtured a Gothic heritage, it took the romantic genius of Sir Walter Scott to broaden medievalism into a popular cult. Scott's achievement was to transform Gothicism from an architectural discipline into a cultural and literary phenomenon. Many years later, the Anglican-turned-Catholic divine John Henry Newman described Scott as the man 'who turned men's minds in the direction of the Middle Ages'. By means of his popularity he reacted on his readers, 'stimulating their mental thirst, feeding their hopes, setting before them visions, which, when once seen, are not easily forgotten, and silently indoctrinating them with nobler ideas which might afterwards be appealed to as first principles'.[8]

As John Britton had professionalised the study of Gothic architecture, so Scott rescued the literary past from its Gothick horror-fantasia. Walpole's *The Castle of Otranto* (1764), Ann Radcliffe's *The Mysteries of Udolpho* (1794) and Matthew Lewis's *The Monk* (1796), with their endless churchyards, creepy houses and gruesome deaths, were widely ridiculed by the early nineteenth century and their pulp-fiction horror style superbly satirised in Jane Austen's *Northanger Abbey* and Thomas Love Peacock's *Nightmare Abbey*. Scott got away from all that and, despite his own occasionally slapdash approach to the historical *vérité*, managed to revive the Middle Ages as a living, breathing era worthy not only of study but active appreciation, even emulation. From his Scottish lair at Abbotsford, he conjured up a dream world of paternalism, gallantry, romantic love, unbounded hospitality and individual triumph. His 'merrie England' was a sumptuous landscape of deep lakes, impenetrable forests and towering castles – just the kind of mental vista to engage listless young men uncomfortable with industrial, urban England, such as Lord Eglinton.

Scott's first substantial novel *Waverley* (1814), helped establish his credentials as a historical author. In its wake came *The Heart of Midlothian*, *The Black Dwarf*, and *Old Mortality*; but it was above all *Ivanhoe* (1819) which brought medieval historicism into the cultural mainstream. It had everything: crusades; a damsel in distress; Robin Hood in his forest; Friar Tuck; an evil Norman baron; and, finally, a brilliant tournament at Ashby de la Zouch with fearsome knights battling for the love of the beautiful Rowena. The very model for Eglinton. The book's characters displayed an immediacy and a pathos which previous historical fiction lacked; their language and personal psychology was uniquely accessible to a broad audience. In the fast-moving world of nineteenth-century culture, *Ivanhoe* proved a runaway success and quickly transferred to the theatre with six different interpretations running on the London stage within a year of its publication. Five years later Rossini would take it to the Paris stage as an opera, while numerous pleasure-garden pastiches took advantage of its high drama. At street markets and even inside the Royal Academy, the novel's heroes and scenic backdrops provided schlock artists with a wealth of portrait ideas, romantic vistas and engravings.[9]

Scott's medievalism portrayed an idealised social state, an organic community of mutual interdependence. His scenes of baronial hospitality and communal faith were a swipe at the atomism and irreligion of the industrialising Britain he so abhorred. Yet Scott himself, despite all the medieval flummery which surrounded his own life, was no nostalgic reactionary. Indeed, in *Ivanhoe*, during the trial of the Jewess Rebecca, he specifically condemns the barbarity of the twelfth century as 'ignorant and superstitious times'. Scott was a student of the 'conjectural model of history', a philosophical approach to the past developed by Adam Smith and others which understood history as a series of progressive, irreversible socio-economic stages culminating in the industrialised present. As he wrote in a scholarly essay on chivalry, 'we can now only look back on it, as a beautiful and fantastic piece of frostwork, which has dissolved in the beams of the sun'.[10] But such historical reservations were lost on the wider audience. Deeply disturbed by the terrible events of the French Revolution and the social anarchy of the Industrial Revolution, Scott offered a highly seductive social model which engrossed his tens of thousands of readers. In 1854, the Manchester Statistical Society revealed that while the Manchester Public Library had loaned Macaulay's *History of England* 124 times over the previous year, Scott's novels had been borrowed on 1,141 occasions.

Despite his highly conservative political implications, the book also crossed social boundaries, enjoying a strong readership amongst artisan and even radical audiences. The early Edwardian communist intellectual T.A. Jackson did not dispute that Scott 'was a shocking old Tory, and a reactionary', but thought there was an undercurrent of political subversion: 'He [Scott] thought kings, lords and gentlemen, had "rights" which it was folly and worse to question: but he thought also, they had "duties" which it was scandalous and worse in them to evade. No radical could be more unsparing than he of the mere "aristocrat".' The future Labour Prime Minister Ramsay MacDonald claimed that Scott 'opened out the great world of national life for me and led me on to politics'.[11] Intriguingly, a passion for Walter Scott is also shared by another Labour Prime Minister, Tony Blair, who revealed to one interviewer that *Ivanhoe* was his favourite novel. Whether Mr Blair was more attracted by the work's conservative or radical message remains unclear.

In Scott's wake, medievalism ran rampant. New editions of Malory were rushed out as well as poor Scott imitations, such as Charles Mills's *History of the Crusades* and G.P.R. James's *History of Chivalry*.[12] Scott's persistent evocation of social harmony through the image of a benevolent castle community entranced aristocratic landowners. In Scotland, the new baronial style became *de rigueur*. At Balmoral Castle, on the banks of the Dee, Queen Victoria and Prince Albert recreated Scott's world with a kilt uniform of dubious provenance, a 'Balmorality' of Highland informality and ethical equality between master and servant (extended to quite scandalous degrees in the relationship between the Queen and John Brown), but all within the context of laird authority. Having cleared their lands of crofters, many Scottish nobles now sought an artificial and mostly aesthetic recreation of their abdicated responsibilities.

The medieval revival extended from architecture and literature to affect Britain's religious sensibilities. In reaction to the anarchic irreligion of industrialising society (so graphically recounted by Dickens, Mayhew and John Shaw), the Church of England fell under the spell of a High Church faction which longed for a return to the authority of the pre-Reformation Church. Centred round a group of articulate, young, fogeyish dons and graduates, the 'Oxford Movement' attacked the Enlightenment 'Usurpation of Reason' and argued instead for a return to the powerful, visible Church of the Middle Ages. Not, it must be emphasised, the Roman Catholic Church but the peculiarly English tradition of Anglicanism as it had existed before the Reformation. They issued their demands for a revived age of faith in a series of 'Tracts', so earning themselves the moniker 'Tractarians'.

The Oxford Movement's spiritual leader, the university's Professor of Poetry John Keble, condemned the 'fashionable liberality' of Victorian Britain. For Keble, the combination of Catholic emancipation, the repeal of discriminatory legislation against Nonconformists, the Great Reform Act and widespread anti-clerical agitation was placing the very survival of the Church of England in peril. The *Via Media* tradition of Anglican Catholicity which stretched back to John

Jewel and Thomas Cranmer was being undermined by the forces of Dissent and Popery – all shamefully sanctioned by an increasingly Erastian, secular state. 'Is Apostasy too hard a word to describe the temper of that nation?', asked Keble. Rather than the Dissent and godlessness of the nineteenth century, Keble championed corporate worship and the symbolic power of the Church.

He was joined in his campaign by the divine and Hebrew scholar, the Revd Edward Pusey, and one of the most controversial Tractarians, John Henry Newman. A gifted middle-class boy from the City of London, Newman possessed a ferocious intellectual ability which quickly shone through, first as an undergraduate at Trinity and then as a Fellow of Oriel College. Coming under the influence of Keble and other revanchist Anglicans, Newman started to bemoan the faithless rationalism of contemporary society. Nowhere was this debilitating liberalism more evident than in post-revolutionary France, which Newman visited during a Grand Tour of the Mediterranean.[13] The precious cleric from Oxford was terrified of being contaminated by the country's shameless atheism. 'A French vessel was at Algiers,' he wrote in his autobiography *Apologia Pro Vita Sua*. 'I would not even look at the Tricolour. On my return, though forced to stop twenty four hours at Paris, I kept indoors the whole time.'[14] The perils of France! The Tractarians took as their model the strong national Church that had prospered under Charles I's Archbishop Laud. The Laudian Church of England had enjoyed both a cohesive role within the community, bringing together everyone under one roof (on pain of prosecution), and a High Church, conservative liturgy. The fact that Laud's policies also brought about civil war was conveniently glided over.

The power of the Church of England had certainly diminished since the 1630s and two hundred years on looked in a relatively parlous state. One of the most serious threats it faced was the growth of Dissenting sects. Between 1800 and 1830 Methodist membership rose by over two hundred per cent, followed closely by the fast-expanding Baptists and

Congregationalists. Within the newly industrialising cities, Nonconformist chapels were taking souls across the social classes. In Liverpool in 1851, Protestant Dissenters constituted 18.3 per cent of the worshipping community; in Manchester the figure was 29.2 per cent; in Birmingham, 34.6 per cent; and in Bradford an extraordinary 45.5 per cent of worshippers stood outside the Anglican Church.[15] Yet the Church of England also faced a worrying shortfall in the physical number of places available for worship. In Liverpool, it was reported that of 95,000 inhabitants the church could only seat 21,000. In Manchester the deficiency was reported to be 68,500. London, Chester and Birmingham were similarly under-resourced. The rural migrants pouring into the industrialising cities could not be accommodated and their souls were quickly lost by the established Church. Such inadequacy comprised not only a spiritual vacuum but also, amidst the turbulence of the Napoleonic wars, a potential threat to the political order. Men not reared in the ethic of the Anglican Church could easily become atheists and then, inevitably, radicals.

The solution pursued by the political and clerical establishment was first to promote Sunday Schools and then to invest heavily in new churches. The early nineteenth century saw a highly aggressive programme of Sunday School enrolment and by 1850 two million, mostly working-class, children were being taught in Sunday School. In 1830s Birmingham some forty per cent of working-class kids were in class. To reclaim the godless streets of the expanding cities, new churches were desperately needed and in 1818 the Church Building Act allocated £1 million (and in 1824 a further £500,000) to flood the urban centres with Anglican churches. In the words of the Speaker of the House of Commons, there was a need to address the deficiency 'which has so long existed, in the number of places of public worship belonging to the established church, when compared with the increased and increasing population of the country'.[16] Between 1835 and 1875 almost four thousand new or rebuilt Anglican churches were consecrated, with the number of churches in Birmingham more than tripling during the first half of the century. In London the battle for souls was energetically led by the Bishop of London, the redoubtable Bishop Blomfield, who sanctioned the building of ten new churches within the particularly godless East End parishes of Bethnal Green and Bow. But despite the vast sums underpinning the Anglican offensive, Nonconformist faiths managed to keep pace with the established Church. In the manufacturing districts of Yorkshire, Lancashire and Cheshire, chapel sittings increased by a monumental 357 per cent between 1800 and 1843.[17]

Simply putting up new churches, so-called 'preaching-boxes', was not enough for the Tractarians. They agitated for a wholesale revival of national faith. They urged not only the construction of Gothic churches, but the recreation of the culture that surrounded the original edifices. In his book *The Christian Year*, Keble advocated the revival of the festivals, fasts and services which constituted pre-industrial society. By charting the cycle of religious celebrations through the year, Keble aimed to restore the lost popular culture of public worship and the spiritual rhythms which accompanied it. Newman too wanted a more cohesive public faith and celebrated the Church, its order and sacraments as the 'keys and spells' by which, through the providence of God, men could be brought into the presence of His saints. He despaired at what might happen to the devotion of the people, 'if we strip religion of its external symbols, and bid them seek out and gaze upon the Invisible?' Many years later, the future Cardinal Newman would realise the personal logic of his spiritual journey, his belief in the function of the clergy and the role of the visible Church, in the bosom of Rome.

Newman's conversion to Catholicism was one of thousands. After decades in the shadows – or more accurately, the shadows of obscure country houses – Catholicism was re-emerging into mainstream British society. Between 1830 and 1850, the period Newman optimistically christened a 'Second Spring', the number of Catholics rose from a quarter of a million to over

700,000. The French Revolution, with its military assault on the Catholic hierarchy, had sparked genuine and widespread sympathy for the traditional religious enemy. The systematic persecution of priests and the destruction of Church property during the Great Terror had shocked even the most resolute anti-Catholic. Meanwhile, the influx of Catholic immigrants and priests gave the old English Catholic tradition a shot in the arm. Religious quietism was no longer an option. In the cities, most especially Liverpool, Manchester and Glasgow, there was also the growing presence of Irish immigrants, who accounted for most of the increase in Catholic numbers. Although the 1829 Catholic Emancipation Act provoked a predictably hostile reaction, by the 1830s the Catholic Church appeared a far more confident, outward-looking body. And with the revival of enthusiasm for Catholicism came a renewed interest in the Catholic Church's cohesive role in society.

This Christian-Catholic revival was as much a European as a British phenomenon. In France, the Catholic polemicist Chateaubriand championed the superiority of Christianity in *Le Génie du Christianisme*. Christianity not only displayed a superior grandeur and beauty in placing mysteries like the Trinity at the centre of its doctrine; it also had superior ethical clout, when its teaching power was compared with different religions.[18] Chateaubriand smugly listed the poetic, aesthetic and literary landmarks of the Catholic faith including such jewels as the Bible, Dante's *Divine Comedy*, Racine's tragedies, and Church ceremonial. But, above all, it was in Gothic architecture that the Christian spirit triumphed. He described his patriotic fervour on entering a Gothic cathedral. For Chateaubriand, 'l'ancienne France semblait revivre'. Gothic, it seems, was a peculiarly promiscuous 'national' style.

In Germany, the passion for medievalism took on a more political than religious tinge. In the early 1800s, inspired by the turbulent *Sturm und Drang* romance of Goethe and Herder, a group of intellectuals and artists developed a coherent critique of modern society. This movement of German Romantics – men such as Schlegel and Novalis – criticised the soulless

philistinism, the isolation and anomie of the modern, bureaucratic world. Instead, like Scott, they looked back longingly
to the faith, compassion and vision of the Middle Ages. But
whereas Scott celebrated individual leadership and the triumphant Romantic hero, the German Romantics revered the
institutions of the medieval past. In contrast to the individualism of the 1800s, they wanted a return to the guilds,
councils and corporations which cemented pre-industrial
society, those myriad secondary political institutions which
held society together – precisely the kind of structures which
critics of the 1835 Municipal Corporations Act thought were
being undermined. Above all, like Chateaubriand and the
Oxford Movement, the German Romantics argued for a return
of the social and political authority of the Church as a unifying
agent in the community. Famously, Novalis stood in wonder
at the symbolic majesty of Cologne Cathedral. The liberalism
of the post-French-Revolution world had produced only the
rootless individualism of the industrial city. What were needed
were the popular institutions of the Middle Ages, the inter-
mediate groups between government and the people, to bring
society back together.

In Britain the ideas of the German Romantics were initially
the elite provenance of Coleridge and the Lake Poets. But
thanks to Thomas Carlyle, they quickly assumed a far larger
audience. Starting with his earliest essay on Jean Paul, month
after month through his journalism and books, Carlyle popularised their thought. And with their harsh criticisms of industrialising society, Romantic ideas found an increasingly
receptive audience. In a talk on 'The Genius and Work of
Thomas Carlyle' to the Manchester Athenaeum in January
1846, the Birmingham-based lecturer and Nonconformist
preacher George Dawson rejoiced in the new popularity of
German culture. 'Our thoughts are becoming impregnated
with its spirit. We are getting German in our phraseology; we
begin to take their authors for our guide.'[19] This German
'spirit' and its corporatist ethic was set to change the very
fabric of the Victorian city.

ii THE MEDIEVAL MANIFESTO

Medievalism was developing into a coherent socio-political programme. The literary, aesthetic and religious tributaries flowed into a political movement demanding credible reforms. For what differentiated the early Victorian medievalists from many of their romantic successors, such as William Morris, was a clear political conviction that it *was* possible to return to the past.[20] There was still a sense that the noble world depicted by Scott, Newman and the Romantics was not irretrievably lost; it offered an eminently achievable, practical ethic for the Victorian world which could be reclaimed. The historian Alice Chandler has summed up that ethic as a 'Dream of Order' – a socially conservative yearning for stability, hierarchy and religious conformity.[21]

One of the first to argue for a policy of medievalism was the utilitarian-baiting Kenelm Digby, a Cambridge graduate who never left the town, opting to greet each day with a bone-shuddering plunge into the river Cam. Often dismissed by historians as little better than a crank, Digby was in fact a widely read figure whose work was studied by Carlyle, William Morris, Benjamin Disraeli and John Ruskin. His unashamed enthusiasm for the Middle Ages made him an easy target for Thomas Love Peacock to satirise as 'Mr Chainmail' in *Crotchet Castle*. 'He is deep in monkish literature, and holds that the best state of society was that of the twelfth century, when nothing was going forward but fighting, feasting, and praying, which he says are the three great purposes for which man was made.'[22]

Digby's grand opus on the ethic of chivalry, *The Broad Stone of Honour: or, The True Sense and Practice of Chivalry*, was a great success, hurtling through four reprints by 1829. It constituted an out-and-out attack on utilitarianism and a defence of the timeless value of chivalry – which he regarded as a permanently valid social code, rather than a purely medieval phenomenon. Chivalry was not something to enjoy for a day at an Eglinton tournament. It was an ethical guide to everyday life and a coherent programme of political action. At its core was faith, and in particular the faith of the holy and apostolic Catholic Church. Echoing Chateaubriand, Digby wondered at the aesthetic triumphs of Catholicism, most notably Ambrogio Lorenzetti's *Allegories of Good and Bad Government* in the Siena Palazzo Pubblico, as well as the works of Raphael and the architecture of Sansovino. For Digby, such genius proved the Catholic Church was 'the bond and the principle of civilization'.[23]

The Poet Laureate Robert Southey, who had so eloquently condemned the industrial city, was an equally keen partisan of the medieval past. In his most articulate commentary, *Sir Thomas More: or, Colloquies on the Progress and Prospects of Society* (1829), the melodramatic Southey stands alone in his library when he receives a saintly visitation from the ghost of the late Lord Chancellor, Sir Thomas More. More, the author of *Utopia*, and more importantly the man who stood up to Henry VIII and his state-sanctioned Reformation, laments all that has passed since his execution. The modern, liberal freedom of city living is to be particularly regretted: 'the independence which has been gained since the total decay of the feudal system, has been dearly purchased by the loss of kindly feelings and ennobling attachments'.[24] In his day, every person had his place. 'There was a system of superintendence everywhere, civil as well as religious.'[25] And in a telling phrase for the looming Gothic Revival, Sir Thomas asks, 'The spirit which built and endowed monasteries is gone. Are you one of those persons who think it has been superseded for the better by that which erects steam-engines and cotton-mills?'[26] In contrast to the glories of Gothicism, the age of steam-engines and cotton mills was a sorry period to live in. What, Sir Thomas later enquires, is to be 'the more melancholy object of contemplation ... the manufactory or the convent?'[27]

Thomas Carlyle developed a similar literary tactic in *Past and Present*, which contrasted the structured, holy world of monastic life in medieval Bury St Edmunds with the fractured atheism of the nineteenth-century workhouse. In the Middle Ages, men understood their connection to each other and involvement within society. 'That any man should or can keep himself apart from men, have "no business" with them, except a cash-account "business"! It is the silliest tale a distressed generation of men ever took to telling one another.' Within the monastery, all appreciated their interconnectedness – even down to the lowliest slave, Gurth. 'Gurth had the inexpressible satisfaction of feeling himself related indissolubly, though in a rude brass-collar way, to his fellow-mortals in this Earth. He had superiors, inferiors, equals.'[28] The liberal notion of freedom could only promise Gurth, as for so many modern factory workers or city dwellers, the liberty to die by starvation in the street unknown and uncared for. The authoritarian Carlyle was convinced the new industrial society did not need greater freedoms, but strong leadership by men as powerful and far-sighted as the monastic leaders of old. Unlike previous ages, the manufacturing era had yet to enjoy the benevolent discipline of authoritarian, social leadership.

The politics of medieval leadership were more successfully taken up by the party of 'Young England' Conservatives. The movement was originally inspired by the aristocrat George Smythe, an incurable romantic who advocated the revival of 'touching' the monarchy as a way of curing scrofula; fought the last duel on English soil in 1852; and was taken early by tuberculosis, marrying an heiress on his deathbed.[29] Together with Lord John Manners, Alexander Baillie-Cochrane and then Benjamin Disraeli, he championed a lost world of feudal benevolence and social solidarity. The programme was simple: the modern industrial elites needed to show as much care for their employees as the old landed aristocracy had for their feudal charges. Indeed, Lord John Manners, heir to the duchy of Rutland and the great Belvoir Castle, thought that the industrial system provided a perfect opportunity for the exercise of such paternalism. 'There was never so complete a feudal system as that of the mills; soul and body are or might be at the absolute disposal of one man, and that to my mind is not at all a bad state of society.'[30] The mill economy provided the perfect opportunity for benevolent social superintendence: the poor could be studiously cared for within the factory rather than left to the bureaucratic whip of the state with its workhouses and Poor Law. The two nations of rich and poor needed to be brought together in a spirit of mutual harmony led by a socially responsible aristocracy. In the House of Commons, the 'Young England' faction opposed Robert Peel and his *laissez-faire* repeal of the Corn Laws. Free trade and legislative let alone would never, they argued, produce a more cohesive society or alleviate the economic conditions of the poorest.

In the country at large, 'Young England' argued for a revival of vertical personal relationships and mutual obligation – in essence, a more proactive role for the landed gentry and the Church. Lord John Manners's pamphlet, 'A Plea for National Holy-Days', echoed the Tractarians in its support for the social purpose of the Church and the natural rhythms of a feudal, Christian existence. His programme of social reforms would also make people far happier than the soulless utilitarianism of the modern city.

> It has of late years been made frequently a source of com-plaint that the English people, who of yore were famous over all Europe for their love of manly sports and their sturdy good humour, have year after year been losing that cheerful character, and, contrariwise, been acquiring habits and thoughts of discontent and moroseness. Nor is this melancholy change, in my opinion, to be wondered at, for although it is true that, in towns, debating clubs, and reading-rooms, and halls of science, and gin-shops have sprung up with a mushroom speed of growth; it is also true we have well-nigh altogether lost sight of those wholesome recreations and cheering influences which formerly obtained among the people, and to which, I firmly believe, those joyous and graceful national characteristics were mainly owing.[31]

It was not enough to offer 'a course of astronomy' or 'a lecture on geology'; Englishmen needed games, maypoles and godly recreation overseen by the national Church. This was even more the case amongst the poor drudges of the factory floor.

The ceaseless literary energies of Benjamin Disraeli catapulted 'Young England' out of the House of Commons and into the public realm. In *Coningsby, or The New Generation* and *Sybil, or the Two Nations* Disraeli savaged the liberal utility of modern conservatism and pushed for the return of the lost ordered world of pre-Reformation England. In *Coningsby*, the future Prime Minister dreamily conjured up the Young England social ideal in the form of Eustace Lyle's St Genevieve manor. Lyle, a Roman Catholic of 'an old Cavalier family' (whose character was modelled on the Catholic nobles Lord Shrewsbury and Ambrose Phillipps de Lisle), had 'revived the monastic customs' by reintroducing almsgiving on his estate. While the utilitarian Lord Everingham is appalled by such indiscriminate indulgence, the hero Coningsby is convinced by this display of paternalistic duty. All around him, in the cities and factories, Coningsby sees that ethic dying. When later he spies one of the greatest Gothic buildings in Europe, King's College Chapel, he asks plaintively: 'Where is the spirit that raised these walls?... Is it indeed extinct? Is this then civilization, so much vaunted, inseparable from moderate feelings and little thoughts?'[32] In *Sybil*, the radical philosopher-guru Walter Gerard poses the same question. In place of monasteries and corporate harmony, all there now stood were gaols, treadmills and workhouses. Without a Church, without a solidifying political fabric, the two nations were in danger of separating yet further. 'Christianity teaches us to love our neighbours as ourself; modern society acknowledges no neighbour.'[33]

The ideology of Young England branched out across the country. In Manchester, the lecturer George Dawson, always a good bellwether of intellectual currents, delivered a lecture to the Mechanics' Institute on 'Old Times and Old Ways'. He condemned the individualism of the modern city and praised his medieval forebears who 'went for unity in the family, the church and the nation; they forgot or ignored individualism ... they could not understand protest, individualism, or self-erection'. Dawson contrasted the liberty which secondary political institutions fostered, the liberty of the guild and the corporation as celebrated by the German Romantics, with the false liberty of the parliamentary system. 'The wheel seems to have turned round, the cry of Europe now is that the over-wrought individualism of modern times wants checking.'[34] At a meeting of the supremely liberal National Association for the Promotion of Social Science, one speaker spoke longingly of the old certainties of the Middle Ages:

> There is something in this state of society so completely in contrast with our own, – there is so much of completeness in its manhood when set against our own fragmentary and imperfectly developed humanity – so much of cohesion and independence in its relation of classes, when compared with our own, separated by yawning chasms and gulfs so awfully hard to bridge over – so much of unselfishness, publicity and mutual bearing of burdens – so much that is noble, and manly, and genial, that it is no wonder if many of those who have studied it closely should become enamoured of it, and see in the disuse of its systems the secret of much that is most deplorable in our days.[35]

Even the most vocal champions of the industrial city fell under the medieval spell. In Liverpool, the architect and civic chronicler James Picton described how the great port city, the cotton and tobacco emporium of the modern age, was not 'quite destitute of the elements of medieval romance. We have had a feudal castle, with its donjon, moat, and subterranean passages. We have possessed an embattled tower, one or more ancient manor houses, and chantry chapels in our church.'[36]

In some cities, the Young England philosophy had already received some form of practical implementation. In Glasgow, the civic reformer Thomas Chalmers had attempted to ease the misery of urbanisation with an array of pre-industrial social policies. A vintage Victorian polymath and leading evangelical (later splitting the Scottish Church), he was described by William Gladstone as 'a man greatly lifted out of the region of mere flesh and blood'. In the 1820s Chalmers watched in shame the growing divisions between rich and poor within the city: 'there is a mighty unfilled space interposed between the high and the low of every large manufacturing city'.[37] After travelling through the pauper districts of Britain's industrial cities, he set out his credo of Christian concern for poverty combined with a Calvinist distaste for legalised charity in *The Christian and Civic Economy of Large Towns*. Chalmers argued for a new urban feudalism through the introduction of pastoral care back into manufacturing communities. By subdividing the cities into parishes, the intimate face-to-face interaction and Christian compassion redolent of the countryside would re-emerge in the cities. Industrial areas could even be assimilated into rural parishes, each with its team of voluntary visitors, deacons and curates. Close attention to homes and families would spur self-help and encourage an ethos of spontaneous concern amongst the better-off. Individual action was everything. 'How few the righteous men were, that would have sufficed to save a city from destruction.' In his own parish of St John's in Glasgow, Chalmers tried rather unsuccessfully to put his ideas to work, while across Glasgow he demanded that evangelicals involve themselves with civic reform and temperance work. It was an influential philosophy, part of the general spirit of rebuilding community ties in the city, and counted Manchester's James Phillips Kay amongst its many admirers.

The Manchester Mechanics' Institute was another civic initiative influenced by the medieval search for corporate harmony. Founded in 1824 by the wealthy Manchester banker Sir Benjamin Heywood and the mechanical engineer Sir William Fairbairn, it took as its guiding principle the notion of social obligation. Fairbairn was a pugilistic pit lad from

North Shields who educated himself in the arts of practical science to become an assistant and colleague to the railway pioneer George Stephenson. He then went on to build up a highly successful mechanical engineering firm specialising in steam engines, waterwheels, boiler construction as well as shipbuilding. One of Fairbairn's most lucrative contracts was to build the steam-powered machinery for Titus Salt's 'Saltaire' woollen mills in Shipley, outside Bradford. The boxer from the pits ended his days a baronet, a Fellow of the Royal Society and President of the British Association. But he always remained committed to elevating Manchester's working classes as he himself had risen.

The Mechanics' Institute took as its creed the fostering of social sympathy between the classes. Heywood, in addition to being partner of Heywood Brothers & Co. (one of many provincial Victorian banks which did so much to energise regional economies), and for a brief spell a Member of Parliament for Lancashire, was President of the Institute. Like many of the Manchester burgher class, he had been taken aback by the conditions of the working class exposed by James Kay's 1832 pamphlet. 'Is it possible, that any one, who is himself in circumstances of ease and comfort, can read those details without an inward stirring to exertion in behalf of his suffering neighbours?' Heywood was determined to promote 'a more kindly intercourse between the different classes of the peoples – more of mutual confidence and regard between the working man and his employer'.[38] And his solution to the class divide seemed lifted straight from the Sir Walter Scott community building handbook.

First, he suggested areas of public recreation where rich and poor could mix. In these enclosed areas there should also be located plots of ground, 'where under proper regulations, some of the manly games of our ancestors might be revived'. Lord John Manners would certainly have approved of such an ambitious plan for Manchester maypoles. Heywood also advocated an extension of city missions (as Thomas Chalmers had suggested), with parish vicars taking a close and personal interest in looking after wayward families. Finally, and most wonderfully, the Mechanics' Institute began a tradition of Christmas dinners to bring Manchester's disparate classes together. As Heywood's record of the 1835 celebration shows, the scene resembled nothing less than a feast from *Ivanhoe*:

> The boar's head and wassail bowl were introduced, with all the ceremonies of ancient observance, not, be it observed, in any unmeaning imitation of the usages of by-gone days, but for the purpose of receiving and preserving, with the hearty old holiday customs of our forefathers, the social and joyous feelings with which they were accompanied; that our kindly and benevolent sympathies might be awakened, and that with us, as with our forefathers on these occasions, there might be hospitality in the hall, and charity in the heart.[39]

iii REWRITING THE CITY

The most telling difference between the glorious Middle Ages and the dissolute nineteenth century could be found in the architecture. The Victorians held it as a truism that building design reflected the cultural sentiments of the age. The health of a people and its civilisation could be charted through its streets, houses, churches and public monuments. Britain's premier design journal, *The Builder*, described architecture as 'the monumental representation of history and civilization – a reflection of the sentiments, manners, and religious belief, of the people practising it'. This was particularly important to understand since 'the architectural embellishment of a city is of much greater consequence in forming the character of the people than some hasty thinkers now-a-days recognize'.[40] And the contrast between the civic architecture of medieval Europe and nineteenth-century Britain's jerry-built conurbations was all too apparent. If by its architecture you shall judge it, the Victorian city revealed a society in an advanced state of collapse.

What emerged out of the medieval enthusiasm of the early 1800s, when combined with concern about the architectural health of the nation, was a full-throttle Gothic Revival. The Christian styles which Britton and Rickman had so painstakingly tried to resuscitate now surged into life across the nineteenth-century city. The urban fabric slowly began to change from Georgian to Victorian as the stylistic hegemony of classicism – seen to such totalising effect in Nash's Regency developments in north London, Newcastle's Grey Street and Edinburgh's New Town – was slowly undermined. In its place came a competing Babel of styles of which Gothic would prove one of the most popular, innovative and durable. No longer dismissed as the plaything of a faddish rural aristocracy amused by grottoes and follies, Gothic was increasingly regarded as a peculiarly urban, civic style. And that process of change was initiated by a little-known Catholic priest called John Milner.

Already renowned for erecting the first chapel in England built in the Gothic style since the Reformation, Bishop Milner secured his title as godfather of the Gothic Revival by authoring *The History of Winchester* (1798; 1809; 1839), which charted the fortunes of Alfred's capital, and by extension those of the nation, with the rise and fall of Catholicism. As Milner guides his readers through the history and topology of Winchester, he contrasts a lost medieval world marked by social institutions and symbols of corporate faith with the civic decay wrought by 'the age of improvement'. Milner's achievement was to translate the political rhetoric of the German Romantics – their championing of secondary political institutions and the social authority of the Catholic Church – into a specifically civic sphere.

The very construction of his book revealed how he understood the city as a text or document able to illuminate certain truths about the values of previous and present societies. Milner re-imagined medieval Winchester as a godly, hospitable community based around a harmonious framework of secondary political institutions. He reconstructed a mental map of the city where every building, monument or statue stood as a civic symbol replete with meaning. Chapter I surveys the 'sacred edifice' of the Cathedral; chapter II, the Hospital of St Cross; chapter IV, the Monks' Cloister; chapter VI, St Elizabeth's College and the Carmelite Convent; chapter IX, the churches of St Michael and St Martin, and the City Cross. These were the civic symbols of a pious society (and the kind of secondary civic institutions the German Romantics supported) that revered brotherhood and practised hospitality – later to be gutted either by the Reformation, or, even worse, some form of utilitarian improvement.

For the age of utility was transposing the city of guilds, town squares and monasteries with the iconography of individualism. And to Milner there was no greater monument to the irreligion and moral decay of the modern town than a gaol. That one was to be built in Winchester upon Hyde Abbey (as it was), the resting place of King Alfred, 'the deliverer of England', was symbolic of a truly dissolute society. 'Thus miscreants couch amidst the ashes of our Alfreds and Edwards, and where once religious silence and contemplation were only interrupted by the bell of regular observance, and the chanting of devotion, now alone resound the clank of the captives' chains and the oaths of the profligate!' Such was the state of its morals that the present age was no less distinguished 'for the erection of gaols and bridewells than many past ages have been for the building of churches and monasteries'.[41]

Milner's history of a crumbling civic order being torn down and replaced by tokens of utility was an arresting vision and his influence can be traced most obviously in the work of Robert Southey. He too contrasted symbols of the modern city with their Gothic forebears to imply that with religious fragmentation inevitably came the dissolution of civil society. When Southey's 'Don Espriella' visits Manchester he compares the city's warehouses to convents, yet they are 'without their antiquity, without their beauty, without their holiness'. Instead of vespers, there is 'the everlasting din of machinery', and when 'the bell rings it is to call wretches to their work

instead of their prayers'.[42] In his later *Essays*, Southey focuses
on the gaol as the most ready civic symbol of the collapse of
community. Previously, society dealt with its own reprobates
in a rough yet local fashion, but there now existed an
unhealthy fetish for state prisons.

In a passage striking for its similarity to Milner, Don Espriella discovers in Chester the same spirit at work as Milner
had witnessed in Winchester. 'The new gaol', he writes mournfully, 'is considered as a perfect model of prison architecture,
a branch of the art as much studied by the English of the
present day, as ever cathedral-building was by their pious
ancestors'.[43] And prison design was certainly a coming form
in Gothic architecture. In Leicester the County Surveyor,
William Parsons, modelled his 1820s New County Gaol on a
medieval castle complete with entrance towers and a mock
portcullis. Later in the century Reading Gaol, Armley Gaol in
Leeds and Holloway Prison in north London all adopted bold,
Gothic castellated styles.

However, what Southey found particularly abhorrent about
the Chester gaol was its Panopticon style. If there was one
symbol of the collapse of society and the triumph of utility, it
was the Panopticon. Originating from a design by Jeremy
Bentham and his brother Samuel, the prison was constructed
in a radial manner, with wings stretching out from the centre
and lit from above. Michel Foucault recovered the principle
behind it. 'At the periphery, an annular building; at the centre,
a tower; this tower is pierced with wide windows that open
onto the inner side of the ring; the peripheric building is
divided into cells ... they have two windows, one on the
inside, corresponding to the windows of the tower; the other,
on the outside, allows the light to cross the cell from one end
to the other.'[44]

A contemporary conservative journal, *Quarterly Review*,
was appalled by the Panopticon idea. The magazine felt particularly sorry for 'the gaoler (the most unhappy wretch of
all)', who 'sits in the centre of his transparent dominion, and
sees to the utmost recesses of its crimes and its filthiness, all

the proceedings of his aggregation of slaves'. With its singled, isolated cells under the ubiquitous eye of the gaoler, the Panopticon comprised a grisly punishment all too typical of the glaring individualism of the age. 'The poets give us a terrible idea of eternal solitude; but eternal solitude is paradise compared to society under such ever lasting inspection.'[45]

The Panopticon became the touchstone edifice of all that was wrong with the industrial city. That it was designed by Bentham, *the* philosopher of social disintegration, made it all the worse. Although the first classic Panopticon was built at the Eastern Penitentiary in Philadelphia, Pennsylvania the idea returned across the Atlantic and aspects of it could be seen at the Millbank penitentiary on the Thames and at Pentonville Prison in north London. But at Chester, Southey thought he had found another. 'The structure of this particular prison is singularly curious, the cells being so constructed that the gaoler from his dwelling-house can look into every one, – a counterpart to the whispering dungeons in Sicily, which would have delighted Dionysius.' The prison does seem suspiciously akin to a Benthamite Panopticon, but Southey was most likely using the Panopticon as a literary device since evidence for such a prison in Chester in the early 1800s is scant.[46]

William Cobbett, the radical Tory demagogue, was quick to join Southey in calling for a revival of the lost certainties of the medieval city. Cobbett was appalled by the spectacle of modern cities, most particularly London. He blamed the 'Great Wen' for fostering 'the Thing': that amorphous collective of the national debt, jobbery, pensions, loans and general financial-imperial corruption he saw destroying the Old England of John Bull, gentlemen farmers and rustic virtue. Cobbett's early days during the 1790s had been spent as a firebrand conservative attacking anyone and everyone, in particular the radical republican Thomas Paine, suspected of sympathising with the ideals of the French Revolution. By the 1820s his reactionary Toryism had transferred to Britain and the whole, stinking system of rotten boroughs, empire-building and paper money. He struck a pose as a modern-day

Cincinnatus railing against the effete corruption of a new Rome from his simple Hampshire farmstead, while his irrepressible egoism, artless bombast and powers of personal promotion ensured his message was heard. His journal, *The Political Register*, sold at its peak some 70,000 copies a week and he emerged as a radical hero following his two-year imprisonment for supporting the rights of the common soldiery.

Like Milner and Southey before him, Cobbett was equally convinced that the fracturing of society, the birth of individualism and political corruption, began with the English Reformation. The 'chief object' of his *History of the Protestant Reformation* (1829), which sold an astonishing 700,000 copies in two years, was to show that the break from Catholicism 'made the main body of the people poor and miserable'; 'that it impoverished and degraded them'; and that in lieu of 'old English hospitality . . . it gave us pauperism'.[47] Cobbett detailed the collapse of civil society by drawing on Milner's history of Winchester. Just as Chateaubriand had done, he listed the glories of medieval Gothic architecture and asked, 'What have we in exchange for these?' In place of monasteries, convents, hospitals and almshouses, with their commitment to helping the poor and unifying society, there were now just miserable workhouses for destitute paupers.

Cobbett pursued this line of analysis with even greater rhetorical effect in his most famous work, *Rural Rides*, an extended rant against all the 'nabobs, negro-drivers, generals, admirals, governors, commissaries, contractors, pensioners, sinecurists, commissioners, loan-jobbers, lottery-dealers, bankers, stock-jobbers' and the rest who have ruined England. According to Cobbett, the damage this corrupt, metropolitan cabal had inflicted on the country could be read in the condition of England's 'noble edifices' – both secular and spiritual. Given the state of immorality and faithlessness in 1830s England, Cobbett was certain that such an architectural wonder as Salisbury Cathedral 'could never be made now'. 'It really does appear that if our forefathers had not made these buildings we should have forgotten, before now, what the

Christian religion was!'[48] What testified to the atomism of contemporary society more than the decay of Christian architecture was what was put in their place. On his trip to Morpeth, Cobbett lamented how 'From cathedrals and monasteries we are come to be proud of our gaols, which are built in the grandest style, and seemingly as if to imitate GOTHIC architecture'.[49] This was the final indignity: symbols of faithless utility dressed up in the garb of a nobler age.

The contrast of the gaol to the cathedral was the perfect symbol for the collapse of any corporate sense of civil society. In Leicester, Cobbett was revolted by Parsons's celebrated gaol. The degraded signs of the times need no more introduction than 'the want of reflection in the people' for the 'self-gratulation which they appear to feel in these edifices'. Instead of expressing shame at these 'indubitable proofs of the horrible increase of misery and crime', they actually boast of them as 'improvements'. 'Our forefathers built abbeys and priories and churches, and they made such use of them that gaols were unnecessary.'[50] Instead, 'their sons' knock down the abbeys and priories, destroy the structures of a godly society and inaugurate gaols as the 'striking edifices' representative of the age.

iv REBUILDING THE CITY

It was another pupil of Milner's, a manic, brilliant Catholic visionary, who moved the debate from lamenting a passing order to a practical programme for building anew the Victorian city. Augustus Welby Northmore Pugin had Gothicism in his blood. His father, Augustus Pugin, had been John Britton's draughtsman for many of his books on Gothic design and had himself published a work on the Christian style, *Examples of Gothic Architecture* (1826). Pugin elder was a French émigré and lapsed Catholic with a good eye for design and an even better one for gently embroidering his past. His claims of noble lineage and ancient blood secured him a beneficial match with a wealthy Protestant Englishwoman.

Though he was brought up along strict evangelical principles, A.W.N. Pugin was a passionate, romantic, rather Byronic figure. He was handsome and serially successful with women despite being universally mocked for his idiosyncratic dress sense. He wore huge, baggy trousers and coats with cavernous pockets for his various sketching implements. Sometimes, he enjoyed dressing like a sailor. An account by one of his numerous sons-in-law affectionately brings out Pugin's general air of mania. John Hardman Powell described him as,

> only just middle height but very strong, broad chest, large hands, massive forehead, nose and chin, well curved flexible mouth, and restless grey eyes, the expression of which turned inwards when in deep thought. His hair was darkest brown, thick, not crisp, and he shaved clean like a sailor. All his movements were rapid, full of mental and bodily energy, showing a nervous and choleric temperament ... He was passionate but believed his anger was always another's fault, honest rages with no malice in them, blowing over without leaving resentment.[51]

What drove Pugin's amazing industry, as well as sending him to an early grave, was a burning desire to reform architecture and revive those sentiments which had first inspired Gothic designers. Gothic was his life passion. He wrote of his twenty-one-year-old third wife, Jane Knill, 'I am married, I have got a first-rate Gothic woman at last, who perfectly understands and delights in spires, chancels, screens, stained glass, brasses, vestments etc.'

But it was no good simply following a contemporary fad and designing in the Gothic style. You needed also to revive the Catholic spirit of those years. 'Yes, it was, indeed, the faith, the zeal, and above all, the unity, of our ancestors, that enabled them to conceive and raise those wonderful fabrics that still remain to excite our wonder and admiration.'[52] Received into the Roman Catholic Church at the age of twenty-two, Pugin retained all his life the fevered zeal of the convert. Whether it was writing pamphlets, designing churches, fashioning the new Houses of Parliament or serving his loyal patron Lord Shrewsbury at Alton Towers (now the site of the gaudy theme park), his life's work was to create conditions for the revival of a truly Catholic society. He reminisced how 'it must have been an edifying sight to have overlooked some ancient city raised when religion formed a leading impulse in the mind of man, and when the honour and worship of the Author of all good was considered of greater importance than the achievement of the most lucrative commercial speculation'.[53] And while there could be no architecture of old without a return to Rome, that journey could be spirited along by refashioning the country with Gothic designs. Pugin wanted to change the face of the Victorian city.

Following the teachings of a school of French rationalist architects, Pugin developed an aesthetic theory based upon 'truth' or the fitness to purpose of the design. The criterion for that judgement was the Christian nature of the art. What made good architecture was the degree of Christian spirit behind it. The reason nineteenth-century cities were so ugly was because of an absence of true faith. The Reformation had undercut public faith and with 'the growth of Protestant principles' came 'the fall of ecclesiastical architecture'. Pugin regarded Birmingham as the pinnacle of this unedifying process, memorably describing it as 'the most hateful of all hateful places, a town of Greek buildings, smoky chimneys, low radicalism and dissent'.[54] Similar points had, of course, been made by Milner, Southey and Cobbett – with all of whom Pugin was familiar – but none had done so either with the same degree of rhetorical venom or with such visual panache.

Pugin's engaging tirade, *Contrasts: or, a Parallel between the Noble Edifices of the Middle Ages and Corresponding Buildings of the Present Day; shewing the Present Decay of Taste,* combined his considerable artistic talents with biting social satire. The book contrasted the civic framework and institutional fabric of a 'Catholic town in 1440' with 'the same town in 1840'. The buildings and institutions of the medieval town present a harmonious and godly community, while the 1840 version exhibits all the faithless utility of an industrialised Victorian city. So, Pugin contrasts the corporate unity of the Catholic churches of St Michael on the Hill, St Cuthbert, St Mary and St John to the competing sects housed in their Baptist Chapel, Unitarian Chapel, Quaker Meeting House and Wesleyan Centenary Chapel. Similarly, whereas the Catholic town has a priory, an abbey and St Edmund's to look after the poor, the industrial city has a 'new gaol'. Needless to say, the prison is a Benthamite Panopticon. More generally, in place of the market cross there is an abstract classical statue testifying to a faithless rationalism; in place of common ground there is enclosed land for the parsonage 'pleasure grounds' (precisely the kind of privilege which infuriated Cobbett); in place of trees, factories; in place of an open bridge, a toll; and in place of churches, a 'Socialist Hall of Science' (the type which Engels frequented on his arrival in Manchester). What strikes the eye most forcefully, though, is the contrast between the 'steeple-chimneys' of the 1840 town and the 'real' church steeples of the Catholic town. In the Catholic town the spires reach towards God, while in the Victorian city they seem only to oppress and pollute.

The purpose of *Contrasts* was to show that medieval civic design not only signified a harmonious, Catholic order but that it also emanated from deeply felt Catholic sentiments. The result was that the works of medieval architects 'bear on their face the indelible stamp of faith, love, and devotion'.[55] However, by the 1830s even the architecture of churches had 'dwindled down into a mere trade'. Just as society had fractured into a host of competing religions and warring individuals, so architecture had descended into a stylistic Babel. 'Private judgment runs riot; every architect has a theory of his own, a *beau* ideal he has himself created; a disguise with which to invest the building he erects.'[56] Nowhere was this stylistic heterogeneity more apparent than at John Marshall's flax-spinning factory, Temple Mills, in the Holbeck district of

Leeds. Even today its extraordinarily garish Egyptian designs, modelled on the temple of Edfu, appear incongruous amidst the otherwise dour millworks surrounding it. And it was precisely such incongruity, which flowed from intellectual inquiry rather than religious faith, which appalled Pugin. Amidst this carnival of styles, even the adoption of Christian architecture is tainted since it comes not from 'principle', 'authority', or 'as the expression of our faith', but instead 'as one of the disguises of the day'.[57]

To renew Catholic architecture and the civic fabric demanded a renewal of faith. Like Digby, Pugin regarded the life of the Middle Ages as neither strange nor impossible, but as a model by which contemporary society could be reformed.[58] The calling of the Catholic architect was to reconstruct the industrial city in such a fashion as to foster the lost corporate spirit of community. 'Companies, Crafts, and Guilds' that 'form the ties of fraternal intercourse and charity' should be celebrated in civic design. The opportunity was too often neglected – as with the London New Exchange. This had been an excellent moment to restore the 'arched ambulatory', 'high crested roofs' and 'lofty clocher or bell tower ... like those which yet remain in Flemish towns, and were formerly to be found in all our cities'.[59] For Christian architecture need not be limited only to church design. Instead, the dream that inspired him and other Gothic revivalists was to reconstruct the entire architecture of those medieval cities in modern settings. 'There is no reason in the world', Pugin suggested, 'why noble cities, combining all possible convenience of drainage, water-courses, and conveyance of gas, may not be erected in the most consistent and yet Christian character.'[60]

Pugin was more than an armchair architect and proceeded to put his principles into practice in numerous churches across England and Ireland. He travelled feverishly, superintending developments, writing articles, pleading for more money from the ever-indulgent Lord Shrewsbury, and designing yet more ecclesiastical edifices. Though disparaging towards the modernity of the railway system, he in fact lived by it, journeying from church to workshop to patron and always grumbling about delays. Along with the Church of St Augustine in his home town of Ramsgate, Pugin's greatest work is commonly acknowledged to be St Giles's, Cheadle, close to Shrewsbury's Alton Towers in Staffordshire. This Roman Catholic church still stands as an almost perfect thirteenth-century recreation complete with acres of stained glass and a screen, piscina and sedilia, its every inch dripping with paint, gold gilding and intimate carvings. Pugin was also proud of his work on St Marie's, Manchester; St Mary's Cathedral in Newcastle; St Barnabas in Nottingham; and St Chad's Cathedral, Birmingham. The latter is unfortunately now hemmed in by a roundabout of traffic whose fumes and noise markedly diminish the sanctity of the site. Those in charge of the interior have not helped much either. In 1967 extensive 'improvements' destroyed Pugin's rood screen and much of the Gothic decoration. Thankfully, the stained-glass windows have remained intact and in a large window in the Sanctuary is depicted a holy figure holding a model of St Chad's. It is Bishop Milner; a worthy nod to the intellectual progenitor of the site.

Pugin's plea for Christian architecture was most enthusiastically taken up by two precocious Cambridge undergraduates, John Mason Neale and Benjamin Webb. In 1839 they established the Cambridge Camden Society, whose purpose was to propagate the 'science' of Ecclesiology, defined as 'the principles which guided medieval builders'. Just as Pugin regarded architecture as testimony to the 'spirit of the age', the Camdenians understood Gothic buildings as the expression of liturgical principles. Churches were not merely places for communal meetings and collective worship, but architectural mediums which proclaimed a theological message. Though both committed Anglicans, Neale and Webb aimed to revive those stylistic principles which had built the great Catholic churches of the thirteenth and fourteenth centuries.

In 1842 the Society launched the *Ecclesiologist* magazine, which set out to establish the correct design of Christian architecture with a fundamentalist doctrinal rigour. From the altar to the baptistery font, every element of worship needed to be arranged appropriately. The magazine attacked the 'liberal principles' that guided modern architecture and which repudiate 'every patriotic and national feeling, view man as a citizen of the world, and consider the architecture of every nation, climate and religion, as equally deserving of imitation'.[61] It was this absence of taste which allowed each architect to have his pet style (such as Egyptian) and had defaced English cities with pagan designs.

With their stringent views and the backing of a highly influential membership, the Camden Society made its voice heard in architectural societies, improvement commissions and ecclesiastical boards across the country. Month by month it turned its attention to different churches and communities, heaping opprobrium upon Liverpool ('great is the mortification in this thriving town, which he, who desires to see his own beloved Communion clothed in the beauty of holiness has to undergo'), joining forces with architectural societies in Bristol to prevent an incorrect restoration of St Mary's Redcliffe, and conversely heaping praise upon ecclesiastical designs in Leeds.[62]

In many cities, the Ecclesiologists were pushing against an open door. Since the 1810s, as Gothic design infiltrated domestic and ecclesiastical architecture, it had started to change the architectural fabric of the Victorian city. Urban churches erected under the 1818 New Churches Building Act were overwhelmingly Gothic; of the 214 new churches, a staggering 174 were built in the 'Christian' idiom. A good example is St Luke's in Chelsea, London. Designed and built by James Savage, it boasts a genuine stone rib-vault complete with flying buttresses covering the whole church. Thomas Rickman, the author and architect who first classified the Gothic styles, oversaw St George's Church in Birmingham, which constituted an impressive rendition of Middle Pointed architecture, as well as the Gothic-designed St George's Church in Everton. His Ramshorn Church, in Ingram Street,

Glasgow (now converted into a student theatre for the University of Strathclyde), is an equally fine if rather more dour display of the Pointed style in action.

Gothic architecture was growing in confidence and nowhere was this more evident than in that most fundamental statement of national identity, the new Houses of Parliament. The old Westminster Palace had been gutted by fire in 1834 and after an initial attempt by the celebrated classicist Sir Robert Smirke to place himself in charge of the redevelopment, the contract was awarded to the Gothicist Charles Barry. Between 1840 and 1860 Barry built one of the most iconic neo-Gothic buildings in Europe which, with its pinnacles, turrets and towers, riding straight up from the ground, is a triumph of medieval picturesque. Famously, Barry was helped in his work by A.W.N. Pugin. Though himself dismissive of the plans for the building ('Tudor details on a classic body'), Pugin typically put his soul into designing the intricate stylised interiors, ensuring that Parliament's carvings, gilding and tracery remain amongst the finest of the nineteenth century. The unrivalled craftsmanship of Pugin became a matter of heated public controversy in 1998 when the then Lord Chancellor, Lord Irvine of Lairg, refitted his Grade I official residence in the Palace at a cost of £650,000. Lord Irvine, a man with as fine a taste for the medieval impulse as Pugin, had already styled himself the 'Cardinal Wolsey' of the Blair administration. And he displayed Wolsey-like grandeur by spending £57,000 on hand-blocked Pugin wallpaper. He explained to a furious House of Commons Select Committee that such skilled craftsmanship simply didn't come cheap. Pugin would certainly have concurred.

Thanks to Pugin and the Ecclesiologists, the Decorated Gothic of the 1300s became the dominant style of the 1840s. All the great architects of the mid-Victorian years – George Gilbert Scott, Richard Cromwell Carpenter, William Butterfield – were members of the Camden Society and the implementation of 'ecclesiological' principles can be seen across British cities. Even though Scott later described the

Ecclesiologists as 'imperious' and recalled how 'any one who had dared to deviate from or to build in other than the sacred "Middle Pointed" well knew what he must suffer', in his St Giles's, Camberwell and Church of St Mary the Virgin in Liverpool he happily accorded with their principles. Similarly, Carpenter's St Mary's Magdalene in Munster Square, London was another 'Middle Pointed' commission, provoking the *Ecclesiologist* to describe it approvingly as 'the most artistically correct new church yet consecrated in London'. Its graceful arches, fine window tracery and generous sanctuary made it an ideal setting for Tractarian worship.[63]

It was during the pastorship of Walter Farquhar Hook and rebuilding of St Peter's Parish Church in Leeds that the aesthetic and political impulses of the Gothic Revival succeeded most spectacularly. Initially sympathetic to the Oxford Movement, Hook was a 'High and Dry' Anglican who believed the Church of England was merely reformed in the sixteenth-century Reformation, not created anew. It was and remained the true Catholic Church. Rising quickly through the clerical ranks he served at Holy Trinity in Coventry and also as a royal chaplain. In 1837 he was elected to the vicarage of Leeds and there faced the bleak task of reinvigorating an Anglican community pincered by Dissent and indifference. His achievements in Leeds would be remarkable and the city's gratitude is today tangible as you leave Leeds railway station and enter City Square to see a statue of Hook in full admonitory flow.[64]

When Hook arrived, Leeds's population was fast approaching 150,000. Yet there were only eight churches in the town besides the parish church, and nine in the suburbs, all of whose attendance figures were pitiful. St Peter's commanded barely fifty regular communicants; meanwhile, the city's Nonconformist congregations were booming, with Methodism leading the way. As the new vicar plaintively remarked, 'The real fact is that the established religion in Leeds is Methodism.'[65] Hook aimed to recharge the Anglican spirit by re-establishing the physical presence of the church in the community. He was disgusted by the state of St Peter's which,

dating from the fourteenth century, had been allowed to fall
into disrepair. Hook described it to his daughter as 'my nasty,
dirty, ugly old church'. In true Camden Society style, he
believed 'a handsome church was a kind of standing sermon'
and began to mobilise support for a substantial renovation.[66]

However, as work progressed parts of the church appeared
ever more fragile. In the end, between 1837 and 1841 the
church was comprehensively rebuilt at an enormous cost of
£30,000. Inspired by the Perpendicular designs of the fourteenth century, most notably York Minster and Fountains
Abbey, the architect R.D. Chantrell created a magisterial
example of Gothic design. The 'tower' was moved from the
centre to the middle of the north wall, which had the dual
effect of opening up the church interior and ensuring St Peter's
had that unique presence along Kirkgate, the principal route
to the church. The south transept was extended, the organ
moved, tracery placed in windows – in fact, according to the
Leeds Intelligencer, 'the whole church has been taken down
and rebuilt, with the exception of a portion of the south wall'.[67]
As physical improvements accelerated, so Hook changed the
internal arrangements by successfully introducing the cathedral form of choral service, placing a choir of laymen in the
chancel. Entering the church today, one is immediately hit by
the majesty of worship which the interior exudes. The heavy
oak carvings, the vaulted ceilings, the ornate choir and carved
pulpit all point to a seriousness of devotion. And despite
being hemmed in by a busy ring road and surrounded by an
unattractive medley of tattoo parlours, dingy pubs and second-
hand clothes shops, the church and its environs manage to
retain a serene, godly air.

The *Ecclesiologist* was delighted with the changes, declaring
the reconstituted St Peter's 'the first large town church to
exemplify their principles'. For the Camdenians it was a
triumph – 'the first great instance of the Catholic feeling of a
church, energising rudimentally – throwing off by a strong,
vigorous mental effort, the mere preaching house, grasping at
the altar as being, rather than the pulpit, the central point of

worship'.[68] The *Church Intelligencer* magazine was equally
enthusiastic. It hoped that Britain would be blighted by 'no
more churches built in the bald and beggarly styles of dissenting meeting-houses'. Instead, designers and clerics should
emulate 'the magnificent church at Leeds which stands a noble
monument to the taste, the sterling Christianity, and the
old-fashioned piety and spirit of Churchmanship of the
town'.[69]

On 2 September 1841 the new church was consecrated in a
distinctly High Church manner. The young Florence Nightingale, attending the ceremony as a sceptical evangelical, was
shocked at this 'gathering of Puseyites from all parts of England'. The clergyman in scarlet, the processions, the superstitious service and the infamous Dr Hook, 'who has the
regular Catholic jerk in making the genuflexion every time he
approaches the altar' – it was all too much for the delicate
Protestant sensibilities of Miss Nightingale.[70] Yet Hook's
impact on Leeds was remarkable. His charismatic sermons
attracted standing-room-only crowds for Sunday worship,
leaving one contemporary chronicler of Leeds life, Benjamin
Barker, to record in his diary for September 1856, 'Went to
Parish Church but could not get in, was full.' The number of
communicants reached 500 on Easter Day compared to the
miserable fifty on his arrival. And following his effective
lobbying, the 1846 Leeds Vicarage Act was passed, dividing
the city into new parishes with resident vicars and new parish
churches. By the time Hook left the city the number of Anglican churches had increased from fifteen to thirty-six. Writing
of the Banquet and Testimonial to celebrate Hook's promotion
to Dean of Chichester in 1859, Barker recorded that 'During
Dr Hook's stay in Leeds of 22 years, there had been built in
the parish 21 out of the 36 churches: at least 30 schools
(Church Schools); and 23 out of the 29 parsonage houses at a
cost of at least £150,000; and a great deal of this work must be
attributed to the self-denying and persevering exertions of Dr
Hook.'[71]

The influence of Pugin and the Ecclesiologists on church

design and the fabric of the Victorian city was profound. By the 1870s it was said that an architect would as soon think of building a church without a chancel, as of building one without a roof. Not only were hundreds of new churches built in the Gothic style during the nineteenth century, but thousands of older, medieval churches were restored or enlarged according to 'Christian' design. In modern British cities that managed to escape the worst 'improvements' of the 1960s, the civic language of Gothic still dots the urban landscape. According to that great twentieth-century critic of Gothicism, Kenneth Clark, 'Probably there is not a church in England entirely unaffected by the Gothic Revival'.[72]

v JOHN RUSKIN AND THE VENETIAN TURN

By the early 1840s there was emerging a strong sentiment in favour of broadening the use of Gothic architecture from the spiritual to the secular. There was a danger, as simply the plaything of Pugin and the Ecclesiologists, that the style was heading down an ecclesiastical cul-de-sac. In *An Historical Essay on Architecture*, Thomas Hope highlighted the use of the Pointed style in civic architecture in the Hanse towns of the thirteenth century. As these cities rose 'in opulence and in dignity', they took pride in building 'in addition to [their] sumptuous cathedrals, halls as magnificent for [their] magistrates and merchants to meet in a body, and even fine houses, for their habitations as individuals'. Although in England 'an idea has prevailed' that Gothic architecture was 'displayed in all its purity and perfection in churches and monasteries alone', on the Continent it was employed extensively in civic and domestic settings.[73]

At the end of the decade, Hope's campaign for a more flexible, secular Gothic received the magisterial endorsement of John Ruskin. Critic, author and patron, Ruskin was perhaps the greatest of that breed of public intellectuals who so energised Victorian social and political life. His precocious criticisms, fierce intellect and uncompromising prose generally appalled the British art establishment, while his starkly original views seemed almost reflected in his appearance. Physically, he was striking. A friend described him as 'a tall, slight fellow, whose piercing frank blue eye lookt through you and drew you to him. A fair man, with rough light hair and reddish whiskers, in a dark blue frock coat with velvet collar, bright Oxford blue stock, black trousers and patent slippers ... The only blemish in his face was the lower lip, which protruded somewhat: he had been bitten there by a dog in his early youth.'[74]

From the mid-1840s, Ruskin appeared to be moving away from the fine art criticism of *Modern Painters* to a greater consideration of architectural issues. In 1848, after a miserable trip around the cathedrals of England, Ruskin took his new wife, Euphemia Gray, to the Continent for a study-tour of Northern Gothic. While the long-suffering Effie sat in gloomy Gothic churches or among blustery abbey ruins, Ruskin documented their journey across France. This holiday, and another, happier one with his parents in the Alps, gave him the material to write his first substantive critique of architectural matters, *The Seven Lamps of Architecture* (1849). In civic terms, the work is best understood as part of the same intellectual trajectory as Milner, Southey and Pugin (although Ruskin always denied he had learnt anything from the latter, mainly out of disgust towards Pugin's Catholicism) and reiterates the message that it was a certain right state of moral feeling that was the essential ingredient for good architecture. Although later in his life Ruskin would question his faith, at this stage he was still working under the powerful influence of his evangelical mother and identified that right state of feeling as ardent religious commitment.

In *The Seven Lamps*, Ruskin lamented the poverty of modern architecture and the spirit of utility which undermined creativity. Like Pugin, he believed in the 'truth' of architecture as serving its function without the sham of deceits and decorations. The Lamp of Obedience stressed the importance of a unitary style – 'the architecture of a nation is great only when it is as universal and as established as its language ... no individual caprice shall dispense with, or materially vary, accepted types and customary decorations'.[75] The beauty of Gothic was found in its adherence to the seven lamps of Sacrifice, Truth, Power, Beauty, Life, Memory and Obedience. The faith of the designer and the builder meant they sacrificed all to produce a more beautiful and truthful edifice than the paganism of classical or Renaissance architecture. It was a unitary style yet it allowed for far greater individual creativity than the despotic equality of classicism, as witnessed by the idiosyncratic catalogue of gargoyles which festooned Gothic cathedrals. The Gothic style demanded freedom, individuality and spontaneity from its workers. For Ruskin it represented a finer, more moral society which ensured a mental as well as physical freedom. 'All architecture proposes an effect on the human mind, not merely a service to the human frame.'

Ruskin's belief in the spiritual ethic of work, individual freedom, and the sham of liberal, contemporary life put him in the same politico-philosophical camp as Thomas Carlyle. In 1855 Ruskin wrote warmly to Carlyle, 'How much your general influence has told upon me, I know not – but I always confess it – or rather boast of it.'[76] He later took to addressing him as 'Master' or 'Dearest Papa'. In turn, Carlyle was a frequent visitor to the Ruskin family home in Denmark Hill, south-east London, and Ruskin himself regularly travelled up to visit the sage of Chelsea at Cheyne Row. The two also shared, in the 1840s, gnawing embarrassments in the marital bedroom with neither showing the slightest sexual interest in his wife.

Ruskin never consummated his marriage to Effie Gray. Whether he was, as legend has it, put off by her pubic hair or menstruation is still open to question. Effie's testimony, six years after the marriage, 'that he had imagined women were quite different to what he saw I was, and that the reason, he did not make me his Wife was because he was disgusted with my person the first evening April 10th' certainly hints at such an interpretation.[77] After this inauspicious start to the marriage, Ruskin retreated into his work while Effie grew miserable, ill and sexually unhappy. She resented both Ruskin's total lack of interest in her and his unnatural proximity to his overbearing, indulgent parents. Effie returned from London to Scotland and the newlyweds separated as Ruskin travelled on the Continent with his parents or shut himself off, lost in his books at Denmark Hill. But to stop damaging rumours circulating among Effie's neighbours in Perth, after nine months apart Ruskin was summoned to Scotland to be reunited with his wife. There, cleverly, Effie suggested Ruskin should show her his beloved Venice, the spiritual retreat he called his 'paradise of cities'. It was an artful attempt to save the marriage. Sadly, the trip did not bring husband and wife any closer, but it did result in one of the architectural epics of the English language.

In 1849 John Ruskin, Effie Ruskin, his valet and her companion Charlotte Ker left England for Boulogne. They caught the train to Switzerland and on through to Milan and Venice. All around them lay the detritus of the abortive 1848 revolution and the Austrian military response which had endangered so much of Italy's artistic heritage. Once in Venice, Ruskin rushed to examine the damage done to the civic fabric by the Austrian bombardment as well as the recent municipal improvement ('*gas lamps!* on each side [of the Grand Canal] in grand new iron posts of the last Birmingham fashion'). The party then decamped to the Hotel Danieli where the Ruskins enjoyed a room with a view of St Mark's Square and the Campanile. And just as Effie had hoped, the couple did indeed grow more affectionate in Venice – but only as they followed ever more separate lives. Effie and Charlotte lost themselves in the society life of the Austrian officer class who lorded it over the defeated city. Dreamily, Effie wrote to her mother, 'I could hardly see less of him than I do at present with his work and think it is much better if we follow our different occupations and never interfere with one another and are always happy.'[78] Mrs Ruskin developed a particular attachment to an attractive, rather suave officer called Charles Paulizza with whom she gently flirted and was accompanied to balls. His charm and chivalry was a welcome, refreshing antidote to her husband's usual habit of argumentative hectoring in polite society. In a lovely irony, it also transpired that it was Paulizza who, as First Lieutenant of the Austrian Artillery, had been in charge of the shelling of Venice and its monuments during the siege. Ruskin, rather nobly, didn't seem to mind.

While Effie was wining and dining her way through Austro-Venetian society, Ruskin was expending all his fragile mental and physical energy on dissecting Venice. Repelled by exploring his wife's body, he found deep satisfaction amidst Venice's catacombs and churches. From St Mark's to the Arsenal to the tombs of Murano, he etched and sketched his way across the city. According to Effie, 'Nothing interrupts him and whether the Square is crowded or empty he is either seen with a black cloth over his head taking Daguerrotypes or climbing about the capitals covered with dust, or else with cobwebs exactly as if he had just arrived from taking a voyage with the old woman on her broomstick. Then when he comes down he stands very meekly to be brushed down by Domenico quite regardless of the scores of idlers who cannot understand him at all.'[79] Children and beggars followed him across the city, while Effie and Charlotte watched in horror. But out of this exploration emerged *The Stones of Venice* (1851–3), a monumental account of morality and aesthetics and one of the most significant texts in the architectural development of the Victorian city.

As Milner had rather prosaically traced the rise and fall of Catholicism through Winchester's changing architecture, so on a grander and more metaphysical scale Ruskin chronicled the decline of Venice as an epic morality tale. 'My Venice, like Turner's, had been chiefly created for us by Byron,' wrote the prudish Ruskin of the great Regency buck. Like his artistic hero, J.M.W. Turner, Ruskin saw in Venice a testimony to aesthetic beauty but also an allegory of ruin. In *Childe*

Harold's Pilgrimage, Byron described the city's descent from what he once called 'the greenest island of my imagination' to a dissolute 'Sea Sodom'. The 'fairy city' became the 'revel of the earth, the masque of Italy', and in Canto IV Byron wanders through a townscape of decay marked only by crumbling palaces and doges declined to dust;

> The very weeds are beautiful, thy waste
> More rich than other climes' fertility;
> Thy wreck a glory, and thy ruin graced
> With an immaculate charm which cannot be defaced.

Ruskin swallowed these Romantic precepts whole. For him, the city's history was a 'warning which seems to me to be uttered by every one of the fast-gaining waves, that beat like passing bells, against the Stones of Venice'.[80] The decline was inseparably linked to the collapse of personal piety 'with a closeness and precision' the work would attempt to expose.[81] This in turn was reflected in the architecture and painting of a city which descended from unrivalled Gothicism to unprincipled Renaissance hybrids. As Ruskin explained in the conclusion, the great principle of the work was to show 'that art is valuable or otherwise, only as it expressed the personality, activity, and living perception of a good and great human soul'.[82] The austere beauty of medieval Venice achieved this, only to be betrayed by the luxury, refinement and paganism of Renaissance Venice.

The glory of medieval Venice, seen to such tremendous effect in the Doges' Palace ('the central building of the world'), was based on designers and builders following the light of the Lamp of Sacrifice and honouring 'something out of themselves'. It was not the festivity of the Renaissance or eighteenth-century Grand Tour Venice (the type of gaiety Effie was enjoying on the side) that built its glories; rather, 'the solemnity of her early and earnest religion'. They built for the honour of God, and 'were content to pass away in nameless multitudes, so only that the labour of their hands might fix in the sea wilderness a throne for their guardian angel'.[83] It was the Lamp of Sacrifice, of Obedience and of Beauty, which produced 'the bright hues of the early architecture of Venice'. So for Ruskin, the Church of St Mark's 'may be seen as a great Book of Common Prayer; the mosaics were its illuminations, and the common people of the time were taught their Scripture history by means of them'. Here he surreptitiously aligns the Catholicism of Venice with the foundation text of English Protestantism while simultaneously, like Milner, deciphering the city as text.

In a famous chapter, 'The Nature of Gothic', which would come to be a set text for generations of future socialists, Ruskin outlined how the beauty of Gothic was found in the liberty of the workman. 'Men were not intended to work with the accuracy of tools', and to force them to do so was to 'unhuman-ize them'.[84] The degradation of the operative into machine produced the vainglorious, self-serving architecture of the modern city. To neuter freedom, 'to banish imperfection is to destroy expression, to check exertion, to paralyze vitality'.[85] This was precisely what was occurring in the industrial city. As Marx and Engels put it in *The Communist Manifesto*, 'Owing to the extensive use of machinery and to division of labour, the work of the proletarians has lost all individual character, and, consequently, all charm for the workman.'[86] The medieval ethic, the Gothic route, could provide happiness for worker and master alike. Together with his political guru Carlyle, Ruskin shared a faith in a Gospel of Work to counter the failings of industrial society.

Only when Venice descended into 'the masque of Europe' did the art and architecture collapse; 'her glorious robe of gold and purple was given her when first she rose a vestal from the sea, not when she became drunk with the wine of for-nication'.[87] Ruskin regarded the Renaissance as playing the same destructive role as Milner, Southey and Pugin had attrib-uted to the Protestant Reformation. It was the self-adulation and luxury of the Renaissance which gradually led Venice to 'the forgetfulness of all things but self' and to a fatal infidelity.[88] In true Carlylian style, Ruskin traced Venice's biblical fall, 'from infidelity to the unscrupulous and insatiable pursuit of pleasure, and from this to irremediable degradation'.[89] A false, more ostentatiously papist Catholicism took hold and painting, sculpture and architecture quickly deteriorated as the waves began to lap (as they now so frequently do) against the crumbling stones of Venice.[90] It was a warning which Ruskin felt was particularly apposite for the mercantile, free-trading nation of his birth; another Venice which had also, as Carlyle put it, 'forgotten God' but hopefully could 'be led through prouder eminence to less pitied destruction'.

While England might not have ingested the full import of Ruskin's moral warning, it certainly welcomed his architectural sermon. Looking back from the vantage point of 1872, Charles Eastlake was unequivocal about Ruskin's influence upon design. 'Never', he wrote, 'has the subject of Gothic architecture been rendered so popular in this country, as for a while it was rendered by the aid of his pen.'[91] Ruskin himself later became horrified by the effect of his work as a tide of Venetian Gothic designs swamped even his house on Denmark Hill. 'I have had indirect influence', he wrote in 1872, 'on nearly every cheap villa-builder between this and Bromley; and there is scarcely a public house near the Crystal Palace but sell its gins and bitters under pseudo-Venetian capitals copied from the Church of Madonna of Health or of Miracles. And one of my principal notions for leaving my present house is that it is surrounded everywhere by the accursed Frankenstein monsters of, *in*directly, my own making.'[92]

Ruskin's achievement was to turn the Gothic Revival in a more civic direction, securing it a wider reception by decoupling its style from Catholicism. It was the liberty of the workmen, and not, as Pugin argued, their Roman Catholicism which provided the magic of Gothic. To a proudly Protestant nation, this separation of design from religion was essential for its move into the arena of public building. And his influence could be charted in the design of courthouses, churches, town halls, Athenaeums, town squares and a plethora of other civic edifices across urban Britain. In the cities, if Ruskin himself was not lecturing there existed a flurry of interest in his work. In October 1853, for example, Mr Huggins led a learned discussion upon 'The Stones of Venice' at the Liverpool Architectural Society. The pages of *The Builder* generously assisted the new fashion in 'Ruskinian Gothic'. In March 1851 the journal printed lavish illustrations of 'Il Palazzo dei Pergoli Intagliati, Venice'. This particular edifice was 'a beautiful specimen of the Gothic architecture peculiar to Venice'.[93] Later in the month a glowing description and illustration of the 'Palazzo Dario' appeared. This was one of the 'numerous small palaces to be found on the Grand Canal', and more importantly, 'Mr Ruskin, in "The Stones of Venice", mentions this palace as one of the earliest specimens of the Renaissance engrafted on Byzantine taste'.[94] In the Free Reference Library and Central Lending Library of Birmingham, Ruskin's *Stones of Venice* proved one of the most popular books along with Macaulay's *History of England* and Murray's *Handbook for the Continent*.[95]

One of Ruskin's most devoted disciples was the Anglican architect William Butterfield, who popularised the practice of 'structural polychromy'. This was the use of multiple coloration or hues in stonework – precisely the kind of style which Ruskin found so attractive in Venice. Slowly, the 'Gothic Revival' was changing from the English Pointed or 'Christian' architecture of the 1840s to the more Venetian idiom of the High Victorian period. According to Eastlake, students now routinely worked elements of Italian Gothic into their buildings: 'churches in which the "lily capital" of St Mark's was found side by side with Byzantine bas-reliefs and mural inlay from Murano; town halls wherein the arcuation and baseless columns of the Ducal Palace were reproduced; mansions which borrowed their parapets from the Calle del Bagatin and windows from the Ca d'Oro'.

At All Saints Church, Margaret Street in London, Butterfield put Ruskin's principles into practice and in an attempt 'to give dignity to brick' designed a consciously urban, Italian Gothic edifice. It mixed the traditional Tractarian requirements of Middle Pointed with a coloration and polychromy derived from San Francesco at Assisi. The English, Anglican precepts of the Oxford Movement were being subtly internationalised. At St Alban's, Holborn he repeated the same feat with his creative use of constructional polychrome in the stonework. At St Mary Abbots, Kensington, and later at the chapel of Exeter College, Oxford, George Gilbert Scott similarly adhered to Ruskin's strictures on polychrome as well as the importance of ornamentation based on natural forms. Oxford's greatest example of Ruskinian Gothic was, of course, the University Museum, as designed by the architects Deane and Woodward. The building seems taken straight from the pages of *The Stones of Venice*. And the use of the celebrated Irish sculptors, James and John O'Shea, to carve freely their way across the façade was as practical an implementation of the 'Nature of Gothic' as had yet been seen.

Far in advance of his peers, George Gilbert Scott was able to transform the Ruskinian ethic into secular civic architecture. Just as the writer Thomas Hope had questioned whether Victorian Britain measured up to the Hanse cities of the thirteenth century, so Scott asked, 'Do our great manufacturing and commercial towns contrast favourably with the ancient seats of industry and commerce, such as were in Flanders and Germany?' The answer was a resounding no. For though Scott and his fellow Victorians had 'thoroughly revolutionized our ecclesiastical architecture, and have brought it back to our true national type', civil architecture remained untouched.

Few things surprise me more than the neglect which pointed architecture has met with among the builders of town-halls. Next to churches, the finest of medieval structures existing are, perhaps, the town-halls of Flanders, Germany, France, and some of the free cities of Italy; yet scarcely an attempt has been made to revive these noble buildings in England, and town-halls are continually being erected in our provincial towns in styles as thoroughly unsuitable as can be conceived.[96]

Although Scott lacked the intellectual sophistication or religious commitment of a Ruskin or Pugin, he nonetheless crafted some of the greatest Gothic icons of the Victorian city. Indeed, he criticised Pugin and the Ecclesiologists for regarding Gothic as an 'antiquarian movement' which seeks 'to revive all that is ancient, instead of being, as is really the case, preeminently free, comprehensive, and practical; ready to adapt itself to every change in the habits of society, to embrace every new material or system of construction'.[97]

Now lost in a cloud of fumes belched up from the Euston Road, and overtaken as a transport site by the mighty King's Cross, the Midland Grand Hotel at St Pancras Station was Scott's great testimony to the secular applicability of Gothic. A red-brick wonder, it brings together French thirteenth-century Gothic designs complete with terracotta, faded yellow stone and a magnificent clock tower. And although the hotel never really prospered, its steeply pitched roof, castellated features and sweeping entrance make it an unmistakable element of London's Victorian heritage; an iconic status only enhanced by the elegant modernism of its near-neighbour, the British Library.

In his Preston Town Hall in Lancashire; his original plans for the new Foreign Office; Leeds Royal Infirmary; the Ypres-inspired Glasgow University building; and, most magisterially of all, his Albert Memorial in London's Hyde Park, Scott continued to bring the medieval ethic to the heart of the Victorian city. With Ruskin, Scott and Butterfield dominating Gothic design its style irreversibly progressed from the old Perpendicular, 'Christian' model of Rickman and Pugin. In its place came the new Venetian Gothic idiom, a style which was to crescendo in the 1860s and 1870s in the great civic edifices of Alfred Waterhouse, Thomas Worthington and John Henry

Chamberlain. And as we shall see in chapter six, the connotations of Venetian Gothic would prove irresistible to the
commercial elites of the industrialising cities.

The Gothic Revival changed the face of the Victorian city. Its
vision of an organic city rebuilt upon faith, with a spirit of
community and brotherhood expressed through a stratum of
guilds, corporations, fraternities and churches, and reflected
in a civic fabric of noble edifices and godly symbols, appealed
intuitively to the bewildered inhabitants of Britain's cities.
Aesthetically, the triumph of Gothic or Christian architecture
was there for all to see. '"Churches without number" have
been erected in it [Gothic]; colleges – both at Universities and
elsewhere; schools – and among others, the one by Mr Barry at
Birmingham; – hospitals, private mansions, etc,' noted *Fraser's
Magazine*.[98] The Young Englander Lord John Manners took
great pride in reading out a long list of Gothic buildings, from
Northampton Town Hall, to 'public buildings at Cardigan', to
the 'Town Hall at Nantwich', to 'corn exchanges at Alston',
and so forth.[99] Bradford City Hall, Halifax Town Hall, the
Royal Courts of Justice on London's Strand and the Assize
Courts and John Rylands Library in Manchester, as well as
numerous public buildings, squares and monuments dotted
across the Victorian landscape, stood testimony to the impact
of Gothic. As Kenneth Clark acidly noted, 'civil architecture
was far more plagued than most of us realise'.[100] Meanwhile
the Gothic Revival enjoyed almost a clean sweep in the construction of new churches.

    However, the triumph of Gothicism was testimony to more
than just an architectural fad. As *The Times* pointed out in
1858, 'The enthusiasm which the revival of the pointed architecture of the Middle Ages has excited in this country is a
great fact, of more importance to us artistically, politically,
and morally than might at first sight be imagined.'[101] The
Gothic Revival signalled a desperate impatience, even fear, of
the new urban world of the manufacturing age. It posed a
brutal critique of nineteenth-century social dislocation and

proffered instead a revival of the old ethical certainties of an idealised medieval past. Hook's High Church reforms in Leeds, Chalmers's urban feudalism in Glasgow and Sir Benjamin Heywood's merrie pastimes at the Manchester Mechanics' Institute were all attempts to solve the problems of the nineteenth century through an ethic of medievalism. The medieval enthusiasm of the early Victorian years extended beyond Walter Scott and John Henry Newman to offer a practical programme as well as a consciously urban approach to changing the nature of Victorian living. Many thinkers had a vision of a reconstituted civic sphere which was more sophisticated than a simple yearning for the order and stability of a lost rural past. Through faith, architecture, and a new understanding of the citizen's social function, Coketown could be dismantled and the bonds of community rebuilt.

The irony was that even as the jeremiads thundered and old Gothic certainties were celebrated, ever greater numbers continued to flood into the industrial cities. New homes went up, new streets were laid and new businesses formed. So surely there was some virtue to be found amongst the dark Satanic mills?

MACAULAY, THE MIDDLE CLASSES
AND THE MARCH OF PROGRESS

On 26 October 1800, the Sierra Leone nation-builder and anti-slave trade evangelical Zachary Macaulay sauntered out for a recuperative ride through the Leicestershire countryside. It was the day after the birth of his eldest son and the exhausted Zachary needed some time away from the gaggle of in-laws at Rothley Temple, the gloomy Tudor mansion where his boy had been delivered. As Macaulay senior trotted idly through the Midlands lanes and fields, his horse became suddenly spooked by the sound coming from inside a nearby cottage. The animal reared up. Zachary was thrown to the ground and both his arms were instantly broken, in the process earning the puritanical Macaulay his first ever rest from work. The noise which had so disturbed the horse was the hum of a spinning-jenny – a sound which was set to become all too common across industrialising Britain.

For the Macaulay family, few augurs could have been more appropriate. With the birth of Thomas Babington Macaulay and the throwing over of Zachary, the brave new world of industrial Britain welcomed in one of its most militant advocates. Whereas Carlyle and Southey had condemned the spinning-jenny as the handmaiden of all that was wrong with the mechanical nineteenth century, the young Macaulay was born to celebrate the machine's liberating potential.

Thomas Babington, the future lawyer, journalist, Parliamentarian, Indian jurist, epic poet, historian of England, and finally Lord Macaulay, would emerge as the Victorians' greatest apostle for progress. 'The history of England is emphatically the history of progress,' he later declared. As a polemicist and politician, he was among the few defenders of industrial Britain able to hold their own against the reactionary diatribes of Carlyle, Pugin and Ruskin. Brought up in the evangelical hothouse of south London's Clapham, Macaulay was a precocious child. While his father caballed with the legendary William Wilberforce and other great men of Church, state and Empire, the young Macaulay worked diligently trying to compose original poems and cantos. At the age of seven, he attempted a universal history from the Creation to the present day – one of the few projects he was later forced to shelve. From Clapham, Macaulay was sent to a school in Little Shelford, Cambridge and a hint of his future sympathy for the benefits of industrialisation is given in one of his earliest letters:

> Poets may talk of the beauties of nature, the enjoyments of a country life, and rural innocence: but there is another kind of life which, though unsung by bards, is yet to me infinitely superior to the dull uniformity of country life. London is the place for me. Its smoky atmosphere, and its muddy river, charm me more than the pure air of Hertfordshire, and the crystal currents of the river Rib. Nothing is equal to the splendid varieties of London life, 'the fine flow of London talk', and the dazzling brilliancy of London spectacles.[1]

At the age of eighteen Macaulay went up to Trinity College, Cambridge, where he again excelled socially and academically. After university he was called to the Bar and then quickly immersed himself in Whig politics, London journalism and anti-slavery activism. By 1824 he was writing for the country's most prestigious Whig journal, the *Edinburgh Review*, and making a name for himself as the liberal elite's brightest young thing.

Every polemicist needs a straw man and in 1829 Macaulay found the perfect counterfoil for his progressive views when he took up cudgels against Robert Southey. As the previous chapter charted, by the late 1820s the revolutionary-turned-reactionary had become one of the most prominent critics of industrial Britain, a writer for whom the nineteenth century could bring little but disaster; a state of affairs nowhere more evident than in the nation's industrialising cities. In a clinical review of Southey's *Colloquies on ... Society*, Macaulay confronted this apocalyptic vision head-on. With all the aggression of youth, he first mocked and then undermined Southey's every proposition. While the latter, as befitted his romantic stature as Poet Laureate, had talked in generalities, Macaulay used all the statistical evidence he could muster from parliamentary returns, philanthropic surveys and parish relief records. 'Mr Southey does not bring forward a single fact in support of these views, and, as it seems to us, there are facts which lead to very different conclusions.'

According to Macaulay, thanks to the beneficence of the manufacturing system mortality rates were falling (a wholly false proposition with regard to inner-city life expectancy), wealth was spreading (defensible in terms of real wage rates but not in any broader conception of standard of living), and employment booming. 'We might with some plausibility maintain, that the people live longer because they are better fed, better lodged, better clothed, and better attended in sickness; and that these improvements are owing to that increase of national wealth which the manufacturing system has produced.' He was scornful of nostalgic yearnings for some halcyon merrie England and noted witheringly Southey's inclination towards 'mortality and cottages with weather-stains, rather than health and long life with edifices which time cannot mellow'. Macaulay the aspirant statesman declared it was just fanciful to believe the nation could be governed along the lines of 'rose-bushes and poor-rates, rather than steam-engines and independence'.[2]

The rhetorical assault continued as he ridiculed Southey's grasp of economics, his authoritarian reverence for state control ('his principle is that no man can do any thing so well for himself, as his rulers, be they who they may, can do it for him'), and his perverse respect for the theology of Charles I and Archbishop Laud. Macaulay was adamant that the progress of modern civilisation, of which manufacturing and industry were such crucial components, had brought Britain and its people many more advantages than drawbacks. Concluding the article with a virtuoso display of Victorian self-confidence, Macaulay suggested that if he were to prophesy (in 1829) that by 1930, 'a population of fifty million, better fed, clad, and lodged than the English of our time, will cover these islands – that Sussex and Huntingdonshire will be wealthier than the wealthiest parts of the West Riding of Yorkshire now are, – that machines, constructed on principles yet undiscovered, will be in every house, – that there will be no highways but railroads, no travelling but by steam ... many people would think us insane'. But for Macaulay such advances in civilisation were all possible given the dynamic potential of progress when driven by the 'prudence and energy' of the English people. And, to his great credit, his predictions were not far wrong.

T.B. Macaulay's article was a call to arms to confront the fashionable but debilitating medieval nostalgia. He was joined in his struggle by the house journal of the utilitarians, the *Westminster Review*, which dismissed the medieval past as an age distinguished only 'by moral depravity and physical wretchedness'. The so-called knightly virtues and spirit of chivalry which Kenelm Digby and others had revered were, in fact, lost amid a surfeit of assassination, torture, rape, arson, pillage and irreligion. Rather than the knights elevating society (as the participants of the Eglinton tournament so ardently believed), 'it was not until very late, and with great difficulty, that the rest of the world could succeed in civilizing them'.[3]

In the provincial press, the Romantic revival was increasingly dismissed as Gothic barbarism, and a barbarism that was in grave danger of derailing the country's progress. In an article upon 'The Political Philosophy of Young England', the

Manchester Guardian dismissed the maypoles and merrie feudalism of the past. The newspaper stressed instead the 'grinding merciless oppression' of the Middle Ages and argued that the defenders of the barbaric past should feel profoundly thankful their lot had 'been cast in the nineteenth century, rather than in the twelfth'.[4] In a speech to the assembled artisans of the Yorkshire Union of Mechanics' Institutes, the Liberal politician Lord Morpeth was eager to denigrate the medieval past. Despite being the future Earl of Carlisle and heir to the great Castle Howard in Yorkshire, Morpeth celebrated the modern era of commercial civilisation in contrast to the aristocratic dominion of old. Where now the mechanics of Victorian Britain came together for self-help and mutual improvement, in medieval times 'the opposite armies of the rival Roses were drawn up in menacing array, and soon mixed in murderous conflict'. A gentle rivalry between competing civic societies was a far better condition than the old 'brawls between the troops of Warwick and the retainers of Clifford'. Thankfully, 'the days of the barons are become the days of the Mechanics' Institutes'.[5]

Hesitantly at first, advocates of manufacturing and the industrial city were entering public debate with greater confidence. The Victorian city started to be defended and even admired as a symbol of progress, prosperity and liberty. The medieval nostalgia of Pugin and Southey was increasingly rubbished by a ready posse of urban industrialists, historians and liberal partisans. Instead, the nineteenth century was championed as the 'Age of Great Cities' and there emerged the first buds of that quintessentially Victorian ethic, civic pride. Here were the people, in George Eliot's phrase, of 'eager unrest' who were 'not convinced that old England was as good as possible'. By 1848, *The Economist* magazine felt confident enough to suggest that 'Modern towns are great wonders and great blessings ... the home of advancing civilization, the abodes of genius, and the centres of all the knowledge, the arts, and the science of our race.'[6]

i The Great Middle Class

Entering the musty confines of the Great Hall up the stairs in Manchester's Town Hall, one is immediately affected by a sense of decay. The room is badly lit, the surroundings dusty and, save the occasional tourist and meandering councillor, eerily empty. However, a closer look around the hall's walls reveals a set of striking frescoes of bewildering determinacy by the self-same author of *Work*, Ford Madox Brown. It is a vibrant cycle chronicling Manchester's mercantile heritage as well as the city's contribution to the advance of civilisation. Among the finest are 'The Establishment of Flemish Weavers in Manchester, AD 1363'; 'The Proclamation Regarding Weights and Measures, AD 1556', which esoterically heralds the introduction of the economically vital notion of quantifiable produce; and 'John Kay: Inventor of the Fly Shuttle, AD 1753'. But the most intriguing is a narrative depiction of 'Bradshaw's Defence of Manchester, AD 1642'. It recounts the city's successful resistance against the Cavalier army of King Charles I during the opening months of the English Civil War. It is a celebration of the struggle for religious devotion and political liberty by what is depicted as a heroic, urban bourgeoisie. And despite its historical subject, it is a picture which beautifully summates a rigidly opposed strand of thinking about the Victorian city to that offered by Young England and their pre-industrial fellow travellers.

With a fervour given to few other historical periods, the Victorians lived and breathed the English Civil War. It was said one was a Cavalier or Roundhead before becoming a Tory or Liberal. The religious struggles and constitutional clashes which enveloped Victorian politics were frequently debated with the Civil War in mind. Macaulay was a keen historian of the 1640s, believing Cromwell 'the greatest prince that has ever ruled England'; Thomas Carlyle was an equally ardent admirer, editing a life and letters of Old 'Nol; while George Eliot modelled the heroine of *Middlemarch*, Dorothea Brooke, on a consciously Puritan lineage. But this passion was not limited to the high politics of Westminster or literary salons of Chelsea. Mechanics' Institutes and Mutual Improvement Societies actively debated the nature of the Civil War and the character of Cromwell. In Oxfordshire in 1852 the Wallington Mutual Improvement Society hosted a debate on the topic which lasted a full seven evenings before eventually resolving that 'a better Christian' than Cromwell, 'a more noble-minded spirit, a greater warrior, a more constant man has scarcely ever appeared on the face of the earth'.[7]

Nowhere was an interest in the posterity of the Civil War and the call of the Good Old Cause more apparent than in the Nonconformist, industrialising cities. Visit any town hall or chapel in a northern city and it will not take you long to discover a statue of Oliver Cromwell or a monument to a fallen Civil War hero. In Huddersfield, local Congregationalists even christened their new church, 'Milton'. During the conflict, the vast majority of commercial towns – Bradford, Birmingham, Manchester, Liverpool – had aligned themselves with the Roundheads. The legacy of that bloody struggle for religious toleration, constitutional propriety and appreciation of the political rights of the middle classes was rekindled in contemporary debates over the virtue of the Victorian city. In Manchester, James Phillips Kay used the motif of the Civil War to author an anonymous pamphlet arguing for electoral reform in which he raffishly cast himself as the descendant of 'an ancient stock of Nonconformists' possessed of large estates during the glorious but all-too-brief days of the Commonwealth: 'a sun which "went down at noon," and left this kingdom to the darkness of a sensual dynasty of hereditary despots'. He went on to celebrate 'the roundheaded, cropeared, and puritanical virtue of the middle classes' before condemning the idea of a Cavalier aristocracy entertaining political power in Manchester.[8]

One of the most influential historians of the English Civil War was the French historian and statesman, François Guizot. A brilliant lawyer, then historian at the Sorbonne, then Prime

Minister, ambassador to London, refugee and finally grand man of letters, Guizot provided some of the most sophisticated and popular interpretations of the seventeenth century. In a series of publications ranging over twenty-five volumes, from *Histoire de la révolution d'Angleterre* to *Histoire de la république d'Angleterre et du protectorat d'Oliver Cromwell*, Guizot stands alongside S.R. Gardiner in putting civil war studies on a scholarly footing. Far more of a cultural and intellectual historian than Gardiner, what Guizot was concerned with was 'the rise of the middle classes', which he regarded as having played a constituent part in the English revolution. Although himself a firm opponent of revolutionary insurgency, having lost his father to the French Revolution and having lived through the turmoil of 1815, Guizot was convinced of the need for the middle classes to assume their rightful place within society – and only a proper appreciation of history could further that.

The French professor attempted to instil precisely such self-knowledge through his teachings at the Sorbonne, which extended beyond the Civil War to a broader account of European history. In a series of lectures delivered in 1828, Guizot trawled through the history of Europe since the Roman Empire to prove that every step on the path to political pluralism, prosperity and religious tolerance was the work of the middle classes. His lectures identified three components of European civilisation (the Roman; the Christian; and the Germanic) which had historically competed for supremacy but never achieved it. And in that very plurality of values lay the ingredient to Europe's extraordinary civilisation. This allowed Europe, unlike stationary societies such as China, to keep developing intellectually and culturally. The middle class or Third Estate was the product of the Roman tradition of municipality and local autonomy. But it was only after the collapse of the Roman Empire that the growth in towns and municipalities fostered the growth of a middle class. 'It has been in the towns and by the operation of municipal liberties,' Guizot later wrote of the eleventh century, 'that the mass of the inhabitants, the middle class, has been formed and has acquired importance in the State.'⁹

This rise of the middle class proved essential in dragging Europe out from its feudal morass. It was the spur to the wealth-creation, cultural achievement and self-government which marked the wondrous history of Europe from the twelfth century onwards. The middle classes created wealth, built glorious edifices and fostered the modern forms of liberal democracy. Through his lectures and books, Guizot umbilically linked the glories of European civilisation to the industry of its middle classes. Even Marx and Engels agreed, as they grudgingly put it at the forefront of *The Communist Manifesto*: 'The bourgeoisie ... has accomplished wonders far surpassing Egyptian pyramids, Roman aqueducts, and Gothic cathedrals; it has conducted expeditions that put in shade all former Exoduses of nations and crusades.'¹⁰

Guizot found a ready audience for his views in Britain. His work was widely published, he toured the country, and became the toast of the country's provincial elite. In the *British and Foreign Review*, George Eliot's husband G.H. Lewes crowned him 'the greatest of living historians' and went on to declare that 'everyone knows and admires the little work on "European Civilization", of which no less than three English translations exist'.¹¹ In the *Westminster Review* he called the work 'the most delightful and important introduction to the study of modern history'.¹² John Stuart Mill was another champion of Guizot's, frequently reviewing his histories and praising his liberal politics. In 1829 *The Athenaeum* reprinted Guizot's lectures on European civilisation with the rejoinder that, 'the name of M. Guizot is too splendidly known amongst us, by researches into our own history ... that we should need to introduce, by any notice of the author, our remarks on this his recent publication'.¹³

Guizot was all the more appreciated in Britain as the middle classes were facing a particularly torrid time during the early nineteenth century. Today, as the Deputy Prime Minister John Prescott (son of a railwayman; himself a ship's steward before entering Parliament as a Labour MP) memorably remarked, we are all middle-class. And it can plausibly be argued that in the twenty-first century the broad mass of British society does indeed belong to a fluid and indeterminate stratum of middle class.[14] But in the early nineteenth century, the language of class was first being applied to what was traditionally known as 'the middling sort' or 'middle rank'. Increasingly, the 'bourgeoisie' (as the French termed them) were identified as a specific class with an aggressive social and political agenda often at odds with the working and the landed classes. In fact, the reputation of the middle class in the early 1800s was fairly bleak. Throughout most of the twentieth century, Western civilisation has generally regarded the middle class as the bulwark of political stability. But as the nineteenth century broke, it stood accused of fomenting the greatest act of political insurgency since 1649, the French Revolution.

Early on in the Revolution, the Scottish lawyer James Mackintosh had bravely praised France's enlightened political reforms. In particular, he singled out the throwing-over of the *ancien régime* and its despotic monarchy as the work of the 'commercial, or monied interest' which had always been 'less prejudiced, more liberal, and more intelligent than the landed gentry'.[15] As the Revolution ground on and the bloodshed of Robespierre's Terror began to temper liberal enthusiasm, Mackintosh performed a dramatic about-turn and instead declared that the Revolution had swung out of control because of the *lack* of an effective, moderating middle class. But the damage was done. Henceforth the French Revolution was seen as a middle-class insurrection. According to a recent study of the image of the middle class, 'a significant legacy of the 1790s debates was the representation of the "middle-class" as prone to political innovation and agitation'.[16] The middle class were caricatured as rootless, money-driven political radicals with no ties to religion, institution or land. They were happy to overthrow all rules and classes in their quest for commercial gain.

Faced with this damaging and persistent slur, liberal thinkers

made a concerted attempt to resurrect the middle-class reputation. Instead of the unpatriotic and irrational money-men of
conservative lore, the liberal polemicists tried to build up a
picture of the middle class as a wise, reasonable and patriotic
rank in society. James Mill protested that the middle class
'contains beyond all comparison, the greatest proportions of
the intelligence, industry, and wealth of the state. In it are the
heads that invent, and the hands that execute; the enterprise
that projects, and the capital by which these projects are
carried into operation ... the men in fact who think for the
rest of the world, and who really do the business of the world,
are the men of this class.'[17]

However, in crafting this benevolent image and condemning
the Terror, many middle-class protagonists remained hopeful
of defending the early principles of the French Revolution.
The attack on the tyranny of Church and monarchy which
inspired the events of 1789 remained a noble calling. In Leeds,
the newspaper publisher Edward Baines described how his
fellow middle-class Dissenters 'were charmed with the broad
principles of civil and religious liberty laid down in France in
the early stages of the revolution, and they continued to hope,
perhaps too long, that that mighty experiment would have a
favourable issue. When disappointed by the crimes and horrors
perpetrated in the name of liberty, they did not abandon their
attachment to liberty itself.'[18] In Liverpool, the banker and
philanthropist William Roscoe celebrated 'the spectacle of a
great nation rising up, as one man, to regain the station and
the happiness from which it had been debarred by centuries
of misgovernment'. And while he was appalled by the later
turn of events, Roscoe and his bourgeois colleagues always
chose to defend the initial ideals.[19]

It was Guizot's achievement to write a history which
allowed the middle classes to look beyond the depredations of
the Terror and celebrate their otherwise virtuous role in the
Revolution. The middle classes did not need to accept that
the only alternative to the monarchical absolutism of Louis
XVI was the violence of popular sovereignty. What they needed

to prove was their own unique suitability for power. Guizot argued that to enjoy the fruits of the French Revolution (the early ideals and high principles of republican liberty) without the Terror which followed, it was essential that the rational and industrious class, the middle class (*'classe moyenne'*), held political power. It was in order to prove they were capable for the task that Guizot set about writing his history of middle-class progress; his task was to persuade the middle class that it was, as one historian has put it, 'descended from a race of heroes' and had the capacity for political power.

As we saw in chapter one, there was no greater symbol of modernity and progress than the industrial city. And the denizens and champions of that new civilisation were the middle classes: the professionals, the merchants, the industrialists, the bureaucrats, retailers, and whole non-manual grouping. The city was a reflection of their virtue, of their contribution to society and political preponderance; it was their civilisation. If the image of the middle classes was to be refashioned, then the image of the city also needed to change. The middle class symbolised the city and the city the middle class. Each had made the other and each was facing an equally wretched reputation. As Bradshaw had so successfully protected Manchester in 1642, so Macaulay, Guizot and their middle-class Ironsides were ready to defend their citadel once more.

ii FAITH IN THE CITY

Almost unique in French political circles (just as true now as then), Guizot was a Protestant. His politically inopportune beliefs led him not only to campaign for religious toleration within France, but also underpinned his historical approach to the English Civil War. Indeed, what attracted him to the history of the seventeenth century was that epoch's struggle for religious liberty. Guizot was the first to describe the Civil War as a 'Puritan revolution' and his account of the period not only positioned the middle classes as a race of heroes, but it also affixed the history of Nonconformity with an equally glorious past – a past which was just as badly needed in the early nineteenth century. For if the middle class as a whole was blamed for the frenzy of the French Revolution, then Dissenters were particularly reviled. The conservative Edmund Burke branded Unitarians a 'political faction' dedicated to the destruction of the Church of England, the subversion of the state and the creation of a political regime modelled on revolutionary France.[20] In 1791, he condemned the 'Phalanx of Party which exists in the body of the Dissenters', and estimated that nine-tenths of these were devoted 'to the principles of the French Revolution'.[21] Dissenters were just as in need of a helpful history of industry and progress which might portray them as a patriotic, loyal and virtuous component of British society.

The English Civil War provided that. For two centuries, Dissenters had been portrayed as the cause of all the misery and maelstrom of the Civil War. But as the pendulum of historical opinion began to swing against the Cavaliers and in favour of the Roundheads, the Good Old Cause once again appeared a tradition to be proud of. The valiant role of the Puritans in fending off Charles I's tyranny, in saving the country from Catholicism and arbitrary government, started to be more confidently celebrated. Indeed, it was tentatively suggested that only because of the stand of the cities and the bravery of the Nonconformist middle class were Victorians able to enjoy their much-lauded civil liberties. The Bradford writer John James pointed out that 'to the Non-conformists, Englishmen are indebted for some of the most valuable prerogatives they enjoy'. The men who 'maintained the right to worship according to the dictates of their own conscience' were also the citizens 'most devotedly attached to the principle of civil liberty'.[22] Such opinions were made in good company, for Bradford was one of the few manufacturing cities where the number of Nonconformists outnumbered Anglicans. But these liberties were gained at a price. In his *Historic Sketch of Bradford*, Edward Collinson described how the city's 'hatred of intolerance and oppression' and 'honest attachment to the cause of civil and religious liberty' caused Bradford to suffer terribly under the 'regal absolutism arrogated by Charles I'.[23] And the city did indeed experience some particularly bloody skirmishes during the wars.

Partly because of the 'memory' of such hard-won liberties, and the martyrology of its victims, little was more insulting to the civic leaders of Victorian cities than the suggestion that urban life was irreligious. The oft-repeated allegation that Coketown was a spiritual wasteland where heathen savages lumbered from factory to slum was an affront to the Dissenting tradition. The Nonconformists of the industrial north were themselves in no doubt they pursued a far more godly life than the red-faced, huntin' and shootin' Anglican clergymen presiding over empty rural parishes. Indeed, they argued that cities, far from being the enemy of religious observance, were in fact essential to Christian practice. Protestantism and urban civilisation, ever since the Reformation had emerged from the city states of Germany, were natural bedfellows. According to one defender of the piety of the Victorian city, 'the strength of Protestantism is a strength on the side of industry, of human improvement, and of the civilization which leads to the formation of great cities'.[24]

It should not be surprising that the most effective advocates of the Victorian city, of its ethos, its history and its values, were the Nonconformist communities. As we saw in chapter three, the manufacturing cities of northern England were becoming increasingly dominated by chapel-goers. By the 1880s six out of ten religious attendees in cities were chapel-goers. What is more, the most influential members of urban civil society invariably belonged to the Nonconformist congregations. And amongst those congregations, it was frequently the Unitarians (Protestant worshippers who denied the Holy Trinity and placed rationality above spiritualism) who stood out as the most articulate champions of civic virtue.

In Manchester, the Unitarian chapels of Cross Street,

Mosley Street and Church Street nurtured the leading figures
of the day: the Heywoods, Kennedys, Potters, Gregs and Hib-
berts. These commercial and manufacturing dynasties often
intermarried with other Unitarian families to create a closely
meshed civic elite. In the first half of the nineteenth century,
nearly 60 per cent of the known marriages of the trustees of
the Cross Street Chapel were to daughters of other Unitarians
in the area.[25] Out of the 22,255 people recorded as being at
worship in Manchester in the religious census of 1851, only
1,670 were Unitarians. But within the Unitarian community
could be counted such influential figures as Sir Benjamin
Heywood, founder of Manchester's Statistical Society, Mechanics' Institute, and sometime MP; and his close friend
William Rathbone Greg, a successful industrialist, social critic
and active figure in the councils and institutes of the Manchester liberal world. Indeed, eleven of the twenty-two men
on the founding committee of the Manchester Mechanics'
Institute were Unitarians.[26]

  In Birmingham, Asa Briggs has described the Unitarian
Church of the Messiah as the 'cultural and intellectual centre
of a whole society'.[27] Amongst its congregation in the 1850s
sat a young industrialist from London called Joseph Chamberlain. In Liverpool, the Renshaw Street Chapel was the place
of worship for the mercantile Rathbone and Roscoe families,
who did more than any other to elevate the city's cultural
standing. In Leeds the Mill Hill congregation played an equally
impressive role in generating a civic elite, while its City Square
Chapel, now little more than a car park and short-cut to
the 'City Square Shopping Plaza', was once the intellectual
fulcrum of the city where a new ethos of civic pride was
promulgated. Meanwhile, in Newcastle the proud heritage of
urban Christianity was outlined most forcibly by the Unitarian divine, the Revd William Turner. His Hanover Square
Chapel became the centre for the city's commercial and cultural leaders from where campaigns for free schooling and a
Mechanics' Society were launched. In his preaching, Turner
consistently emphasised the historical mission of the city in

defending religious toleration and civil liberty. On his death in 1854 at the ripe age of ninety-three, his successor spoke of how Turner regarded religious liberty 'as the foundation and pillar, the security and bulwark of all true freedom, the precursor to the attainment and enjoyment of all civil rights and enlightened civil independence'.[28] And those civil liberties could only properly be safeguarded in the city.

Turner could have further stressed the religiosity of the city by pointing to the multitude of places for worship in Newcastle. In addition to the large number of Anglican churches fronted by the fourteenth-century St Nicholas's, there was his own Hanover Square Chapel, the Wall Knox Meeting House for the Scottish Presbyterians, the Meeting House of Friends for the Quakers, the Clavering Place Meeting House for the United Secession Church, the Zion Chapel for the Independents, the Brunswick Place Chapel for the Wesleyan Methodists, *ad infinitum*. This competitive market for souls was replicated across other Victorian cities. Nottingham's Dissenting community boasted the Castle Gate Chapel, Sion Chapel, St James's Street Chapel, Friar Lane Chapel – as well as Baptist chapels, Methodist chapels, and a Quaker Friends Meeting House. By the mid-century, Bradford had 11,500 Nonconformist worshippers practising in forty different chapels. Such Christian fervour prompted one Congregationalist to comment that 'so far is it from being in the nature of the system of manufactures to render men indifferent to religion, that where that system obtains, much more is manifestly done to uphold and diffuse religion than is done in neighbourhoods of a different description'.[29]

Manchester was, of course, just as well endowed as Bradford. In 1842 the Nonconformist writer Benjamin Love produced *The Handbook of Manchester*, which combined history, topography, liberal politics and handy facts. Chapter ten was entitled 'Conditions of Morals – Crime – Religious Institutions – Places of Worship', and Love took great pride in listing the 'many institutions which have for their praiseworthy object the spread of moral principles'. Of particular note were the immense sums recently subscribed 'for the erection of churches in various destitute parts of the town'. After listing the myriad chapels, he noted how 'The places of worship in Manchester are numerous.'[30] This view was seconded by William Cooke Taylor during his 1841 tour of the manufacturing districts, during which he was thoroughly impressed by Manchester's 'zeal for religion, charity, and science', citing as evidence the massive amounts subscribed to the fund for building churches and to the Methodist Centenary Fund.[31]

By the mid-century, the Nonconformist congregations were increasingly active in constructing new chapels or embellishing existing structures. As the Church of England tried to regain the spiritual initiative in the city, Dissenting communities responded in kind with a massive building programme underwritten by the ability of the manufacturing and mercantile Nonconformist congregations to mobilise large resources quickly. In Leeds, the august East Parade Congregational Chapel was erected at the cost of £15,000 – of which over £1,000 came from the opening services.[32] When the Great George Street Congregationalist Church in Liverpool burned down, the church elders decided to rebuild immediately. On the very day of the disaster the congregation managed to raise the enormous sum of £3,762 before the embers were cold. The church was rebuilt and continues to stand today as one of Liverpool's most sumptuous classical buildings – although it now resounds to the organised chaos of a local community centre and kids' club known as 'The Blackie' (because of the soot on the original building), rather than the earnest injunctions of Nonconformist preaching.

In his fulsome defence of urban religiosity, *The Social, Educational, and Religious State of the Manufacturing Districts*, Edward Baines recorded that in Lancashire, while the population had increased 104 per cent between 1801 and 1841, there had been an increase in church and chapel room of 241 per cent. And of the churches and chapels built since 1801, the voluntary donations of the public had subscribed nine times as many as the state. Nationally, the figure was even starker. 'Since 1815 the Ecclesiastical Commissioners have built 281 churches, out of the public money, throughout all England and Wales; but since the year 1800, voluntary zeal has built 1,178 churches and chapels in these Manufacturing Districts alone![33] The Congregationalist Robert Vaughan was quick to remark on the lesson of the Nonconformist self-help spirit. 'It is found in such places [manufacturing cities], that the edifices raised both by the state and by the more wealthy of the land for public worship, are not so numerous as are those which owe their existence to the voluntary effort of the people themselves.'[34]

For Dissenters, this forest of churches and chapels was a sign of a healthy spiritual community. Pugin had abhorred the multiplication of faiths in the Victorian city and in his *Contrasts* provocatively countered the sublime unitary faith of the Roman Catholic Church against the Babel of a Baptist chapel, Unitarian chapel, Quaker Meeting House, and Wesleyan Centenary chapel. Pugin meant this as an insult – indicative of the false choice of modern existence – but to Dissenters it was a compliment. There could only be true piety where the individual could make a voluntary, rational choice over whether and where to worship. Forcing the individual to attend church through state sanctions was not the sign of a godly society but a theocratic tyranny. As Macaulay argued in his 1829 essay, 'Mr. Southey thinks that the yoke of the church is dropping off, because it is loose. We feel convinced that it is borne only because it is easy, and that, in the instant in which an attempt is made to tighten it, it will be flung away.'[35] Victorian cities, with their mass of new chapels and churches, provided a far more spiritual arena than their medieval forebears. Through the pages of the *Edinburgh Review*, Baron Mounteagle made the liberal position clear. If, he asked, we believe that 'a greatly increased number of churches, and of ministers of religion, and religious zeal promote the well-being of a people', then it was quite clear that 'it is among our commercial communities that these principles of good have been brought into the most vigorous activity.'[36] Baines was even more bullish:

> Comparing these seats of Manufacture, then, either with the great Metropolis of the land, – with the selectest portions of Westminster, in the very presence of the throne, the legislature, the aristocracy, and the hierarchy, – with the Arcadias of Dorsetshire and the South – and I may add, even with the learned shades of Oxford, – I maintain that we have no need to blush or hang our heads, whether you make the comparison in regard to Education, Morality, Religion, Industry, or Order.[37]

iii CITY AIR MAKES YOU FREE

What Bradshaw had supposedly fought for in Manchester in 1642 (modern scholarship suggests Colonel Rosworm played a more important role in the city's defence), and what Ford Madox Brown had articulated in his Town Hall frescoes, was a conception of liberty, political as well as religious. The famous German aphorism *Stadtluft macht frei* (city air makes you free), applied even amongst the polluted smog of industrial Britain. Like its predecessors, the modern city was taken to be a symbol of liberty which enjoined upon it a historic mandate to further the call of political, religious and social freedom. Throughout history, the urban middle classes had played a central role in the struggle for political liberty against the despotism of the landed interest. It was the wealth of the burgher class in cities which had allowed it to challenge feudal backwardness and elevate Britain to its commercial and imperial supremacy. Guizot's histories had purposefully opposed the interests of the feudal class to that of the burgher or middle class. Across the pages of the *Edinburgh Review* Baron Mounteagle praised Guizot's work, deriding the 'jealousy felt towards the commercial and manufacturing interests' as little more than a love for 'the feudality of ancient times' and a passionate desire 'to restore the full dominion of the sceptre, the sword, and the mitre'.[38] The battle for the city was a struggle between the sunlit uplands of modern liberty and the dark ages of feudal-clerical tyranny, and 'it is in the annals of great cities, of their commercial inhabitants, that we trace the growth of civilization'.[39]

This choice was driven home by the businessman turned radical politician, Richard Cobden. By the early 1830s, the London-born Cobden had progressed from being a clerk in his uncle's warehouse in the capital to a wealthy calico printer in Manchester. As his business flourished, Cobden worked himself into the centre of the city's expanding social world. As befitted his commercial stature, he became a member of the Statistical Society, was appointed Vice President of the Literary and Philosophical Society, and helped to establish the city's staunchly liberal Athenaeum club. He also became more deeply involved in politics as he watched aghast the prodigious excesses of British foreign policy. With all the caricatured myopia of a Manchester man, Cobden railed against the cost of an interventionist foreign policy which only benefited the aristocratic classes while hitting the middle classes through loss of trade. In 1835 he published *England, Ireland and America*, condemning the principles of British foreign policy in contrast to the ecumenical commercialism of America. 'The middle and industrious classes of England can have no interest apart from the preservation of peace. The honours, the fame, the emoluments of war belong not to them; the battle-plain is the harvest-field of the aristocracy, watered with the blood of the people.'[40]

However, it was events closer to home which drew Cobden more actively into the political arena. The 1835 Municipal Corporation Act had begun the modern era of local government by ending the old system of unelected corporations which had previously controlled civic affairs and introducing instead a degree of local elections for councillors. However, because Manchester was not governed by a corporation, it was unaffected by the legislation. Defoe's 'greatest mere village in England', the European epicentre of the Industrial Revolution where de Tocqueville, Engels and the world of public opinion had been drawn, was governed by a cacophony of competing authorities some of which emanated from bygone juris- dictions. For Cobden, the fact that Manchester's affairs were still controlled by a feudal lord of the manor, in the form of the Mosley family, was an embarrassment all too typical of British middle-class diffidence. In contrast to their Con- tinental peers, the kowtowing of the middle classes was humiliating. 'Our countrymen, if they were possessed of a little of the *mind* of the merchants and manufacturers of Frankfurt, Chemnitz, Elberfeld, etc. would become the de Medicis, and Fuggers, and De Witts of England, instead of glorying in being the toadies of a clod-pole aristocracy, only less enlightened than themselves.'[41]

In 1838, he began a campaign to free the city from these feudal apron-strings and demand the kind of civic self- governance Manchester's position and wealth deserved. In writing 'Incorporate Your Borough – By a Radical Reformer', Cobden produced one of the great Victorian paeans to middle- class virtue. The tract condemned the 'landlord interest' and the town's barbarous ancestors, who 'used to make excursions from their strongholds to plunder, oppress, and ravage, with fire and sword, the peaceable and industrious inhabitants of the towns'.[42] It was the creative, prosperous and tolerant middle classes who had built Manchester and it was time their contribution was recognised. Unlike Engels, who had depicted the 'bourgeoisie' as an economic class, Cobden chose to define middle-class identity in moral, political and, above all, urban terms. The 'intelligent and wealthy community of Man- chester' needed to unite in battle against monopoly and priv- ilege and, just like their burgher ancestors, 'resist the aristocratic plunderers'. Incorporation and middle-class self- government would restore the vitality of the town and secure its future prosperity. It was, argued Cobden, vital that Man- chester was placed beyond 'the control of a booby squirearchy, who abhor us not for our love of political freedom than for those active and intellectual pursuits which contrast so strongly with that mental stupor in which they exist – I had almost said – vegetate'.[43]

The campaign was a success and in 1838 Manchester was incorporated, with the victorious Cobden as one of the city's new aldermen. The campaign had produced in Cobden a taste for politics and he now set off to counter a more debilitating form of economic servitude. Introduced in 1815 to protect the landed classes from suffering during the post-Napoleonic-War depression, the Corn Laws had managed to stay on the Statute Book for another thirty years, restricting wheat imports and artificially inflating the price of bread. While 'Young England' regarded them as a necessity for rural estate-holding and social cohesion, for the Manchester middle classes the Corn Laws were a symbol of the aristocratic corruption of the state and an indefensible subsidy to the country's richest landowners. In 1838 Britain experienced one of the worst harvests of the nineteenth century and prices rocketed. Renewed opposition to the Corn Laws spread through the northern cities and in September at the York Hotel, Manchester an Anti-Corn-Law Association was established. By the following year it had become the Anti-Corn-Law League, with Richard Cobden at its head.

The League understood itself as part of the historical mission of the urban bourgeoisie to take on the vested interest of the landed elite. They were fulfilling the dynamic calling of the middle classes throughout European civilisation. In biblical, liberation language, Cobden spurred on his followers by describing their struggle as a 'Hanseatic League against the feudal Corn-Law plunderers'. In a rhetorical flourish, drawing on the same history of European progress which Guizot had outlined, he described how 'The castles which had crowned the rocks along the Rhine, the Danube, and the Elbe, had once been the stronghold of feudal oppressors, but they had been dismantled by a League; and now they only adorned the landscape as picturesque memorials of the past, while the people below had lost all fear of plunder, and tilled their vineyards in peace.' One of the League's greatest orators, the Unitarian

minister W.J. Fox, told a mass meeting in Covent Garden in
1843 that the League's most important asset was 'the power of
great cities, the agency of civilization; of great towns and cities
that first reared their towers as landmarks when the deluge of
barbarism in the middle ages was beginning to subside'. The
battle could only be won if the towns and cities of Britain
actively mobilised against the iniquitous tax. And what did the
great urban middle class have to fear? 'Landlords! They built
not this magnificent metropolis – they covered not these 40 sq.
miles with the great mass of human dwellings that spread over
them – they crowd not our ports with shipping – they filled not
your city with its monuments of science and of art'.[44]

   In 1846 Sir Robert Peel granted the League its wish by
confronting 'Young England', splitting the Tory Party, and
repealing the Corn Laws. Prices fell, imports surged and the
diet of the working classes was transformed as the Manchester
middle classes celebrated a defining cultural moment. In com-
memoration of the victory, a Free Trade Hall was erected in
the city centre. Modelled on the Gran Guardia Vecchia in
Verona, which the architect Edward Walters had visited on a
Continental tour, it was, in A.J.P. Taylor's wonderful phrase,
'dedicated, like the United States of America, to a proposition –
one as noble and beneficent as any ever made ... It was difficult
to sit in the Free Trade Hall, and still more difficult to speak
from its platform (as I once did), without recalling its political
significance. The men of Manchester had brought down the
nobility and gentry of England in a bloodless, but decisive,
Crécy. The Free Trade Hall was the symbol of their triumph.'[45]
The venue is now anachronistically being transformed into a
'Radisson Edwardian' hotel. Described as a 'deluxe hotel on
one of the city's most historic sites', it seems an appropriate
if rather vulgar updating of the free trade ethic.

iv INDUSTRIAL MARVELS

The 'Manchester school', as it first became known as a slur
by Benjamin Disraeli and then subsequently worn as an ideo-

logical badge of honour, was adamant that economic liberty was necessary both in international trade but also in internal regulation. It was the liberty allowed to the manufacturers which had produced the successes of the Industrial Revolution and, in that perpetual defence of inaction, it was alleged that whatever restricted industry only ended up hurting the working man and his family. To counter the baleful impression of industry which so many 'in the South of England' retained, the Leeds journalist Edward Baines aimed to legitimise modern manufacturing by crafting for it as glorious a historical narrative as Guizot had offered the middle classes. At the beginning of his *History of the Cotton Manufacture in Great Britain* (1835), Baines suggested that such a study was of far greater worth than 'the annals of wars and dynasties or ... nineteen-twentieths of the matters which fill the pages of history'.[46] What followed was a fast-track account of the progress, technical inventiveness and success of the British cotton industry from Edward III up to the 1830s, when it was able to beat India at its own game. Baines then embarked on a page-by-page rebuttal of the allegations levelled against factory-owners and cotton manufacturers. To critics who complained of slave wages, Baines rejoined that there were 'thousands of spinners in the cotton districts who eat meat every day, wear broad cloth on the Sunday ... furnish their houses with mahogany and carpets'. He went on to praise the philanthropy of the cotton lords and the social and educational benefits of child labour. As for the slurs of James Phillips Kay and C. Turner Thackrah, that hours of repetitive labour were harming the physical development of the workers, it was simply untrue:

> It is scarcely possible for any employment to be lighter. The position of the body is not injurious: the general attitude is erect, but the children walk about, and have opportunity of frequently sitting if they are so disposed. On visiting mills, I have generally remarked the coolness and equanimity of the work-people, even of the children, whose manner

seldom indicates anxious care, and is more frequently sport-
ive than gloomy.[47]

Indeed, Baines later argued that the factory worker should
think himself lucky since he had a chance to experience
first-hand 'the benefit of the most perfect and most expensive
tools in the world – all the splendid inventions of Arkwright,
Hargreaves, Crompton, Cartwright, Watt, and many others,
combined and arranged in an admirable series, within one
building'.[48] His conclusions were supported by the social
critic Sir George Head, whose hagiographic *Home Tour
Through the Manufacturing Districts of England* was an
elegy to the new industrial elite. Head would hear no
nonsense about an exploited working class. Rather, he celebrated the community spirit of the cotton mill compared to
the domestic solitude of the rapidly dying-out weaver. 'I saw
around me a crowd of apparently happy beings, working in
lofty well-ventilated buildings, with whom a comparison
could no more in fairness be drawn with the solitary weaver
plying his shuttle from morning to night in his close dusty
den, than is the bustle and occupation of life with soul-
destroying solitude.'[49]

Others followed in Head's wake. By far the most significant
was Robert Vaughan's *The Age of Great Cities: or, Modern
Society Viewed In Its Relation To Intelligence, Morals, and
Religion* (1843). Vaughan was both a first-rate historian, with
a Chair at the University of London, and a leading Congregationalist, later combining the roles as Principal of the
Lancashire Independent College which was established to
train the Nonconformist ministry. Vaughan saw Nonconformity and urban living as inseparable states and an attack
on one constituted an affront to the other. He was as passionate
a defender of the nineteenth century as Macaulay and saw the
greatest evidence of progress in the fast-expanding cities of
mid-Victorian Britain. Almost every aspect of urban living was
a testimony to progress. And like Edward Baines, Vaughan
had no patience with the malicious allegations of Kay and

Thackrah. 'That the vices chargeable on our manufacturing population have been greatly exaggerated, and that the high moral qualities which belong to a large portion of them have been greatly overlooked, we have no sort of doubt.'[50] He went on to defend the factory system for 'taking the young out of harm's way', imbuing them 'with regular, orderly, and industrious habits', as well as offering 'considerable' earnings.[51] This must have been reassuring to the rickets-ridden wage slaves of the northern mill towns.

Defenders of the industrial city were even willing to counter the irrefutable charges of ugliness and pollution levelled against manufacturing. Instead, they praised its unique aesthetic. According to Joseph Cowen, the brick manufacturer, proprietor of the *Newcastle Chronicle* and Liberal Member of Parliament, you just needed to look beneath the surface. Strip away the ugly exterior and behold instead a thing of beauty. What Cowen really admired was the hum of the city. While de Tocqueville and Southey were appalled by its terrible noise, it was music to Cowen's ears. 'Behind the dull roar of our machinery, the bellowing of our blast-furnaces, the panting of our locomotives, and the gentle ticking of the electric telegraph ... we can hear the songs of children who are fed and clad, and the acclaim of a world made free by these agencies.'[52] Those sensible enough to 'dip beneath the surface' would be able to trace 'the broad outlines of a mighty poem ... in those bellowing blast-furnaces and grimy workshops'.[53] In Bradford, the local historian John James spoke with pride of the 'hundreds of clacking power-looms and thousands of whirring spinning-frames [which] din the ear'.[54] And in Leeds, Edward Baines used the pages of the *Leeds Mercury* to explain how, beneath the 'huge, unsightly mills, unwashed artifices, smokey towns, and streams running as black as ink', there could be found 'the strong sinews of a nation's strength, the deep mine of her treasures, the bulwarks of liberty, the fountain of intelligence and public spirit'.[55] Even de Tocqueville was willing to admit that Manchester's supreme ugliness hid wonders. 'From this foul drain the greatest stream of human industry flows out to fertilise the whole world. From this filthy sewer pure gold flows.'[56]

The factories, chimneys and mills which dominated the civic vista and so appalled Pugin started to be appreciated for their sublime, almost grotesque beauty. They too had a 'Gothic' appeal. *The Builder*, a fervent supporter of new development, remarked how cities were no longer scarred by 'gloomy feudal retreats', but were instead edified by 'markets, quays, storehouses, and magazines, all united to show the peculiar resources and features of the times'. Above all, in the provinces, a visitor would find 'vast manufactories, chimneys of surprising height, roofs of metal supported upon trusses of iron of astonishing span, girders, columns, bridges both of arch and suspension of the same material', all indicating the progressive spirit of the industrial city.[57]

In similar fashion, Benjamin Love's *Handbook of Manchester* urged readers not to be put off by the stench of the city's ink-dyed rivers and bubbling streams of refuse, but to 'take a walk among the Mills of Manchester; and although his notions of smoke and darkened waters, may not be the most agreeable, still, these will soon vanish, and feelings of wonder take their place'.[58] He went on to describe the glories of the cotton mills, and in particular the awful magnificence of one of modern Manchester's industrial marvels: the Messrs Birley and Co.'s multi-storey mill. And Love was right; there does remain something awesomely impressive about the great Victorian mills. Despite its decrepit state, a visit to the vast Manningham Mills in Bradford's Heaton Park or indeed the Saltaire mills in Shipley gives a sense of how overpowering these buildings must have been when surrounded by the low-level housing and winding roads of the mid-nineteenth century. The sheer extent of the buildings, their arching towers and vast gates constituted a thunderous defence of the manufacturing ethic.

Alongside the celebration of factories and the power of industry, there was an almost giddy pleasure found in the desecration of the countryside for urban development. Factories planted on fields, rivers diverted, forests cut down were all favourable signs of progress. One history of Bradford lovingly listed the dismembering of the surrounding environment. 'Its green fields turned into thickly-studded streets of elegant and spacious warehouses; its streamlets that flowed by the side of mossy banks, hidden from the view and covered with a variety of structures.' The author was particularly glad to see the collapse of the eighteenth-century system of 'putting out', or domestic cottage-work, in favour of the factory; 'the domestic loom and ancient distaff exchanged for the prodigious steam-impelled machine, with its vast power of production'.[59] This despite the mass unemployment and hardship such progress entailed.

In much of this anti-rural rhetoric there was a strong anti-feudal flavour. A mid-century history of Blackburn described the heavily populated, commercial city as a tribute to the perseverance and industry of the middle classes. There were no longer 'fields lying waste, or forests preserved for the barbarous sport of the wild hunter'. The lazy feudal barons of the shire had been 'elbowed off the scene, by the sons and daughters of honourable industry'. To symbolise the triumph of energy over lethargy, 'the axe of times has levelled every vestige of the ancient forests for the good and noble purpose of man'.[60]

Like Guizot and Cobden before him, the radical Joseph Cowen regarded the Victorian middle classes as involved in a historic mission to battle the landed elites. In a speech in Middlesbrough he explained how the battle between country and city was an extension of that fight. The hillsides of Middlesbrough used only to resound 'to the cry of the hunter's hounds, and the crack of the sportsman's gun' (a dreamily improbable scenario for today's inhabitants of the borough), but now they were filled with 'beneficient [sic] activity' – such as the thud of the forge hammer and the scream of the steam engine. By challenging the old aristocratic imperium, Middlesbrough and other industrial towns were acting out their historic function as citadels of freedom curbing 'the pretensions

of the barons'. While this might not please those who could
only detect beauty in pastoral pursuits or sentiment 'in struggling streams and dreamy sunsets', the hive of activity in the
industrial city offered a deeper, more significant beauty. The
pollution of Middlesbrough was remarked upon by another
visitor, a sceptical member of the Darlington Board of Health
who obviously had little time for nannying interference. 'If
I go to Middlesbrough I see large works there sending out
thousands and thousands of cubic feet of gas and smoke close
to private residences. I ask the individuals who live there
if they do not suffer in their health. They say "No, it is all
good for trade, we want more of it, we find no fault with
smoke."'[61]

v Highly Civil Society

For many inhabitants of the Victorian city, their most tangible
liberty was an unprecedented sense of social freedom. The
licence of city living, which had so appalled Southey and
Carlyle, was regarded as a great benefit. And what most spectacularly marked out the growing conurbations was their intellectual and social vibrancy, apparent in the mushrooming
number of civic associations. Once again, much of the ration-
ale for active social participation in city life could be traced
back to the legacy of the English Civil War.

The Nonconformist communities of the industrialising
cities, and above all the Unitarians, believed fervently in the
authority of rational truth. Their belief system was partly
inspired by the thought of the philosopher John Locke, who
had proposed that knowledge should not be dependent on any
authority but only on the individual's own personal perceptions. Adhering to this thesis, Dissenters looked to the
power of reason to discover truth. In matters religious, this
meant obeying the word of the Bible rather than the arbitrary
edicts of a man-made Church. Since there was no single,
simple truth to which all men could adhere, Dissenters
demanded the liberty of judging for themselves. In Liverpool

the Unitarian William Roscoe spelt out the creed. 'The asser-
tion and defence of truth is incumbent upon everyone, and
particularly upon every teacher of religion; but there is one
truth, paramount to all the rest, which is the very basis of
religious enquiry ... that every person, in his spiritual concerns, has a right to adopt such opinions as appear to him to be
right.'[62] No one should be compelled to worship in a particular
fashion; each man must come to God through his own journey.
The alternative to private judgement was the kind of theocratic tyranny which Southey and the Tractarians were urging.
For the Dissenters, the role of the state was not to inflict a
specific programme of worship but to allow the conditions for
its free and spontaneous practice.

This vision of personal liberty extended from the religious
to the secular realm. From the right to judge the Bible privately
followed the right to think, read and write as the individual
saw fit. The personal search for reason was the dominant
motivation in any rational human's life and should never be
impeded. Yet with this emphasis on individual intellectual
growth came also a strong belief in sociability, in human
contact as a vital part of human nature. For man to flourish
he needed to be involved in a series of social, voluntary and
civil relationships. He needed to talk, debate, argue and social-
ise. Rational Dissenters believed that free association and
companionship with fellow men was absolutely essential to
human sustenance. According to the historian Knud
Haakonssen, civil and political associations were regarded as
the surest means to realising 'the natural moral community
to which humanity was providentially disposed'.[63]

Such philosophical precepts tallied with the deeply held
Nonconformist conviction in the creation of a public sphere
outside the control of the state. Centuries of state-sanctioned
violence against them had instilled a wary fear of government. The ejection of Puritan ministers in 1662 from the
Church of England as well as the 1791 attack on the Nonconformist scientist Joseph Priestley by 'Church and King'
mobs in Birmingham was part of the collective memory of

Dissent. More damagingly, Nonconformists were legally dis-
criminated against until the repeal of the Test and Corporation
Act allowed them to reintegrate back into mainstream cultural
and political life. The British state had not served them well
and many were keen to form a voluntary culture free from
government interference. The societies, institutes and Athenaeums which began to proliferate across the Victorian city
were part of a rational public sphere built by self-help and
diametrically opposed to the authority of the state and the
established Church.

Across university faculties, government departments and
fashionable think-tanks, the terms 'civil society' and 'social
capital' are now sociological buzzwords referring to the social
space which exists between the family and the state. Regions
with a healthy civil society display strong public participation
in voluntary societies, political parties and neighbourhood
groups. According to the American political scientist Robert
Putnam, strong civil society is the product of high levels of
social capital. And by that he means those communities where
neighbours know each other's first names, involve themselves
in local schools and events, and famously prefer to go ten-pin
bowling in organised sports leagues rather than to go bowling
alone. Commensurably, those areas with active sports leagues,
choral societies and other social networks are more likely to
be engaged politically and enjoy a strong civic culture. But
across Western Europe and America, Putnam points out, social
capital is collapsing as people disengage from civil society,
stop joining political parties, watch TV, and live alone.[64]

Long before Professor Putnam started to quantify social
capital, Victorian civic leaders were generating a highly developed civil society. It is one of the intriguing paradoxes of
the Victorian city that a culture universally criticised for its
anomie and isolation – a world of crossing-sweep Joes and
rootless individuals – also enjoyed a rich network of clubs,
societies and institutes. According to a chronicler of mid-
nineteenth-century Ipswich, 'the tendency to association is
one of the great characteristics of the age'.[65] Such bodies ranged

from the elite Literary and Philosophical Societies to the artisan Mechanics' Institutes to working-class Friendly Societies to newspaper reading rooms. They were testimony, many believed, to the progressive moral and political purpose of the modern city. Or as the *Bradford Observer* put it, 'Nothing more vividly marks our civilization than the multiplication of separate societies and agencies religious, charitable, political, economic, educational, professional, friendly, recreative, and what not.' This liberal spirit of voluntary participation was symbolically contrasted to the social tyranny of medieval city life with its despotic Catholic Church and highly restrictive guilds.

There is an underlying presumption in many accounts of Victorian civil society to regard the defining purpose of these clubs and institutes as an attempt to undermine the inherent radicalism of an industrial proletariat. By endowing centres for rational education and debate, civic leaders were surreptitiously indoctrinating the elite working class with a belief in private property and the principles of capitalism. As one voguish historian put it, the Institutes' purpose was 'to integrate the lower orders into the cultural hegemony of capital'.[66] The lower middle class, artisan and working classes might have thought they were educating themselves, but in truth they were being instilled with ideas which would ultimately hinder their political development.

While it is certainly true that many of the institutes (most notably the Mechanics' Institutes) had an ideological edge, the problem with this historical interpretation is that it excludes the religious and political motivations which inspired many of the urban middle class. It ignores the progressive underpinnings of much of the Nonconformist approach to civil society. For this was the age of England's urban enlightenment and its leading players believed, above all, in the value of sociability, rational knowledge, voluntary association and a strong civic culture outside the confines of the state. The visiting French intellectual Hippolyte Taine could only marvel at such an independent culture:

> I have the greatest admiration for the spirit of all these
> institutions, and for the generous and sensible initiative of
> those private citizens who voluntarily and at their own
> expense set about improving the commonwealth, for-
> warding the State's business without having recourse to the
> State ... Many of the servitudes to the State which we
> accept would seem intolerable to them; whatever smacks
> of the barracks, of regimentation, is repugnant to them.[67]

These ideals were as much the driving force as any attempt to
quell the radicalism of the urban working class.

As a part of this progressive civic ideology, women were
also offered a new role within the public realm as middle-class
actors. The urban wife or mother was not necessarily the
cowed, domesticated figure of Victorian mythology. Instead,
new research suggests a significant female presence within
civil society at lectures, concerts and exhibitions. In the mid-
Victorian years, women rarely took a lead role in the governance of civic bodies (women-only institutions would
emerge later in the century), but were nonetheless expected
to be engaged with the city's 'culture' as an element of their
middle-class identity and as testimony to the city's modern
sociability. It was anticipated that ideas and attitudes gained
in a public sphere would then be reintroduced to the domestic
setting. Meanwhile, urban society was thought to gain from a
civilised, female presence which constituted further dem-
onstration of its cultural supremacy over the boorish, male
bastions of the countryside.[68]

Standing at the apex of the nineteenth-century city's social
and intellectual milieu was the Literary and Philosophical
Society. Over two hundred were active by 1800 and the majority owed their establishment to the Nonconformist tradition
of scientific inquiry. They took as their model the celebrated
Royal Institution in Mayfair and Society of Arts in Charing
Cross. The *Quarterly Review* described how 'the lectures
delivered ... are calculated to diffuse amongst the higher and
middling classes a taste for liberal studies, and a spirit of

philosophical investigation'.[69] Despite their title, most societies rarely discussed either literature or philosophy and instead focused on new advances in science – specifically, chemistry, mechanics and geology. The abiding spirit was one of rational amateur endeavour and Joseph Priestley, who carried out his experiments into oxygen (or 'dephlogisticated air' as he called it) in his home-made laboratory, was the cult hero of this democratic culture of inquiry.

The Manchester Literary and Philosophical Society was established in 1781 with 'the purpose of uniting the pursuits of science and literature with commercial opulence'. Most of its founder members had links with the old Nonconformist Warrington Academy (where Priestley had taught), which later became Manchester New College. While James Phillips Kay was an enthusiastic member of the Society, the figure most publicly associated with the institute was the celebrated chemist John Dalton. It was through the pages or *Memoirs* of the Manchester Literary and Philosophical Society that Dalton revealed his extraordinary advances in understanding atomic theory and creating the framework for the modern periodic table. Brought up a Quaker, he spent his early years as a schoolmaster teaching in Kendal where he participated in a sadistically strict regime. John Dalton would hold the boys while his brother Jonathan would flog them. Traumatised by the brutality of the regime (which makes one wonder about the poor pupils), Dalton immersed himself in studying meteorology, reading barometers and catching butterflies.

By the time he joined Manchester New College in 1793, his life was devoted to natural philosophy. Living the austere life of a bachelor as a paying guest in a friend's family house, Dalton applied all his time to chemistry. 'If I have succeeded better than many who surround me', he later remarked in a conscious echo of Isaac Newton's remarks about standing on the shoulders of giants, 'it has been chiefly, nay, I say almost solely from unwearied assiduity.'[70] As his experiments startled the scientific world, so he enjoyed the extraordinary honour of having laboratories housed in the Society before later being elected President. He received a Fellowship of the Royal Society and the French Academy of Science, and became a figurehead for the Manchester tradition of democratic, Dissenting science. On his death in 1844, his remains were placed in the Town Hall and in the course of one day over 40,000 visitors filed past the body. By 1855, a public subscription had raised over £5,000 for a statue of Dalton. Together with a bronze James Watt, the two scientists dominated Piccadilly Esplanade for over a hundred years – until the City Council decided to replace Dalton with an electricity substation.

Leeds was rather late in establishing its own Literary and Philosophical Society. Although Leeds had long enjoyed a 'Reasoning Society' for like-minded Nonconformists, the success of Manchester's and then Liverpool's Literary and Philosophical Society (established in 1812 by local Dissenters) spurred the city into action. Through the pages of the *Leeds Mercury*, Edward Baines senior led the charge for Leeds to hold its own against the Lancashire foe. And in 1818 Baines, together with the surgeon and critic of industrial cities Dr Thackrah and the liberal manufacturers John Marshall and Benjamin Gott, duly established a 'Lit. and Phil.' for the edification of the city. It was described later in the century as 'a little torch of culture burning in the midst of the darkness of provincial Philistinism'.[71] In the struggle for culture, the Society was soon supplemented by a Conversation Club, a Curfew Club and other voluntary associations all of which, according to the city's historian R.J. Morris, helped to unify any political or religious differences and define a viable middle-class identity.[72]

In Newcastle, thanks to the efforts of the Revd Turner, the city's Society was one of the country's largest with over 800 members by 1830. In contrast to the other more philosophical societies, Newcastle's 'Lit. and Phil.' was determinedly pragmatic, stressing the importance of commercial application as much as academic inquiry. It issued a ceaseless flow of scientific papers helpful to the surrounding coal and lead industries. In an act of classic Victorian prudery, it also voted by a majority of twenty to one to ban Byron's *Don Juan* from the library.

For members of Manchester's middle class of a less scientific bent, there was a wealth of other institutes available. The city was positively awash with sociability. In 1806 the Portico Library was established on Mosley Street, with Peter Mark Roget of Thesaurus fame as its first Secretary. William Gaskell, the minister of the Unitarian Cross Street Chapel, was its long-time Chairman while his wife, the novelist Elizabeth Gaskell, made extensive use of the library's collection. Today the library manages to retain an eirenic calm amidst its elegant Mannerist architecture, despite the fact that its lower floor has now been leased to a Forgery & Firkin public house. In 1815 the library was joined by the Manchester Literary Society, in 1821 by the Natural History Society, followed quickly by the Manchester Royal Institution, then in 1825 by the Mechanics' Institute, in 1829 by the breakaway New Mechanics' Institute, in 1834 by a Statistical Society, and in 1838 by the Manchester Geological Society; not to mention the Manchester Society for the Promotion of Natural History, the Union Club, the Phrenological Society, the School of Design, the Botanical and Horticultural Society, the Medical Society, the Architectural Association, the Royal Victoria Gallery for the Encouragement of Practical Science, and a rich array of musical groups from the Madrigal Society to the Harmonic Society.

The city's Royal Institution, also located along Mosley Street, was housed in a stately neo-classical building fronted by an imposing set of Doric columns designed by Sir Charles Barry. Now the location for Manchester's City Art Gallery, the Institution offered a more cultural and artistic programme than that provided by the Literary and Philosophical Society. Established in 1823 by the ubiquitous Sir Benjamin Heywood with his fellow Unitarian businessman George Wood, its ambition was to promote 'the interests of literature, science and the arts, and the obtaining of a channel by which the works of meritorious artists might be brought before the public'.

It would diffuse literature and art through 'the discordant elements of society' and in turn foster 'a pervading emotion of friendly sympathy and mutual satisfaction'. The Institution undertook an extensive project of civic patronage with exhibitions, prizes and scholarships. Outside lecturers were invited to deliver talks with such didactic titles as 'On the Influence of Commerce on the Progress of Civilization and on the Happiness of Nations' or 'The Rise and Progress of Civil Society'. The virtuous role of the middle classes and the beneficial contribution of cities figured heavily in both. Tellingly, the Institution's pragmatic agenda was revealed in the building's motto: *Nihil pulchrum nisi utile* (Nothing beautiful unless useful).

The city also had an increasingly developed working-class civic culture. In addition to the street life of 'rough' sports, gambling, singing salons and pubs ('the public house is for the operative, what the public square was for the ancients', reported Leon Faucher),[73] there was an increasingly sophisticated network of burial societies and savings banks. The celebrated Manchester Unity Friendly Society Independent Order of Oddfellows grew to become the country's leading friendly society. By 1860, it had over 300,000 members in affiliated societies contributing weekly payments of a few pence in return for the promise of sick allowance, medical help and if need be funeral costs. Today its success continues, with the society retaining over 100,000 members and £130 million under management. Unfortunately, the other great equitable societies of the nineteenth century have not fared so well as carpetbaggers and a lack of capital have led to their successive takeover by commercial banks.

If Manchester was the capital of friendly societies, then Liverpool enjoyed the distinction of running one of the most successful burial societies. As part of the city's booming insurance industry, the Liverpool Liver Burial Society was established in 1850 and could boast 55,000 members by 1872, located mainly in Glasgow and Liverpool, all earnestly insuring themselves against the indignity of a pauper's burial.

Today, as the Royal Liver Assurance, it has millions of members as well as an iconic portside headquarters. More broadly, nineteenth-century Liverpool enjoyed an equally vibrant civil society with an obligatory Literary and Philosophical Society, a Lyceum (now the main Post Office on Bold Street), an Academy of Art, a Botanical Garden, a Liverpool Institute and School of Art (currently the site of the Liverpool Institute for the Performing Arts, more widely known as 'Sir Paul McCartney's *Fame* School'), a Polytechnic Society, Union-Rooms, a Medical Society and, most importantly of all, a Royal Institution. Founded by William Roscoe and the local Tory MP and corn merchant John Gladstone (father of the future Prime Minister, William Ewart Gladstone), the Institution went on to spawn a Natural History Museum, its own Art Gallery, classical and mathematical schools, and finally a School of Design.

Despite being the site for the most prestigious social club of the Industrial Revolution, the Lunar Society of scientists and industrialists held at Matthew Boulton's Soho House, mid-nineteenth-century Birmingham lacked the merchant prince patronage which underpinned the big civic institutions. The Birmingham economy of workshops and small manufacturing did not produce the same disparities in wealth as Manchester or Liverpool. Instead, the city fostered more democratic modes of civic engagement such as friendly societies, trade unions and mutual improvement societies. The first modern building society was established in 1843 as the Birmingham Building Society, Number 1. Between 1842 and 1865 nearly £2.5 million was paid, chiefly by the working and lower middle classes, into building and freehold land societies across the city. In addition, there were savings clubs, clothes clubs, building societies, burial clubs; in 1835 a civic history estimated that there were upwards of 400 benefit clubs in Birmingham, containing in excess of 40,000 members. Birmingham's community of friendly societies was particularly rich, including the Sick Man's Friendly Society; the Abstainers' Gift; the Society of Total Abstinence; the Honourable Knights of the

Wood; the Royal Dragoons; and even the Modern Druids. According to the *Morning Chronicle*, 'There is perhaps no town in England in which the principle of association for mutual benefit, real or supposed, is carried to so great an extent as in Birmingham.'[74] It was this world of working-class civil society which led one visiting Austrian politician to comment, 'England is at present the theatre of a gigantic development of associated life, which gives to her labour, her education, her social intercourse, nay, to the entire development of her culture, a pronounced direction, a decisive step. The tendency towards the union of forces and the working of this union are nowadays more powerful in England than ever, and more powerful than anywhere else.'[75]

Glasgow, on the other hand, had a high-profile elite of extremely wealthy merchants and industrialists who mixed together in predominantly professional or commercially oriented societies located around George Square. It was through the Merchant House, the Trades' House, Royal Exchange, Stock Exchange, Chamber of Commerce, Institution of Accountants and Actuaries, or Faculty of Procurators that their civil society was thickened. The Glasgow elite also liked to appoint each other in an endless corporate merry-go-round onto the boards of the city's leading banks, cotton companies, railways firms and engineering works. Opportunities for bonding were further available in the vast number of public dinners and ritual processions which dominated the civic calendar. If it wasn't a Free Trade dinner with special guests Richard Cobden and John Bright, then it was a ceremony to unveil a statue for a dead dignitary or the laying of a foundation stone for yet another professional institute.

Languishing beneath the academic echelons of the Literary and Philosophical Societies and beneath the professional middle-class clubs lay the most popular and radical institute of the Victorian city, the Mechanics' Institute. Pioneered in turn-of-the-century Glasgow by Dr Birkbeck, Mechanics' Institutes swept through Britain's civic centres. Edinburgh followed Glasgow in 1821 with a Mechanical School of Arts and in 1823 Birkbeck joined forces with the populist Whig politician Lord Brougham to establish an Institute in London. Almost 2,000 people flocked to the Crown & Anchor Tavern on the Strand to witness its launch. The Institute can be found today just off London's Gower Street, where it continues its tradition of public education under the name of Birkbeck College as part of the University of London. In 1826 there were already twenty Mechanics' Institutes in towns and cities in Lancashire and Yorkshire alone. By 1850 the number of Mechanics' Institutes and kindred societies in the two counties had grown to 700, with a total membership of over 120,000 people.

As their numbers grew, the aims and ambitions of each institute multiplied. Brougham and Birkbeck believed in the technical education of the working man to enable him to pursue his professional calling; conservative supporters regarded the institutes as a means of educating the working class about the dangers of radicalism; more practical voices argued that in an era of unprecedented technical advance, it made economic sense to train up an artisan workforce. In the industrial cities, backers of the Mechanics' Institutes seemed to have a dual agenda. First, they wished to elevate the working class from their ignorant and sensual existence through the diffusion of useful knowledge. A classic Mechanics' Institute programme of classes, lectures and earnest reading material would open the artisans' eyes to the wonders of education and the economic advantage of technical expertise. Yet the tuition would also instil the virtues of capitalism, personal industry and private property. The Institutes could happily combine both a philanthropic and more aggressive class agenda. But as the working classes themselves began to take control of the Institutes, the ideological objectives of the founding fathers were often jettisoned.

As I outlined in the previous chapter, Manchester received its own Institute in 1824 when the mechanical engineer Sir William Fairbairn attempted to counter the middle-class dominance of the Manchester Royal Institution with a more working-class-focused society. With funds from Sir Benjamin Heywood and the involvement of James Phillips Kay among others, the Manchester Mechanics' Institute was established to teach young men 'the application of science to mechanical and manufacturing art'. For this was very much an industry-led operation with the focus on skills and training as Manchester's commercial elite attempted to fight the looming threat of French and American competition. The Institute would teach the mechanic a greater knowledge of his business and show how to improve his productivity. In the words of Hippolyte Taine: '"Self-help" again, that is the key word which is so little understood in France. From the same personal impulse come forth all those associations, unions and institutions which are so numerous here.' The classes and lectures were of a fairly high calibre and the Board were enormously proud that works by Kant, Fichte and Hegel were frequently borrowed from the Institute's library. Whether they were then read is perhaps a different matter.

The chronic problem which the Manchester Mechanics' Institute faced was that very few mechanics actually turned up. The majority of members were either lower-middle-class or upper-working-class. The solid artisan stayed away or joined the rival New Mechanics' Institute. This was partly the product of the Institute's constitution whereby honorary members (i.e., the civic elite of Fairbairns and Heywoods) ran the club with little input from the constituent working class. As a result, the lecture programmes and classes were frequently criticised as dry and impractical. Slowly the Institute democratised and broadened out its syllabus from its early, technical precepts. In Carlisle, the Mechanics' Institute underwent a similar process since, although it was 'well managed and liberally supported', according to one member, the Institute was deemed to have 'failed somewhat in its mission, mainly, as was thought, through the reluctance of the weaver in his clogs and fustian jacket to meet in the same room with the better clad, and possibly better mannered, shop assistants and clerks of the city. So these new places were made purely democratic, having no master, and not permitting even any in the management but such as lived by weekly wages.'[76]

The Leeds Mechanics' Institute had similar origins and outlook to Manchester. It was founded in 1824 under the instigation of Edward Baines thanks to the early financial generosity of the industrialist Benjamin Gott. The Institute was moulded by the city's Unitarian civic elite, introduced hopelessly narrow scientific courses, and had a non-artisan governing board. Unsurprisingly, it too had to change its ways and operate a more popular, recreational programme which included annual *Soirées* where the great and the good (often Charles Dickens or Lord Morpeth) offered the city artisans pearls of wisdom. In Birmingham, the city's Mechanics' Institute also suffered from low attendance and closed in the mid-1840s after barely twenty years in operation. In Glasgow the Mechanics' Institute and, south of the Clyde, the Gorbals Popular Institution proved more successful with their classes, debates and literary societies. By 1838, some 1,200 workers and their families were attending weekly Saturday night concerts and socials in the Mechanics' Institute hall.[77] Yet even Glasgow, home to the Mechanics' Institute movement, succumbed to the need for lower-brow Athenaeums.

Despite the emergence of the more populist Athenaeums and Lyceums in reaction to the rigorous strictures of the Mechanics' Institutes, the movement begun by Brougham and Birkbeck had a valuable legacy. Though the Mechanics' Institutes were frequently controlled by middle-class oligarchies and the courses often had a strong ideological bent, they nonetheless helped to democratise knowledge and ideas. The Institutes' finest historian, Mabel Tylecote, concludes, 'They played a part in campaigns for social betterment and in the battle for popular enlightenment and culture. To many humble persons, living under conditions of great cultural impoverishment, they were almost the sole means of access to new experience and to the cultivation of their mental powers.'[78]

More generally, defenders of the Victorian city argued that such civil associations indicated a healthy sense of rational endeavour and were a vital component in strengthening the city. Robert Vaughan told an audience at the Manchester Athenaeum that 'the most marvellous thing in modern history, was the influence which institutions such as Athenaeums and Mechanics' Institutes had exercised over the community'. He favourably contrasted the sense and reason of present-day Manchester with the 'tumultuous masses' of twenty years ago, who could be worked into a dangerous frenzy on the slightest pretext. The speaker following him explained how the Athenaeum was a glowing testimony to the power of intellectual association. An isolated human being was merely a shadow, but a man 'connected, associated, co-operating with others', was a force to be reckoned with. The great commercial city of Tyre fell because it failed to grasp the importance of association – 'the power of combination; that power by which man exercises the strength of a community, and in which his individuality is lost in that great combination which enables him to effect the wonderful changes which we see around and about us'.[79]

In expressing these sentiments both speakers were echoing the thoughts of Alexis de Tocqueville. Given the isolation of modern democratic society, de Tocqueville regarded associations as essential for protecting individual rights against the state and ensuring a healthy civil society. The civic fabric needed to be bound together through a network of voluntary associations, educational institutions, political activism, newspapers, and the other elements that made up vigorous urban communities. An 'association for political, commercial, or manufacturing purposes, or even for those of science and literature, is a powerful and enlightened member of the community', which cannot easily be disposed of and which by defending its own rights against the encroachments of the government, saves the common liberties of the country'.[80] 'What strength can even public opinion have retained', he asked, 'when no twenty persons are connected by a common tie, when not a man, nor a family, nor chartered corporation, nor class, nor free institution, has the power of representing or exerting that opinion?'[81] Without these kinds of institutional affiliations, ever greater power would accrue to the state, culminating in the kind of autarkic, centralised system which had set the scene for the French Revolution.

Mechanics' Institutes, Athenaeums and Lyceums were more than political bulwarks against the threat of an over-mighty state; they were also indicative of the liberality and intellectual superiority of city life. Whereas Southey and Pugin understood community as a series of limited, established face-to-face relationships and condemned the isolation of the manufacturing age, others heralded the easy interaction and diffuse unity of the city. According to Robert Vaughan, the 'tendencies of manufacture, and of commercial pursuits' led to an 'equality of condition' as men were freed up from their old feudal ties. The city fostered a spirit of 'independence' and 'self-reliance' at odds with the outmoded serf–lord relationship.

Self-confident champions of the modern city set out to prove that the growth of large towns necessarily led to greater intelligence. In a lecture on the cotton trade to the Blackburn Mechanics' Institute, the manufacturer and evangelical churchman Alderman John Baynes declared that in the city, 'There is an interchange of thought, mind is brought into contact with kindred mind, and made brighter and sharper by the friction. It is according to the order of society ... that the growth of large towns should be co-incident with progress, and the development of intellectual superiority.'[82] Progress and civilisation were inextricably linked to personal and intellectual liberty. Robert Vaughan described how 'each man stimulates his fellow, and the result is a greater intelligence. The shop, the factory, or the market-place; the local association, the news-room, or the religious meeting, all facilitate this invigorating contact of mind with mind.'[83] The city was a symbol of civilisation. 'Policy, polity, politeness, urbanity, civility, derive their names as well as their nature from city life, while the terms rustic, savage, heathen, pagan, indicate the rougher and more backward tendencies of the herdsmen and cultivators of the ground,' reasoned the Liverpool architect James Picton.[84] The rural contrast was one Edward Baines was keen to pursue. 'No one', he suggested, 'will venture to compare the agricultural labourers with the manufacturing in point of *intelligence* and *information*.' Although he did grudgingly concede those working outside factories tended to live longer.[85]

Crucial to the citizen's intellectual development was the prevalence of a thriving newspaper industry. Vaughan was adamant that if Britain's great cities disappeared, 'the freedom of the press, and nearly the whole system of liberty of which that freedom is a part, must also disappear'.[86] Across the Victorian city, municipal presses boomed – and even more so after the repeal of stamp duties on newspapers in 1855. And, as ever, the Unitarian community was at the forefront of this vital civic industry. A free press independent of state censorship was a core component of the Nonconformist political agenda. The *Newcastle Chronicle*, *Tyne Mercury*, *Leeds Mercury* (published and edited by the Baines family), *Hull Rockingham*, *Sheffield Independent*, *Liverpool Times* and *Manchester Guardian* were all built up by Unitarians.[87]

Manchester had a highly developed newspaper market. According to one German visitor, 'In this city are published five or six of those colossal English morning newspapers, of which the simple German reader wonderingly asks himself, how anybody can read them from beginning to end over his after dinner pipe!'[88] With newspapers came news rooms and libraries for the free perusal of the press. The 'News Room' at the Manchester Exchange received on a daily basis some 140 periodicals. Carlisle boasted twenty-four reading rooms by the 1850s containing over 4,000 volumes and subscribed to by 1,400 members. Even more gratifyingly, the Bradford library was said by the missionary traveller John Shaw to 'have a better stock of daily and periodical literature than some of the reading rooms, where officers of the army and navy, and gentlemen of the professions, resort in the fashionable town of Cheltenham'. It seemed that 'under the rough exterior of these working men' could be found 'well cultivated intellects' able to 'put to flight, in sound and well reasoned argument, those who ride in carriages and dwell in mansions, in Bath, Cheltenham, Leamington, or Brighton'.[89]

This was the progressive middle-class vision of the city. Not the spiritual and political tyranny of the church, the cross and the stocks, but the liberal community of the news room and factory. In a paper read before the Manchester Statistical Society, the speaker waxed lyrical on the intelligence, commerce and mechanical ingenuity of the circle of Manchester: 'the minds of men are in a state of electric communication of ideas; their political sentiments indicate the restless vigour of a rising and sturdy people; their religious opinions are full of fervour and of piety'.[90] In contrast to the mental stupor of a French peasant, Hippolyte Taine was taken by the city's intelligent working class. The Manchester artisan 'has more ideas in his head, more notions of all kinds, more intelligence in social, political, and religious matters, in short a wider horizon. He is accustomed to hear important topics and remote things and places discussed; he reads the newspapers, and his mind is open to curiosity. In Manchester recently a travelling biographer delivered two lectures on Macaulay, charged an entrance fee of 18p, and the hall was filled by working men.'[91]

A diary from the period gives an insight into the self-improving world of the urban mid-Victorian. Born in 1837, the son of a woollen manufacturer, Benjamin Barker lived a modest middle-class life just outside Leeds in Bramley. From the mid-1850s he started to keep a diary which combined his precocious thoughts on world events (most notably the Crimea) with a record of his social and civic activities. A keen organist and music buff, Barker flitted from Methodist chapel to Leeds Parish Church and sometimes to St George's Hall in Bradford or the Music Hall in Leeds for concerts. He was an active member of the Bramley Mechanics' Institute and frequenter of evening lectures, such as 'Science and Literature, their connection with religion' by the Revd Punchon of Leeds whom Barker found 'eloquent beyond the powers of description'. November 1858 was a typically frenetic month:

> 2nd November 1858. Came down to Leeds by 7.59 train and went to a 'Conversazione' in the Town Hall to celebrate the closing of the Industrial Exhibition. There was a splendid company, full dress.
>
> 13th November 1858. Went to the 1st People's Concert in the 'Victoria Hall' in the Town Hall, the Principals were Misses Whitan, Newbound, Messrs. Inkersall and Delaventi, with a full Band of forty performers.
>
> 20th November 1858. Went to Improvement Society, afterwards called at Public Meeting at Mechanics' Institute – about beginning the Institute again.[92]

This idea of growing intelligence emerging through the social whirl of the city became a valuable political tool in debates over extending the right to vote during the 1867 Second Reform Bill. Supporters of household franchise argued that the growth of cities had given more men the chance for intellectual reflection and a greater understanding of politics. One pro-reform advocate explained how urban 'intercourse and experience, the collision of mind with mind and class with class', bear fruit in an open-mindedness and width of sympathy unknown in a less active society; and these enable men to 'pass sometimes beyond the sphere of their immediate circumstances, and give their minds to questions involving principles of justice or of policy'.[93] The growth of cities and a more urbane civilisation since the last Reform Act of 1832 required a broadening of the franchise. Similarly, the lack of such intellectual challenge in the small boroughs which still sent unrepresentative MPs to Westminster necessitated their abolition. 'Where there is no circulation for a series of good lectures, no chance of a meeting at which leading public men will be present, there is really no counter-acting influence to operate toward the enlargement of the mind, or the puri-

fication of the sense of public morality.' In these circumstances, allowing such a borough to return an MP, 'only
augments the evil'.[94]

The radical John Bright made a series of speeches, in the
House of Commons and in cities across the country, setting
out the case for reform in all of which he heaped similar
praise upon the 'great cities' and the working men who had
constructed them.[95] In Birmingham he told a crowd at the
opening of the New Exchange buildings that 'merchants and
manufacturers' were becoming more important in the world
than 'soldiers and statesmen'. 'It is obvious to me that the
power of these heretofore great authorities is waning, and that
in every part of the world the power of the great industrial
interests is considerably waxing.' And he argued, as Cobden
had done before, that historically it was not from 'monarchs
or lords of the soil' but from towns and cities 'has come
whatever there is of social, or civil, or religious, or industrial
freedom to the inhabitants of this country'. The intelligence
and industry of Victorian city dwellers had earned them a
place in the constitution.[96]

vi URBS TRIUMPHANT

The superiority of the Victorian city was most clearly dem-
onstrated in its culture of civic benevolence and philanthropy.
While the medieval city might have been awash with churches
and priories, the nineteenth-century urban world projected its
civilisation through a flurry of charitable institutions and
societies. Vaughan for one was convinced that city inhabitants
displayed a 'higher tone of moral feeling'. It was only in cities
that one could find 'spontaneous efforts in the cause of public
morals, and in aid of the necessitous, made in such manner as
to embrace voluntary association, and large sacrifice of time,
thought, and property'.[97] Across Britain new infirmaries, hospitals and schools were graciously endowed. One of the most
effusive of Victorian back-slappers, G.R. Porter, believed that
'the hospitals of this country, so numerous and so liberally

supported, are among the most honourable of our national monuments'.[98] Between 1820 and 1860, London saw three times as many specialist hospitals (over forty) opened as in the previous four decades.[99] Increasingly, they focused on such specialisms as eye and ear complaints, consumption and children's diseases. Institutes and hospitals for the deaf, dumb and blind proved particularly popular. The mid-Victorian years also witnessed the campaign led by Charles Dickens to build one of London's most loved children's hospitals, Great Ormond Street.

William Hutton, the loyal Birmingham propagandist, described in his history of the city a panoply of new institutions: the Free School, Charity School, Dissenting Charity School, Deaf and Dumb Institution, as well as the News Room, Mechanics' Institute and Society of Arts. Liverpool could boast a Ladies Benevolent Society, Dorcas Society, Strangers' Friend Society, Blind School, Charitable Society, Charitable Institution House, Catholic Orphans' Society and numerous other worthy causes.[100] In an article for the conservative *Fraser's Magazine*, the Manchester clergyman Robert Lamb systematically listed his city's 'benevolent institutions' as symbols of growing civility. Modern Manchester was delineated not by feudal anachronisms, the monasteries and priories which Southey and Pugin revered, but by such symbols of progress as 'an Infirmary', 'a Dispensary', 'an Asylum for the Deaf and Dumb, and one also for the Blind', 'a Hospital for the board and education of orphan children', 'a Grammar School of considerable eminence', and 'a Library of 10,000 volumes for the free use of the people'.[101] These were the symbols of the rational and virtuous middle class of the manufacturing city. Similarly, Benjamin Love's handbook of Manchester gave over a whole chapter to 'Benevolent Institutions' and another to 'Education and Educational Institutions'. Such philanthropic concerns were the product of Manchester's generous mercantile class who subscribed in their thousands to local causes. 'No town', Love confidently suggested, 'possesses a greater number of charitable and benevolent commercial men;

and the charity and benevolence of Manchester tradesmen are commensurate with the scale of their commercial transactions.'[102] After visiting Manchester's Peel Park, the museum, the library and the Mechanics' Institute, Hippolyte Taine concluded that 'Rich people give money for useful purposes on an enormous scale here.'[103]

In Glasgow, there existed a more active culture of involvement in the city's charitable institutions.[104] The commercial and industrial elite immersed themselves in appeals, infirmaries and civic philanthropy. While the city's women took to 'calling' on fallen families and organising charity bazaars, the male elders liked to devote their efforts to more ostentatious, capital projects. For to be active in the great philanthropic endeavours of the day was essential to rising in public esteem. It also made commercial sense as Glasgow's merchant princes networked and socialised through their charitable causes. Leonard Gow, for example, combined his profession as a prosperous ship-owner with duties as a director of the Merchant House, Clyde Trust and Chamber of Commerce as well as involvement in the Western Infirmary, the Charity Organization Society and the National Bible Society for Scotland. The Glasgow merchant William Campbell devoted much of his time to the Royal Infirmary, the Glasgow Native Benevolent Society and the Free Church. Andrew MacDonald was a Scottish railway baron who took a lead role in Glasgow's Royal Technical College, Royal Infirmary, and House of Refuge.

Few in Glasgow could outdo the energetic involvement of James Lumsden in matters philanthropic. A successful wholesale stationer and Lord Provost of the city, Lumsden's main achievement was to secure the finances of the city's Royal Infirmary. But his commitments did not end there. According to one contemporary biographer, 'It is scarcely possible to name a single local cause, or event of a public nature, with which the name of Mr Lumsden is not intimately associated. He was the builder of the Model Lodging-Houses, the founder and patron of the Glasgow Native Benevolent Society, the active and efficient promoter of every public improvement.'

The author goes on to offer a wry account of a wealthy civic elder working an entire city:

> He could hardly at any time walk fifty yards in any of our leading thoroughfares without speaking to twenty people. The sight of any acquaintance seemed instantly to recall some special thing he had to say to him. He had always a dozen irons in the fire, and every one of them he appeared to keep at white heat. Every day he might be seen in the street or on 'Change, gnawing his thumb anxiously, or urging forward some object, public or private, with his impatient voice and emphatic shrug of the right shoulder; and anon, catching some passer by perhaps to extract a couple of guineas for the Royal Infirmary, of which he was treasurer.[105]

The moral virtue of the city was reflected in its architecture. Hugh Gawthrop, author of *Fraser's Guide to Liverpool*, regarded the city's Assize Court and St George's Hall with extra reverence since there was 'no drawback to damp the ardour of enthusiastic admiration'. The buildings' stones 'are not cemented with the blood of Negroes; these ornaments and decorations are not insulting trophies of grinding oppression; this massive pile has not been raised by successful appeals to demented superstition – extracting the hard-earned coin through fears of supernatural terrors'. On the contrary, the financing of the building was 'unpolluted'; 'it is a temple erected to the genius of Commerce – bartering fairly, justly, freely – guided by the sanctifying influences of an enlightened Christianity'. The massive St George's Hall was a symbol of the prosperity of modern civilisation and a testimony to how the spirit of commerce immeasurably improved the condition of mankind. When, argued Gawthrop, you added to this the improved roads, the new Albert Docks, the Customs House, canals, bridges and railways of Liverpool, 'we are almost induced to believe that the day of modern civilization is at its acme'.[106]

The contribution of the middle classes to Victorian civic

life began to be more confidently celebrated as the century progressed. A new literary genre emerged which began to triumph the stories, adversity and 'character' of the Victorian middle class as surely as earlier generations had written of the deeds of generals, statesmen and clerics. The middle classes, actively differentiated from the idle upper classes and sensuous working classes, began to take on the type of heroic role which Guizot had first outlined for them in his Sorbonne lectures. Yet this was not a heroism of martial valour, discovering new continents, or leading revolutions; rather, the steady, earnest, responsible industry of a class which had quietly built up the strength of mid-Victorian Britain. As James Kay put it, 'Our hours are not wasted in "ennui", in friendly dissipation, in exhausting excitement, in plotting factions in clubs'.[107] In her *History of England During the Thirty Years' Peace*, the liberal intellectual Harriet Martineau sang the praises of 'the great middle class, of which history has told so little', who 'busy about their private affairs, their manufactures and their commerce, – busy about their local affairs, their magistracy', had founded England's urban civilisation while the 'idle and indifferent' carried out the plunderous wars 'of which history tells so much'.[108] In doing so she provided a template for the wondrously understated ending of George Eliot's *Middlemarch*. As Dorothea settles down to her new, quiet life with Will Ladislaw, Eliot remarks how 'the growing good of the world is partly dependent on unhistoric acts; and that things are not so ill with you or me as they might have been, is half owing to the number who lived faithfully a hidden life, and rest in unvisited tombs'.[109] Yet middle-class hagiographers were increasingly keen to shed light on some of those hidden lives.

A flood of city histories engulfed the Victorian literary market. Wealthy towns keen to legitimise their newly minted pasts churned out histories drawing on Roman, Saxon and Norman chronologies. Manchester celebrated its Briton roots as the ancient settlement of Mamecestre. Other cities cooked up equally dubious historical lineages. William Hutton clearly understood his task in recounting Birmingham's past, for 'she has never manufactured an history of herself, who has manufactured almost everything else'.[110] The end of these new histories culminated in a glorious account of local civic heroes. Usually entitled 'Biographical Notes', 'Biographical Anecdotes' or 'Great Men', these achingly worthy chapters stressed not aristocratic endeavours but the more liberal achievements of the commercial middle class in the city's history. Here was an aggressive attempt to develop an autonomous civic culture independent of metropolitan bias. In his life of the Leeds doctor and civic worthy John Heaton, the author T. Wemyss Reid complained how

> Biography has nothing to say of the men who have had most to do with the building up of the fortunes of Birmingham and Manchester, of Liverpool and Leeds. The local representative must acquire the stamp of metropolitan approbation before it is thought worthy of notice even by the most thoughtful of social students. Thus it comes to pass that in English literature and English thought, a great and useful class of men are systematically ignored.[111]

The new breed of civic biographers were determined to change that. Henry Smithers, in his account of Liverpool, proudly described how fame used to be based on warfare and other martial virtues, but it now owed as much to wealth creation, the liberal arts and civil government.[112] John James's *History and Topography of Bradford* frankly admitted that Bradford had not, 'like some Attic soils in the kingdom', given birth to men who had challenged the admiration and eternal gaze of posterity. But it had produced talented and memorable individuals who had worked hard, prospered, and no doubt added something to 'the never-fading page of literature and science'.[113] James Wheeler's *Manchester: Its Political, Social and Commercial History, Ancient and Modern*, provided an extensive biography of 'great Manchester men'. Whilst it inevitably mentioned Lord de la Warre and the Duke of Bridgewater, the section allocated much greater space to those industrious middle-class heroes John Dalton, Sir Robert Peel and Thomas Percival.[114] William Wylie's history of Nottingham was even more categorical. 'Nottingham is at present remarkable for the number of self-made men which it contains – men who from the humblest positions, have by their professional ingenuity and perseverance reached the highest honour which their own can bestow'.[115]

The Leeds dignitary Sir Edward Baines did particularly well as his son, the more outspoken Edward Baines junior (heir to the editor's chair at the *Mercury*), wrote a lengthy, loving biography of his father. It is a classic example of the kind of virtuous middle-class literature which proved so popular in mid-Victorian Britain. 'The aim of this Memoir is to do good,' Baines declared on the opening page. 'Rich as is our literature in the lives of statesmen, warriors, and men of genius, such biographies are perhaps less calculated for practical usefulness than that of one who may be held up as a model to our active and intelligent middle classes.'[116] Born in the Ribble Valley a mile from Preston in 1774, Baines moved to Leeds to study as a printer's apprentice. He worked hard, saved and prospered, living the embodiment of a Victorian morality tale. 'Whilst still receiving weekly wages, he practised a prudent economy. He was ambitious to improve his condition, and he took the only effectual means to do it by saving as much as he could of the fruits of his industry. His tastes were simple, his habits strictly virtuous, and his companionships virtuous.'[117] As a good Nonconformist, he joined the local 'Reasoning Society' where he animatedly entered discussions about civil and religious liberty before marrying the sister of a fellow Reasoner. Baines continued to prosper and in 1801 organised a consortium of leading Unitarian notables (including the textile manufacturer John Marshall) to buy out the *Leeds Mercury*. Taking sales from 700 in 1801 to 10,000 by 1840, Baines transformed it into Britain's leading provincial paper. At the same time, he nurtured the Baines dynasty by securing his family and friends influential posts on the *Liverpool Times*,

Sheffield Independent and *Bradford Observer*.

Edward Baines junior described his father as a man 'self-harnessed to the car of progress' – and it was a commitment to a Victorian ideal he was determined to incorporate into the life of Leeds. As we have seen, he became a leading civic figure, involving himself with the Literary and Philosophical Society, the Mechanics' Institute and the Leeds Temperance Society. In 1834, he achieved his finest hour when he was proudly returned as MP for 'the city he had entered as an apprentice'. At which point his self-conscious industriousness only accelerated. 'When I tell you that I presided at the Baptist Irish Society at seven o'clock this morning,' he informed one unfortunate correspondent, 'that I was at the Sheffield Gas Committee at mid-day, and that I have to attend on Mr Buxton's motion in the House of Commons this evening, as well as to take the chair at the Irish Evangelical Society at six o'clock, you will conclude that I have not much time for correspondence.' The Baines biography is an account of commercial and social success achieved through nothing but hard grind, persistence and the display of sturdy middle-class character.

Given such a shining exemplum, perhaps it is no coincidence that precisely those virtues of self-help, duty, character and thrift caught on in mid-century Leeds. And no one propagated them with quite such enthusiasm as the radical Leeds lecturer-turned-writer, Samuel Smiles. It was in a series of talks to mutual improvement societies held in an old cholera hospital during the 1840s that Smiles brought together the material for his most famous work, *Self-Help*. Prior to its publication in 1859, Smiles had already written *The Life of George Stephenson*, which predicted many of the themes of hard work, self-improvement and control which *Self-Help* dwelt on at such length. Smiles was thus part of a broader literature on middle-class morality and self-improvement, but he was by far and away the most popular.

Self-Help sold 20,000 copies in the first year, climbing to 55,000 after five years before being translated across Europe and the Far East. Its creed was simple: God helps those who help themselves. And by reading a catalogue of great lives, the lowliest individual could see the fruits of self-help and rise to the greatest heights. 'The valuable examples which they furnish of the power of self-help, of patient purpose, resolute working, and steadfast integrity, issuing in the formation of truly noble and manly character, exhibit ... what it is in the power of each to accomplish for himself.'[118] The lives of James Watt, Richard Arkwright, Josiah Wedgwood, John Dalton, Charles James Fox and many others Smiles held up as beacons to guide the honest working man through his labours. But Smiles also included lesser-known figures in his industrious pantheon. He too was intent on democratising greatness, on collecting a cycle of bourgeois heroes outside the traditional confines of Parliament, the Church and Army. Whereas Thomas Carlyle had declared that history was 'at bottom the History of the Great Men who have worked here', Smiles aimed to resuscitate the lost voices of the industrious class. 'Many are the lives of men unwritten, which have nevertheless as powerfully influenced civilisation and progress as the more fortunate Great whose names are recorded in biography.' It was Smiles's ambition to bring those forgotten names to light and in so doing, 'illustrate the efficacy of self-respect and self-reliance in enabling men of even the humblest rank to work out for themselves an honourable competency and a solid reputation'. For in the world of Smiles there was no such thing as genius: all progress, all achievements were the product (as Dalton protested) of hard grind and ceaseless energy. Even the extraordinary genius of Michelangelo and William Wordsworth was reduced by the Leeds lecturer to little more than the fruits of a healthy dose of hard work and fair play. *Self-Help* was a cruel combination of mind-numbing banality and the crushingly obvious. According to Smiles, Nicolas Poussin's motto was, 'Whatever was worth doing at all was worth doing well.' And that for Smiles was at the root of his brilliance.

By the 1900s, Smiles's work was deemed unfashionable and

he was thankfully unable to find a publisher for his final book, *Conduct*. The Puritanism of *Self-Help* did not sit well with the decadence of Edwardian England or an emergent socialist ethic. A labour leader once warned the socialist philosopher Robert Blatchford away from the text; 'It's a brutal book; it ought to be burnt by the common hangman. Smiles was the arch-Philistine, and his book the apotheosis of respectability, gigmanity, and selfish garb.'[119]

Three-quarters of a century later, Smiles would return to fashion under the patronage of his most gifted twentieth-century acolyte, the Conservative thinker and politician Sir Keith Joseph. As an Oxford-educated scion of a wealthy construction family, Joseph was an unlikely fan of the earnest Leeds lecturer. Yet in Smiles, Joseph thought he had found the greatest champion of entrepreneurship – the economic elixir which was to lift Britain out of its post-war decline. In 1986, Joseph wrote a new introduction to the book which had been reissued through the Penguin 'Business Library' series. There he argued that 'of all the economic histories ever written, it is Smiles' *Self-Help* that most explicitly and vividly portrays, celebrates – above all, *understands* – the entrepreneur and the virtues that make him what he is'.[120] The apostle of mutual improvement and working-class self-amelioration had been transformed into an apologist for Thatcherite *laissez-faire* and the ethics of 'trickle-down'. But then again, there was no one who celebrated *petit bourgeois* morality quite like Mrs Thatcher.

By the mid-nineteenth century, the commercial middle classes were more respected and more powerful than ever. They had built the civilisation of the Victorian city; this was truly the age of great cities. Macaulay saw Victorian urban civilisation as more religious, more humane and more virtuous than any that existed before. The rich civic fabric of chapels, associations, institutes and infirmaries testified to a nation at the pinnacle of conscientious prosperity. Today, in the Mechanics' Institutes, Lyceums and Athenaeums which now house post offices, Halifax building societies or, in the case of London's Cobden Club, a fashionable private members' bar, we can see the shell of that rich civic fabric. But still the middle classes were not happy. The city, their cities, lacked something. Despite the wealth, the political power, the vibrant civil society, even the laudatory biographies, there remained a nagging fear. A fear of vulgarity; a fear that the Victorian city was, in Matthew Arnold's biting terminology, a crucible of philistinism. It is to the debate over the Victorian city and its *cultural* purpose that we now turn. A debate that would be resolved through the raising of some of the greatest town halls and municipal edifices ever built.

PART TWO

TRANSFORMING THE CITY

[5]

MAMMON AND THE NEW MEDICI

In the summer of 1857, the city of Manchester played host to the greatest art exhibition in Europe. Under one glass roof, Michelangelo's *Virgin and Child with St John and Angels* competed with Raphael's *Large Cowper Madonna*; grandiose portraits by Van Dyck hung alongside the landscapes of Turner and Constable. Works by Holbein, Titian, even Giotto, the most sacred of Italian Renaissance masters, jostled for position among some 1,800 canvases. The galleries of fine art were supplemented by glittering exhibits of Venetian glass, Flemish tapestry, Indian ivory and Chinese fabric. There were cabinets from Urbino, enamels from Limoges, and porcelain from Sèvres. The zealous visitor could enjoy over 16,000 *objets d'art* herded to Lancashire from across the Empire and beyond. According to *The Times*, Manchester's 'Art Treasures Exhibition' was 'an event almost unique in the history of art in England or perhaps the world'.[1]

Located a short train ride from the city centre, the exhibition was sited in the grounds of Manchester Cricket Club in Old Trafford Park. Where today towers modern Manchester's most famous edifice of civic pride, the Old Trafford Stadium 'Theatre of Dreams', there stood the largest collection of public and private art ever seen in Europe. And where crowds from across the north of England now pay homage to Manchester United Football Club, in the 1850s they came in their hundreds of thousands to marvel at a treasure trove of cultural artefacts. Special train services were laid on from Birmingham, Liverpool and Macclesfield as employers were cajoled into

granting days off and subsidising cheap tickets. The engineering magnate William Fairbairn provided special entry for
800 mechanics from his workshops. From Titus Salt's textile
works in Saltaire arrived a party of 2,500 employees in thirty-
seven carriages, dressed in their Sunday best and accompanied
by their own drum-and-fife band. And, needless to say, the
Leeds culture vulture Benjamin Barker was not going to miss
out on such a spectacle:

> Rose at 6.30, went to Leeds by 7.14 train. Started to Man-
> chester by a special train at 8.35 by Huddersfield, got to Art
> Treasures Exhibition at 12.40, got lunch outside (took it in
> my pocket), went in at 1, inspected Museum of Ornamental
> Art until 2 o'clock. 2 to 3 in Water Colour Gallery, 3 to 4
> Photographs, and the drawings by ancient Masters, 4 to 5
> Ancient and Modern Masters, at 5.5 [sic] went out to the
> train, got in, started for home at 5.25, got to Leeds at 9.40,
> could not get to Bramley until 11 o'clock train...[2]

The citizens of Manchester were engrossed by this cultural
behemoth on their doorstep. Elizabeth Gaskell wrote to her
publisher, George Smith, demanding he and Mrs Smith 'pay
us a visit before our beautiful Exhibition is closed. It really is
beautiful, – even after Italy. Indeed, I think Italy makes us
enjoy the pictures of our old friends, the great Masters, even
more.'[3] Even the cynical Friedrich Engels, who enjoyed such a
turbulent relationship with the city, was seduced by the public
enthusiasm. He wrote to his old friend Marx, 'Everyone up
here is an art lover just now and the talk is all of the pictures
at the exhibition ... you and your wife ought to come up this
summer and see the thing.'[4]

The exhibition was a huge success and during the six-month
display attracted over one and a half million visitors. Unlike
the Millennium Exhibition at London's Greenwich Dome in
2000, it was a distinct mark of social cachet to have walked
the aisles of the Art Treasures Exhibition. Among those drawn
to Trafford Park were the towering figures of the Victorian

era: Lord Palmerston, the French Emperor Louis-Napoleon (Napoleon III), Charles Dickens, Benjamin Disraeli, Alfred, Lord Tennyson, the American diplomat Nathaniel Hawthorne, the Queen of the Netherlands as well as Queen Victoria herself. With this array of distinguished patrons, the exhibition helped to launch a series of celebrated careers. The artists of the Pre-Raphaelite Brotherhood, most notably Holman Hunt and Henry Wallis, enjoyed unprecedented attention, as did the Charles Hallé Orchestra, which performed almost daily under the glass canopy. For one glorious year, Manchester became the fulcrum of the artistic world; for a brief moment, the Victorian Bilbao.

But what on earth was Manchester doing hosting such an ambitious cultural showcase? Manchester – the notorious 'Cottonopolis', the shock city of the Industrial Revolution; a city instinctively associated with vomiting chimneys, belching factories, and a subliminal disinterest in anything Giotto, Titian or Constable had to offer. As even the supremely loyal *Manchester Guardian* was forced to admit, 'If the English are held to be a nation entirely of shopkeepers, Manchester is supposed to be always behind the counter, and to view men and measures through an atmosphere of cotton.' Mancunians were popularly ridiculed for following a 'money-making life', allowing their bodies and souls to become absorbed 'in [the] pursuit of material wealth and practical utilities'.[5] And in that reputation lay an answer to this urgent desire to edify the Victorian city.

i PHILISTINISM

Despite their growing economic sovereignty and political authority, there remained a gnawing undercurrent of cultural disquiet among the Victorian middle classes. Above all, the architects of the new industrial civilisation were sensitive to the charge of philistinism; that their cities, these testimonies to their wealth and influence, were little more than reflections of materialism and acquisitive individualism. Unlike the great urban civilisations of ancient and medieval Europe, the Coke-town and 'Cottonopolis' of the nineteenth century were reviled as places of muck and brass that had little capacity for intellectual or aesthetic endeavour.

The new manufacturing cities were indeed condemned by contemporaries, not simply for their utilitarianism, their phys-ical ugliness, their irreligion, their moral depravity, but also for their crass money-grubbing vulgarity. William Cooke Taylor, a supporter both of manufacturing and urbanisation, in his *Notes of a Tour in the Manufacturing Districts of Lancashire* described Manchester as 'essentially a place of business, where pleasure is unknown as a pursuit, and amusements scarcely rank as secondary considerations. Every person who passes you in the street has the look of thought and the step of haste.'[6]

W.H. Jones, in his pseudonymous *Gimcrackiana, or Fugitive Pieces on Manchester Men and Manners*, was even more withering. 'The all-absorbing feeling of the bulk of the inhab-itants, is a desire to acquire wealth; and everything is deemed worthless in their estimation, that has not the accom-plishment of this object for its end. Now, this insatiable passion for gain cannot co-exist with a love of literature or the fine arts'.[7] In a further example of the nineteenth-century fascination with the relationship between noise and industry, Jones dwelt upon the vulgar ear of the Manchester man who 'hears more music in the everlasting motion of the loom than he would in the songs of the lark or the nightingale. For him philosophy has no attraction, poetry no enchantment; mountains, rocks, vales and streams excite not his delight or admiration; genius shrinks at his approach.' 'One reads figures, nothing but figures on all the faces here,' remarked one German visitor.[8] Another, Friedrich Engels, explained how it was 'self-interest and especially money gain' which motivated the unremittingly vulgar Mancunian bourgeoisie. Once, when he tried patiently to explain to a fellow businessman about the city's terrible housing conditions and manifest social ills, 'The man listened quietly to the end, and said at the corner where we parted: "And yet there is a great deal of money made here; good morning, sir."[9]

Even the staunchly urbanist *Leeds Mercury*, in a lead article entitled 'The Spirit of Public Improvement', lamented how such cities as Leeds, Bradford and Liverpool had 'in the midst of the arduous pursuits of industry ... neglected almost everything except the making of individual fortunes'.[10] This absence of cultural achievement affected the industrialists' own confidence. According to Taylor, the manufacturers of the modern industrial city lacked any sense of communal identity or civic pride. While it was easy to discover the achievements of the German burgomasters and medieval Italian merchants, 'the manufacturers act as if they were ashamed of themselves and their order, and sought to hide the disgrace of their existence under some fashionable name'.[11]

The assault on urban materialism culminated with Matthew Arnold's biting essay, *Culture and Anarchy*. With its criticism of the 'bad civilization of the English middle class', this historically mesmerising work brutally encompassed over forty years of distaste for what Arnold termed the 'Hebraism' of the Victorian middle-class 'Philistines'. It was as much a denunciation of their Dissenting, religious denomination as their dependence upon the new industries of the manufacturing age. For he dated the malaise of English life not from the Industrial Revolution of the late eighteenth century, but from the emergence of Puritanism in the mid-seventeenth century and its domination of English bourgeois culture. The Civil War heritage, which the Nonconformists were so proud to identify with, he branded 'the prison of Puritanism'.[12] As such, Arnold drew upon the critique developed by John Stuart Mill in *On Liberty* (1859), whose attack on the 'despotism of custom' and 'tyranny of the majority' was an implicit challenge to the emergence of a suffocating, Nonconformist narrow-mindedness.

Arnold's lofty contempt for the vulgarity of the Dissenting middle classes, huddled together in John Bright's 'great cities', was summed up in his account of the suicide of Mr Smith, 'secretary to some insurance company'. The unfortunate Mr Smith had put an end to his life fearing bankruptcy and consequently the threat of eternal damnation. This prompted Arnold to reflect how 'The whole middle class have a conception of things, – a conception which makes us call them Philistines ...the concern for making money, and the concern for saving [our] souls!'[13] This conception of life led them not only to ignore the good life of 'sweetness and light', but 'even prefer to them that sort of machinery of business, chapels, tea-meetings, and addresses from Mr Murphy [a notorious anti-Catholic lecturer], which makes up the dismal and illiberal life on which I have so often touched'.[14] It was, of course, a wholly preposterous proposition when seen in the light of Benjamin Barker's diaries, for example, and his rich appreciation of fine art, music and intellectual debate. But for Arnold, the Nonconformist manufacturers of the 'great towns' had too limited an understanding of man's spiritual range. Their lives, oriented around Mammon and the parochial, Dissenting fear of damnation, were devoid of any proper appreciation of man's cultural calling. The money-grubbing, narrow Hebraism of the urban middle classes stood in stark contrast to the eternal values of Arnold's upper-middle-class 'Hellenism'.

It was the desire to escape from the shadow of philistinism into Arnold's sweetness and light that would lead Victorian industrialists, merchants and manufacturers to strive so energetically to position themselves as the Medici of the mechanical age. This was not, as some historians have suggested, an act of reactive, class genuflection – a desperate attempt to achieve aristocratic approbation by emulating some kind of upper-class ethic. Instead, the civic elites hoped to craft their own proudly urban, often Dissenting, necessarily bourgeois culture with its endogenous heroes and traditions. In their quest to show there was more than Mammon to the industrial cities, they set about manufacturing their own cultural history and identity. And while Arnold contrasted their philistine 'Hebraism' with his own cultured 'Hellenism', it was, ironically, Hellenism which first offered the urban middle classes an escape from this wounding critique.

ii Hellenism

During the long eighteenth century, Austria, southern France, Greece and Italy had all provided a favoured tramping-ground for the aristocratic excursions of the Grand Tour. For decades, noble young men, or *milords*, enjoyed a debauched rite of passage stretching from Calais to Rome. This came to an end with the French Revolution which, followed by the equally disruptive Napoleonic wars, made travel to the Continent (as today's Foreign Office might put it) 'inadvisable for British subjects'. It took the crushing of Bonaparte and the Peace of Amiens to open up Europe and the Mediterranean once more to British tourists. With the travel ban lifted, they came in their thousands. And in the early 1800s, Greece rapidly became the destination of choice for all cultured travellers.

Lady Shelley reacted in typically fulsome style to the reopening of the tourist season. 'Every wish of my early years had centred on a tour of the Continent ... The change in the political world in 1814, at last promised to gratify my wishes in that respect.'[15] The frenzy following the arrival of the Elgin Marbles in 1803 led to a cascade of guidebooks and travel writing. The romance of the Greek War of Independence (1821–4), the lustre of which was greatly augmented by Lord Byron's tragic death at Missolonghi, only added to the Hellenic fashion. Among the most celebrated tourists' tracts were those by the topographers Colonel Leake (*Topography of Athens; Travels in Northern Greece*) and Sir William Gell (*Topography of Troy; Argolis: the Itinerary of Greece*). Gell himself was a leading light in the Society of Dilettanti, which organised countless expeditions to Greece and Asia Minor, plundering and recording the ancient civilisations. As the Tory journal the *Quarterly Review* put it in a review of Leake's work, 'No one is now accounted a traveller who has not bathed in the Eurotas and tasted the olives of Attica.'[16] And ever greater numbers did indeed wish to count themselves as travellers.

After the conclusion of the Napoleonic wars, an excursion around the Mediterranean was decreasingly the preserve of the aristocracy. Middle-class industrialists and professionals from the Victorian cities began to make their presence felt in Italy, Greece and Turkey.[17] With Gell's book in their hand (as a generation later would have their Murray and then Baedeker), they pounded a well-trodden route through Athens and the romantic Delphi ruins. One of those exploring the tourist trail was the young architect William Wilkins. Entranced by what he saw in Greece, Asia Minor and Italy he returned to England to design Downing College, Cambridge, the National Gallery and University College London. Another middle-class visitor was Edward Baines junior who spent his early twenties touring the requisite monuments of ancient and Renaissance Europe. A more tragic example of this expansion in the corps of the travelling public was the son of the wealthy Leeds woollen merchant, Benjamin Gott. Benjamin junior had already journeyed extensively through the Low Countries in 1814, providing his father with intelligence both on potential customers for their Armley Mill produce as well as opportunities for artistic purchases. Yet his 1817 trip through Italy and Greece ended in disaster, for he died from fever in the Athenian port of Piraeus and was then buried in the Temple of Theseus at Athens. Back in Leeds, his distraught father commissioned Greek landscape watercolours, Athenian cityscapes and abundant classical statues in memory of his lost son.[18]

With unprecedented numbers of middle-class tourists returning from Greek expeditions, Hellenism became the fashion of the day. Periclean Athens was heralded as the apotheosis of Western civilisation. 'We are well aware, that to a large class of persons, any attack upon the Greeks, or the ancient republics, amounts to a crime little less than sacrilege,' commented the *Quarterly Review*.[19] Just as the Mediterranean had been removed from the ghetto of the Grand Tour, so the Athenian cult was no longer limited to the sophisticated world of London and Oxbridge, of clerics, civil servants and dons.

English philhellenism was as much a bourgeois fashion as an aristocratic cult. If, as one leading historian of Victorian culture has suggested, the Victorians saw the Greeks 'in themselves', they did so just as much in Leeds as in London.[20] According to another historian, 'In architecture, dress, furniture, sculpture, painting and poetry, Grecian was the style. Greekomania had gripped the British public.' One advertiser in *The Times* cynically hoped to exploit the market by merchandising a 'Grecian Volute Headdress', 'formed from the true marble models, brought into this country from the Acropolis of Athens by Lord Elgin.'[21]

A brief glance over the lectures held at the Leeds Literary and Philosophical Society gives some indication of the burgeoning interest. In April 1822, the future *Leeds Mercury* editor Edward Baines junior delivered a paper 'On the Rise and Progress of Art, Science, and Literature among the Athenians'; in April the following year, Baines lectured again, 'On the Elgin Marbles, and the Causes of Excellence of Grecian Sculpture'; in March of 1832, Christopher Kealey presented a talk 'On the comparative beauties of Grecian and Gothic Architecture'; in January 1835, H.J. Marcus lectured 'On the Classical Period of Greece, compared with the revival of letters in modern Europe', and in March 1837, 'On the comparative advantages of a state of civilization and literature over a state of barbarism'. In April 1845 the Revd Charles Sangster took up the theme once again with a talk entitled 'On the Character of the Athenians', and in December 1854 William Osburn concluded the Society's classical interest with a lecture 'On Greece'.[22]

Apart from the sea, the sun and the romance of a lost civilisation, why was nineteenth-century civil society so bewitched by Greek heritage? Asa Briggs has suggested there existed an envious fascination with a time and a place that had not been 'swallowed up in industrialisation'. Periclean Athens was among a number of 'older historic places' to which the middle class could retreat away from the social and economic strains of industrialisation. It was a mythical 'place' to contrast against 1800s Britain.[23] Yet the evidence points in a very different direction. For the industrial cities, Athens was not a Hellenic paradise – the Arcadian retreat of so many Grand Tour travel writers. Nor was it simply a lost world of antiquity and archaeology – the realm of discovered tombs and the Elgin Marbles. It was not a place of refuge, but rather an ideal to emulate. For the Victorian civic elite saw in the Greek city states both an ideal of urban living and an answer to the slur of philistinism.

The city republics of classical Greece had combined the civic ideals of the urban middle class: local self-government, internal liberty, a culture of rationalism and, crucially for civic identity, the combination of commercial success with aesthetic vibrancy. The Athens of the statesman Pericles, the architecture of the Tower of the Winds, the commerce of Piraeus, and the intellectual circle of Plato and Sophocles revealed the heights to which a prosperous urban community could accede. The Athenian combination of industry, art and science provided a ready defence against any ignorant, metropolitan charges of philistinism. As *The Builder* put it, the commercial city of Athens, 'not much larger than Liverpool or Bristol', managed to produce within two centuries 'a greater number of exquisite models in war, philosophy, patriotism, eloquence and poetry; in the semi-mechanical arts, which always accompany or follow them, sculpture and painting; and in the first of the mechanical, architecture – than in all the remainder of the universe in 5,000 years'.[24]

iii CITIES OF MINERVA

One of the more eccentric English visitors to the Continent during the summer of 1830 was the dandyish novelist and fashionable man of letters, Benjamin Disraeli. Together with his Oxford friend George Meredith (who was then engaged to Disraeli's sister), the two young bucks embarked on a glorious sixteen-month traverse which took them from Spain to Egypt via Corfu, Albania, Greece, Turkey and the Holy Land. Disraeli cut his usual raffish figure. In Gibraltar his clothes were, he claimed, 'the admiration and envy of many subalterns', while he was, rather magnificently, the first person to carry both a morning and evening cane, changing them over when the gun fired. Sailing from Malta to Corfu, Disraeli as ever paid close attention to his sartorial condition. 'You should see me in the costume of a Greek pirate', he wrote to his brother Ralph. 'A blood-red shirt, with silver studs as big as shillings, an immense scarf for girdle, full of pistols and daggers, red cap, red slippers, broad blue striped jacket and trousers.'

While the future Prime Minister paraded aboard yachts, flirted with ambassadors' wives and bowed to the Grand Vizier, it was the chance to witness the great urban civilisations of the Mediterranean that proved the most formative influence on his political thinking. After visiting Corinth, Argos and Mycenae, Disraeli and Meredith arrived at last in Athens. There they lost themselves in the romantic wonders of a fallen civilisation and claimed to be the first Englishmen to whom the Acropolis had been opened in nine years. From Athens they sailed for Constantinople ('An immense mass of buildings, cupolas, cypress groves, and minarets') and then Jerusalem. 'I was thunderstruck,' Disraeli wrote. 'I saw before me apparently a gorgeous city ... Except Athens I never saw anything more essentially striking.'[25]

Disraeli's sense of the exotic, his hazy Oriental affection for 'the great Asian mystery', were all indulged by the wonders of Jerusalem. However, it was Athens that had made the most powerful impact and back in England he returned again and again in his writings to the legacy and import of that city – most notably in *Coningsby*. At the beginning of Book IV, the eponymous hero travels to Manchester ('the great metropolis of machinery') to understand the brave new world of manufacturing and industry. Disraeli takes this opportunity as narrator to offer some broader thoughts on the nature of urban civilisation. 'A great city, whose image dwells in the memory of man, is the type of some great idea. Rome represents Conquest; Faith hovers over the towers of Jerusalem; and Athens embodies the pre-eminent quality of the antique world – Art.'

But the world was changing and a new civilisation upon us: 'What Art was to the ancient world, Science is to the modern; the distinctive faculty. In the minds of men the useful has succeeded to the beautiful. Instead of the city of the Violet Crown, a Lancashire village has expanded into a mighty region of factories and warehouses. Yet rightly understood, Manchester is as great a human exploit as Athens.'[26]

This was the classic embodiment of the image of Manchester as the 'shock city' of the nineteenth century – an urban emblem of the new world of industry, steam and factories. Yet Disraeli also had a different message. Like his young hero, he too travelled to Manchester in 1844 and at the newly opened Athenaeum delivered a lecture entitled 'The Value of Literature to Men of Business' containing a very different moral to that which *Coningsby* had suggested. To the city's assembled worthies, he challenged Manchester to be known for more than just its science and industry. It should yearn to emulate ancient Athens: to marry commerce and culture, manufacturing and intellect.

Disraeli began by sharing with the audience the wonders of Athens, 'that citadel fame of ineffable beauty ... a brilliant civilization developed by a gifted race more than 2,000 years ago'. Whilst Manchester had made great strides in moving from an 'assemblage of manufacturers' to a 'great mercantile emporium', it still devoted too much energy to utility. However, he sensed a keen dissatisfaction amongst his Mancunian hosts, that 'amidst the toil and triumphs of your scientific industry' there had come upon the manufacturers of the Cottonopolis, 'the irresistible yearning for intellectual refinement'. As a result Manchester merchants had constructed 'an edifice consecrated to those beautiful emotions and to those civilizing studies' – the not accidentally named Athenaeum. He exhorted the assembled industrialists to go further in their refinement and 'direct in every way the formation of that character upon which intellect must necessarily now exercise irresistible influence'. The leaders of Manchester should look upon the Athenian precedent to understand how business and commerce need never be an obstacle to intellectual and cultural advancement.[27]

At the Athenaeum's annual *Soirée* (a portentous, back-slapping gathering of the city's great and good), the Chairman and historian Archibald Alison echoed Disraeli's comments:

> There is a natural connection which has made itself mani-fest in every age between commerce and intellectual emi-nence ... And we shall find that the genius, the taste and the fancy which have rendered the city of Minerva immortal – which have caused its name, after the lapse of 2,000 years, to be adopted by an institution animated by a similar spirit – was owing to the combined efforts of commerce and intel-lect, to the vicinity of the harbour of Piraeus to the temples of the Acropolis.[28]

The theme was continued at the following year's *Soirée* when Lord Mahon (Earl Stanhope) declared the modern indus-trial cities of Britain were, to paraphrase *Coningsby*, 'as great an exploit' as ancient Athens. He too conjured up the image of 'that renowned city' as it had stood since antiquity and played upon his audience's tacit cultural bond, emboldened by a shared experience of Greek travel and literature. Who, Mahon demanded, 'has not sought to familiarise his mind with those scenes' of classical Athens? Principally, 'that majestic temple which crowns the Acropolis ... superior to any other structure in the zenith of its splendour, and fresh from the sculptor's hands?' Mahon expanded liberally on the 'marble columns', the 'sunny heights', and 'in the distance, the azure expanse of the Aegean Sea'. Whilst modern industrial society might have outrun the early Athenians in 'some branches of modern science, and many other branches of human know-ledge', it had yet to rival them in sculpture, oratory, or phil-osophy. Then, Mahon came to the crux of his argument:

> ... in ancient Athens the study of arts and the acquirements of literature were united with, and made to flourish by, the

pursuits of commerce. For while these great speculations in philosophy were being pursued in the groves of the Academy, and while Phidias was raising the master-pieces of his art – at that very time, ships from every clime known were crowding the wealthy port of Piraeus. And thus it was that with these people the pursuits of commerce were not only joined with, but formed a foundation to, the super-structure of art and literature which still continues to excite our wonder and admiration.[29]

What ancient Greece taught the wealthy Victorian elites was that not only could art and culture flourish in a com-mercial environment, but that economic success was in fact essential to fostering aesthetic excellence. The manufacturers and industrialists of Manchester were simply on the verge of a turning point in the socio-economic cycle: the move from wealth-creation to artistic patronage. Furthermore, the history of ancient civilisation showed that truly great art, architecture and philosophy flowed not from courtly patronage or country houses but from mercantile and industrial wealth.

In his powerful urban polemic, *The Age of Great Cities* (1843), the Congregationalist and historian Robert Vaughan took up that theme by disparagingly contrasting baronial and courtly art with the triumphs of civic patronage. It was a remarkable fact, he believed,

> ... that the states of Greece, which knew nothing of her-editary distinctions, which were not possessed of large wealth, which consisted of so many city communities, and were pervaded generally by the spirit of republicanism, col-onization, and commerce – that it was given to those states to supply to all subsequent time the models of the wonderful in science and art, models which the proudest empires have done well to imitate, which they have rarely equalled, and never surpassed.[30]

Vaughan went on to demonstrate how commerce and creativity were inseparably linked; 'society becomes possessed of the beautiful in art, only as cities become prosperous and great'.[31] This stood in dramatic contrast to the awful boorishness of the county squirearchy. 'In short, a flourishing Greek city exhibited society in the highest state of mental and moral improvement to which it has been found possible that man should attain.'[32] A popular, contemporary history of Liverpool similarly concurred that 'the arts did not attain meridian splendour in Greece or Italy until after they had been enriched by successful commerce'.[33] For, 'when the arts are liberally encouraged and science meets due reward, commerce and wealth must have poured from their tributary streams into the golden tide'.

The intellectual energy of the Athenian state extended beyond fine art to an entire culture of intelligent, rational discussion. As we have seen, the Victorian city was honeycombed by an array of clubs, institutes, societies and fellowships. And the civic leaders who presided over the Literary and Philosophical Societies, Mechanics' Institutes and, most obviously, Lyceums and Athenaeums, consciously emulated their classical forebears. They discovered in the academies of ancient Athens precisely the type of intelligent, Socratic discourse they took to be the hallmark of the industrious bourgeoisie. The directors of the Manchester Athenaeum were frank in acknowledging its cultural heritage. 'Minerva herself presides over its halls, its libraries and its literary entertainments; with her placid and benign countenance she invites and welcomes the young men of Manchester to all her literary and scientific treasures which she spreads before them in the greatest profusion'.[34] The city's middle-class, male elite seemed increasingly able to locate their power and understand the nature of their urban civilisation within an appropriate historical framework.

Yet for some the classical world was too antique a society for emulation. The slavery, the overwhelmingly agricultural economy, and the martial valour did not seem to provide a terribly useful urban model. Instead, they turned toward a society that made its money from cotton and finance, combined democracy with civic leadership, and exercised an even more impressive aesthetic patronage.

iv William Roscoe and the Italian Renaissance

After a series of catastrophic investments in mining and property ventures, in 1816 the Liverpool bank of Messrs J. and W. Clarke finally crashed. The shock inflicted by this collapse on Liverpool's booming economy was short-lived; but the benefits that accrued to the city's civic culture can still be felt today. For flooding into the auction rooms from one of the lead partner's elegant villas came a library of rare European literature and a gallery full of High Renaissance art. Up for sale were canvases by Andrea del Sarto, Ghirlandaio, Bellini, and even Leonardo da Vinci. With them came Italian prints, Venetian *objets*, and fifteenth-century Renaissance tracts.

This incredible treasure chest of rare cultural artefacts was painfully extracted from the beautiful but bankrupt home of Liverpool's most cultured citizen: the Parliamentarian, author, anti-slavery activist, man of letters and now ruined banker, William Roscoe. As merchant and patron, Roscoe stands as a cultural lynchpin in the development of the Victorian city. His historical publications and aesthetic patronage were instrumental in developing a new appreciation of the architectural and aesthetic importance of the Italian Renaissance across British urban culture.

Roscoe was born in 1753, the son of a hale and hearty publican-cum-market-gardener in Mount Pleasant. At the age of twelve he left school to help his father sell potatoes before being articled to a firm of Liverpool solicitors. As he immersed himself in the miserable grind of the law, Roscoe found a personal outlet in literature. In one of the many inspiring examples of artisan auto-didacticism which litter the late eighteenth century, he taught himself Italian and embarked upon numerous embarrassing attempts at poetry, urging his

fellow townsmen to pursue more liberal pursuits than
Mammon:

> Ah! Why, ye sons of wealth, with ceaseless toil,
> Add gold to gold and swell the shining pile?
> Your generous course to happiness ye bend,
> Why, then, to gain the means, neglect the end?[35]

To stimulate this broader, artistic culture among his commercial peers, Roscoe founded a Society for the Encouragement of the Arts of Painting and Design and then, as a
practising attorney, a Literary Society with fellow professionals. At the same time his scholarly interest in Italian
literature developed as he started to research a life of Lorenzo
de' Medici. With Liverpool's commerce prospering he shifted
his professional concerns from law to finance and moved
to rustic Toxteth Park. Notorious in the early 1980s for its
deprivation and inner-city race riots, to Roscoe it was charming. 'The principal attraction of this residence was the immediate vicinity of a small but beautiful dingle, leading to the
shores of the Mersey, and presenting many delightful prospects
of the river and the country beyond.'[36] From there he progressed on to Birkenhead and then Allerton Hall, where he
could indulge (as a rational child of the Enlightenment) his
Linnaean passion for botany. Indeed, his love for plant science
and agricultural improvement was such that in 1802 he established Liverpool's Botanic Gardens. Suffused in the world of
plants and animals, he was moved to write that sublime
nursery classic, *The Butterfly's Ball and the Grasshopper's
Feast*, depicting a harmonious botanic netherworld.

It was, however, Roscoe's *Life of Lorenzo de' Medici, Called
the Magnificent* which earned him national and international
acclaim.[37] First published in 1796, it went through three
reprints by 1799 before being edited into an even more popular
version by William Hazlitt. An unashamedly hagiographic
work, it established the intellectual contours for the Victorian
relationship with the civic Renaissance past.

His analysis of the glory of Florence was unapologetically bourgeois. It was the honest toil of the middling, industrious classes displayed 'in the pursuits of commerce, and the improvement of their manufactures' which built the city's aesthetic marvels. It was not the Church or feudal barons who patronised the city's artists, architects and writers. Rather, it was thanks to the political tranquillity and creative spirit of the bourgeoisie itself. The Florentine commercial class – and here was Roscoe's central contention – never lost sight amidst its money-making and manufacturing of the cultural ends of existence. They were 'earnest in the acquisition of wealth' and 'indefatigable in improving their manufactures', but they knew that 'the true dignity of man' resided in his cultural output.

It was also widely appreciated that such creativity required nurturing. It was up to civic leaders to provide encouragement to the cultural community, and few had done so with such aplomb as Lorenzo de' Medici. His purchase of Greek sculpture and antiquarian *objets*, his creation of public museums, his patronage of Brunelleschi and other leading architects accelerated Florentine arts years beyond its city state rivals. Above all, it was his creation of an academy to promote the fine arts which cemented the greatness of Florence. 'To this institution, more than to any other circumstance, we may, without hesitation, ascribe the sudden and astonishing proficiency which, towards the close of the fifteenth century, was evidently made in the arts and which, commencing at Florence, extended itself in concrete circles to the rest of Europe.'[38] It was this spirit of the enlightened, liberal philosopher-king which would come to inspire Liverpool's merchant princes – the Rathbones, Heywoods, Ewarts and Gladstones – to reinvigorate Merseyside's civic culture.

Ironically, it was the loss of Roscoe's own art collection that initially spurred them to establish a Medici-style academy. As bankruptcy loomed, Roscoe was forced to part with his library and art collection which were immediately bought up for the public good. William Rathbone, scion of the Unitarian business dynasty, purchased the entire book stock and placed it in the Athenaeum; to this day, it provides the basis for Liverpool's Picton Reference Library. Meanwhile, a further consortium of Rathbone, Benjamin Heywood and William Ewart (friend of the Liverpool merchant John Gladstone, who would later honour their companionship by christening his son William Ewart Gladstone) bought Roscoe's thirty-seven pictures for £760. With this 'Series of Pictures illustrating the Rise and early Progress of the Art of Painting in Italy, Germany etc.', they began the programme of exhibitions and talks which merged into the Liverpool Royal Institution, the aim of which was to burnish the same creative spirit that had marked fifteenth-century Florence and to produce a home-grown Michelangelo. According to Roscoe, this constituted nothing less than 'An attempt to institute in the midst of a great trading city a place which should be a perpetual focus for every intellectual interest, a perpetual radiator of sane and lofty views of life, a perpetual reminder of the higher needs and aspirations of men in the midst of the fierce roar of commercial competition and the clangorous appeal of those surroundings to the vulgar lust of money.'[39]

At its opening in November 1817, the culturally bereft Roscoe bravely delivered the inaugural address (in front of, among others, the eight-year-old W.E. Gladstone) in which he traced the fruitful history of commerce and creativity. 'In every place where commerce has been cultivated upon great and enlightened principles, a considerable proficiency has always been made in liberal studies and pursuits.' It was the role of bodies such as the Royal Institution to ensure the continuing harmony of utility and pleasure, 'for those who, amidst the duties of an active profession, or the engagements of mercantile concerns, wish to cultivate their intellectual powers and acquirements'.[40]

In 1948 the collection of the Royal Institution was subsumed into the Walker Art Gallery. Today, as you visit the gallery (passing through a portico which depicts Michelangelo on one side, Raphael on the other, and Commerce resting above

them), Roscoe's eye for a Renaissance master is instantly
apparent in Room 1 where most of his bequest remains on
display – from a serene Perugino to a majestic Simone Martini
to Ercole de' Roberti's tortuous *Pietà*. Unfortunately, Roscoe
himself did not fare as well as his cultural legacy. The bank
never recovered from the 1816 crash and in 1820 J. and W.
Clarke was still unable to pay off its creditors. His beloved
Allerton Hall was taken into receivership and the great civic
benefactor was left to survive on the proceeds of his literature
and the charity of his generous friends. But his place in the
city's history was secure. At his burial at Renshaw Street
Unitarian Chapel in 1831, the Liverpool press spoke proudly
of how the city 'once only known for its enormous commercial
wealth' had given birth 'to the most distinguished of the
historians of Europe'. 'From this great mercantile city, as from
a second Florence', there had issued works of extraordinary
cultural maturity.[41] For that was Roscoe's achievement: providing Victorian cities with the cultural confidence to celebrate their commercial pre-eminence.

Built upon mercantile wealth flowing from the cotton,
woollen and banking industries, the prosperous and beautiful
republics of Florence, Pisa, Lucca, Siena as well as Venice were
quickly adopted as an aspirational paradigm for the middle
classes of the Victorian city. 'It was in the *manufacturing city*
of Florence', Archibald Alison informed the members of the
Manchester Athenaeum at their annual gathering, 'that a rival
was found in Dante to the genius of ancient poetry; in the
mercantile city of Venice that painting rose to its highest
lustre on the canvas of Titian; Genoa sent forth that daring
spirit which first burst the boundaries of ancient knowledge,
and exposed to European enterprise the wonders of another
hemisphere'.[42] The city republics effortlessly inspired the
imagination of the Victorian civic leaders with their enticing
history of bourgeois confidence and identity; their unembar-
rassed celebration of the virtue of trade and industry; with the
extraordinary renaissance of art and architecture fostered by
mercantile patronage; and finally their federal political struc-

ture, which safeguarded a flourishing municipal base devoid of centralisation.

Similarly, the northern European city republics of Bruges, Ghent and Antwerp, founded upon an equally aggressive commercial basis and just as renowned for their art and architecture, offered an engaging if less celebrated precedent. 'It is in the North', continued Alison, 'that the chief triumphs of the alliance between commerce and intellect are to be found.'[43] The enormous wealth derived from the woollen and worsted industries and the ready display of that wealth in architecture, fabrics and fine art constituted a beguiling model for the Victorian *nouveaux riches*. The Venetian Gothic style of much of the architecture in Flanders and the Dutch Republic provided an obvious appeal for the warehouse aesthetic of the northern cities. And for the Dissenting elites who held such sway in Manchester, Leeds, Bradford and Birmingham the proud history of Protestantism – heroically displayed during the birth of the Dutch Republic – made these cities even more attractive. Yet the fundamental appeal of the city states was class- rather than denomination-based. Civic republican history – in Italy as well as the north – provided one of the clearest testimonies to the creative and prosperous potential of a powerful, ascendant middle class.

The language of seduction and enticement is not inappropriate, for the early Victorians did in some peculiar manner 'fall in love' with Italy. As with Greece, the number of middle-class visitors to Italy, and in particular to Tuscany, rose dramatically following the end of the Napoleonic wars. They began that great middle-class affair with the Italian nation that continues to this day, with legions of 'gap year' students studying language courses across Florence and Perugia, rivalled only by the ceaseless incursion of the wealthy English into the 'Chiantishire' countryside of Siena. And then, as now, the cry from the *cognoscenti* was of an Italy ruined by the tourism.

Lord Byron, who had done so much to romanticise Venice

and the Italian republics in *Childe Harold*, complained as
early as 1817 of how Rome was 'pestilent with English'. 'A
man is a fool who travels now in France or Italy, till this tribe
of wretches is swept home again.'[44] Henry Matthews, in his
1820 *Diary of an Invalid*, was equally horrified. 'The English
swarm everywhere', he wrote of Rome. 'It seemed like a
country town in England at assizes.'[45] By the 1840s, Florence
welcomed over 5,000 British visitors each year. Lady Lyttelton
described how, when she arrived there in 1819, 'we found this
town up to the brim with English, and with difficulty found a
place to put our heads in'.[46] There was even an English-
language newspaper, the *Tuscan Athenaeum*, catering for the
Anglophile market, while Anglican churches received congregations of up to 800 in Florence and Rome.[47] The Italian
city republics became tourist centres glorified by the poetry
of Samuel Rogers and clinically deciphered by an explanatory
literature of middle-class guidebooks. The profusion of Murray's *Handbooks* in the 1840s for tourists with restricted time,
limited means and little historical knowledge set the tone.
Sir Francis Palgrave, who edited the Murray *Handbook for
Travellers in Northern Italy*, self-consciously differentiated it
from an earlier edition which he rather pejoratively termed 'a
description of what used to be called the "grand tour"'.[48]

Holidays to Italy and the Continent were becoming increasingly the currency of the newly wealthy middle class from
across Britain's cities. The French chronicler Hippolyte Taine
described in tones of some astonishment his railway com-
panions on a trip from York to London:

> In the same carriage as myself was a Newcastle family,
> the husband, his wife and her mother, lower-middle-class
> townsfolk, quite well dressed in new clothes. They were on
> their way to Venice, for pleasure, yet they cannot have been
> rich for they were travelling third class ... My three fellow-
> travellers were making conscientious preparations for their
> trip: they were studying a Murray, an Italian phrasebook,
> and a special guide, full of figures, for the crossing of the

Alps ... they were sensible folk, capable of learning and who, although they may not appreciate painting, will bring back a good deal of information and many useful notions.[49]

Inevitably, Dickens (who visited Italy in 1844) also wielded his gently mocking pen on this vulgarised passion for Continental travelling. In *Little Dorrit*, he described the Twickenham home of the quintessentially middle-class Meagles as packed with souvenirs from Egypt, Venice, Tuscany, and 'morsels of tessellated pavement from Herculaneum and Pompeii'.[50] Perhaps the most famously *déclassé* visitors to Florence in English literature emerged early in the twentieth century: the father-son combination of George and Mr Emerson ('She knew that the intruder was ill-bred, even before she glanced at him. He was an old man, of heavy build, with a fair, shaven face and large eyes') who cause such a stir in the Pensione Bertolini at the start of E.M. Forster's *A Room With A View*.

Among all classes, rapture for the Italian city republics was universal. Samuel Rogers's popular *Italian Journal* was typical in its description of Florence. 'A heavenly day. Walked on the Arno ... Saw the Chapel de' Medici, and the tombs of the Medici in the Chapel de Depositi, by Michael Angelo ... As we approached Florence we saw the dome, the belfry, and the watch-tower of the Palazzo vecchio – with many other turrets – black against the evening sky. The dome magnificent!'[51] In Mariana Starke's *Travels on the Continent* (1820), she offered the disclaimer that, 'It is scarce possible to discover the magnificent edifices of Venice floating, as it were, on the bosom of the deep, without exclaiming; Singular and beautiful city! of whose appearance imagination can form no idea, because no other work of man is like this.'[52] In 1845, the *Manchester Guardian* published a lengthy, glowing account of Florence for the discerning Mancunian tourist entitled, 'Letters on Italy'.[53] *The Times* meanwhile heralded Florence 'the most eligible of human abodes' for those whose aim in life is enjoyment. The newspaper's Tuscan correspondent listed the beauties of 'the quaint turrets, the lofty domes, the gay pinnacles, the frowning battlements'. In short, 'if any town surpasses Florence in magnificence none equal it in variety and originality'.[54] Ruskin's *Mornings in Florence* would only accelerate the tourist trend – much to the author's horror.

Inspired by works such as Roscoe's history of Lorenzo, the emergent passion for Italy was reflected in a broader, intellectual interest in Italian Renaissance history. After Roscoe, one of the most widely-read accounts of the Renaissance was by the Swiss historian and political economist J.C.L. Sismondi. A seminal intellect in nineteenth-century Europe, his technical work on political economy was used extensively by Marx but his elegiac narratives of the Tuscan city states entranced the British reading public. According to the historian E.A. Freeman, a narrative of Italian history was 'accomplished in a manner perhaps as nearly approaching perfection as human nature allows in the immortal work of Sismondi'.[55] His purple prose conjured up a glorious image of the prospering, independent and creative municipalities of Renaissance Italy.

> Stone bridges of an elegant and bold architecture were thrown over rivers; aqueducts carried pure water to the fountains. The palace of the *podestas* and *signorie* united strength with majesty ... The prodigies of this first-born of the fine arts [Michelangelo] multiplied in Italy: a pure taste, boldness, and grandeur struck the eye in all the public monuments, and finally reached even private dwellings; while the princes of France, England, and Germany, in building their castles, seemed to think only of shelter and defence.[56]

Reprinted numerous times and then converted into one of Lardner's pocket Cabinet Cyclopaedias, his books could be found in the libraries of most urban Athenaeums or Mechanics' Institutes; both the Newcastle and Liverpool Literary and Philosophical Societies held copies. For Sismondi's analysis was attractively clear: it was the industrious, patriotic, rational and benevolent sensibilities of the Italian bourgeoisie that had underpinned the glories of the Italian Renaissance. The greatest era in Europe's aesthetic history was the work of a class branded in Victorian Britain as Hebraic and philistine.

The middle classes were the heroes of the republics. Conversely, Sismondi criticised the irresponsibility and *faux* chivalry of the Italian aristocrats who had hindered their advance, sowed faction and discord, and frequently ensured the exile of the cities' most brilliant artists and authors, not least Dante. The glories of the Italian Renaissance were constructed upon the ethic of citizenship and a change in the moral outlook of the individual: from selfishness to community. 'The sympathy existing among fellow-citizens', he wrote, 'from the habit of living for each other and by each other – of connecting everything with the good of all – produced in republics virtues which despotic states cannot even imagine ... how rich in virtues was Italy in the twelfth Century, when covered with republics, and when every city simultaneously fought for liberty!'[57] It was these virtues – the 'republican spirit now fermented in every city' – which gave the republics their civic glory.[58]

By the mid-century, the British middle class had gained a solid grounding in Italian art, architecture, politics and history. Those who went abroad came back, in Taine's words, with 'many useful notions', while the establishment of the Society of the Friends of Italy in 1851, the writings of Mazzini and the freedom-fighting romance of Garibaldi only increased public fervour at home. This was particularly the case in the Liberal-led northern cities who powerfully identified with the Risorgimento struggle for liberty. In Newcastle, the Liberal MP and newspaper owner Joseph Cowen was a vigorous supporter of Italian self-government. He helped to smooth things over between Mazzini and Garibaldi (who visited him during a tour of the Tyne) and even deployed his industrial and media contacts within Europe to assist the Italian revolutionary cause.

v Manufacturing Culture

The republic which most successfully married commercial prowess with aesthetic excellence was, of course, Florence. As a democrat and as a radical, Roscoe had first and foremost expressed his admiration for the political activism which was such a hallmark of Renaissance Florence. According to Roscoe, the 'singular pre-eminence' of the Arno republic was due to its 'nature of government';[59] not principally because of the form of government it produced, but because of the creative *métier* of the citizens which flowed from their passionate love of liberty. The 'active spirit' which had called forth the 'talents of individuals' to preserve their liberties and municipal autonomy was, in times of peace and security, channelled instead into creative uses. The 'defence of freedom' nurtured in the Florentine people faculties and strengths that were instrumental in its later prosperity. For when 'the active spirit of its inhabitants' was not engaged in defending its liberty, it 'displayed itself in the pursuits of commerce, and the improvement of their manufactures'.[60] In addition, the popular nature of its system of self-government fostered a broad range of skills amongst its citizens. 'Where the business of government is confined to a few, the faculties of the many become torpid for want of exercise; but in Florence, every citizen was conversant with, and might hope, at least, to partake in the government; and hence was derived the spirit of industry which, in the pursuit of wealth and the extension of commerce, was, amidst all their intestine broils, so conspicuous and so successful.'[61]

Sismondi also made Florence the heroine of his history, but subtly differed in his depiction of Lorenzo de' Medici, whom he regarded as little more than a tyrant whose arbitrary governance was contrary to the Arno spirit. For Florence was 'the city where the love of liberty was the most general and the most constant in every class; where the cultivation of the understanding was carried furthest; and where enlightenment of mind soonest appeared in the improvement of the laws'.[62]

The city's tradition of liberty and self-government obviously appealed to a Victorian civic elite who keenly guarded their municipal autonomy from Westminster. In a speech at the Leeds Philosophical Hall, the former Whig Chancellor of the Exchequer, Thomas Spring-Rice, reminded his audience how 'we ought not to forget how much freedom, industry, literature and civilization are indebted to Florence, to Venice, Genoa, and the other Italian republics'.[63] *The Builder* magazine celebrated the aesthetic of self-government with a long description of the Renaissance cities' *palazzi pubblici* dating from 'the palmiest days of the Italian republics of the thirteenth and fourteenth centuries'. But the journal was keen to stress that these buildings were more than just medieval town halls; they were 'as it were the parliamentary houses of small though highly-civilised territories'.[64]

The admiration was reflected in the number of tourists. Together with Rome, Florence consistently drew the highest visitor numbers and became the subject of numerous laudatory histories. Amongst the finest was Henry Edward Napier's *Florentine History*. Published in 1846, the year in which England's landowning classes were dealt a symbolic blow by the repeal of the Corn Laws, it followed Roscoe and Sismondi in locating the origins of Florence's greatness in its system of local self-government and the dynamism of its middle classes. Florence, for Napier, was a very good example 'of the power which even a petty state may attain by the innate force of free institutions acting on a manly energy of character'.[65] Civil society, or 'free institutions', left the 'natural faculties and activity of the people' unfettered and so produced a 'considerable expansion of mind and domestic industry'. The glories of Florence were achieved for the most part by 'a self-governed nation of shop-keepers'. The history of Florence was a tale of the potential of the middle classes left to govern themselves. 'Florentine taste and genius first generated artists ... for whatever evils spring from a turbulent democracy ... it was on the whole a more noble and impressive condition, more in unison with the dignity of man than the forced tranquillity and painful submission of their lord-bestridden neighbours'.[66]

Along with the freedom, the self-government and the middle-class workfulness, what the Victorians really admired in Florence was its wealth: its unabashed pursuit of monetary gain through trade and industry. The Renaissance republics provided a perfect, legitimating narrative for the new wealth of the northern industrialists. The history of the Medici, the Sforzas, the Vecchi, the Brancacci and numerous cotton, silk and woollen merchants provided Victorian magnates with the precedent they felt they needed. Sismondi's Italian history had early on stressed the great wealth of the republics. Their 'city manufactures', particularly woollen stuffs, were 'renowned through the western world'. The city state merchants were the 'greatest capitalists of Europe' with counting-houses 'scattered through-out the commercial parts of the world'.[67] Similarly, Napier chronicled the Florentine 'love of enterprise' and 'acute mercantile spirit'. This sentiment pervaded society so deeply that 'he who was not a trader, or who had not made a fortune in foreign parts, had little consideration at Florence'.[68] Napier rejoiced in the intimate connection between 'commerce, manufactures, and political power' which helped the corporations acquire 'vast riches and influence'.[69]

Most ambitiously of all, the Bradford historian John James intimated at the striking parallels between Florence 'under the administration of its illustrious Merchant Prince, Lorenzo de Medici' and the industrial squalor of 1850s Bradford. Both, he repeated, contained a large number of artisans 'especially employed in the manufacture of clothing'.[70] In a similar vein, Lord Morpeth praised English mercantile progress towards the glimmering Florentine ideal. He told an audience suitably gathered together in the Free Trade Hall, Manchester, how he rejoiced 'that English commerce seems in these our days to be rising to the real heights of its position, and to fill the dignity of its calling. – But this the Tuscan, this the Genoese, this the Venetian men have done.'[71]

The popularity of Roscoe's work on Lorenzo had indicated

early on that it was in the battle against the charge of materialism that the civic elite of the industrial cities found greatest
use for the legacy of the Renaissance republics. From the
patronage of Lorenzo to the tapestries of Ghent, it was now
claimed that commerce had always proved the truest friend of
art. In Birmingham, the ultra-philistine John Bright described
how it was that, 'in the States of the north of Italy commerce
was attended by arts and letters, and freedom and civilization,
to an extent which ... is beautiful to contemplate and most
remarkable'.[72] It was, in the succinct words of Disraeli, 'a
merchant of Venice that called forth the genius of Titian'.
Emboldened by their knowledge of the Renaissance past, civic
leaders suggested that not only could a city be just as significant an arena for aesthetic creativity as a country house –
but, in fact, that trade and commercial wealth were pre-
requisites for a vibrant cultural environment.

In a speech to the Manchester Athenaeum in 1843 entitled
'The Liberalizing Tendencies of Commerce and Manufactures', Disraeli tackled the defamatory conjunction of mercantile wealth with philistinism. On the contrary, he declared
that 'the pages of history' have shown that 'literature and the
fine arts ... have ever discovered that their most munificent
patrons are to be sought in the busy hum of industry'. Disraeli
championed the industrialists and merchants of Venice who
had nurtured the work of Titian and Tintoretto and had raised
those 'noble palaces' that commemorate the genius of a Sansovino or a Palladio. Similarly, in the Netherlands it was the
'manufactures of Flanders, dwelling in such cities as Bruges,
and Ghent, and Mechlin' who had fostered the painting and
fabrics of the region. Disraeli dismissed the notion that a
consequence of 'commerce and manufacture' was to neglect
'those more intellectual and highly refined pursuits' at the
apex of civilisation. In fact, the act of commerce and art of
manufacture sympathises with the inventiveness and skill
needed in artistic creativity. Disraeli concluded by announcing
he was certain a future as great as the Florentine past was
'destined for those great cities of Lancashire'.[73]

Three years later, Lord Ebrington similarly stirred his Mancunian audience to help rid the country of the 'feudal prejudice' that trade was incompatible with cultured pursuits. He
urged them to look to 'the merchant princes of Florence, and
those illustrious traders, the Medici, the patrons of trade, and
fosterers of literature'. It was Ebrington's contention that 'the
honourable pursuit of trade and of manufacture, so far from
being incompatible with refinement of mind, and elegant
accomplishments, has done ... far more to promote it than all
the over-vaunted glories of war or the pursuits of ambition'.
The history of commerce and manufacture had ever been the
history of intelligence and of civilisation.[74]

It was a message designed to please. For more than any other
Victorian city, Manchester took the Florentine ideal to its
heart. Thomas Worthington, one of the city's most successful
architects, would late in his life describe Manchester as 'the
Florence of the nineteenth century'.[75] From high up in their
seven-storey warehouses towering over Mosley Street, Portland Street and Princess Street, the wealthy cotton and
woollen lords were determined all should realise that they
stood as Europe's modern Medici. But unlike the Medici of
old, they had not yet been accorded the cultural respect their
status warranted. If Manchester men preened themselves as
the greatest merchants, they in turn were thought of as the
basest philistines. It was the duty of Manchester's mercantile
elite, the 'Cotton Lords' or 'Millocrats', to redeem their city's
miserable reputation. In a stinging editorial, Manchester's
liberal journal, the *Athenaeum Gazette*, explained how 'our
manufacturers' have 'an intellectual and a moral, as well as a
material or merely utilitarian mission to fulfil'. Manchester
should be celebrated not only for its 'numerous seats of pro-
ductive industry', but should also become 'distinguished for
its centres of mental development and of true "intellectual
enjoyment".'[76] It was the responsibility of the city's wealthy
industrialists to follow the tradition of merchants through the
centuries and assume the role of cultural patrons.

So it was that by the mid-1850s, as the jibes reached uncomfortable levels, Manchester's civic leaders decided to confront their critics in a suitably grand style. The mid-century witnessed a rage for exhibitions. As London and then Dublin and Paris had all held Great Exhibitions celebrating their commercial and industrial prowess, so Manchester decided it would do the same. But instead of a trade fair (which would be too obvious an event for Manchester to host), the city would hold an art exhibition; not just art, but fine art; and not simply a large fine art exhibition, but the largest Europe had ever witnessed. It would also serve as a testimony to a culture independent of metropolitan approbation; a culture inspired by the Industrial Revolution and the Nonconformist traditions wholly distinct from the fashions of London and the southeast.

Art exhibitions had already proved popular in the industrial towns as a means of generating an indigenous artistic culture. Leeds had hosted a series of 'Polytechnic Exhibitions' in 1839, 1843 and 1845 organised jointly by the Mechanics' Institute and the Literary and Philosophical Society. These public exhibitions of 'Works of Art, Science, Natural History and Manufacturing Skill' offered fine art to the untutored at competitive prices, partly in an attempt to quell the equally hurtful slurs of materialism. According to the Leeds civic worthy and wool merchant George Goodman, 'The splendid paintings ... showed that a high degree of civilization and improvement was taking place in the town.'[77] But what Manchester planned would be far, far grander.

The driving force behind the Art Treasures Exhibition was a German art historian, Gustav Waagen, a wealthy cotton manufacturer, J.C. Deane, and one of Manchester's most well-connected civic philanthropists, Sir Thomas Fairbairn. Sir Thomas was the son of the mechanical engineer, Sir William Fairbairn, and had remained in the family firm of boiler-making and shipbuilding while working equally conscientiously to position himself at the heart of Manchester civic society. He worshipped at the city's Unitarian Church Street Chapel, involved himself with the Literary and

Philosophical Society and held the position of Lancashire Deputy Lieutenant. He was a citizen committed to over-hauling Manchester's maligned public image while at the same time celebrating the city's liberating principles and developing an autonomous cultural heritage.

The Art Treasures Exhibition was designed to complement the empowering values which had secured the incorporation of Manchester Council, overturned the Corn Laws, built the Free Trade Hall and sent the *laissez-faire* ideals of *das Manchestertum* around the world. The idea was simple: the organisers would ask all the great art-holders in the country to throw open their collections, lending their finest works to the people of Manchester. As Manchester had economically liberated the country by pioneering the Industrial Revolution and abolishing the restrictive practices of the Corn Laws, so now its mission was to liberate culture as another step in freeing Britain from its feudal past. Art would be transferred from the closed-off world of aristocratic country houses (of which Waagen had made a detailed critique) to the open vista of an iron-and-glass venue designed to enlighten the pro-ductive, industrious classes.

On the whole, the request for loans proved a success. Local landowner the Earl of Ellesmere immediately offered up twelve paintings, including a highly valuable Van Dyck. Thou-sands of other loans came in from country houses, museums and even the Royal Collection. Not everyone was so generous. The request for a contribution led one indignant duke to demand, 'What in the world do you want with Art in Man-chester? Why can't you stick to your cotton spinning?'[78] But that was precisely the point. As the *Guardian* put it, to collect all the scattered treasures of art 'in this utilitarian city' would redound greatly to the credit of Manchester and show that 'here, amongst us, is the proper soil in which to plant a great idea for the encouragement of art and the refinement of taste'.[79]

The exhibition would also help to elevate the industrial working class through a cheap and accessible display of morally uplifting art.[80] 'To wake the soul by tender strokes of art' were the lines from Pope emblazoned on one end of the gallery. Fairbairn, along with some of his enlightened business peers, believed in the moral force of art and became one of the city's most committed patrons. The riches his father had strenuously saved up as a boiler magnate now flowed into the profligate pockets of the decidedly anti-industrial Pre-Raphaelite community. As a devout Nonconformist, much of the work Fairbairn commissioned offered spiritually didactic lessons, most notably William Holman Hunt's *The Awakening Conscience*. It is a Pre-Raphaelite classic showing a kept woman (with plenty of rings on her fingers, but none signalling marriage) struggling from the embraces of her lover. Her hallowed, beatified face as she rises from her lover's unwanted petting depicts the redemptive power of Christianity in a fallen world. Today it still holds the attention in London's Tate Britain Gallery. The paternalistic, improving Fairbairn was keen to have such morally didactic pieces at the centre of the exhibition and ensured that many of the other pictures intended for display, such as Holman Hunt's *The Hireling Shepherd*, showed similarly stringent messages of Christian duty.

The idea of the Manchester show was easily sold to Prince Albert, still flush from his success in championing the 1851 Great Exhibition. He agreed to open the exhibition and promised that Queen Victoria herself would put in an appearance. With royal support secured, all that was needed was a building to house the flow of exhibits. In a conscious echo of Hyde Park, a vast Crystal Palace-like structure was commissioned with all costs met from individual subscriptions. Following a public meeting in Manchester Town Hall, thirty-two city worthies subscribed £1,000 each and a further sixty committed themselves to £500 a head. In a superb display not only of mid-Victorian wealth, but also the intense civic pride of the mercantile class, the overall costs of £72,000 were quickly and painlessly raised. And in an equally impressive display of Victorian engineering can-do, standing at over six hundred feet long and fifty-six feet tall, the building was designed and built within eight months.

In 1857 Manchester's Art Treasures Exhibition opened to rapturous acclaim. For its organisers, the moral of the exhibition was clear: it conclusively proved the happy union of art with commerce, that Manchester was not a cultural desert and, in the supportive words of the *Leeds Mercury*, that 'appreciation and love of the fine arts are not confined to great landed proprietors ... but that they exist in those who have been classed among the disciples of the most rigid utilitarian school'.[81] The *Illustrated London News* concurred that the exhibition showed Manchester could now 'hurl back upon her detractors the charge that she is too deeply absorbed in her pursuit of material wealth to devote her energies to the finer arts'.[82] Fairbairn, Deane and the other organisers at last enjoyed the longed-for analogies with the great mercantile patrons of the past. The official magazine of the event, the *Art Treasures Examiner*, claimed that Manchester now 'steps forward in her aggregate character to emulate the glorious example of Florence of old, under her prince-merchants the de' Medici, to display to the world the richest collection of works of fine art the resources of the county allow'.[83]

Into this contented, almost self-satisfied scene stepped a figure entirely at odds with the ethos of the Exhibition. A man who, at this stage of his complicated political journey, described himself as a 'violent Tory of the old school' and had made his name publicly reviling everything the 'Manchester school' stood for: the individualism, the mechanisation, the *laissez-faire* economics. He derided the Manchester ethos as 'the "Let alone" principle', which is, 'in all things, which man has to do with, the principle of death'.[84] Taken as a whole, he thought Manchester could in fact 'produce no good art and no good culture'. In their boundless quest for cultural respectability, the organisers of the Art Treasures Exhibition had made the awful mistake of inviting John Ruskin to deliver two lectures.

By 1857 the thirty-eight-year-old John Ruskin was a national figure. The success of *The Seven Lamps of Architecture* and *The Stones of Venice*, as well as his numerous works of polemical journalism, had made him a star on the public lecture circuit. Packed audiences in London, Bradford, Edinburgh and, of course, Manchester crowded out civic institutes, galleries and Athenaeums to hear his cerebral, visceral critique of contemporary morality and its architectural representation. Precious, biting and utterly convinced of the divine worth of his aesthetic mission, Ruskin's difficult personality frequently jarred with that of his provincial bourgeois audience.

In *The Stones of Venice*, Ruskin had already made clear his views on the ethic of the modern industrial city: 'And the great cry that rises from all our manufacturing cities, louder than their furnace blast, is all in very deed for this, – that we manufacture there everything except men; we blanch cotton, and strengthen steel, and refine sugar, and shape pottery; but to brighten, to strengthen, to refine, or to form a single living spirit, never enters into our estimate of advantage'.[85] In a speech to the Bradford School of Design, entitled 'Modern Manufacture and Design', he broadened his critique to suggest that virtually no artistic value could come from modern cities. He damningly contrasted the life of a designer living in the thirteenth century, taking an afternoon stroll in medieval Pisa, with that of a contemporary in Victorian Rochdale. The former, let us call him 'Nino Pisano', would have seen on each side of a bright river

a line of brighter palaces, arched and pillared, and inlaid with deep red porphyry, and with serpentine. Opening on each side from the river were gardens, courts, and cloisters; long successions of white pillars among wreaths of vine; leaping of fountains through buds of pomegranate and orange ... Above all this scenery of perfect human life, rose dome and bell-tower, burning with white alabaster and gold: beyond dome and bell-tower the slopes of mighty hills, hoary with olive; far in the north, above a purple sea of peaks of solemn Apennine, the clear, sharp-cloven Carrara mountains sent up their steadfast flames of marble summit into amber sky ... What think you of that for a school of design?

By contrast, the unfortunate Rochdale aesthete battled with an urban environment characterised by uninhabited houses with gardens

blighted utterly into a field of ashes, not even a weed taking root there; the roof torn into shapeless rents; the shutters hanging about the windows in rags of rotten wood; before its gate, the stream which had gladdened it now soaking slowly by, black as ebony and thick with curdling scum; the bank above it trodden into unctuous, sooty slime; far in front of it, between it and the old hills, the furnaces of the city foaming forth perpetual plague of sulphurous darkness; the volumes of their storm clouds coiling low over a waste of grassless fields...[86]

If the organisers of the Art Treasures show, wealthy civic dignitaries such as Fairbairn and Deane, had expected a warm pat on the back, a message of congratulation for bringing art to the cultural wastelands of the north, they were in for a shock. The more attuned might have spotted hints of Ruskin's intent in the title he chose for his lecture, 'The Political Economy of Art'. The work was later reprinted as *A Joy for Ever*, the motif ironically taken from John Keats's 1818 poem *Endymion*:

A thing of beauty is a joy for ever:
Its loveliness increases; it will never
Pass into nothingness

The Art Treasures Exhibition had emblazoned this message on the front of their Old Trafford glasshouse. But Ruskin's point was that the entire exhibition, like its 1851 predecessor, signalled the precise opposite of eternal beauty. It lasted a mere six months and had no intention of fostering 'a joy for ever'. Instead, according to Ruskin, the purpose of the show was 'to encourage the production of works of art, which the producing nations ... only hope to sell as soon as possible'.[87] Production, producing – this was Manchester's crime. They had no understanding of the true, timeless nature of art or the spiritual function of artistic endeavour as work. Art could not fit into their narrow world of political economy, of profit and loss, or the cash-nexus. 'You have always to find your artist, not to make him; you can't manufacture him, any more than you can manufacture gold.'[88] Ruskin proceeded to deliver this lesson with a parable brutally honed to appeal to the Manchester merchant princes' *amour propre* as he turned the Medici ideal on its head.

He regaled his audience with the story of how, during the height of the Renaissance, Florence's greatest plutocrat, Pietro de' Medici, ordered Michelangelo to carve him a statue – out of snow. At the 'period of one great epoch of consummate power in the arts', Pietro committed the crime of impatience, and it was this thoughtless impatience which now bedevilled all modern patronage.[89] The superficiality of Victorian art and design were the result of this self-defeating transience. Talent and creativity were squandered by artists working in perishable materials; by wasting their time on illustrating journals or newspapers; and by neglecting the skills which the old trades fostered. The demands of industrial patronage, the hustle of nineteenth-century commercial life were corrupting a necessarily timeless aesthetic culture. Ghirlandaio, Michelangelo and Leonardo da Vinci's transformation into artists was a long and arduous one. Ruskin reminded the audience that they worked and trained for years as goldsmiths patiently understanding their craft, learning an appreciation of the function of art before becoming painters. It was an ethic which Ruskin would try to revive with his own artisan movement, the Guild of St George.

There never was, he later wrote in his preface to the lecture, 'nor can be, any essential beauty possessed by a work of art,

which is not based on the conception of its honoured permanence'.[90] In short, art was not something to be thrown
together in a hastily constructed glasshouse on the edge of
Manchester for the vulgar gratification of a fundamentally
materialist audience. It was the loving product of careful work
carried out not for profit or fame but for the glory of God.
The hard work of Deane and Fairbairn to rebrand industrial
Manchester as a cultural emporium, to cast the businessmen
of Mosley Street as the new Medici, had not it seemed convinced everyone.

Displaying the kind of mettle which had earned Britain its
position at the fulcrum of the Industrial Revolution, the civic
elite of the Victorian city were not to be so easily dissuaded
from their task of manufacturing a new cultural identity.
Increasingly they turned their attention to a branch of design
with Ruskinian levels of permanence. Exhibitions might come
and go, but the urban fabric, the architecture of the city, would
last for generations. And as they directed their wealth into
transforming the face of the industrial city, the Victorian
merchant princes were more determined than ever to cast it
afresh in their own image.

[6]

MERCHANT PRINCES
AND MUNICIPAL PALACES

'I do not care about this Exchange because you don't!' John
Ruskin was at it again. Kindly invited by the burghers of
Bradford to judge a design competition for their new wool
exchange, he turned on his audience of civic worthies with
typical flourish. Over ninety long minutes, in a room 'filled
to its utmost corner', he delivered a 'good and true sermon
against our greedy lust for gold'.[1] First, he scolded the west
Yorkshire burghers for their slavish obedience to the 'great
Goddess of "Getting On"': 'She has formed, and will continue
to form, your architecture, as long as you worship her.' It was
their reverence toward this false idol that had produced the
bleak, functional mills dominating Bradford's cityscape, 'a
quarter of a mile long, with one steam engine at each end, and
two in the middle, and a chimney three hundred feet high'. To
punish the city's moral incapacity, Ruskin then melo-
dramatically refused to judge the entries. 'You cannot have
good architecture merely by asking people's advice on occasion. All good architecture is the expression of national life
and character; and it is produced by a prevalent and eager
national taste, or desire for beauty.'[2] None of which Bradford,
or indeed any other industrial city, seemed to possess. And
so was it any wonder that the state of modern design was
in such a poor state? Eventually, Ruskin came to the
conclusion that in fact 'for a city, or cities, such as this *no
architecture* is possible – nay, no desire of it is possible to
their inhabitants'.[3]

But Ruskin was wholly misguided in accusing his audience

of disinterest. For what so markedly distinguished the middle-class moulders of the Victorian city was their deep concern with aesthetic styles and the nature of design. High-profile public competitions, angry newspaper broadsides, and even parliamentary debates were testimony to a civil society passionate about civic architecture and its symbolic representation. Indeed, even as Ruskin stepped up to the podium, Bradford was in the midst of a brutal feud between supporters of Renaissance, English Gothic and Venetian Gothic Exchange designs, all played out across the letters page of the *Bradford Observer*.[4]

For while few might have been willing to swallow Ruskin's dismissal of Victorian architecture as a reflection of its getting-on materialism, his contention that urban design reflected social and moral values had by the mid-century become a widely accepted nostrum. The Liverpool architect Sir James Picton confirmed the point in a paper which drew upon the design of the city states of old. 'The commercial cities of antiquity, Carthage, Tyre, Palmyra, Alexandria, erected their magnificent monuments, many of which remain to this day, to attest their greatness. The cities of Middle Age commerce, Venice, Florence, and Genoa, expended their wealth in vying with each other in adorning their cities in the spirit of honourable rivalry.'[5] Those advocating grandiose civic projects similarly stressed how closely architecture mirrored the spirit of the age. 'The architectural embellishment of a city is of much greater consequence in forming the character of a people than some hasty thinkers now-a-day recognize. The constant contemplation of fine forms, or the reverse, has a powerful effect upon the mind,' commented *The Builder*.[6] A later article on 'The City and Its Structures' concluded that 'every great city is characterised by its public buildings'. That was why Florence, Milan, Bologna and Venice all 'record the fame of their projectors, and instruct posterity in arts to be lost no more'.[7]

In the light of this aesthetic consensus, the state of the industrial city was regarded with ever greater public embarrassment. In the Victorian cities the mood amongst civic 'improvers' became increasingly concerned with beautifying the urban fabric. The *Birmingham Daily Press* suggested that it 'hardly need point out the desirableness of making our great towns as comely as possible'. Just as a beautiful city would excite a virtuous civic pride amongst its inhabitants, so 'an ugly, squalid place will give its character to the people'.[8] These sentiments were more acutely felt in Leeds. In 1850, the fiercely improving *Leeds Mercury* complained that the city did not yet boast a single edifice 'deserving to be shown to a stranger as ornamental to the town, either from its architecture or from its containing monuments or works of art deserving of admiration'.[9] This was to be deprecated since 'the general tone of thinking and feeling of a population, their taste, and their manners, are likely to be refined and improved by the amplitude, the symmetry, and the elegance of their public building'. This poverty of architectural display stood in stark contrast to the Renaissance cities of Antwerp, Bruges, Ghent and of medieval Italy, which all displayed 'town-halls of extraordinary beauty and noble dimensions', as well as wonderful public buildings, monuments and statues. In short, Leeds had reached 'that stage of opulence and that amount of population, which justify and demand great efforts for the improvement of the town'.[10]

Buoyed by this groundswell of political opinion, the mid-nineteenth century witnessed a marked increase in what would now be termed 'prestige developments', symbolic, ostentatious new structures designed both to beautify and glorify the industrial cities as crucibles of modern civilisation. But, as if still in awe of Ruskin's magisterial denouncements or perhaps inhibited by the modernist tenets of twentieth-century architecture, historians have been all too slow in realising the full wonder of Victorian architecture and its successful transformation of the urban fabric. It was an omission that assumed the status of historical gospel when enunciated by the great Whig chronicler G.M. Trevelyan:

Urban and suburban life in modern England made no appeal
through the eye to the imagination, as had the old village
life of our island, or the city life of ancient and medieval
Europe. Civic pride and civic rivalry amongst the industrial
towns of the North were almost entirely materialist and
not at all aesthetic. The pall of smoke and smuts in itself
was enough to discourage any effort after beauty or joy in
the visible aspect of life.[11]

Wandering in Trevelyan's shadow, Sir Peter Hall, one of
Britain's most respected urban historians and planners,
recently described the British of the nineteenth century as 'a
nation of shopkeepers' who 'were always inclined to count the
cost of everything; not for them the Roman traditions of
grands travaux, which flourished on the other side of the
Channel'.[12] However, when one reads the history and looks at
the raw architectural evidence, it is difficult to see how such
a conclusion could be reached. The Victorian city became a
veritable patchwork of *grands travaux* – a sizeable proportion
of which were designed in the classical, the Venetian Gothic
and Renaissance styles.

Just as the merchant princes of the industrial cities had
attempted to develop a cultural identity by aligning themselves with the commercial heritage of Athens and Florence,
so now they transferred it to the architectural realm. Across
the Victorian civic landscape, the urban elite refashioned their
cities in the texture of the Greek city states and Italian republics. Just as rhetorically they had defended their wealth and
power as part of the virtuous 'purpose' of the middle classes,
so aesthetically they constructed a civic identity around the
mercantile symbols of classical and Italianate architecture.
The urban aesthetic of Athens, Venice, Florence and Siena –
as well as Antwerp, Bruges and Ghent – was plundered to
express a new pride in the power and prosperity of these
modern merchant princes.

And, much as Ruskin might have demurred the consequences, the styles dominating the city owed much to his

scholarship. The popular affection for Italian architecture, so richly augmented by *The Seven Lamps of Architecture* and *The Stones of Venice*, produced an eclectic mix of 'Italian' designs from Venetian Gothic to Italianate, from an austere Romanesque to a gaudy *palazzo*. As Sir George Gilbert Scott put it in his memoirs, 'the introduction of the foreign element . . . came on shortly after the publication of his "Seven Lamps." This undoubtedly set people upon Italian Gothic.'[13] To Ruskin's dismay, the Gothic style had by the mid-century developed a flexibility which allowed it to be employed in any number of styles and myriad buildings quite beyond his strictly defined aesthetic criterion.

Ironically enough, Ruskin's influence was even felt at the Bradford Wool Exchange. Despite his barrage of abuse, the worsted and woollen merchants of south Yorkshire honoured the Ruskinian tradition by choosing a design straight from the pages of *The Stones of Venice*. After a long and involved public debate, the submission by the Bradford architects Lockwood and Mawson, described as 'Venetian Gothic freely understood', went up along Market Street. Though now darkened by pollution and overshadowed by unsympathetic developments, one hundred and fifty years on the building still instantly speaks of St Mark's and the Doges' Palace. Much to Ruskin's chagrin, he had brought polychromy stone, Romanesque windows and an elegant, Venetian balcony into the heart of 'Worstedopolis'. Today, the Exchange also boasts one of the finest examples of renovation. It has been sliced in half with a modernist, glass design housing a Waterstone's bookshop which has successfully managed to retain the dignified, civic feel of the original. Not least because they have kept a Victorian statue of Cobden preaching – albeit in the children's fiction section.

i MONUMENTS TO MERCURY

But to begin with it was Athens not Venice. Far exceeding the attraction of Grecian art and civic institutes was the early

Victorian passion for classical architecture. Looking back from
the relative calm of the 1850s, *The Builder* jokingly recalled
the early century's frenzied obsession with 'the beauties of
Grecian architecture': 'The public admiration thus excited
speedily assumed the character of a mania, or rage. Greek
architecture was adopted in all possible and some almost
impossible situations. Shop-fronts, porticos of dwelling-
houses, banks, gin-palaces – everything was to be modelled
from the Parthenon, the Erectheum, or the temple on the
Ilyssus.'[14]

Led by architects such as William Wilkins, C.R. Cockerell,
and Alexander 'Greek' Thomson, the Greek Revival began to
shift the nineteenth-century civic landscape. What so engaged
the architectural community was the Greek belief in generous
civic patronage. They built to celebrate the glory of their city.
According to William Wilkins, the wonder of their buildings
could be attributed to the attention to which 'the Athenians
were directed by their rulers to the acquirement of a taste for
everything great in science and in art'.[15] Above all, there was
a tradition of grand monuments to elevate the communal,
public sphere. Robert Vaughan stressed the modesty of the
Athenian private dwellings and enviously praised how 'the
wonders of Greek architecture, and the most memorable pro-
ductions of Greek art, were all contributions dedicated to
the honour of religion, or to the majesty of the state'.[16] The
historian Theodore Buckley, in his *Great Cities of the Ancient
World*, explained that the Athenian 'public spirit' intended
works of art not for 'adorning the staircases of the nobility,
but as votive offerings, or gifts to the public'. These gems of
art and architecture were then placed in religious sanctuaries,
'or in the public buildings where every man might admire, as
he trafficked in the ordinary business of life'.[17] Even high-
ranking members of the Church of England were not immune
to the attractiveness of pagan public architecture. At the
opening of Manchester Town Hall in 1878, the Bishop of
Manchester celebrated Waterhouse's municipal palace within
the tradition of the classical city state:

We did sometimes spend too much money on our homes, entertainments, and the like, and he desired to see the day when English people would be proud of their public institutions and their public buildings, and at the same time be led to cultivate greater simplicity, which was the mark of true refinement, in all the social habits and intercourse of life. The old Greeks when they had any citizen whom they specially delighted to honour used to invite him to a banquet in their Town Hall, and to be entertained at the public expense in the Town Hall was the acknowledged reward of high and meritorious public services.[18]

Classical architecture became intimately associated not only with the commercial and cultural ideals of the Greek city states, but also with a more philosophical celebration of the public sphere. The classical idiom was removed from the uniquely metropolitan connotations of Nash's Regency London. To build in the Greek style indicated a confidence in the values of urban living and the ethic of citizenship. Nineteenth-century civic leaders were determined to emulate that ideal by erecting structures that similarly celebrated the wealth, benevolence and virtue of their cities. The purpose of such monumental architecture was to arouse the individual from his mundane, everyday concerns and realise his good fortune to be a citizen of such a splendid *civitas*. Unlike today, when central and local government cower in fear of being accused of 'wasting' taxpayers' money, the Victorians started to think that public designs deserved to be bold, portentous and expensive.[19]

Liverpool, in particular, a port city like Piraeus (as well as with a history of slavery), witnessed a steady accumulation of classical architecture. Much of this was down to Cockerell; a veteran Mediterranean traveller who worked hard to bring the Greek Doric style to Britain's cities. He was assisted by the Liverpool Corporation Surveyor, the architect John Foster. In this highly skilled environment all was Greek. The 1815 Wellington Rooms in Mount Pleasant caught the fashion by displaying a façade consisting of a circular Greek temple with an adaptation of the Athenian monument of Lysicrates which had been illustrated by Stuart and Revett in their *Antiquities of Athens*. Similarly, John Foster's Oratory mortuary chapel of St James's Church, now overshadowed by the gargantuan Liverpool Cathedral, was modelled on a Greek temple with a correct portico of six Doric columns at each end and four internal Ionic columns supporting the ceiling.[20] By far the grandest of Foster's classical monuments was his 1828 Custom House, a massive dockside edifice symbolising Liverpool's status as a global commercial power and rightful heir to Athens's mantle. Bombed during World War II and subsequently demolished, it boasted a vast dome, thunderous Ionic columns, and a suitably august portico. Not far along the waterfront, Jesse Hartley would soon come to design the city's Albert Dock with a similar (if less sumptuous) acknowledgement of Liverpool's classical aspirations; the cast-iron, unfluted Doric columns offered an engagingly brutal marriage of commerce and culture. On into the twentieth century, when the three dockside offices of the Royal Liver, Cunard and Port of Liverpool Authority went up they became popularly known as the 'Three Graces' – the city's architectural answer to the original Three Graces, Aglaia, Euphrosyne and Thalia, of fifth-century Athens. Now that Liverpool is set to be European Capital of Culture 2008 the waterfront has been nominated as a World Heritage site and there is talk of constructing a twenty-first-century 'Fourth Grace'.

Back in the nineteenth century, away from the docks, Cockerell was working equally hard to lay the architectural foundations for a latter-day city state. This vigorous champion of classicism had already made his name designing a superb Literary and Philosophical Society in Bristol (modelled on the Temple of Vesta at Tivoli) as well as the Parthenon-inspired National Monument on Carlton Hill, Edinburgh. In Liverpool, along Castle Street, he crafted an elegantly classical three-storey branch building of the Bank of England complete with portico and reassuringly sturdy Doric columns. However, his finest work still stands today as a definitive testimony to civic pride. Put out by the Town Hall already under construction in the centre of Birmingham, the Liverpool Corporation decided they required as beautiful a public edifice to reflect the city's commercial and civic status. And contrary to what Trevelyan suggested, this civic rivalry was almost wholly aesthetic. An architectural competition was announced for a concert hall to be paid for by public subscription and to which a set of Assize Courts were later added. Amazingly, the prize of erecting this civic landmark was won by the unknown but highly gifted twenty-five-year-old London designer Harvey Lonsdale Elmes, who immediately set to work on building one of the great classical edifices of the nineteenth century. Yet tragically the contract proved too much for him. The indecisiveness and political chicanery of the Corporation, combined with the complex design problems posed by heating, lighting and simply constructing such a vast edifice, destroyed his health. In 1847 he died of consumption, with the work still uncompleted.

It was left to Cockerell to finish the job and he did so magnificently. Even today as you step out of Liverpool's inhospitable Lime Street Station, the raw classical mass of St George's Hall, with its huge portico of sixteen Corinthian columns, remains instantly impressive. Described by Pevsner as 'the freest neo-Grecian building in England and one of the finest in the world', it is a testimony both to Liverpudlian self-confidence and the early-nineteenth-century dominance of classicism. Inside, the Hall manages to fuse an almost Roman sense of space – with its huge, inset columns, marble and gold-leaf detailing and arching coffered vault – with intricate Greek details including the coloured Minton tiles on the floor and the almost exotic Concert Room balcony. The classical feel is further augmented by the array of sculptures of eminent Liverpudlians carved to resemble Socrates or Caesar. Sir James Picton, the herald of civic pride, celebrated the Hall 'as a design at the head of our public buildings, and worthy to take rank with those of the purest age of Grecian art'.[21] But for some the classicism went too far. A contributor to *The Builder* was aghast at the pagan imagery of the Hall's pediment. 'May I be permitted to ask', he enquired, 'what Liverpool has to do with Mercury, and whether for the chief decoration of the chief provincial town of a Christian country, no better source of inspiration can be found than the fabled creation of Paganism?'[22]

Despite the barbs, classicism continued to thrive in Liverpool long after it had fallen from fashion in other cities. Spilling out from St George's, the Liverpool Museum and Library, and then the Walker Art Gallery and finally the Picton Reading Room were all modelled in a brooding, classical motif. The city's Lyceum Club came to resemble a Greek temple, while a statue of Minerva watched over the comings and goings in the Town Hall. For many cultural commentators Liverpool's architectural blossoming was as extraordinary as it was welcome. If the city's ambition was to shed the philistine slur, then it was all but achieved according to *Tait's Edinburgh Magazine*: 'In this large city, we shall surely find many public structures and private mansions exhibiting improved taste; and we shall be induced to prolong our stay here for a few days, to mark and note the progress of art amongst this busy, prosperous, and enterprising community.'[23]

Liverpool was not alone in its classical fetish. In Glasgow, Alexander 'Greek' Thomson worked successfully to give the Clydeside city that magical, rather incongruous classical air it has enjoyed ever since. For somehow the city's classicism had to be more esoteric, more original than the old rival Edinburgh – the celebrated 'Athens of the North'. And it had to tell a story of Glasgow's cultural identity as a city of global commerce and imperial power. As Thomson himself put it, the purpose of art was the 'furnishing of our minds with correct images'.[24] The architect David Hamilton had already begun the process by turning a private Georgian tobacco mansion into a faithful product of neo-classicism, complete with Corinthian portico and roof-top temple, for the city's Royal Exchange. Thomson continued the fashion with a mar-

vellously eclectic range which can be seen most readily in his
ecclesiastical architecture.

Unlike Cockerell or Wilkins, Thomson had never witnessed
at first hand the wonders of ancient Greek architecture but
managed nonetheless to produce a series of striking classical
buildings prominent across the Glasgow skyline for their dramatic, jutting towers. His own United Presbyterian Church,
where he worshipped until his death, still dominates the Cale-
donian Road, resisting persistent attempts to demolish it. His
other works for the Presbyterian Church on St Vincent Street
(now a decaying edifice overshadowed by office blocks) and
also in Queen's Park combine simple neo-classicism with a
trademark rectangular block tower crowned with an intricate
spire. Meanwhile, along the city's west end, safely upwind
of the pollution and smog from the textile and engineering
industries, a new *civitas* of broad terraces and set-back villas
modelled almost wholly in the classical style was taking
shape. What became Kelvingrove Park was surrounded by
terraced buildings of which Thomson's own Great Western
Terrace would prove one of the most durable. The Glaswegian
middle class could now live Grecian, worship in Grecian
churches, and, if they passed their days within the hubbub of
the Royal Exchange, even work Grecian.

If Liverpool and Glasgow were the most affected by the
classical turn, few cities escaped unscathed from the Grecian
craze. In Nottingham, the new Mechanics' Institute was 'supported on fluted columns of the Corinthian order of architecture, imitated from the temple of the Sybil at Tivoli'.[25] In
Manchester, the Manchester Royal Institution was designed
by Charles Barry in a rich classical vein complete with Doric
columns, classical friezes, and atrium. In Newcastle, whose
Grey Street offers one of the most complete classical urban
vistas, a local historian praised the newly developed County
Courts for emulating 'the stability and grandeur of a Grecian
temple'.[26]

The Athenian idyll had been made concrete. Just as in Periclean Athens, commerce had been turned into culture and a

vibrant, competitive municipal base was energising the political and public sphere.

ii URBAN RENAISSANCE

It was the Italian city republics of the fourteenth and fifteenth centuries which were to prove the most favourable model for Victorian emulation. Like Athens, they too had nurtured a tradition of expressing their civic pride through a culture of public architecture. As Sismondi put it in his history of Italy, 'The citizens allowed themselves no other use of their riches than that of defending or embellishing their country.' As a result, 'every city built public palaces for the Signoria ... and prisons; and constructed also temples, which to this day fill us with admiration by their grandeur and magnificence'.[27]

Nowhere was this practice of public edification more admired than in the mercantile emporium of Manchester; a city still desperate to shed the philistine tag and display a cultural ambition through its civic fabric. As it embarked on a city-wide reconstruction, the number of practising architects expanded from nine in 1825 to 164 by 1900, while the construction industry stood second only to the cotton mills as a source of male employment. Yet the city's first Renaissance landmark was designed by a predominantly London-based architect and inspired by a quintessentially metropolitan design.

In between rebuilding the Palace of Westminster in that rampantly Gothic idiom, Charles Barry found time to wander up Whitehall and along Pall Mall to oversee plans for the new Reform Club. Established as a Whig haunt to further the progressive ideals of the 1832 Reform Act, Barry modelled the new establishment on the kind of imposing Renaissance palace which studded the streets of Florence and Siena. He had already attempted this design in an earlier Pall Mall clubland venture, The Travellers' Club, but the Reform marked its perfection – and with it the start of the transition from the Greek Revival of the Regency to the Italianate *palazzo* of the

Victorians. With its statuesque front, high-vaulted (complete with perimeter balcony) interior and tessellated court floor, milled over by gossiping civil servants, journalists and politicians, the club still retains a mercantile, Florentine feel. And it was exactly the type of design the Manchester money-men were after.

Barry employed the same Renaissance formula to design the city's new Athenaeum building. Housed on Mosley Street, around the corner from his neo-classical Royal Institution (the two have now been joined together as the Manchester Art Gallery by a pioneering steel-and-glass pavilion), its Italianate style marks a distinctive break from the old Doric designs. Athens was giving way to Florence. Inscribed with a frieze adapted from Raphael's Palazzo Pandolfini in Florence, it began the *palazzo* craze which was most promiscuously adopted in the construction of the city's proliferating warehouses.

Right through the Industrial Revolution, Manchester retained its eighteenth-century heritage as a trading city and as a result invested just as much in its warehouses as its factories or mills; indeed, more so. According to one recent estimate, the city's 1,450 warehouses absorbed over forty-eight per cent of property asset investment by 1815 as opposed to a mere six per cent in factories, a trend that only accelerated with the later development of the Manchester Ship Canal.[28] And as places of prestige, commercial emporiums designed to woo potential clients as well as simply store goods, the warehouses became the focus of intense architectural competition.

Once again, medieval mercantile states provided the inspiration. As George Gilbert Scott explained, 'The medieval builders had no notion of the seats of commerce and manufacture being given up to unsightliness, nor of their buildings, however utilitarian, being allowed to disfigure their cities. We find, accordingly, that their warehouses were as nobly treated as any other of their buildings. The finest warehouses in existence are probably those remaining in the old commercial cities of

Germany.'[29] In the event, inspired by the elegance of Barry's Athenaeum, it was Italy not Germany which provided the model.

Along the commercial district of Mosley Street, Portland Street and Princess Street, firms competed like modern banks with their towering skyscrapers to raise the most striking edifice. Now destined for apartment conversions and over-looked in the rush towards the nearby 'Gay Village' along Canal Street, the mid-century warehouses must have pre-sented an awesome spectacle. First up was a warehouse con-structed for that champion of Manchester commerce and middle-class suzerainty, Richard Cobden. Designed by Edward Walters, No. 15 Mosley Street paid an obvious homage to Barry with its trenchant Renaissance styling. But the Cobden warehouse was only a trial run for Walters's greatest com-mercial design, the J. Brown and Son Warehouse of 1851. This was a mighty Italianate *palazzo* rising six storeys from the street and offering as great a testimony to the power of trade and commerce as any modern Medici could hope for. Walters would once more celebrate the great progressive ethic of com-merce when he designed the Free Trade Hall. He finished his commercial work in Manchester with his 1860 Manchester and Salford Bank, again in Mosley Street and again styled in a determinedly Renaissance fashion. The memory of the Italian city republics was being succinctly positioned at the heart of Manchester's civic fabric.

Working alongside Walters was the architect John Edgar Green, who was an equally loyal disciple of the Renaissance precepts established by Barry's Athenaeum. In 1848 he designed Sir Benjamin Heywood's Bank in St Ann's Square in a more simple *palazzo* style than Walters, but lacking nothing in elegance. In 1854, he moved from Heywood's financial to philanthropic concerns when he began work on the new headquarters for the Mechanics' Institute. Located amongst the warehouses of Princess Street, it blended seamlessly with their grandiose Italianate styling – surreptitiously inculcating the mechanics and artisans of the industrial city with the progressive, commercial ethic of the mercantile elite.

The Renaissance style was equally popular in non-commercial buildings. The most successful Manchester designer of civic and municipal works in the Italianate idiom was the Unitarian architect, Thomas Worthington. A committed social reformer who spent much of his life championing working-class housing and public utilities, his first significant work was symbolically enough the Overseers' and Churchwardens' Office. Modelled on the Renaissance grandeur of Sansovino's St Mark's library, Venice, it hinted at a shift from Florence to Venice and the mixing of pure Renaissance with Ruskin's Venetian Gothic. He followed it up with public baths designed for the working classes in Greengate, Salford and New Store Street, Manchester. The styling and intricate detailing Worthington put into these works indicated a Ruskinian ardour for workfulness and an equally Ruskinian belief in elevating the masses through beautification. To contrast these ornate, elegant municipal baths with the public swimming pools of today is to chart a sorry story of civic collapse.[30]

Worthington's fusion of Florentine Italianate and Venetian Gothic is seen to best effect in his sumptuous Albert Memorial close by his even more Venetian-inspired Memorial Hall (built as an act of remembrance to the great ejection of Nonconformists in 1662, it now hosts an unpuritanical pub, The Albert Square). Dominating Albert Square and facing the Town Hall in the centre of Manchester, the Albert Memorial is a worthy tribute to the Prince who opened the Art Treasures Exhibition and blessed the city's Renaissance ambitions. The work provided George Gilbert Scott with the basis for his even grander, gilded affair in London's Hyde Park crowning the South Kensington 'Albertopolis'. Worthington's memorial was inspired by the Santa Maria della Spina in Pisa, while *The Builder* described it as belonging to 'that period of medieval architecture which prevailed in Florence between the ages of Giotto and Brunelleschi'.[31]

Marvellously, Worthington extended his passion for Renaissance design into the field of industry. In Salford he attempted to camouflage a furnace chimney as a Sienese campanile – a feat rivalled by the Birmingham-based architect J.H. Chamberlain's 'Giotto-esque chimney' designs for a local warehouse. In Leeds, the Tower Works on Globe Road actually achieved it with a beautiful Florentine campanile complete with a sister edifice modelled on the Lamberti Tower in Verona. Seen from Leeds train station, the glimmering Renaissance towers still retain their beauty amidst the sprawl and carparks of Holbeck. Finally, even *The Builder* got in on the act, producing a wonderful series of 'Designs for Furnace Chimney-Shafts', all of which could easily have been mistaken for the towers of San Gimignano. There could be no greater symbol both of the confidence of the industrial elite in celebrating their mercantile heritage and of the fashion for Renaissance styling.

The Victorian memory of the Italian republics was infective and few cities escaped its draw. In Halifax, Charles Barry modelled the Town Hall on Sansovino's library of St Mark's. In Blackburn, the new Covered Market House of 1848 was built in the style of an early Italian *palazzo*. In Nottingham, the Guild Hall was built with a Florentine stucco which, 'supported by ten wooden pillars of the Tuscan order', formed an Italian *piazza*. This was in addition to the 'Venetian' Exchange.[32] The tower of the Keighley Mechanics' Institute was an imitation of the Palazzo Vecchio, Florence.

In Birmingham, Chatwin styled his bank commissions on Venetian *palazzi*, and Charles Edge designed Italianate villas in the elegant Edgbaston suburb. Indeed, in Birmingham the Italianate style influenced even the design of grocers' shops. An article in *The Builder* on 'Recent Architecture in Birmingham' described a shop which 'calls to mind the famous Loggia by Orcagna, on the Piazza Vecchia, Florence; and the porch of a Venetian church we recollect'. However, the 'conspicuous use of bricks of different colours' reminded the reviewer more 'of those well-known edifices of the older parts of Genoa'. The article concluded that in the Italian palatial style of the Renaissance, 'Birmingham might boast of some excellent examples – both in stone and stucco'.[33] Similarly,

'The Styx of this new Hades.' River Irwell and its environs, Manchester, 1859.

St George's Dock, Liverpool, c.1895.

Polemicist and prophet, Thomas Carlyle, 1865.

'Look upon this picture, and on this.' A.W.N. Pugin marks the decay of a Christian nation by contrasting a 1440s town (above) with an 1840s town.

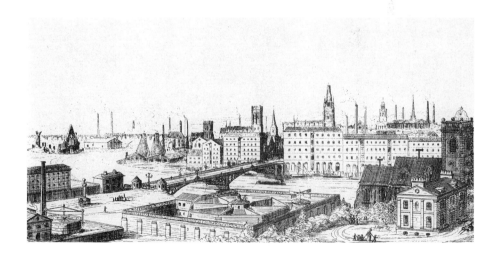

Above: Exterior of
Ducal Palace, Venice,
by John Ruskin, 1851.

Left: St Marks, Southern
Portico, from *Examples of
the Architecture of Venice,*
by John Ruskin, 1851.

Above: Arabian windows in the Campo Santa Maria Domini, from *Examples of the Architecture of Venice,* by John Ruskin, 1851.

Right: For John Ruskin (1865), the city's history was 'a warning which seems to me to be uttered by every one of the fast-gaining waves, that beat like passing bells, against the Stones of Venice.'

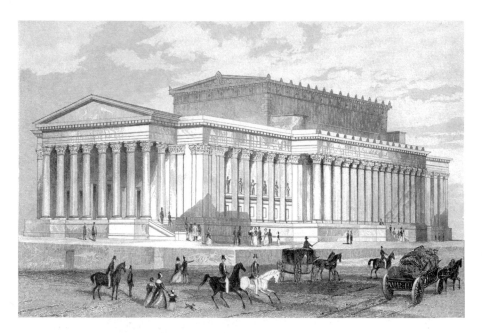

Above: 'The freest neo-Grecian building in England.' Liverpool's St George's Hall, c.1840.

Left: A sense of the *agora*. Liverpool's St George's Plateau.

'Dedicated, like the United States of America, to a proposition.'
Manchester's Free Trade Hall, 1880.

'Not inferior to those stately piles which still attest the ancient
opulence of the great commercial cities of Italy and Flanders.' Leeds
Town Hall, 1858.

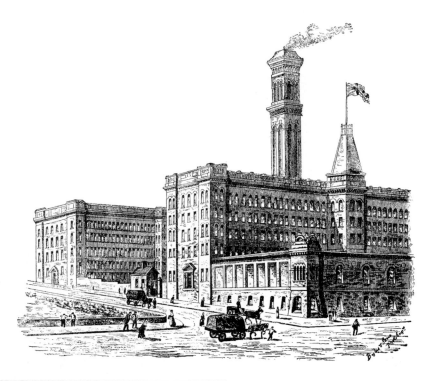

Above: An incongruous campanile. Manningham Mills, Bradford.

Left: 'Next to churches, the finest of medieval structures existing are, perhaps, the town halls of Flanders, Germany, France and some of the free cities of Italy.' Detail of the Midland Grand Hotel at St Pancras, designed by Sir George Gilbert Scott.

parts of Glasgow rebelled from the classical dominance of 'Greek' Thomson with a series of strikingly eclectic, Venetian-inspired designs. The Stock Exchange in the commercial centre of West George Street (now Nelson Mandela Place), along with the Clydesdale Bank, stand out against their classical neighbours. The most famous Venetian edifice remains John Stewart Templeton's extraordinary carpet factory overlooking Glasgow Green. Designed by William Leipers, it is a rather free act of homage to the Doges' Palace complete with Venetian Gothic windows and polychrome colouring inset with a garish blue mosaic.

iii LIFE AND SOUL OF THE CITY

Contemporary reaction to Manchester's architectural renaissance was uniformly adulatory. As early as 1836, one contributor to the proceedings of the Manchester Statistical Society felt able to declare that the city boasted 'richly stored streets of warehouses and factories, and palaces of merchants worthy of the ancient and better days of Florence'.[34] It was heralded as the city *par excellence* of the Italian Renaissance, while *Building News* remarked how 'One can scarcely walk around Manchester without coming across frequent examples of the grand in architecture. There has been nothing to equal it since the building of Venice.'[35] *The Builder* agreed that after a long period of depression, 'art in Manchester has sprung into vigorous existence'.[36] The new architecture and prevailing good taste was down to 'the tide of prosperity' which had swept the city. For the proof that warehouses could be designed for both utility and beauty, 'we need not now point exclusively to the commercial cities of Italy'.[37] Ten years on, in an editorial on 'Proposed New Public Buildings in Manchester', the journal expressed the hope that 'the "merchant princes" of Manchester' who displayed 'such spirit in the erection of palatial warehouses' would now display an equal liberality in designs for the town hall and other public buildings.

Thankfully, the Manchester merchants took up the

challenge and created one of the most iconic civic edifices of Victorian Britain. By the mid-nineteenth century, the growth in activities by the newly incorporated municipal authorities, combined with an expanding need for criminal courtrooms, led to a flurry of town hall developments. The financial autonomy which the councils enjoyed meant they had the ability to raise rates or subsidise investment with their profits garnered from utility ownership. Alternatively, new construction could be funded from public subscription, drawing on the community's buoyant civic pride. Town hall construction offered a moment to define the identity of the industrial city; to show London the dignity and historic grandeur of these regional capitals. Sir Charles Barry voiced the motive perfectly: 'A town hall should in my opinion be the most dominant and important of the municipal buildings of the city in which it is placed. It should be the means of giving due expression to public feeling upon all national and municipal events of importance. [It should serve] as it were the exponent of the life and soul of the city.'[38]

Curiously, Manchester's civic guardians felt that the 1857 Art Treasures Exhibition had still not quite nailed the Coketown lie and they needed an even grander testimony to their cultural conscience. A magnificent town hall would also celebrate Manchester's position within the country's political firmament: a reminder of the power of the self-governing 'little republics' which existed outside the ambit of Westminster's imperial Parliament. The prime movers in the campaign for a new town hall were two Nonconformist liberal businessmen. Abel Heywood was a radical publisher who in a classic display of self-help and earnest endeavour had educated himself through the Mechanics' Institute to become the Mayor of Manchester. He was joined on the New Town Hall Committee by a leading light in Manchester's cultural circles, the cotton manufacturer and later Chairman of the City Art Gallery, Joseph Thompson. Looking back after its successful construction, Heywood openly admitted his priorities: 'By universal admission, the Town Hall is a worthy monument to the industrial greatness of Manchester and an outward and visible sign to the world that we are not wholly given up to Mammon and that the higher culture is not neglected among us.'[39]

In true Renaissance fashion, an architectural competition was announced and from it emerged the victorious design of the anonymous 'Mr Valentine', later revealed as Alfred Waterhouse, the designer of the Venetian Gothic Binyon and Fryer Warehouse as well as the greatly admired Assize Courts. Happily, Waterhouse was a Lancashire Nonconformist (a Quaker) and equally committed to burying the Mammon slur. He was an avid admirer of Ruskin with a particular affection for *The Seven Lamps of Architecture*. And in good Ruskinian style, he had spent his apprenticeship touring the Continent filling his notebook with sketches of St Mark's and Torcello in Venice, and Santo Spirito and Giotto's Campanile in Florence.

Within a notoriously difficult site, Waterhouse managed to erect an edifice which speaks of an incredible moment of Mancunian municipal ardour. Rising up from the cobbled Albert Square, the Town Hall mixes Christian Gothic (seen to greatest effect in the Westminster-like Great Hall) with a more Ruskinian, Venetian Gothic to produce an air of authority and grandeur. As one enters through the carved, wooden doors, the Hall has the spirit of St Mark's, with its tessellated floor, low ceilings and gold rimming. But instead of Byzantine iconography, one is immediately placed between statues of the scientist John Dalton and his pupil, the physicist James Joule, both heroes of the city's rational scientific tradition. The ground floor has a calm, cloistered feel as Gothic arches interplay with statues of civic icons: William Fairbairn, Joseph Heron, Oliver Cromwell and Richard Cobden – who would no doubt be delighted at a plaque celebrating Manchester's historic 1980s achievement as 'Britain's First Nuclear Free Zone'.

The Hall's civic iconography is loyal to the precepts of the Manchester school, with the city's mercantile heritage not hidden or deprecated but rudely celebrated. It is apparent as you first step into the building on the mosaic floor which

displays alternating rows of bees heralding the city's indus-
triousness. The message is consolidated on the passage floor
where the cotton flower proudly states Manchester's business.
Edward III stands prominent as the monarch who brought the
Flemish weavers to England and began the textile industry.
His statue is joined by the Tudor merchant Sir Humphrey
Chetham, while the free-trade campaigner and Manchester
MP John Bright guards the stairway. This unashamed approach
to Manchester's commercial identity crescendoes with the
Ford Madox Brown frescoes decorating the Great Hall. Brown
had no compunction in championing the history of the cotton
trade, industrial mechanisation, and economic growth. And it
was this civic cycle, which so obviously recalls the work of
Ambrogio Lorenzetti in the Sienese Palazzo Pubblico, that
Samuel Barnett must have had in mind when he later spoke
of future cities having 'the Municipal Offices, with its Town
Hall, on which panels an artist will have painted scenes from
the city's history, and where the citizens will throng in their
thousands to hear great speeches or to listen to great music'.[40]

The Town Hall opening in 1878 witnessed Manchester's
most impressive civic gala since the Art Treasures Exhibition.
The programme involved a 45,000-strong procession of Manchester tradesmen who marched by the Lord Mayor, regal in
scarlet, to the sound of ringing bells and the National Anthem.
Every possible civic association was represented, from the
Operative Bricklayers' Association to the Working Men's Club
Association to the United Society of Boilermakers – all carefully watched over by troops from the 106th Regiment along
with mounted cavalry. Here was the full, rich tapestry of
Victorian civic society on display. After the Town Clerk had
presented Mayor Heywood with a gold key to the Town Hall,
the speeches started.

Heywood himself, having been a councillor for some forty
years, remarked poignantly on the differences between the old
unreformed corporation run by Cobden's 'booby squirearchy'
and the improving activism of the 1860s administration. He
was followed by the guest of honour, John Bright, MP, who,

typically, saw the Town Hall as a personal vindication of his public life. It was a testimony to the 'forces of liberality, forces of generosity, and of freedom, municipal freedom'. As to the Town Hall itself, 'it is truly a municipal palace. There is nothing like it so far as I know ... There is what abroad they call the *hotel de ville*, or what London people call the Mansion House, or what you call your Town Hall, but I doubt whether there is a building equal in costliness and grandeur to this.'

Yet, just as the weary reservations of Ruskin chilled the optimism of the Art Treasures Exhibition, so his shadow was not far from the sumptuous Town Hall opening. In an indication of the cultural 'memory' which Waterhouse's architecture evoked, Bright warned Manchester's citizens that decline could come at any moment, as it had done to the crumbling stones of Venice:

We must bear in mind that great cities have fallen before Manchester and Liverpool were known; that there have been great cities, great mercantile cities, on the shores of the Mediterranean – Phoenecia [*sic*], Carthage, Genoa, Venice. The poet has said of the people of Venice –

'Her daughters had their dowers
From spoils of nations and the exhaustless East
Poured in her lap, all gems in sparkling showers.'

But what were the lines with which he concluded –

'Venice, lost and won
Her thirteen hundred years of freedom done,
Sinks like a seaweed into whence she rose.'[41]

Manchester's Town Hall was by no means the first municipal palace. The cities of Yorkshire had been working just as hard in trying to elevate their industrial towns into equally grandiloquent testimonies to commercial civilisation. Bradford was amongst the first, with its new status as capital of the worsted trade requiring a suitably grand civic edifice. What emerged was the stately, classical St George's Hall, which was a rapidly constructed imitation of Elmes and Cockerell's rather more magnificent Liverpool original. Initiated, designed and built over the course of eighteen months, it was financed by the city's great and good (including Titus Salt), for the very speed of its inception was meant to reflect the dynamism as well as the civic pride of the new industrial elite. A long way from its founding earnestness, it now hosts concerts and comedy nights.

More than a little piqued by Bradford's new status symbol, the burghers of Leeds came together to demand their own town hall to trump their Yorkshire junior. Leading the call was the doctor, social reformer and civic elder, John Heaton. A bookseller's son and Leeds Grammar School boy, Heaton had spent the early 1840s travelling the Continent and returned to Leeds determined to elevate urban life to the same civilised heights he had experienced amongst the heirs to the medieval Italian and German communes. Outside his surgery, he positioned himself at the centre of the city's Literary and Philosophical Society, and as Secretary to the Leeds Improvement Society agitated determinedly for a new municipal edifice. According to his memoirs, he believed that 'if a noble municipal palace that might fairly vie with some of the best Town Halls of the Continent were to be erected in the middle of their hitherto squalid and unbeautiful town, it would become a practical admonition to the populace of beauty and art, and in course of time men would learn to live up to it'.[42]

Years of lobbying paid off when in 1851 a committee of the Town Council was appointed to make inquiries into building a new town hall.[43] By 1853 the foundation stones were being laid and, as in Manchester, it was readily apparent that municipal vainglory was the driving motive behind the project. In the words of the committee chairman: 'the town council intend, in the first place to erect a building which will improve the public taste, and give an improved architectural appearance to the town of Leeds ... We are about to erect this town hall, first, as an ornamental building, and in order that the local or municipal business of the borough may be concentrated in one building, and thereby be done better and cheaper than it could be were it otherwise.'[44] Providing offices for the expanding municipal bureaucracy came a very poor second to besting Bradford.

Not everyone was convinced of the necessity of a new town hall and especially one at such a prodigious cost. Throughout the 1850s, Heaton had to remind grumbling ratepayers that the Town Hall was essential if they were to shed their provincial image as an aesthetic wasteground. The building was intended 'to show that in the ardour of mercantile pursuits the inhabitants of Leeds have not omitted to cultivate the perception of the beautiful and a taste for the fine arts, and to serve as a lasting monument of their public spirit and generous pride in the possession of their municipal privileges'. And typically, Heaton appealed to a Renaissance precedent to make his point; for, 'the citizens of free towns in the middle ages erected for their public meetings, and as the seat and outward symbol of their public government, the most sumptuous buildings'.[45]

Heaton won the battle for the Town Hall – but he still had a fight on his hands over the addition of an ornate tower. There quickly emerged an open struggle between the functionalist ratepayers and the more visionary improvers. Luckily, Heaton and the improvers were backed by the *Leeds Mercury*, which rounded on critics for their lack of civic pride. If Leeds was to rise to its true historical glory it needed a beautiful tower, since 'they are found on the town-halls, cloth-halls, and market-houses of Belgium and Holland, and on the castles and palaces of Italy'. Bruges, Brussels and Ghent all had towers, as did the Palazzo Vecchio of Florence, the Palazzo Pubblico in Siena and the Castello Vecchio in Ferrara.[46] The newspaper concluded its campaign by demanding that the city corporation, 'leave an edifice which may tell the world that the people of Leeds have not had their taste utterly destroyed by factories and warehouses, or lost their liberality in incessant money-making, but that they know what is due to the public claims of the community, and that they have the spirit to adorn this great seat of industry with buildings worthy of themselves and of their country'.[47]

Dr Heaton and the *Mercury* corralled and bullied the recalcitrant Council and what finally emerged was Cuthbert Brodrick's magnificent monument to nineteenth-century Leeds. In 1858, with the city festooned in 'flags, triumphal arches, poles and flowers, in the very best possible style', the Queen opened the Town Hall. Obviously, Benjamin Barker was there, exultant that 'for a time, if only for a few hours, the borough became the seat of empire of the greatest monarchy of the earth'.

> At the Town Hall the crowds were so great that the barriers bent cracked and splintered before the immense pressure ... At twenty minutes to 12 o'clock the Royal cortege entered the great square in which the Town Hall is built. The scene here quite defies all attempts to describe it in words. The cheers literally seemed to rend the air ... The Great Hall was thronged by all rank and fashion of the county of York; the varied dresses of the Choir at the north end of the hall in the orchestra was like a garden; while the body of the Hall was filled with ladies in beautiful dress (my mother was among them) and many gentlemen in uniforms ...[48]

Looming across the Leeds skyline at ninety-two feet tall, the Town Hall stands as a vast temple to the Victorian municipal spirit; 'an edifice', according to its proud organising committee, 'not inferior to those stately piles which still attest the ancient opulence of the great commercial cities of Italy and Flanders'.[49] Though surrounded by Corinthian pillars, its style is essentially Renaissance: a huge *palazzo* designed in the Barry mode – which was not surprising given that Brodrick was an earnest protégé of Sir Charles. The imposing lion statues in the shadow of the huge, folly-like clock tower only add to the brazen, civic self-confidence. Here at last was a proper response not only to Bradford, but also to Liverpool and Birmingham.

The Leeds municipal bureaucracy long ago moved to the modernist 1930s Civic Hall, but Brodrick's building was never meant for officialdom. It was meant to stamp Leeds on the map as the economic powerhouse and cultural fulcrum of Victorian West Riding, and today its sheer might still dominates the urban fabric. Though fraying at the edges (with the glorious lions eroded by car fumes), the interior Great Hall remains startling in its breadth. As remarkable are the morally uplifting, quintessentially Victorian messages which circle the hall's ceiling: 'Goodwill Towards Men'; 'Honesty is the Best Policy'; and 'Labor Omnia Vincit'. Sadly, as a site of communal endeavour and active citizenship its days are gone. Instead, the building now houses the Council's 'leisure services' and the Great Hall is available for hire for events ranging from 'the International Concert Season to Conferences, Dinner Dances, Light Entertainment, and Prayer Meetings'.

iv Battle of the Styles: the Foreign Office and Northampton Town Hall

The civic leaders who commissioned both the Manchester Town Hall and Leeds Town Hall expressed broadly similar views when it came to the buildings' styles. The same cannot be said either for the Foreign Office in London or the new Town Hall in Northampton. Architecture was becoming an increasingly controversial issue, with political values being attached to historical styles: Liberals favoured Italianate, opposed by the Tory prejudice for Gothic. The consequence was an often rancorous party divide when it came to allocating contracts, nowhere more so than in the case of the new government offices for Whitehall.

The story of the buildings which now dominate King Charles Street is an amusing but complicated tale best told through the *Personal and Professional Recollections* of

George Gilbert Scott himself. It sheds light on a time when government Ministers were interested, passionately, in urban design and when architecture itself had a contentious polemical significance. In 1859, the battle stood evenly matched between Lord John Manners, the 'Young England' Conservative who had already shown his inclinations by rebuilding Belvoir Castle in High Gothic fashion, and Lord Palmerston, the bawdy Liberal populist, who was a fierce advocate of an Italianate design and all the connotations of imperial destiny it signified. Unfortunately for Palmerston, he was not in power and Manners was. As the Minister in charge of public works, Manners sanctioned the construction of a new India Office and Foreign Office to be designed by Scott in the High Gothic style he later brought to St Pancras and to Glasgow University. But then in May 1859 Lord Derby's government fell; out went Manners and in came Palmerston.

Barely disguising his glee, one of Palmerston's first acts as Prime Minister was to send for Scott. Whereupon, he 'told me in a jaunty way that he could have nothing to do with this Gothic style, and that though he did not want to disturb my appointment, he must insist on my making a design in the Italian style, which he felt sure I could do quite as well as the other. That he heard I was so tremendously successful in the Gothic style, that if he let me alone I should Gothicize the whole country, etc., etc.'[50] Scott was crestfallen but refused to be sacked. 'To resign would be to give up a sort of property which Providence had placed in the hands of my family.' He returned to the drawing board and started to introduce some elements of 'the Byzantine of the early Venetian palaces' into the initial Gothic design. The new design was to be 'Byzantine toned into a more modern and useable form'. Whatever it was it did not please Palmerston, who bluntly informed Scott that he thought it '"neither one thing nor t'other – a regular mongrel affair – and he would have nothing to do with it either"'.[51]

With his never very great patience now wearing thin, Palmerston insisted on Scott 'making a design in the ordinary

Italian' or else be removed from the project. Scott cracked. 'I made up my mind ... bought some costly books on Italian architecture, and set vigorously to work to rub up what, though I had once understood pretty intimately, I had allowed to grow rusty by twenty years neglect.'[52] Together with his co-architect Digby Wyatt, he produced for Palmerston an orthodox Italianate design. And while Palmerston was delighted, the new design had still to receive the sanction of the House of Commons.

Over the course of 1861, the new designs were subjected to a lengthy parliamentary scrutiny – the type of architectural and aesthetic debate which would never now be heard in Westminster. Scott's Italianate design was regarded by his original Gothic backers as a wretched betrayal, with Lord John Manners valiantly refusing to accept defeat. He made an impassioned plea for the Gothic style, listing its many architectural triumphs (including Waterhouse's Assize Courts in Manchester) while declaring it to be the true national style. Others were ruder, suggesting Scott's submission was more suitable to the Doge and Senate of Venice rather than a department of state of the English Commonwealth. Speaking in support, a Mr Cowper, MP defended the designs on the grounds that 'the association to be desired was that of the period in which we lived, and the Italian style was that which by its breadth, simplicity, and symmetry best represented modern sentiment and aims'. William Tite, the architect, President of the Royal Institute of British Architects (RIBA) and MP for Bath, was equally in favour, quoting extensively from Ruskin to support the case.

Finally, Palmerston rose and began his speech with a typically bravado attack on Manners and the Gothic School. While Manners had listed Gothic successes, Palmerston asked him 'to look at Leeds. Does the noble Lord forget the large and handsome building which is so justly considered the ornament of that town, and which is also of the Italian style?' He then ridiculed the idea of Gothic as a national style. 'But is the Gothic national? I never heard of the Goths, the Vandals, or the Saracens doing much in this country.'[53] On the contrary, the work of Inigo Jones and Christopher Wren suggested that Italianate had just as proper a claim to the title. Moreover, our current cultural sentiments were more in tune with the Renaissance than the Middle Ages, a view endorsed by *The Builder*. In an article on this raging 'Battle of the Styles', the magazine was similarly disposed to Scott, since it regarded 'our present position, habits and requirements as so much more nearly allied to those of the Italian republics in the days of their prosperity' than to the English Gothicism of abbeys, colleges and monasteries.

Palmerston won out and the result is the Italianate campanile which now looks out from the Foreign Office across St James's Park towards the symbol of a previous era of London improvements, the Georgian monstrosity of Buckingham Palace. Housing the sumptuous Locarno Room and dripping with Venetian iconography, the Foreign and Commonwealth Office still stands as Whitehall's finest departmental building. It was a battle worth winning. But a hundred miles north of Westminster an intriguingly similar battle of the styles was just beginning.

By the mid-1850s, the leading burghers of Northampton, the Midlands market town originally built around the footwear trade but now encompassing a growing amount of proto-industrial commerce, had begun to sense that their city's wealth and significance demanded some kind of monumental edifice to reflect its burgeoning status. The old Guildhall had outlived its purpose and the site of the existing Corn Exchange was too limited for the civic aspirations of the Northampton municipal worthies. In September 1860, the town voted to adopt William Ewart's pioneering 1855 Public Libraries Act, which permitted the levying of a rate to fund municipal libraries and museums. The Council agreed to impose a one-penny rate to fund the construction of a new town hall.

Even before the levy was fixed a pre-emptive ratepayer reaction had begun. In a letter to the editor of the *Northampton Mercury*, a Mr Hilary Healtop complained that the town was simply 'not in a condition to incur the very large outlay which such a building would necessitate'. What with local taxation and the 'Improvement Rate', the good citizens of Northampton were 'in some danger of being improved off the ground altogether'.[54] At a Council meeting following the decision to proceed with the building, numerous councillors complained both about the cost and the fear that a large town hall would simply encourage unwanted political protest and party agitation.[55] The key issue, however, was the style of the building. The Council, as was the tradition of the time, decided upon an architectural competition. It would then draw up a shortlist of the submissions and finally ask the RIBA President and Ruskin admirer, the busy William Tite, to decide upon the final design. Councillor Shoosmith had wanted to invite John Ruskin himself to deliver the adjudication but was overruled. The open architectural competition meant Northampton was set to enjoy its very own 'Battle of the Styles'.

The opening salvo took the form of a letter to the *Mercury* from 'Gothic – But No Goth'. The anonymous author believed that in building a guildhall for 'one of the oldest corporate bodies in England', the design should 'lead us back to the Feudal, the Monastic, the Chivalric, the good old times, the days of merrie England'. Northampton should follow in the tradition of the rich architectural monuments those ages had left behind – 'the Abbeys, Monasteries, Castles, the Baronial Hall, the grand old English Gothic'. In tones reminiscent of Pugin, the Goth pleaded with the Council to inflict 'no Parade or Drapery Banks, no Mechanics' Institute, no Classic, Italian, Grecian, Renaissance, Mongrel Puppy shop fronts upon us'. Northampton needed a building where 'the spirit of old Simon de St Elizabeth will not blush to greet his brother burgesses in; wherein Thomas à Becket might have looked with pleasure'.[56]

True to his task, William Tite rapidly produced a shortlist of three designs, of which two were serious contenders. The first model, by the anonymous 'Circumspice', was a grandiose Italianate design in the style of Scott's redesigned Foreign Office. The second, designed by 'Non Nobis Domine' (Edward

Godwin), was Gothic – but the Ruskinian Gothic of Venice and Waterhouse rather than the Early English style advocated by the *Mercury*'s 'Goth'. The designs were opened up to debate, with Councillor Hessman championing 'Circumspice'. For while Gothic was all very well for a church, 'for a public hall the prevailing style of architecture seems to be the Italian or Grecian'. However, the mood of the Council was against him and Godwin's design won out. The *Mercury*, in a bravura leader column on the virtues of industrious municipalities, backed the Council's decision. 'Not because it may remind us of monasteries (seeing that we have no monks); or of Abbeys (having no Abbots); or of Castles (which costly and picturesque nuisances have become happily obsolete); or of Baronial Halls, (not meaning to revive old feudal orgies); but because the style is associated with the history of our Municipal Institutions'. [57]

The Town Hall iconography consciously appealed to the English tradition of municipal self-government and the city's local history of autonomy. The eight statues on the upper storey included Richard I, who gave Northampton its first charter; Henry VII, who granted the town a further charter in 1495; Edward I, who allowed Northampton two MPs, who were amongst the country's earliest parliamentary representatives; Queen Victoria; and St Michael, the patron saint of the town. The tympana on the ground-floor windows were the construction of a civic narrative with events including the trial of Thomas à Becket and the execution of Mary Queen of Scots. The heads of the arches of the four windows included the granting of a charter of incorporation by Henry VI. Below the ground-floor windows were a series of heraldic shields representing both the prominent civic leaders and the important crafts of the town. [58]

However, this was only part of the stylistic tale. The Town Hall also directly appealed to the glorious tradition of the self-governing Italian republics with which the Northampton civic elite were keen to ally themselves. Godwin's Town Hall is a testimony to the currency of Ruskin's edict that there should not be a single ornament put upon great civic buildings without some intellectual intention. Godwin took his admiration for Ruskin so far as to divide the ground floor into seven bays of slightly varying widths in imitation of St Mark's, and to design the ground-floor façade with illustrations from the second volume of *The Stones of Venice*. The building is dotted with iconography celebrating in a consciously Renaissance or 'civic republican' fashion the town's history of commerce and local self-government. In a skilled prequel to Manchester Town Hall, the sculptures around the four lower windows focused upon the commercial and industrial history of the city and its heroic workers and merchants. In an intriguing echo of Ruskin's title for his Art Treasures Exhibition lectures, the *Mercury* described the building as 'a thing of beauty, and a joy for ever'.[59]

The design was enormously popular. At the ceremony for the laying of the foundation stone, the Mayor reeled out familiar platitudes about the people of Northampton being alive 'to the duty of improving the spiritual, social and intellectual condition of the people'. But it was Lord Henley, MP who showed just how powerfully the Italian civic heritage (in its broadest sense) had become associated with the Victorian city by claiming that the Venetian Gothic style was somehow intrinsically English. It was, he said, most agreeable to see an English public building constructed in the style 'in which England erected her buildings in the ancient and most interesting periods of our history'.[60] Venetian Gothic had become the 'national' style of the English municipality.

Through its urban architecture and monuments, the new middle class of the industrial cities showed that commerce bred creativity, that it was the industrious bourgeoisie who since Periclean Athens and Medici Florence had fostered the aesthetic triumphs of European civilisation. It was they who were the harbingers of Arnold's 'sweetness and light'. The merchants of Manchester and Liverpool stood as the respectful heirs of Lorenzo the Magnificent, carrying forward his legacy into the industrial world.

*

Unfortunately, the industrial society of Victorian Britain presented greater challenges than the idealised Tuscan past and amongst its most pressing remained the sanitary state of the cities. Was it not grotesque to be expending vast sums on vainglorious edifices as sickly children continued to perish from cholera in dank basements? In Bradford, a Mr Illingworth thought the new Wool Exchange a grotesque folly; 'his opinion was that before they attempted considerable improvements in the town they ought first to improve its sanitary condition by giving their attention to the removal of the canal and other nuisances'.[61] The sanitary reformer Edwin Chadwick was equally appalled by the priorities of wealthy, unhealthy Liverpool, the city that could gorge tens of thousands of pounds on civic monuments while cesspools and sewage still lined the streets. 'A parsimony for objects of such importance as the saving of pain and misery would ill become Liverpool, where there is in course of expenditure, for splendour, on one single edifice, St George's Hall, upwards of £100,000; a sum which would, if so applied, serve to sweep and cleanse in perpetuity, and make decent, the filthy by-streets of upwards of 23,000 houses, out of the 45,000 houses, which are under the corporation jurisdiction.'[62] For many sanitary reformers, it was time the municipal spirit was transferred from the town hall to the street, from the civic to the sanitary.

SEWAGE, SAXONS AND SELF-GOVERNMENT

As a rule, Queen Victoria did not like to leave Balmoral. Indeed, the idea of leaving her Highland retreat to open Glasgow's new waterworks could hardly have appealed to her less. Yet such was her devotion to Prince Albert and his engineering enthusiasms that on 14 October 1859 Her Majesty stood ready for duty on the sodden banks of Loch Katrine. Amidst weather of 'a truly Highland character', the royal party embarked upon the *Rob Roy* steamer (complete with glass viewing pavilion) to travel across the loch to the newly constructed aqueduct tunnel. Welcomed by Glasgow's Lord Provost and a thousand-strong crowd of loyal subjects, braving the mists and foggy rain, the Queen listened patiently to the speeches before hastily flicking the index-lever to set the hydraulic engines in motion. Hungry as ever, Her Majesty then quickly retreated to the Commissioner Cottages, decorated with 'a chaste green, diaper pattern, with imitation oak pilaster, hatched in gold', for a hearty roast lunch.

As Victoria and Albert chewed on their *boeuf rôti* with *dindon sauce aux huîtres*, cannon were fired from Stirling Castle and bells rung from every steeple in Glasgow to celebrate the opening of this engineering marvel. As the royal wines were decanted, outside the pure Highland water surged through the Loch Katrine sluices, rushing down the thirty-four miles of tunnels, aqueducts and iron pipes, via a reservoir at Mugdock Castle, to deliver Glasgow its first fifty million gallons – a volume of fresh water the city would now receive every day from the Loch Katrine works.

After nine years of planning and at a final cost of some £1.5 million, Glasgow's civic leaders had swapped the source of their city's water supply from the deadly quagmire of the Clyde to the healthy, soft-water lochs of the Highlands; and in so doing, according to the Water Commission secretary, had completed economically 'one of the largest and most comprehensive schemes for the supply of water which has yet been accomplished'. This was, in the characteristically Scottish words of the *Glasgow Daily Herald*, 'a fact most highly appreciated by a community thirsty for good water on the one hand and abhorrent of high taxing rates on the other'.[1]

Six years later it was London's turn. But after the tragic death of Prince Albert, the widowed Queen was in no mood for any more engineering excursions. Instead, it fell to the Prince of Wales to open an even more impressive testimony to Victorian urban enterprise. Joseph Bazalgette's amazing system of multi-levelled intersecting sewers, whisking away surface water and waste from Hampstead to Stratford, Pimlico to the Isle of Dogs, made Loch Katrine seem positively elementary.

The Great Stink of summer 1858 had given Bazalgette his moment. As the thermometer hit ninety-five degrees, Old Father Thames appeared in Disraeli's words as 'a Stygian pool reeking with ineffable and intolerable horrors'. When the library windows were open, MPs had to retreat from their brand-new Houses of Parliament with handkerchiefs covering their faces in flight from the river's stench. 'Gentility of speech is at an end,' declared the *City Press*, 'it stinks: and whoso once inhales the stink can never forget it, and may count himself lucky if he live to remember it.'[2] Having ignored the mounting problem of the capital's sanitation for decades, the Government immediately charged the Metropolitan Board of Works with cleaning up the river's noxious cargo.

Wisely, this board of mainly obdurate time-servers appointed the brilliant Bazalgette as their chief engineer. His genius was to combine the city's natural gravitation with the old sewage system, while also constructing a set of new beam engines to create a network of sewers and pumping-stations. Supported by a metropolitan army of contractors and labourers, Bazalgette excavated 3.5 million cubic yards of earth, used 318 million bricks and laid some eighty-two miles of sewer. At a cost of over £4 million, the completed network was able to carry out fifty-two million gallons of sewage to a distance some fourteen miles beyond Tower Bridge – where it was then carried out a further twenty-six miles by the tides.[3]

The network was inaugurated in 1864, but it was only in 1870 when Prince Edward opened the new Victoria Embankment that the true marvel of the scheme was revealed. Stretching along the north side of the Thames from Blackfriars to Westminster, this vital London artery elegantly concealed London's new system of low-level east–west sewers. Bazalgette had achieved far more than cleaning the streets; he had mastered the Thames. He had tamed its tides and reclaimed thirty-seven acres of land to form the northern and southern, Victoria and Albert, embankments. The lugubrious, waterside London of Pepys and Canaletto had been replaced by the sturdy, concrete metropolis of Bazalgette and Empire.

Glasgow's Loch Katrine works and London's new sewage system are both testimonies to one of the most enduring popular memories of the Victorian age: the days when the British got on and built things which worked. It is recalled as an era of enormous technological self-confidence and unhampered vision which found its clearest voice in the extraordinary life and work of another half-French engineer, Isambard Kingdom Brunel. His intuitive designs for railways, tunnels, bridges and ships spoke of a society enjoying a ready relationship with science, engineering and progress. A relationship that appears irreversibly to have broken down in twenty-first-century Britain.[4]

The physical construction of the Victorian city – its infrastructure of roads, railways, sewers and bridges – is a part of that elegiac memory. When modern London traffic averages at less than ten miles per hour, roads are ceaselessly and carelessly dug up by competing utility companies, and any new building is subject to the most stringently bureaucratic planning process, the pioneering resolve and swift actions of the mid-Victorian urban engineer are 'remembered' longingly. And in the space of a phenomenal decade of graft, which saw the capital transformed into a vast building site, London gained a swathe of impressive thoroughfares and smart shopping streets: Southwark Street (1864); High Holborn (1867); High Street Kensington (1869); Queen Victoria Street (1871); and the vital sanitary works which lay hidden beneath the sweeping Victoria and Albert Embankments. Much of the old medieval City was torn apart for new roads and rails in what the *Illustrated London News* called 'the "time to pull down"'. The polluted mire of London had to be cleansed, its fêted arteries opened up with new roads, drains and sewers. But it was not just the capital, as similar improvements disrupted cities across the country.

For the Victorians themselves, the question of urban infrastructure and, above all, urban sanitation, was far more than just an issue of science and technology. Living in the days of the Great Exhibition, such displays of engineering bravado were of less moment than to us who walk in the shadow of the Greenwich Dome and the 'Wobbly' Millennium Bridge. Rather, the question of who was in control of urban sanitation, how new sewage systems were to be funded, and which authority decided upon their medical necessity cut to the quick of Victorian conceptions of civic identity and even British history itself. Relatively arcane arguments over the differing roles of central and local government in overseeing sanitary improvements prised open a vigorous debate about the nature of British cities and their role in the great island story. Under the guise of legislative and polemical disputes over sewage and cesspools, the city was perceptibly aligned to Victorian conceptions of just what it meant to be British. Increasingly, national identity was understood as an uniquely urban identity. The British people were not a rural race, a people of village lanes and plough teams, but from their earliest Saxon origins a people of cities.

i Romancing the Saxons

The lurid accounts of the Jacobin Festivals of Reason emanating out of 1790s Paris only served to accelerate a deepening impatience with the excesses of Enlightenment. By the early 1800s, the rational cosmopolitanism of the Age of Reason – with its language of universal human rights and ceaseless progress – was losing ground in the wake of the Terror and Napoleon Bonaparte's imperial ambitions. The zealous theories of the *philosophes* and the *idéologues*, along with the cold, Cartesian reason of Leibniz and Condorcet, had seemed to deliver only revolution and warfare.[5] It was increasingly clear that reason alone was not the path to happiness.

Across Europe, 'Romantic' writers and thinkers reacted by encouraging the growth of pointedly nationalist ideologies. Localism, patriotism and superstition began to acquire a new force against the backdrop of the bleak utility of the eighteenth century. Traditional beliefs, which had seemed so ridiculous to the Newtonian mechanics of Bentham, Voltaire and the apologists of the French Revolution, gained fashionable currency. Historical interest in different languages, peoples and cultures – in contrast to the idea of universal human sensationalism – expanded rapidly. As Hugh Trevor-Roper put it, 'The old, customary organs of society, the old established beliefs, which had seemed so contemptible to the rationalists of the *Encyclopaedia*, now acquired a new dignity.'[6]

The philosopher of the day was no longer the brilliant Voltaire but the shamefully sentimental Edmund Burke. The renegade Whig turned Conservative apostle celebrated the 'wisdom of unlettered men' above the theorising of 'sophisters, oeconomists, and calculators'; he venerated the achievements of antiquity above the 'metaphysical abstractions' of natural rights and social contracts. The entire thrust of his *Reflections on the Revolution in France* was an attack on the 'mechanical philosophers' of the French Revolution, who had dissolved all the bonds of experience, law and tradition which had historically held the state together. For Burke, the lesson of 1789 was never to abandon national customs and experience in favour of a 'geometrical and arithmetic constitution'. In the unseen, geological strata of the ancient constitution there existed intelligence and wisdom far beyond the fanciful ideas of clever intellectuals.[7]

Burke's diatribe was received most readily on home soil – this despite the fact that Britain, unlike France and other war-ravaged European countries, had no need to invent some lost, pre-revolutionary heritage. The glorious constitution so perfectly assembled in 1688 had allowed it to avoid any of the bloody disjunctures which so disfigured the Continent. British history had flowed in a seamless, Whiggish progression bar the unfortunate events of the 1640s. Nonetheless, the Romantic spirit was abroad and the search was on to discover Britain's 'true' national character.

Incrementally, the quest had been going on since the mid-eighteenth century, starting with James Macpherson's researches into the oral tradition of the Celtic past and Thomas Percy's work on English ballad culture. Despite their somewhat questionable use of manuscript evidence, Macpherson's tribal epic, *Ossian*, and Percy's slightly more scholarly *Reliques of Ancient English Poetry* sparked a series of investigations into the lost languages and cultures of the British Isles. While the ambition of the Jacobins had been the elimination of patois and the hope of the Enlightenment was a universal language of human understanding, the Romantics celebrated the uncouth and frequently incomprehensible tongues of primitive cultures. It was a fashion which would encompass the wizened dialect of Samuel Taylor Coleridge's 'bright-eyed Mariner' as well as the *Lyrical Ballads* of Words-worth and Coleridge. However, the British Romantics were also affected by a broader, more European cultural current.

Ironically, one of the first to have taken up the Burkean banner and championed the wisdom of custom was the metropolitan intellectual and high-powered salon hostess, Madame de Staël. Daughter of Louis XVI's minister of finance, Jacques Necker, Germaine de Staël had spent the post-revolutionary years flitting between Switzerland, England and Germany. And it was her trip to Germany in 1803 which resulted in one of the epochal works of the Romantic movement. Entertained by such figures as Goethe, Schiller and both the younger and the elder Schlegel, Mme de Staël fell for the Teuton sprit and declared barbaric Germany one of the foundation cultures of European civilisation.

In her ensuing work, *De l'Allemagne*, she set about tracing the competing origins of modern European national identity. While Italy, France and Spain had their roots in the Roman family, she declared that the Germans, the Swiss and the English belonged to the Teutonic. Mme de Staël went on to list the characteristics of the Teutonic nations, their manners, poetry, politics and morals. Here was a clear exposition both of unique national characteristics but also of the trans-national bond of Saxon heritage which linked Britain to a Continental ancestry. It was no accident, she appreciatively noted, that 'German literature is much better known in England than in France', and that the English poets, having consumed the work of their German counterparts, 'do not fail to perceive that analogy which ought to result from one common origin'.[8]

Published first in Paris and then in London in 1813, Mme de Staël's *Germany* strengthened an already influential strand of cultural thinking that the British people were a Saxon people. Despite the centuries of Roman rule, despite the waves of Viking invasions, despite the totality of the Norman Conquest, despite even the native Celts and Picts, it was the Germanic tribes of the Angles, the Jutes and the Saxons that swept into Britain in the late fifth century who, fourteen centuries on, still commandeered the national psyche. This fulsome interpretation of the Saxon heritage became the dominant motif of the Romantic histories of the early nineteenth century which sought to weave together a national narrative of an island race.

A keen student of Thomas Percy's English studies, the historian Sharon Turner began the genre with his *History of the Anglo-Saxons* (1795–1801; 2nd edn, 1823), which was followed

up by a *History of England* (1814–23). Turner's Romantic
refashioning of the national story was carried on by John
Lingard's *History of England* (1819), Henry Hallam's *View of
the State of Europe during the Middle Ages* (1819), Sir Francis
Palgrave's *The History of the Anglo-Saxons* (1831), and, later,
John Kemble's masterly *The Saxons in England* (1849) – his
very title indicating a trans-national, racial reading of British
history. Indeed, Kemble was particularly sensitive to national
cultures and traditions. He had spent his early life studying
German philology with the Brothers Grimm of fairy tale fame
and he went on to edit the first English edition of the Anglo-
Saxon epic *Beowulf*.

Nourished by this academic literature, there started to
emerge a popular interest in the Saxon past. Publishers specialising in Anglo-Saxon reprints enjoyed unprecedented
demand and in 1838 Joseph Bosworth brought out his *Oxford
Anglo-Saxon Dictionary* which systematically explained the
Teutonic roots of the English language. Meanwhile the country's baptismal fonts were swamped with a new generation of
mewling Aelfrics and Alfreds. Between 1834 and 1849 an
estimated twenty-nine national historical societies were
established in England as archaeological associations began
to dig up the ruins of Wessex, Essex and Mercia.[9] The rich
tapestry of Victorian civil society fell headlong for the new
medieval enthusiasm. Members of the Leeds Literary and
Philosophical Society enjoyed numerous lectures on medieval
life and architecture. In March 1849 the Society played host
to a paper, 'On the Saxon Institutions of England', by John
Holmes; and in the following month the Alfred the Great
Society annual meeting was held in Leeds.[10] In November
1847, members of the Manchester Royal Institution enjoyed a
conversazione upon 'The Commerce of the Anglo-Saxons'.
The following year, a Mr Scott delivered a paper at the RMI,
'On the Existing Elements of English Society', in which he
explained how 'the ground-work of our character, happily for
us, has continued to be the Saxon'. This, thankfully, endowed
the Englishman with straightforwardness, realism, yet also

'the most vivid and striking imagination'. In November 1852, the Rosicrucians convened in Manchester to hear a paper upon the history of the Anglo-Saxon system of governance – as well as an extended reading from Kemble's *The Saxons in England*. Not to be outdone, in February 1853 the Lancashire and Cheshire Historic Society entertained the Revd William Throber and listened no doubt attentively to his work upon 'Traces of the Saxons and Danes in the Foreland of the Fylde'.[11]

The new histories of Saxon England proved a great hit in the provincial capitals. In the introduction to later editions of *The History of the Anglo-Saxons*, Sharon Turner noted how 'the taste for the history and remains of our great ancestors has revived and is rapidly increasing'. This was certainly the case in Newcastle, where the 1829 Catalogue of the Library of the Literary and Philosophical Society boasted the works of John Lingard, Sharon Turner and Henry Hallam.[12] The same works could be found in the libraries of numerous civic institutions and societies across the country. But as we saw in chapter three, it was the novels of Sir Walter Scott which achieved the most remarkable success in popularising the Saxon past. Scott himself garnered most of his historical information from Turner's histories, but the dreamy image of Saxon England which he conjured up in *Ivanhoe* did more to connect the Victorian imagination with its Saxon heritage than any number of Teutonic philologies.

This welter of pro-Saxon propaganda only strengthened the Teutonic account of British history first offered by Mme de Staël. The great Oxford Professor of History, William Stubbs, magisterially summed up the consensus in his *Constitutional History of England*. 'The English are a people of German descent in the main constituents of blood, character, and language, but most especially in the possession of the elements of primitive German civilisation and the common germs of German institutions.'[13]

Before their Romantic resuscitation, the Saxons had never enjoyed that enviable a reputation within British historical circles. Their rude manner and aesthetic insensibility had made them easy prey for the refined intellectuals of the Enlightenment. In his *Decline and Fall of the Roman Empire*, Edward Gibbon was scathing about the destruction which the Saxons had wreaked on the civilised Roman Empire they inherited. 'The arts and religion, the laws and language, which the Romans had so carefully planted in Briton, were extirpated by their barbarous successors.'[14] David Hume's epic *History of England* was equally contemptuous of the barbaric Teutons, dismissing them as 'a rude, uncultivated people, ignorant of letters, unskilled in the mechanical arts, untamed to submission under law and government, addicted to intemperance, riot, and disorder'.[15] In his Whiggish narrative, the Norman Conquest brought only benefits to the British Isles; an opinion shared by Thomas Carlyle, who asked what would have become of England without the Normans. 'What had it ever been? A gluttonous race of Jutes and Angles capable of no grand combinations; lumbering about in pot-bellied equanimity; not dreaming of heroic toil and silence and endurance such as leads to the high places of this universe, and the golden mountain tops where dwell the spirits of the dawn.'[16]

However, for a majority of Victorians the Saxons offered an ideal of something altogether more heroic. Their rule was increasingly imagined as a lost golden age which had secured for Britain its finest characteristics. By far the most significant was the notion of local self-government – a complicated bundle of assumptions perhaps best expressed by the notoriously inexpressive character of Mr Thornton in Elizabeth Gaskell's 'Condition of England' novel, *North and South*.

After much affectionate jibing at the hands of the newly arrived Oxford cleric Mr Hale and his refined daughter Margaret, the sullen northern mill-owner is forced to defend his ugly home town of Milton (read, Manchester). Contrasting Milton man's workfulness to the classical scholarship and flippancy of the Oxonian, Thornton reminds Mr Hale that 'we are of a different race than the Greeks', whose decadence led to a lingering decline. Instead, Mr Thornton points to the moral rectitude of his Saxon genealogy. 'I belong to Teutonic blood; it is little mingled in this part of England to what it is in others; we retain much of their language; we retain more of their spirit; we do not look upon life as a time for enjoyment, but as a time for action and exertion.' By far the most telling sign of Milton man's Saxon lineage was his unwavering belief in the virtue of municipal autonomy. 'We are Teutonic up here in Darkshire in another way. We hate to have laws made for us at a distance. We wish people would allow us to right ourselves, instead of continually meddling, with their imperfect legislation. We stand up for self-government, and oppose centralization.'[17]

This sense of freedom, this spirit of local self-government was seen as the defining attribute of the Saxon bequest. It was a principle of governance they grafted onto the ordered Roman civic system to produce the unique constitutional harmony of local self-government and municipal autonomy. 'The self-government which is a peculiarity of the Anglo-Saxon race', as the *Birmingham Daily Press* put it, was 'brought out of their old German forests, and planted here' and 'has been the basis on which we have erected our glorious edifices'.[18] This freedom-loving spirit inevitably entailed a profound hostility toward any signs of central control. In the words of the Professor of Ancient and Modern History at the University of London, Sir Edward Creasy, 'The chief element of our nation is Germanic, and we have good cause to be proud of our ancestry. Freedom has been its hereditary characteristic from the earliest times at which we can trace the existence of the German race.'[19]

There did exist one rather fundamental problem with this historical interpretation. Since the Roman author Cornelius Tacitus first described the Saxon tribes in his great work, *Germania; or, On the Origin and Situation of the Germans*, one of their most notable characteristics had been a deep hostility towards cities. They were an earthy people who were happiest amongst the mystical wilds of the massive Hercynian forest. They revered wood above marble, soil above civility. It was a naturalist heritage which enjoyed a revival during the eighteenth century when the Saxon forest became once again a symbol of German national identity. Johann Gottfried Herder contrasted an indigenous culture of Romantic forestry folklore against the effete classicism of the French-led Enlightenment. Similarly, when the Brothers Grimm began to collect their anthologies of medieval German poetry, ballads, legends and folklore they chose to publish them in a collection significantly entitled, *Altdeutsche Wälder* ('Old German Forests'). Forests and freedom, not towns and civility, were the Saxon way.[20]

Faced with this difficulty, there emerged a fairly tortuous historical attempt to prove how the Saxons adapted themselves to the existing network of Roman cities in Britain. The medievalist Sir Francis Palgrave argued that the Teutons simply dropped their old habits and took over the Roman sites. As soon as the Saxons 'planted themselves on Roman ground', they managed to forget their 'ancient maxims'. Occupying the Roman *municipia*, 'they pursued their conquests from these points of defence, and enriched themselves with the spoils of wealth and civilization'.[21] Others suggested that because of the different natures of Roman and Teuton civilisation, the Saxons felt compelled to establish completely new urban settlements.

Common ground was eventually reached with municipal historians suggesting the Saxons retained their original autonomous, tribal spirit when they conquered Britain but somehow, providentially, managed to graft it onto the Roman inheritance. The consensus view was voiced by the former Ancoats physician and now President of the National Association for the Promotion of Social Science (NAPSS), Sir James Kay-Shuttleworth (he had added the Shuttleworth), in an address of 1859: 'The right of self-government seems to have been more easily transferred with the tithing and hundred to the *burh*, and the Saxon institution displaced the Roman'.[22]

Either way, the Saxons established across Britain a 'dispersed, not centralized' civic base, which stood in sharp contrast to the imperial control of the Romans. 'All over England', according to Kemble, 'there soon existed a network of communities, the principle of whose being was separation, as regarded each other: the most intimate union, as respected the individual members of each.'[23] The country devolved into a series of self-acting little republics gently watched over by a wise, hands-off monarchy. The conservative magazine, *Fraser's Magazine*, described this as 'Alfred's system', 'under which England flourished so long and free'. Its guiding principle was 'to multiply the centres of government, so that the energies of all were brought into play'.[24]

This was the basis of the Saxon bequest: a spirit of self-government and civic autonomy which lasted down the centuries. The ragged independence nurtured in the forests of Saxony was transplanted wholesale to the municipalities of Britain – and centuries on still governed the Victorian city. According to *The Times*, 'Local self-government is the most distinctive peculiarity of our race and has mainly made England what she is, while the nations of continental Europe are still held in tutelage by their rulers.'[25]

With self-government came political stability. The Germanic system of decentralised *mark* settlements (areas of land held in common by the freemen of the community) forged the seamless Whig constitution that marked out Anglo-Saxon Britain from its Continental neighbours. A diffuse civic structure with numerous urban centres prevented an excessive concentration of political power and instead provided the basis for a stable polity. Henry Hallam called 'the long and uninterruptedly increasing prosperity of England', 'the most beautiful phenomenon in the history of mankind'. Not a little of this was due to the decentralised system of local self-government, the 'spirit of the laws' which ensured the 'characteristic independence' of the nation.[26] As the *Westminster Review* put it, 'The cause of the stability and healthy development of English order and liberty [is] easily found in that remarkable local or self-government, which is the distinguishing feature of our political organisation.'[27]

The foundations of that political stability were also rooted in the Saxon tradition of civil society and active citizenship. It was the Saxons, according to Henry Hallam, who had first introduced into England the guilds (from the Saxon verb *gildan*, to pay or contribute) and 'voluntary associations, sometimes religious, sometimes secular' which were to become such a hallmark of the Victorian city.[28] The myriad Friendly Societies and Oddfellow clubs which so embodied the nineteenth-century spirit of civic association eagerly welcomed a heritage which extended back to some hoary Saxon origin. In turn, political theorists saluted the clubs' and guilds' subtle contribution to the British state's stability. Their strengthening of community identity and calendar of civic functions were regarded as part of the political release-valve which helped to prevent more fundamental constitutional clashes.

With a prosperous civil society came a culture of engaged citizenship. Active participation in the democratic process was early on claimed as an intrinsically Teutonic attribute. Their original administrative structure of shire-gemots, hundreds, tythings and wapentakes was the fruit of their ancient forest settlements: that system of *folc-moot* democracy redolent with images of warriors sitting round the oak tree, an ideal which Walter Scott brought brilliantly to life in *Ivanhoe* with his description of Locksley's egalitarian, woodland assemblies. Under an 'oak-tree of enormous magnitude, throwing its twisted branches in every direction', Locksley's band of honest yeomen, ironically made outlaws by the Norman 'forest laws', practised their Saxon heritage of self-government.[29] As it had been in Tacitus's *Germania*, the forest was once more a symbol of freedom.

The ascending system of *mark*, *weald* and ultimately *Witenagemot* (the closest Saxon approximation to a national parliament) allowed for the political contribution of all citizens willing to pay *scot* (tax) and bear *lot* (carry out civic duties). According to one history of Anglo-Saxon governance, it was the positive duty of all responsible citizens to involve themselves in political debate. 'It was the duty of every man, and enforced by penalties, to attend his proper folk-mote, in order to discharge there the duties and responsibilities that attach to him as a member of the State.'[30] It was these conditions, in the words of another medieval historian, which 'made every Saxon answer for the rest of his brothers, and be cared for somewhere'.[31] This culture of active political participation wisely prevented the cumulative consolidation of power in a single individual or authority.

This rather esoteric historical argument about Saxon citizenship assumed a polemical significance in the debates surrounding the 1835 Municipal Corporation Bill. Supporters of the Bill argued that the corruption inherent in unreformed, closed corporations betrayed the nation's Saxon heritage. Originally, the case for reform was framed in openly Saxon terms with some of the Bill's advocates talking of a return to the early *folc-moot* ideals of Saxon self-government. When the Saxons first started ordering their towns, the voters consisted of all 'the permanent free inhabitants of the boroughs'. Anyone 'performing their duties, and enjoying their privileges; paying scot and bearing lot' had the right to vote.[32] Only when Henry VI began establishing municipal corporations (with Kingston-upon-Hull as the first) did the cancer of self-selection and closed elections corrupt the democratic process. Down the centuries, the situation deviated ever further from its virtuous Saxon origins. To rebuild that national combination of municipal vibrancy and political stability, it was essential that 'every resident and responsible householder' should possess the same democratic rights which their Germanic forefathers had held centuries previously. For the history of England's free municipalities provided 'as fine a lesson in social progress and political science, as the experience of the past in any age can give; for these institutions long embodied all that could be called national in spirit or in form, and were the chief sanctuaries of those political feelings which have distinguished England from every continental state'.[33]

The genius of the British political system came from its untamed, Germanic roots. From the wilds of the Saxon forest emerged all that was unique about the admirable ennui of the constitution. As the popular Birmingham lecturer George Dawson put it, in the Teutonic tradition of self-government can be seen 'the gem of all of our present institutions. Enfolded in this, like the oak in the acorn, our parliaments, conferences, trials by jury, local self-government, and all the other customs of which we are so proud.'[34] Towards the end of the century, J.R. Green, the sublimely Whiggish historian of 'the English people', was even more elegiac in his praise:

> It is with a reverence such as is stirred by the sight of the head-waters of some mighty river, that one looks back to these tiny moots, where the men of the village met to order the village life and the village industry, as their descendants, the men of a later England, meet in Parliament at Westminster, to frame laws and do justice for the great empire which has sprung from this little body of farmer-commonwealths in Sleswick.[35]

ii WHATEVER HAPPENED TO THE NORMAN CONQUEST?

Given the Victorian veneration for their Saxon legacy, their celebration of its timeless wisdom as well as contemporary utility, it might appear that the events of 1066 had rather slipped their mind. And numerous Victorian authors did indeed strive surreptitiously to airbrush the Norman Conquest and defeat of hapless King Harold from the island story. Yet despite regret for this historical calamity, the Victorians were in fact acutely conscious that the invasion saw the arrival of a wholly new, foreign race into the British Isles. A race with very different ideas about the relationship between central and local government and the right of self-governing municipalities.

Race and the ideology of racism were nineteenth-century constructions, and the categorisation was employed as much to describe the tribes who had cumulatively inhabited Britain as the newly subjugated peoples of Empire. The Romantic quest for signs of national differentiation, for unique identities and origins, was readily applied to the warring races who had met at Hastings in 1066. In *Ivanhoe*, Walter Scott specifically envisioned the Saxons and Normans as two distinct races, 'the vanquished distinguished by their plain, homely, blunt manners, and the free spirit infused by their ancient spirit and laws; the victors, by the high spirit of military fame, personal adventure, and whatever could distinguish them as the flower of chivalry'.[36]

His cast of Front-de-Boeuf and de Bracy effortlessly fulfilled the historical role of the rapacious Norman, whilst Rowena, Ivanhoe and Cedric (who 'stands up so sternly for the privileges of his race')[37] played the parts of virtuous Saxons with equal finesse. The Normans were portrayed as a despotic, Catholic and ultimately corrupt race who cruelly terrorised the benign, free-spirited Saxons. Scott graphically indulged his anti-Norman readership with lurid accounts of the actions of King Stephen's lordly entourage, who 'suffocated some in mud, and suspended others by the feet, or the head, or the thumbs, kindling fire below them. They squeezed the heads of some with knotted cords till they pierced their brains, while they threw others into dungeons swarming with serpents, snakes, and toads.'[38] Here was the tyranny of the 'Norman Yoke' in all its terrible glory. As the court jester Wamba riskily joked to his audience of assembled Normans,

> Normans saw on English Oak,
> On English neck a Norman yoke;
> Norman spoon in English dish,
> And England ruled as Normans wish;
> Blythe world to England never will be more,
> Till England's rid of all the four.[39]

Scott determined the dominant paradigm for ensuing interpretations of the Norman invasion. When, thirty years later, Edward Bulwer-Lytton produced *Harold, the Last of the Saxon Kings*, the model was already well established. In the figure of Harold, Bulwer-Lytton aimed to sketch 'the pure Saxon character' marked by 'patient endurance, love of justice and freedom – the manly sense of duty rather than the chivalric sentiment of honour'. And while Bulwer-Lytton professed to be 'as lenient as justice will permit' on the Norman duke, he found it 'as impossible to deny his craft, as to dispute his genius'.[40]

Amongst Scott's most influential disciples was the French historian Augustin Thierry, who penned an even more fundamentalist history of the period. His *Histoire de la Conquête de l'Angleterre par les Normands* (1825) took great relish in depicting the harsh punishments of those Saxons who dared to resist William the Bastard. 'The most prominent were tried and condemned with some show of form; the remainder were handed over to the discretion of the foreign soldiers, who made them serfs on their domains, or massacred them'.[41] In turn, amongst those who read Thierry's history and absorbed its colourful interpretation of the Normans' programme of ethnic cleansing was Benjamin Disraeli.

In chapter two, I discussed how Disraeli's idea of the 'Two Nations' of the rich and the poor posited a deeply antagonistic, class analysis of industrial British society. However, as so often with Disraeli, there was more to it. Perhaps unsurprisingly given his Jewish background and the opprobrium it attracted in Anglican political circles, Disraeli was bewitched by race. His own Jewish heritage and interest in the racial divisions of the Orient were tortuously explored in *Tancred, or the New Crusade*. And in *Coningsby*, the quixotic Sidonia portentously announces that 'All is race; there is no other truth.' *Sybil* is also a tale of race. It is a story of how the nineteenth-century descendants of the conquering Norman aristocracy continued to live off the illegally plundered wealth of dispossessed Saxons. So it is the Normans who are 'The Rich' and the miserable Saxons, now reduced to the state of factory hands, who are 'The Poor'. The work is as much a racial as a class analysis of British societal divide. The young aristocrat Charles Egremont is a Norman and the radical

Chartist Walter Gerard is a Saxon; they are 'formed by a different breeding, are fed by a different food'. In one hackneyed scene, Sybil, the Saxon 'daughter of the people', even reads chapters of Thierry's history of the Conquest to her father, Gerard. The tale of the noble Harold moves her to ask, 'Why have we not such a man now?' The more downbeat Gerard seeks solace by indulging in 'a cup of the drink of Saxon kings'.[42]

More recently, commentators have observed that social divides continue to be based along similar racial lines. The humorist John O'Farrell described how when canvassing for the Labour Party in mid-1980s London, 'It struck me that the classes in Britain were still basically divided along the lines of Normans and Saxons. The Normans of Fulham still drank wine and owned land in France and the Saxons of Fulham still drank ale, used "Anglo-Saxon" vocabulary and tended small strips of land behind the playing fields.'[43]

The historical assumption that the Norman Conquest brought nothing but terror and misery to the benighted Saxon people became undisputed terrain in Victorian understandings of the past. John Lingard's *History of England* was unrelenting in its account of how 'foreign' Norman barons overran the country. 'Contempt and oppression became the portion of the natives, whose farms were pillaged, females violated, and persons imprisoned at the caprice of these petty and local tyrants.'[44] Sir James Kay-Shuttleworth in his speech to the NAPSS voiced the educated view. 'No tyranny could be more absolute, cruel, and relentless', he told the gathering of academics, civil servants and professionals, 'than that with which the Norman king and his nobles crushed the spirit of the Saxon people into subjection.'[45] Macaulay concurred. The 'tyranny of the Norman race' ensured that the subjugation of a nation had 'seldom, even in Asia, been more complete'.[46]

One of the most telling signs of the foreignness or 'otherness' of the Norman invaders was their hostility towards local self-government. King William brought with him a baronial class with no respect for the concept of civic autonomy or burgher citizenship. Their background was feudal, not municipal, and the Norman elite rapidly dismantled the Saxon system of little republics in favour of a centralised state administered through baronial agents. The bureaucratic intrusion of the Domesday Book was an affront to the liberal, self-governing tradition of Alfred's reign. Victorian historians recounted with horror the steady erosion of Saxon civic liberties. Homersham Cox, in his history of the British Commonwealth, described how 'the attempt was made in England, after the Norman Conquest, to destroy the independent political organization of the shires and boroughs'.[47] Instead of elective Saxon shire-reeves or borough-reeves, the Norman despots imposed viscounts to rule the shires and tyrannical bailiffs to govern the towns. Edward Creasy, in his analysis of the English constitution, described the impact of the petty tyranny of the Norman bailiff over the 'oppressed citizens' who were used to their own 'old elected port-reeve or borough-reeve'. He concluded that, 'By no class was the effect of the Conquest felt more severely than by that of the citizens and burgesses.'[48]

Yet the sturdy Saxon spirit, which had seen off the might of the Roman Empire, did not submit meekly. Beneath the boot of the bailiff and tax demands of the viscount, the Saxon heart continued to beat. And it was in the towns and cities that resistance was formulated to the Norman takeover. The brave Saxon boroughs defended the now-'English' love of self-government against the introduction of a corrupt Norman centralism. Independently of the Norman elite, the medieval cities began to grow and prosper and soon challenged the authority of their feudal rulers. In the words of Kay-Shuttleworth,

> For a time the feudal institutions were strengthened – personal independence and the spirit of local government were depressed. But the germ of local and national representative institutions survived in the traditions, customs, and provincial constitution of the country, and the mixture of race gradually infused that moderation into the exercise of feudal

power which tempered the fierceness of the first military occupation of the country.[49]

Gradually, the cities and boroughs grew in power thanks to their trade and commerce. The Saxon mettle of enterprise and self-government managed to struggle through the dark days of the eleventh and twelfth centuries. The radical *Westminster Review* described how the spirit which had 'animated their forefathers at Hastings, was now directed to the jealous defence of their rights against encroachments'.[50] And in 1215, King John was at last forced to confirm their 'ancient liberties and free customs by land and water' in the sacrosanct words of the Magna Carta. The story of the towns as the natural harbours of the resilient Saxon spirit appealed to a Victorian urban readership hungry for a historical identity. That the cities had then managed to prosper and confront a Norman aristocracy partly through the wealth of their industry was an extra source of pride for a commercial middle-class audience. And the struggle of that burgess class, explained the antiquarian Thomas Wright, 'in defence of their municipal liberty during the Middle Ages, ended in securing for us the popular freedom which all classes of society now enjoy'.[51] Imperceptibly but irreversibly the myth was born that somehow the Saxon character – its temperament, institutions, and love of self-government – managed to survive the totality of the Norman Conquest. Despite the brutality of the invasion and the hegemony of baronial rule, despite the litany of cruelty and rapacity listed by Thierry and Creasy, the Saxon legacy of free, democratic involvement lived on, ready to be ignited at any moment.

The historian Sir Francis Palgrave reduced 1066 to little more than a titular *coup d'état* which created new institutions at the top of the English polity but left Anglo-Saxon institutions and customs intact on the ground; for the Teutonic spirit had been tilled into the very soil of the nation and rooted almost beyond the possibility of being pulled up. The Normans were but temporary impostors overseeing the higher echelons of the state. Just as Mr Thornton had boasted of his Teutonic blood, so Mrs Markham's populist *History of England* concluded her narrative of 'England from Egbert to Harold' with a charming scene in which a mother explains to her daughter, 'Your papa and I are Saxons.' When the child expresses her surprise – 'Why I thought you were an Englishwoman!' – the mother gently recounts, 'So I am: but, as the Saxons continued in the country after the Conquest, and were much more numerous than the Norman settlers, we are still almost all of us of chiefly Saxon descent; and our language, and many of our habits and customs, sufficiently declare our origin.'[52]

In his massive *History of the Norman Conquest of England*, the liberal historian Edward Freeman went one step further. While he admitted the Conquest brought with it an extensive foreign infusion, 'which affected our blood, our language, our laws, our arts', it was only a 'temporary overthrow of our national being'. For the fundamental elements within the English nation survived and within only a few generations the Saxons surged back from defeat. They now 'led captive our conquerors' and 'England was England once again'. Bizarrely, the Conquest was now regarded as having only served to strengthen and preserve the essential Saxon temper of the British Isles.

The Victorians indulged themselves in a collective act of historical amnesia. They dispensed with their Norman past to forge an ancient Saxon identity which placed towns, cities and a belief in self-government at its core. The Saxon spirit, that belief in self-government, defined the British nation. And what made this discourse so relevant to the mid-Victorian public was that many saw the same divide between Saxon and Norman apparent in the cultural differences between nineteenth-century France and Britain.

iii A TALE OF TWO CITIES

The French nation had also been the victim of a brutal foreign conquest. But while the Saxons had somehow managed to dilute the impact of the Norman Conquest, the defeated Gauls had offered only minimal resistance to the invading Franks. In turn, the Franks took over the political structures which had been established by the Romans. Crushing the old self-governing Gallic tribes, it was the Franks and then the Normans who planted the seeds of the centralised, feudal structure which came to dominate the French state.

One of the most perceptive observers of the cultural chasm which divided Norman France from Saxon England was the Manchester *voyeur*, Alexis de Tocqueville. On his first visit to England in 1833, he noted down the views of the British political classes as to precisely what value defined their national political identity:

> Dr Bowring [a Benthamite MP and editor of the *Westminster Review*] said to me today, 'England is the country of decentralisation. We have got a government, but we have not got a central administration. Each country, each town, each parish looks after its own interests ... It is not in the nature of things that a central government should be able to watch over all the needs of a great nation. Decentralisation is the chief cause of the substantial progress we have made in civilisation.'

It was a sentiment which the sanctimonious Mr Podsnap was happy to endorse in Charles Dickens's *Our Mutual Friend*. When questioned over Britain's lax system for poor relief, he immediately sensed 'what you are driving at. I knew it from the first. Centralization. No. Never with my consent. Not English.'[53] Simple as that.

De Tocqueville never drifted far from Podsnap's homespun wisdom. The difference between France and England, Norman and Saxon was one of central authority. In his *Democracy in America* and *The Ancien Régime and the French Revolution*, de Tocqueville enviously chronicled the Anglo-Saxon self-governing spirit in contrast to the deleterious effects of French centralisation. For de Tocqueville, the rot had set in during the eighteenth century when French monarchs garnered ever greater power, so undermining the foundations of municipal autonomy. All the intermediary institutions of civil society – towns, Church, nobility, or business – submitted themselves to the microscopic rule of the Sun King. Central officials, the much reviled *intendants*, crawled over every decision made or grant allocated in every municipality or region which dared to act on its own initiative. Even village fêtes were routinely audited. 'Under the old government, as in our time, there was not a town, borough, village, not even the smallest hamlet in France, neither hospital, factory, convent, or college, which could have an independent will in its own affairs, or administer its own property and pleasure. Then, just as it does now, the administration kept all the French in tutelage'.[54]

As every guild, corporation or municipality was neutered, a dangerous gulf emerged between the individual citizen and the monarchical state. The vast Versailles court paraded itself atop a barren civic fabric, a withered honeycomb ready to crumble on the flimsiest of pretexts. And so when the moment came, the Revolution was awesome. As the *Edinburgh Review* put it in a review of de Tocqueville's work, 'this new and central power [the state] had reduced to insignificance or nothingness all local powers, and had thus slain all provincial life and all municipal action – for to this more than to any other cause is attributable the sudden and avalanche-like character of the Revolution'.[55]

The tragedy of the Revolution, however, was that it only accelerated the momentum for centralisation. Rather than rebuild civil society or encourage self-government, the Jacobins grabbed even further authority for the state. Political liberty in any liberal, pluralist sense never emerged. Instead, 'beneath the seemingly chaotic surface', there developed 'a vast, highly centralised power' which proceeded to undermine any residual elements of autonomous power. The inevitable consequence of this concentration of authority was a recurring political instability which subjected France to ceaseless revolution. The chief reasons 'for the collapse of all the various governments that have arisen in France during the past forty years are administrative centralisation and the absolute predominance of Paris'. Governments and monarchies could come and go with a quick dispatch of personnel in Paris.[56]

De Tocqueville's analysis fitted in well with an emergent national and racial identity predicated on an emotional attachment to decentralisation and municipal autonomy. The unequivocal enemy of the piece was Paris: an otiose, decadent, corrupt capital which had sucked the life out of France. 'Centralism has given to Paris an importance', according to Francis Lieber, 'which no capital possesses in any other country. The French themselves often say, Paris is France.' *The Economist*, a devoutly anti-European journal (no change there), similarly concurred with de Tocqueville over the nefarious over-governance of France. 'Every license [sic] is granted by the central authority. Every official through-out the empire – every prefect, mayor, notary, tobacco dealer, through-out France, is appointed by a minister at Paris, and can be dismissed by him'.[57] Edward Freeman, in an essay on the medieval history of Paris, suggested that 'Paris is to France not merely its greatest city, the seat of its government, the centre of its society and literature. It is France itself; it is, as it has been so long, its living heart and its surest bulwark. It is the city which has created the kingdom, and on the life of the city the life of the kingdom seems to hang.'[58]

Paris's gain was France's downfall. Its beauty and brilliance suckled the revolutionary upheavals of 1789, 1815 and 1830. In the words of the populist historian of cities, Theodore Buckley, 'Such has been Paris: too gay to be stable; too fickle to remain content; ever the prey of new rulers; ever the centre of spurious patriotism.'[59] Without the political safety valves of provincial meetings, local elections, or the activity of municipal institutions, revolution was the only corrective against Parisian centralisation. 'To the French imagination', *The Economist* commented, 'the simplest, shortest, and easiest way of conquering their liberty, when oppression has become

unbearable, has always been to seize upon the reins of power.'
While other nations negotiate concessions from their governments, 'the French "cashier" their governors and become
governors themselves'.[60] To the Victorian imagination, Paris
was the city of perpetual Revolution.

> A great city then may present many objects of interest and
> be even architecturally grand, yet its grandeur be the screen
> of its deformity. Witness Paris, for instance, the centre of
> modern civilisation; walk through the streets in the very
> neighbourhood of the Louvre, and the Palais Royal, with
> their shelving pavements, the gutter in the middle, their
> narrow streets, no place for foot passengers, the lamps
> hanging from ropes and making you think you still, as
> in the Revolution, hear the cry. Away with him to the
> Lantern![61]

Britain by contrast was blessed with a stability secured by
its diffuse urban base. Britain was far more than London; it
was a land of great cities, each one playing a part in the
political process and preventing the unstable accumulation of
too much power in the capital. Celebrating the hosting of
the National Association for the Promotion of Social Science
congress in Birmingham, the *Birmingham Daily Press* eulo-
gised the importance of England's provincial capitals. 'On the
other side of the Channel Paris is France, but no such rule
applies with us.' In Britain, 'Birmingham, Manchester, Liverpool, Glasgow, and other towns must be asked their opinion'
before any great decisions are taken.[62] London, according to
The Builder, is not England. 'Intelligence, wealth, and power,
dwelling in fine cities, and carrying out noble institutions, are
to be found in every quarter of our island, and make up an
extraordinary aggregate.'[63]

The strength of the British constitution lay not simply in
its willingness to devolve power to the cities, but also in the
involvement of those urban citizens in the national political
process. The British civic system educated its people for the

mature responsibility of governance. Having wondered at the New England system of town meetings, de Tocqueville stressed the vital importance of municipal self-government for the health of the body politic. 'Town meetings are to liberty what primary schools are to science; they bring it within the people's reach, they teach men how to use and enjoy it. A nation may establish a free government, but without municipal institutions it cannot have the spirit of liberty.'[64]

Local government had to act as the primary school for national politics – it was there to inculcate the principles of democracy and citizenship. 'Real and efficient, not merely nominal municipal institutions, seem essential to instruct and practise a people in habits of self-government', expounded *The Economist*.[65] Towns as the playground of municipal politics were the foundations of the unique attributes of the British constitution. Alderman Baynes, in a lecture to the Blackburn Literary, Scientific, and Mechanics' Institution, explained that a town council was like a miniature parliament and so, 'an excellent training school to fit men for the higher and more responsible office' of national representation. In addition, it is opposed to centralisation, 'the bane of continental governments', and instead 'fosters a love of freedom'. 'It teaches the people to rely upon their own exertions, to think and act for themselves, and that is the characteristic of a free people.'[66]

The contrast was complete: between the centralising, revolutionary, despotic instability of Norman France and the self-governing, diffuse, empowering stability of Saxon Britain. And then right on cue, as if these prejudices required any further enforcement, revolution once more engulfed Paris.

In February and again in April 1848, Paris erupted into anarchy as the monarchy of Louis-Philippe collapsed and the capital played midwife to the birth-pains of the Second Republic. Barricades went up along the capital's narrow streets and some 1,500 lives were lost in the street fighting until the election of Louis-Napoleon returned the country to calm. For smug observers across the Channel the swift change of government effected by the Parisian mobs was everything they had come to expect. In the midst of the uprisings, *The Economist* blamed the turmoil on Parisian vainglory. France's history of centralisation had left it vulnerable to 'despotism, disorder, and ruin ... under the dictation of a small party in Paris' whilst the provincial cities – bludgeoned into apathy after years of central control – did nothing. The difference to England could not be more striking. 'Will our correspondents consider for one moment what would have been the acts, and the state of Manchester, Liverpool, Birmingham, Glasgow, Edinburgh, and the whole of the provinces of this country, had an attempt been made to enact such scenes in London...?'[67]

When Paris again exploded in April 1848, the magazine returned to the same theme, demanding to know how 'a few citizens, a small mob, a little knot of bold adventurers' could seize power in Paris and then hold the entire country to ransom. 'No such thing could happen either in England or in the United States. The Mayor of Liverpool, or the Provost of Edinburgh, would not at once recognise a government issuing orders in the name of Mr Feargus O'Connor or Mr Ernest Jones. He would not on the authority of telegraphic despatches ... proclaim a republic by orders from London.' In France, however, the government had established a 'complete central authority' in Paris which meant that 'whoever, therefore, can get hold of the bureaus and the palace becomes master of France'.[68] For *The Economist* the moral was clear. 'Thank God! We are Saxons!'[69]

iv SAXON SANITATION

There did exist one drawback to the Saxon way. The difficulty with leaving cities free to do what they liked was that quite often they didn't do very much. Self-government slipped easily into no government and the result for Victorian Britain was a continuing and deleterious decline in public health standards during the first half of the nineteenth century. A cultural attachment to self-government combined with an ideological fixation with economy conspired to preclude the active involvement of local government in public health reform. And all the while the stresses on the Victorian city grew ever greater: immigration accelerated, heavy industry boomed, the sanitary infrastructure crumbled, and the quality of housing became even more overcrowded and unhealthy.

In chapter one, I outlined the shocking sanitary conditions which deformed the industrial city. In 1841, life expectancy at birth was 26.6 years in Manchester, 28.1 years for Liverpool, and twenty-seven years in Glasgow. These bleak figures indicated a disturbing reversal of previous improvements in public health and life expectancy during the early 1800s. Instead, by the mid-century there existed a marked expansion of inequality both in life expectancy and in quality of life. Indeed, industrialisation and urbanisation arguably cemented levels of inequality which Britain has never truly shed; for while the families of peers lived no longer than the national average at the start of the eighteenth century, by the 1850s they were living a full fifteen years longer. Death was no longer the great leveller, as class and occupational status significantly affected life expectancy. Intriguingly, it could also affect how tall you were. One of the more unexpected academic breakthroughs of recent years has been the charting of variations in average height levels, which is taken to be a very good indicator of nutritional status and general healthiness. And the statistics indicate an obvious deterioration in the average male height for those born in the late 1830s through to the early 1850s. Victorian urban life was not only shortening lives, it was also making life shorter for those who lived.[70]

At least the issues were starting to be addressed, however. Following his many years in the political wilderness, Edwin Chadwick's voice was at last being heard. In 1840 the House of Commons established a Select Committee on Health of Towns chaired by the Liberal MP for Shrewsbury, Sir Robert Slaney. After taking evidence, the Committee recommended an ambitious plan for the reform of cities, including a General Building Act to end back-to-back housing; a General Sewage and Building Act; and a General Act to aid local improvements embracing cemeteries, public baths, water supply, lodging-houses and parks which were 'essential' to the health and comfort of the urban poor.[71]

In the wake of the Select Committee came an even grander Royal Commission for Enquiring into the State of Large Towns and Populous Districts. The Commission's brief was to help foster 'a gradual improvement in the moral and physical condition of large numbers of Your Majesty's poorer subjects', and with their unprecedented powers of investigation and summons they looked at everything from land drainage to building ventilation to water supply to fire hazards. More importantly, with the Duke of Buccleuch, the Earl of Lincoln and the hugely wealthy London developer William Cubitt serving as Commissioners, its activities gave a personal, political momentum to the question of sanitary reform – especially as many of them would end up vomiting on street corners during their insalubrious fact-finding missions. The evidence presented by Liverpool's medical health officer, Dr William Henry Duncan, was typical in its account of the state of the city's courts, alleys and tenements.

> I do not know of a single court in Liverpool which communicates with the street or sewer by a covered drain. The fluid contents, therefore, of the overcharged ash-pits too frequently find their way through the mouldering walls which confine them, and spread a layer of abomination over the entire surface of the court. In some instances it even oozes through into the neighbouring cellars, filling them with its pestilential vapours, and rendering it necessary to dig wells to receive it, in order to prevent the inhabitants being inundated. One of these wells, four feet deep, filled with this stinking fluid, was found in one cellar under the bed where the family slept.[72]

Outside the formal political structure, there also emerged new non-governmental bodies demanding improvements to the state of the Victorian city. By far the most influential was the Health of Towns Association (HTA). Established in 1844 by the Marquis of Normanby, its board of the great and the good included Benjamin Disraeli, Edward Bulwer-Lytton, Earl Derby and Lord Morpeth. By 1847, following the successful conclusion of the Anti-Corn-Law League's activities, it emerged as the most powerful lobby in the country, with branch associations in Edinburgh, Liverpool, Manchester, York and Derby. The Association's remit was clear: 'To diffuse information as to the physical and moral evils that result from the present defective Sewerage, Drainage, Supply of Water, Air, and Light, and Construction of Dwelling Houses; and thus to facilitate the work of Legislation, and prepare the Public for the reception of a sound and comprehensive sanitary measure.'

To achieve its objectives the Association employed all the familiar tools of a modern pressure group. This included a sophisticated PR machine which issued 'Weekly Sheets of Facts and Figures', 'with the object of presenting at short intervals of time, and in a form to attract attention and offer facilities for quotation, some of the more striking facts which have been recently placed before the public'.[73] By far their most effective publicist was the London physician Hector Gavin. Wandering the streets of 1840s Whitechapel, Mile End, and Bethnal Green, and minutely noting down the miserable sanitary conditions, Gavin produced a classic of mid-Victorian social commentary. He entitled it, rather whimsically, *Sanitary Ramblings*.

DIGBY-ST., GLOBE-ROAD. 19. – In this most dirty street, exists one of the most atrocious nuisances which it is possible to create ... the whole of the area is filled with every variety of manure in every stage of offensive and disgusting decomposition; the manure is piled up to a considerable height, and is left to dry in the sun; but, besides this table mountain of manure, extensive and deep lakes of putrefying night soil are dammed up with the more solid dung, and refuse, forming together, mountain and lake, a scene of the most disgusting character... The decomposing organic particles which are ever being set free from this putrescent mass, are wafted by each wind that blows, over a population to whom they bring disease and death, as surely as, though more insidiously than, the deadly simoom.[74]

In Stratford, Gavin found a factory for evaporating 'Gas liquor',

the stench of which is so foetid that, even when the poor poisoned victims, living near, are confined to their rooms by typhus fever, consumption etc., they *dare not, and cannot* open a window, as it almost suffocates the inmates, particularly when the wind blows the fumes in that direction. The poor creatures have even been driven out by the intolerable stench into the main road, where they have asked *what were they to do*? To which it was replied, that if they could become *pigs or oxen*, and were killed, the law would punish the proprietors of these nuisances by making them pay their value; but as they were only *women and children* the law did not trouble itself about them.[75]

Headed by a cabal of evangelical aristocrats, the HTA's guiding principle was an elevated Christian idealism. The cities needed to be cleaned so the people could be cleansed. 'The health, the tranquillity, the morality, nay, the Christianity of the people of this country are nearly concerned in the sanitary condition of these towns,' declared one of its lead advocates, Viscount Ebrington.[76] Living in filth, the people lived in sin. According to Gavin, 'It is most assuredly a truth, that unless the physical and social condition of the people be amended, no great progress can be made in spreading the doctrines of morality or religion.'[77] The Christian socialist Charles Kingsley, author both of *Two Years Ago*, a bleak novel about poor sanitation and the threat of cholera, and the clean-water utopia of *The Water-Babies*, similarly made the link in a lecture entitled 'Great Cities and Their Influence for Good and Evil'. It was only by abolishing 'foul air, foul water, foul lodging, overcrowded dwellings' that morality and decency could be embedded. 'You may breed a pig in a sty, ladies and gentlemen, and make a learned pig of him after all; but you cannot breed a man in a sty, and make a learned man of him.'[78]

The philosophy of the Association was an early indication of a retreat from the former hardline assumptions that crime, sin and intemperance were the sole product of character failure. Increasingly, the environment was accounted as an influence upon social behaviour, an argument most cogently developed by the Bishop of London as he introduced the 1846 Public Baths and Washhouses Bill into the House of Lords. The Bill enabled local authorities to levy a rate to fund the construction of baths and washhouses specifically designed for the urban poor. By encouraging cleanliness, the measure would not just assist the struggle against infectious diseases; it would also allow the individual to rise out of the mire of the Victorian city. The issue thus 'concerned the moral as well as physical welfare of the humbler classes of the population, affecting their moral welfare through their physical state'. The Bishop urged his fellow peers to help 'elevate the poor man from extreme destitution – they must take off from him the urgent pressure of misery before they could assail him, as a moral agent, with any chance of success'.[79]

And on these criteria, the Act was an enormous success. Liverpool was the first to take advantage of its provisions and by 1857 Birmingham, Manchester, Leeds, Glasgow, Edinburgh, Bolton, Coventry, South Shields, Preston and Nottingham had all followed suit. At a meeting of the NAPSS, the Act was heralded as one of the great social reforms of the mid-century, responsible for diminishing infection, decreasing the charge on public rates and even cutting crime. 'Few institutions for the improvement of the social and moral condition of the industrious classes have been more thankfully received by those for whose benefit they were intended, than "baths and washhouses".'[80]

What emerged from the myriad inquiries into sanitary conditions and the mounting pressure for political action was a
greater scientific rigour in the approach to questions of disease
and public health. Above all, there was at last the realisation
that it was not the mythical 'miasma' but poor sewerage and
contaminated water supplies which were the deadliest killers.
Dr Southwood Smith (who himself would suffer three bouts
of typhus) noted in his report to the Poor Law Commissioners
that, 'in every district in which fever returns frequently, and
prevails extensively, there is uniformly bad sewerage, a bad
supply of water, a bad supply of scavengers, and a consequent
accumulation of filth'. Where proper sewers had been laid,
fever was almost absent.

The return of cholera in 1846 and 1848 heightened the
sanitary impetus. And although it would not be until 1884
that it was finally accepted that the cholera *vibrio* could be
water-borne, there was certainly a keener awareness of the
dangers of impure water. In Soho, London, the pioneering
physician Dr John Snow analysed the mortality levels of
various water pumps across the capital and discovered a clear
link between polluted water and outbreaks of cholera – an
invisible menace whose deadly potential was rapidly enhanced
by the decision of the London authorities to flush out all the
galleys and drains into the Thames in the hope of dispelling
atmospheric impurities. By the late 1840s, with cholera knock-
ing on the door of middle- and working-class districts alike,
the cry for sanitary reform was unstoppable. But so far local
authorities, the historic trustees of Saxon self-government,
had failed to make safe their cities.

v The Shopocracy

Responsibility for sanitary reform in the Victorian city was
not a clear-cut issue. A Babel of competing boards, authorities
and surveyors exercised control over various different aspects
of the urban infrastructure. There were paving boards and
lighting boards, highway surveyors and turnpike trusts, ves-

tries and Poor Law guardians, magistrates, police boards and even lords of the manor. None of them co-ordinated their actions with one another and each jealously guarded their own administrative patch. The inevitable result was that when a disease like cholera came to pay its respects, city authorities had minimal chance of organising a coherent response.

Those municipal corporations faced with pressing public health concerns reacted by submitting Improvement Bills to Parliament. These private bills, which applied only to the sponsoring city, gave local authorities the right to levy rates for certain purposes, rationalise the public health bureaucracy and even borrow money (a philosophical crime in mid-Victorian Britain). The 1842 Leeds Improvement Act allowed the Council to pave, light and cleanse the streets, to construct a new system of sewage and drainage, to impose building regulations and control smoke pollution. To fund the improvements the Council was sanctioned to levy three rates and borrow £100,000. In 1844 Manchester introduced its own Borough Police Act and in 1846 Liverpool submitted to Parliament its Sanitary Bill. When passed, the Act co-ordinated the city's public health authorities under a single Health Committee and allowed for the appointment of an inspector of nuisances, a borough engineer and a medical officer of health – the post to which William Duncan was appointed on a salary of £300 a year.[81]

Although these local Acts often delivered improvement in sanitary administration, they were still hopelessly inadequate to the pestilential problems facing the Victorian city. First, there was the difficulty of actually getting the legislation through Parliament: it was expensive and time-consuming and only the largest authorities were able to marshal the requisite resources. Liverpool was thought to have spent almost £100,000 on its 1846 Act. The legislation which then emerged was often highly restricted in its powers and frequently subject to challenge. In fact, the Royal Commission on the State of Large Towns regarded local improvement Acts as little short of hopeless. 'Several of the local Improvement

Acts confer no jurisdiction beyond the public highways, and
give the authorities no powers to drain or cleanse the courts,
alleys, and closes inhabited by the poorer classes... In many
towns the powers given are neglected, and in most of them
imperfectly exercised.'[82]

There also existed political problems with sanitary reform
within the municipality. The nature of Victorian local authority finance meant that a quite disproportionate amount of
political power was vested amongst the petty bourgeois shopkeeper class who practised a unique form of irresponsible
economy. Until the extension of the franchise enjoined in the
1867 Second Reform Act, local authorities were dominated by
the rate-paying small property-owner. They were the constituents who regularly voted and elected themselves onto the
Council. Not wealthy enough to move out to the suburbs, but
liable as the owners of small property interests within the
city, they fought vigorously against any urban improvements
which necessitated an increase to the rates. And given the
very limited options available to local authorities to raise
money, any sanitary reforms usually did necessitate an extra
levy upon property-owners. As the poor typically rented their
tenement dwellings and the wealthy often lived outside the
city in plush villas (or were wealthy enough to pay), any rate
hike typically fell most perceptibly upon the lower-middle-
class *rentier* businessman who had invested in a little property.[83]

In numerous cities requiring a programme of public health
works, the local shopkeepers, innkeepers, small property-
owners and petty capitalists formed themselves together into
Ratepayer Associations and Protection Societies to fight off the
threat of extra municipal expenditure. This was the 'Economy
Party'; the Shopocracy. Throughout the 1840s and 1850s, this
vocal lobby exercised their grip on local government by time
and again blocking improvement plans. Rarely could they be
seduced into voting for projects that might actually save their
lives. Instead, in language frequently littered with appeals
to their Saxon heritage, they defended their right to self-

government; their right to be dirty but free. As ever, Charles Dickens deftly satirised the hypocrisy when he imagined an election address in the fictitious town of Cess-cum-Poolton, 'Ratepayers: Cess-cum-Poolton! Rally around your vested interests. Health is enormously expensive ... Be filthy and be fat. Cesspools and Constitutional Government! Gases and Glory! No insipid water!!!'[84]

Political and legal obstacles to cleaning up the Victorian city came together with bruising momentum in the case of London. The hindrances to sanitary reform apparent in the provincial cities were magnified by a factor of ten in the filthy, stinking capital. There was first of all the problem that London was made up of a labyrinthine collection of competing political authorities. In the middle sat the six hundred acres of the City of London. Divided into twenty-six wards and housing 12,000 to 15,000 resident freemen ratepayers, it was run as a medieval city state by the Doge-like Corporation of London. The resident freemen elected the Court of Common Council which existed alongside a host of other Byzantine institutions (such as the Court of Wardmote and Court of Aldermen), all presided over by the Lord Mayor. Separate from the Corporation, but equally influential players in the back-door world of City government, were the rich and extremely secretive City Companies or Guilds. It constituted a network of back-scratching financial and professional clubs which to this day exert a wholly unreformed power over the modern City of London.

Outside the City, there existed historic Westminster along with the counties of Middlesex, Kent and Surrey. At local level, London was governed by a web of parish vestries of varying democratic nature and equally variable size: from the truly, locally democratic right up to the 60,000-strong vestry of St George's, Hanover Square. In theory, the parishes were responsible for the paving, lighting and cleansing of their streets; however, the fluid nature of public health requirements meant that their authority was frequently superseded by individual Acts of Parliament as well as the powers over

roads and water wielded by turnpike trusts. Even further up
the bureaucratic chain wallowed the eight Metropolitan Commissioners of Sewers, many of whom still operated under a
1532 Act of Parliament. Needless to say, the Bumbledom
Commissioners were involved in a ceaseless bureaucratic war
with one another – as well as the parish vestries and medical
establishment. According to one London historian, 'Jobbery,
extravagance, and gross technical incompetence were almost
everywhere the rule.' Until 1817 the Westminster Commission did not even possess a plan of its own drains.[85]

Aside from fighting amongst themselves and supping turtle
soup, what the Commissioners did do was regularly flush the
entire content of London's sewers into the Thames. Whilst this
tactic might have been just about acceptable when cesspools
contained most human waste and sewers were merely chan-
nels for surface water, it was most certainly not after Mr
Thomas Crapper ('a certain flush with every pull') began
making his presence felt. The popular take-up of the Water
Closet (WC) from the 1830s onwards, combined with a London
population swelling to two million, substantially increased
the amount of household waste as well as the demand for
water. Sewers now turned into cesspools, and with ninety
million gallons of raw sewage entering the Thames daily the
journalist George Godwin feared, 'the entire excrementation
of the Metropolis ... shall sooner or later be mingled in the
stream of the river, there to be rolled backward and forward
around the population ... From the polluted bosom of the
river steam up, incessantly though unseen, the vapours of a
retributive poison.'[86] As excrement lined the banks of the
Thames, London fell victim to wave upon wave of typhus and
cholera. Needless to say, despite the obvious requirements
for quite elementary sanitary regulations, London's chaotic,
competing authorities were wholly disinterested in working
together.

Not least, this was because the rhetoric of local self-government found its most confident voice in the vestries of
London and amongst the self-selecting elites of the City Cor-

poration. Nowhere was the historic right of local authorities to look after themselves more celebrated than amongst the bubbling cesspools of Finsbury, Holborn and St Pancras; and nowhere was the Saxon bequest more venerated than amongst the open latrines of the City of London. The City steadfastly blocked any projects to clean up the capital which could be interpreted as trespassing on those precious civic liberties wrest from the grasp of King John. The political power and commercial muscle wielded by the corrupt Corporation condemned innumerable Londoners to an early death. And it was only going to get worse. For in 1845 the advocates of local self-government gained their most persuasive advocate.

On 18 December 1845, the lawyer and historian Joshua Toulmin-Smith was having dinner with his wife and daughters at his elegant home in Highgate, north London. As the family ate their meal in a picture of Victorian bourgeois domesticity, there was a rap at the door. There then intruded upon this Englishman's castle an excise officer armed with a search warrant backed up by an assortment of burly assistants. Alerted by an anonymous letter to the presence of an illegal still within the Toulmin-Smith household, the officer set about searching the premises. The sanctity of the household, the *sine qua non* of the British constitution, had been breached. According to Toulmin-Smith's later statement of complaint, 'the officers treated the females of his family very roughly; and [that] his wife had never recovered from the shock she received'.[87] From that moment on, Toulmin-Smith dedicated his life to challenging at every turn the growing might of the nineteenth-century state. In doing so, he became the spiritual leader of the shopocracy.

Born in 1816 in Birmingham, Joshua Toulmin-Smith's quixotic life and breadth of intellectual interest define him as a quintessential, if somewhat forgotten, Victorian figure. He was an expert phrenologist, pioneering geologist, Norse linguist, and respected Anglo-Saxon scholar – while his day job was as a barrister. What Toulmin-Smith believed, above all else, was that local self-government was the defining attribute of the English people, established in this country 'by men free when roaming the forests of Germany, and no less free when landing on the shores of England'. Whereas many advocates of self-government were happy to decentralise down to the municipality, Toulmin-Smith argued that the parish provided the most virtuous unit for governance. It was the true inheritor of the Saxon tything and hundred, and any removal of powers from parish authority constituted a dangerous step along the road to centralisation. As the *Birmingham Daily Post* put it in an obituary following his untimely death in a bathing accident, 'The apostleship of parochialism, the praise of local self-government, the untiring advocacy of purely English precedents as opposed to French philosophies and German government, was the ruling passion of Mr Toulmin-Smith's useful, honourable, and patriotic career.'[88]

French-sounding and French-spirited, centralisation was the enemy of honest Anglo-Saxon government eating away at the moral fabric of society. 'No interference by any central authority can be permitted without a necessarily consequent sacrifice of independence, self-reliance, and efficiency.' Centralisation was anathema to progress as it 'destroys every incentive to effort at improvement; and damps every ardor for the progressive development of resources'. There was no need for self-help when the state would do everything for you. Once shackles were placed on the 'true and free action of all Institutions of Local Self-Government', then 'zeal and energy are thus killed out, and the continual impulse to advance is quelled as far as possible'. 'In short, the system of centralization is demoralizing, degrading, and inconsistent with a spirit of freedom.'[89]

Through books with engaging titles such as *Local Self-Government and Centralization*, pamphlets and speeches, Toulmin-Smith made the historic case for local autonomy and outlined the multiple evils of a centralising state: the kind of state which allowed excise officers to storm an Englishman's home on little more than an anonymous tip-off. More specifically, he railed against the collectivist evils of public health legislation and sanitary reform which dared to take power out of the hands of the parish. It was a message of short-sighted economy dressed up as noble Saxon rectitude which found a receptive audience amongst hard-pressed *petit bourgeois* ratepayers.[90] As a Londoner, and later a member of the Hornsey vestry, he proudly championed the capital's fragmented and deadly system of governance. For Toulmin-Smith even the unreformed canker of the Corporation was a model of propriety, 'possessing in its character of an associated community and body corporate full powers of local self-government'. To his credit, the arch anti-centraliser was undoubtedly a man of principle, defending London's archaic vestry system even as the 1848 cholera made its way up to the airy environs of Highgate Hill.

Yet as the inadequacies of Britain's sanitary infrastructure became ever more glaring, advocates of reform were at last beginning to make the ideological case for intervention. The Saxon heritage of self-government and the modern spirit of *laissez-faire* started to be challenged. In a Health of Towns Association pamphlet, Viscount Ebrington declared that *laissez-faire* was in fact a foreign intervention which emerged from the nihilism of 'Voltaire and his school': 'Everything would take care of itself if it only were left to itself.'[91] But the human price of this foreign philosophy was verging on the criminal. Samuel Smiles voiced the danger with rare anger:

> When typhus or cholera breaks out, they tell us that Nobody is to blame. That terrible Nobody! How much he has to answer for. More mischief is done by Nobody than by all the world besides. Nobody adulterates our food. Nobody poisons us with bad drink. Nobody leaves towns undrained … Nobody has a theory too – a dreadful theory. It is embodied in two words: laissez-faire – let alone … When people live in foul dwellings, let them alone, let wretchedness do its work; do not interfere with death.

The HTA even plucked up the courage to take on the Saxon argument for self-government. In their view, it was little more than an excuse for corrupt vested interests, inefficient jobbery and misguided notions of economy. 'Whence proceeds this outcry against interference with local self-government and Saxon institutions? Is it from the labouring classes, the largest portion of the community, inhabiting the courts and alleys? ... Or is it not rather from Paving Boards, and from local officers, whose works, apart from the question of economical administration, are proved to be the most inefficient and the most wasteful in the country?'[92] Where would this passion for outmoded Saxon government lead us, demanded one of Chadwick's protégés, since we 'might as well demand at once a return to the heptarchy; or claim for Marylebone and St Pancras the right of declaring war against each other, or against France'.[93] This was exactly the scenario which G.K. Chesterton later explored in his satirical squib *The Napoleon of Notting Hill*, in which the peculiar, frock-coated civil servant Auberon Quin is bizarrely anointed King of England and immediately reinstitutes 'the arrogance of the old medieval cities applied to our glorious suburbs'.

> All these boroughs where you were born, and hope to lay your bones, shall be reinstated in their ancient magnificence – Hammersmith, Kensington, Bayswater, Chelsea, Battersea, Clapham, Balham, and a hundred others. Each shall immediately build a city wall with gates to be closed at sunset. Each shall have a city guard, armed to the teeth. Each shall have a banner, a coat-of-arms, and, if convenient, a gathering cry.[94]

vi DIRTY BUT FREE

By the mid-1840s, the case for public health reform was becoming unanswerable and the new Liberal government which entered office under Lord John Russell in 1846 was determined to legislate. Their case was strengthened by the looming threat of further cholera as well as by the presence of numerous HTA members on the parliamentary front bench. The only question was what form the legislation would take.

With the passing of the Baths and Washhouses Act in 1846 and more importantly the Nuisances Removal and Diseases Prevention Act, a model for central–local relations had already been established. The principle was to devolve as much power as possible to the municipality while encouraging a reliance upon expert opinion and retaining some authority for executive boards of guardians. Central government had to encourage local authorities to reform while also making a great show of their rights of self-government. As Russell put it to Edwin Chadwick, who with his Liberal patrons now in power was fast pushing for radical measures, 'They will not bear a Prussian minister, to regulate their domestic affairs, so that some faults must be indulged for the sake of carrying improvements in the mass.'[95]

After numerous false starts, what emerged was the Public Health Bill of 1848. Championed by Lord Morpeth, the HTA member and now First Commissioner of Woods and Forests (which curiously put him in charge of public health), the Bill cut through the decades of Local Acts and Improvement Commissions. In their place, it proposed that either the Town Council or an elected Local Board of Health should administer all aspects of public health within the municipality. Most controversially, it also established a centrally staffed General Board of Health with the power to force localities to form a Local Board if a petition was received by one-tenth of ratepayers or the death rate from all causes had reached the figure of twenty-three per thousand. The Boards could ensure that no new house was built without proper drainage or privies; that the local water supply and sewage system were clean and effective; as well as exercise powers over insanitary 'nuisances', highways, burial grounds and public parks. A new system of rates was introduced, but most significantly of all Local Boards could raise money for works of a permanent nature by borrowing against the rates for up to thirty years.[96]

Morpeth's Bill was a truly innovatory piece of legislation which, while encouraging local initiative, ceded new powers to central officials and established the national principle that no municipality had the prescriptive right to be dirty. Unsurprisingly, defenders of local self-government and Britain's unique Saxon heritage were appalled and attacked the proposals as a nefarious attempt at centralisation which threatened to undermine the ancient virtues of the Saxon municipality. It was part of an underhand agenda to introduce Continental systems of governance into the British way of life. And, unfortunately for Morpeth, it was his task to introduce the Bill into Parliament just as the Continent was descending into yet another bout of revolutionary turmoil. With Paris in flames, critics of the legislation did not hide their glee.

Edward Baines of the *Leeds Mercury* set the tone by protesting that while his paper was 'most anxious that every town in the kingdom should have the benefits of good sewerage and pure water', they 'could not consent to purchase these blessings by a permanent infringement of the rights of municipal bodies, and, through them, of the people at large'. But as the situation on the Continent began to deteriorate, Baines's opposition to the Bill became more pointed: 'The only acknowledgment claimed by the authors of the Public Health Bill for this magnificent promise, is that the people shall quietly stand by while their municipal institutions – the boast, the characteristic of England, and the bulwark of her liberties – are offered up a holocaust on the altars of that newest of ideas – centralization.'

In March, Baines called again upon all admirers of 'free municipal institutions' to mobilise quickly against the Bill. He juxtaposed his appeal with an extended, scaremongering lead column on the anarchy dismembering Paris. In a series of articles worthy of today's *Sun* newspaper, Baines ran a full-page analysis of why England was different from the

Continent. Of all the European countries, England was most free from the threat of internal convulsion because of its peaceful capacity for improvement and reform. One of the reasons for this was its avoidance of centralisation and the strength of its municipal institutions.[97] The *Manchester Guardian* followed suit with lead articles on the 'Revolution in France' and 'Lord Morpeth's Bill for Promoting the Public Health'. If the Bill passed unmodified, the *Guardian* warned, 'it will go far to destroy the independence of local government altogether'.[98]

But it was *The Economist* which most potently linked the events in France with the spectre of active government under the guise of sanitary reform. As the French nation spiralled out of control, the leader columns filled up with minute analysis of what had brought France to this sorry state. Over-regulation, over-centralisation, too great a dominance of Paris, too many bureaucrats, absence of local self-government – all figured highly in *The Economist*'s hall of shame:

> They have stifled manufactures, they have checked the growth of a town population, they have prevented hands being drafted from agriculture to new arts, and have much contributed to bring on the present condition of France, even including the revolution. In truth it is impossible to calculate all the consequences of interfering with the useful employments of the people; and those must be deaf to the voice of experience, who, in spite of such warnings, now propose to import into England something like the absurd regulations of France.

Morpeth's Bill would destroy Britain's thriving civic base and betray the country's Saxon heritage. As one of the most militant defenders of the rights of local self-government, *The Economist* was quite happy to argue for bad sanitation rather than the moral degradation of centralisation. The 'mental imbecility which is everywhere produced in the masses by such subversion', when one man in Whitehall is made responsible for the governance of millions, would 'seem to us far greater evils than the perpetuation of bad smells, and generation of partial diseases, suppose they were the inevitable consequence of non-interference by authorities with the dwellings of the multitude'.

British cities, the magazine continued the following week, did not need the meddling of imperfect legislation to improve their health. For, 'whatever may be said on the score of unhealthiness against Liverpool, London, Manchester, Birmingham, and Sheffield, the spirit of improvement is alive in them ... it has altered the whole face of them within the memory of man, and requires only to be enlightened by science, not impeded by quackish legislation'. The consequences of such benevolent law-making as the Public Health Bill were mental and moral stupor. 'We warn our readers in all the great towns of the empire, that they may bid *adieu* to neighbourly peace, enterprise, and individual improvement', if the Bill became law. To centralise power in the quest for general political uniformity, 'is little better than a covert plan for despotism'. Yet precisely that process – as symbolised by the Public Health Bill – was something 'now happening amongst us'. Far better to be dirty and free.[99]

Similar arguments linking the Bill with the Continental and especially French revolutions were made during its passage through the House of Commons. Radicals and Tories alike mangled Morpeth's legislation. Charles Pearson, MP warned that the Bill would deprive cities and local authorities 'of the independent conduct and action which was the glory of our Saxon institutions, and, like rickety children, be placed in the go-cart of central Government'. An MP who had supported the Bill when Morpeth first introduced it in 1847, he now had a change of heart. 'He confessed he had once been partial to the system of centralization, but recent events had shown him its rotten and dangerous character; and he should, therefore, give the Bill every possible opposition.' Even the Government seemed conscious of the intellectual case of the opposition. As the Chancellor of the Exchequer, Charles Wood, later put it to Lord John Russell, it was evidently wise 'to put as little on the Government whose overthrow causes a revolution as you can and to have as much as you can on the local bodies which may be overthrown a dozen times and nobody be the worse'.[100]

David Urquhart, MP, the maverick anti-centralisation campaigner and ally of Joshua Toulmin-Smith, argued that sanitary reform was just that – a politically dangerous measure of centralisation. The Public Health Bill 'was an usurpation by the Government of the powers of local bodies, and a destruction by the general Executive of local rights. The people of England loved and possessed municipal government, and they would not suffer themselves to be jockeyed out of it.' He regarded the 'results' happening in other countries as the 'inevitable tendency of placing inordinate power in the hands of Government'. In particular, the fate of the late government of France 'should be a warning to the would-be centralizers in this country'.[101] Toulmin-Smith himself could not contain his anger at the Bill's betrayal of the British tradition. 'No scheme more demoralizing and mischievous, in every respect, was ever introduced by the enemies of human freedom and progress.' Not only would the legislation destroy improvements in sanitation that the institutions of local self-government were implementing, but 'mental and moral elevation, social well-being and responsibility, political independence, commercial freedom' were all to be sacrificed at the shrine of centralisation.[102]

Despite the howls of Saxon indignation, the measure was passed and the first effective steps along the road to better public health were tentatively travelled. But the reformers didn't have it all their own way. London remained an impassable obstacle. From their power base at the General Board of Health, Chadwick and Morpeth (along with Lord Shaftesbury) wielded unprecedented powers over provincial cities, but they were impotent to improve the capital surrounding their Gwydyr House headquarters. With great rhetorical assistance from Toulmin-Smith, the Corporation of London had fought an impressive rearguard action against the 1848 Bill and managed to exclude the City from its provisions. Chadwick had to make do with the 1848 Sewers Act which tinkered with the Metropolitan Commission of Sewers and at least provided for a Medical Officer of Health in the City (a fierce supporter of local self-government, Dr John Simon, received the appointment). London's local administration continued to be carried out by 300 different bodies deriving their powers from 250 Local Acts of Parliament. It would not be until the 1855 Metropolis Management Act and the creation of the Metropolitan Board of Works that there emerged a coherent metropolitan administration annulling all the overlapping commissions, vestries and trusts. And yet even then, the City was excluded. For by the mid-1850s the Saxon spirit, which had survived the Norman Conquest and could certainly outlast a bit of sanitary legislation, had resurfaced with a vengeance.

vii Revolving Despots: Chadwick and Haussmann

With his knees lodged under the table at Gwydyr House, Edwin Chadwick had used his executive position on the Board of Health to harry, humiliate and bludgeon into place a proper public health strategy. Displaying his usual Stakhanovite industry, Chadwick rolled out sanitary reform across the country. By 1858 the Public Health Act measures had been adopted in 219 places, with sewers laid and cesspools cleaned out. Chadwick, however, was a Benthamite: a man driven by the logical, rational need for human improvement guided only by expert advice. As such, he was blind to politics as the art of the possible and his brusque, antagonistic manner, combined with his unrelenting ardour for personal feuds, rapidly diminished the General Board of Health's ministerial support. Even his great patron and ally Lord Morpeth could not put up with Chadwick's ways and resigned from the Board. And the situation was not helped by Chadwick's misguided decision during the 1849 cholera epidemic to flush out London's sewers into the Thames in an attempt to eliminate 'miasmatic' deposits.

So when the General Board of Health's term came up for renewal in 1854 the omens were not promising. Indeed, the lead-up to the event turned into an anti-Chadwick witch-hunt. Even Lord John Russell turned on the man who had inspired one of his government's greatest legislative successes, telling the Commons 'that he [Chadwick] did not take sufficiently into account the habits of self-government of this country, and the desire there was in all local bodies to continue that government in their own hands'.[103] There was also admiration across the political divide for the improvements which John Simon had achieved in cutting cholera rates in the City of London without any interference from central government. Simon had shown how the voluntary principle, the self-governing principle could work in practice. For perhaps the first time in his public career, Chadwick sensed the direction the political wind was blowing and, with his health visibly suffering after years of highly personal criticism, tendered his resignation. *The Economist* did not exactly wish him well. 'He is essentially a despot and a bureaucrat,' they remarked in a valedictory piece. 'He thinks that people ought to be well governed, but does not believe in the possibility of them governing themselves well. He would coerce them to their own good.' The magazine suggested he might prosper in a Russian court where the principles of self-government were not so familiar.[104]

With him went the rest of the Board. In its place emerged a distinctly neutered creature headed by the local self-government enthusiast, Sir Benjamin Hall (of Big Ben fame). The Board's powers of central authority were slowly stripped while the arch-localiser John Simon was appointed Medical Officer. The *coup de grâce* was delivered by the 1858 Local Government Act, which wound up the General Board and signalled a return to the old ways of doing things. The reforms were in fact part of a broader impatience with central

bureaucracy which flowed from Whitehall's disastrous handling of the Crimean War campaign. To Toulmin-Smith and
others in his highly active Anti-Centralization Union the governmental blunders and 'functionarism' exposed by the
hapless war effort were testimony to the dangerous fallacy of
centralisation. Balaklava had shown what could happen when
the constitutional principles of self-government were so systematically flouted. The late-1850s legislation sought to
redress the balance and stay the hand of governmental growth.
Local authorities were now free to adopt public health provisions or not as they, and they alone, saw fit. The Saxon spirit
had won out.[105]

Lord Morpeth's 1848 Bill might then be regarded as a somewhat pyrrhic victory for Chadwick and the public health
movement; a momentary advance in sanitary reform cruelly
overturned by the 1858 self-government backlash. But in
reality there were bureaucratic and political forces now at
work which meant the role of central government in setting
guidelines and enforcing standards would only expand. In fact,
it was the 'dirty party' who were on the defensive. Helped by
a new cadre of doctors and health inspectors co-ordinated
by the Local Government Act Office, cities began slowly to
improve their sanitary infrastructure. This was the start of
Loch Katrine and the Bazalgette era, the era of public works
and mid-Victorian can-do engineering. By 1864, a further 268
towns had established local Boards of Health – although now
of their own volition. Meanwhile, medical and sanitary advice
offered by expert opinion in London was regularly sought by
municipal authorities.

Central government did not wither on the vine. Instead,
each time a major public health crisis hit Britain and each
time the voluntary principle was seen to fail, there were calls
for an extra degree of government superintendence. The purity
of the Saxon bequest was gently undermined by every municipality which failed to rise to the responsibility of self-
government. In response, the 1865 Sewage Utilisation Act,
the 1866 Sanitary Act, the 1875 Artizans' and Labourers'

Dwellings Act, and the 1875 Public Health Act encroached further upon civic autonomy, giving government the power to discipline negligent authorities and enforce minimum sanitary standards. The mid-century compromise over social and public health policy was reached with central government assuming an expert supervisory role and local government ostentatiously exerting its right to implement the requisite measures. Britain's Norman and Saxon blood, the spirit of centralisation and local self-government, were finally united in a tempestuous union under the banner of the 1858 Local Government Act Office.

The Norman–Saxon relationship was changing in another direction as well. Not only as the century progressed and the British Empire began to blossom did the virtues of the conquering Norman seem previously undervalued; there was also a noticeable change in attitudes towards that grotesque epitome of Norman centralism, Paris. The capital city which had condemned France to decades of revolution, which had sucked the nation's life-blood from it, and which was the symbol of all that was vain and fickle about urban life became subject to a mounting trickle of praise. As early as the mid-1840s, in a statement which must have won him few friends, the Liverpool physician William Duncan expressed his admiration that in France, 'the promotion of the public health is a constant object of solicitude, both with the government and the municipal councils'. He was particularly impressed with the Parisian approach to public health and the importance attached to that city's 'Council of Health'.[106] Yet the Parisian golden age was only just beginning.

On 30 June 1853, the bullish figure of Georges-Eugène Haussmann was appointed *Préfet* of the Seine *Département* in the new administration of Emperor Louis-Napoleon. Over the next twenty years, the feverish energy of Baron Haussmann turned the city of revolution into the city (as Peter Hall memorably put it) of perpetual public works. He built seventy-one miles of new road, laid 400 miles of pavement, doubled the number of trees to 100,000, laid sixty miles of sewers (still

twenty-two miles short of Bazalgette), demolished 27,000 and
built a further 102,000 houses – as well as thirteen new
churches, two synagogues, five town halls, six barracks and
five theatres.[107] He redecorated the Louvre, repaired Notre-
Dame, covered the Canal of St Martin with an arch, restored
the church of St Etienne du Mont and reconstructed the The-
âtres Lyrique and the Cirque. His *grands boulevards* cut
through the revolutionary working-class districts, while his
great public spaces and proliferating public parks made Paris
a fit monument for the empire of Napoleon III. The old medieval city of de Tocqueville's *ancien régime* was taken apart
courtyard by courtyard, arrondissement by arrondissement.
'My Paris, the Paris in which I was born, the Paris of the
manners of 1830 to 1848, is vanishing, both materially and
morally', noted the brothers Edmond and Jules Goncourt in
their journal of 1860.[108] And the historian François Guizot, for
one, was appalled. 'The history of Paris is the history of France.
There was not a street that had not been the scene of some
important event. The new Rue de Rivoli and Boulevard de
Sebastopol, are fine communications, especially for military
purposes, but they are hateful to the historian and to the
artist.'[109]

Haussmann's disembowelling had removed the fermenting,
insurrectionary urban wilderness. In its place, the Paris of the
Second Empire was becoming a city of social spectacle, peopled
by Baudelaire's *flâneurs* strolling the arcades and promenades.
'The crowd is his domain, just as the air is the bird's, and water
that of fish. His passions and his profession is to merge with
the crowd. For the perfect idler, for the passionate observer it
becomes an immense source of enjoyment to establish his
dwelling in the throng, in the ebb and flow, the bustle, the
fleeting and infinite.'[110] Haussmann's aggrandising verve was,
of course, exactly what the Victorians had come to expect of
Paris, unaware that the inspiration for much of his vision
had come from Nash's redevelopment of Regency London.
Haussmann's Paris fitted perfectly with a conception of the
city's flashy, wealthy and ultimately corrupt character. Louis-

Napoleon was merely continuing the centralising traditions begun by Louis XIV, accelerated by Robespierre and crowned by Napoleon I. And no doubt soon the Parisian mob would rise again.

But, curiously, many in mid-Victorian Britain did not display their traditional Saxon opprobrium for the changes going on. Instead, there was something approaching jealousy. *The Builder* magazine compared London unfavourably with the Seine city and actively praised the 'improvements in the French capital', especially in the field of 'practical hygiene or sanitation'. Despite Bazalgette's strenuous efforts, 'the British capital is far behind the French in general effect of architecture in streets and public places; and the difference in this particular alone contributes to that which exhibits itself in comparative mortality'.[111] Others admired the ability of a city to develop an urban plan and then stick to it – an altogether novel habit for the Victorians.

By the 1860s there was a festering impatience with the classic, Victorian way of doing things: of voluntarism, civic association and muddling through. Since the 1835 Municipal Corporation Act, local councils had been placed in nominal charge of their towns and cities and yet very little seemed to have been achieved by them. Instead, it was the churches, business leaders and friendly societies which had run the city. The result was the kind of institutional disorder which afflicted everything from sanitary reform to welfare provision to building regulations. The romance of the *folc-moot* was waning as Paris showed what could be achieved by a dynamic municipal leadership directing the city's strategy. 'Mark how differently they do things in Paris,' commented *The Times*. 'The programme of palaces to be decorated, theatres to be removed, libraries to be transformed, churches and cavalry barracks to be built, to say nothing of the little item "all the old boulevards to be reconstructed", has something of the magical in its character.'[112] Many now looked to Haussmann's Paris as a model of achievement. One of the numerous English visitors impressed by the city's aesthetic transformation was a screw salesman from the Midlands called Joseph Chamberlain. If Paris could do it, why couldn't Birmingham?

[8]
JOSEPH CHAMBERLAIN
AND THE MUNICIPAL GOSPEL

'How clearly, how vividly, he stands out in memory! The mass of iron-grey hair heavily streaked with white, nearly covering his ears, quite covering his broad, low forehead; bushy eyebrows nearly straight, and beneath them dark brown eyes that twinkled and flashed and blazed and melted; the nose straight or nearly so; the mouth partly hidden by a straggling beard, – firm, but not so firm that it could not curve with scorn or quiver with emotion.' There he stood. The Revd George Dawson, resplendent in his trademark velvet coat and colourful cravat, ready once more to inspire the city with his uniquely beguiling oratory. Behind him was Birmingham's newly built Free Reference Library, another testimony to the growing civic ambitions of the 'hardware village', and in front of him an expectant crowd of thousands. The preacher, acclaimed by Charles Kingsley as 'the greatest talker in England', did not disappoint.

His speech was a *tour de force*, effortlessly seducing the Brummie audience, playing shamelessly to their roaring cultural aspirations. Dawson declared that the Library's opening amounted to a new era in Brummagem civic life; the 'expression of a conviction on your part that a town like this exists for moral and intellectual purposes'. He went on:

There are few places I would rather haunt after my death than this room, and there are few things I would have my children remember more than this, that this man spoke this discourse at the opening of this glorious library, the first

fruits of a clear understanding that a great town exists to
discharge towards the people of that town the duties that a
great nation exists to discharge towards the people of that
nation – that a town is a solemn organism through which
should flow, and in which should be shaped all the highest,
loftiest and truest ends of man's intellectual and moral
nature.[1]

Standing amongst that crowd so bewitched by Dawson's
rhetoric was a young businessman from the local screw-
manufacturing firm of Nettlefold & Chamberlain. The company's ambitious marketing director, Joseph Chamberlain, had
arrived in Birmingham twelve years earlier and had since then
come to love his adopted city. But he too felt it was worthier
of a greater ambition; that Birmingham could achieve more
for its people and posterity beyond metal-banging and button-
making. Dawson's words struck a chord in the young industrialist's imagination. Year later, he reached the conclusion
that the only way a city could effectively shape the destinies
of its citizens was through the actions of its municipal authority. The moral purpose of the city lay in its council.

As Chamberlain was pondering the civic future of Birmingham, a contingent of Glaswegian city elders were making
their way from the drizzle of the Clyde to the resplendent
banks of the river Seine. Lord Provost Blackie, Glasgow's
reforming Mayor, along with the City Architect John Carrick
and the Medical Officer of Health, Dr William Gairdner, had
embarked on a fact-finding mission to investigate the much-
lauded improvements of Baron Haussmann. In their own
words, they went to gather information on the 'recon-
structions ... and great works which it was understood have
been, and still are in progress to improve the sanitary condition, as well as the external aspects of the city'.

The visitors were certainly impressed by the sewage infrastructure and public health planning under development; but
it was the glistening appearance of Louis-Napoleon's Paris
which wowed them. They wandered the wide boulevards

carved through the medieval arrondissements; admired the broad public spaces prised open for civic preening; marvelled at the new housing apartments; and, as products of Glasgow's internecine civic politics, could only envy Haussmann's unitary authority over the city. They returned embarrassed at the miserable state of Clydeside and committed themselves to mirroring the Haussmann miracle: 'we have much to learn from Paris ... and particularly modern Paris'.[2] In practice this meant a determination to gut the crumbling Old Town and impose a cohesive civic style across a remodelled city. And the authority which was to design and implement this work was not going to be the usual patchwork of voluntary societies, railway developers, and civic guilds. Instead, it would be the Town Council.

The sanctity of *laissez-faire*, of legislative let-alone and governmental non-interference, had been progressively (if haphazardly) undermined by growing local and central intervention through the 1840s and 1850s. Concerns over urban sanitation and public health slowly augmented the power and reach of town councils. Part of the consequence of that change was a conceptual shift in perceptions about what the nineteenth-century city stood for. At the beginning of Queen Victoria's reign, Britain's filthy, booming cities resembled the dark angels of industrialisation. They symbolised the shock of the Industrial Revolution: the new working conditions, the social disjuncture, the wealth, the poverty and the dark Satanic mills. The northern cities at the hub of modern textile production became inextricably defined by industry and its deleterious human by-products. Manchester, as we have seen, was 'Cottonopolis'; Bradford, 'Worstedopolis'. This reverence for commercial enterprise as well as a belief in the virtue of voluntarism dominated the urban culture. As chapter three explored, this was the era of civic voluntarism: that fabric of friendly societies, Athenaeums and Mechanics' Institutes which dominated the mid-Victorian city. Yet by the time Dawson celebrated the opening of Birmingham's Library, those organisations and the exclusive ethos they embodied were being forced to share the civic terrain with an increasingly confident set of democratic town councils.

The instinctive identification of unbridled commerce and voluntary self-help with city life was beginning to shift. The reforms which Birmingham and Glasgow embarked upon from the late 1860s forged a different understanding of the city which linked urban identity with popularly elected municipal authority. Cities became known not just by the activities of their businesses or the culture of their civil society, but also by the reforms and rhetoric of their councils. The vision of the city which George Dawson enunciated and elected councillors attempted to deliver, presented an alternative understanding of urban life. In time, this approach to city governance would gain the title of 'gas and water' or 'municipal' socialism. But what eventually became known as collectivism began as something more akin to tooth-and-claw capitalism. And the first steps along this putative trek towards socialism were taken by one of the most enterprising, buccaneering capitalists of mid-Victorian Britain.

i JOSEPH CHAMBERLAIN: UNITARIAN AND BUSINESSMAN

The political career of the Chamberlain dynasty begins and ends with Oliver Cromwell. Joseph Chamberlain first shuffled into public life by opposing the motion 'That the Character and Conduct of Oliver Cromwell do not entitle him to the Admiration of Posterity'. Unfortunately, his fellow bright young things at the Birmingham and Edgbaston Debating Society did not share his respect for the late Lord Protector and the motion was carried by fifteen votes. Eighty years on, the ghost of Cromwell returned to haunt the Chamberlains when his son Neville lost the premiership in that vital debate of May 1940 after Leopold Amery bellowed Old Nol's words from the back benches, 'You have sat here too long for any good you have been doing. Depart, I say, and let us have done with you. In the name of God, go!' And with that the

Chamberlains were gone; the only twist in the tale being that Leopold Amery's son, Julian, would go on to complete the first substantive biography of Neville's father, Joseph.

Given Joseph Chamberlain's lineage, it was not surprising he had chosen to champion 'the good old cause' in that initial Birmingham debate. The Chamberlain clan (on the female side) were descendants of Richard Sergeant, a Nonconformist minister who suffered in the great ejection of Puritans from the Church of England in 1662. Emboldened by this martyrdom, the radical heritage continued down the generations and by the nineteenth century the Chamberlains were proud Unitarians of the practical, rational variety who held the scientist Joseph Priestley as their guide. Joseph Chamberlain's father (also called Joseph) was said to introduce himself with the not altogether welcoming phrase, 'Yes, sir, Joseph Chamberlain and a Unitarian'.

The Chamberlain business was not, at this stage, screws but cordwaining, a form of shoe manufacturing using new leather. Following his father, and his father before him, Joseph Chamberlain senior was a member of the prestigious Cordwainers' Company and expected all his six sons to join him in their City of London firm. Close to the workshop, under the shadow of St Paul's, stood the Carter Lane Chapel where the Chamberlains worshipped with other upwardly mobile Unitarians. It was an active congregation which concerned itself with the present as much as the future life by supporting a mission in the East End. There, amongst the poverty and violence engendered by the casual labour of London's docks, the young Joseph Chamberlain taught (secular) Sunday School classes. He never forgot the tough social environment his pupils struggled with and how those conditions could cripple their life chances.

Joseph junior was the first-born, entering the world in July 1836 at the family home in the then genteel south London village of Camberwell. Later, the by now quite sizeable Chamberlain clan moved to Highbury in north London, a location which would become synonymous with the Chamberlains and after which Joseph would later name his own house in Birmingham. He was a happy child, cared for by loving parents, affectionately teased by doting sisters, and well liked within the broader Unitarian community of cousins and family friends.

Snapshot moments from these early years give us something of the engaging psychological make-up of a man who would come to transform Victorian civic life as well as British politics. At his primary school in Camberwell, he founded a Peace Society – but immediately started fighting with his fellow pacifists. As he later recalled, 'It was to be a charitable society, and we had a fund of 5 pence half penny to distribute, of which I contributed the largest share, for I remember my uncle gave me a four penny bit. The quarrel was as to what should be done with so large a sum. Eventually, after long consideration, it went to a crossing sweeper near the school, and that was the end of the peace society.'[3] The youthful Chamberlain also developed a passion for the works of Charles Dickens as well as a precocious interest in amateur theatricals. Both perhaps pointed to his later love of political drama and weakness for sartorial flair.

At fourteen, Chamberlain was sent to University College School. Established as a junior component of the new University College, the school was specifically created by the radical triumvirate of Jeremy Bentham, James Mill and Henry Brougham to educate children of the Nonconformist middle class. In contrast to the Anglican obscurantism of the great public schools, the ethos was profoundly rational and determinedly unsectarian. Mathematics, science and French were taught in a culture of progressive modernism which engendered an impatience with the *ancien régime* mentality of Oxbridge, Westminster and Windsor. Chamberlain blossomed in the studious environment and even sought extra learning by attending lectures at Polytechnic Institutions during school vacations. A successful academic career was his for the taking.

Unfortunately, Joseph Chamberlain senior had other ideas. Unable to afford to send all his sons to university, he had come to the steadfastly egalitarian decision to send none at all. So after two years at UCS, Joseph was taken from the rarefied environs of Gower Street to learn his trade at the cordwainer's bench in the City. Characteristically stoical about this change in fortune, he began at the bottom of the business, mastering the ancient craft and understanding the principles of book-keeping and commercial management. However, Chamberlain learnt more than just the family business. Amongst the Chartists and reformers who made up the company's artisan core, he also picked up an early taste of radical party politics to supplement his theoretical education.

Despite his forced enthusiasm, Chamberlain was not destined for cordwaining. In one of those intriguing quirks of history, an American inventor named Thomas J. Sloan had patented a machine for the fully mechanised production of wood screws. First displayed at the 1851 Great Exhibition, Sloan's invention promised to revolutionise the British screw-making industry. One businessman particularly exercised by this breakthrough was Joseph Chamberlain's uncle, John Sutton Nettlefold. The husband of Chamberlain senior's sister, Martha, Nettlefold had built up a moderately successful wood-screw manufacturing company based in Birmingham. When he saw the Sloan invention in Hyde Park, Nettlefold realised instantly he would either have to buy up the patent before his competitors or face a lingering commercial decline as other firms mechanised. Nettlefold opted to fight and made a bid for the machine. However, the costs of the patent as well as the extra capital required to start up full-scale manufacturing were too much to afford on his own. He was forced to seek a partnership with his wealthy brother-in-law, who agreed to invest in Nettlefold but with the proviso of sending his son to watch over the new enterprise.

In 1854, Joseph Chamberlain arrived in the West Midlands. That year saw the start of a relationship between the family and the city which would, through the extended Chamberlain family and more specifically the political career of his sons (Austen and Neville, like their father, both represented

Birmingham in the House of Commons), last well into the mid-twentieth century. It has been described as the city's 'Chamberlain tradition'.[4] At his death in 1914, *The Times* remarked how 'Mr Chamberlain's work in Birmingham and his unresting devotion to the city of his adoption, and Birmingham's almost passionate loyalty to him through every phase of his public life, make up a unique tale of services mutually, gratefully, and affectionately rendered ... To a degree unparalleled in modern British politics he and Birmingham were synonymous.' And the lead article noted in conclusion that, 'As the head of a large, prosperous, cultivated, and public-spirited clan of relatives and connexions, his position in Birmingham grew to be almost patriarchal.'[5]

Chamberlain could not have arrived in the city at a better time. The mid-Victorian boom of the 1850s and 1860s benefited few cities more obviously than 'the hardware village'. With the Crimean War raging and the widespread introduction of steam-power into factory production, the scene was set for sustained growth in the armaments, button and small metal industries that constituted Birmingham's commercial base. Nettlefold and Chamberlain surfed the economic wave utilising their technological advantage to dominate the screw-making market. Joseph Chamberlain proved himself a master of corporate strategy: he pressurised rival firms to sell out and those that refused he aggressively undercut before racking up prices. As inspired in his commercial marketing as he would later prove in politics, Chamberlain operated a sophisticated battery of discounts and promotional ruses. In the back-room, he also worked hard on the numbers, developing a familiarity with commercial finance which would later prove vital when he took on the city's utility companies.

Chamberlain established his entrepreneurial zeal most spectacularly during the Franco-Prussian War. With an unwavering eye for the mark-up, he realised that the 1871 siege of Paris meant the capital's screw manufacturers would be unable to supply their customers. Displaying an ease with European language and culture unknown among his fellow Birmingham businessmen, Chamberlain set off for a tour of France to capture this virgin export market. Thanks to his entrepreneurialism, Nettlefold & Chamberlain rose to control seventy per cent of Birmingham's screw output and by the early 1870s employed some 2,500 workers in sites across the city. As one of the firm's cashiers matter-of-factly put it, 'Money was made very rapidly after Mr Joseph came.'

In his first years in Birmingham, Chamberlain lived the life of a committed bachelor. He took lodgings in Edgbaston and became an active member of the Debating Society despite a legendary haplessness at public speaking. It was said he relied too heavily on notes and displayed a showy propensity for French quotations. At work, he brought with him the ethos of Carter Lane by fostering a culture of rational self-improvement amongst the workforce with reading evenings, a French class, a Debating Club, a Benefit Club and even a Working Men's Institute. But he was his father's son and on his arrival in Birmingham, he had joined the city's premier congregation at the Church of the Messiah. There he found himself in familiarly earnest, upper-middle-class surroundings with the elite of Birmingham's Nonconformist community: around him sat the great commercial and intellectual clans of the Kenricks, Nettlefolds and Martineaus. It was amongst this congregation that he met his first wife, Harriet Kenrick, daughter of the influential West Bromwich businessman Archibald Kenrick. Their marriage in 1860 cemented Joseph Chamberlain's remarkable ascent through Birmingham's social and commercial landscape.

ii Easy Row and the Municipal Gospel

There was another Birmingham. As Joseph Chamberlain walked his daily journey from Edgbaston to his offices on Broad Street, he passed a bleak industrial landscape of crumbling housing, insanitary streets and grinding deprivation. Mid-Victorian Birmingham was in a sorry state. The city had traditionally prided itself on its close-knit, artisan-based

cohesiveness. In contrast to the fractious distance which separated the Manchester factory-owner or Liverpudlian merchant from their proletariat, Birmingham's small-scale
metalworks had created a different urban culture. There was a
high degree of job specialisation which in turn led to extensive
interdependence of craftsmen across different trades. Richard
Cobden ascribed the town's social and political state to 'the
fact that the industry of the hardware district is carried on by
small manufacturers, employing a few men and boys each,
sometimes only an apprentice or two; whilst the great capitalists in Manchester form an aristocracy... There is a freer
intercourse between all classes than in the Lancashire town
where a great and impassable gulf separates the workman from
the employer.'[6]

Since the 1830s and the days of the Birmingham Political
Union (one of the pioneer campaigns for electoral reform),
the city had also been renowned for its radical, democratic
sentiments. However, the initially progressive aspirations of
Thomas Attwood and his fellow reformers had since been
channelled into far more conservative directions. Powerful
petit bourgeois hostility towards civic governance combined
with an absence of truly wealthy 'merchant princes' to produce
a civic infrastructure in a state of almost total collapse. It was
not just that leading Birmingham ratepayers systematically
resisted sanitary or civic improvements (which they did);
worse, the opponents of improvement were actually in charge
of the Council. The city was held to ransom by a uniquely
reactionary shopocracy.[7]

In 1842, in an extraordinary display of negative civic pride,
Birmingham conservatives prepared a petition pressing the
government to revoke the city's Charter of Incorporation
(passed only four years earlier) in the hope of reducing the
rates. As central government forced cities to assume ever
greater civic responsibilities, Birmingham resisted with ever
greater fury. Council revanchists blocked the purchase of Birmingham Waterworks Company, refused to sanction a new
Improvement Bill, and as a result had their overdraft from the

Birmingham Banking Company halted, leading to the cancellation of a number of infrastructure projects. As a late-Victorian chronicler of the city described it, 'Birmingham some thirty years ago was considerably under the influence of men of the unprogressive tradesmen class... In their private businesses they were not accustomed to deal with big transactions and high figures, so that spending large sums of money, if proposed, filled the brewer, the baker and candlestick maker with alarm. They were careful and economical, but their care in finance was apt at times to be impolitic, and their economy has in several cases proved to have been somewhat costly.'[8]

In the mid-1850s the situation deteriorated further when a group of 'Economist' tradesmen, victuallers, shopkeepers and small manufacturers took control of the newly empowered Council. This shopkeeper cabal was headed by the old-school radical and tabloid hack Joseph Allday, a man renowned across Birmingham as much for his wife's tripe shop as his own particularly scurrilous news-sheet, the *Argus*. True to every caricature, one of the Economists' first acts was to dismiss the borough engineer and replace him with his assistant at half the price. They then slashed spending on roads by fifty per cent within the year. With their eye trained on the rates, they viewed the institution of the Council (which had only come into full being in 1852) with a wary hostility. In the Economist world view, the city of Birmingham was most certainly not, as Dawson put it, a solemn organisation through which flowed man's truest and loftiest ends. Rather, it was a random amalgamation of individuals who were unaffectionately joined together mostly for purposes of business. The role of the municipal authority was to ensure a light policing of the streets, a respect for contracts and that was about it.

To show his rich contempt for the institution of the Council, Allday convened meetings in the rowdy, smoky and purposively disrespectful venue of the Woodman Tavern on Easy Row. Neither the conduct nor the venue in which the councillors governed their city was designed to foster any sense of pride or purpose in municipal activities. The attitude of the

Economist councillor was adeptly satirised by the pro-reform paper the *Town Crier*, in the figure of 'Gideon Bagsworth':

> Gideon is strongly possessed with the notion that every-thing local and provincial is of necessity vulgar, and that to become a Town Councillor is nothing less than to undergo a voluntary degradation... To this disgraceful prejudice, Gideon adds an enormous dead weight of indolence in all matters unconnected with his own particular business, or his own domestic life, and more than all, he 'devotes' himself to these two objects with a perfect fanaticism, a fanaticism which he only does not recognise as pure selfishness, because it is sufficiently expansive to include wife and family. When he has subscribed to those insti-tutions which other Bagsworths subscribe to, he considers that he has amply fulfilled the duties of citizenship, and that he is thereby exempted from any obligation to take the slightest real personal interest in the well-being of the town in which he lives, moves, and makes his money.[9]

This contempt for municipal activism, this absence of faith in the function of the city and its Council, was reflected in Birmingham's urban environment. It was a disgusting city. Thomas Carlyle characteristically sank his teeth in: 'As a town it is pitiful enough – a mean congeries of bricks, including one or two large capitalists, some hundreds of minor ones and perhaps, 120,000 sooty artisans in metals and chemical produce. The streets are ill-built, ill-paved, always flimsy in their aspect – often poor, sometimes miserable. Not above one or two of them are paved with flagstones at the side ... Torrents of thick smoke, with ever and anon a burst of dingy flame, are issuing from a thousand funnels.' John Thackeray Bunce, the influential editor of the *Birmingham Daily Post*, described how the city centre was 'so poor and neglected ... that Bir-mingham people, jealous of the credit of their town, were ashamed to show it to visitors as the heart of Birmingham'.[10] This was the miserable vista which greeted Joseph Chamberlain twice a day as he walked his way to and from work; a sight which made him ever more determined to raise the city from this mire.

A cohesive case for improving Birmingham was first voiced not by newspaper editors, businessmen or politicians but from the pulpit of the Church. One of the curiosities surrounding the philosophy of municipal socialism is that its origins are located in Christian doctrine – the very belief system which socialism had originally attempted to subsume. More specifically, it was the work of three Nonconformist ministers – George Dawson, Robert Dale and Henry Crosskey – who commandeered late Victorian Birmingham with all the civic fury of nineteenth-century Savonarolas.

At the front was Dawson. Born in 1821 the son of a Baptist schoolmaster, he was early on trained up for the ministry. After attending Glasgow University, he returned briefly to teach at his father's school before taking up a position at Birmingham's Mount Zion Chapel in 1844. However, what he had ingested as a student at Glasgow had begun to bear fruit. Slowly, the German Romanticism, the philosophical Idealism and, above all, the work of Thomas Carlyle which he had studied as an undergraduate inched away the mental constraints of Baptist doctrine. Dawson found himself increasingly unhappy with the formal teachings of the Church. He was a literary, romantic man who discovered that Carlyle's passion, spleen, and unerring faith in humanity seemed to speak to a more fundamental belief than any formal orthodoxy. Among his first sermons at Mount Zion was a series entitled 'Signs of the Times' – the biblical title of Carlyle's most inspired essay.[11]

Unfortunately for Dawson, the congregation at Mount Zion did not take so kindly to his theological free-wheeling and in 1847 he was forced from the chapel. Yet such was the impact and affection he had generated within sections of his flock, many helped to fund and then to follow Dawson over to his new Church of the Saviour on Edward Street. Drawing on certain aspects of German biblical criticism as well as the radical Unitarian teachings of James Martineau, Dawson created his own unique doctrine distinct from the evangelical Nonconformity of his fellow ministers. But no one had to sign up to it, as the Church of the Saviour demanded no creedal basis for membership.

For it was not the rigorous theology which drew the crowds to Dawson's pulpit, rather the brilliance of his preaching. Kingsley's 'greatest talker' was one of the most inspired lecturers of the mid-Victorian generation. Described with a sneer by the *Spectator* as 'a kind of literary middleman between writers like Carlyle and Ruskin and those ordinary English manufacturers, or merchants, or tradesmen, who like thought but like it well illustrated', he was sought across industrial cities for his lectures on Cromwell, Coleridge, German poetry, Italian history and any other subject which took his fancy.[12] This same intellectual heterogeneity and ease of oration inspired his ministry. In Birmingham, he was loved by his congregation for his homely manner of preaching (as well as his fine looks). 'In speaking, whether in the pulpit or on the platform, he spoke as he might have spoken to half a dozen friends gathered round the fireside. The style was easy, natural, intimate, unstudied, and direct ... It was talk – talk at its best; it was not declamation. And the talk was never hazy, but always clear.'[13] Above all, it was the practical applicability of his day-to-day theology which drew in the crowds. The Dawson gospel was perfectly attuned to the aspirant mentality, the easy-going commerciality, of Birmingham's Nonconformist bourgeoisie. His fellow minister and political ally, Robert Dale, described the style.

> Quickly descending from generalities to the particular, he would talk to his congregation about Avery's scales, and about yard measures, about tea and sugar, about adulterated mustard and about butter half of which was fat, about stocktaking and long credit ... about all the details of the doings of a scoundrel who had been tried a day or two before for

his transactions in connection with a fraudulent joint-stock company; about dress and jewellery; about dinners and evening parties; about all the follies and sins and vanities of the day. This made his sermons effective. Men of business knew what he meant when he talked about honest trading. Women knew what he meant when he talked about simplicity of living. Masters and servants, parents and children all had their turn, and could hardly miss the intentions of his lessons.[14]

So, what was Dawson's message? What was the sermon he preached? At its emotional core was an idea of community drawn from the works of Goethe, Schiller and other German Romantics. He imagined the modern city as an organic whole whose purpose was to secure an ideal of the good life for all its citizens. 'To him a city meant something besides the policeman and the scavenger: it had larger and higher functions than to maintain public order and to provide for the public health,' explained one contemporary biographer. 'For a city, as he conceived it, was a society, established by the divine will, as the family, the State, and the Church are established, for common life and common purpose and common action.'[15] Birmingham was more than just a random conglomeration of individuals as Allday and his fellow Economists suggested. It was, in fact, the modern incarnation (with all its theological connotations) of the institutions which had traditionally bound civic society together: the guilds, the Church, the old associations. In language which no doubt made his Mount Zion worshippers shudder, he described the city as the new corpus. 'This then was the new corporation, the new Church, in which they might meet until they came into union again – a Church in which there was no bond, nor text, nor articles – a large Church, one of the greatest institutions yet established.'[16] At the emotional and spiritual core or nave of this new Church was the elected municipal authority: the Council.[17]

Elements of this conception of the city as a vast, non-doctrinal church were drawn from intellectual currents

fashionable on the Continent. Like other internationalist liberals, Dawson passionately backed the idealistic nationalism
sweeping Europe, even visiting Paris with parts of his congregation in the aftermath of 1848. He raised funds and
organised rallies in support of Mazzini's struggle for Italian
self-government and Lajos Kossuth's campaign of liberation
in Hungary against the Austrian Empire. The insight Dawson
took from these visitors and the cause they championed was
a sense of reverence for the nation. In Hungary, Italy, as well
as Austria and France, partisans of self-government developed
an almost mystical sanctity about the idea of nationhood: the
nation as embodiment of the spirit and character of its people.
Dawson transferred that idealism from the nation to the city,
investing the civic realm with equal religiosity. In his schema,
the city bestowed the same duties and deserved the same
patriotic affiliation as the nation. The municipality was the
rightful recipient for modern feelings of *patria*.

Continental radicals also gave Dawson a broader understanding of what modern liberalism might entail, an idea of
liberalism which did not necessarily equal a radical hostility
to the state as an agent of political oppression, but rather as a
beneficent force for society. Through intervention and regulation, the state and the municipality could be an agent of
progress. For Dawson, the old radicalism of Cobbett – of an
instinctive hostility towards political power as a source of
corruption and domination – appeared increasingly redundant.
It was a political approach which he shared with a former
member of his congregation and subsequently minister of
Carrs Lane Chapel, Robert Dale. In a speech to the Birmingham Junior Liberal Association, Dale described the shift
in thinking:

> In my early years, and when I began to think about politics,
> one chief article in the creed of extreme Radicalism was
> this – that the powers of government, municipal and
> national, should be restrained within the narrowest possible
> limits; that government should do nothing for us except

protect us against force and against fraud . . . But Radicalism has gradually come to discover that with political power in the hands of the people, municipal and national government may contribute very much to the positive development of national life. . .[18]

What all this meant in practice was a wholly new approach to the philosophy and functions of municipal government. It was a municipal gospel.[19] It was a belief that municipalities could in fact achieve more than Parliament in helping their communities; and a firm belief that, in contravention of years of separation between the earthly and the divine, between the vale of tears and the life ever after, it was a Christian duty to intervene through municipal authority to alleviate life on earth. In Dale's vision of city life, brought together in his aptly titled *The Laws of Christ for Common Life*, it was municipalities which had the power to redress the inequalities of the human condition. The duty of every Christian man was thus to put himself forward in the services of the Council. This was the practical import of the municipal gospel: an unparalleled advocacy of the virtue of the town councillor. The position which Allday and his fellow Economists held only in order to prevent civic improvements, a position which through the spirit of the Woodman Tavern had been systematically denigrated, was now elevated to almost worshipful heights.

In Dale's secular theology, civil authority was nothing less than a divine institution and the actions of the Christian man were as much judged in the civic arena as the spiritual, for the two were commensurate. 'The man who holds municipal or political office is "a minister of God." One man may have just as real a Divine vocation to become a town councillor or an MP as another to become a Missionary to the heathen. In either case it is at a man's peril that he is "disobedient to the heavenly vision."'[20] It was a Christian duty to agree to serve on the sewage committee or watch committee or even accept the mayoralty. Those who declined to wield political power were guilty 'of treachery both to God and to man'.[21] Dawson backed up Dale in typically less clerical language by denouncing those who thought they were somehow 'above' municipal service. 'And how many are there who don't meddle in these matters, and with whom the affectation of superiority, with which they decline to do so, is a simple cover for indolence? How sweet it sounds – this philosophical indifference and superiority! How mean it really is! By it and through it, the government of towns and nations sinks down into the hands of the vulgar, the self-seeking, and the mean.'[22]

This was exactly the form of governance that Birmingham was labouring under. Dawson and Dale together with Henry Crosskey, the Unitarian minister at the Church of the Messiah (where Chamberlain worshipped), were determined to change this. These three turbulent priests entered public life with the verve of political street brawlers. Not only did they preach politics from the pulpit, they came down from on high and canvassed their cause on the street. Week after week they fought the Economists and reactionaries. Week after week they spoke of a new Jerusalem, a new city on the hill to be built there in Birmingham along the lines of their municipal gospel. It was time for all good men to stand for election and for the Council to understand its mission and fulfil its duty. 'All the year through', explained Crosskey's biographer, 'whenever there was a chance of preaching the municipal gospel, he pleaded with pathetic earnestness and with passion for the new policy. When the contests were on, he went to two or three meetings night after night in the obscurest parts of the town, and appealed, as for his own life, for the return of the right men. His intensity was astonishing. He spoke as if the whole fate of the town depended on the result of the ward election.'[23]

Other clerics became worried for the triumvirate's spiritual health. 'Dale, when do you mean to quit politics and look after your soul?', waspishly enquired the Roman Catholic Canon O'Sullivan. Of course, for Dale municipal activism was as much the work of God as any penitence or confession.

The message slowly seeped through. Battered by the relentless propagation of the municipal gospel, the Nonconformist elites who took up the pews in the chapels of the Saviour, the Messiah and Carrs Lane began to involve themselves in the life of the Council. They began to stand for the Council and gradually the governance of Birmingham changed – with quite remarkable consequences. As the son of Robert Dale eloquently described it:

> It began, as all such movements do, in the dream of solitary and silent hours. Then it made its way into the minds of a few men of kindred spirit. And the dream became an ideal; and the ideal grew into a conviction; and conviction flamed into enthusiasm; and enthusiasm took shape in policy, and passed from the study and the club to the platform and the pulpit, and swept through the wards of the city, and fired men's minds and kindled their hearts, until the ideal that had once been a dream had become a reality. Those years in which the new gospel began to spread and to prevail – those glorious hours of crowded strife – can we ever forget them?
>
> Bliss was it in that dawn to be alive;
> But to be young was very heaven.[24]

iii Gas and Water

The politician destined to implement this vision, to take the municipal gospel from an ideal to a reality, was Joseph Chamberlain. He drank deep at the well of Dawson and listened keenly to the admonitions to service uttered by his own minister, Crosskey. Looking back, early historians of the Birmingham civic renaissance described how Dawson and Chamberlain worked as a dynamic double-act. The preacher infused the minds of the people with municipal reform, while Chamberlain, 'the cool, calm man of business, the long-headed, persevering, patient, yet acute politician', had the guile to see it through.[25] His spirit of worldly Unitarian engagement, which had inspired him to work in the East End Sunday Schools as a young man, was now drawn to the cry for civic improvement. Widely respected in Birmingham civil society and personally prosperous from the success of Nettlefold & Chamberlain, he now had the time and inclination to involve himself in matters outside business. As a good entrepreneur, he also sensed the moment was ripe for a constructive engagement in municipal life.

Frustratingly, the actual chronology is not so clear-cut. For what drew Chamberlain into active political life was not initially urban renewal, but education reform. In 1867 Chamberlain was invited to a meeting held by Birmingham's newly elected Mayor George Dixon to discuss the state of the city's schooling. There he first encountered the circle of Liberals and Nonconformists who would prove the vehicle for his political ascendancy, chief amongst them John Thackeray Bunce and the Unitarian ironmonger and councillor, Jesse Collings. At the time, education reform was felt to be particularly pressing as that year's Second Reform Bill had, by doubling the electorate from 1,430,000 to 2,470,000, enfranchised a great mass of the urban upper working class. If these future masters were not educated, then political meltdown and social anarchy were regarded as only a matter of time. Chamberlain himself was more sanguine. From his arrival in Birmingham, he had taught night classes both at the Nettlefold & Chamberlain works as well as at the Messiah Chapel. He championed education not out of trepidation, but from a conviction that it remained the finest mechanism both for working-class self-improvement and for broader class harmony.

Chamberlain quickly proved himself to be the most committed and indeed eloquent advocate of the need for free and universal schooling. When Dixon, Collings and the other Birmingham Liberals then established a National Education League, loosely modelled on the Anti-Corn-Law League, to campaign for a universal system of elementary education funded by rates and managed by local authorities, Chamberlain manoeuvred himself into the post of Chairman. In an early taste of the machine politics which would come to be the hallmark of his public life, Chamberlain soon had a nationwide campaign up and running complete with hundreds of branches, a sophisticated publicity system and an effective lobbying operation. And they needed it. For waged against the League was the imposing figure of 'their' Liberal Prime Minister, W.E. Gladstone.

The issue, as so often with Gladstone, was one of religion. While the Grand Old Man was willing to introduce universal elementary education, as a staunch Anglican he was adamant that the children should be educated in the tenets of the Church of England. Chamberlain and the other members of the predominantly Nonconformist League were appalled: to be forced to pay for their children to be educated in an alien religion was anathema. The Puritan blood still flowed in Chamberlain. Freedom of religion was (as his ancestor Richard Sergeant had borne witness) a matter of conscience and he was determined not to fund state-sanctioned Anglicanism. The League demanded instead a system of non-denominational religion. To press their case, they arranged a meeting with Gladstone at No. 10 Downing Street where, fearing a haemorrhaging of Liberal support in the Nonconformist heartlands, the Prime Minister and his Education Minister W.E. Forster responded to the League's concerns with their 1870 Education Act.

Despite their success in Westminster, back in Birmingham the League had hopelessly misread the direction of legislation. They assumed the Education Act would give control over schools to the elected local authority. Consequently, the League mobilised hard in the 1869 elections to get their men onto the Council. Among the successful candidates was Chamberlain himself who took the predominantly working-class St Paul's ward with a healthy majority – no doubt helped by the large number of Nettlefold & Chamberlain employees in the district. Yet thanks to a last-minute back-bench intervention, the 1870 Forster Act allocated responsibility for schooling to directly elected boards and not the Council. The League had misplayed its hand and at the subsequent school board elections lost heavily.

But Chamberlain was now on the Council. And while concerns over education policy might have first drawn him into municipal politics, the speeches of Dawson and the sermons of Crosskey soon expanded his horizon. He too started to express his faith in the almost limitless virtue of local government. In contrast to the Parliament at Westminster, concerned with lofty matters of Empire and war, he celebrated the immediacy of local government to the people. Its actions had the capacity to change people's lives substantially for the better by transforming the urban environment. 'By its means you will be able to increase their comforts, to secure their health, to multiply the luxuries which they may enjoy in common, to carry out a vast co-operation system for mutual aid and support, to lessen the inequalities of our social system, and to raise the standard of all classes in the community,' he later declared.[26]

With a new faith in the authority and functions of the Council came a resolute belief in the duty of service. Chamberlain ingested the municipal gospel and, while he never suggested office was a divine calling, he certainly strove to elevate the reputation of councillors both by his own service and by encouraging his peers. He shared with Dawson the view that there was little more contemptible than sophisticated condescension towards those willing to stand for election or (even worse) the narrow-minded hostility of the *petit bourgeoisie* to men of means and vision trying to improve the city. 'I do not think there is any sneer more undeserved than that directed against men who were willing unselfishly to devote their best energies and services to the town in which they lived, and I have always thought those who professed to think themselves above such work were infinitely beneath it. There is no nobler sphere for those who have not the opportunity of engaging in imperial politics than to take part in municipal work, to the wise conduct of which they owe the welfare, the health, the comfort, and the lives of 400,000 people.'[27]

For this was what attracted Chamberlain into office: the potentiality of power. As permissive legislation granted local authorities ever greater sanction to intervene within the city, the capacity of councils grew ever more varied. According to Chamberlain, 'If a man has leisure, and wants occupation, his taste must be difficult indeed if he cannot find some congenial employment in connection with the multifarious duties of the Town Council of Birmingham.'[28] With Chamberlain into office came a cadre of leading businessmen and professionals inspired by the preaching of the municipal gospel and excited by the opportunity of power. The grip of shopkeepers and the ethos of the Woodman Tavern was beginning to wane. The proportion of substantial businessmen on the Council grew from 7.8 per cent in 1862 to 23.4 per cent in 1882, while tradesmen and small businessmen declined from 32.8 per cent to 17.2 per cent over the same period.[29]

With the city's most celebrated ministers preaching an ethic of municipal service and civil society's most fashionable figures standing for office, it became a mark of social cachet to belong to the Council. The tripe-eating caricature of Gideon Bagsworth seemed a world away from the high-flying, confident yet proudly Brummie entrepreneurs now in charge of the city. The Times suggested that, 'Perhaps no such capable and enterprising men have ever met together on an English public body as gathered round Mr. Chamberlain on the Birmingham Council.'[30] Dale, partly responsible for the birth of this avant-garde civic spirit, waxed lyrical on its incredible effect:

> It now became the ambition of young men, and cultivated men, and men of high social position to represent a ward and to become aldermen and mayors ... The November Ward meetings assumed a new character. The speakers, instead of discussing small questions of administration and of economy, dwelt with glowing enthusiasm on what a great and prosperous town like Birmingham might do for its

people. They spoke of sweeping away streets in which it
was not possible to live a healthy and decent life; of making
the town cleaner, sweeter and brighter; of providing gardens
and parks and music; of erecting baths and free libraries, an
art gallery and a museum ... Sometimes an adventurous
orator would excite his audience by dwelling on the glories
of Florence, and of the other cities of Italy in the middle
ages, and suggest that Birmingham too might become the
home of a noble literature and art.[31]

At the forefront of it all was Chamberlain. He used the
political experience he had garnered in the Education League
to mould a Liberal Association machine, run by his loyal
Prussian organiser Francis Schnadhorst, which time and again
swept the Birmingham elections. Helpfully, Chamberlain had
the backing of much of the local press with his most vocal
cheerleader, John Thackeray Bunce, holding the chair of the
Birmingham Daily Post. The previously diffident debater from
Edgbaston now revelled in all the high drama of public life,
taking to the crowds, controversy and electioneering with
relish. And in a clean sweep in 1873, he secured the Liberals
not only the Council but also the directly elected school
boards. 'We have given the Beer and Bible Tories a smashing
defeat – polling 291,000 votes to their 195,000', he wrote
to his friend John Morley. Others in Birmingham were less
sanguine about Chamberlain's hegemonic control over commerce, media and Council. 'Now, me Lads, let us be equal,
and I will be your King', was the message which adorned one
hostile cartoon during the 1873 campaign.

Despite the criticism, Chamberlain had won through and
his prize was the mayoralty. He handed over control of Nettlefold & Chamberlain to Joseph Nettlefold (just as the mid-
Victorian boom was coming to a bumpy end) and left business
for politics, determined to make real the lofty ideals of the
municipal gospel. 'In twelve months by God's help the town
shall not know itself,' he announced with Cromwellian flourish.[32]

Like Napoleon's generals, the best political careers demand luck. And Chamberlain entered local politics at precisely the right moment. The Second Reform Act of 1867 along with the Municipal Franchise and Assessed Rate Act of 1869 had eased the hold of the economist ratepayers, of the shopocracy, over municipal activities. In terms of urban local government elections, the electorate approximately quadrupled bringing in some sixty per cent of working-class men. Many of these new voters were not owner-occupiers, but tenants and wage-labourers. Known as 'compounders', they did not pay rates directly in person but rather as a part of their rent through the landlord. What this meant in political terms was a large constituency far less sensitive to the costs of civic improvement and municipal intervention than the pre-1867 narrowly property-based electorate. Together with these new voters Chamberlain struck up a serially successful political alliance. It was a mutually beneficial match between an urban patriciate and an urban proletariat which left only the *petit bourgeois* ratepayer to pick up the tab.[33]

Yet even Chamberlain, with his *de haut en bas* approach to matters fiscal, realised his grandiose plans were often more than the ratepayers could bear. As the Council's duties inexorably expanded in the early 1870s, and as Chamberlain fully developed his municipal ambitions, it was apparent that a new source of funding was required. Chamberlain's solution would become known as 'Gas and Water' socialism. The municipal ownership of utilities could bypass the Council's limited tax base by using profits which would have gone to private shareholders to fund instead civic improvements or even reduce the rates. In turn, a sustained programme of investment in improving sanitation and civic infrastructure could alleviate the most expensive forms of urban degeneration and, in a virtuous cycle, reduce the burden on ratepayers.

'Municipal reformers look to Birmingham as the eyes of the faithful are turned to Mecca,' declared one adulatory analysis of Birmingham Council in 1895.[34] But despite the well-worked self-image of Chamberlain as a municipal pioneer, the precedent of Victorian councils providing gas and water was already well established. The pre-incorporation Manchester street commissioners had built a city gasworks as early as 1817 and by 1870 there were some forty-nine municipal gas undertakings including civic rivals Leeds and Glasgow. Similarly, many other cities had already taken control over their own water supply. Glasgow had its Loch Katrine, but Manchester, Cardiff and numerous others had also acquired local utilities – many doing so in the 1860s as Birmingham still laboured under the Economists' reactionary regime. As Asa Briggs has noted, Birmingham was not only not ahead but stood in fact quite far behind the times.[35]

Even if Birmingham was not the first, it was Chamberlain's achievement to give a philosophical voice to the growing momentum towards municipalisation. He elevated the policy above sheer pragmatism and invested the dull business of utility ownership with a profoundly ethical dimension. Chamberlain set out two clear principles to guide Birmingham's programme. He believed that 'all monopolies which are sustained in any way by the State ought to be in the hands of the representatives of the people, by whom they should be administered, and to whom their profits should go. In the second place, he was inclined to increase the duties and responsibilities of the local authority, in whom he had so great a confidence, and would do everything in his power to constitute these local authorities real local parliaments, supreme in their special jurisdiction.'[36] Both precepts guided his first foray into municipalisation.

Birmingham's gas was supplied by two happily complacent private companies: the Birmingham Light and Coke Company (est. 1819) and the Birmingham and Staffordshire Gas Light Company (est. 1825). Each had an equally fractious relationship with their largest single customer, the Town Council, and Chamberlain was determined to buy them out. As he had shown by his successful expansion of Nettlefold & Chamberlain, he was convinced of the benefits in economies of scale brought by amalgamation. Chamberlain aimed to combine the two companies together, but with the Council in charge. And as a municipal body, its rates of interest on borrowing would be far lower than those available to the private sector.

However, the Council would still have to raise the borough debt from £500,000 to a staggering £2.5 million. While these sums might well have put off the old Economist faction of tradesmen and shopkeepers, Chamberlain kept his nerve. Timidity would prove a false economy. Even after paying interest, Chamberlain calculated that the Council would begin making an annual profit of £14,800 which would rise to £50,000 per annum after fourteen years without increasing the cost of gas to the public. In addition to the commercial case, Chamberlain also argued the proposition in terms of the inherent virtue of municipal control. The scheme was, he suggested, 'practical evidence of the sincerity of the high opinion which he had always held and expressed of municipal institutions, and of the advantages to be derived from local self-government'.[37] The Council voted in favour of the initiative by a margin of forty-six to one.

In January 1874 Chamberlain entered negotiations with the gas utilities and in August 1875 the Birmingham (Corporation) Gas Act received the Royal Assent. As Mayor and architect of the scheme, Chamberlain placed himself as Chairman of the new Gas Committee. The Council had bought the companies out for £1,953,050 18s 11d and it now waited anxiously for the gas-into-money miracle to bear fruit. Nervous councillors didn't have to wait long. The first year's profits more than doubled the projected £14,800 to over £34,000. And it kept growing from there. Thanks to the scheme's extraordinary profitability, by 1879 some £80,000 had been allocated towards rate relief, £50,000 to the reserve fund and £35,000 to the sinking fund. In addition, by 1884 the price of gas had come down by thirty per cent while the city had gained a new recreation ground by the conversion of ten acres of derelict gas company land. Here was the municipal gospel in all its practical glory.[38]

While the municipalisation of the gasworks was intentionally profitable, Chamberlain made the case for controlling
the water supply not on the basis of future earnings, but because
of the benefits to be reaped by the different values inherent in
municipal rather than private control. Chamberlain argued
'that a private company must needs look to profits, whereas a
Corporation, having public funds at its command, would be
able to improve the quality of the water, and give an abundant
supply, irrespective of commercial return'. The case for
municipalisation was one of public health and social good.[39]

Because of its geographic location, Birmingham was a com-
paratively healthy city for industrialising Britain. However,
the effect of the Economist governance and their sustained
opposition to any investment in the urban infrastructure
meant that by the 1870s the death rate had risen to 25.2 per
thousand, which was some three per cent above the national
average. The city's sanitary state was particularly shameful.
A ratepayer reaction in the early 1850s had blocked the purchase of the local waterworks and with little municipal over-
sight, the monopoly supplier continued to operate along
aggressively commercial lines with minimal concern for
public health. As a result, the majority of the Birmingham
poor drew their water from filthy and often deadly local surface
wells rather than from piped water. Sewage and refuse facilities
remained backward, with a network of overflowing cesspools
which provided perfect conditions for a flourishing array of
zymotic diseases.

After the success of the gas municipalisation, selling the
water scheme to the Council was not tricky. Chamberlain's
fellow councillors supported the resolution without a vote,
the requisite Bill flew through Parliament, and by January
1876 a not-for-profit committee was in charge of the Birmingham water business. The success or otherwise of the
scheme was never meant to be charted through profits.
Instead, its very real achievements could be marked through
the cleansing and purifying of the city and by the number of
lives saved. By the early 1880s, the death rate had fallen from

25.2 to 20.7 per thousand. As Chamberlain memorably put it, 'We shall get our profit indirectly, in the comfort of the town, and the health of the inhabitants.'

As Chamberlain launched ever more ambitious plans for reform, he transformed the status of Mayor from benign dignitary to hands-on political leader. Employing the same mastery of tactics and familiarity with low cunning which gave Nettlefold & Chamberlain its powerful market share, Chamberlain foiled his opponents with speed, procedure and will-power. Economist councillors were forced to vote on resolutions as they tried to move an amendment; motions were carried as they were about to make a speech. In one correspondence, Chamberlain was even brash enough to boast of holding 'almost despotic authority here, and being able to carry out innumerable schemes'.[40] Although not yet sporting his trademark orchid (usually a Cattleya), his political confidence and substantial personal wealth were reflected in his *flâneur* styling. He was described at the time as wearing 'a black velvet coat, jaunty eyeglass in eye, red neck-tie drawn through a ring, very smart indeed'.[41] On occasion, he might turn up with a seal-skin top hat. Buoyed up by these municipal triumphs, Chamberlain made a crass tactical mistake by standing in 1874 as the Liberal parliamentary candidate for Sheffield. Despite embarking on a rhetorical swing to the Left in the hope of marshalling the city's radical artisan vote, he lost heavily. The normally supportive *Town Crier* could not resist a crack at Chamberlain's moonlighting with a ribald 'Impromptu on Our Mayor's Return':

> Joe Chamberlain, my Jo, Josh,
> When you to Sheffield went,
> You never dream't how quickly
> You homeward would be sent.
> You thought you'd put the 'screw' on,
> So 'forward' you did go,
> You're quite 'advanced' enough, Sir,
> Joe Chamberlain, my Jo.

Joe Chamberlain, my Jo, Josh,
Of the School-Board keep the chair,
Be humble and contented,
In the parlour of the Mayor.
You've now learnt how to cut, Sir,
You're very sharp, I know;
But Sheffield blades are sharper,
Joe Chamberlain, my Jo.[42]

With gas and water in Council hands, the political foundations of municipal socialism were laid. Chamberlain's energetic successes in Birmingham would soon spur other councils to take private utilities into public ownership. Yet the irony was that this 'socialist' endeavour proceeded from quintessentially capitalist principles: chiefly, the desire of large corporate businesses to have secure and cheap energy supplies. Such an impetus was not surprising given the hold business exercised over the city Council. Chamberlain the industrialist was not alone. Between 1860 and 1891, businessmen provided some fifty-five per cent of Birmingham's sixty-four councillors.[43] An American journalist of the time described how 'Birmingham is above all else a business city, run by business men on business principles'.[44] The business ethos was pointedly blessed by Dale, who delivered reverential eulogies on the lives of Birmingham's industrial elite and declared the mutual compatibility of commerce and religion. 'The 11th Commandment is that thou shalt keep a balance-sheet', was one of his favourite sermon sound bites.

No one more instinctively believed in the precepts of what might be termed 'municipal capitalism' than Chamberlain himself. As an avowed corporatist, he was an advocate of big business, rationalisation, and the beneficial interchange between municipal authority and private commerce. His outlook was, in fact, remarkably antithetical to the traditional Birmingham ethos of small manufactories with its radical suspicion of political intervention. He regarded his stewardship of Birmingham not in the tradition of John Bright or

Thomas Attwood, but as a modern chief executive. In an article for the American magazine *The Forum*, Chamberlain spelt out his philosophy in signally un-socialist language. 'The leading idea of the English system may be said to be that of a joint-stock or co-operative enterprise in which every citizen is a share-holder, and of which the dividends are receivable in the improved health and the increase in the comfort and happiness of the community. The members of the council are the directors of this great business, and their fees consist in the confidence, the consideration, and the gratitude of those amongst whom they live.'[45] And judged on those terms, his mayoralty hit all its budgetary targets. Another American visitor to the city was full of admiration for Chamberlain's fiscal management. 'Viewing the expenditure as a whole, it has been made more advantageously by far than any private firms or companies could have effected it, and the community, as individuals and as a corporate body, is the richer at least by two or three dollars for every dollar of the forty or fifty millions that the corporation has dared to borrow and invest.'[46] It was, as a celebrated magazine article put it, 'the best-governed city in the world'.

iv IMPROVEMENT

Chamberlain was interested in more than just maximising shareholder value; he was determined to leave a permanent imprint of his reforming administration. The Mayor was also convinced that the regeneration of the city's housing and urban infrastructure was essential to improving the standard of living amongst Birmingham's poorest. There could be precious little substantive social reform given the state of the social and civic environment. Chamberlain was determined to 'improve' the city: its streets, its houses, its civic fabric. Yet, as with the city's municipalisation programme, Birmingham was not the pioneer. Instead, that honour belongs to the city which had dispatched its councillors to learn the lessons of Haussmann's Paris back in 1866.

'There was in the very heart of the city one of the foulest ulcers that ever disgraced a modern city. Every approach to the old University was through a moral sewer of a most loathsome description, crowded with population, showing by its physique the extent to which the human form divine could be degraded by drunkenness and every attendant form of vice and profligacy.'[47] That was how one sanitary investigator described the miserable state of Glasgow's medieval city centre. The population of Clydeside had increased five fold between 1801 and 1861 and, while the middle classes had trekked west to escape the pollution and overcrowding, the Old Town had been left to crumble. Some 50,000 of the most unskilled and unfortunate working classes were crowded together in barely eighty-eight acres of courts and 'wynds' where typhus and cholera roamed freely. It was an area of viciously low life expectancy focused around heavy industries and blighted by a culture of what government Ministers might today term 'anti-social behaviour'.

The Old Town was an affront both to Glasgow's civic ambitions as the second city of Empire as well as the traditional Kirk impulse for paternal control of the feckless poor. It was also a scene of such desperate social misery to inspire even the most granite-hearted councillor to work for its improvement. In the early 1860s the mercantile Liberal elite who controlled Glasgow initiated some suitably ameliorative steps. The city's Medical Officer of Health, the Glasgow University professor William Gairdner, introduced new municipal facilities to combat fever and prevent unnecessary sanitary infections. At the same time, the Glasgow Police Act initiated a crackdown on tenement overcrowding by introducing minimum space-per-head requirements for houses of less than 2,000 cubic feet. The Sanitary Department established 300 cubic feet per adult, and half that for children under eight, as the health minimum. Outside premises suspected of multiple occupancy, a metal plate or 'ticket' was attached indicating the official capacity and the maximum number of residents permitted. This practice of ticketing gave the city Council an unprecedented capacity for domestic interference. The knock on the door from the municipal sanitary inspector became a regular ritual of Glaswegian life right through to the twentieth century; in 1904 alone, over 15,000 people were still living in ticketed houses.[48]

Ticketing was only a palliative. The Council realised it needed to embark upon more fundamental reform if it was going to counter the worst horrors of the slum. Attention focused increasingly on the kind of comprehensive demolition and co-ordinated redevelopment pursued with such success in 1850s Paris. Glasgow had already witnessed a certain amount of slum destruction; but, just as in London and other city centres, this had been driven by the commercial imperatives of railway companies with little regard for regeneration or rehousing displaced inhabitants. What the city required was a programme of improvement focused on public health priorities established by the Council and controlled by municipal officials. 'Our need was the sorest', declared one history of the city, 'for that a deadly gangrene was eating into the very heart of the City was obvious, clear also it was that the evil could be alleviated only by the strenuous surgery that had been exercised.'[49]

The 1866 City of Glasgow Improvement Act launched the most comprehensive plan of civic improvement in the nineteenth century; it aimed to transform Glasgow as Haussmann had remade Paris. Its provisions established an Improvement Trust with the Lord Provost (in this case, the staunchly pro-improvement Provost Blackie), the magistrates and Council as trustees with the authority to purchase and demolish whole districts deemed as health hazards. In practice, this meant the eighty-eight overcrowded acres of central Glasgow around Gallowgate, Trongate, Saltmarket and Glasgow Cross. Having cleared the congested slums, they then embarked on the construction of thirty-nine new streets as well as reshaping a further twelve. While the Improvement Trust laid the foundations for renewal, it was initially left to private enterprise to pursue commercial opportunities for reconstruction. Even so, private developers were to be subject to strict planning guidance. Glasgow's City Architect, John Carrick, had been particularly impressed by Haussmann's imposition of a unitary style and drew up similarly uniform guidelines for street widths, building heights, and even architectural idiom.

The cost of improvement was not cheap. To finance redevelopment, the Trust levied a rate across Glasgow of 6d in the pound for five years followed by 3d in the pound for a further ten years as well as borrowing a massive £1.25 million. The price of the scheme was most acutely felt by Lord Provost Blackie, who lost his seat on the Council as soon as the rate was introduced. But improvement continued without him and by 1874 some seventy-seven acres had been purchased by the Trust and over 15,000 homes destroyed while new streets were laid, sewers installed and houses erected. By 1876 over 28,000 people had been moved out of the blighted areas. Clause 28 of the Improvement Act required that no more than five hundred people could be removed every six months unless new accommodation was available. However, the terms were more honoured in the breach and although new lodgings and working-class estates were developed at Oatlands and Overnewton (to the south and west of the city centre and quite distant from most places of work), tens of thousands of Old Town residents were made homeless by the destructive speed of the city centre improvement.

Despite working-class criticisms (which would increase markedly during the 1880s), the Glasgow improvements were heralded as a model for urban renewal. Council officials, charities and journalists all came to witness the great Glaswegian experiment. Among the most enthusiastic was the London housing reformer Octavia Hill, who was pressing for the reforms in Glasgow to be repeated nationwide. 'As I looked over the official photographs of these "wynds", dark and dirty, and in every way degraded, and the Chairman and Secretary of the Trust which has had the workings of the Act kept saying, "This is still standing – but *that* is gone," and "That is taken away, and that and that comes down next month," I could not help feeling how proud and glad these men must be to have achieved such reforms.'

Ever the hands-on philanthropist, Hill walked the new streets of Glasgow.

> The next morning I went to see what remains of the old 'wynds' and closes. I found that here and there a house, here and there whole sides of a close or alley, had been taken down, to let in the brightening influence of sun and air. The haggard, wretched population which usually huddles into dark out-of-the-way places, was swarming over the vacant ground for years unvisited by sun and wind. Children were playing in open spaces who had never, I should think, had space to play in before. I felt as if some bright and purifying angel had laid a mighty finger on the squalid and neglected spot. Those open spaces, those gleams of sunlight, those playing children, seemed earnest of better things to come – of better days in store.[50]

Thanks partly to Octavia Hill's sustained lobbying, Glasgow's improvements caught the eye of Benjamin Disraeli's new administration. As the city's proud historians put it, in many of 'the important modifications of social legislation the towns and cities have been pioneers'.[51] In language replete with Octavia Hill's Manichaean tinge, the Tory Home Secretary, Richard Cross, introduced in February 1875 the Artizans' and Labourers' Dwellings Bill. 'I ask you on these dens of wretchedness and misery to cast one ray of hope and happiness; I ask you on these haunts of sickness and of death to breathe, at all events, one breath of health and life; and on these courts and alleys where all is dark with a darkness which not only may be, but is felt – a darkness of mind, body and soul – I ask you to assist in carrying out one of God's best and earliest laws, – "Let there be light."'[52]

It was a good example of Victorian national legislation drawing on local experimentation, and the Act followed Glasgow's lead by empowering Medical Officers of Health to declare a district within a town unhealthy, so forcing the local authority to take action. After an official inquiry, and further approval from the Local Government Board, a council could gain powers to buy condemned property by agreement or arbitration but without paying any extra price for a compulsory sale. Following its purchase, the local authority could destroy unfit habitations, sell the land on after infrastructural improvements, or arrange for the construction of new housing. As in Glasgow, what the Act did not allow without special permission was for municipal authorities to act as house-builders in competition with commercial constructors. Councils were to provide the conditions for private enterprise to flourish.

With the still unrectified problem of slum life as well as the destruction and homelessness wrought by unregulated railway development, the so-called Cross Acts were a step forward in co-ordinating urban planning and positioning the municipal authority rather than private enterprise as the dominant partner. In an ever-widening field of activity, the council was now regarded as the most responsible, the most relevant civic body for running British cities.

One of the first to utilise the Artizans' and Labourers' Dwellings legislation was one of its most vocal backers, Joseph Chamberlain. For the state of inner-city Birmingham rivalled anything Glasgow had to offer. The death-rate in the central St Mary's ward stood at almost twenty-six per thousand – double that of the thirteen per thousand enjoyed in Edgbaston. 'But besides this high death-rate', according to Bunce, 'there existed in consequence of the unhealthy condition of the district, a generally low condition of health amongst the population, leading to indulgence in stimulants, and to other vicious habits, and predisposing to various forms of illness, epidemic and otherwise.' As the political campaign for improvement began, pro-reform councillors made the case for demolition and reconstruction in provocatively gruesome style. 'In one case a filthy drain from a neighbouring court oozed into their little back yard,' was how Councillor William

White depicted conditions in the district under examination; 'in another, the sitting room window could not be opened, owing to the horrible effluvia from a yawning midden just under it; in another case, the fireside of the only sitting room had to be deserted, owing to the noxious percolation from a privy penetrating the wall within a foot or two of the easy chair ... it is quite time that the Council should endeavour, now that we have greater facilities given to us for battling with these evils, to bestir ourselves in every possible way, and to leave no stone unturned by which all or part of such evils may be removed.'[53]

City centre improvement allowed for further affirmation of Dawson's municipal gospel. Faith and charity were not enough to alleviate this miserable state; what was needed was direct action by the city Council to provide the conditions for man's moral fulfilment. As Chamberlain saw it, there could be no individual self-improvement amidst the grime and insanitary contamination of St Mary's. Setting out his staunchly activist, New Liberal credentials, Chamberlain told a sanitary conference in Birmingham, 'What folly it is to talk about the moral and intellectual elevation of the masses when the conditions of life are such as to render elevation impossible! What can the schoolmaster or the minister of religion do, when the influences of home undo all he does?'[54] Making the case for slum demolition and the provision of wholesome dwellings, the Mayor asked 'if the members of this Council had been placed under similar conditions does any one of us believe that he should have run no risk of the gaol or the hangman? For my part, I have not sufficient confidence in my own inherent goodness to believe that anything can make headway against such frightful conditions as those I have described.' The question was simple. 'The town must pay for this state of things in meal or in malt. We must pay in our health, or with our money.' And in true Chamberlain style, he went on to cost the city's high death rate and preponderance of preventable diseases in terms of lost wages and medical attendance at some £54,000 per annum. This lost revenue was, he calculated, more than enough to pay for the cost of improvement two or three times over.[55]

With its artisan economy built along canals, Birmingham had traditionally likened itself to the great commercial emporium of Venice. But it was Paris which provided the model for improvement. Chamberlain was only seventeen when he first saw Paris, but as he revisited it over the years during marketing trips he was each time impressed by the capital's steady transformation. Like the Glaswegian councillors, he too wanted to mirror some of the Haussmann magic. Chamberlain spoke of running 'a great street, as broad as a Parisian boulevard, from New Street to the Aston Road', opening up the centre for commerce and transport. His ally, Councillor White, enviously described 'the leafy verdure' of Paris, 'its healthy look, and its broad streets and boulevards, and charming flowery open spaces in every direction'.[56] Chamberlain might also have had in the back of his mind not the Paris of Haussmann, but the anarchy of the 1871 Paris Commune. In a later article on 'Labourers' and Artisans' Dwellings', Chamberlain warned that 'if something be not done quickly to meet the growing necessities of the case' then the people might well succumb to wild socialist theories.[57]

With the go-ahead from the medical and sanitary authorities, Chamberlain proposed clearing forty acres of slums, building eight acres of new streets and opening up the fetid medieval city quarters to the light of new offices and commercial space. The St Mary's ward, which lay to the west of Bull Street and south of St Philip's Cathedral, was to be cleared and to have driven through it a spanking new road christened Corporation Street. The historic slums, with their crime, immorality and infection, would be replaced by breezy boulevards reflective of Birmingham's new municipal dignity. Chamberlain worked hard to convince the Council to back his scheme of 'sagacious audacity'; and after the Mayor's Midas touch with gas and water they could not but concede.

What is all the more extraordinary is that Chamberlain managed to push the development through the Council at a time of intense personal grief. Following the death of his first wife, Harriet, during childbirth, Chamberlain had transferred his affections to another member of the influential Kenrick clan, her first cousin, Florence. She was a vivacious, radical Nonconformist who encouraged Chamberlain's more liberal policies and to whom he became completely devoted. Yet the punishing schedule of childbirth he insisted upon eventually undermined her never very robust constitution. Florence died in 1875, followed in quick succession by the other great female figure in Chamberlain's life, his mother. This double blow was almost too much for Chamberlain as he sank into depression, questioned his Unitarian faith and attempted to resign from the Council. In the end, he returned to his municipal work with a typically Victorian intent to see off low spirits with some hard grind.

In 1876 the Birmingham Improvement Act received the Royal Assent. Work started two years later after the Council had bought up £1.3 million of property for levelling and redevelopment, in the process expelling some 9,000 inhabitants. Out of the rubble of St Mary's came the new commercial emporium of Chamberlain's Birmingham, still apparent today along the broad, shop-lined streets and office blocks of Corporation Street, New Street, Hill Street and up to Victoria Square itself. For this was the beauty of the scheme. Improvement was not simply a matter of sanitary reform, it was also a very attractive commercial proposition. At an initial annual cost to the Council of only £12,000, Chamberlain planned to make Birmingham 'the retail shop of the whole of the midland counties of England' by turning the centre into a shopping Mecca. In doing so, he hoped to deliver the Council another revenue stream beyond municipalisation. By leasing out the compulsorily purchased and newly erected buildings on seventy-five- rather than ninety-nine-year leases, Chamberlain ensured the Council received a lucrative income source from valuable town centre properties – a source which would only grow, he assumed, because of the improved nature of the retail district. He spoke majestically of providing an 'unearned increment' for future councillors fifty years hence.[58]

In terms of sanitary health, civic commerce and municipal finances, the Chamberlain improvement scheme was a success. Bunce was typically upbeat. 'Slums and rookeries, pestilential morally and physically, have disappeared as if by magic, and have given place to streets and buildings worthy of occupying the centre of a great town.'[59] Mortality rates declined sharply in the city centre, businesses boomed, and (after a substantial period of debt and high rates) the Council began to collect a profit. But it took a long time coming. There were first of all complaints that the commercial side of the development was overshadowing the sanitary. In a subtle inversion of the Parisian analogy, critics spoke sarcastically of Corporation Street as a self-aggrandising 'Rue Chamberlain'. Many thought Chamberlain had finally got too far ahead of himself. 'His daring and dash almost dazed his fellow towns-folk, for, like Napoleon, he rushed on from one exploit to another with a rapidity that astounded his friends and confused and overwhelmed his foes.'[60] While streets and houses were merrily demolished, very little provision had been made for those thrown out of the old slums. This problem only inten-sified when the 1880s economic downturn put off private developers, while the Council was still prevented from build-ing its own houses by the terms of the Cross Acts. The poor had been driven out of the city but not until the 1890s was any co-ordinated Council provision made for their rehousing. The Haussmann analogy, the city despot who drove the poor from their Parisian homes to the suburbs of Montmartre, seemed to work both ways.

The Mayor himself was unabashed. In June 1876 he wrote to his friend Jesse Collings, 'I think I have now almost com-pleted my municipal programme and may sing *nunc dimittis*. The Town will be parked, paved, assized, marketed, Gas-and-Watered and *improved* – all as the result of three years' active work.'[61]

Chamberlain's vision of improvement extended beyond the

utilitarian business of housing and shopping; it was as much a matter of cultural as commercial achievement. He followed keenly the teachings of George Dawson that urban man does not live by bread alone. 'This means that the city which is a city must have its parks as well as its prisons, its art gallery as well as its asylum, its books and its libraries as well as its baths and washhouses, its schools as well as its sewers: that it must think of beauty and of dignity no less than of order and of health.'[62]

Housed in a seventy-foot by thirty-foot room inside the Central Library was the 'Corporation Art Gallery'. Opened in August 1867 with a collection of only fifty-six paintings on loan from private collectors and the Birmingham and Midland Institute, it proved an instant success. By December, almost 35,000 people had been to visit the gallery. Its popularity increased dramatically after a selection of choice artefacts from the 1851 Great Exhibition were put on show, followed by a collection of Turner paintings lent by the National Gallery in London. With substantial bequests from leading industrialists including Chamberlain, the glass manufacturer Thomas Clarkson Osler and, most generously of all, the engineering brothers Richard and George Tangye, the gallery embarked upon a series of eye-catching acquisitions. The latter donors were driven as much by concerns over the state of technical design and manufacturing skill as any purely philanthropic urges. By the mid-1870s, visitor numbers had swelled to nearly 300,000 and the gallery's popularity made it too large for the library site.

After a series of disastrous out-of-town relocations which saw attendance figures plummet, a new venue was decided upon which uniquely symbolised the Chamberlain municipal ethic. In the late 1870s, the widening responsibilities and growing income of the city Gas Committee forced it to look for new offices. It was Richard Chamberlain, Joseph's brother who followed him (after Jesse Collings) into the mayoralty, who came up with the innovative solution that the money from gas should be used to fund a central art venue. While the bureaucracy of the gas department would occupy the ground floor, the wonders of fine art would reside on the upper storey. It was a fitting symbol of the municipal gospel; a perfect mix of municipal capitalism and progressive, liberal governance. Gas financed a building filled with improving art bought with industrial largesse – while the ratepayer was compelled only to subsidise the maintenance and insurance costs.

In 1881 Richard Chamberlain laid the foundation stone of the City Museum and Art Gallery. Over the next five years an ornate testimony to resplendent civic classicism designed by the architect H.R. Yeoville Thomason rose up to dominate the piazza later known as Chamberlain Square. On one corner jutted forth that great symbol of Victorian Birmingham, the 'Big Brum' tower, a doughty Venetian challenger (modelled on San Marco) to Westminster's Big Ben. Inside the museum, a marble stairway replete with Corinthian pillars swept the culture-hungry citizens upstairs to the vestibule past a substantial bronze relief of the philanthropic Tangye brothers. Under the guidance of the newly appointed curator, Whitworth Wallis, the Birmingham gallery built up an impressive array of British, European and Persian art, with particularly fine collections of jewellery, brass-work, glassware and some wondrous Pre-Raphaelite paintings which still hang in the building's high-ceilinged Round Room. The motto emblazoned on the entrance hall memorial stone said it all: 'By the Gains of Industry We Promote Art.'

The triumphant style and construction of the Art Gallery was the conclusion of a greater programme of civic development all aimed at honouring the new municipal spirit. It was a monumentalist architecture, much of which was predicated on clearing out the old slums to make way for these sanitary, even sanitised spaces, which heralded the virtue of the municipal ethic. Whole communities were ushered out for wide streets, open squares and portentous official buildings designed to unite the city under one civic identity and create an environment for public man (but not yet the unaccompanied woman). The Birmingham Liberal J.T. Bunce argued that municipal government should be carried out with 'such stateliness of manner as to dignify the corporate life'. These symbolic spaces were precisely the forum for that public ritual of openings, foundation-stone layings, banquets and ceremonies which constituted the 'civic religion' of the Chamberlain tradition in late-Victorian Birmingham.[63] Through a range of rhetorical and visual strategies, the council was incrementally associated with civic and economic progress. The pageantry, the processions and monumental buildings all combined to celebrate a narrative of Urban Liberalism.[64]

The grandest of these civic landmarks was the symbolically named Council House in Victoria Square. Built in the mid-1870s around the corner from the Art Gallery site, this was an earlier Corinthian masterpiece from the studio of Yeoville Thomason designed to complement the quintessentially classical Town Hall of Joseph Hansom. At a ceremony for the laying of its foundation stone, Joseph Chamberlain made one of his greatest Birmingham speeches extolling the virtue of public buildings for the dignity of municipal life.

> I have an abiding faith in municipal institutions, an abiding sense of the value and importance of local self-government, and I desire therefore to surround them by everything which can mark their importance, which can show the place they occupy in public estimation and respect, and which can point to their great value to the community. Our corporations represent the authority of the people. Through them you obtain the full and direct expression of the popular will, and consequently, any disrespect to us, anything which would depreciate us in the public estimation, necessarily degrades the principles which we represent. Therefore, just as in past times we have provided for our monarchs and our princes palaces in which to live, just as now we provide magnificent edifices for our great State departments and have found a worthy home for the Imperial Legislature itself, so now I think it behoves us to find a fitting habitation for our local Parliament, to show the value we put upon our

privileges and our free institutions. Let me remind you that those old communities from whom we derive the model of our municipal institutions were never behind-hand in the discharge of this duty. We find in the old cities of the Continent – of Belgium, and Germany, and Italy – the free and independent burghers of the Middle Ages have left behind them magnificent palaces and civic buildings – testimonies to their power and public spirit and munificence, memorials of the time when those communities maintained the liberties and protected the lives of the people against the oppression, and the tyranny, and the rapacity of their rulers...[65]

Few buildings of Victorian Britain announce the dignity of municipal institutions and the debt owed to former urban civilisations with more gusto than the Council House. At 150 feet long and 162 feet tall, complete with Grand Dome and portico relief depicting 'Britannia Rewarding the Birmingham Manufacturers', it stands as a nineteenth-century Venetian palace with Victoria Square acting as its St Mark's. It is a bricks-and-mortar memorial to the municipal gospel. And, thankfully, Victoria Square has recently been renovated and cleaned, with new fountains and paving helping to re-establish its credentials as a civic piazza. The Council House itself stands as one of the defining monuments to Victorian civic pride, but among its statues of Joseph Chamberlain, Neville Chamberlain, Victoria and Albert, John Bright and James Watt (a scientific icon claimed by both Glasgow and Birmingham) you have to look hard for the intellectual origin behind this municipal movement. But there it is. Hidden behind the security guard's desk in the entrance hangs a delicate 1879 oil painting by local artist E.P. Thompson of 'George Dawson and Friends', depicting the founding members of the congregation of the Church of the Saviour. It was the congregation which built the Council.

Across Birmingham, a new urban architecture which drew heavily on the Venetian Gothic popularised by John Ruskin started to transform the civic fabric. The rebuilt Central Reference Library (cruelly demolished in the 1960s), the Birmingham School of Art behind the Art Gallery, and the extensions to the Birmingham and Midland Institute all testified to what J.T. Bunce called 'a municipal life nobler, fuller, richer than any the world has ever seen'. The architect of choice in late-Victorian Birmingham was the Mayor's namesake, J.H. Chamberlain. Although no relation, he shared the liberal values of the municipal gospel and expressed it most readily for the city's inhabitants in the forty board schools he designed, complete with polychromatic brickwork and Ruskinian styling. From the Council House to the local library to the community school, the values of civic pride and Council activism were celebrated with almost Soviet-style Realism in their architecture and iconography. Nowhere was this more the case than in J.H. Chamberlain's most celebrated commission: the 1880 Chamberlain Memorial in Chamberlain Square.

A beautiful Gothic spire standing at over sixty-five feet tall, it celebrates with a portrait medallion, mosaics and fountains the achievements of Joseph Chamberlain as Councillor and Mayor. Watched over by statues of James Watt and Joseph Priestley, it is a shrine to the 'Chamberlain tradition'. For, aside from the symbolic designs, what was so quintessentially Chamberlainite about the Memorial fountain was the plan for its water supply. While the Council budgeted for five million gallons yearly for the fountain (at a cost of £150 per annum), they discovered that by spending £300 they could recycle some of this fountain water for use in the local markets, 'and allowing 5% on the capital outlay, the cost of the water used would thus be reduced to about £50 p.a'.[66] Chamberlain could not have hoped for a more appropriate memorial to his mayoralty.

Sadly, the demolition of the sympathetic Victorian architecture which surrounded the Memorial and its replacement in the 1970s by John Madin's horrendous ziggurat concrete library (famously described by the Prince of Wales as looking 'like a place where books are incinerated') rather lessens the impression today. Once a shrine to public service, it is now sullied by the glaring neon lights of a McDonald's and the tat of second-rate retailers. Chamberlain steadfastly believed in the marriage of commerce and civic values, but in the 1870s it was always the dignity of public space and municipal life which superseded the frequently grotty requirements of business.

By the time the Chamberlain Memorial fountains started to pump their municipal waters, Birmingham was a new city from the one that had greeted the young London apprentice back in 1854. The shopocracy had been defeated, men of stature lured into Council office, and the municipal gospel of Dawson and Dale made real. There remained unresolved problems of slum-dwelling, stark social inequality and industrial unrest, but the achievements of the Chamberlain tradition cannot lightly be discounted. As ever, it was Chamberlain himself who was most ready to trumpet them.

> During a little over half a century the town has been transformed and ennobled. Formerly it was badly lighted, imperfectly guarded, and only partially drained; there were few public buildings and few important streets ... But now, great public edifices: not unworthy of the importance of a midland metropolis have risen on every side. Wide arteries of communication have been opened up. Rookeries and squalid courts have given way to fine streets and open places. The roads are well paved, well kept, well lighted, and well cleansed. The whole sewerage of the town has been remodelled, and the health of the people is cared for by efficient sanitary inspectors. Baths and wash-houses are provided at a nominal cost to the users. Free libraries and museums of art are open to all the inhabitants; free schools and a school of art, together with facilities for technical instruction, are provided for their education.[67]

While the reforms of Chamberlain and his Council were very welcome for the people of Birmingham, Chamberlain's greatest achievement was to position the elected Council as the motor and repository of civic pride. Urban identity was no longer commensurate with the charitable voluntarism of merchant princes occasionally bestowing gifts on a grateful municipality. Instead it belonged to the city's municipal institutions. There emerged from this philosophy a new belief in the activities of city councils.

In a marvellously evocative passage in his history of Birmingham, J.T. Bunce described the municipality as a 'complex machine' which kept the city functioning. And he listed in loving detail the municipal day which began at dawn when, as 'the town awakens, the waterworks come into full activity'. There then emerge 'a little army of scavengers from the wharves and yards of the Public Works Department, to cleanse the streets from dirt and refuse, to water them, to repair the roadways and footpaths'. They in turn are followed by 'the inspectors of nuisances, who visit the courts and houses, cleanse and repair the drains, search out causes and cases of infectious diseases'. Just as vital for the functioning of the city are the five hundred constables walking the beat, the firemen ready at the watch, and the law courts ready to sit. 'So, day by day, year out, year in, the vast machinery of local administration, as we have it in our town, works steadily and silently on, "unhasting, unresting", without pause, or hitch, or serious flaw'.[68] This picture of the town needing to be watered, cleansed and watched over echoes Dawson's earliest evocation of Birmingham as an 'organism' – a living, breathing entity with the municipality as its heart.

v RED CLYDESIDE

As with any decent gospel, the municipal word spread. It enjoyed by far its warmest reception in the city of Dawson's education and site of the original improvement policy. Glasgow Council had already put itself in charge of gas and water, with remarkable results in provision and price. 'No other city in the world, at least outside of Scotland, can at all compare with Glasgow in the universality of the use of gas in the homes of the working classes.'[69] The city authorities now began to jettison the sacrosanct principle of the Cross Acts by starting their own house-building programme. Shocked by the persistence of slum life some twenty years after the Improvement Act, the Council decided it could wait no longer for private-sector development. Hundreds of municipally constructed tenements and business premises sprang up across the city as the Council tried to build its way out of the property slump. To help tenement dwellers get to their places of employment, the municipality then set its eye on the tramway system. As with the Cross Acts, government legislation regarding tramways had allowed municipalities to own the infrastructure but preserved operational contracts for commercial business. Glasgow again broke rank; tired of the inefficient service and pressured by union demands for better conditions for drivers and conductors, the Council took the service into municipal control. The result was better working conditions, cheaper fares, more user-friendly routes, and even a healthier operating profit. 'The handsomer and more comfortable cars, on which the City Arms are gaily emblazoned, and the happier appearance of the men ... complete the satisfaction with which the Glasgow citizen at present regards the latest addition to municipal business.'[70]

Gas, water, housing, tramways – Glasgow's ambitions did not end there. Emulating Chamberlain's Birmingham, the Council wanted to celebrate the municipal ethos behind this ownership by extending their remit beyond the utilitarian. In October 1883, Lord Provost Ure laid the foundation stone of the Municipal Building, Glasgow's answer to the Birmingham Council House and now home to the City Chambers. Some 60,000 spectators, led by the Freemasons and marshalled by a vast contingent of trade guilds, packed into George Square for the ceremony. Here was the civic religion in full flow: a rapturous celebration of the municipal spirit. 'The arches, the Venetian masts, the statues in the square, the numerous flags and decorations exhibited on hotels and business premises, the brilliant uniforms of the military, and the vari-coloured attires of the tens of thousands assembled – all these combined presented a spectacle excelling in magnificence and interest anything that has been witnessed in the city of Glasgow within the memory of living man.' Provost Ure spelled out the obvious significance of the Municipal edifice. 'The magnificent mass which is soon to rise where we now stand is no State-aided institution, to be placed under surveillance of Government officials. It is the citizens' own, to be bought with their money, to be dedicated exclusively to their uses, to pass under their executive control. Could there, therefore, be found a surer index of this people's devotion to its municipal institutions, and faith in their permanence...?'[71] Astonishingly, when the sumptuous Renaissance building was finally opened by Queen Victoria in 1888, the public's enthusiasm remained undimmed. Some 400,000 marched through the Romanesque loggia, admired the tessellated mosaic depicting the city's coat of arms, climbed the granite and marble staircases, and stood in awe of the vast banqueting chamber – evidence, according to one architectural critic, that 'the people of Glasgow are proud of their city, and show it enthusiastically when occasion requires'.[72] A sentiment rightly bestowed on the City Chambers which to this day, despite being marooned by the George Square roundabout, retain a marvellous sense of civic dignity.

At Kelvingrove, in Glasgow's west end, the city's aesthetic ambitions were equally on display with the erection of a grand public exhibition to raise funds for a new art gallery. On 8 May 1888 the Prince and Princess of Wales drove through cheering crowds to open the exhibition building, dubbed 'Baghdad by Kelvinside', designed in Oriental and Moorish garishness by the architect James Sellars. The city's answer to Manchester's 1887 Royal Jubilee Exhibition and Edinburgh's 1886 International Exhibition,the Kelvingrove monstrosity contained all the extravagant requisites of these quintessentially Victorian events. There were galleries of fine art, industrial expertise, interior luxuries, engineering marvels, and, as the second city of Empire, imperial exoticisms all watched over by a statue of Sir Walter Scott (who might well have been turning in his grave at the scene's vulgar commercialism). Aside from two gondoliers imported from Venice, popularly christened 'Signor Hokey' and 'Signor Pokey', by far the greatest novelty of the exhibition was the Fairy Fountain illuminated by that new addition to Victorian city life, electric lights. 'By day, with bands playing and well-dressed crowds of promenaders, the scene is one of gaiety and brightness, and when night falls, and the electric light shines brilliantly, and from the fairy fountain the many-coloured waters climb into the sky, the sober-sided citizens of Glasgow can hardly believe that some spirit of enchantment has not transformed their own grey, steady-going town into the like-ness of Paris on a fete day.'[73]

The exhibition reaped a profit of £46,000 which went straight into funding a new museum and art gallery – a Scottish response to London's South Kensington museums. Today, the striking, sandstone edifice of Kelvingrove Art Gallery and Museum remains one of Glasgow's most distinctive Victorian icons. For many civic commentators in the late nineteenth century, what marked out the planned new galleries was not the Spanish Baroque skyline but their municipal nature. Unlike ever before, the artefacts belonged through the Council to the entire city.

> The facts of history show that the ruling powers have, in all times, been the collectors of rare and costly things, of the treasures of art, the triumphs of human ingenuity and skill, and the wonders of science. But the aim of these ruling collectors in earlier times was entirely different from the purposes for which the modern municipal authorities form their museums. Among ancient potentates the collection and hoarding of treasures were the principal means of storing and preserving accumulated wealth ... so it was with the emperors and kings, with the ruling families, the Medicis and other Italian tyrants ... Now that it is the

turn of the municipalities to exercise democratic rule and authority over the people, they, in their turn, have become collectors; but their modest museums ... are for the instruction and the gratification of the people at large. The modern ratepayer has the satisfaction of knowing that, while he pays for the support of museum and art gallery, the institutions are his property and dedicated to his service; his ancestor equally paid for the collections of the potentates of his time; but the gathered treasures were neither his nor for him.[74]

There could be no clearer denunciation of the merchant prince model, nor any more obvious shift away from the mid-Victorian Florentine ethos of the Roscoes, Rathbones and Heywoods. Even more so than in Birmingham, Glasgow's Council elders championed a belief in public service and the virtue of the municipality. On Clydeside, civic pride was commensurate with municipal pride. The Council and city were as one. According to one author, it was not the philanthropic industrialists of Manchester and merchants of Liverpool who had revived the civic republican model, but the determined municipalism of Glasgow. The activity of the city authority had gone beyond the protection of private property, and instead 'now renders services to the citizens which they cannot render to themselves or to each other, and exacts from them the performance of certain duties whose sanction is in the interests of the community. And the general result seems, without exaggeration, to be that the modern City is reverting in importance to the position of the City-state in classical antiquity.'[75] Here was an almost Spartan ethos of civic devotion.

In some British cities the tradition of Renaissance homage would continue right into the twentieth century, although by then it had been suitably municipalised. Growing up in 1940s Leeds, the future playwright Alan Bennett was struck by how

the arms of the City of Leeds are embossed on public library books and on the exercise books we write in at school; they are emblazoned on the side of the trams and on the dustcars; any public celebration sees medallions with the arms of the city fixed to lamp-posts and public buildings and even strung across the street in the city centre... The arms could even be found growing in Roundhay Park where, together with the Floral Clock, the owl and the lamb are painstakingly planted out in alyssum and lobelias by the Corporation Parks Department. Thus it is that a child is reminded of the identity of the city at every turn, much as a 15th-century citizen of Florence or Venice was reminded in the same way.[76]

But it was the totality of Glasgow Council's ambitions that differentiated the city from Bennett's Leeds or Chamberlain's Birmingham. There was a deeper historic trend apparent in the Glaswegian approach. Since sizeable urban communities began to form in mid-eighteenth-century Scotland, the town had always been a place of order in contrast to the wilds of the countryside. Within the Scottish burgh tradition, there was an expectation of strong control and civic order far in excess of that projected by Midlands Nonconformity. Yet the Birmingham–Glasgow difference was as much political as religious. The emergence of a clique of elected Labour councillors (known as the 'Stalwarts') and the development of a popular socialist culture fed by trade unions produced a far stronger dynamic towards collectivism. There was an ideological commitment to the public control of utilities and services beyond a Birmingham business interest in practicality or economic potential.

By 1902 Glasgow city owned 2,488 houses, seventy-eight lodging-houses, 372 shops, eighty-six warehouses and workshops, twelve halls, two churches, a bakehouse, a thousand-acre farm, a golf course, a telephone service, and the local electricity supply. This was in addition to gas, water, markets, baths, washhouses, slaughterhouses, parks, botanic gardens, art galleries, museums, libraries, tramways, 'houses of refuge', and industrial and other schools.[77] *The Times*, realising the philosophical implications of this control, was aghast at the city's unprecedented reach. 'There is, in fact, hardly any limit to the activity of Glasgow's local rulers; and, if any city in earth could be made perfectly happy, prosperous, and contented by means of an extreme resort to municipal enterprise, municipal trading, municipal Socialism – call it what you will – that city should be Glasgow.'

vi FROM MUNICIPAL GOSPEL TO MUNICIPAL SOCIALISM

By the late 1880s, the municipal gospel was metamorphosing into municipal socialism. A civic movement which had initially been codified around the capitalist interests of Birmingham's commercial elite was now identified with the values of the Paris Commune and other socialist currents infiltrating from the Continent. The nightmare vision of militant working-class control, which many early municipal gospellers thought their actions were working against by promoting social harmony, was now a possibility in the political landscape ushered in by the 1867 and 1884 Reform Acts. The tools of municipal activism were increasingly found in the hands of an urban working class whose ambitions were not always the same as their wealthy, liberal predecessors. What George Dawson had begun, James Keir Hardie would conclude. And the change in tenor can arguably be traced back to a select London dinner party held in 1883.

At the age of twenty-five, the young Beatrice Potter, cerebral high-society daughter of the railway and timber industrialist Richard Potter, first encountered the forty-seven-year-old widower Joseph Chamberlain. In her diary, she described her impression of the former mayor and now leading Liberal politician as a 'Curious and interesting character, dominated by intellectual passions, with little self-control but with any amount of purpose.' For the socially acquisitive Ms Potter, the power and the passion were a dangerous but attractive combination. Chamberlain himself, who liked young brides, was enamoured by his daughter's new friend. So there began, much to the embarrassed annoyance of Mr Potter, a highly ambiguous courtship between Joseph Chamberlain and his daughter. The 'romance' was based to a strong degree on mutual attraction, but at the same time hindered by Beatrice's astute reservations about Chamberlain's domineering personality. 'By temperament he is an enthusiast and a despot. A deep sympathy with the misery and incompleteness of most men's lives, and an earnest desire to right this, transforms political action into a religious crusade; but running alongside this genuine enthusiasm is a passionate desire to crush opposition to his will, a longing to feel his foot on the neck of others, though he would persuade himself that he represents the right and his adversaries the wrong.'

In the end, after a merry-go-round of dinners, picnics and visits, Beatrice's concerns about his authoritarian nature (which must have been even worse in private than public life) forced her to reject his offer of marriage. 'I shall be absorbed into the life of a man whose aims are not my aims; who will refuse me all freedom of thought in my intercourse with him; to whose career I shall have to subordinate all my life, mental and physical ... The woman's nature has been stirred to its depths ... I have loved and lost.' The misery of parting was awful. 'Will the pain never cease?' she asked herself. 'If Death comes it will be welcome – for life has always been distasteful to me.' A sentiment which only worsened in 1887 when Chamberlain announced his engagement to the daughter of the United States' Secretary of War.

Beatrice tried to battle her depression by throwing herself into charitable activity in the East End and then helping her cousin Charles Booth on his pioneering sociological study of the capital's poor, *The Life and Labour of the People of London*. Yet the misery only lifted in 1890 when a certain 'Sidney Webb, the socialist, dined here to meet the Booths. A remarkable little man with a huge head and a tiny body, a breadth of forehead quite sufficient to account for the encyclopaedic character of his knowledge. A Jewish nose, prominent eyes and mouth, black hair, somewhat unkempt, spectacles and a most bourgeois black coat shiny with wear. But I like the man.' So much so that she married him.[78]

Beatrice's amorous transition from Joseph to Sidney is, on the one hand, little more than intelligentsia high jinks, but it can also be read as an intellectual shift from the municipal gospel of Chamberlain's Birmingham to the municipal socialism of Webb and the Fabians. In the 1880s, socialism was still regarded as a fundamentally utopian venture with only a minority following. Its name conjured up images of Charles Fourier, Henri de Saint-Simon and Robert Owen along with their plans for hopelessly idealistic communities which, when actually put into practice, typically dissolved into disarray and acrimony within months; or, in the far more real case of the Paris Commune, dangerous insurgency. The works of Marx and Engels were neither translated nor widely read and so socialism was rarely understood as a practical political programme. While there were calls for land nationalisation and fiscal redistribution, much of this was proposed as a way to *avoid* socialism. For its supporters, socialism generally denoted a form of ethical idealism: a distant society of shared property and benevolent sentiments towards which all developed humanity should ultimately aim but which was not necessarily achievable through political action. Socialism was a religion of humanity and not yet about the raw politics of the means of production.

For many active socialists, this was deeply frustrating. The point was not to interpret the world, but to change it. And to an increasing degree, they focused their attentions on the municipality as a model for displaying the applicability of socialism. The 1900 International Socialist Conference in Paris was clear:

The Congress declares: That it is a duty of all Socialists ... to make clear to all the value of municipal activity, to recognize in all municipal reforms the importance which attaches to them as 'embryos of the Collectivist State', and to endeavour to municipalize such public services as the urban transport service, education, shops, bakeries, medical assistance, hospitals, water supply, baths and washhouses, the food supply and clothing, dwellings for the people, the supply of motive power, public works, the police force, etc., and to see that these public services shall be model services as much from the point of view of the community as from that of the citizens who serve it.[79]

The Independent Labour Party was equally of the opinion that 'The practicability of Socialism is shown in no better way than by recent advances in municipalization. The great point which experiments in municipalization have proved beyond dispute is that public authorities can organize labour and provide for the needs of the people ... very much better than private capitalists.'[80] Municipal ownership thus became a step along the road not to a better functioning of the city or some kind of Liberal equanimity, but socialism itself. In the view of the ILP, it was *the* best way to improve the lives of the British working class. And, according to the Labour pioneer Keir Hardie, the battle over municipal socialism was another episode in the great historical struggle between borough and baron.

The battle now waged around municipal trading is but the renewal of a struggle carried on for two hundred years against king, cleric and lordling ere yet there was a Parliament in being ... As the burghers triumphed then, so will they now. Already property of the estimated value of £500 million has passed from private to public ownership. The citizens of our time are beginning to realize the benefits which follow in the train of common ownership. On every side can be seen the dawning of the idea that were the means of producing the fundamental necessaries of life – food, clothing, shelter – owned communally, as many of the conveniences already are, the problem of poverty would be solved.[81]

Poverty could be alleviated not only through the cheap provision of necessities, but also through an enhancement of city employees' working conditions. Municipal control of utilities and businesses allowed for increases in wages, cuts in working hours, and proper health and safety regulation.

Nowhere was this policy more actively pursued than in London. In 1888, the undemocratic and now widely reviled Metropolitan Board of Works was replaced with an elected London County Council. Although a marked improvement on Board governance, the LCC's writ did not include second-tier district and vestry Boards nor the all-important City Corporation. Nonetheless, in 1889 an optimistic 'Progressive' alliance took control of the Council after winning seventy-three of the 118 seats contested. Among those elevated into office were the Dock Strike leader John Burns (Battersea), and an intellectual keen to put theory into practice, Sidney Webb (Deptford). Here if anywhere were the conditions ripe for the fully-fledged implementation of municipal socialism.

The Progressive LCC adopted a two-pronged strategy of municipal intervention and model employment which aimed to construct a new political and social order for London. As in Glasgow, the Council was determined to raise the living standards of the working classes through an extensive social welfare programme. John Burns described their goals as 'to do for all what private enterprise does for a few. It is the conscious ordering of the city, through ownership of public services, of its own comfort, happiness and destiny.'[82] Perpetually trying to expand their responsibilities, the LCC gained control of working-class housing, parks and open spaces, street improvements, building regulations, the tramways, and a number of key infrastructure developments including the Holborn Kingsway and the Blackwall Tunnel. Much to its continuing frustration, the Council never gained control of gas, electricity or the water supply. But there was little political hesitation about extending municipal power right down to everyday life. The Labour Progressive Will Crooks boasted of bringing the Council into the home: 'We not only protected poor tenants from house spoilers and extortionate water companies, we gave a helping hand to the housewife. We saw that the coal-sacks were of proper size, that the lamp oil was good, the dustbin emptied regularly, that the baker's bread was of proper weight, that the milk came from wholesome dairies and healthy cows, that the coster in the street and the tradesman in the shop gave good weight in everything they sold.'[83]

Combined with the municipal activism was an unparalleled policy of direct employment by the Council. After further victories in the 1892–3 elections, the Progressives converted the Stores Department into a Works Department which became the largest single public works operation in the world. As the employer of some 12,000 workers by 1904, the LCC ran a deliberate policy of 'fair wages' along with shorter hours and secure employment. The rights and conditions which Glasgow had achieved for its tram-workers, the Progressives won for all their municipal employees. John Burns celebrated the Works Department as 'the biggest thing yet done for Collectivism' and, along with the ILP, used it to show his trade union confrères how the state and the municipality could deliver socialism.[84]

Through municipal intervention and direct employment, the Progressives hoped to bind the identity of the capital ever closer to the actions of the Council. It was suggested London's lack of civic pride had, in contrast to Birmingham or Glasgow, always hindered the capital's social progress. There was none of that fierce loyalty to the municipal *patria* which had done so much to transform the northern industrial cities. The socialist firebrand Henry Hyndman feared Londoners had 'less public spirit than the citizens of any other great capital'. It was all the more strange given that 'the people of other metropolitan cities, far inferior in wealth and population, have never been by any means wanting in municipal pride'.[85] In his Fabian manifesto, *The London Programme*, Sidney Webb voiced the complaint most eloquently and in so doing highlighted an intriguing shift in understanding of the example of the Italian city republics:

'A great city . . . is the type of some great idea.' A thoughtful, affected Benjamin Disraeli photographed at Osborne House 'by command
of H.M. The Queen', 1878.

Alfred Waterhouse at work, c. 1891.

Top: 'Truly a Municipal Palace.' Manchester Town Hall, designed by Alfred Waterhouse, c. 1890.

Above: A celebration of the city's industry. Bees line the Town Hall's mosaic floor.

Right: One of the magnificent staircases in the Gothic interior of Manchester Town Hall.

'The cool, calm man of business, the long-headed, persevering, patient, yet acute politician.' Joseph Chamberlain, complete with orchid.

Chamberlain Square, Birmingham, with the Chamberlain Memorial, 1897.

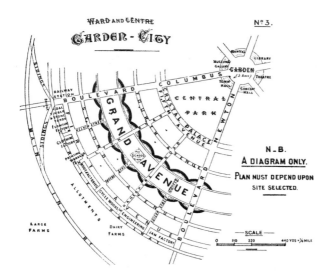

American urban influences are obvious in this early plan for the garden city. Illustration from *Garden Cities of Tomorrow* by Ebenezer Howard, 1902.

'Town and country must be married, and out of this joyous union will spring a new hope, a new life, a new civilization.' Letchworth Garden City, 1938.

Priestley's Bradford. Manningham Mills, c. 1920.

Industrial archaeology. Post-war Leeds.

The Midlands Metropolis. The new Selfridges building at the redeveloped Bull Ring, Birmingham.

The greatest need of the metropolis is, it may be suggested, the growth among its citizens of a greater sense of common life. That 'Municipal Patriotism' which once marked the free cities of Italy, and which is already to be found in our own provincial towns, can, perhaps, best be developed in London by a steady expansion of the sphere of civic as compared with individual action ... We should 'municipalize' our metropolis, not only in order to improve its administration, but as the best means of developing the character of its citizens.[86]

The *communes* of the Italian Renaissance were thus no longer pinnacles of private enterprise and mercantile pride, but rather examples of highly active councils. In Webb's schema, civic pride was now dependent upon, and the product of, municipal actions.

London's persistent inability to develop any kind of municipal patriotism was ultimately the product of a failure of political representation. The villain of the piece was the City Corporation, which for some eight hundred years had undermined nascent civic sentiments. In an inflammatorily titled article, 'The London County Council: Towards a Commune', John Burns described how the Corporation 'could have been the heir of all the civic ages, the nexus of all the traditions and historical associations of the *civitas* of a free people', but instead it 'had become hypnotised by vested interests, nepotism, and feasting'. Criminally, it missed the opportunity to provide a lead for the fast-expanding metropolis and so generate any kind of municipal ardour. It was now the duty of the LCC to bring to life 'a revivified municipal ideal'. And until their ejection by aggrieved ratepayers in 1907, the Progressives tried to do precisely that.[87]

The rhetoric and policies of the Glasgow Council and the LCC meant that municipal socialism was regarded as offering more than just a route to working-class amelioration. It was also a new way of conceptualising urban life. The city was regarded as much as a social as an industrial ideal; a vehicle for democratic engagement and political reform. Sidney Webb bitterly criticised the nineteenth century's tradition of 'local patriotism', which was almost entirely confined to 'the fortunate minority of prosperous businessmen'. Unable to resist a dig at his old rival Chamberlain, he described how the merchants of Liverpool, the manufacturers of Manchester, and the 'proprietors of the great Birmingham combinations in hardware and machinery' had hijacked the identity of the city. 'In their leisure hours, and from their surplus income, these public-spirited citizens sought to build up the corporate life of "their" city; to enrich it with public buildings, with picture galleries, with open spaces ... But in the slums of Liverpool and Manchester and Birmingham – even in the crowded cottages of the artisans and clerks, who together made up two-thirds of the population – anything like municipal patriotism or civic pride remained almost unknown.'

It was the challenge of municipal socialism to return the city to its people; to ensure that the city, through its council, reflected the aspirations of its citizens. In the Webbs' schema, only by a sustained programme of municipal intervention – in everything from gas and water to music and drama – could you hope to revive 'civic patriotism'.[88] The municipal socialist vision of the city was not one of guilds and churches or voluntary societies and self-governing Mechanics' Institutes – and most certainly not one of merchant princes and philanthropic patronage. Rather, it was the creation of an ethical socialist community through public ownership and public control. 'It may well prove to be the case that, in a Socialist Commonwealth, as much as one-half of the whole of the industries and services would fall within the sphere of Local Government.'[89]

While many local authorities eschewed the politically charged rhetoric of the Webbs, they did accept the creed of municipal socialism. For if the late nineteenth century witnessed little acceptance of the dread word 'socialism', it happily welcomed collectivism. When Sir William Harcourt announced 'We are all Socialists now', what he meant was a broad appreciation of collectivist politics. The atomistic individualism of the mid-Victorian era was ebbing away as government encroached further in social and economic policy, and nowhere more so than in local government. The American journalist Albert Shaw was startled how, 'In the theory and art of modern city-making collectivism has a large and growing place. The municipal corporations, until recently rather passive as political and social organisms, are now becoming highly conscious of their organic entity, and highly active in extending old functions and assuming new ones.'[90] Meanwhile *The Times*, by far the most acerbic critic of municipal socialism, commented on 'the evident willingness on the part of so many local rulers to adopt the Socialistic Idea, though not accepting the Socialist name'.[91]

The numbers spoke for themselves. Between 1884 and 1914, annual expenditure on municipal trading in gas, water, electricity and tramways rose from some £8.5 million to over £42 million. Apart from the Ship Canal, by 1905 Manchester alone had invested £7.4 million in water, £2.6m in gas, £2.3m in electricity supply and £2m in tramways. In 1909, of the seventy-four county boroughs in England and Wales, fifty-three owned their water undertakings, thirty-three the gas supply, sixty-five electricity, and fifty the tramways. Of the 253 non-county boroughs, 179 supplied water, seventy-three gas, eighty-three electricity, and twenty-four controlled tramways. Millions now received their most essential utilities through the aegis of the municipality. It cleaned them, fed them and carried them to their place of work. This extraordinary extension of authority came at the cost of marked increases in municipal borrowing. In 1874–5 the proportion of local authority borrowing to the total national debt stood at just over twelve per cent, but by 1896–7 it had exceeded thirty-nine per cent. The growth in municipal borrowing and expenditure certainly accounts for the great rise in local government expenditure in the late-Victorian period. The local authority share of all forms of government expenditure rose from thirty-two per cent in 1870 to a historic high of fifty-one per cent in 1905.[92]

Municipal socialism contained a momentum of its own. A self-generating bureaucracy continued to develop while councillors championed the obvious rationality of expanding their dominion. There appeared little subversive or even party-political about delivering 'best value' services. As George Bernard Shaw surreptitiously put it in his aptly titled *The Common Sense of Municipal Trading*, 'Municipal trading seems a very simple matter of business.'[93] Even the great socialist John Burns, who wanted to transform London into a commune, described his vision of the LCC as a 'joint-stock company, with the ratepayer as shareholder'. It was simply a quest for efficiency and cheapness and should, in Burns's view, be a 'non-political' question.

For committed socialists, this was the wonderful subterfuge of municipal socialism. It was socialism by the back-door: carried out by unsuspecting councillors under the noses of Conservative ratepayers. Sidney Webb, in a wonderful passage in his *Socialism in England*, exposed the political ratchet by which self-consciously Conservative councillors were inadvertently facilitating the emergence of a collectivist, even socialist state.

> The 'practical man', oblivious or contemptuous of any theory of the Social Organism or general principles of social organisation, has been forced by the necessities of the time into an ever deepening collectivist channel. The Individualist Town Councillor will walk along the municipal pavement, lit by municipal gas and cleansed by municipal brooms with municipal water, and seeing by the municipal clock in the municipal market that he is too early to meet his children coming from the municipal school hard by the county lunatic asylum and municipal hospital, will use the national telegraph system to tell them not to walk through the municipal park but to come by the municipal tramway, to meet him in the municipal reading-

room by the municipal art gallery, museum and library, where he intends to consult some of the national publications in order to prepare his next speech in the municipal town-hall, in favour of the nationalization of canals and the increase of the government control over the railway system. 'Socialism, Sir,' he will say, 'don't waste the time of a practical man by your fantastic absurdities. Self-help, Sir, individual self-help, that's what made our city what it is.'[94]

Not all were fooled. *The Times* urged municipal electors to 'wake up' and not allow 'British local government to drift too much into the hands of men who, if not Socialists themselves, are willing to act in strict accord with socialistic aspirations'. This warning was followed up by a letter to the newspaper from a Mr Eastlake of Sutton Coldfield, who noted how 'practical' schemes for the municipalisation of water and gas were simply 'the practical work for which Socialists have been long theorizing'. Furthermore, 'if our misguided town councillors and aldermen persist in their present course there will be no need for Socialists to trouble themselves about the carrying out of their schemes – that part of their work will all be done for them by the "level-headed" business men who preponderate upon city councils'. Eastlake suggested that Webb's description of the individualist town councillor be pinned to every council chamber in Britain as a warning of the consequence of their undertakings. In some cases, even greater wariness was required to counter the socialist infiltration. According to one councillor from Folkestone, 'In every town council the socialistic element is to be found, it may be present to a large and considerable extent, or it may exist but in a small and apparently insignificant degree. But whether its representatives be many or few, the organization remains well nigh perfect ... They work steadily, compactly; often silently, but they ever work on.'[95]

As the interests of municipalities expanded and their threat to private enterprise grew more apparent, an influential contingent of vested interests rallied to counter the slide to

socialism. Critics pointed to the dangerous debts now being
accumulated by councils. What progressive councillors lauded
as pioneering investment, the less charitable regarded only
as irresponsible financing. By 1903–4, total local authority
indebtedness had risen from £80 million in the early 1870s to
near £400 million – enough to imperil the nation's credit
rating, according to worried Treasury officials.⁹⁶ More immediately, the increase in municipal trading was threatening to
crowd out private enterprise. Gas and water utilities had long
ago surrendered to the councils, but now electricity, tramway
and omnibus companies were all threatened by municipal
ambition. Businesses were destroyed by power-hungry councillors, while opportunities for capital investment were threatened by fears that sectors could be subject to arbitrary
municipalisation. Lord Avebury, a peer with substantial business interests, led the defence against this attack on private
enterprise. 'Who will risk his money in competition with
Town Councils, which have the bottomless purse of the ratepayers to draw on, and have not to face any risk to themselves?'
he asked.⁹⁷ The situation was at its bleakest in Glasgow, which
stood in danger of being converted from 'a free city, where
every man has liberty to carry on his occupation or his industry
under the protection of his local rulers, into a communistic
society where those rulers would have all industries under
their own control, and deprive him alike of any opportunity
for independent enterprise and of any incentive to individual
exertion'.⁹⁸

There were also concerns that the mushrooming of municipal enterprise was affecting the fabric of local authorities. In
a curious inversion of the Chamberlain thesis that a council
with real power attracts the finest minds, now the fear was
that the sheer breadth of civic responsibility was putting the
best people off. The multiple burdens of council office meant
that it could no longer rely on the public service ethos of
businessmen and leading professionals, but instead was
dependent upon altogether less dynamic figures with time
on their hands. The result was a collapse in the quality of

councillors just at the moment when they wielded unprecedented power and required the most astute candidates. In
the London borough of Poplar, *The Times* was appalled to
discover, council authority lay in the hands of an iron foundry
labourer, a chemical works labourer, a gas-stoker and a brick-
layer. They must, the newspaper contended, be 'as helpless as
children when they are called upon to deal with thousands or
hundreds of thousands of pounds'. More worryingly, this
woeful lack of experience was in a local authority with one of
the most advanced programmes of municipal enterprise in the
country.[99]

With little personal wealth to be lost through rate increases
and even less appreciation of the necessity of economy,
working-class councillors were accused of undermining all
attempts at financial probity. Perversely, the Victorian spirit
of civic pride was now to be deprecated. Commentators expressed concern about 'undue rivalry between neighbouring
towns' and the dangerous disposition 'that every new public
building put up should be of so elaborate a character as to be
"worthy" of the real or supposed "importance" of the town,
that one locality must not allow itself to be "behind" its
neighbour'. The tradition of emulation which had fostered the
construction of Liverpool's St George's Hall and Manchester
Town Hall was now condemned as spendthrift irresponsibility.
The Times revelled in exposés of councillor extravagance
which the ratepayers of 1990s Doncaster would find familiar:
of fact-finding missions abroad of dubious provenance;
unnecessarily expensive, self-congratulatory dinners; and
inexcusable misallocations of resources on civic aggrand-
isements. Perhaps the greatest indictment was the discovery
by the Liverpool auditor that during a visit of the Council's
Tramways Committee to inspect electric cars in Preston, the
deputation spent £18 6s on expenses – including £7 3s on
thirteen bottles of champagne and £1 16s on cigars.

The new breed of working-class councillors did not just look
after themselves, they also looked after their own. With the
LCC Works Department leading the way, critics became

alarmed at increases in the city payroll, the cosy relationship between the councils and the unions, and the whole sleazy architecture of municipal employment which would later fall under the rubric of 'jobs for the boys'. Socialist councillors in Battersea were accused of gerrymandering for trying to buy votes with the promise of Council jobs. 'Not only is it regarded as the special prerogative and function of the Labour member to find work for his friends and electoral supporters, but he himself cheerfully accepts the task because it is by increasing the volume of municipal work, and by ensuring for the workers the best possible conditions, that he makes certain of getting their votes when the time comes round for him to seek re-election.'[100] It is not difficult here to find an early echo of so many of the accusations levelled against incompetent and irresponsible Labour councils – most notably Derek Hatton's Liverpool in the 1970s and 1980s. The consequence in both periods was a renewed call for central government intervention to protect ratepayers from extravagant council expenditure and ensure the maintenance of municipal democracy, a reaction which only resulted in an emasculation of local government whether it was deemed 'responsible' or socialist.

More optimistic voices ignored the warnings of massive debt, jobbery, political venality and commercial ruin. Instead, they argued not for retrenchment but a sustained expansion of the municipal dominion. In a series of Tracts, the Fabians set out their agenda for the municipalisation of docks and warehouses, slaughterhouses and hospitals, pawnshops and steamers, and, most magnificently of all, bakeries. 'Bread is as much an article of universal consumption as water. A municipality, after all, is but a corporate association of bread consumers. Why should it not produce what it consumes?'[101]

The more avant-garde wing of the municipal socialist movement was represented by the Bolton-based magazine, *The Municipal Reformer and Local Government News*. Every issue was fronted with a sketch of a 'Municipal Reformer' and the first issue's pin-up boy was, appropriately enough, Sidney

Webb. Less excitingly, Webb was followed in the second issue by Mr S. Norbury Williams, the Citizens' Auditor from Manchester. The *Municipal Reformer* argued for a new civic settlement beyond politics, one in which all aspects of public welfare would be placed under public control. In an ordered, evolutionary progress the magazine proposed the full communal ownership of the municipality by its people as the surest means to promoting their future health and happiness. It constituted a different, elegiac vision of municipal socialism; a proto-communist new Jerusalem distinctly at odds with the buccaneering entrepreneurialism of Joseph Chamberlain and his acolytes. 'Municipal reformers have an ideal city in their minds. They dream of a glorious life of citizenship that is to come. They see that a new fellowship will grow, indeed, is growing, in which all men will be friends and neighbours and brothers. City life is to evolve into this as isolated country life cannot. Men will learn to bear each other's burdens, to care for and protect each other in ways yet unknown; and citizenship will be a perennial joy.'[102]

William Morris's *Clarion*, the journal of his Socialist League, similarly looked forward 'to the time when joy will be considered as much a necessity in a city as anything else'. When that epoch was reached, municipal ratepayers 'will not fail to demand that this great necessity of joy, or . . . the means of joy, be also supplied by their local councils'.[103] Joy was now a council priority.

This was where the municipal gospel of Dawson and Chamberlain concluded – in language increasingly focused not on the city as a paternalist force complete with a historic mission to liberate the individual and energise society, but instead as a self-sustaining community conceptualised as distinctively separate from Victorian urban values. The organisational municipal gospel would ultimately become an irrelevance in a self-governing system in which council authority would wither on the vine. The gospel was a victim of its own success: if all accepted its precepts then the need for the enforcing authority was redundant.

The eclipse of the Chamberlain vision was only one aspect of a broader impatience. Despite some sixty years of reform, the cities of late-Victorian Britain still retained some of their initial industrial fault-lines. And now the poverty, the crime, the pollution, the insanitariness were exacerbated by further immigration and a sustained economic downturn. One city, one monstrous Babylon of corruption and dissolution, became the prime focus of late-Victorian urban anxieties. Out from the rookeries of St Giles, the slums of Bethnal Green and the pubs of Whitechapel arose the plaintive cry of Outcast London.

PART THREE

FLEEING THE CITY

[9]

LONDON: THE WHITED SEPULCHRE OF EMPIRE

We were now about three hundred yards from the village of Ujiji, and the crowds are dense about me. Suddenly I hear a voice on my right say, –

'Good morning, sir!'

Startled at hearing this greeting in the midst of such a crowd of black people, I turn sharply around in search of the man, and see him at my side, with the blackest of faces, but animated and joyous: –

'Who the mischief are you?'

'I am Susi, the servant of Dr Livingstone,' said he smiling and showing a gleaming row of teeth.

'What! Is Dr Livingstone here?'

'Yes, sir.'

... I pushed back the crowds, and, passing from the rear walked down a living avenue of people until I came in front of the semicircle of Arabs, in the front of which stood the white man with the grey beard. As I advanced slowly towards him, I noticed he was pale, looking wearied, had a grey beard, wore a bluish cap with a faded gold band round it, had on a red-sleeved waistcoat and a pair of grey tweed trousers. I would have run to him, only I was a coward in the presence of such a mob – would have embraced him, only he being an Englishman, I did not know how he would receive me; so I did what cowardice and false pride suggested was the best thing – walked deliberately to him, took off my hat, and said: –

'Dr Livingstone, I presume?'

'Yes,' said he, with a kind smile, lifting his cap slightly.[1]

With that legendary greeting, Henry Morton Stanley transformed David Livingstone into a transatlantic celebrity and
an icon of British understated stoicism. Livingstone's lonely
jungle death soon after the publication of Stanley's self-serving
account, *How I Found Livingstone* (1872), elevated him only
further towards secular Victorian sainthood. For popular
culture in the late nineteenth century revered the explorer
with the same raw enthusiasm previous decades had reserved
for the industrialist or soldier. This was the age of Burton
and Speke, Livingstone and Stanley, the Royal Geographical
Society and the London Missionary Society. It was, above all,
the age of Africa: the terrible, 'dark continent' riddled with
savage mystery, untold riches, and cannibalistic tribes.

At the same time as Livingstone was making his way across
Lake Tanganyika and Stanley traversing the Congo, brave
souls were exploring similarly treacherous terrain slightly
closer to home.

> In these pages I propose to record the result of a journey into
> a region which lies at our own doors – into a dark continent
> that is within easy walking distance of the General Post
> Office. This continent will, I hope, be found as interesting
> as any of those newly-explored lands which engage the
> attention of the Royal Geographical Society – the wild races
> who inhabit it will, I trust, gain public sympathy as easily
> as those savage tribes for whose benefit the Missionary
> Societies never cease to appeal for funds.[2]

The journalist George Sims's journey into 'horrible London'
produced accounts of godlessness, barbarism and suffering as
graphic as any jungle tales Stanley had to offer. And his reports
for the *Daily News* were consumed as avidly as Stanley's
breathless dispatches for the *Daily Telegraph*. Accompanying
Sims into the 'Wilds of London' was the foolhardy author
James Greenwood, who described with all the verve of a colonial pioneer his trip to the East End docklands:

Everybody addicted to the perusal of police reports has read of Tiger Bay, and of the horrors perpetrated there – of unwary mariners betrayed to that craggy and hideous shore by means of false beacons, and mercilessly wrecked and stripped and plundered – of the sanguinary fights of white men and plug-lipped Malays and ear-ringed Africans, with the tigresses who swarm in the 'Bay', giving it a name. 'God bless my soul!' remarks the sitting magistrate, as evidence of a savage assault in the shape of an ear snapped off a human head by human teeth, and decently wrapped in a cool cabbage-leaf, is exposed to his gaze, along with a double-handful of towzled female hair, tendered on behalf of the defendant as proof of provocation – 'God bless my soul! It must be a very shocking neighbourhood'.[3]

Greenwood took the reader yet deeper into the canopy: to an 'Evening at a Whitechapel gaff' as well as 'Amongst the Music-Hall Luminaries'; 'An Exploration into "Jack Ketch's Warren"'; and 'A Dustman's Tea-Party'. It was becoming a crowded terrain. When, in 1890, Stanley hammered out *In Darkest Africa*, a two-volume work describing his heroic conduct during the rescue of the Governor of Sudan, General Booth of the Salvation Army responded with *In Darkest England and the Way Out*. For William Booth, the dismal nether-worlds of Africa and England were shamefully alike:

while brooding over the awful presentation of life as it exists in the vast African forest, it seemed to me only too vivid a picture of many parts of our own land. As there is a darkest Africa is there not also a darkest England? ... May we not find a parallel at our own doors, and discover within a stone's throw of our cathedrals and palaces similar horrors to those which Stanley has found existing in the great Equatorial forest? ... Darkest England, like Darkest Africa, reeks with malaria. The foul and fetid breath of our slums is almost as poisonous as that of an African swamp ... A population sodden with drink, steeped in vice, eaten up by

every social and physical malady, these are the denizens of
Darkest England amidst whom my life has been spent...[4]

Late-Victorian society was becoming as shocked by the
exposure of its cities as it was excited by the 'Scramble for
Africa'. And what made the burgeoning literature of urban
exploration all the more disturbing was its focus on London,
'the heart of Empire'. The exotic customs and strange hap-
penings which Sims, Greenwood and Booth exposed seemed a
world away from the contented mid-Victorian urban scene of
civic pride, artisan self-help or even municipal socialism. For
time and again it was portrayed as another world: a world of
dangerous swamps and violent savages more readily suited to
the jungles of Angola than the backstreets of Bethnal Green.
It was imagined as an alien civilisation which the age of
progress had all but forgotten.

In turn, the late-Victorian rediscovery of London produced
a culture of anti-urban sentiment that contributed markedly
to a breakdown in British civic pride. Concern followed by
fear over the state of this lost London was channelled into an
intellectual retreat from the city. The Victorian ideals of urban
living – be it the municipal gospel of Chamberlain, the middle-
class ethos of Cobden and Bright, or the guild vision of Pugin
and Cobbett – were quietly jettisoned. The city was decreasingly regarded as an arena to be celebrated, reformed, or rebuilt
along ideological or aesthetic principles but instead as a mode
of existence best rejected altogether.

i THE CAPITAL OF CORRUPTION

London was the pre-eminent global city of the late nineteenth
century. Boosted by wave upon wave of national and international immigration, its population expanded exponentially
during the latter years of Queen Victoria's reign. At the time of
the 1851 Great Exhibition, Greater London's entire population
stood at 2.5 million. By 1871 that figure had grown to 3,890,000
and in 1901, the year of Victoria's death, it reached 6,586,000.

Extraordinarily, almost one-fifth of the population of England and Wales lived in London by the close of her years. Sidney Webb, the London County Council representative and leading municipal socialist, described the capital as 'more than a city: it is a whole kingdom in itself, with revenues exceeding those of mighty principalities. With its suburbs it exceeds all Ireland in population ... the three next largest cities in the world could almost be combined without out-numbering its millions.'[5]

Public opinion, politics and literature, which had through-out the mid-nineteenth century been so mesmerised by the industrialising cities of northern England, returned its focus to Cobbett's 'Great Wen'.[6] Yet the London of the late-Victorian era was no longer interested in dominating the precious Home Counties of Cobbett's childhood; it was now at the centre of a global imperium occupied more with India, Australia and South Africa than Winchester or the Sussex Weald. As *The Economist* famously put it, 'London is often more concerned with the course of events in Mexico than with what happens in the Midlands, and is more upset by a strike on the Canadian Pacific than by one in the Cambrian collieries.'

This was the London of the Stock Exchange, the docks, Mansion House, and a cast of international financiers beau-tifully embodied in Trollope's baroque crook Augustus Mel-motte: 'He could make or mar any company by buying or selling stock, and could make money dear or cheap as he pleased.' It was the London of an army of black-coated clerks populating the endless offices of commerce, banking, insur-ance and real estate businesses. This capital was the global financial hub, or in Joseph Chamberlain's words, 'the clearing house of the world', which funded railways in Peru, mining in New South Wales and tea plantations in India. Between 1870 and 1914, the United Kingdom was responsible for forty-four per cent of global foreign investment (compared to 19.9 per cent by France). With the capital flowed the ships and steamers out of the Thames into the Empire – sitting on board one of which was Joseph Conrad's traumatised Marlow, ready once more to venture out 'into the heart of an immense darkness'. In their place came millions of tons of raw goods: furs from Canada, tea from China, spices from Ceylon. Occupying twenty-six square miles of wharves and warehouses and employing over 30,000 men, the Thames docklands constituted a remarkable civilisation in itself.

Late-Victorian and Edwardian London was, in Asa Briggs's apposite phrase, 'a world city'. But more specifically, it was an imperial city. The businessman and future chronicler of London's poor, Charles Booth, described the capital as not only 'an unrivalled national emporium and world-market' but also as 'the Mother-City of the Kingdom and of the Empire'.[7] The Liberal politician and essayist C.F.G. Masterman called it 'The Heart of the Empire' from which Britain governed some twenty-five per cent of the earth's population. However, empire was not something Britain simply *did* to the rest of the world. It was a reflexive process that impacted equally upon the metropole and the colonies. London was as much formed by the imperial exchange as Calcutta and Colombo. Indeed, this imperialist context, suggests a recent history, suffused the entire city. 'Imperialist sentiments appeared in the wrappers and advertisements of cigarette packets, soaps, teas, medicines, drinks, and a thousand other items. They were celebrated in textbooks read by London's schoolchildren and on the maps the children studied. They could be discerned in London's very architecture, in its public spaces, its buildings, shops, factories and offices.'[8]

The same was true of Glasgow, the 'Second City of Empire', where colonial iconography coursed through Clydeside's global commerce. Adverts for Tennent's India Pale Ale, Camp coffee or Thomas Lipton's Ceylon tea ('Direct from the tea garden to the tea pot') drew on a host of exotic imperial imagery including elephants, plantation scenery, docks and ships. Meanwhile, the city itself was re-imagined as a microcosm of the Empire with street names such as Virginia, Havannah, Jamaica, Tobago and West Nile. Glasgow's financial infrastructure – the banks, merchant houses, and shipping headquarters – rarely failed to advertise their imperial remit with lavish architectural symbolism.[9]

But the urban equality of the mid-Victorian era was fading: London was the new Rome. Civic architecture and iconography of the capital – Cleopatra's Needle, Trafalgar Square, the Royal Exchange, and ultimately Holborn Kingsway leading down to Australia House, India House and Africa House – helped to forge a determinedly imperial *mentalité*, an identity which was cemented by popular entertainment and urban amusements, the themes of which seamlessly traversed the classes. While the bawdy music halls hosted 'Nigger minstrels', the middle classes received only a slightly more sophisticated interpretation of the benefits of Empire from events such as the Colonial and Indian Exhibition at the Imperial Institute. London was presented as the dynamic heart of a Christian people selflessly devoted to spreading commercial wealth and civilised values across the world.

What of the city itself? 'We have read of the magnificence of the hidden cities of the East', wrote the journalist J.A. Ingham, 'and are told that London is the clearing house of Europe, the Nineveh and Babylon of modern times, the wealthiest city on record, whose merchant princes, bankers and capitalists pay income tax on twenty millions per year to the national exchequer. We do not ask, Is she beautiful? Is she healthy?'[10] According to a growing body of opinion, the answer was a worrisome 'no'. Behind the glitter, behind the pomp and majesty lay a desperate capital on the verge of moral collapse and violent social disorder. It was a prospect T.B. Macaulay had toyed with, in a 1840 review of Von Ranke's *History of the Popes*, when he had forewarned of a still flourishing Catholic Church even as 'some traveller from New Zealand shall, in the midst of a vast solitude, take his stand on a broken arch of London Bridge to sketch the ruins of St. Paul's' (so providing a mental vista of decay which Gustave Doré so memorably realised in print).[11] Like 'The glory that was Greece/The grandeur that was Rome', this London Babylon, this capital of Empire, was facing an apocalypse brought on by luxurious indulgence and class divide. In a letter to *The Times*, the East India Company civil servant Sir Charles Trevelyan spelt out the fears.

> London is the metropolis, not only of the United Kingdom, but also of an empire upon which the sun never sets, including the vassal continent of India, itself an empire. London is the foremost city of Christendom ... Yet this London is a whited sepulchre, which, indeed, appears beautiful outward, but within is full of dead men's bones, and of all uncleanness. It is a gigantic laboratory of corruption and crime; and, while it aspires to Christianise the heathen, it exercises a far more direct and effectual influence in heathenising Christians, and in dragging the rest of England down to its own level.[12]

What so unnerved the commentators and politicians was the dangerous gulf within the city between the respectable classes of the civilised West End and the dissolute residuum of the East End. As the divide deepened (especially after the collapse of the Thames shipbuilding industry in the later 1860s), the East End became a *terra incognita* as unknown and as dangerous to the clubs of the West End as the Great Lakes of central Africa. With none of the fashionable chic which now envelops the East End, the dilapidated communities of Whitechapel and Hoxton, Mile End and docklands constituted for the Victorian public a jungle of pauperism, immorality and criminality which few dared to encounter. Originally reclaimed from drained marshes, the East End was now once more reimagined as a giant swamp where moral miasmas lurked just as deadly as their sanitary counterparts. It was a heathen quagmire peopled by Jews, drunks, prostitutes and criminals all threatening to undermine the elegant foundations of imperial London. It was a district ultimately codified for contemporaries by the frenzied, sexually charged murders of Jack the Ripper – a savage monster the type of which only the backstreets of Whitechapel could produce. Disraeli had described 1840s England as constituting 'Two Nations'; that appellation was now widely applied to late-nineteenth-century London. And it was a divide which seemed to become ever more dangerous as the poor started to assume subhuman attributes.

London first discovered its underclass through the pioneering journalism of Henry Mayhew. In the pages of the *Morning Chronicle*, he had given a voice to the pure-finders, costermongers, crossing-sweepers and dustmen who had previously shuffled unremarked through the capital's streets. The library of imitative literature which followed Mayhew's *London Labour and the London Poor* could never equal him in sophistication or sympathy. In fact, the fashion was quite the opposite. Rather than individualising characters, writers returned to portraying the London poor as an unrecognisable mass of the nameless and faceless, comparable in their backwardness to the animal kingdom. Thomas Beames, an assistant clergyman at St James Church, Westminster, described the notorious 'rookeries' of Holborn, Jacob's Island and St Giles's off New Oxford Street in his best-selling account of the capital's underworld, *The Rookeries of London*.

> Doubtless there is some analogy between these pauper colonies and the nests of the birds from whom they take their name; the houses for the most part high and narrow, the largest possible number crowded together in a given space ... Other birds are broken up into separate families – occupy separate nests; rooks seem to know no such distinction. So it is with the class whose dwellings we are to describe. We must speak of the dwellings of the poor in crowded cities, where large masses of men are brought together ... We must speak of human masses pent up, crowded, crammed into courts and alleys...[13]

Beames went on to talk of one rookery as a 'honeycomb' or 'hive' in the centre of which could be found 'the famous thieves' public house', called Rat's Castle. In full sensationalist flow, the London poor became indistinguishable from rats, bees and rooks. The *Pall Mall Gazette* reported how in the slums and alleys of London 'men, women and children are herded together in filthy styes'.[14] George Sims believed that 'only the ferocious instincts of the brute are fostered by the state of existence' prevalent in the capital.[15] In these animalistic conditions there inevitably arose animal urges: 'men and women are brought together in the same apartment whom no marriage tie unites, and who have no other bond than that of common want'.[16]

With little soul contained within their animal bodies, the London poor also displayed minimal need for God. Whereas Mayhew had once sorrowfully described his meeting with a nine-year-old mudlark who 'didn't know what religion his father and mother were, nor did know what religion meant', others were less forgiving in their approach to the capital's godless masses.[17] The *Pall Mall Gazette* spoke of 'colonies of heathens and savages in the heart of our capital'.[18] It was a catchy phrase which General Booth later repeated as he demanded why 'the existence of these colonies of heathens and savages in the heart of the capital should attract so little attention!'[19] With godlessness there inevitably followed hostility to political authority and social order. The London poor, like an animalistic mob, were more than capable of turning on their masters. Thomas Beames reported how it was 'on record that during the combats in Paris in 1848 ... multitudes of strange figures issued from these lurking places, distinguished by their appearance from the rest even of the poor population. They bide their time; the agitator calls, and "they will come when he doth call."'[20] Fears of a London insurrection only grew after the revolutionary events of the 1871 Paris Commune. Widely and graphically reported in the British press, the Commune not only confirmed the image of Paris as a volcano of perpetual revolution but also emphasised the instability inherent in large cities which contained such fissures between rich and poor. 'This mighty mob of famished, diseased, and filthy helots is getting dangerous, physically, morally, politically dangerous,' warned George Sims. 'Its fevers and its filth may spread to the homes of the wealthy; its lawless armies may sally forth and give us a taste of the lesson the mob has tried to teach now and again in Paris.'[21]

ii Outcast London

One writer particularly exercised by the godless state of London's pauper classes was the Secretary of the London Congregational Union, the Revd Andrew Mearns. In 1883, he combined the existing strands of criticism of the capital into a blunt, brilliant diatribe. *The Bitter Cry of Outcast London* was a coruscating indictment of the policies of Church and state alike for failing to alleviate 'the great dark region of poverty, misery, squalor and immorality', as a result of which, 'in the very centre of our great cities, concealed by the thinnest crust of civilization and decency, is a vast mass of moral corruption, of heart-breaking misery and absolute godlessness.'[22] With the passion of a dedicated reformer, Mearns vented his fury at how the boom years of mid-Victorian growth had left behind the denizens of outcast London. 'Few who will read these pages have any conception of what these pestilential human rookeries are, where tens of thousands are crowded together amidst horrors which call to mind what we have heard of the middle passage of the slave ship.'

As James Phillips Kay and Friedrich Engels had done previously in 1830s Manchester, Mearns publicised the wretchedness of internal overcrowding. 'Here are seven people living in one underground kitchen, and a little dead child lying in the same room ... Here is a mother who turns her children into the street in the early evening because she lets her room for immoral purposes until long after midnight'. The baneful consequence of these density levels was the iniquitous mixing of the honest poor with the criminal classes. 'Often is the family of an honest working man, compelled to take refuge in a thieves' kitchen.' But most shocking of all were the moral consequences. In a phrase that would jolt Victorian political culture and secure his pamphlet acres of lurid coverage, Mearns declared 'Incest is common.' Moreover, 'no form of vice and sensuality causes surprise or attracts attention. Those who do appear to be married are often separated by a mere quarrel, and they do not hesitate to form similar companionships immediately.'[23] When these reports were followed up in the *Pall Mall Gazette* by W.T. Stead's exposé of child sexual slavery, sensationally headlined 'The Maiden Tribute of Modern Babylon', outcast London truly resembled a latter-day Babylon on the verge of moral combustion.

Mearns located the roots of outcast London in the housing crisis which, decades in the making, had engulfed the capital during the early 1880s. For the prosperity of the 1850s and 1860s had not in fact omitted the urban poor but ploughed straight into them. The transformation of London into a modern capital, with new roads, rails, buildings and monuments, had created a chaotic landscape from which the working classes had been forced to flee. In his great London novel, *Dombey and Son*, Charles Dickens gave a taste of the anarchy visited by railway development when it scythed through Camden Town (Staggs's Gardens). 'The first shock of a great earthquake had, just at that period, rent the whole neighbourhood to its centre. Traces of its course were visible on every side. Houses were knocked down; streets broken through and stopped; deep pits and trenches dug in the ground; enormous heaps of earth and clay thrown up; buildings that were undermined and shaking, propped by great beams of wood.' Six years later, when the dying Paul Dombey returned to visit the Gardens, it was unrecognisable. 'It had vanished from the earth.'[24]

The cutting of railway lines, underground tunnels and sanctioning of improvement legislation (the great panacea for Birmingham and Glasgow inner-city regeneration) proved disastrous for the casual workers and tenement dwellers of central London. As Victoria Station, Charing Cross, Farringdon Street, Liverpool Street, as well as Euston and St

Pancras, were scythed through the city an estimated 120,000 of the 'labouring classes' were evicted from their homes between 1840 and 1900. In the frenetic period 1859–67 alone, some 37,000 displacements took place. And up until 1874 there existed absolutely no requirement upon railway companies to rehouse the homeless. 'Where are they all gone, sir?', asked an onlooker in 1866. 'Why, some's gone down Whitechapel way; some's gone in the Dials; some's gone to Kentish Town; and some's gone to the Workus.'[25]

The chaos wrought by the unregulated railway companies was exacerbated by the activities of the vestries and later the Metropolitan Board of Works. Bazalgette's sewers, along with the construction of such major 'arteries' as Victoria Street, New Oxford Street, Commercial Street and Shaftesbury Avenue, displaced a further 100,000 between 1820 and 1880.[26] Many of these developments were regarded as purposefully ideological: designed like Haussmann's boulevards to expose the dangerous rookeries and culs-de-sac of a potentially revolutionary urban proletariat. *The Times* was convinced that 'as we cut through our woods and roads through our forests, so it should be our policy to divide these thick jungles of crime and misery'.[27] Whereas Nash and earlier developers had used roads as shorelines to hem in the poor, to hide them behind a stage set of Regency wonder, the ambition now was to drive straight through, opening up the dreaded rookeries. Friedrich Engels, watching the transformation of London from his new perch in Regent's Park, saw the bourgeoisie involved in a nefarious strategy he too termed 'Haussmann'.

> By the term 'Haussmann' I do not mean merely the specifically Bonapartist manner of the Parisian Haussmann – breaking long, straight and broad streets through the closely-built workers' quarters and erecting big luxurious buildings ... By 'Haussmann' I mean the practice which has now become general of making breaches in the working-class quarters of our big towns, and particularly in those which are centrally situated, quite apart from whether this is done

from considerations of public health and for beautifying the town ... No matter how different the reasons may be, the result is everywhere the same: the scandalous alleys and lanes disappear to the accompaniment of lavish self-praise from the bourgeoisie on account of this tremendous success, but they appear again immediately somewhere else and often in the immediate neighbourhood.[28]

This was indeed the difficulty. Evictions did not lead to a general dispersal to healthier areas but simply the transfer of overcrowding from one district to another. Even the implementation of such intentionally ameliorative legislation as the Artizans' and Labourers' Dwellings Act (which Chamberlain used to effect in Birmingham), only aggravated the problem. According to the Tory leader Lord Salisbury, '"improvements" on a vast scale have been made, and those improvements, in too many cases, have only meant packing people tighter'.[29] Old houses and unsafe dwellings were destroyed, but new ones were not erected in the same location or number. When replacement buildings were finally constructed, most former tenants had either long dispersed or new rents were typically far in excess of previous arrangements.

With their slums razed to the ground, the dispossessed poor were meant to move out to the suburbs. But this presumption was based on a wilful misreading of the capital's casual economy with its small-scale production and strong seasonal variations in employment. Those employed in the service industries were unable to relocate outside the city (assuming they ever could afford it) as they needed constantly to be on site and available for work. As even *The Times* acknowledged, 'the dock and wharf labourer, the porter and costermonger cannot remove. You may pull down their wretched homes; they must find others, and make their new dwellings more crowded and wretched than their old ones. The tailor, shoemaker and other workmen are in much the same position. It is mockery to speak of the suburbs to them.'[30] The result of 'improvement' was a huge hike in inner-London rents, dramatically increased levels of overcrowding and all the pestilential and moral problems which went with it.

The publication of *The Bitter Cry of Outcast London* segued into a broader debate about the long-term health of Britain's urban populace which had been running since 1859. Coming on the back of a series of revelations concerning evolutionary progress, Charles Darwin's *On the Origin of Species* helped to uproot the entirety of Victorian social and cultural thought, from religion to business to Empire. Despite its widespread impact, many people found the theory of evolution by natural selection a complex theory to grasp and in its wake there emerged a mini-industry in popular translations. One of the most successful at bringing Darwinian ideas more intelligibly before a general audience was the journalist and essayist Herbert Spencer. As well as popularising aspects of evolutionary philosophy, he also explored his own ideas about natural competition and the necessity of progress to create a school of thought known as 'Social Darwinism'. In its most basic form Social Darwinism portrayed human society as involved in a perpetual struggle for the 'survival of the fittest' with the weakest being progressively eliminated. When Spencer's theory was in turn combined with ideas circulating about race, degeneration and biological determinism it produced some disturbing interpretations about the deleterious impact of London on the nation.

As politicians and clergymen occupied themselves with the threat of political revolution and sexual immorality, Social Darwinians started to express concern about the deterioration of the Anglo-Saxon stock in Britain's cities. The social reformer Lord Brabazon asked his reader to take a walk through the streets of London. 'Should he be of average height, he will find himself a head taller than those around him; he will see on all sides pale faces, stunted figures, debilitated forms, narrow chests, and all the outward signs of a low vital power.' 'Nature is stern', Brabazon intoned in full Spencer mode, 'she has no compassion – as men sow, in like manner shall they reap.'[31] The physician G.B. Longstaff concurred in this vicarious diagnosis of the crisis. 'The narrow chest, the pale face, the weak eyes, the bad teeth, of the town-bred child are but too often apparent. It is easy to take an exaggerated view either way, but the broad facts are evident enough; long life in the towns is accompanied by more or less degeneration of race.'[32]

Eminent medical experts suggested that city dwellers might be biologically incapable of sustaining an urban life down the generations. In a paper entitled *The Effects of Town Life on the General Health*, Dr Williams-Freeman contended that 'London is so unhealthy a district that the Anglo-Saxon race is incapable of becoming acclimatized to it. It can exist for two or three generations, when, if not recruited by fresh blood, it dies out.' Haplessly the Londoner could only struggle against the awful ratchet of evolutionary progress. 'Finding himself at a disadvantage in competition with the immigrant, he goes through many stages before he is finally eliminated. Irregular labour, odd jobs, sweaters' dens, prostitution, subsistence of charity, agitation, "demonstrations" and riot, are only some of the struggles of the dying Londoner before he pays the debt of nature, whose laws he has had no power to obey.' Before they eventually died out, the city dwellers exhibited curious behavioural signs which were the unique product of their urban environment. Williams-Freeman interpreted them in predominantly psychological terms:

> The first effect of the bustle of town life on the nervous system is a sensation of unnatural exaltation and excitement of all the faculties, amounting sometimes to an unpleasant irritation ... sooner or later come the signs of nervous exhaustion, restlessness, nervousness, insomnia, a craving for more excitement which never satisfies the mind, with loss of concentration, of judgement, of sense of proportion ... leading in individuals to a lowering of mental tone more distressing than many forms of physical ill-

health, and in communities to a loss of morale and a prone-
ness to excitement, passion, or scare.[33]

All of which might have been bearable if this filthy breed
was not attempting to drag the rest of the race down with it.
While Social Darwinians were content to see the elimination
of an unfit residuum, the problem with this degenerative class
was that it was infecting what remained of the healthy stock.
The disease was spreading as fast as the cities were growing.
With a total population approaching twenty-six million, over
seventeen million now lived in towns, with just over 8.5
million remaining in the countryside. London was expanding
faster than ever by sucking in migrants from across the British
Isles. Between 1841 and 1881 it took in an estimated 1.1
million new inhabitants, primarily from Ireland, central
Europe, but, above all, from the British countryside.[34] 'The
census of 1881 has shown Englishmen that they are rapidly
becoming a population of town-dwellers,' announced Lord
Brabazon. 'Every seventh Briton is a cockney by residence, and
only one in three lives in the country.'[35]

Rural labourers and yeomen, the bulwark of the Anglo-
Saxon race, were being drawn in ever greater numbers into the
degenerative mire of London's East End. The 'Great Depression' of the 1870s and 1880s saw a marked downturn in the
fortunes of British agriculture as an influx of cheap American
and Russian grain imports undermined national cereal production. Agricultural prices collapsed, unemployment soared
and Britain's rural communities faced the hard times which
Thomas Hardy so brilliantly evoked. In *Tess of the D'Urbervilles*, Hardy recounted the process of agricultural depopulation; how 'families, who had formed the backbone of the
village life in the past, who were the depositories of the village
traditions, had to seek refuge in the large centres: the process,
humorously designated by statisticians as "the tendency of
the rural population towards the large towns", being really
the tendency of water to flow uphill when forced by machinery.'[36] For many of the rural unemployed, the only solution

was to seek a new livelihood in the city. To those concerned with the racial health of the nation, no prospect could have been more disastrous.

The situation brought about by the whited sepulchre of London had become so fraught that imperialists thought the 'heart of the Empire' was in danger of undermining the Empire itself. 'With a perpetual lowering of the vitality of the Imperial Race in the great cities of the kingdom,' warned Masterman, 'no amount of hectic, feverish activity on the confines of the Empire will be able to arrest the inevitable decline.'[37] A decline which many feared was being exacerbated by the tens of thousands of Russian and East European Jews entering the capital from the 1880s. Represented as physically enfeebled and possessing a low 'standard of living', the 100,000-odd Jews making their home in London's East End impacted precariously upon fears of Britain's imminent international decline.[38] Of course, the most famous blood-sucking, central European arrival was not a Jewish refugee but a Transylvanian aristocrat who seduced fashionable London, as recounted by Bram Stoker in his *Dracula* (1897). The cycle of degeneration needed somehow to be broken, if not for England then for the sake of the Empire and its dependent, untutored races. Again, the spectre of Rome haunted the late-Victorian imagination. Its empire fell precisely because of the luxury, racial mixing, and physical decline that inevitably accompanied mass urbanisation. As one satirical pamphlet on 'The Decline and Fall of the British Empire' (purportedly published in 'Tokio, 2005'), later put it, 'The first sign of decadence in a Nation appears when it forsakes the calm delights of the country to live amid the depressing splendour of dreary towns.' The same cycle of decline that undermined the Roman Empire could not be allowed to happen to the British.[39] It was a call which united parties of Left and Right. In his *London Programme*, Sidney Webb argued for Fabian policies of reform 'if only for the sake of the rest of the Empire'.[40]

Imperial fears about the effect of outcast London shot up the political agenda when the Army started to reject applicants on grounds of physical incapacity. Of 64,000 men recruited for the Army as early as 1884, claimed Lord Brabazon, no fewer than 30,000 were turned away on account of physical weakness. The peer feared 'large numbers of the inhabitants of our cities are physically unfitted, though in the prime of life, to defend the country in time of war'. Britain was faced with an evil which 'would ultimately lead to degeneration of the race and to national effacement'. When the government needed to enlist soldiers for the Boer War, Brabazon was proved horribly right as tens of thousands were prevented on medical grounds. And as the British forces were outmanoeuvred in the Transvaal, imperialists were quick to lay the blame for the reverses on the disparity between the weak-chested London squaddie and the healthy, country-bred Boer. Such was the level of official concern, the government set up an Interdepartmental Committee on Physical Deterioration to suggest remedies for this alarming threat to national security.

In the light of increased German industrial, military and diplomatic competition, the debate about London and other British cities assumed a strategic significance. British national efficiency, its place in the hierarchy of nations, was being placed in jeopardy by the state of its cities. The town planner T.C. Horsfall voiced the worry when he unfavourably contrasted the divergent paths taken by the two Saxon races. 'The German towns contain a much larger proportion of tall, well-developed men and women than do the English towns, and in no large German towns is it possible to find such masses of undersized, ill-developed and sickly-looking people as are to be found in the poorer districts of London, Manchester, Liverpool, Birmingham, and all other large British towns.'[41] The Germans lived in well-planned, well-built environments, underwent regular physical exercise both in school gymnastic classes and adult military training, and, most interestingly of all, their social classes shared the same civic space. There was no West End/East End divide in the great German towns. Instead, rich and poor mixed alike and the result was a healthier urban community and a threateningly more powerful race.

iii THE COLONIAL SOLUTION

Momentum for the cleansing of outcast London had been growing before the German threat appeared. The bitter cry of outcast London had echoed as far as the turrets of Balmoral Castle from where Queen Victoria dispatched a note to her Prime Minister, Gladstone, expressing distress at 'all she has heard and read lately of the deplorable condition of the Homes of the Poor in our greatest towns'.[42] When Trafalgar Square and the West End came under attack from East End 'roughs' in 1886 and then again in 1887 (so-called 'Bloody Sunday'), fears of revolution, echoes of the Paris Commune, gripped the political classes.

Official approaches to the problem of urban poverty had traditionally placed great faith in the practical work and doctrinal announcements of the housing reformer Octavia Hill, along with the generally uncharitable Charity Organisation Society. Both asserted that the difficulties facing the casual poor were generally self-made and boiled down to questions of character and moral fibre. Poverty and mass unemployment were not the issue; the challenge was to counter the process of 'demoralization' by training the poor in habits of punctuality, thrift and respectability through a series of highly controlled housing projects. The poor needed to be helped to help themselves. Here in all their glory were the 'Victorian values' of Thatcherite lore.[43]

The focus on character and emphasis on moral uplift produced one of the most celebrated and durable social experiments of the period: the Settlement Movement. Pioneered by Edward Denison but made famous by Samuel Barnett's Toynbee Hall in Whitechapel, the movement settled middle-class, Christian volunteers in the immoral wastelands of the East End. Through the personal involvement of these high-minded graduates in the community, settlements aimed to curb the self-destructive habits of the poor. At the movement's emotional core was a profound distaste for impersonal, bureaucratic charity and a strong belief in class interaction, the unifying of the West End and East End, as the route to social reform. As Barnett proudly claimed in his curiously entitled work *Practicable Socialism*, 'The poor have learnt to help themselves, and have found self-help a stronger bond by which to keep the home together than the dole of the relieving officer or of the district visitor.'[44] The beguiling figure of Samuel Barnett, along with his glamorous wife Henrietta, attracted a flurry of bright young things down from Oxford to the slums of Whitechapel. Hundreds of future social reformers passed through its doors, including the godfather of the welfare state, William Beveridge, as well as the future Labour Prime Minister Clement Attlee. Attlee became Secretary of the Settlement – but, rather wonderfully, 'still attended the Haileybury House Club whenever possible'.[45]

However, by the later 1880s Toynbee Hall and the COS no longer seemed enough. Instead, there emerged within elements of middle-class opinion a different attitude towards combating poverty. Beatrice Webb described it as 'a consciousness of sin ... a growing uneasiness, amounting to conviction, that the industrial organisation, which had yielded rent, interest, and profits on a stupendous scale, had failed to provide a decent livelihood and tolerable conditions for a majority of the inhabitants of Great Britain'.[46] The old evangelical certainties of Hill and the settlement ethos of Barnett appeared outdated, even misguided in the light of more rigorous sociological and economic analyses. Whether it was sin, guilt or fear, politicians and social reformers began to emphasise the role of the environment (as the Health of Towns Association had done so many years beforehand) and economic conditions in circumscribing the fate of the poor. Amidst the terrible blight of the Great Depression, the collapse of industries, changes in market structures and overcrowded housing were at last appreciated as playing a more decisive role in the emergence of poverty than individual moral failings.

Pressure for reform multiplied after the publication in 1889 of the first part of Charles Booth's encyclopaedic study of the East End, *Life and Labour of the People in London*. A successful shipping magnate from a prosperous Unitarian family in Liverpool, Booth originally began his researches into the capital's poor (helped in part by his younger cousin, the ubiquitous Beatrice Potter) after hearing statistics put about by the left-wing Social Democratic Federation (SDF) that one in four Londoners lived in abject poverty. Dismissive of such socialist propaganda, he aimed to put them right with an array of objective data garnered by the most advanced methods of social analysis. After years of trawling through school board visitor reports, Poor Law statistics and police data, as well as walking the streets of Whitechapel and Mile End, Booth and his team discovered the proportion living in poverty was most certainly not the SDF figure of twenty-five per cent; it was, in fact, something approaching thirty-five per cent. Booth found that of 900,000 people in the district, some 314,000 were poor while over 100,000 suffered from acute 'distress'. Moreover, the cause of poverty in outcast London was not idleness, drunkenness or thriftlessness but in the vast majority of cases unemployment, low pay, large family dependency or sickness.[47]

Stung by criticisms of inaction, a new spirit of intervention was abroad and it extended right up to the high priest of conservatism, Lord Salisbury himself. In the wake of *The Bitter Cry*, he supported a Royal Commission on the Housing of the Working Classes. The Tory Prime Minister (who succeeded Gladstone into Downing Street in 1885) then followed it up with the 1885 Housing Act, which empowered the Metropolitan Board of Works to build and let homes for the working classes. It was a clear admission of the failures of private enterprise and charity to provide properly for the complex needs of the urban poor.

Other urban commentators advocated an altogether more sinister solution which took the Social Darwinian analysis of racial degeneration to an unedifying conclusion. The late 1880s heard ever more voluminous calls for the sterilisation of the urban residuum in the name of national efficiency. Charles Booth, whose research did so much to underpin the progressive case for government action, unashamedly argued for the extirpation of the casual poor, the social group he termed 'Class B'. 'They render no useful service, they create no wealth: more often they destroy it. They degrade whatever they touch, and as individuals are perhaps incapable of improvement.'[48] He suggested they be sent to compulsory labour camps or the poorhouse, where their children could be nurtured under less degrading influences so as to break the degenerative cycle. By eliminating the class which dragged down all those surrounding it, Booth believed the deserving, working poor would then be able to rise up the social scale. He called it 'individual socialism'. The writer Arnold White did not proclaim any such lofty ideals. He simply urged 'the extermination of the unfit as a class'.[49]

What the majority of these political solutions to the problem of outcast London had in common was a willingness to engage with the problems of the city. Octavia Hill's housing trusts, Samuel Barnett's Settlement Movement, the Royal Commission on Housing, the Metropolitan Board of Works redevelopment, and even some of the eugenic proposals all aimed to reform the functioning of the city. And this reforming impulse was very much the spirit with which the London County Council initiated its own social programme in 1889. However, there existed alongside this strategy a very different set of solutions. One that suggested the capital's level of racial degeneration, social disintegration and populous overcrowding signalled a need to flee the city altogether.

The economist Alfred Marshall was one of the first to outline a rejectionist template. In an article for the *Contemporary Review*, he praised the foresight of the industrialist Sir Titus Salt for moving his works from inner-city Bradford to the wholesome country air of Shipley. Saltaire combined all 'the advantages of town and country ... it had cheap rents, fresh air, wholesome outdoor amusements for young and old; the nerves are not overwrought, and the physique does not degenerate'. Marshall proposed a similar policy for London: the removal of large sections of the working population into industrial colonies outside the degenerative filth of the capital. Manufacturers would gain from low rents and the workers would thrive in a healthy environment. There was no longer any point in trying to reform London. It was beyond saving. 'Surely time and money devoted to helping the feeble and timid to move and carry their work with them, are better spent than in diminishing some of the evils of their lives in London. In London, even when their houses are whitewashed, the sky will be dark; devoid of joy, they will still tend to drink for excitement; they will go on deteriorating'.[50]

General Booth's scheme for rescuing the submerged tenth from the urban jungle of darkest England was composed along similar lines. The Salvation Army intended to establish a series of colonies 'for all and any who have been shipwrecked in life, character, or circumstance'. Some of these would be urban, but a larger number would be located 'in the provinces' as part of an attempt to reverse the tide of rural migration and its attendant misery. 'As the race from the Country to the City has been the cause of much of the distress we have to battle with, we propose to find a substantial part of our remedy by transferring these same people back to the country, that is back again to "the Garden!"' What this meant in practice (or rather, in theory) was a self-contained estate of a thousand acres populated with a series of teetotal agricultural villages. Working the land, the urban poor would garner new skills, undergo a godly reformation of character, and ultimately be transformed into model employees ready for labour in a string of new colonies abroad. Booth hoped this linear process of personal regeneration might well lay the foundation, 'per chance, of another Empire to swell to vast proportions in later times. Why not?' For those working families left behind in cities, the Salvation Army proposed their transfer to a series of 'Industrial Settlements' in the countryside. These new villages would be lined with 'cottages of suitable size and construction', have close railway links to the capital and operate an affordable system of rents and train fares 'for the families of working-men'.[51]

The intellectual retreat from London was gathering pace. The task of reforming the city was too great. Self-sustaining colonies, villages and industrial settlements free from pollution, drink and urban immorality provided an answer. Marshall, Booth and the other contributors in this field might have had competing ideas over the precise model for these town-country communities, but all held firm to two key tenets. First, London needed to be abandoned; but second, the remedy did not lie in the tentacle of suburbs now encircling the capital.

iv In Suburbia

'Why should I not publish my diary? I have often seen reminiscences of people I have never even heard of, and I fail to see – because I do not happen to be a 'Somebody' – why my diary should not be interesting. My only regret is that I did not commence it when I was a youth.' So began George and Weedon Grossmiths' sublime spoof of the suburban ingénue Charles Pooter. Published in *Punch*, *The Diary of a Nobody* was a brilliant satirical assault on the social mores and upward aspirations of London's burgeoning suburbia. 'My dear wife Carrie and I have just been a week in our new house, "The Laurels", Brickfield Terrace, Holloway – a nice six-roomed residence, not counting basement, with a front breakfast-parlour... After my work in the City, I like to be at home. What's the good of a home, if you are never in it? "Home, Sweet Home", that's my motto ... There is always something to be done: a tin-tack here, a Venetian blind to put straight, a fan to nail up, or part of a carpet to nail down.' Filled with cringing accounts of his daily battle against surly tradesmen, his passion for home improvements, and endless, needless social difficulties, it remains a peerless comedy of manners.

[At the theatre in Islington] ... I was leaning out of the box, when my tie – a little black bow which fastened on to the stud by means of a new patent – fell into the pit below. A clumsy man not noticing it, had his foot on it for ever so

long before he discovered it. He then picked it up and
eventually flung it under the next seat in disgust ... To hide
the absence of the tie I had to keep my chin down the rest
of the evening, which caused a pain at the back of my neck.[52]

Pooter's suburbia was a miniature landscape of humorous
embarrassment. In reality, London's suburbs comprised in
scale and sophistication a planning phenomenon and social
movement instinctively hostile to the precepts of Victorian
civic pride. The ethos of suburbia constituted a sustained
assault on the nineteenth-century urban tradition.

The growth of suburban London had been going on for some
one hundred years before the Pooters moved into Holloway.
Since the late eighteenth century, the space between inner
London and its surrounding villages (Islington, Hackney, Highgate, Clapham, and so on) had been slowly filling up with
housing along the main arterial roads. The creation of St
John's Wood in north London was arguably one of the first
consciously suburban developments, artfully mixing the benefits of urban proximity with a villa aesthetic. There quickly
followed in its wake the less elegant Kentish Town, Gospel
Oak, Primrose Hill and the other London neighbourhoods
which started to submerge the old villages into one larger,
unitary metropolis. Dulwich, Camberwell and Hampstead
now became high-end commuter settlements as the appellation 'suburb' lost its previously plebeian connotations. Then
in the 1880s came a step-change in development.

'The greatest advance of the decade is shown', reported
Sidney Low in 1891, 'not in the cities themselves, but in the
ring of suburbs which spread into the country around them
... The centre of population is shifting from the heart to the
limbs. The life-blood is pouring into the long arms of bricks
and mortar and cheap stucco that are feeling their way out to
the Surrey moors, and the Essex flats, and the Hertfordshire
copses.'[53] Between 1891 and 1901 the outer-ring suburbs of
London expanded by forty-five per cent.[54] By the end of the
century, the population of Lambeth stood at almost 300,000,

up from a mere 28,000 in 1800. Similarly, Camberwell boasted some 250,000 inhabitants, compared to the 7,000 with which it began the century; and the vast majority of that growth occurred from the 1880s onwards. The contemporary compiler of these figures thought 'the expansion of London ... is in itself a fact unparalleled in the history of cities'.[55] Of course, it was not just London. Headingley in Leeds, Bowden and Ellesmere Park near Manchester, and Edgbaston and Handsworth outside Birmingham all experienced marked increases in population, but none of them to the same extent as the booming south-east.

In any urban setting there has always existed a certain conceptual flexibility about where precisely suburbia begins, but late-Victorian London rightly sensed it was being encircled by a markedly more conscious form of suburban civilisation. 'There is a great flood', declared *Building News*, 'which has overtaken London and our great cities with houses and dwellings for the middle and working-classes. Go where we will ... the fungus-like growth of houses manifests itself, stretching from town to suburb and village ... This is one of the social revolutions of the age.'[56] Part of the revolutionary nature of modern suburbia was precisely its democracy. The benefits of out-of-town living were being extended to the previously excluded lower-middle and labouring classes. 'The habit of living at a distance from the scene of work has spread from the merchant and the clerk to the artisan,' reported *The Times*, 'and one has only to observe the substitution of small houses for large in the older suburbs, and the streets of cottages in new extensions, to realize that the suburb is now mainly the residence of the family of small means.'[57]

The changing constitution of the suburb was principally due to advances in London's transport provision. The 1883 Cheap Trains Act compelled railway companies to provide some form of workmen's trains at suitable fare levels. Great Eastern was the first to take the lead and in so doing opened up Edmonton and Walthamstow as some of the capital's first working-class suburbs. Connections to Stoke Newington,

West Ham and Lewisham followed. Altogether the number of workmen's trains increased from 1,807 in 1890 to 6,490 in 1904 and reached 12,318 by 1912. With the lines came the property developers and row upon row of terraced housing. The railways also opened up more lofty, distant sites for the middle-class commuter, acting as much like pioneers of human settlement as the trans-continental lines of North America. Meanwhile, the electrified London Underground network (beginning with the Metropolitan Line) and the city's tram system were extending the compass of domestic development. London was spreading its tentacles.[58]

While the dominant impression of suburbia may be one of staid conformity – a world of stifling regularity where innovation is anathema – the process of its construction was anything but. The rapid developments of the 1880s left Londoners feeling utterly bewildered at the pace of change. Descriptions of the time bring to mind modern accounts of deforestation in the Amazon rainforest: a morass of roads, building sites and wilful destruction. 'The speculative builder descends upon green fields,' reported The Times, 'cuts straight roads through them, and plants as many houses on a given space as he thinks he can let.'[59] In The New Machiavelli, H.G. Wells's narrator describes his memory of childhood in the London suburb of 'Bromstead' (for which read Bromley) during the late nineteenth century as full 'of digging and wheeling, of woods invaded by building, roads gashed open and littered with iron pipes amidst a fearful smell of gas ... of hedges broken down and replaced by planks, of wheelbarrows and builders' sheds, of rivulets overtaken and swallowed up by drainpipes'. Wells, who grew up in Bromley, regarded the encirclement of his small Kent village by London as 'a sort of progress that had bolted; it was change out of hand, and going at an unprecedented pace nowhere in particular'.[60]

What this disordered, suburban machine was destroying in its wake was the network of detached, scattered villages which had for centuries comprised London's outer ring. Neighbourhoods which had traditionally backed onto open countryside were now swamped by the suburban tsunami. In south London, Walter Besant recorded in anguish the slow evisceration of the beautiful Battersea and Wimbledon of his youth. 'It is difficult, now that the whole country south of London has been covered with villas, roads, streets, and shops, to understand how wonderful for loveliness it was until the builder seized upon it.'[61] Anyone visiting today's Wandsworth or Stockwell might find such a leap of the imagination equally arduous. It was not just the paving-over of the countryside which dismayed the critics, it was also what went up in its place. The new suburban developments, the monotonous and tightly packed terraced housing spilling out across the city, were uniformly condemned as vulgar, cheap and dreary. Even those attempting sophistication with a Gothic frontispiece or Doric door were ridiculed for their suburban affectation. According to the supremely hostile *Times*, suburbia was 'a district of appalling monotony, ugliness, and dullness'. In his bilious squib, *The Suburbans*, the reactionary poet T.W.H. Crosland was even more vicious: 'in the whole arid area of Suburbia you shall not find a building that meets the eye graciously, or that does not bespeak a vile taste and a stingy purse'.[62]

Even greater contempt was reserved for the ethic of suburbia. For during the late nineteenth century the suburban way of life first emerged as the subject of that intense cultural fascination which continues to this day, sustained by perpetual reruns of *Terry and June* and *The Good Life*. For middle-class suburbia has always been far more a state of mind than a geographical location; its defining attributes mental rather than physical. In the words of one historian, it is a 'bourgeois utopia': a world of privacy and seclusion which celebrates the family unit and is consciously separated off from the public (male) domain of work and civic culture. 'Its power derived ultimately from the capacity of suburban design to express a complex and compelling vision of the modern family freed from the corruption of the city, restored to harmony with nature, endowed with wealth and independence yet protected

by a close-knit, stable-community.'[63] Consequently, suburbia
reveres the house and the garden and the individual, domestic
pursuits which surround them. Towards the final entries in
his *Diary of a Nobody*, Charles Pooter's son looks set to enter
the same City firm as him. For Pooter it is a dream of familial,
domestic bliss come true. 'My boy in the same office as
myself – we can go down together by the 'bus, come home
together, and who knows but in the course of time he may
take great interest in our little home. That he may help me to
put a nail in here or a nail in there, or help his dear mother to
hang a picture ... In the summer he may help us in our little
garden with the flowers, and assist us to paint the stands and
pots.'[64]

Masterman regarded this new tribe of Pooters as a totally
homogenous civilisation – 'detached, self-centred, unosten-
tatious'. 'It is a life of Security; a life of Sedentary occupation;
a life of Respectability ... Each boasts its pleasant drawing-
room, its bow-window, its little front garden, its high-sounding
title "Acacia Villa", or "Campderdown Lodge" – attesting
unconquered human aspiration. There are many interests
beyond the working hours: here a greenhouse filled with chrys-
anthemums, a bicycle shed, a tennis lawn.'

It was this otiose reverence for domesticity which corrupted
the suburban mind, its mental stupor reflected in and
reinforced by the fashion for reading low-grade journalism,
'personal paragraphs, descriptions of clothes, smile, or
manner'. This tittle-tattle produced, in turn, 'a vision of life
in which the trivial and heroic things are alike exhibited, but
in which there is no adequate test or judgment, which are the
heroic, which the trivial ... This is the explanation of the so-
called "snobbery" of the suburbs.' H.G. Wells was similarly
exercised by the frivolous suburban mentality. He denounced
'Bromstead' as 'a dull useless boiling-up of human activities,
an immense clustering of futilities'.[65] It was the futility of the
existence which led to the enormous expenditure of energy
on 'keeping up with the Joneses' or pursuing what Masterman
regarded as the staple ingredient of suburban life, low-grade

neighbourhood vendettas. 'So into a feud with a neighbour over a disputed garden fence ... or a criticism of manners and fashion, dress and deportment, will be thrown force and determination which might have been directed to effort of permanent worth, in devotion of one of the great causes of the world.'[66] And this even without the great *casus belli* of modern-day suburbia – fast-growing leylandii.

The most iniquitous consequence of suburban life was its assault on the public ethos of the city. The individualism, the domesticity along with the obsessive emphasis on privacy was anathema to the ethos of Victorian civic life. As Donald Olsen has remarked, the flight to the suburbs involved the conscious rejection of the rest of society beyond the immediate family; the most satisfactory suburb was that which gave the maximum of privacy and the minimum of outside distraction.[67] The civic pride which drove William Roscoe to found the Liverpool Royal Institution, inspired the *conversazione* of the Manchester Athenaeum, or encouraged the brightest and best to offer themselves as candidates for Birmingham City or London County Council was quietly abandoned for mowing the lawn and a bit of tinkering in the garden shed. The great achievements of the Victorian civic spirit were progressively undermined by a string of outwardly innocuous green suburbs.

Indeed, their very design thwarted the public life of urban man; there was no civic space, no *agora* for political or economic debate. Victorian civil society, the urban spirit which had made the nineteenth century the 'age of great cities', was being suffocated by stealth. The Athenaeums, the Mechanics' Institutes, the chapels and town halls were being exchanged for bow windows and well-bordered lawns. South London was typical:

It is a city without a municipality, without a centre, without a civic history; it has no newspapers, magazines or journals; it has no university, it has no colleges, apart from medical; it has no intellectual, artistic, scientific, musical, literary centre – unless the Crystal Palace can be considered as a centre; its residents have no local patriotism or enthusiasm ... it has no theatres except of a very popular or humble kind; it has no clubs, it has no public buildings, it has no West End.[68]

The consequence was a diminution in public life or greater sense of an urban responsibility beyond the domestic sphere. There existed instead a carefully protected myopia with regard to municipal or civic duties. An Englishman's house was now his castle and he showed decreasing interest in lowering the drawbridge. Masterman thought the situation approached one of moral corruption:

Suburban life has often little conception of social services, no tradition of disinterested public duty, but a limited outlook beyond a personal ambition ... What remains? A public spirit in local affairs which is deplorably low, which sends a minute percentage of voters to Council or Guardian Elections, and accompanies a perpetual contempt for present municipal mismanagement with a refusal of the personal effort required to make that management clean and efficient.[69]

Commuting between city and suburb, spending the day in crowded offices, reading the sensationalist press, avidly following professional sport, and happy to live in a state of blissful political and social ignorance, the modern suburban man was as much a threat to British civilisation and Empire as the lowliest Whitechapel slum dweller. This dreadful weakening of civic fibre convinced the majority of urban reformers that despite the health benefits of airy living, despite the enormous popularity of suburban housing, outcast London could not be saved by creating a nation of Bromsteads.

But if the fate of London did not lie in its encircling suburbs, what was the future for Britain's urban civilisation? With cities growing ever mightier, the race declining, poverty deepening, and even national security at risk, viable solutions to outcast London (as well as outcast Manchester, Liverpool, Leeds and Glasgow) were required more urgently than ever. One man thought he had the answer. And it lay not in the city or suburb, but in the garden. The dark continent of 1880s London would lead not to the cleansing of the capital's rookeries, but instead spark a flight from the city to the garden and with it a devastating disavowal of the Victorian civic spirit.

GARDEN CITIES AND THE TRIUMPH OF SUBURBIA

Among the swarm of commuters making their daily journey from the sprawling suburbs of Victorian London into the city centre was a middle-aged gentleman of medium height and sturdy build dressed in all the dignified accoutrements of nineteenth-century office employment. Sporting a small moustache and greying hair, Ebenezer Howard 'was the sort of man who could easily pass unnoticed in a crowd'. Every morning, this anonymous shorthand writer caught the train from his modest home in Dulwich the five miles to the Houses of Parliament where he spent the day transcribing the verbose pronouncements of MPs and Peers. And while they debated the reform of working-class housing, the cleansing of outcast London, and the terrible blight of suburban development, up above them in the shorthand gallery was working away this unprepossessing figure who knew that he held the single answer to all these problems.[1]

To Ebenezer Howard, along with a growing body of influential opinion, the state of Britain's cities had deteriorated beyond reform; they needed to be deserted or razed to the ground, with resources transferred to creating new communities free from the existing detritus of city life. Given the very real threat cities posed to the state of the race, as well as to political stability, the moral well-being of the British people depended vitally on their being liberated from the Victorian urban heritage. These sentiments of civic revulsion inspired a search for new forms of settlement which were able to retain the social vibrancy of urban living but united with the sanitary health and clean living of the countryside. And by far the most successful solution was that proposed by Howard. But contrary to his expectations, rather than renewing urban life the implementation of his vision would fatally undermine it. Ebenezer Howard's bequest would not be a reformed urban civilisation, but a new planning consensus which spurned the legacy of the nineteenth-century city and posited instead a miserable town-country suburbia which one hundred years on still blights our public space and belittles our civic sense.

i Ebenezer Howard and the Windy City

Ebenezer Howard was born in 1850, the son of lower-middle-class, Nonconformist shopkeepers in the City of London.[2] He spent his early years living in a series of small country towns – Ipswich, Sudbury, Cheshunt – where he attended local Dissenting academies. Never a scholar, he left school at the age of fifteen and signed up as a City clerk, where he displayed a natural aptitude for shorthand transcription. When he reached twenty-one, Howard unexpectedly deserted the dreary confines of his City post and headed off for the rolling plains of middle America. In March 1871, he arrived with two friends in the perennially bleak state of Nebraska and took control of a 160-acre plot complete with a one-room log cabin. A long way from Sudbury, around him lay the desolate Midwest prairies. One of Howard's future acolytes, the town planner F.J. Osborn, always remained bemused by this outback period. 'Those who knew him in later years will find it delightful to picture him as a frontiersman, a slight figure wearing glasses for short sight, carrying a revolver and an Enfield rifle lest he should meet Indians (he met only one, and "nothing happened"), planting with his own hands maize, potatoes, melons and cucumbers, and occasionally preaching at the distant Ebenezer Church.'[3]

Nebraska was not a success. After a terrible winter and barely a year on the land, Howard fled the farm for the urban safety of Chicago, Illinois. But he found Chicago in an even worse state. A monstrous fire in 1871 had destroyed twenty-eight miles of streets, some 2,000 acres of the downtown district, putting 100,000 people out of their homes and wiping out one-third of the city's value. Arriving just as the 'Great Rebuilding' was getting under way, from his post as a shorthand writer on La Salle Street, Howard saw the new Chicago of planned boulevards and towering office blocks take shape around him. Perhaps more importantly, from his lodgings on Michigan Avenue he also enjoyed the rambling Lake Shore Park, which stood as a buffer between the densely packed city and the icy expanse of Lake Michigan. Before it was the 'windy city' (so-called for its politics rather than chilling winds), Chicago was known as 'the garden city' because of its extensive parks and open spaces. Even today – with the glitzy Lincoln Park in the north and the less salubrious Lake Shore Park in the south – the city remains, outside the downtown district, a surprisingly green conurbation.

After five years in America, Howard returned to a London buffeted by the Great Depression, the rural influx, and the working-class housing crisis. But after the austerity of Nebraska and the ruins of Chicago, Howard enjoyed his life back in the capital. He took up a shorthand position with a firm of parliamentary reporters, fell in love with a tradesman's daughter, Elizabeth Ann Bills, and revelled in the daily excitements of the teeming city. 'The crowded streets – the signs of wealth and prosperity – the bustle – the very confusion and disorder appealed to me, and I was filled with delight.'[4] What really excited him were the radical political and religious ideas circulating through the capital. During his years in America, Howard had developed a keen interest in transcendentalism as well as that quintessential late-Victorian pursuit, the relationship between science and religion. Back in Britain, he joined the heterodox debating group, The Zetetical Society, which included in its membership George Bernard Shaw and Sidney Webb, where he spent earnest evenings discussing these matters with fellow free-thinkers.

With the publication of Andrew Mearns's *The Bitter Cry*, Howard was inevitably drawn to the debate about housing and the fate of London. However, while he might have worked in the same building, even listened to their debates, he moved in a very different sphere to the Establishment circle of Alfred Marshall, Lord Brabazon and the Marquis of Salisbury. Howard's world was a clerks' domain of Nonconformist chapels, free-thinking discussion groups, and the odd intellectual's lecture. But as he sat transcribing the policy prescriptions of Brabazon and Salisbury, one thought began to occupy his mind with ever greater fervour: the deleterious effects – which he had first witnessed in Chicago after fire damage had destroyed accommodation and escalated housing costs – that city-centre land values exerted over the progress of society. He started to believe that the myriad problems of urban Britain were predicated on an inequitable and outmoded form of real estate valuation.

It was not of itself a novel contention. Indeed, the politics of land had become a *cause célèbre* in radical London following the arrival in 1881 of the American reforming firebrand, Henry George. In his heretical work *Progress and Poverty*, George argued that since no man created the land, it was wrong for its wealth to be alienated from the general population by private appropriation. Moreover, increases in rental value accruing to landlords were rarely the product of individual initiative but rather the by-product of general economic growth. Accordingly, this 'unearned increment' was the rightful property of the nation at large and not individual landlords. The answer to this unsustainable economic condition, which was hindering progress towards socialist harmony, was the restoration of the social value of the land to the public by means of a single land tax. Ultimately, it was hoped this would lead to the nationalisation of the land and the equitable distribution of its wealth amongst the public. With the creation of the Land Restoration League, the Land Nationalisation Society and the adoption of the single land tax by various embryonic socialist organisations, the issue of land reform became a central component of late 1880s political thinking.

But then, amidst the political turbulence of this transatlantic debate, on 30 May 1887 Julian West fell into a deep sleep. He woke up after 113 years in 2000 and saw beneath him a totally changed city from the Boston of his slumbers:

> At my feet lay a great city. Miles of broad streets, shaded by trees and lined with fine buildings, for the most part not in continuous blocks, but set in larger or smaller enclosures, stretched in every direction. Every quarter contained large open squares filled with trees, among which statues glistened and fountains flashed in the late afternoon sun. Public buildings of a colossal size and an architectural grandeur unparalleled in my day, raised their stately piles on every side. Surely I had never seen this city nor one comparable to it before.

The hero of Edward Bellamy's futuristic novel, *Looking Backward: 2000–1887* (1888), had been transported from the urban squalor and social iniquity of 1880s America to an utopian socialist commonwealth in which technological advance had eliminated degrading toil and all men were equal. An industrial army, working in harmony harnessing employment to aptitude, had taken over the rational organisation of the economy and the result was a society of abundance. In true Henry George fashion, the land, both agricultural and urban, was held in trust for the community. But Bellamy's futuristic Boston was not some Arcadian rural commune. The society of *Looking Backward* was industrial, urban and technologically sophisticated. It was tightly ordered, economically regimented and consequently free of crime, greed and poverty; all of which was reflected in its modern, open, urban design marked by a combination of Haussmannesque boulevards, extensive parklands as well as a consciously civic architecture. For one enthusiastic British reader, this picture of a cohesive rural-urban, egalitarian society was bewitching.

> I was transported by the wonderful power of the writer into a new society, which, having solved for itself the industrial elements of the social problem, had its face turned towards the problem of the higher life ... I shall never forget the next morning's experience. I went into some of the crowded parts of London, and as I passed through the narrow dark streets, saw the wretched dwellings in which the majority of the people lived, observed on every hand the manifestations of a self-seeking order of society, and reflected on the absolute unsoundness of our economic system, there came to me an overpowering sense of the quite temporary nature of nearly all I saw, and of its entire unsuitability for the working life of the new order – the order of justice, unity, and friendliness ... the writer had permanently convinced me that our present industrial order stands absolutely condemned and is tottering to its fall, and that a new and brighter, because a juster order must ere long take its place.[5]

In fact, Ebenezer Howard was so taken by Bellamy's utopia that he arranged for the English publication of the novel at his own expense. However, not all his compatriots were so convinced by Bellamy's rather Fordist future. The aesthete and socialist William Morris was scathing about the utopia's soulless mechanism. 'His scheme may be described as State Communism, worked by the very extreme of national centralisation ... a machine-life is the best which Mr Bellamy can imagine for us on all sides.'[6] Morris responded with his own socialist utopia, outlined in the punningly entitled *News from Nowhere* (1891). His former mentor John Ruskin had already provided the intellectual foundations for the Arts and Crafts approach to town planning when he described how it was impossible 'to have any right morality, happiness, or art, in any country where the cities are clotted and coagulated together'.

Instead, 'you must have lovely cities ... limited in size, and
not casting out the scum and scurf of them into an encircling
eruption of shame, but girded each with its sacred pomoerium,
and with garlands of gardens, tall blossoming trees, and softly-
guided streams'.[7] Although not quite as uplifting as Ruskin,
the Richard Jefferies novel, *After London* (1885), which
depicted a capital reclaimed by its marshes ('a vast stagnant
swamp, which no man dare enter, since death would be his
inevitable fate'), was a further source of inspiration.

In *News from Nowhere*, Morris drew upon these utopian
and dystopian traditions while adding in a touch of class war.
Set in the London of the future, Morris (who had fought in
the 'Bloody Sunday' riots of 1887) depicted a society where
capitalism and parliamentary governance had been overthrown by violent revolution.

> 'Tell me one thing, if you can,' said I. 'Did the change ...
> come peacefully?'
> 'Peacefully?', said he. 'What peace was there amongst
> those poor, confused wretches of the nineteenth century? It
> was war from beginning to end: bitter war, until hope and
> pleasure put an end to it.'[8]

Standing in place of 'the world city' was a rural Elysium
where artisans (dressed in fourteenth-century garb) lived in
small communes and worked in self-governing craft guilds,
where the Houses of Parliament had been converted into a
giant dung-heap, and factories and suburbs had been replaced
by forests and meadows. The Thames landscape was a very
different place. 'The soap works with their smoke-vomiting
chimneys were gone; the engineer's works were gone; the lead
works were gone; and no sound of riveting and hammering
came down the west wind from Thorneycroft's.'[9] Morris
depicted an epoch of rest after the socialist revolution; a land
of beauty and art which would teach a desire for a better life.
It was an aggressively anti-urban picture which, coming in the
wake of Arnold Toynbee's intellectual assault on the Industrial

Revolution, sought to reject the entire ethos of the Victorian city. The nineteenth-century urban world was recast as a symbol of greed, misery and destructive competitiveness. There could be no more attempts at gradual reform; it had to be destroyed and reborn as a different society.

Morris and Bellamy's violent interjection of the country into the city became a popular literary and political conceit. From his ultra-urban settlement in Whitechapel, Samuel Barnett composed a tract entitled *The Ideal City* in which he described how in future a socially minded citizenry would 'lay out open spaces, raise and decorate their public buildings. They will endow the bands which play in the parks and the halls. They will employ the artists who will make the streets a very gallery of pictures.'[10] In *Merrie England* (1895), the great socialist polemicist Robert Blatchford outlined a utopian future of 'towns rebuilt with wide streets, with detached houses, with gardens, and fountains and avenues of trees'. Sidney Webb even invoked the 'windy city' as he outlined how the Fabians would transform the capital along similar if more politically viable lines than Morris. 'The parks, indeed, will be tremendous affairs. The new towns in the suburban belt will, as at Chicago, be connected by shady avenues, expanding at intervals into a ring of parks intersected by winding country lanes, bought up and preserved by a generation to whom Rye Lane and Lisson Grove serve as hideous warnings of the consequences of neglect.'[11]

At the same time as the country seemed to be making its way into the city, schemes for new settlements had ceased being the stuff of pipe dreams. On the outskirts of Birmingham and Liverpool they had become a reality.

ii CORPORATE COMMUNITIES: BOURNVILLE AND SUNLIGHT

Not far from the Edgbaston suburb where Joseph Chamberlain had first settled in Birmingham was a pretty little area known as Bournbrook. It was to this site, four miles south of the city, that in 1879 the brothers George and Richard Cadbury decided to move their cocoa and chocolate product business from its central Broad Street location. They christened their new headquarters Bournville in an attempt to exploit the vogue for French names given to high-quality food.

Of good Quaker pedigree, with a long record of involvement in the community, the Cadburys remained appalled by the miserable state of Birmingham's working-class housing despite all the 'improvements' which had been promised by Chamberlain. Like many of his fellow reformers, George Cadbury was convinced that improving the housing of the poor was the key to their social betterment. So when the new Bournville site was erected he ensured sixteen affordable houses went up with it designated specifically for the company's solid, thrifty working classes. As demand intensified a Building Estate was then established, open to anyone who wanted to live on the site. By 1900 the Estate consisted of 330 acres and 313 cottages, along with various educational and civic institutes including non-denominational schools, a Ruskin Hall for arts and crafts, and a Friends' Meeting House.

With houses spaced at no more than eight to an acre (twenty to a hectare), Bournville's design signalled a blanket rejection of the high-density urban living which had been such a signal component of the Victorian city. The Estate architect, Alexander Harvey, instigated a fairly uniform model drawn from local Worcestershire styles but allowed just enough differences in front elevation to give the impression of individual variety. Light and airy, the houses typically consisted of a parlour, living room and kitchen downstairs, with three bedrooms upstairs. Bathrooms came later. Most importantly of all, the Bournville resident was surrounded by parks, forty-two-foot-wide tree-lined roads and unprecedentedly spacious gardens back and front. Fruit trees were planted at the far end of the garden and tenants were expected to grow vegetables, with remedial gardening classes offered for the young and horticulturally challenged. More bizarrely, the very first residents

on the Estate were given a copy of George Cadbury's Rules of
Health which included such essential advice as 'use oatmeal
porridge for breakfast'; 'Apples should be used freely, both raw
and cooked'; 'Breathe through the nostrils with the mouth
closed, especially at night'; and 'Furnish your sleeping apartments with single beds; double beds are now little used in
civilised countries except in the United Kingdom.'[12]

Despite Cadbury's benevolent quirks, the estate was a
success, quickly attracting a substantial waiting-list for new
applicants – as well as a steady flow of admiring visitors. One
journalist from *The Municipal Reformer* reported that he was
'charmed with the place ... I felt how different is the lot of
these Cadbury girls compared with many thousand of their
enslaved and sweated sisters dragging on a jaded and hopeless
existence in our large manufacturing towns and cities'. In a
sight which would have been welcomed by Lord Brabazon and
others concerned about the declining state of the race, 'the
spacious recreation grounds we passed indicated that there is
every thought for physical exercise and athletics of various
kinds'.[13]

Along with the confectionery trade, another late-Victorian
growth industry was soap manufacture. By the 1880s, the
marketing skill and technological expertise of the Liverpool
firm Lever Brothers had turned their 'Sunlight' business into
the undisputed brand leader. In a similar vein to George
Cadbury, the Lever Brothers Chief Executive William Hesketh
Lever combined commercial acumen with a strong desire to
raise the standing of his industrious employees through
housing reform. So when high rents and heavy port duties
forced his business out of Liverpool, Lever turned his back on
the city and decided to build a new factory complete with
model village on the banks of the Mersey. In 1888 the first sod
of 'Port Sunlight' was cut by Mrs Lever, while her husband
explained how it was his hope 'to build houses in which our
workpeople will be able to live and be comfortable – semi-
detached houses, with gardens back and front, in which they
will be able to know more about the science of living than in

a back slum, and in which they will learn that there is more enjoyment in life than the mere going to and coming from work, and looking forward to Saturday night to draw their wages'.[14]

What Port Sunlight turned into was a display of domestic architecture and suburban design utterly at odds with the Liverpool of St George's Hall and the Albert Docks. Despite its commercial origins, the Sunlight village was not a celebration of mercantile wealth or civic pride but an architectural wonderland of 'Old English' houses and Arts and Crafts décor. The houses, solely allocated to Port Sunlight employees, combined materially decent conditions and individual styles amidst the same amount of green, open space as at Bournville. Front gardens were allowed but no garden gates, which might delineate individual properties and hinder a communal spirit. 'There is an air of emancipation in the very appearance of its beautiful houses and spacious, clean-cut front gardens,' declared *The Municipal Reformer*. 'What a happy inspiration the word "Sunlight" was with regard to a distinctive brand of soap! ... But the name seems still more happy as applied to the openness and beauty of a model village.' It was small wonder that 'Messrs. Lever should themselves testify that their workpeople are better, more efficient, and that their families are healthier and happier amidst such surroundings, and enjoying such superior advantages.'[15]

This was the intellectual atmosphere in which Ebenezer Howard set about thinking of a new form of civilisation able to unite country and city. He admired the developments at Bournville and Port Sunlight, but his ambitions were broader than creating model villages for factory employees. He was drawn to the writings of Morris and Bellamy, but as a good Victorian was reticent about Bellamy's collectivist impulses and opposed to Morris's class war. Instead, what the shorthand writer from Dulwich was interested in was nothing less than the spiritual renewal of society through the gradual establishment of a series of new settlements he called Garden Cities.

iii GARDEN CITIES OF TOMORROW

In 1898, after a decade of cogitation, Ebenezer Howard entered the national debate with the publication of *Tomorrow! A Peaceful Path to Real Reform*. At its emotional core, according to one Howard acolyte, was 'nothing less than a vision of a transformed English industrial civilization'.[16] He began *Tomorrow!* (subsequently reprinted as *Garden Cities of Tomorrow*) with a damning quotation from the leader of the London County Council, Lord Rosebery:

> There is no thought of pride associated in my mind with the idea of London. I am always haunted by the awfulness of London: by the great appalling fact of these millions cast down, as it would appear by hazard, on the banks of this noble stream, working each in their own groove and their own cell, without regard or knowledge of each other ... Sixty years ago a great Englishman, Cobbett, called it a wen. If it was a wen then, what is it now? A tumour, an elephantisis sucking its gorged system half the life and the blood and the bone of the rural districts.

This was followed up by a statement from Dean Farrar complaining how cities were destined to become 'the graves of the physique of our race' as rural villages stood 'stationary or receding'.[17] Howard's vision was a product of its times, emerging from a context of fears over the enormity of London, the health of the nation's race, the depopulation of the countryside, and an amorphous *fin de siècle* worry about the spiritual well-being of the British people. He addressed these themes but did so by turning to a tradition of colony and settlement literature dating back to the 1850s' vogue for model villages which could themselves be traced back to Robert Owen's experiment at New Lanark. Most notably, he drew upon the work of the Christian radical politician and journalist James Silk Buckingham, who had formed extensive plans for his highly structured community of 'Victoria'. More usefully,

there was 'Hygeia', an 1876 pamphlet by Benjamin Ward Richardson which outlined a healthy community based on
advanced sanitation, green spaces, low densities and well-
designed houses. Dedicated to Edwin Chadwick, it detailed
the size, population and town planning requirements of a
settlement designed to counter the deadly diseases of the
modern city.[18]

But Howard was more than just a town planner. The spiritualism he first discovered in Chicago always coloured his
thinking and his hope for a future of Garden Cities was as
much about the human condition as anything as pedestrian
as pavement widths. With his first chapter opening with the
familiar lines from Blake's 'Jerusalem' and the ensuing text
scattered with quotations from Tolstoy, Goethe and Ruskin,
it is apparent that *Tomorrow!* was involved in a more metaphysical ambition of reform than anything Marshall or Richardson ever proposed. The problem facing modern man was
his alienation from the land and yet few wanted to retreat
back to rural unemployment or indeed the cloying social life
of a village. In his plan for a Garden City, Howard believed he
had discovered the 'Master Key' which could square the circle,
simultaneously alleviating urban squalor and rural depopulation.

As Howard saw it, the challenge facing society was: 'The
People. Where will they go?' The answer was to look beyond
town and country to a third alternative 'in which all the
advantages of the most energetic and active town life, with all
the beauty and delight of the country, may be secured in
perfect combination'. He illustrated his theory with a diagram
of Three Magnets (now the name of a large pub on Letchworth
Garden City high street) representing Town, Country and
Town-Country, all competing for the individual needle or
person. 'The town is the symbol of society – of mutual help
and friendly co-operation, of fatherhood, motherhood, brotherhood, sisterhood, of wide relations between man and man – of
broad, expanding sympathies – of science, art, culture, religion.
And the country! The country is the symbol of God's love and

care for man. All that we are and all that we have comes from it.'

Each magnet also had its drawbacks: the high rents, excessive hours, bad health, and slums of the town; the low wages, lack of amusement, and minimal public spirit of the country. Only in Town-Country were all the advantages and none of the faults of town and country on offer. 'Town and country must be married, and out of this joyous union will spring a new hope, a new life, a new civilization.' The Garden City would be able to combine social intercourse alongside the beauties of nature; higher wages together with lower rents; prospering business opportunities but not at the expense of the environment; total freedom yet all the joys of co-operation and mutual sympathy. 'The certainty of being able to live this life will be the magnet which will produce the effect for which we are all striving – the spontaneous movement of the people from our crowded cities to the bosom of our kindly mother earth, at once the source of life, of happiness, of wealth, and of power.'[19] How was it all to be achieved?

For Howard it was simple. What was required was the purchase of 6,000 acres at a cost of £40 per acre, with the £240,000 price tag raised on mortgage debentures bearing interest at an average rate of four per cent. At the centre of this estate would be 1,000 acres where the Garden City would be sited in circular form with a three-quarter-mile circumference. The town would accommodate an upper limit of 30,000 inhabitants housed in 5,500 lots averaging twenty by a hundred and thirty feet, with the minimum space being twenty by a hundred feet. The surrounding 5,000 acres would be taken up by a green belt of agricultural land which would also contain quasi-urban institutions such as reformatories and convalescent homes. This would house a further 2,000 people, taking the total up to 32,000.

The true wonder of the Garden City came in its design.

Six magnificent boulevards – each 120 feet wide – traverse the city from centre to circumference, dividing it into 6

equal parts or wards. In the centre is a circular space containing about 5½ acres, laid out as a beautiful and well-
watered garden; and, surrounding this garden, each standing
in its own ample grounds, are the larger public buildings –
town hall, principal concert and lecture hall, theatre, library,
museum, picture-gallery, and hospital.

A plethora of public buildings looked onto green open spaces in
a style highly suggestive of the parks and avenues of Chicago.
Within his 1,000 acres of English countryside, Howard
attempted to cram in all the Midwest spaciousness of Lake
Shore Park and Michigan Avenue. After a nod to Chicago came
a homage to New York, as Howard christened his centrifugal
five-acre garden 'Central Park' and the town's encircling boulevards 'Fifth Avenue', 'Fourth Avenue', 'Third Avenue', and so
on. His appeal to the language and styles of such symbolically
urban metropolises as Chicago and New York showed that
Howard was never interested in building pretty suburbs, let
alone another Bournville.

In a further attempt to insinuate the hustle and bustle of
urban life into the country, Howard designed a central
shopping precinct modelled on Paxton's Great Exhibition
glasshouse. The Central Park was to be ringed with an 1851-
style 'wide glass Arcade called the "Crystal Palace"... Here
manufactured goods are exposed for sale, and here most of
that class of shopping which requires the joy of deliberation
and selection is done.' One of the Garden City's essential
selling points was its clear separation of industry from
residential areas. The distance to work was walkable, but
residents could leave behind the Victorian practice of living
amidst the waste, filth and pollution of the belching factory
or stinking tannery. Meanwhile, all the streets were tree-
lined, large gardens were standard, and every house individually designed.[20]

This departure from the contemporary model village style
was matched by an equally radical approach to land ownership,
the issue which had first drawn him to urban planning.

Howard agreed with Henry George that the 'unearned increment' of landlords was an inequitable concentration of wealth which bore no relationship to productive effort. And it was, more often than not, simply the result of higher densities – hence the marked differences between town rent and agricultural rent. Howard wanted to ensure that any increased value of land in the Garden City benefited the whole community rather than private landlords. Consequently, his 6,000-acre Estate would be legally vested in the name of four gentlemen 'of responsible position and of undoubted probity and honour' who held the freehold on behalf of the Garden City inhabitants. With no private landlords ratcheting up prices, rents would initially be on the low side. All ground rents, based on the annual value of the land, would be paid to the trustees who would use the money to service the four per cent interest charges, create a fund to pay off the £240,000 capital and devote the rest to public purposes. According to Howard, it was as much a rate as a rent. 'That part of the rent which represents interest on debentures will be hereafter called "landlord's rent"; that part which represents repayment of purchase-money "sinking fund"; that part which is devoted to public purposes "rates"; while the total sum will be termed "rate-rent."

The theory of 'rate-rent' was fundamental to the Garden City. Ultimately, the capital would be paid off along with the interest charges, leaving all funds available for investing in municipal works such as schools, roads, parks, entertainment and sporting infrastructure. But as a good Liberal, Howard was adamant that the Garden City would not fall prey to the kind of municipal socialism undertaken by the London County Council. Instead, Howard hoped the Garden City would foster voluntary and charitable activities, with inhabitants 'enjoying the fullest rights of free association and exhibiting the most varied forms of individual and co-operative work and endeavour'.[21] Unlike the rigidity of Bellamy's *Looking Backward*, Howard wanted a vibrant civil society and culture of political pluralism outside the confines of the municipal authority. The

Garden City would retain the healthy custom of debate and intellectual variety which had always been a defining element of city life.

This emphasis on individual initiative extended beyond politics to economics. What marked out the Garden City from its utopian predecessors was Howard's belief in private property. There was going to be no smash-and-grab nationalisation of the land as Henry George and the Land Nationalisation Society had proposed. 'The change required would be simply a change of landlords. Separate ownership would merge in the joint-stock ownership of the public.'[22] Howard was keen to differentiate his plan from previously discredited attempts at communal living. 'No reader will confuse the experiments here advocated with any experiment in absolute Communism.' This stress on wealth-generation extended to the Garden City's business strategy. The man who had farmed maize in the Nebraskan outback understood the crucial importance of commerce and manufacturing to any successful settlement. Seduced by the same low rents which had led the Cadbury brothers out to Bournville, and attracted by a healthy workforce, Howard had no doubt that a bustling district of factories, warehouses, markets, coal and timber yards would quickly fill up their allotted site on the outskirts of the residential area. The industrial outlets, all powered by pollution-free electricity, would be linked to a railway line which encircled the business sector, separating it off from the broader agricultural belt.

One of the intellectual cornerstones of the Garden City was that it was not a suburb; indeed, according to Lewis Mumford, it was imagined as 'the antithesis of a suburb'. Howard aimed to create a self-sustaining community, not a dormitory, residential zone dependent upon a nearby city for employment or civic spirit. It had to have its own ethos, economy and political autonomy. So when a town reached its limit of 32,000 residents there was no question of allowing development to seep into the agricultural belt. The *raison d'être* of the Garden City was the proximity of town to country, giving people the ability to walk to work while enjoying rural life; creeping suburbs would negate that entirely. The next step in the peaceful reform programme was thus to multiply the number of Garden Cities, 'each town in the cluster being of different design from the others, and yet the whole forming part of one large and well-thought-out plan'. These 'social cities', with a population similarly capped at 32,000, would be grouped around one Central City and be linked together by a futuristic transit system of inter-municipal railway.

The consequence of these new developments for the old, over-crowded cities, most notably London, would be fatal. As people fled the old urban centres for the beauties of the Garden Cities, ground values and rents would collapse. The cities' municipal debts would fall on fewer and fewer people, resulting in even steeper rent increases and accelerated depopulation. Slowly, slums would be pulled down and (in an echo of William Morris) their sites occupied by parks and gardens. 'Elsewhere new cities are being built; London then must be transformed. Elsewhere the town is invading the country; here the country must invade the town.'

London's loss was society's gain. The proliferation of 'social cities' would act as 'the stepping stone to a higher and better form of industrial life generally throughout the country'. In clusters of Garden Cities where town and country, freedom and order, individualism and socialism all happily combined, a new civilisation would be born. Real reform would emerge as socially and spiritually enlightened citizens escaped the moral quagmire of the Victorian city. 'These crowded cities have done their work; they were the best which a society largely based on selfishness and rapacity could construct, but they are in the nature of things entirely unadapted for a society in which the social side of our nature is demanding a larger share of our recognition – a society where even the very love of self leads us to insist upon a greater regard for the well-being of our fellows.'[23]

The implicit message of the Garden City was a wholesale rejection of the unplanned chaos of the nineteenth century. In

the same vein as Edward Bellamy and William Morris, Howard
wanted to replace the destructive, enervating anarchy of the
industrial city with a highly structured urban plan. 'A town,
like a flower, or a tree, or an animal, should, at each stage of
its growth, possess unity, symmetry, completeness, and the
effect of growth should never be to destroy that unity, but to
give it greater purpose.'[24] Garden City ideologues rewrote
the previous hundred years of urban design as a grotesque
display of money-grabbing utility which needed to be
replaced by a system of co-ordinated town planning and
'social cities'. Every industrial city was depicted as a Coketown as the civic architecture and public ethos of the
nineteenth century were systematically traduced. 'In our
modern towns there is very little beauty of design, almost
no glory of architecture. Buildings, streets, have been erected
on the barest utility basis: cramped in order to get as much
property on as small a space as possible: thus punishing the
present and robbing the future in that narrow economy
which is in the end the silliest extravagance.'[25] The Victorian
urban world, 'the age of great cities', was no longer a mark
of civilisation to be proud of. The Industrial Revolution was
rewritten as a bad dream interrupting the natural civic flow
from the elegant, urbane eighteenth into the town-country
twentieth century.

The Garden City thus constituted an affront to Victorian
civic thought. Its conjunction of the rural and the urban would
have appalled Richard Cobden, who understood the city in
clear opposition to the country. Its focus on domestic architecture and the private sphere of the family was a retreat from
the urban confidence of Macaulay back to the age of Southey
and his weather-stained cottages. It has been suggested by
some historians that Ebenezer Howard's town-country utopia
was a product of his Nonconformist background, but there
appears little in common between the consciously middle-
class, fiercely pro-urban ethos of the Manchester or Leeds
Unitarians and the esoteric, spiritual humanism of the Garden
City. And, as we have seen, Howard wanted little to do with

the municipal gospel of Birmingham or the LCC. What Howard proposed was not the reform of the city, but flight from the city. The question was, could he ever manage to realise this new Jerusalem?

iv LETCHWORTH GARDEN CITY

The Times was predictably sceptical.

> Mr Howard is not content with half measures; like Sir Thomas More, he builds a Utopia – a charming 'Garden City' of 32,000 people in the midst of a little territory, all owned, planned, built and generally directed by the community itself. The details of administration, taxation, etc., work out to perfection, and it is quite evident that if Mr Howard could be made town clerk of such a city he would carry it on to everybody's satisfaction. The only difficulty is to create it; but that is a small matter to Utopians.[26]

It was not a small matter for Ebenezer Howard. He was determined to differentiate the Garden City from the whimsical utopias of the past by actually building it. He regarded *Garden Cities of Tomorrow* more as a prospectus than an ethical tract. And encouraged by the wide coverage and not wholly hostile reviews, Howard embarked on a national lecture tour to sell his vision project to potential investors.

The progressive Left were generally unresponsive to the call. He received no help from the Independent Labour Party, the trade unions or the Co-operative Movement; the Fabian Society was actively hostile, arguing that resources would be better used alleviating conditions in existing cities not building new ones. George Bernard Shaw, his colleague from the Zetetical Society, ridiculed 'Ebenezer the Garden City Geyser' – before surreptitiously investing in a number of developments. A similar air of weary cynicism was apparent in Howard's own household. Struggling to keep the family fed and housed as Ebenezer travelled the country, Elizabeth

Howard plaintively wrote to her husband, 'I could wish that the good Lord who made you a Social Reformer had also given you the wherewithal to reform on.'[27]

Despite the personal barbs and financial difficulties, Howard pressed on and by mid-1899 he had established a Garden City Association (GCA) to put the ideas into practice. It boasted a strong executive in the form of Chairman Ralph Neville, a lawyer and former Liberal MP, and Secretary Thomas Adams, an ideologically committed Scottish surveyor. Above them sat an advisory board of the great and the good complete with Earl Grey and George Cadbury and supported by the *Daily Mail* proprietor Alfred Harmsworth. It was up to Neville to sell the project to the finance houses in the City of London – the very site Howard ultimately hoped to force into insolvency. As the GCA attempted to extract £300,000 from a conservative business community, Howard's radical ambitions to transform society were gently played down. Instead, Neville stressed the financial opportunities of a Garden City development and resuscitated the racial arguments for thinning the cities. In his first speech as Chairman, he described how 'a physical degeneration was proceeding':

> Nothing could prevent the ultimate destruction and decadence of the race if they did not see that the mass of the people led lives which were inconsistent with sound physical development ... Looking at it as a question of national rivalry, there were reasons for saying that unless they discovered some means of mitigating the evil, of restoring healthy conditions of life, they were inevitably doomed to failure in the fierce rivalry which they had to undergo.[28]

The language must have appealed to the patriotic sense of the Edwardian boardroom and by 1903 the First Garden City Ltd was issuing shares and searching for a suitable location. It quickly became apparent, however, that what the investors envisaged and what Howard had outlined in *Garden Cities* were not wholly complementary. Questions over the role of the Board of Management, the power of shareholders, the rates of dividend, the degree of freehold and the extent of rent-ratepayer democracy slowly strangled the initial idealism. Ebenezer Howard himself was marginalised as his occasional outbursts about remaking the human spirit tended to frighten the financial horses. When at last the company decided on the tiny hamlet of Letchworth in rural Hertfordshire as its prospective site, Howard feared it was simply going to be another Bournville and not the first step along a peaceful path to real reform. Rather than transforming the capitalist way of life, with its business backing and staid objectives, the Garden City looked in danger of endorsing it.

One of the few bright points was the appointment of Raymond Unwin and Barry Parker as consultant architects. A keen disciple of Ruskin and Morris, Unwin was a believer in the Garden City aesthetic. 'One who was privileged to hear the beautiful voice of John Ruskin declaiming against the degradation of *laissez-faire* theories of life, to know William Morris and his work... could hardly fail to follow after the ideals of a more ordered form of society, and a better planned environment for it, than that which he saw around him in the 1870s and 1880s.'[29] Unwin had held the post of Secretary at the Manchester branch of Morris's Socialist League and striven to transfer his hero's Arts and Crafts idiom into architecture – or 'civic art', as he called it. An early supporter of town planning, he was contemptuous both of the destructive incoherence of the Victorian city as well as the amorphous vulgarity of the suburb. His civic philosophy signalled a return to the cohesion of medieval communities similar to the type which Pugin and Southey once championed.

The [medieval] village was the expression of a small corporate life in which all the different units were personally in touch with each other, conscious of and frankly accepting their relations, and on the whole content with them. This relationship reveals itself in the feeling of order which the view induces. Every building honestly confesses just what it is, and so falls into its place ... It is this crystallisation of the elements of the village in attendance with a definitely organised life of mutual relations, respect, or service, which gives the appearance of being an organic whole, the home of a community, to what would be a mere conglomeration of buildings...[30]

He advocated a design model based around 'squares and quadrangles' where 'the spirit of co-operation will find a congenial ground from which to spring'. He too wanted a marriage of the urban ambience with the health and space of a rural setting. Offered the chance to work on Letchworth, Unwin immediately accepted, expressing faith that the Garden City 'will have in its life something more worthy to be expressed in its architecture than mere self-centred independence and churlish disregard of others, which have stamped their character on our modern towns'.[31]

Let loose on the Hertfordshire hills, Unwin and Parker planned out their design for Letchworth in ferocious detail. They studied the contours, walked the fields and mugged up on their *Garden Cities of Tomorrow*. With virgin land before them they wanted to create a totally cohesive urban design which stayed true to the diagrammatic sketch set out by Howard. To their credit, they almost achieved it. They laid out a town centre with an open square and radial avenues just as Howard had envisaged. One of these was even called 'Main Avenue'. There were formal street layouts with a clear grid structure and a plethora of open spaces and parks. In Letchworth's domestic architecture, Unwin and Parker equally made their mark, designing an impressive collection of Arts-and-Crafts-style houses which set a lofty tone for the entire community. With their low density of twelve houses per acre (thirty per hectare), complete with large private gardens, early Letchworth had the spacious feel of a colonial settlement. But it was not to last.

The finances of the Garden City Company remained tight and, much to the indignation of Parker and Unwin, key elements of Howard's plan had to be shelved. It was too expensive to put the railway round the edge of the town, so instead it passed through the middle. Rather than being placed on the outskirts, the non-pollution-free industrial quarter was located in the north-east quarter to take advantage of prevailing winds. The combination of the railway and siting of industry managed to split the town between a working-class north and a more middle-class south. This divide was further exacerbated by the construction of a huge corset-making Spirella Factory bang in the middle of the northern residential area. Even greater damage to the town's founding style occurred when the Company directors decided Parker and Unwin's housing provision was too expensive and too slow. A further economic downturn in the early 1900s had made affordable housing all the more necessary if Letchworth was to survive. In 1905 a cheap cottage competition was held which involved the construction of 121 new houses, all of them an affront to Unwin's Arts and Crafts sensibilities. In response, he tried to concentrate on the southern half of the town but even here his unified plan was under attack as the Company allowed for ever more idiosyncratic individual house designs at the price of aesthetic cohesion. In the end, Unwin indignantly withdrew his affections from the Garden City and headed south for a new development planned outside Hampstead.[32]

As Unwin was leaving Letchworth, a series of light industries began to arrive, attracted (as forecast) by the low rents and large sites on offer. With them came a trickle of skilled workers enticed by the prospect of decent, affordable housing in healthy surroundings. The first commercial lessees in Letchworth were Ewart and Son, a firm of hotwater geyser manufacturers (an ironic choice given Bernard Shaw's nickname for Howard). They were followed by the printers J.M. Dent and Son as well as the Spirella Company, which managed to bring with it a number of light engineering and manufacturing firms, all combining to create a sustainable economic base. With prospering businesses and an expanding workforce, Letchworth's population reached nearly 9,000 by the outbreak of the First World War.[33]

Letchworth was also a magnet for a very different kind of migrant from the light engineering chief executive. From its inception, Edwardian England's avant garde had fallen head over heels for the Garden City. Its design, its ethos, its founding principles could hardly have appealed more to the 1900s Bohemian set. 'Friendliness – freedom from class distinction,' wrote one early champion of the Garden City, 'the "policy of the good neighbour", co-operation, public spirit, community service, a sense of fellowship with nature and all natural things have been characteristic of Letchworth from the beginning.'[34] Free-thinkers, radicals and simple-lifers made their way to Hertfordshire to partake of the celebrated 'Letchworth spirit' wickedly satirised by John Betjeman in his poem 'Group Life: Letchworth'.

> Tell me Pippididdledum,
>   Tell me how the children are.
> Working each for weal of all
>   After what you said.
> Barry's on the common far
>   Pedalling the Kiddie Kar.
> Ann has had a laxative
>   And Alured is dead.
> Sympathy is stencilling
>   Her decorative leatherwork,
> Wilfred's learned a folk-tune for
>   The Morris Dancers' band.
> I have my ex-Service man and
>   Mamie's done a lino-cut.
> And Charlie's in the *kinderbank*
>   A-kicking up the sand.
> Wittle-tittle, wittle-tittle
>   Toodle-oodle ducky birds,

What a lot my dicky chicky,
  Tiny tots have done.
Wouldn't it be jolly now,
  To take our Aertex panters off
And have a jolly tumble in
  The jolly, jolly sun?[35]

There were Esperanto clubs, vegetarian banquets, folk dancing, May Day marches, adult education groups, pantomimes in Howard Hall, football clubs and a pub – which was teetotal. Instead of providing alcohol, it offered intellectual libation in the form of improving talks by the likes of Bertrand Russell, Lloyd George and George Bernard Shaw. For 'one of its own idealisms' was that Letchworth should 'become a kind of popular university where young people can grow up with sound ideas of what a city should be – not from hearing lectures, but from seeing a few thousand people living a "good life" – which was constituted by, 'dances, dinners, concerts, camping, clubs innumerable, debates, card-parties, sewing-parties, receptions, public lectures . . .. Strong social life is one of the main attractions of the Town and has borne out Mr Howard's anticipation that the sense of a common civic interest would prove a unifying factor.'[36]

Much to the horror of the Company's fund-raisers, the typical Letchworth citizen was regularly caricatured in the popular press as a vegan crank. He dressed in knickerbockers and sandals, was a keeper of tortoises, a member of the Theosophical Society, and an ardent student of William Morris, H.G. Wells and Leo Tolstoy. The Garden City resident became a stock literary figure depicted as a counter-culture subversive and political revolutionary ready, beneath his handwoven flannel, to undermine the state at a moment's notice. It was a reputation which could only have been enhanced by the decision of the Russian revolutionary V.I. Lenin to stay in Letchworth when he attended the 1907 conference of the Russian Social Democratic Party in London.[37] And the large number of conscientious objectors (among them the Labour Party Deputy Prime Minister, Herbert Morrison) during the First World War did not help to dispel the image. Twenty years later, when George Orwell passed through Letchworth on the road to Wigan Pier, the stereotype was still an easy target:

> One sometimes gets the impression that the mere words 'Socialism' and 'Communism' draw towards them with magnetic force every fruit-juice drinker, sandal-wearer, sex maniac, Quaker, 'Nature Cure' quack, pacifist and feminist in England. One day this summer I was riding through Letchworth when the bus stopped and two dreadful looking old men got into it. They were both about sixty, both very short, pink and chubby, and both hatless. One of them was obscenely bald, the other had long grey hair bobbed in the Lloyd George style. They were dressed in pistachio-coloured shirts and khaki shorts into which their huge bottoms were crammed so tightly that you could study every dimple. Their appearance created a mild stir of horror on top of the bus. The man next to me, a commercial traveller I should say, glanced at me, at them, and back again at me, and murmured, 'Socialists', as who should say, 'Red Indians'. He was probably right – the ILP were holding their summer school at Letchworth. But the point is that to him, as an ordinary man, a crank meant a socialist and a socialist a crank ... If only the sandals and the pistachio-coloured shorts could be put in a pile and burnt, and every vegetarian, teetotaller and creeping Jesus sent home to Welwyn Garden to do his yoga exercises quietly![38]

Wandering through the Garden City today, it is still possible to breathe the 'Letchworth spirit'. Vasanta Hall houses the superbly Edwardian Theosophical Society, which continues to put on a regular programme of events and lectures. Round the corner is the 'Liberal Catholic Church' which describes itself as 'an independent Church which combines the ancient form of sacramental worship with the utmost liberality of thought, it leaves its members free in matters of belief'. There is a certain air of meditation and an elderly gentleness which hangs over the parks, leafy lanes and recreation areas. Perhaps the 'Letchworth spirit' lives on most successfully in St Christopher School. Since its foundation as a progressive institution in 1915 the town school has been entirely vegetarian, with lunches typically consisting of 'no fewer than 16 different kinds of freshly made salad' including 'olive and couscous, sweetcorn and spring onion ... and a particularly nice one with penne and wild mushrooms'.[39]

Yet outside these faithful pockets of resistance, there is little sign of Howard's pioneering vision in modern-day Letchworth. His hope had been to go beyond town and country in a third direction 'in which all the advantages of the most energetic and active town life, with all the beauty and delight of the country, may be secured in perfect combination'. This lofty ideal is now barely recognisable in Letchworth or its Hertfordshire bed-mate and successor Welwyn Garden City. Neither of them has the excitement or thrill of city life; their high streets filled with identikit brands are no different from a provincial town, while the heavy traffic tends to suffocate any nascent rural sensibilities. What they represent more than anything else is a slice of prosperous suburbia; beautiful, green and carefully designed with a remarkable collection of well-tended private gardens, but suburbia nonetheless. Combined with its fast rail links to central London and Cambridge, Letchworth has managed to become everything Howard did not want: a wealthy, dormitory commuter village. Poignantly, the Spirella Factory, long ago converted into offices, now has space to let.

Writ large, this transition to suburbia was the historical tragedy of the Garden City movement. It did not create a new way of living, a path to real reform, free from city, country or suburb. Instead, it opened the floodgates for a new, far more nefarious breed of suburbia which came to swamp inter-war Britain.

v Hampstead Garden Suburb and the Death of the City

> Nina looked down and saw inclined at an odd angle an
> horizon of straggling red suburb; arterial roads dotted with
> little cars; factories, some of them working, others empty
> and decaying; a disused canal; some distant hills sown with
> bungalows; wireless masts and overhead power cables; men
> and women were indiscernible except as tiny spots; they
> were marrying and shopping and making money and having
> children. The scene lurched and tilted as the aeroplane
> struck a current of air. 'I think I am going to be sick', said
> Nina.[40]

The disfigurement of Britain, which so horrifed Evelyn
Waugh's Bright Young Things, began harmlessly enough. After
storming out of Letchworth, Raymond Unwin discovered a
new patron in Henrietta Barnett. Protégée of Octavia Hill and
wife of Samuel Barnett, Henrietta was a macassar oil heiress
described acidly by Beatrice Webb as 'pretty, witty, and well-
to-do [marrying] the plain and insignificant curate who was
her fellow worker in the Parish of St. Marylebone; not solely
... because he had won her admiration and affection, but also
as a way of dedicating her life to the service of the poor'.[41]
However, helping out in the lowly slums of Whitechapel could
be a thankless business and at weekends Henrietta and Samuel
used to retreat from the depths of Toynbee Hall to the heights
of Whitestone Pond on Hampstead Heath. In their elegant
Heath End House, the couple entertained like-minded reformers and recharged themselves for East End duties by rambling
across the Heath. Their idyllic lifestyle was unhappily disturbed in 1902 when plans were announced to extend the
Northern Line from Golders Green up to Edgware. Henrietta
Barnett realised that the Underground's expansion would inevitably be followed by housing development, landing Heath
End House with a 'Bromstead' right on its doorstep.[42]

A lady who loved to campaign, she quickly rallied together an influential committee to lobby the Fellows of Eton College to sell them the surrounding land. Barnett planned to scupper any private developers by getting in first and building a *garden* suburb, the aim of which was 'to house people of many different incomes, and which will be free, it is hoped, from the evils of monotony and inertia which invariably exist where one class only congregates'. Hampstead Garden Suburb was to be a vast, permanent teetotal Toynbee Hall where all classes would mix freely, not in miserable terraced rows but in beautiful homes surrounded by airy environs.

> In the Garden Suburb Estate it will be an essential condition of building that the dwellings of all classes be made attractive with their own distinctive attractions, as are the cottage and the manor house of the English village; the larger gardens of the rich helping to keep the air pure, and the sky view more liberal; the cottage gardens adding that cosy, generous element ... The houses will not be put in uniform lines, nor in close relationship, built regardless of each other, or without consideration for picturesque appearance. Each one will be surrounded with its own garden, and every road will be planted with trees, and be not less than forty feet wide.[43]

Eton College duly sold up its 265 acres to the recently floated Hampstead Garden Suburb Trust and in 1907 the first sod was cut by Barnett herself just off the Finchley Road. The trustees then had to secure a Private Act from Parliament to give the Suburb exemption from local planning laws allowing it to go ahead with its uniquely low-density levels of eight houses per acre (twenty per hectare), fifty-foot spaces between houses, special building by-laws and series of culs-de-sac. Allowed far greater financial and artistic licence than he had enjoyed in Letchworth, the overjoyed Unwin produced a cohesive design for the entire site

untroubled by factory locations or railway tracks. He imple-
mented a plan with precisely the kind of self-contained,
organic ethos he had originally hoped for at Letchworth.
The roads were narrow and tree-lined with large grass
margins, the houses redolent of the domestic architecture
of Norman Shaw and Philip Webb, and a series of round-
abouts and dead-ends consolidated the village feel. Few
designs could have been more antagonistic to the dominant
traditions of Victorian urban planning.

What emerged from Unwin's drawing-board was a decidedly
beautiful, *faux*-rustic suburbia which rapidly became one of
London's most exclusive suburbs. One hundred years on, it
remains a decidedly affluent neighbourhood with very little
trace of the Christian socialist impulse which inspired it. For
while Henrietta Barnett might have achieved her aesthetic
ambition for a rural Heathside community, she never reached
her social goal. The East End working classes remained unper-
suaded by the expensive and inaccessible housing, not to
mention the stifling middle-class paternalism, on offer. But
while labourers might have stayed away, the leaders of Labour
were drawn in ever-increasing numbers toward the Suburb.
The future Labour Party Prime Minister Harold Wilson,
Foreign Secretary Patrick Gordon Walker, War Minister
Emanuel Shinwell and Labour Whip Will Howie all made their
homes in Barnett's model settlement. Many of them no doubt
were watched over by their near neighbour Sir Martin Fur-
nival-Jones, Director General of MI5. Further down the road
was Mary Mandelson, the daughter of the Letchworth conscientious objector Herbert Morrison, along with her son
Peter. The more self-consciously intellectual Labour politicians, such as Hugh Gaitskell, Douglas Jay and Michael
Foot, tended to remain on the other side of the Heath in
Hampstead proper.[44]

Ebenezer Howard shared the Frognal set's distaste for Barnett's settlement. He saw Garden Suburbs for what they were:
highly dangerous manipulations of the Garden City principle.
'They are rather dormitory districts with little or no provision

for work, except, indeed, for work in the garden, and they tend to diffuse the corporate sense over so wide an area that in its diffusion that sense is apt to become largely lost.'[45] There was no attempt to inculcate an urban spirit, let alone industry or entertainment, into the Garden Suburb; it was simply a more rarefied district within the city suburbs. More damagingly, it served to accelerate rather than counter the suburban trend. For it was not long before every ambitious family wanted to live in a suburb of large gardens, green lanes and generously proportioned houses endlessly advertised in newspaper puff pieces. And it was not long before the political establishment cravenly responded.

The 1909 Town Planning Act marked an unqualified shift away from high-density, Victorian civic planning by making the low-density, large houses of the Garden Suburb the template for future town planning. Henceforth, the nineteenth-century tradition of civic architecture, of public spaces and grand urban *projets*, was abandoned for private houses and the anonymity of the suburb. This policy revolution was further endorsed after the First World War, when the government decided the style of the homes fit for wartime heroes would also conform to Garden Suburb proportions. In a highly influential polemic, *Nothing Gained by Overcrowding* (1918), Raymond Unwin passionately made the case for low-density, green-spaced Garden Suburbs as something approaching a political right. The concerns of conservationists and urban planners were drowned out as policy makers and architects unleashed a tide of concrete, utterly oblivious as to what the long-term effects of their policy would be when placed in the hands of private developers and in the context of a fast-expanding car culture.

The results were all too apparent all too quickly. The inter-war years witnessed a housing boom that irreversibly scarred the British landscape and marked a total rejection of the virtue of civic life. The nineteenth-century city was vilified with the same level of venom Lytton Strachey directed towards his eminent Victorians. A citizen of the West Riding, a burgher from Bradford, but J.B. Priestley voiced the 1930s consensus when he described how the nineteenth century 'had found a green and pleasant land and had left a wilderness of dirty bricks. It had blackened fields, poisoned rivers, ravaged the earth, and sown filth and ugliness with a lavish hand... What you see looks like a debauchery of cynical greed.'[46] Nowhere was this ethic more readily apparent than in the city. As Victorians had heralded their wealthy conurbations as representing the spirit of the age, so critics concurred. The Industrial Revolution became a 'bad dream'; the nineteenth-century city, 'ugly'.[47]

In place of dense, vibrant cities or even vaguely cohesive Garden Cities, government and business now planted a mangled, sprawling suburbia. An average of 300,000 houses were built every year during the 1920s and 1930s, with 1936 seeing a peak of 350,000. Funded first of all by the state and then by private developers buoyed up by strong housing demand on the back of historically low interest rates, the inter-war period saw four million houses go up with ninety per cent in newly developed or existing suburbs. In a vast transhumance, the British people made their way from the cities to the low-density (on average twelve to an acre; thirty to a hectare), low-rise housing springing up between train stations, along arterial and country roads and in vast housing estates situated outside the urban centres. Becontree to the east of London, Kirkby near Liverpool, Longbridge on the outskirts of Birmingham: these were the new edifices of sub-urban Britain.[48]

Some seventy years previously, in a speech entitled 'Great Cities and Their Influence for Good and Evil', Charles Kingsley had urged precisely this movement: the charge of city into the country. He wanted to see 'a complete interpenetration of city and of country, a complete fusion of their different modes of life, and a combination of the advantages of both'.[49] In 1900 H.G. Wells, who had seen this process happen to his childhood village of Bromley, warned more bleakly of a similar scenario.

Practically, by a process of confluence, the whole of Great Britain south of the Highlands seems destined to become an urban region... As one travels through the urban region, one will traverse open, breezy, 'horsey' suburbs, smart white gates and palings everywhere, good turf, a grand-stand shining pleasantly; gardening districts all set with gables and roses, holly hedges and emerald lawns ...The same line of reasoning that leads to the expectation that the city will diffuse itself until it has taken up considerable areas and many of the characteristics, the greenness, the fresh air, of what is now country, leads us to suppose that the country will take to itself many of the qualities of the city. The old antithesis will indeed cease, the boundary lines will altogether disappear; it will become, indeed, merely a question of more or less population. There will be horticulture and agriculture going on within the 'urban regions' and 'urbanity without them'.[50]

By 1928, it was upon them. In *England and the Octopus*, the conservationist Clough Williams-Ellis recorded the encircling tentacles of the suburb: the bungalows, the villas, the 'ribbon development'. Williams-Ellis bitterly lamented the decision to save the country from the Germans only to destroy it ourselves. Worst of all, just as Kingsley had demanded and Wells had feared, Britain was becoming an entirely urban region with no apparent difference between town and country. 'We plant trees in the town and bungalows in the country, thus averaging England out into a dull uneventfulness whereby one place becomes much the same as any other – all incentive to exploration being thus removed at the same time as the great network of smoothed-out concrete roads is completed.'[51] As Kenneth Grahame so memorably described it in *The Wind in the Willows*, the stoats and weasels of modern suburbia were destroying the England of his childhood – on the back of Toad's motor car.

In the process, the English were losing their urban nature. The nation which had once prided itself on being the country

of 'great cities' with its multiplicity of urban centres in contrast to Paris's hegemonic domination of France; the English
people who had self-government coursing through their Saxon
blood; the country which had produced the first cities of the
modern age was now in danger of succumbing to suburbia. By
1929, D.H. Lawrence was deeply perplexed about England's
civic consciousness:

> The English character has failed to develop the real *urban*
> side of man, the civic side. Siena is a bit of a place, but it is
> a real city, with citizens intimately connected with the city.
> Nottingham is a vast sprawling place towards a million, and
> it is nothing more than an amorphous agglomeration. There
> is no Nottingham, in the sense that there is Siena... The
> English are town birds through and through, today, as the
> inevitable result of their complete industrialization. Yet
> they don't know how to build a city, how to think of one,
> or how to live in one. They are all suburban, pseudo-cottagy,
> and not one of them knows how to be truly urban ... as
> citizens of splendid cities they are more ignominious than
> rabbits.[52]

The Italian city republics, once a source of urban emulation
for Victorian merchant princes, were now just a sore point of
contrast.

Social and psychological investigation of suburbia, the new
anti-civic world of bypasses, filling stations and Hoover
Factory buildings, became a literary sport. Its most lucid
chronicler was J.B. Priestley who along his *English Journey*
expressed the sense of a lack of virtue which surrounded the
suburban, inter-war Britain 'of arterial and by-pass roads ... of
giant cinemas and dance-halls and cafes, bungalows with tiny
garages, cocktail bars, Woolworths, motor-coaches, wireless,
hiking, factory girls looking like actresses, grey-hound racing
and dirt tracks, swimming pools, and everything given away
for cigarette coupons'.[53] George Orwell was equally sniffy
about the 'celluloid, rubber, chromium-steel everywhere, arc-

lamps blazing all night, glass roofs over your head ... everything cemented over' civilisation of the 1930s. In *Coming up for Air*, he depicted the miserable existence of the insurance salesman George Bowling who lived in Ellesmere Road, West Bletchley – a street like any other 'all over the inner-outer suburbs'. 'Just a prison with the cells all in a row. A line of semi-detached torture-chambers where the poor little five-to-ten-pound-a-weekers quake and shiver, every one of them with the boss twisting his tail and the wife riding him like the nightmare and the kids sucking his blood like leeches.'[54]

Despite this cultural hostility and a voluminous snobbery, by some imperceptible but tragic process the suburbs were increasingly imagined as the natural home of the English people. The English were no longer regarded as an urban race, who had created some of the great civic wonders of Europe, but an innately semi-rural tribe who felt most at ease in the burgeoning suburb. The Conservative Prime Minister Stanley Baldwin thought nothing more touching than 'to see how the working man and woman after generations in the town will have their tiny bit of garden if they can ... The love of these things is innate and inherent in our people.'[55] On his *English Journey*, Priestley passed along a road into Swindon 'lined on each side by tiny semi-detached houses of red brick'. What marked the houses out was their extraordinary profusion of flowers: dahlias, Michaelmas daisies, bright geraniums. According to Priestley, this was a natural, indigenous trait. 'There is this to be said about the English people: give them even a foot or two of earth, and they will grow flowers in it ... Here we take leave of the country reluctantly, and with infinite gradations, from the glory of rosebeds and the full parade of hollyhocks to the last outposts, among grimy privet and grass where perhaps a sooty aster still lingers.'[56] Indeed, suburbs instinctively appealed to our national psyche, our belief in compromise, balance, and the blurring of boundaries allowing us 'one foot in the city and one in the country'. George Orwell's ceaseless quest for the national spirit led him also to speak of 'the English' as 'great lovers of flowers, gardening and "nature", but this is merely part of their vague aspiration towards an agricultural life'.[57]

The Britain of Manchester, Bradford, Glasgow and Leeds was on the way to becoming a nation of invincible green suburbs. As Lawrence predicted, the urban side of the Englishman was withering on the vine. The appointment of John Betjeman – who once boasted of his desire to give up poetry to become manager of the Ongar overland station – as Poet Laureate marked the official conjunction of national identity with suburban values. In a welter of verse broadcast across the country on the Home Service, Betjeman celebrated the dormitory homelands of Ruislip and Pinner, Harrow and Neasden and the other glorious suburban settlements of Middlesex and Buckinghamshire.

> Gaily into Ruislip Gardens
> Runs the red electric train,
> With a thousand Ta's and Pardon's
> Daintily alights Elaine;
> Hurries down the concrete station
> With a frown of concentration,
> Out into the outskirt's edges
> Where a few surviving hedges
> Keep alive our lost Elysium – rural Middlesex again.

However, even the Homer of 'Metro-Land' could not bring himself to love the apotheosis of twentieth-century soulless suburbia, Slough. Victorian civic pride finally died among the bogus Tudor bars of the Reading basin.

> Come, friendly bombs, and fall on Slough
> It isn't fit for humans now,
> There isn't grass to graze a cow
> Swarm over, Death!
>
> Come, bombs, and blow to smithereens
> Those air-conditioned, bright canteens,

Tinned fruit, tinned meat, tinned milk, tinned beans
Tinned minds, tinned breath.

Mess up the mess they call a town –
. . .[58]

EPILOGUE

STILL WAITING
FOR THE ROVER?

In the honeyed aftermath of Manchester's successful hosting of the 2002 Commonwealth Games, the 'northern editor' of what was once the *Manchester Guardian* reported how in the north of England, 'self-confidence is back to the Victorian days of big city power; that sense of zest when Manchester and Leeds felt unfettered by a restraining hand down south.'[1] In media circles, it was a common enough opinion. The revival of 'Cottonopolis' from its post-industrial slump, along with its maturing from the 'Madchester' days of the late 1980s, was just one among many easily digestible stories of civic renewal. With its redeveloped Bull Ring and effective stewardship of the 1998 G8 Summit, Birmingham was also praised for reviving its nineteenth-century heyday. Even Liverpool, described in 1982 as 'a "showcase" of everything that has gone wrong in Britain's major cities', appeared to be resuscitating its fortunes thanks to Irish property developers, an innovative council and a large tranche of European subsidy.[2] London's society bible, *Tatler* magazine, went so far as to anoint the city 'the capital of cool' in an issue entirely devoted to 'a place where tradition meets cutting edge'.[3]

This national narrative of reawakened civic pride culminated during the competition for title of 'European City of Culture 2008'. City rivalry was reborn in a 'Renaissance of urban England' as Birmingham competed with Cardiff and Liverpool with Newcastle-Gateshead – each flaunting their rediscovered aestheticism in the hope of garnering the same riches Glasgow had enjoyed following its successful year as

Capital of Culture in 1990. The former Deputy Prime Minister, Michael Heseltine, went so far as to suggest that Britain was witnessing, 'the biggest investment and regeneration of [its] cities since the Victorian age'.[4]

But beyond the PR spin, beyond Gateshead's Baltic Arts Centre and Manchester's Gay Village, was it, is it true? After seventy years of near total decline, after decades of sustained depopulation, suburbanisation, industrial depression, cultural collapse, and political castration, could it really be that British cities are starting to revive their long-lost Victorian ethic? Does Britain stand on the verge of reclaiming its heritage as 'a land of great cities'?

i The Road from Wigan Pier

On 8 February 1936, the Wigan electrician Joe 'Jerry' Kennan received a knock on the door. " 'We were just having tea. I opened the door and there was this tall fella with a pair of flannel bags on, a fawn jacket, and a mac.' "[5] It was Eric Arthur Blair, better known as George Orwell. He had come to Wigan – after visits to Manchester, Barnsley, Sheffield and the Liverpool docks – to explore the condition of the north of England during the industrial depression of the 1930s. To write about the unemployed and the dispossessed, Orwell needed to be amongst them. 'To study unemployment and its effects you have got to go to the industrial areas. In the South unemployment exists, but it is scattered and queerly unobtrusive ... It is only when you lodge in streets where nobody has a job, where getting a job seems about as probable as owning an aeroplane and much less probable than winning fifty pounds in the Football Pool, that you begin to grasp the changes that are being worked in our civilization.'[6] And just as he had assumed the life of a tramp in all its unedifying grime to write *Down and Out in Paris and London*, so now he mucked in with the fractured proletariat – sharing their food, taking their entertainment, and staying in lodging houses, doss-houses or (in the case of Wigan) above a tripe shop.

What emerged from Orwell's trip was perhaps his greatest work of social anthropology and political advocacy, *The Road to Wigan Pier*, bringing to the attention of a southern middle-class audience the conditions ravaging industrial cities during the inter-war depression. Orwell's prose mixed hard facts with ready emotion to expose the plight of the towns which had once earned Britain the title of 'workshop of the world'. 'The total population of Wigan is a little under 87,000; so that at any moment more than 1 person in 3 out of the whole population – not merely the registered workers – is either drawing or living on the dole. The 10- or 12,000 unemployed contain a steady core of from 4–5,000 miners who have been continuously unemployed for the last seven years. And Wigan is not especially badly off as industrial towns go.'[7]

For while the nineteenth century had blessed them, the twentieth-century economy was not kind to Britain's great cities. The threat of German, American, and French competition, the changing financial configuration of Empire, the weakness of our technical and educational infrastructure, and the financial disinterestedness of the City of London in British industry could all be safely ignored before the First World War as the sun never set and the economy still prospered. Even as global markets retracted, international competition increased, and Britain's low productivity became apparent in the inter-war years, still government and industry failed to act. Over-reliant upon single industries, hampered by outmoded equipment and bedevilled by restrictive labour practices, by the time the 1929 Wall Street crash sent world trade into free-fall the northern cities looked like sitting ducks.

The staple industries of shipbuilding, coal, textiles, engineering, iron and steel – the trades which had sustained the Victorian cities – collapsed. In 1912 Britain exported 7,000 million square yards of cloth but by 1938 that figure had fallen to less than 1,500 million taking with it tens of thousands of jobs. And while the closure of Palmer's shipbuilders in Jarrow pushed the town's jobless rate up to an extraordinary seventy-three per cent, such incidences of mass, structural unemployment were not uncommon. At the peak of the depression in the early 1930s, some thirty-five per cent of coalminers, forty per cent of cotton operatives, forty-eight per cent of steelworkers, and sixty-two per cent of shipbuilders were out of work.[8] Alongside the manufacturing jobs, there crumbled the traditional port and dock economy. The collapse in world trade combined with the retreat of Empire to leave the commerce of the Mersey and the Clyde high and dry. The once global emporiums of Liverpool and Glasgow started cruelly to turn in on themselves.

The south of England prospered with its light industries, food retail, and electrical engineering (the world of by-passes and Hoover factories conjured up by J.B. Priestley), as the north of England, with its 'Special Areas' and unemployed marches, stultified. This was Priestley's 'nineteenth century England'; the decaying England of 'coal, iron, steel, cotton, wool, rail-ways; of thousands of rows of little houses all alike, sham Gothic churches, square-faced chapels, Town Halls, Mech-anics Institutes ... sooty dismal little towns, and still sootier grim fortress-like cities. This England makes up the larger part of the Midlands and the North and exists everywhere; but it is not being added to and has no new life poured into it.'[9] The North–South divide was born and for the once hegemonic Victorian cities, the cities nurtured by the Industrial Revo-lution, it was a devastating reversal of fortunes.

One of the most damaging consequences of this economic shift was the demise of a substantial financial sector inde-pendent of London. The provincial banks, which were at the centre of so much Victorian civic culture, progressively suc-cumbed to metropolitan conglomeration. In 1914 there had been thirty-eight joint-stock banks, but by 1924 there were only twelve, of whom the 'Big Five' (Midland, National Pro-vincial, Lloyds, Barclays, Westminster) dominated the field. With the banks went the provincial stock exchanges, a major source of long-term finance for industry before the First World War. Manchester remained buoyant during the 1920s, but along with Birmingham, Cardiff, Sheffield, Newcastle,

Glasgow and Bristol it would eventually fall under the shadow of the London Stock Exchange. As bankers and stock-brokers headed to the capital, so provincial industry found it all the more difficult to raise funds, while regional culture and civil society became all the poorer in the absence of mercantile patronage. The old Manchester Stock Exchange building is now a restaurant, called 'Stock'. The Glasgow Royal Exchange is a modern art gallery.

The wartime demands of the 1940s offered some respite for the industrial heartlands, but Britain's economic centre of gravity was ineluctably shifting southward. Yorkshire, Lancashire, Cheshire, Wales, and Scotland did indeed seem to belong to the nineteenth century. The true state of affairs was hidden by 'Butskell' booms and the golden age of 1950s and 1960s global capitalism. But beneath the consumer durables, the televisions, cars and 'never had it so good' washing machines, the British economy was continuing its post-industrial paralysis. Economic growth during the 1960s was typically one half of our European competitors (and nearly one quarter of Japan's). Shorn of its Empire, Britain's share of world exports of manufactures declined from 25.5% in 1950 to 9.3% in 1975.[10]

The oilshock of 1973 finally wrenched the country out from its post-war, imperial complacency. By then the party was well and truly over as unemployment ratcheted upwards and the dawn of monetarism meant Westminster would no longer spend its way out of recession. It was left only to Mrs Thatcher and her Chancellor of the Exchequer, Geoffrey Howe, to deliver the *coup de grâce*. The politically motivated depression of the early 1980s saw unemployment reach 3.3 million. 'Most of the jobs lost were in manufacturing industry; most of them were full-time; most of them were held by men; most of them were in unionized plants; most of them were in the traditional industrial areas.'[11] And most of them were in Victorian cities.

Since that social nadir, the economic base of many of the former Victorian cities has progressed quietly along the same, bleak trajectory. Technological change and globalisation has caused the steady erosion of the manufacturing sector as skilled and semi-skilled jobs are exported to newly indus- trialising countries. Between 1991 and 1996, Manchester saw a ten per cent and Liverpool a twenty-five per cent cut in the proportion of its workforce employed in manufacturing and construction.[12] Currently, fifty-five per cent of working-age people in Liverpool have jobs compared to a national average of seventy-five per cent. Studies undertaken by the Joseph Rowntree Trust indicate that Britain's twenty leading cities lost over 500,000 jobs between 1981 and 2001, while the rest of the country gained at least 1.7 million.[13]

Along with the jobs went the residents. The 2001 census revealed that in the decade since 1991 Manchester lost 39,900 people taking the city's population down towards 390,000. Liverpool shed a relatively greater 36,100 (taking its popu- lation to some 440,000 from 700,000 in the 1960s) and Bir- mingham a less substantial 27,400 (cutting its population to 980,000). Leeds and Bradford both managed to buck the trend, but it was London which was the real winner. Between 1981 and 2001, the north-east lost five per cent of its population and the north-west some three per cent while London proper grew by more than five per cent and the south-east of England as a whole by ten per cent. Currently, some twenty-six per cent of the UK population lives in London and the south-east.

Yet behind these dispiriting figures there are signs of hope. The most recent data point to an upsurge of urban residency between 1999 and 2001 (particularly in Manchester, Bir- mingham and Leeds) as well as sustained job creation, growing wages and higher house prices. This is not just thanks to the much maligned service or retail sector but emerging know- ledge-based industries. A global economy where competitive advantage is based on technology, branding and creativity might allow Britain's cities to exploit both their unique human assets and their historically metropolitan outlook. According to a recent government report, 'there is evidence that many of the largest cities have begun to turn around their employment prospects and have succeeded in capitalising on the "new"

economic sectors linked to IT, tourism, cultural industries
and industries linked to Research and Development'.[14] Indeed,
'a process of urban renaissance is taking place ... The Core
Cities have been through their worst period and are recovering
economically.'[15]

Innovative research universities are proving essential to
this process. Encouragingly, successful universities, such as
Manchester (as well as UMIST), Liverpool, Leeds, Birmingham, Sheffield and Glasgow, have begun to 'spin-out'
increasing numbers of high-wage, high-skill jobs in their host
cities. Many of these universities are now forming partnerships to share innovations and lever north some of the
research funds which are still heavily focused on southern
universities. Manchester and Liverpool are currently trying
to establish a 'biotech corridor' between the cities bringing
together the universities, hospitals and emergent bio-
technology cluster in the north-west. The universities of Sheffield, Leeds and York have formed the 'White Rose partnership'
to incubate a series of knowledge- based technology businesses
in the Yorkshire cities.[16]

Sectors traditionally regarded as 'soft' – media, design, technology, education – are now appreciated as increasingly crucial
to post-industrial prosperity and they find their natural homes
amidst the buzz of the city. The leading advocate of this
approach to urban regeneration is the US economist Richard
Florida. His influential book, *The Rise of the Creative Class*,
makes a compelling statistical case that generating a tolerant,
creative environment is crucial for building a sustainable
urban economy.[17] In 2003, he drew up a 'creativity index' of
Britain's cities which Manchester topped 'as a result of its
mix of ethnic diversity, gay friendliness and technological
innovation'.

However, the historic challenge Britain's post-industrial
cities face is re-connecting a commercial elite with its civic
environment. Joseph Chamberlain's fealty toward Birmingham was built around Nettlefold & Chamberlain's social
investment in the city. Similarly, the involvement of Cobden

in Manchester, Rathbone in Liverpool, and Marshall in Leeds
was predicated upon their commercial interests. But this style
of personal, provincial capitalism quickly proved at odds with
the demands of twentieth-century corporate finance. Limited
liability and depression-era restructuring saw the removal of
firms from their local base. The introduction of punitive taxation systems and the growth of large public credit companies
meant that provincial cities were increasingly left only with
branch offices. Now, globalisation and the emergence of
powerful multi-nationals has further accelerated the trend.
Currently, some ninety per cent of the UK's biggest companies
are London-based, compared to sixty per cent in 1964, while
others are managed from abroad.[18] All of which can leave
city authorities at the whim of corporate decisions made in
London, Tokyo or Detroit and does little to thicken any sense
of commercial civil society. To walk round Leeds City Square
with its towering corporate sky-scrapers, housing Price-
WaterhouseCoopers and NatWest, or Glasgow's Royal
Exchange, with its Borders, coffee chains, and cloned shops
reminiscent of an airport terminal, is to bear witness to the
damaging dislocation between commercial wealth and civic
identity.

However, despite the evident prosperity of Glasgow city
centre, or Birmingham's Selfridges and Manchester's Trafford
Centre; despite the new jobs in media, technology, culture,
and IT; despite the 'New York style' loft conversions and
football wealth, the economic state of Britain's cities still
remains precarious. They continue to produce less GDP per
head than the EU average, and less than the UK average.
Meanwhile, London continues to expand with all the monstrous energy of Cobbett's Great Wen. It generates eighteen
per cent of the United Kingdom's GDP and is responsible
for an astonishing four million jobs outside the capital. Its
productivity is twenty-five per cent and its average earnings
over thirty per cent higher than the national average.[19] The
elite bank Coutts might well be setting up a branch in Liverpool to cater for the multi-millionaires of Heswall, but the

south-east contains two-thirds of the nation's millionaires, while 509 of the 1,000 people featured in the *Sunday Times* rich list are based in London.[20] 'Our conclusion is that the country is being split in half,' revealed a study by Sheffield University of the 2001 census. 'To the south is the metropolis of Greater London, to the north and west is the "archipelago of provinces" – city islands that appear to be slowly sinking demographically, socially and economically.'[21] Such stark analysis only underscores the conclusion that if we are to return to the more equitable economic geography of the nineteenth century, with a proper dispersal of wealth across the nation, then the Victorian cities still have a long way to go to reclaim their place in the pumproom of British prosperity.

ii Manufacturing Culture

With London's twentieth-century supremacy came a renewed cultural arrogance. 'All England is in a suburban relation' to London, declared the novelist Henry James as early as 1905. And the succeeding hundred years saw only an acceleration of that deleterious trend. The corporate and financial stampede southward was quickly followed by the political parties, the media (including the *Manchester Guardian*), the professional establishment (from lawyers to doctors to accountants to architects), the cultural elite, even the representatives of organised labour. In 'The English People', a 1945 essay described by George Orwell as 'a piece of propaganda for the British Council', the erstwhile Wigan denizen lamented the cultural over-centralisation of England. 'Not only is the whole of Britain in effect governed from London, but the sense of locality ... has been much weakened during the past century. The ambition of the farm labourer is usually to get to a town, the provincial intellectual always wants to get to London.' Indeed, Orwell could not think of a single 'important literary or artistic movement that is truly independent of London and the university'.[22] It was a sentiment echoed sixty years later in a letter to the *London Review of Books* in response to

Alan Bennett's nostalgic recollections of 1940s Leeds. The correspondent, Mr Maurice Marks, similarly recalled the great municipal governments of the mid-century and how, in his case, 'Sheffield looked after you.' 'And what did I do for Sheffield? Bugger off as soon as I could to Manchester and then London.'[23]

How different today's provincial insecurity is from the confident civic world of Benjamin Barker, the excitement of the 1857 Art Treasures Exhibition, the music of the Halle orchestra, the art of the pre-Raphaelites, the architecture of Worthington, Walters and Yeoville Thomason, the literature of Elizabeth Gaskell, the intellectualism of the Literary and Philosophical Society, the history of William Roscoe, the journalism of Edward Baines, even the political culture of John Bright, Richard Cobden, and Joseph Chamberlain. Depressingly, Britain in the twentieth century retreated to an eighteenth-century model where the capital once again pioneered the fashion before dictating it to her civic satellites in Oxbridge, Bath, Bristol, and Brighton. 'When a man is tired of London, he is tired of life,' opined Samuel Johnson.

In the Victorian era, that metropolitan imperialism appeared outdated as the great northern civilisations established themselves as core components of the cultural firmament. J.B. Priestley remembered how before World War I, there was 'a kind of regional self-sufficiency, not defying London but genuinely indifferent to it'. His father read the *Yorkshire Observer*, rarely saw a national newspaper and believed that 'what happened "down south", outside politics, was no concern of his'.[24] Similarly, in a 1957 article for *Encounter*, A.J.P. Taylor described how Manchester had once 'looked at southern England in Cobden's spirit. It cared little for what was going on "down there". London was not expected to provide either ideas or material direction.'[25] And yet it was so short-lived. By the 1920s, Manchester, Liverpool, Bradford, and Birmingham had become 'the provinces' as London resumed its dominance.

The cultural disintegration of the Victorian city owes much

to the decline of Nonconformity. Not only were the Unitarians and Congregationalists typically at the forefront of nineteenth-century civic culture, but the very identity of the industrial city was often predicated upon a sense of being part of the Puritan elect. The Dissenting vision which had sustained Nonconformity since the English Civil War, and had then been channelled so energetically into building the new Jerusalem of the Victorian city, was now withering on the vine. By the early 1900s, Nonconformist congregations were starting to dwindle. In 1900 the celebrated East Parade chapel in Leeds, the place of worship for generations of Baineses, was demolished. When in 1933 J.B. Priestley visited a Nonconformist chapel in Birmingham, the city of the 'municipal gospel' whose achievements were inspired by the preaching of Dale, Dawson, and Crosskey, he doubted 'if there were half-a-dozen men under thirty five in the chapel ... I suppose that in my chapel-going days, there would actually have been twice the number of people at this service. And though there was a certain amount of nodding and smiling before, and some hand-shaking after the service, I did not gather the impression that for most of these people this chapel was the centre of their social life ...'[26]

Alongside the decay of the Puritan spirit went a belief in the unique attributes of the middle class. Arraigned as revolutionaries, traitors, atheists, philistines, capitalists, and even socialists during the long nineteenth century, it was their sense of persecution and belief in the virtue of their social mission which had helped to create the city. Attacked on all sides, the middle class had a keen understanding of their own identity: neither the boobyish squirearchy of the land nor the intemperate, manual working class. If they had a creed, it was called Liberalism. The middle class were the industrious class, the heroes of *Self-Help* who since the eleventh century had been the architects of Europe's commercial, political and cultural progress. The Victorian city was but the latest manifestation of their urban identity; civic pride a testimony to bourgeois self-confidence. But by the early twentieth century the defined contours of what constituted the middle class were being muddied. Together with the strange death of liberal England vanished the defining attributes of provincial middle-class culture.

Puzzlingly, Orwell described in 1941 how 'the tendency of advanced capitalism has [therefore] been to enlarge the middle class and not to wipe it out as it once seemed likely to do'.[27] The Marxist revolution never happened and instead the bourgeoisie triumphed – but, ironically, in the process laying the seeds of their own cultural extinction. The historian Jurgen Kocka has described the 'built-in tendency to universalisation' in bourgeois culture. When with rising real-term incomes ever-increasing numbers could afford the signifiers of a middle-class life (now understood in terms of leisure and consumption, rather than moral certainty or political beliefs), the sense of election was lost. 'The middle class proved stronger than its opponents. It won. Its culture and principles have spread widely to all parts of the *classes superieures*, and to a certain extent to the shrinking rural population, to the middle masses that used to be called "the lower middle class", and even to parts of the working class ... [But] in this victory the middle class lost much of its identity.'[28] We are, as John Prescott put it, all middle class now.

As part of this cultural dissolution, the relationship between the middle classes and the city suffered a near terminal disjuncture. The cultural signifiers of a middle-class life – the semi-detached home, the garden, the social set – were now to be found in the suburbs. And as power slowly receded from the industrial city, the social and professional circles of the upper middle-class elite widened and their identification with the city waned. The Baines and the Marshalls departed from Leeds, the Chamberlains and Kenricks from Birmingham, the Phillipses and Heywoods from Manchester. The urban world as a specific place and generic category played a rapidly decreasing part in middle-class identity.[29] Historians have long debated whether this amounted to a 'gentrification' of the middle class: a collective betrayal of bourgeois identity as the aspirant middle classes aped upper-class mores, sent their children to public school, shunned industry, and exchanged an urban culture for the gentrified world of Oxbridge, London, finance and the professions. In place of hard-edged, middle-class northern grit there emerged a southern, refined upper middle class more interested in London-led 'society' than industrial capitalism with disastrous results for Britain's economic competitiveness. But while the thesis has certainly been overplayed, the first half of the twentieth century indubitably witnessed the draining of civic leadership and cultural confidence from Britain's cities.

In his 1957 essay, A.J.P. Taylor described how Victorian Manchester, the city of his birth, had once stood as 'the last and greatest of the Hanseatic towns – a civilisation created by traders without assistance from monarchs of territorial aristocracy'. The city had been 'the symbol of a civilisation', 'an ambition of mankind', but was now 'little more than a historical curiosity'. Mournfully, he noted, 'The merchant princes have departed. They are playing at country life in Cheshire or trying to forget Manchester in Bournemouth and Torquay. There are no more dinner-parties, no more bustle of social occasions.'[30] J.B. Priestley remarked how in the modern West Riding, 'the wealthier industrialists are busy turning themselves into country gentlemen ... Now they are gone, and their places have not been taken by other families.'[31] The fate of provincial bourgeois culture was sealed, confirms a recent cultural history, 'in the inter-war period by the development of a mobile, national upper middle class and by the concentration of key national cultural institutions in London'.[32]

All of which makes the re-emergence of 'culture' as one of the defining elements of Britain's urban renaissance the more intriguing. For if the likes of Liverpool, Newcastle, Glasgow, and Manchester have focused their regeneration strategies on a single quality, it is culture. Birmingham sells itself on its Symphony Hall, Royal Ballet, New Gallery Walsall, and Repertory Theatre; Manchester its Lowry Centre, Art Gallery and even a museum dedicated to the concept of city life, URBIS; Newcastle-Gateshead meanwhile has its Baltic Centre for Contemporary Art, Sage Music Centre and the public architecture of the Millennium Bridge and Angel of the North. As it was for the Victorians, it is again suggested that culture is the pillar of an urban civilisation. But there is a difference. Whereas nineteenth-century civic culture was more often than not the indigenous product of a Nonconformist conscience, the culture of today's cities appears more of a branding and marketing tool than a reflection of civic identity. It is frequently the work of quangos and urban regeneration consultants rather than the organic outcome of any home-grown civic sentiment.

That said, culture can prove highly successful as an economic strategy. Popularly known as the 'Bilbao Effect', after the northern Spanish city which transformed itself from post-industrial malaise into a regeneration showcase on the back of its Frank Gehry-designed Guggenheim Museum, it is premised on an understanding of cultural policy as a valuable tool in diversifying a crumbling economic base, attracting knowledge-based 'cultural industries', and marketing the city as an attractive location for mobile international capital and specialised professionals. The more exciting and interesting the civic environment, the greater chance of bringing in investment and jobs from footloose global capital.[33] Richard Florida has urged cities to pursue a policy focused precisely around this idea of 'quality of place'. Only those cities that succeed in attracting creative talent by fostering a 'people climate' will enjoy appreciable growth. And what the creative class looks for, Florida suggests, is ready employment opportunities, high-quality cultural and leisure amenities, exciting spaces for social interaction, diversity, and an authentic civic environment. All of which play to the traditional strengths of the British city.

The European Commission long ago alighted on the significance of cultural renewal as a route to urban regeneration and established the Capital of Culture and then City of Culture

competition to encourage its proliferation. In 1990 it was
Glasgow's turn. And there is little doubt the city's year as
Capital of Culture helped it emerge from its seemingly perennial post-industrial depression. Before it became 'Miles
Better', Glasgow in the 1980s was popularly imagined as a city
of heroin, razor gangs, Easterhouse, the Gorbals, industrial
militancy and economic collapse – most of which could be
encapsulated in the drug-related killing spree of the mid-1980s
'ice-cream wars'. The Culture title eased those perceptions as
Clydeside's cinema, art, theatre, music and wondrous Victorian architecture were rediscovered after a half-century
hiatus. In addition to the international rebranding, estimates
suggest that the actual events of 1990 generated up to 5,580
new jobs and a very rounded £1 billion return in public and
private investment into the regional economy. Theatre attend-
ances rose by forty per cent, the number of foreign visitors by
fifty per cent, and conferences held in the city doubled. The
cultural effects were later consolidated as the city gained a
Royal Concert Hall, a modern art gallery, new museums and
film theatres. Shopping and commerce surfed on the back of
the cultural wave, the city's universities became increasingly
sought-after as exciting locations to study, and Glasgow's new
image helped in the development of a successful media and
design industry.

Other cities took note and across the post-industrial landscape what were once icons of the Industrial Revolution were
surreptitiously exchanged for manufactories of culture. In Liverpool, the Albert Dock, once the gateway to Empire, was
transformed into a home for Tate Liverpool, Granada TV and a
Beatles heritage centre. In Shipley, on the outskirts of Bradford,
Saltaire mill was converted with the help of David Hockney
into an arts and crafts emporium complete with swish restaurant, bar, bookshop and fine art gallery. The surrounding
streets, once home to Titus Salt's mill-hands, now provide
some of the most expensive real estate in the Bradford suburbs.
In Salford, site of the classic slum of the early twentieth
century, urban renewal is being driven by the glimmering

metallic edifice of the Lowry Centre. Located amongst the
redeveloped quays, this massive cultural complex encom-
passes two theatres for performing arts as well as providing a
gallery for L.S. Lowry's grimy cityscapes. Over the bridge, in
nearby Trafford, there is a less spectacular example of the
Bilbao phenomenon. An unsympathetic, headline-grabbing
development by architect Daniel Libeskind houses the Imperial War Museum North which, compared to its metropolitan
parent, is a poor offspring.

The most successful cultural enterprises rightly announce
themselves with an architectural statement, but they also
draw on indigenous traditions which appeal to the city's self-
identity. Yet many of them suffer from a common dependency
upon Lottery and state funds which ensures that so much
cultural regeneration is dangerously dependent upon political
fashion and consumer trends. And as the sorry story of the
Pop Museum in Sheffield and the precarious state of the Royal
Armouries in Leeds have shown, grandstanding, high-prestige
developments funded by outside quangos usually falter if there
is no local talent or support networks behind them. The Victorian civic leaders built and financed their civic emblems
independently through private subscriptions or a levy on rates.
They were proud their municipal edifices and cultural centres
were free of government interference. With a Coutts in
Liverpool, millionaires commuting into Manchester from
Cheshire villages, and lawyers earning a mint in Leeds, it might
be time for cultural entrepreneurs to start thinking more creatively about tapping the private wealth of the new urban elite
rather than appealing for more funds from state bodies.

The apotheosis of the new urban aestheticism was reached
during the Capital of Culture competition. With each city
eager for the hundreds of millions of pounds of investment,
thousands of jobs, and prospect of international brand recognition there came forth a frenzy of well-packaged culture.
'Be in Birmingham', said the hardware village; 'Liverpool: The
World in one City', announced the marketing men in Merseyside; 'Newcastle-Gateshead buzzin', was the message from

the north-east. Along with Cardiff, Bristol and Oxford, each city had expended a large fortune on endowing museums, renovating dilapidated docksides, commissioning fashionable architects, and pump priming the media. Metropolitan cynics carped at these provincial upstarts pronouncing themselves worthy heirs of Barcelona or Florence. But their Victorian forefathers had only claimed the same. Recalcitrant leftists, on the other hand, regarded the culture industry as little more than a 'carnival mask' hiding social inequalities and offering only low-wage, low-skill jobs in hospitality. The city had become a place of play; just another terrible manifestation of 'heritage Britain'.

In 1987, with Liverpool approaching its slough of post-industrial despond, local historian Tony Lane predicted that in the twenty-first century the conurbations of the north would be transformed into 'open cities of tree-lined streets, coppiced corners and wooded hollows':

> Of all the Northern cities, Liverpool will be reckoned the richest. It will be celebrated for the completeness of its range of Victorian and Edwardian architecture, for its unrivalled concentration of neo-Grecian public buildings, for its arts treasures and museums, for its playwrights and poets, its artists and musicians... Liverpool, with its superb endowment of river and undulating terrain, its chain of parkland cutting through the city, its electric social history and its thriving cultural life will make York and Chester look as prettily twee as they actually are. Liverpool's first new future will be as one of the new cultural capitals of Northern Europe.[34]

In 2003 this remarkably prescient vision came true as Liverpool took the City of Culture accolade for 2008. As a signal of support for the city's regeneration, the cultural commissars backed the optimistic, multi-racial message of the world city bid. And with an estimated 14,000 new jobs, £2 billion of public and private investment, and some 1.7 million extra visitors predicated on the outcome, it was a welcome boost to a city still shedding work and residents. Part of the reason behind its success was, according to the judging Chairman Sir Jeremy Isaacs, 'a greater sense there that the whole city is involved in the bid and behind the bid'. For what marked Liverpool out was the close involvement of the Council rather than the abdication of cultural leadership to private-sector culture and heritage consultants. It was a welcome reassertion of municipal legitimacy.

Government Ministers suggested the very bidding process, the jobs and regeneration it kick-started, ensured that all the cities were winners. And despite the triteness, it was true. Civic rivalry ensured councils gave the go-ahead to long-delayed plans for urban renewal, the publicity surrounding the competition attracted investment and visitors, and new jobs were created or kept. As a result of the Newcastle-Gateshead bid, John Goddard, the Vice-Chancellor of Newcastle University, told the *Guardian*, 'We are finding it much easier to recruit students and senior staff.'[35] But for its critics, such a process could never be regarded as 'culture' in any meaningful sense. If Ruskin had been appalled at the Manchester Art Treasures Exhibition, then he was turning in his grave at the City of Culture entries. 'You have always to find your artist, not to make him; you can't manufacture him, any more than you can manufacture gold.' Here was manufactured culture, drawn up by regeneration specialists and regional development advisers, at its most blatant. The architectural critic Jonathan Glancey took up Ruskin's cudgels by suggesting that Victorian cities had created an urban culture on the back of their trade and industry, but 'today it is the other way around. Instead of culture springing from the inner workings of our cities, we see it as the way to make our cities work.' Unlike on the Continent, culture in Britain had been separated off from economic activity and now we were trying hopelessly 'to reinvent a magic wand by which our old cities will be made to shine again'.[36]

But the culture of the Victorian cities was just as carefully manufactured as the 2003 bids. The difference then was that it was an indigenous circle of middle-class civic patriots who coordinated the function, whereas all too frequently today culture is generated by metropolitan professionals, characterised by one newspaper as 'men in rectangular glasses with business cards', with only the loosest of ties to the civic environment. Cultural policy is essential to regenerating post-industrial cities, but urban culture will only emerge with local talent and local patronage. And for that to happen people need to move back to the cities and stay there.

iii REGENERATING JERUSALEM

'Suppose we are entering the city by way of the Great Park. Our fast car takes the special elevated motor track between the majestic skyscrapers: as we approach nearer, there is seen the repetition against the sky of the twenty-four skyscrapers; to our left and right on the outskirts of each particular area are the municipal and administrative buildings; and enclosing the space are the museums and university buildings. The whole city is a Park.'[37] This was how the influential inter-war architect Le Corbusier envisioned the dream metropolis he called Radiant City. A modernist, car-focused bastardisation of Ebenezer Howard's vision, Le Corbusier's 'vertical garden city' was an anti-civic dystopia of flyovers, skyscrapers and soulless, disparate green spaces. In her masterful work, *The Death and Life of Great American Cities*, the community activist and author Jane Jacobs showed how this template seduced the architectural establishment and went on to destroy much of the nuanced social fabric of the US inner city. During the latter half of the twentieth century, a similar tragedy befell Britain's cities as all too many planners tried to turn Le Corbusier's dreams into reality.

The scene was set by the voguish 1940s commentator Thomas Sharp who in his influential polemic, *Town Planning*, blamed the Industrial Revolution for destroying the English civic tradition as represented by Cheltenham, Bristol, Bath and Brighton. 'In foul slums and in deserts of dreary byelaw-standardised streets, in the sun-obscuring murk of factory chimneys, the very conception of the town *as a town* disappeared from English minds. By the end of the nineteenth century, so vilely had English towns been built in the period of their greatest extension, the whole conception of the town as a home ... had vanished into the anything but thin contemporary air.'[38] What emerged from this viscerally anti-Victorian context were the New Towns of the 1950s and with them some of the most doctrinaire acts of homage to modernist design.

Stevenage, Harlow, Basildon, Bracknell and, of course, Milton Keynes were laid out in thrall to the ring road and concrete walkway, if not the high densities, of the new town-planning paradigm. It was a world of the car, the deserted city centre, and a demarcated home and office community. All the 'organized complexity' of the city – the congenial space for unofficial interaction, diversity, vibrancy – were planned out of these anti-urban developments. Hugely popular in their day as spillover sites for Birmingham, London, Glasgow and other cities, fifty years on many of these towns face a spiral of decline caused by poor housing, bad public transport and crumbling civic amenities. Bracknell Council has decided to confront its problems head on by destroying its entire city centre and rebuilding along more people-friendly principles.[39]

Unfortunately for Britain's urban base, Le Corbusier's writ extended from the New Towns into the Victorian cities. As historians lambasted the social consequences of the Industrial Revolution and progressives demonised Victorian prudery, planners seized the post-war opportunity to scythe through the 'gloomy' nineteenth-century civic fabric. In an act of vandalistic revenge, the children and grandchildren of the Victorian civic pioneers began to kill off the nineteenth-century city. What the Luftwaffe had missed, the planners invariably hit. 'Year by year we are pulling down the older parts of our cities with a savage and undiscriminating abandon which will not earn us the gratitude of posterity. If the detailed study of

Victorian cities is not pursued at this perilous moment in time
... it may be difficult to pursue it at all,' wrote Asa Briggs in
the 1963 Introduction to his seminal work, *Victorian Cities*.[40]

Birmingham, a city previously renowned for the intimacy
of its social networks, became a martyr to urban 'progress'
with a 'concrete collar' of underpasses and fly-bys desolating
the centre. Glasgow's M8 motorway ploughed through the
streets of Clydeside while Leeds, Liverpool and Manchester
suffered similar desecrations. Even as Asa Briggs was pleading
for its conservation, the pile-drivers and wreckers' balls were
swinging into operation across the post-industrial north.
Euston arch fell, but with the passing of the 1968 Town and
Country Planning Act the rate of demolition at least began to
slow.

In more recent years, the destruction has relented as architects, planners and councils have at last come to appreciate
some worth in the achievements of their Victorian forebears.
Ironically, given the fierce autonomy of the nineteenth-
century municipality, the inspiration behind much of this
urban renaissance has emanated from central government.
The need to build a further 3.8 million homes over the coming
twenty years (thanks to changing social habits), and the political inability to do so entirely on greenfield sites, has meant
Whitehall has finally been forced to confront the suburban
sprawl and its low-density ethic. For despite the construction
of New Towns as an attempt to rescind suburbia, the last fifty
years have seen the concrete tentacles extend ever further.
The hundreds of thousands who have fled the cities have
headed either into suburbia or back into the countryside.
Indeed, the last fifty years, according to Peter Hall, have witnessed 'the repopulation of the English countryside'; a trend
which only gathers pace today fuelled by TV programmes and
Sunday supplements extolling the good life of country living.[41]

The death of cities and the easy proliferation of monotonous
housing estates has been exacerbated by the failure to control
housing densities. Ebenezer Howard's spacious Garden City
was built at a density of thirty dwellings per hectare (about

one eighth of the density of the traditional city street), but
during the 1990s average density for new housing developments stood at an extraordinarily low twenty-three dwellings per hectare – a figure even lower than that reached during
the inter-war suburban sprawl. But this type of detached home
with a garden on monotonous, Barratt-style housing estates is
where people seem to want to live. A 1992 survey for the
Department of the Environment revealed a clearly inverse
relationship between satisfaction with housing and population
density. At densities of less than five persons per hectare sixty-
eight per cent of residents claim to be 'very happy', whilst at
forty persons per hectare the figure falls to thirty-seven per
cent. It was also discovered that ten times more people pre-
ferred houses to flats and sixty-four per cent thought having a
garden 'very important'.[42] More recent government research
has only confirmed these trends, revealing that 'the more urban
the area the more likely the residents are to be dissatisfied, to
report problems and to live in poor quality neighbourhoods'.
In 1998–9 some sixteen per cent of heads of household in urban
areas expressed dissatisfaction with their area, compared to
seven per cent of households in suburban areas and three per
cent of households in rural areas. Many elements of this urban
discontent are poverty-related, with knock-on effects to do
with schooling, crime and healthcare provision, but a substantial component of dissatisfaction is the product of the
environment: public space, pollution, noise, safety.[43]

Armed with these findings the government has pursued a
dual approach. In addition to anti-poverty programmes, it has
followed the analysis of the architect Richard Rogers (himself
heavily indebted to the work of Jane Jacobs) and opted for
design-led urban renewal.[44] The 1999 'Urban Task Force',
which Rogers chaired, advocated building better environments
and rebuilding poorly developed ones as a prerequisite for
regenerating Britain's cities. 'Promoting sustainable lifestyles
and social inclusion in our towns and cities depends on the
design of the physical environment.'[45] Despite their curious
contention that the Victorian period made 'an indelible mark

on the British attitude towards the role and function of the city [which] ... marked a departure from the Continental attitude towards urban development and urban living', the Task Force produced a series of viable recommendations for reviving the city.[46] Not all of Rogers's prescriptions became policy (such as his desire for a minimum of fifty dwellings per hectare) with the 2000 Urban White Paper regarded as something of a mixed bag. In addition to a government target of sixty per cent of all future development on recycled, brownfield sites, the White Paper did at least introduce new planning policy guidance for inner-city development, tax credits and capital allowances for urban regeneration, funds for cleaning up contaminated land, and a scheme to reward excellent public design and civic spaces. Unfortunately, beaten down by the Treasury, it signally failed to levy VAT on new greenfield estates and abolish it for urban developments.

More encouraging has been the creation of the Commission for Architecture and the Built Environment (CABE), tasked with improving standards in public design. For there can be little doubt that compared with Continental nations, British post-war public architecture has been of a consistently low quality. Think of the social security office, the hospital, even the town hall; Richard Rogers's finest work was not for a council, health authority or government department, but the quintessentially private-sector Lloyd's of London. It is indicative that in England less than ten per cent of all architects are employed by local authorities, while the figure is thirty-seven per cent in Germany.[47] After decades of neglect of the public sphere, after misplaced faith in the sole ability of the private sector to deliver urban renewal and living cities, there has been a slow realisation of the role of municipal and national authority in improving civic life. As the CABE 'statement of values' puts it, 'We believe that good architecture, landscape architecture, urban design and spatial planning breathe life back into places suffering from economic and social decline, restoring community identity and civic pride and attracting investors and visitors.'

One of the Commission's more exciting initiatives was to join up with the London-based think-tank, the Institute for Public Policy Research (IPPR), and the Royal Institute of British Architects (RIBA) to launch an architectural competition for a new generation of town halls. As councils were transformed during the postwar decades into administrative conduits for central government fiat, town halls came to resemble little more than office blocks. The resplendent iconography, the triumphant self-confidence of the Victorian municipal palace were exchanged for the architecture of bureaucracy. We lost an understanding that public buildings shape the public realm and that local government is inevitably devalued when it is located in shoddily designed office blocks catering to the needs of staff above citizens or councillors.

Yet in an age of demotic equality and universal franchise, there is no enthusiasm for returning to the elite opulence of the Victorian town hall. When Glasgow Council built its City Chambers in the 1880s, the designers provided forty-four seats in the public gallery for a population of some 500,000. Nonetheless the City Chambers, Manchester Town Hall and particularly Bradford City Hall all remain as urban icons commanding affection and offering a ready source of civic identification amongst residents. Whilst most of the new designs submitted to the 'Designs on Democracy' competition suggested novel approaches to reinvigorating civic democracy (open debating chambers, giant web monitors etc.), the best submissions also understood the importance of retaining an element of the aura, the majesty of governance, in the designs. For despite its elite provenance, the Victorian town halls commandeered a respect for the office of local government and the public sphere.

The new political and professional emphasis on design, on the importance of civic space and public architecture, is finally managing to undo some of the worst excesses of the 1960s. Inspired by the American-led school of New Urbanism, Britain's architects, planners and civil servants have started to concentrate on creating walkable, mixed-use communities which value rather than obliterate the authentic, historic city-scape. Indeed, many planners have returned to the very precepts that guided the Victorian city. Joyously, the greatest sinner has proved the most ardent in its repentance. The city of the Spaghetti Junction has rediscovered Chamberlain's Parisian boulevards and municipal piazzas. 'We are witnessing something of a renaissance in the creation and use of public space in (sharp intake of breath) Birmingham,' reported the *New Statesman*. 'Since the 1990s, a new Birmingham has emerged, marked not by underpasses, fly-bys and junctions, but by open squares and broad pedestrian streets. New Birmingham has been built around public space. You can now walk, unchallenged by the motor car, over the canals in Brindleyplace, through the mall of the new Symphony Hall, into Centenary Square, Paradise Forum, Chamberlain Square, Victoria Square and on to the central shopping district.'[48] Birmingham's pedestrianisation scheme has changed the entire feel of the city, bringing businesses and professionals, tourists and citizens, back into the centre. Even the monstrous Bull Ring shopping centre is being redeveloped as a part of which a colossal new Selfridges department store has been built complete with a highly distinctive 'skin' of 15,000 aluminium discs.

Across the Victorian cities, a similar story of design-led renewal is apparent. Leeds has rebuilt its city square from little more than a roundabout and created a vibrant public space in the Millennium Square to the north of the city. It must now do the same with the constant traffic jam on Westgate outside the Town Hall. Manchester has enjoyed an array of civic improvements: from numerous warehouse conversions to residential blocks in Deansgate to the redeveloped Arndale centre and pedestrianisation round the Corn Exchange and Shambles district. The Manchester Art Gallery on Mosley Street, by the firm Michael Hopkins and Partners, has rightly been recognised as a superb piece of innovative architecture. All of which has produced an unexpected turnaround in Manchester downtown residency. The resident population in the core of the city has risen from less than 300 in 1995 (the year prior to the devastating IRA bomb) to some 3,000 by 1998 and currently stands at nearly 15,000. Over the next two years, it is expected to top 20,000. In Liverpool the city centre population has similarly grown from 2,000 to more than 9,000.[49]

Credit for the seeds of this civic renewal must partly lie with Government decisions and the emergence of a more sophisticated approach to regeneration than the Enterprise Zones and Development Corporations of the 1980s. But the Labour administration now appears ready to disregard the results of this successful strategy by planning to build a further four new towns in the south-east of England. The Thames gateway towards Stansted in Essex, Ashford in Kent and Milton Keynes (again) are all the targets of a massive and ill-considered house-building project. As residents still flee the old industrial cities, as streets in Oldham and Ashton and Salford lie boarded up and derelict, the Government stands ready to pump-prime the south-east with yet more infrastructure. The new developments might not repeat the mistakes of the last New Towns but the money would nonetheless be far better spent on subsidising urban renewal, rebuilding 'design-led' neighbourhoods or offering venture capital to urban entrepreneurs in the struggling cities, rather than over-heating the London catchment area. The decision resembles a terrible hangover from the discredited policies of predict and provide, of clumsy central government dictat which so badly served the Victorian city during the twentieth century.

iv WAITING FOR THE ROVER

The Labour Minister and founding father of the National Health Service, Aneurin Bevan, liked to tell the story of how he first became involved in politics. His protégé and biographer, Michael Foot, recounted it best:

> 'Very important man. That's Councillor Jackson,' his [Bevan's] father had said to him. 'What's the Council?' he

asked. 'Very important place indeed and they are very powerful men,' his father had replied. 'When I get older I said to myself; the place to get to is the Council. That's where the power is. So I worked very hard and, in association with my fellows, when I was about twenty years of age, I got on the Council. I discovered when I got there that power *had* been there, but it had just gone. So I made some enquiries, being an earnest student of social affairs, and I learned that the power had slipped down to the County Council. That was where it was and where it had gone to. So I worked very hard again and I got there and it had gone from there too.'[50]

Where it had gone was Westminster. The twentieth century witnessed the steady emasculation of civic autonomy; the draining of power and influence from local councils to national government. Chamberlain's 'noble sphere' of municipal politics became increasingly devoid of the ambitious young men who so transformed Birmingham. A sign of the times was revealed in 1907 when Winston Churchill indignantly rejected a Cabinet position at the Local Government Board. 'I refuse to be shut up in a soup kitchen with Mrs Sidney Webb.' Clearly, the world of the town hall was losing its ardour. 'There is no place in the Government more laborious, more anxious, more thankless, more cloaked with petty and even squalid detail, more full of hopeless and insoluble difficulties,' he later explained to Prime Minister Asquith.[51]

The rot had set in during the early 1900s. This was not due to Lord Avebury and *The Times*'s campaign against spendthrift municipal socialism, but rather the result of a growing trend in Edwardian politics from local voluntarism to national obligations. Watching aghast the steady improvements of the German state and shamed by the lacklustre condition of Britain's working classes (seen to such embarrassing effect during the call-up for the Boer War), demands for 'national efficiency' inevitably expanded the remit of national government. The great municipal experiment in education, begun by W.E.

Forster in 1870 and which placed Chamberlain on the Birmingham school board, was ended with the 1902 Education Act and the abolition of directly elected school boards. Health and welfare became a matter for national politicians. In the course of a debate over school medical inspection in 1906, the politician H.A. Tennant tellingly remarked, 'we ought not to allow the local authorities to differ from the nation in a matter in regard to which the nation has already decided'.[52] The old Victorian framework of friendly societies, philanthropy and self-help no longer seemed appropriate to the global struggle of the twentieth century. In 1911, Lloyd George killed off the voluntarist ethic with the passing of National Insurance while, in the face of ratepayer reactions, councils were beginning to retreat from the socialist ambitions of the 1890s.

The demands created by the First World War extended the reach of the state which then never quite receded. But it was the aftermath of the Second World War which sealed the fate of local self-government. Beveridge's moral crusade to rid Britain of his Five Evils, along with Attlee's political conviction that the failed promises of the First World War could not be repeated for the heroes of 1945, produced a state-driven determination to build a 'New Jerusalem' of universal welfare provision. The two alumni of Toynbee Hall set about dismantling what remained of Victorian civic autonomy. A system which secured geographic social equality necessitated the elimination of regional and civic disparities. The nationalisation of health, welfare and housing, along with the gas, water and electricity utilities, might have been the route to socialism but its unforeseen casualty was a tapestry of local council provision. None of which seemed to bother Aneurin Bevan, the former councillor from Tredegar and Monmouthshire, who happily bulldozed the NHS over the objections of the Friendly Societies' Medical Alliance. From now on, as Douglas Jay infamously remarked, the man in Whitehall knew best. As the Empire receded and the Westminster Parliament focused more keenly on domestic affairs, local authorities became subject to unprecedented levels of central control.

So much so that at the 1946 Association of Municipal Corporations conference, an indignant Alderman Roberts from Grantham warned that 'You have only to look around the world today and find that efforts are being made to govern countries without local authorities, and we want to avoid that by all means in this country.'[53]

Unfortunately such respect for municipal autonomy was not passed on to his daughter, Mrs Thatcher, who in the 1980s delivered an equally comprehensive assault on local democracy. What was once nationalised was now privatised. Michael Heseltine bypassed elected councils with his private-sector Urban Development Corporations, which in the event proved 'bloodily successful' in the regeneration of London Docklands and Liverpool Docks, as well as his less successful Enterprise Zones and City Challenge schemes. Yet that was only a taster. By the mid-1980s, councils offered one of the few tiers of resistance to the Conservative administration with the antics of Ken Livingstone at the Greater London Council (GLC), Margaret Hodge in Islington, Derek Hatton in Liverpool, and Bernie Grant in Haringey infuriating the Tory high command. Their response was the 1984 Rate Act, depriving local authorities of a freedom which stretched back to the sixteenth century: the ability to set their own rates.[54] High-spending authorities would henceforth be subject to a Whitehall-dictated rate-cap. This historic assault on local democracy was followed up by the 1985 Local Government Act which abolished six metropolitan county councils along with the GLC – to be replaced by the wholly undemocratic London Residuary Board. John Burns's dream of bringing 'a revivified municipal ideal' back to the capital was finally dead.

The 1980s marked a sustained *political* assault on local government with a bewildering array of central government agencies and quangos, the establishment of an Audit Commission to pick through local government finances, and the implementation of Compulsory Competitive Tendering for local authority services. In office, the journalist Simon Jenkins remarked, Mrs Thatcher 'had treated British urban government in the manner she most deplored in Brussels' treatment of her. Local sovereignty had been infringed, meddling regulations imposed and democratic assemblies bypassed. Town halls were deluged with Whitehall paper and visitations by government regulation and inspectors.'[55] And she did so at a time when the rest of Europe was dismantling its postwar centralism. Formerly fascist regimes in Portugal, Spain and Greece were devolving powers to the locality, the city and the region just as the British were suffocating what was left of civic self-government. Even France, the centralist *bête noire* of the Victorians, now offered a more pluralist polity following the Mitterrand government's transfer of extensive executive responsibilities to the ninety-five local *départements*. In Britain, the woman in Whitehall seemed to think she knew best – until, at least, she introduced the Poll Tax.

The political rhetoric might have softened during the 1990s, but the strangulation of local government did not. By the end of the century, Britain's councils were a ghost of their Victorian progenitors. Local government expenditure as a proportion of total government expenditure had risen from thirty-two per cent in 1870 to an unprecedented fifty-one per cent by 1905 as councils uniformly expanded their functions. But after eighty years of Whitehall interference local authority spending had been whittled down to twenty-eight per cent of government expenditure in 1979 and by 1998–9 it had sunk to a historic low of twenty-four per cent.[56] As councils' financial remit had been curtailed, so their revenue became ever more dependent upon central government grants. The removal of the business rate from local authority hands in 1990 deprived city government of a source of locally determined revenue that was available to virtually every local authority across Europe. It destroyed the relationship between councils and business and shifted power even further to the centre. In the year 2001–2, only twenty-five per cent of local authority budgets was raised from local taxation while seventy-five per cent came from government grants. Some nine per cent of that government grant was itself ring-fenced for specific policy areas designated by Government Ministers. The rest was delivered through an almost unfathomable process called the 'standard spending assessment' involving an enormously complicated equation to carve up the national cake.[57] All of which made it very hard work for any modern, enterprising Joseph Chamberlain to finance new schemes, raise revenue or even invest in infrastructure by servicing a substantial debt. It seemed the modern political masters were far more 'Victorian' than the taxing, spending, indebted Victorians themselves.

However, the problem local authorities often face is a depressing absence of modern Chamberlains stepping forward for office. With the rescinding of power from local politics, talent has often headed straight for national and European politics. Municipal leaders have fallen from popular view. At least in the 1980s the controversies surrounding Derek Hatton, Shirley Porter, even David Blunkett in Sheffield brought civic politics into the national arena. Now only five per cent of the population can name their local councillor, while turnout in council elections is less than thirty per cent.[58] This is partly a product of the size of our council wards. In Germany, the ratio of councillors to electors is 1:250, in France it is 1:110, and in the UK it is an altogether unwieldy 1:1,800.[59] At the same time, local communities are being slowly stripped of their grass-roots democracy. In the 1890s, Londoners elected some 12,000 citizens to serve on the councils and committees running their health, transport and education. Now we have 36,000 appointed members of quangos in the UK deciding on crucial parts of our civil society such as schools and hospitals with deleterious consequences for political decision-making and democratic leadership. The situation had become so bleak for local representatives that in 2001 the Institute for Public Policy Research (IPPR) issued a pamphlet entitled, 'In defence of councillors'.

Despite the change of administration in 1997, and the arrival into office of politicians (such as David Blunkett) whose careers were founded in local government, the pressures on

councils grew even worse. A new threat emerged in the form
of an over-energetic state determined to run the country from
the centre with almost Jacobin rigour. A chaotic centralism
developed in which initiative after initiative was launched by
ministers hungry for social change after being excluded from
office for eighteen years. The result was that councils became
subject to a dizzying raft of schemes as well as a greater
Whitehall control from ring-fenced grants. By my estimates,
local authorities were soon having to cope with the following initiatives, partnerships, zones, funds and programmes:
Community Empowerment Funds; Community Chests;
Community Champions Fund; Neighbourhood Manage-
ment Pathfinders; Neighbourhood Renewal Fund; Business
Improvement Districts; Home Zones; Education Action
Zones; Employment Zones; Health Action Zones; Learning
Zones; Sports Action Zones; Urban Regeneration Companies;
Millennium Villages; Regional Development Agencies; Town
Improvement Schemes; Local Tax Reinvestment Programme;
Excellence in Cities; Healthy Living Cities; New Deal for
Communities; Single Regeneration Budget; Local Public Services Agreements; Comprehensive Performance Assessment;
and Local Strategic Partnerships – the last ironically billed as
a policy tool to make sense of overlapping schemes in the
area. Local Public Services Agreements (PSAs) constituted a
particularly revanchist approach to civic autonomy detailing
the duties of councils in everything from education to transport to social services. A typical Local PSA was 'to increase
the number of looked after children who are adopted by at
least 66% between 1999/2000 and 2003/4'.[60]

In *The History of Civilization in Europe* (1828), François
Guizot had mused on how a twelfth-century burgher would
react to an eighteenth-century borough. 'The inhabitants tell
him, that beyond the wall there is a power which taxes them
at pleasure, without their consent ... He learns that the affairs
of the borough are not decided in the borough; but that a man
belonging to the king, an *intendant*, administers them, alone
and at a distance.' Conversely an eighteenth-century burgher

visiting a twelfth-century town would find a model of local self-government. 'The burghers tax themselves, elect their magistrates, judge and punish, and assemble for the purpose of deliberating upon their affairs ... In a word they govern themselves; they are sovereigns.'

Along similar lines, it would be interesting to wonder how a Victorian civic elder would cope in the current *dirigiste* environment. In 1870s Birmingham, Joseph Chamberlain enjoyed the freedom to raise rates, municipalise utilities, take out vast loans, and freely allocate city funds. Today he might wait anxiously for a ministerial Rover and spend the day shuffling a Parliamentary Under Secretary of State around crumbling city 'no go areas' in the hope of obtaining some beneficence from Whitehall departments. And were he to be successful, he would then suffer the added indignity of being forced to sign his Local PSA committing himself to do exactly as Treasury civil servants dictated if he wanted any hope of future funds. Actions which Guizot would not necessarily regard as sovereign.[61]

To its credit, the Government has recently begun to see the error of its ways. The introduction of referenda for directly elected mayors and the creation of more dynamic council cabinets has started the process of re-energising local government. A mid-term study by the New Local Government Network of the first twelve mayors showed a remarkably positive outcome. Mayors were regarded as less partisan, more representative of their communities, more prominent in local leadership and likely to win re-election.[62] Amidst talk of a 'new localism', the government seems ready to return more powers to municipal authorities. The 2001 local government White Paper, *Strong Local Leadership – Quality Public Services*, extolled 'the magnificent municipal achievements of the nineteenth century' before admitting the necessity 'to increase councils' room for action, giving them the powers and freedom they need to innovate and shape services in ways that respond to and meet local needs'.[63] A further official report has confirmed the necessity for decentralisation by charting how Continental cities that enjoy greater fiscal and political independence are 'more proactive, more entre-preneurial and probably more competitive'.[64] Unfortunately, Ministers chose to ignore the findings. The unwelcome re-emergence during 2004 of Whitehall rate-capping and the passing of a crudely centralist Planning Act indicated there was still quite some way to go in understanding the principle of municipal autonomy.

Nonetheless, after decades of centralisation, democratic dis-integration, and fiscal restrictions, local government is slowly regaining some of its nineteenth-century attributes. Even Vic-torian civil society, the mosaic of voluntary organisations and self-help institutes which were such a source of contempt for the 1945 welfare pioneers, is being looked at afresh. As the inefficacy of the state as the sole welfare provider is becoming ever more apparent, and as policy-makers search for the elusive 'social capital', that thick network of clubs and societies which underpinned the Victorian social fabric is increasingly admired. The former Labour Leader Neil Kinnock once described Victorian values as 'cruelty, misery, drudgery, squalor and ignorance', but Chancellor of the Exchequer Gordon Brown now speaks highly of the nineteenth-century's 'civic patriotism' and reminds the Labour Party that it 'grew out of voluntary organisations, friendly societies and mutual aid organisations'. He has even suggested that whereas once 'we thought the man in Whitehall knew best . . . now we know the woman from the playgroup might know better'.[65]

However, if the Labour Government is truly committed to local autonomy and civic renewal then it needs to reassess the spirit of 1945 and its adherence to a uniform, geographical equality of public service. If councils are to be successful, they need to be free to innovate and allocate resources where they see fit which could mean a local prioritisation on schools rather than adoption, transport rather than mental health. Good local government will bring diversity in service delivery, along with healthy civic competition, but also the risk of disparity. Without necessarily jettisoning in its entirety the progressive advances of the welfare state, it is perhaps time to think more imaginatively about precisely which equities are sacrosanct and which diversities worthy of encouragement. Reconciling, or finding a new equilibrium for these competing values, represents a pressing ideological decision. This is the great political challenge: for Ministers to know where to let go and allow local people armed with the vote the maturity of self-government.

v The Victorian Revival

'One thing is pretty certain, and in its way comforting, that however far the rage for revivalism may be pushed, nobody will ever want to revive the nineteenth century,' Leslie Stephen was wont to remark as he led the charge away from the Victorians. But one of the putative merits of studying history is to be able to learn from the past. So, beyond the points of contrast and disparagement, is there anything which can usefully be taken from the Victorians for the future direction of Britain's cities? First indications suggest that our twenty-first-century society and systems of civic governance would not willingly return to the glory days of Chamberlain's Birmingham or 1880s Glasgow. Electoral reforms to the franchise, progressive advances in attitudes towards deference and class, and changes in gender and race politics suggest that the unitary white middle-class fabric which underpinned those cities' civic renaissance is no longer feasible. For good or bad, society is now far too democratic and egalitarian to allow a Joseph Chamberlain clique to hijack city government.

However, the recent surge of interest in the nineteenth-century urban world indicates there is some virtue in thinking about the applicability of certain Victorian civic ideals to the modern city. The fundamental question comes down to one of identity: how do you re-engage a notion of civic patriotism or civic pride with an individualistic society with only the loosest of affiliations to nation, region and class let alone to the city? The achievements of the Victorian municipal leaders were often premised upon a popular level of civic identification which only began to wane from the early 1900s. To identify with the city demands not only employment ties and physical location, but a sense of pride in the achievement and image of the *polis*. Which is why, despite the clichéd barbs, the City of Culture competition, and the cultural industry more generally, is an important component of re-energising civic identity. But the next stage is to try to ensure urban culture is a truly indigenous product and not simply a high-end marketing tool. For that civic leaders need to think more creatively about generating a stronger ethic of commercial and philanthropic patronage whether through off-setting parts of the local business rates or a system of civic honours. It needs to become a mark of social cachet to endow a new wing of the local museum (rather than contributing to another British Museum fighting fund) as well as to invest in the local football team. Government might also look into the idea of twice yearly civic lotteries to generate funds for cultural projects and to help remove some of the lottery pot from London's sticky fingers.

Part of the civic energy of the Victorian city often boiled up in the frequently bitter fights over architectural competitions, and modern local authorities could certainly think more innovatively about generating broader debate on controversial city centre redevelopments. Proper town hall meetings and the use of local media – rather than a model available for viewing at the bottom of the council offices on a Tuesday afternoon – might help to encourage citizens to engage pro-actively with their urban environment. The new architecture of the city must form part of a renewed commitment to public design of the highest quality. It must work to embed a new conception of the city as a civic space commensurate with an ideal of citizenship which extends beyond a neutral setting for individual acts of commercial exchange. Our cities need to regain their civic setting. The next generation of iconic civic architecture should not be a Selfridges or Harvey Nichols, but libraries, town halls, and municipal gardens. And they in turn should be adorned with civic monuments. Today, too few of our cities fund the type of statues, plaques or monuments which all serve to generate, at however residual a level, some form of civic identity.

The decline of the city has, of course, proceeded indelibly with Britain's post-industrial transition. Yet the new world of the information age and Knowledge Driven Economy surely offers a route to regeneration. Contrary to expectation, the New Economy has not killed off geography. In fact, locations and community are more important than ever. And the skills, historic fabric, culture, and urban edge of the British city presents a compelling economic case. Universities, creative clusters and Business Improvement Districts (BIDs) will hopefully provide a magnet for growth, while attractive civic environments and, more importantly, a well-trained labour pool will encourage international investment. But without losing the benefits of a competitive environment, there is a need for some way of tying companies more closely to the locale. This is the work of public opinion and the municipal bully-pulpit: to infiltrate an identification with the city into commercial decision-making. For in the long run, building up strong local brands tied to the city can only be beneficial both for business and civil society.

Vibrant, living cities depend crucially upon people residing in their centres. The challenge for the former Victorian cities is to ensure that when singles become couples and have children they do not instinctively fly to the suburbs. With the pollution, noise, and traffic of the city some families will inevitably seek a quieter life elsewhere, but there are many who would be willing to stay if it was not for the state of inner-city schooling. According to a recent government report, 'People living in urban areas are more likely to be dissatisfied with schools.'[66] While the poor condition of many urban comprehensives is partly the product of ingrained local poverty, there is an enormous amount which central and local government could do in increasing resources, improving teaching, and cutting class sizes specifically for urban areas. Lest it be forgotten, Joseph

Chamberlain first became involved in local government because of Birmingham's schools.

To encourage a new generation of Chamberlains to enter public office, power and money need to be returned to councils. The Council Tax system requires urgent reform with cities given greater charge of local funds as well as power over the business rate. There also needs to be a broader debate about introducing local sales, tourism and entertainment taxes both to diversify the local authority tax base and revive a tangible element of urban democracy.[67] Whitehall must steady itself for a leap of faith and revive the nineteenth-century model of entrusting local authorities with their own responsibilities. At first, no doubt, there will be well-publicised accounts of mismanagement as municipalities relearn the skills and mentality of self-governance. But power attracts talent and when communities have the opportunity to run themselves, when individual mayors or council leaders have the chance to govern Liverpool, Birmingham, Manchester and Glasgow with the same authority and public gaze enjoyed by their Continental and American counterparts, then it is only a matter of time before politicians of calibre re-enter municipal government. Already, Ken Livingstone in London and Ray Mallon in Middlesbrough are making a difference as directly elected mayors to the political culture of their cities. Britain's centralist political culture remains almost unique among most Western developed nations where political leaders rise time and again from urban and regional power bases to assume national office. Herbert Morrison was arguably the last person to take that road to Westminster – as long ago as the 1930s.[68]

Not only does power need to flow back to the cities, but within civil society there exists a similar urgency for renewed grass-roots democracy. The dead hand of the quangos must be lifted and their authorities returned either to elected councils or, in the case of schools and hospitals, locally elected boards. Even with devolution, Britain still suffers from a terrible over-representation at the national level and under-representation at the local which has not necessarily produced the finest process of decision-making. The age-old trouble is that once bureaucrats and politicians gain power they are very rarely interested in rescinding it. It will take an act of great political courage to alter that mindset.

But if the Victorian city is to live again, it will take more than politicians. The nineteenth-century urban world entailed a vision of the city and citizenship which now appears almost moribund. Initially developed by an elite coterie of middle-class Nonconformists, it was an appreciation of the virtue of an urban life and the historic, liberating mission of the city. Even amidst the smog, filth and poverty of the industrialising north there existed an understanding of the city's purpose as a political and cultural entity. The idea of Britain as a 'land of great cities' has vanished and instead we are left with the mirage of a 'green and pleasant land' retreating ever further into the concreted distance. To save the *rus* and the *urbs* we need to renew our perception of Britain's urban identity and learn to love, hate, reform, rebuild, but, above all, debate the city, 'dark Satanic mills' and all.

NOTES

PREFACE: MANUFACTURING CITIES [pp 1–9]

[1] George Eliot, *Felix Holt: The Radical* (1866) (London, 1995), pp. 3–7
[2] Daniel Defoe, *A Tour Through the Whole Island of Great Britain* (1724–6) (London, 1971), pp. 392; 482; 536
[3] *ibid.*, p. 544
[4] John Byng, *Rides Round Britain* (1782–93) (London, 1996), pp. 187; 196–7; 422
[5] Hansard, XXVIII (1835), col. 559
[6] See Peter Ackroyd, *Blake* (London, 1996)
[7] Ferdinand Braudel, *Capitalism and Material Life* (London, 1973), p. 382
[8] See E. Soja, *Postmodern Geographies: The Reassertion of Space in Critical Social Theory* (Oxford, 1989)

1: THE NEW HADES [pp 13–44]

[1] Quoted in R.J.W. Selleck, *James Kay-Shuttleworth* (Ilford, 1994), p. 25
[2] George Bell, *Day and Night in the Wynds of Edinburgh* (1849) (Leicester, 1973), p. 6
[3] J.P. Kay, *The Moral and Physical Condition of the Working Classes Employed in the Cotton Manufacture in Manchester* (1832) (Manchester, 1969), p. 8
[4] Arnold Toynbee, *Lectures on the Industrial Revolution in England* (1884) (Newton Abbot, 1969), pp. 93; 189–91. Toynbee's was the dominant, negative image of the Industrial Revolution until free-market economists in the 1950s, led by Friedrich von Hayek, began to celebrate the era's revolutionary spirit of enterprise. In more recent years, the Industrial Revolution has undergone something of a popular revival as the art and architecture of the early 1800s has returned to fashion. Paintings by Joseph Wright of Derby now regularly command over £1 million, while the Derwent Valley Mills, Saltaire and New Lanark have all joined Britain's list of UNESCO World Heritage sites. See Tristram Hunt, 'Industrial Evolution', *Guardian*, 12 January 2003.

⁵ Peter Clark (ed.), *The Cambridge Urban History of* Britain, vol. II: 1540–1840 (Cambridge, 2000), pp. 473–4

⁶ See David Feldman, 'Migration', in Martin Daunton (ed.), *The Cambridge Urban History of Britain, vol. III: 1840–1950* (Cambridge, 2000)

⁷ See W.D. Rubinstein, 'The Victorian Middle Classes: Wealth, Occupation, and Geography', *The Economic History Review*, XXX, 4 (1977)

⁸ Archibald Alison, *Principles of Population and Their Connection with Human Happiness* (London, 1840), I, p. 529

⁹ See S. Gilley and R. Swift (eds), *The Irish in the Victorian City* (Chatham, 1985), p. 15

¹⁰ Robert Southey, *Letters from England: by Don Manuel Alvarez Espriella* (London, 1808), II, p. 59

¹¹ *ibid.*, II. p. 71–2

¹² Kay, *Moral and Physical Condition* (1969), p. 35

¹³ Quoted in L.D. Bradshaw (ed.), *Visitors to Manchester* (Manchester, 1987), p. 25

¹⁴ Leon Faucher, *Manchester in 1844* (Manchester, 1844), p. 16

¹⁵ Parliamentary Papers VII (1843), 'Select Committee on Smoke Prevention. II. Minutes of Evidence', p. 62

¹⁶ *The Collected Letters of Thomas Carlyle and Jane Welsh* (North Carolina, 1970–), XXVIII, p. 54

¹⁷ Hugh Miller, *First Impressions of England and its People* (London, 1847), p. 38

¹⁸ Quoted in Anthony Wohl, *Endangered Lives* (London, 1983), p. 235

¹⁹ Henrietta Barnett, *Canon Barnett. His Life, Work and Friends* (London, 1921), p. 197

²⁰ Friedrich Engels, *The Condition of the Working Class in England* (1845) (London, 1987), pp. 124–5

²¹ Quoted in Bradshaw, *Visitors to Manchester* (1987), p. 35

²² William Strange, *Address to the Middle and Working Classes on the Causes and Preventions of the Excessive Sickness and Mortality Prevalent in Large Towns* (London, 1845), p. 28

²³ Quoted in Wohl, *Endangered Lives* (1983), p. 81

²⁴ Toynbee, *Industrial Revolution*, (1969), p. 189

²⁵ Southey, *Letters from England* (1808), II. p. 59

²⁶ Thomas Carlyle, 'Chartism', in *Selected Writings* (London, 1986), p. 211

²⁷ Alexis de Tocqueville, *Journeys to England and Ireland* (1835) (London, 1958), p. 94

²⁸ *ibid.*, p. 107

²⁹ C. Turner Thackrah, *The Effects of the Principal Arts, Trades, and Professions, and of Civic States and Habits of Living, on Health and Longevity* (1832) (London, 1959), pp. 5–6

30 W.H. Jones, *Gimcrackiana, or Fugitive Pieces on Manchester Men and Manners* (Manchester, 1833)
31 Hippolyte Taine, *Notes on England* (1872) (London, 1957), p. 219
32 See Hugh Pennington, *London Review of Books* (2001), 23, 3
33 See E.P. Thompson, 'Time, Work Discipline and Industrial Capitalism', *Past and Present*, 38 (1967); for a critique see J. de Vries, 'The Industrial Revolution and the Industrious Revolution', *Journal of Economic History*, 54 (1994)
34 Southey, *Letters from England* (1808), II, p. 83
35 Quoted in Bradshaw, *Visitors to Manchester* (1987), p. 54
36 See M.W. Flinn, 'Introduction', to Edwin Chadwick, *Report on the Sanitary Condition of the Labouring Population of Great Britain* (1842) (Edinburgh, 1965)
37 Quoted in Andrew Gibb, *Glasgow: The Making of a City* (London, 1983), pp. 107–8
38 J. Shaw, *Travels in England* (1861) (London, 1985), p. 200
39 Bell, *Day and Night* (1973), p. 10
40 Parliamentary Papers XXXIV (1836), 'Royal Commission on the State of the Irish Poor in England', p. iv
41 *ibid.*, p. 457
42 *ibid.*, pp. xi–xii
43 Kay, *Moral and Physical Condition* (1969), p. 35
44 De Tocqueville, *Journeys* (1958), p. 104
45 Carlyle, 'Chartism', in *Selected Writings* (1986), p. 171
46 Quoted in Hector Gavin, *Unhealthiness of Towns and the Necessity of Remedial Measures* (Health of Towns Association, 1847), p. 10
47 Edwin Chadwick, *Report on the Sanitary Condition of the Labouring Population of Great Britain* (1842) (Edinburgh, 1965), p. 98
48 *ibid.*, p. 111
49 Southey, *Letters from England* (1808), p. 89
50 Chadwick, *Report* (1965), p. 92
51 Szreter and Mooney, 'Urbanization, Mortality and the Standard of Living Debate: new estimates of the expectation of life at birth in nineteenth century British cities', *Economic History Review*, LI, 1 (1998), pp. 84–112
52 Chadwick, *Report* (1965), p. 78
53 Quoted in Frank Smith, *The Life and Work of Sir James Kay-Shuttleworth* (London, 1974), p. 20
54 Viscount Ebrington, *Unhealthiness of Towns, Its Causes and Remedies* (London, 1846)
55 Szreter and Mooney, 'Urbanization, Mortality, and the Standard of Living Debate', *Economic History Review* (1998), pp. 84–112
56 Gavin, *Unhealthiness of Towns* (1847), p. 11
57 See Simon Szreter, 'Urban Fertility and Mortality Patterns', in Daunton (ed.), *Cambridge Urban History of Britain* (2000)

[58] Engels, *The Condition of the Working Class in England* (1987), p. 67
[59] *ibid.*, p. 69
[60] *ibid.*, p. 64
[61] *ibid.*, p. 89
[62] *ibid.*, p. 87
[63] *ibid.*, p. 89
[64] *ibid.*, p. 100
[65] *ibid.*, p. 170
[66] *ibid.*, p. 98
[67] *ibid.*, p. 125
[68] Gareth Stedman Jones, 'The First Industrial City? Engels's Account of Manchester in 1844.' Unpublished paper.
[69] Engels, *The Condition of the Working Class in England* (1987), p. 290

2: CARLYLE AND COKETOWN [pp 45–74]

[1] Charles Dickens, *Hard Times* (1854) (London, 1987), p. 65
[2] Lewis Mumford, *The City in History* (London, 1961), pp. 459; 450
[3] See, for example, *Daily Telegraph*, 1 May 2001
[4] J.S. Boone, *The Need of Christianity to Cities* (London, 1844), pp. 13, 14–15
[5] Bell, *Day and Night* (1973), p. 29
[6] Charles Dickens, *Oliver Twist* (1838) (Oxford, 1982), p. 49
[7] *ibid.*, p. 130
[8] See Harold Perkin, 'An Age of Great Cities', in D.N. Mancoff and D.J. Tela (eds), *Victorian Urban Settings* (London, 1996)
[9] Henry Mayhew, *London Labour and the London Poor* (1861–2), (London, 1985), pp. 6–7; 273
[10] *ibid.*, p. 211
[11] Kay, *Moral and Physical Condition* (1969), p. 63
[12] Shaw, *Travels in England* (1985), pp. 179; 189
[13] Quoted in Trevor Fisher, *Prostitution and the Victorians* (Stroud, 1997), pp. xxiv; xxiii
[14] William Wordsworth, *Prelude* (1850) (London, 1979), VII
[15] Southey, *Letters from England* (1808), p. 88
[16] *Report from the Select Committee on the Health of Towns* (New York, 1968), p. xiv
[17] Chadwick, *Report* (1958), pp. 198; 193
[18] *ibid.*, p. 193
[19] *ibid.*, p. 147
[20] Peter Gaskell, *Artisans and Machinery: the Moral and Physical Condition of the Manufacturing Population* (London, 1836), p. 89
[21] Walter Scott, *Familiar Letters* (Edinburgh, 1894), II, p. 78
[22] R. Parkinson, *On the Present Condition of the Labouring Poor in Manchester* (Manchester, 1841), p. 85

23 William Cooke Taylor, *Notes of a Tour in the Manufacturing Districts of Lancashire* (1841) (London, 1968), p. 164
24 Toynbee, *Industrial Revolution* (1969), p. 190
25 Benjamin Disraeli, *Sybil, or The Two Nations* (1845) (Oxford, 1988), p. 66
26 Gareth Stedman Jones (ed.), *The Communist Manifesto* (1848) (London, 2002), p. 222
27 Baron d'Haussez, *Great Britain in 1833* (London, 1833), p. 34
28 Faucher, *Manchester in 1844* (1844), p. 126
29 Robert Mudie, *London and the Londoners: Or a Second Judgement of Babylon the Great* (London, 1829), II, p. 209
30 Robert Southey, *Sir Thomas More: or, Colloquies on the Progress and Prospects of Society* (London, 1829), p. 94
31 Thomas Carlyle, *Past and Present* (1843) (New York, 1965), p. 271
32 Charles Dickens, *Bleak House* (1853) (London, 1985), p. 683
33 Virginia Woolf, *The Death of the Moth and other essays* (New York, 1942), p. 20
34 Quoted in Raymond Williams, *The Country and the City* (London, 1973), p. 215
35 Thomas de Quincey, *Confessions of an Opium-Eater* (London, 1823), p. 79
36 Quoted in Gary Messinger, *Manchester in the Victorian Age* (Manchester, 1985), p. 12
37 De Tocqueville, *Journeys* (1958), p. 108
38 Taylor, *Notes of a Tour* (1968), p. 9
39 *Bentley's Miscellany*, VI (1839), p. 597
40 Faucher, *Manchester in 1844* (1844), p. 26
41 Harriet Martineau, *History of England During the Thirty Years' Peace* (London, 1850), II, p. 704
42 T. Pinney (ed.), *Essays of George Eliot* (London, 1963), p. 213
43 See Fred Kaplan, *Thomas Carlyle* (Cambridge, 1983); Rosemary Ashton, *Thomas and Jane Carlyle: Portrait of a Marriage* (London, 2002)
44 Thomas Carlyle, 'Signs of the Times', in *Selected Writings* (1986), p. 71
45 'Nature has placed mankind under the governance of two sovereign masters, pain and pleasure. It is for them alone to point out what we ought to do, as well as to determine what we shall do.' Jeremy Bentham, *An Introduction to the Principles of Morals and Legislation* in A.J. Ayer & J. O.'Grady (eds), *A Dictionary of Philosophical Quotations* (Oxford, 1992), p. 46
46 Thomas Carlyle, *Sartor Resartus* (1833–4) (Oxford, 1987), pp. 127; 146
47 Carlyle, 'Signs of the Times', in *Selected Writings* (1986), p. 77
48 *ibid.*, p. 151

⁴⁹ Carlyle, *Past and Present* (1965), p. 148
⁵⁰ Kenelm Henry Digby, *The Broad Stone of Honour* (London, 1829), book 4, p. 30
⁵¹ Kay, *Moral and Physical Condition* (1969), pp. 63–4
⁵² Taylor, *Notes of a Tour* (1968), p. 164
⁵³ Benjamin Disraeli, *Coningsby* (1844) (London, 1963), p. 199
⁵⁴ *The Times*, 25 June 1835
⁵⁵ Sidney and Beatrice Webb, *English Local Government*, vol. IV: *Statutory Authorities for Special Purposes* (1922) (London, 1963), p. 425
⁵⁶ *Blackwood's Edinburgh Magazine*, XXXVII (1835), p. 965
⁵⁷ Hansard, XXVIII (1835), col. 1005
⁵⁸ J.S. Mill, 'Bentham', in John Stuart Mill and Jeremy Bentham, *Utilitarianism and Other Essays* (1838) (London, 1987), p. 172
⁵⁹ Disraeli, *Sybil* (1988), p. 65
⁶⁰ Faucher, *Manchester in 1844* (1844), pp. 24–5
⁶¹ Kaplan, *Carlyle* (1983), p. 430
⁶² Peter Ackroyd, *Dickens* (London, 1990), p. 301
⁶³ Kaplan, *Carlyle* (1983), p. 260
⁶⁴ John Forster, *The Life of Charles Dickens* (1872–4) (London, 1969), II, p. 122
⁶⁵ For an excellent discussion of Coketown see F.S. Schwarzbach, *Dickens and the City* (London, 1979)
⁶⁶ Lewis Mumford, *The City in History* (London, 1961), p. 447
⁶⁷ Peter Hall, *Cities in Civilization* (London, 1999), pp. 611
⁶⁸ *ibid.*, pp. 704–5

3 : PUGIN *VERSUS* THE PANOPTICON [pp 75–127]

¹ Benjamin Disraeli, *Endymion* (Leipzig, 1880), II, p. 30
² See Ian Anstruther, *The Knight and the Umbrella* (Gloucester, 1986)
³ See Charles Dellheim, *The Face of the Past* (Cambridge, 1982)
⁴ Charles Dickens, *Dombey and Son* (1848) (Oxford, 1982), p. 324
⁵ Disraeli, *Coningsby* (1963), p. 117
⁶ See J.M. Crook, 'John Britton and the Genesis of the Gothic Revival', in J. Summerson (ed.), *Concerning Architecture* (London, 1968)
⁷ George Gilbert Scott, *Remarks on Secular and Domestic Architecture* (London, 1857), pp. 16; 9
⁸ John Henry Newman, *Apologia Pro Vita Sua* (1865) (London, 1994), p. 108. Reverence for Scott was common among the Tractarians. See J.H. Keble's laudatory article, 'The Life and Writings of Sir Walter Scott', *British Critic*, XXIV (1838), pp. 423–83
⁹ For a broader discussion of Victorian historical culture, see Peter Mandler, *The Fall and Rise of the Stately Home* (Yale, 1997), pp. 21–38

[10] *The Miscellaneous Works of Sir Walter Scott Bart* (Edinburgh, 1870), VI, p. 124

[11] Quoted in Jonathan Rose, *The Intellectual Life of the British Working Classes* (London, 2001), pp. 40–41

[12] See Mark Girouard, *The Return to Camelot* (New Haven, 1981)

[13] It might be useful to define what Newman meant by Liberalism. He defined it in *Apologia Pro Vita Sua* as follows: 'Now by Liberalism I mean false liberty of thought, or the exercise of thought upon matters, in which, from the constitution of the human mind, thought cannot be brought to any successful issue, and therefore is out of place. Among such matters are first principles of whatever kind; and of these the most sacred and momentous are especially to be reckoned the truths of Revelation. Liberalism then is the mistake of subjecting to human judgement those revealed doctrines which are in their nature beyond and independent of it, and of claiming to determine on intrinsic grounds the truth and value of propositions which rest for their reception simply on the external authority of the Divine Word.'

[14] Newman, *Apologia* (1994), p. 49

[15] See E.P. Hennock, *Fit and Proper Persons* (London, 1973), p. 357

[16] Hansard, XXXVII (1818), col. 1117

[17] See Standish Meacham, 'The Church in the Victorian City', *Victorian Studies*, XI, 3 (1967–8)

[18] Stephen Bann, 'Romanticism in France', in R. Porter and M. Teich (eds), *Romanticism in National Context* (Cambridge, 1988); D.G. Charlton, *The French Romantics* (Cambridge, 1984)

[19] *Manchester Guardian*, 21 January 1846

[20] See Boyd Hilton, 'Disraeli, English culture, and the decline of the industrial spirit', in L. Brockliss and D. Eastwood (eds), *Union of Multiple Identities* (Manchester, 1997). See also S.A. Skinner, *Tractarians and the 'condition of England': the social and political thought of the Oxford Movement* (Oxford, 2004)

[21] Alice Chandler, *A Dream of Order* (London, 1971)

[22] Thomas Love Peacock, *Crotchet Castle* (1831) (London, 1986), p. 163

[23] Digby, *Broad Stone of Honour*, (1829), book 4, p. 587

[24] Southey, *Sir Thomas More: or, Colloquies on the Progress and Prospects of Society* (1829), I, p. 60

[25] *ibid.*, p. 94

[26] *ibid.*, p. 158

[27] *ibid.*, II, p. 242

[28] Carlyle, *Past and Present* (1965), pp. 282; 211

[29] See Robert Blake, *Disraeli* (London, 1969), pp. 167–190

[30] Charles Whibley, *Lord John Manners and his Friends* (London, 1925), I, 106

[31] Quoted in *British Critic*, XXXIII, 66 (1843), p. 411
[32] Disraeli, *Coningsby* (1963), p. 221
[33] Disraeli, *Sybil* (1988), p. 65
[34] *Manchester Guardian*, 13 November 1850
[35] Tom Taylor, 'On Central and Local Action in Relation to Town Improvement', *National Association for the Promotion of Social Science* (1857), pp. 474–5
[36] J.A. Picton, *Memorials of Liverpool* (London, 1873), pp. 1–2
[37] Thomas Chalmers, *The Christian and Civic Economy of Large Towns* (Glasgow, 1821), p. 29
[38] Sir Benjamin Heywood, *Addresses delivered at the Manchester Mechanics' Institute* (London, 1840), p. 120
[39] *ibid.*, p. 82
[40] *The Builder*, 131, 9 August 1845
[41] J. Milner, *The History of Winchester* (London, 1798), II, p. 226
[42] Southey, *Letters from England* (1808), II, p. 97
[43] *ibid.*, p. 103
[44] M. Foucault, *Discipline and Punish* (London, 1991), p. 200
[45] *Quarterly Review*, X (October, 1813 and January 1814), p. 489
[46] *ibid.*
[47] William Cobbett, *A History of the Protestant Reformation* (1829) (London, 1994), p. 13
[48] *ibid.*, p. 324
[49] William Cobbett, *Rural Rides*, ed. G.D.H. Cole and M. Cole (London, 1930), p. 728
[50] *ibid.*, p. 663
[51] Quoted in P. Atterbury and C. Wainwright (eds), *Pugin: A Gothic Passion* (London, 1994), p. 3
[52] A.W. Pugin, *Contrasts* (1840) (Leicester, 1969), p. 6
[53] A.W. Pugin, *The True Principles of Pointed or Christian Architecture* (1841) (London, 1973), p. 51
[54] Quoted in M.W. Brooks, *John Ruskin and Victorian Architecture* (New Brunswick, 1987), p. 235
[55] *The Builder*, 372, 23 March 1850
[56] A.W. Pugin, *An Apology for the Revival of Christian Architecture in England* (1843) (Oxford, 1969), p. 1
[57] *ibid.*, p. 2
[58] See Kenneth Clark, *The Gothic Revival* (London, 1995)
[59] Pugin, *An Apology* (1969), p. 19
[60] Pugin, *True Principles* (1973), p. 39
[61] *Ecclesiologist*, I (1842), p. 161
[62] *ibid.*, VI (1846), p. 202
[63] See Gavin Stamp and Colin Amery, *Victorian Buildings of London* (London, 1980)
[64] For an excellent account of W.F. Hook and St Peter's Church, see

Christopher Webster, *The Rebuilding of Leeds Parish Church 1837–41* (London, 1994)

[65] Quoted in Clyde Binfield, *So Down to Prayers* (London, 1977), p. 60

[66] *ibid.*, p. 7

[67] *Leeds Intelligencer*, 28 August 1841

[68] *Ecclesiologist*, VIII (1847), p. 132

[69] *Church Intelligencer*, 11 September 1841

[70] Quoted in Webster, *The Rebuilding* (1994), p. 19

[71] 'The Diary of Benjamin Barker of Bramley, near Leeds', Thoresby Society, MSS XI, Box 2 and 3

[72] Clark, *The Gothic Revival* (1995), p. 9

[73] Thomas Hope, *An Historical Essay on Architecture* (London, 1840), p. 398

[74] E.T. Cook and A. Wedderburn (eds), *The Collected Works of John Ruskin*, VIII, (London, 1903), p. xxxiv

[75] John Ruskin, *The Seven Lamps of Architecture*, in Cook and Wedderburn (eds), *Collected Works*, VIII (London, 1903), p. 252

[76] *Correspondence of Carlyle and Ruskin* (California, 1982), p. 63

[77] Mary Lutyens, *Millais and the Ruskins* (London, 1968), p. 155

[78] Mary Lutyens, *Effie in Venice* (London, 1965), p. 133

[79] Quoted in John Julius Norwich, *Paradise of Cities* (London, 2003), p. 82

[80] John Ruskin, *The Stones of Venice*, in Cook and Wedderburn (eds), *Collected Works*, X (London, 1903), p. 17

[81] *ibid.*, X, p. 27

[82] *ibid.*, XI, p. 201

[83] *ibid.*, X, p. 67

[84] *ibid.*, X, p. 192

[85] *ibid.*, X, p. 203

[86] Marx and Engels, *The Communist Manifesto* (2002), p. 227

[87] Ruskin, *The Stones of Venice*, in *Collected Works*, X (1903), p. 177

[88] *ibid.*, XI, p. 120

[89] *ibid.*, XI, p. 134

[90] The independence of the Venetian Church from the Papacy was a much-needed argument for Ruskin to obscure the otherwise problematic Catholicism of medieval Venice.

[91] Charles Eastlake, *The Gothic Revival* (1872) (Leicester, 1970), pp. 277–8

[92] Ruskin, *The Stones of Venice*, in Cook and Wedderburn (eds), *Collected Works*, X (London, 1903), p. 459

[93] *The Builder*, 423, 15 March 1851

[94] *The Builder*, 425, 29 March 1851

[95] J.A. Langford, *Modern Birmingham and Its Institutions* (Birmingham, 1873), p. 343

[96] Scott, *Remarks on Secular and Domestic Architecture* (1857), p. 198

[97] *ibid.*, p. viii

[98] *Fraser's Magazine*, XXVIII (1843), p. 597

[99] Hansard, 3rd series, vol. 164 (1861), col. 530

[100] Clark, *Gothic Revival* (1995), p. 9

[101] *The Times*, 16 January 1858

4: MACAULAY, THE MIDDLE CLASSES AND THE MARCH OF PROGRESS [pp 128–185]

[1] Sir George Otto Trevelyan, *The Life and Letters of Lord Macaulay* (London, 1959), p. 41

[2] *Edinburgh Review*, L (1829), pp. 539–40

[3] *Westminster Review*, VI (1826), p. 66

[4] *Manchester Guardian*, 20 August 1845

[5] *Leeds Mercury*, 4 May 1844

[6] *The Economist*, 13 May 1848

[7] See Blair Worden, *Roundhead Reputations* (London, 2001); Raphael Samuel, 'The Discovery of Puritanism', in *Island Stories*, II (London, 1998)

[8] J.P. Kay, 'A Letter to the People of Lancashire, concerning the Future Representation of the Commercial Interest, By the Return of Members for its New Boroughs to the Reformed Parliament' (London, 1831), pp. 4; 16

[9] S. Mellon (ed.), *François Guizot: Historical Essays and Lectures* (Chicago, 1973), p. 74

[10] Marx and Engels, *The Communist Manifesto* (2002), p. 222

[11] *British and Foreign Review*, 16 (1844), p. 100

[12] *Westminster Review*, XXXVI (1841), p. 280

[13] *The Athenaeum*, LXV (1829), p. 37

[14] See S. Gunn and R. Bell, *The Rise and Sprawl of the Middle Class* (London, 2001)

[15] Quoted in Dror Wahrman, *Imagining the Middle Class* (Cambridge, 1995), pp. 23–4

[16] *ibid.*, p. 152

[17] Quoted in Brian Simon, *Studies in the History of Education* (London, 1960), p. 78

[18] Edward Baines, *The Life of Edward Baines* (London, 1859), p. 26

[19] Henry Roscoe, *The Life of William Roscoe* (Edinburgh, 1833), p. 105

[20] John Seed, 'Rational Dissent and political opposition, 1770–1790', in Knud Haakonssen (ed.)., *Enlightenment and Religion* (Cambridge, 1996), p. 157

[21] Quoted in 'Introduction', Edmund Burke, *Reflections on the Revolution in France* (1790) (London, 1986), p. 27

[22] John James, *History and Topography of Bradford* (London, 1841), p. 152

[23] Edward Collinson, *History of the Worsted Trade* (London, 1854), p. 113

[24] R.D.D. Vaughan, *The Age of Great Cities* (London, 1843), p. 78

[25] See John Seed, 'Theologies of power: Unitarianism and the social relations of religious discourse, 1800–50', in R.J. Morris (ed.), *Class, Power and Social Structure in British Nineteenth-Century Towns* (Leicester, 1986)

[26] John Seed, 'Unitarianism, Political Economy and the Antinomies of Liberal Culture in Manchester, 1830–1850', *Social History*, VII, 1 (1982), pp. 5; 12

[27] Asa Briggs, *Victorian Cities* (London, 1990), p. 204

[28] George Harris, *The Life and Labours of the late Rev. William Turner* (Manchester, 1859), p. 15

[29] *ibid.*, p. 319

[30] Benjamin Love, *The Handbook of Manchester* (Manchester, 1842), p. 144

[31] Taylor, *Notes of a Tour* (1968), p. 10

[32] See Clyde Binfield, *So Down to Prayers* (London, 1977), p. 74

[33] Edward Baines, *The Social, Educational, and Religious State of the Manufacturing Districts* (1835) (London, 1843), p. 19

[34] Vaughan, *Great Cities* (1843), p. 319

[35] *Edinburgh Review*, L (1829), p. 553

[36] *Edinburgh Review*, LXXVII (1843), p. 202

[37] Baines, *State of the Manufacturing Districts* (1843), p. 61

[38] *Edinburgh Review*, LXXVII (1843), p. 204

[39] *ibid.*, pp. 201–3

[40] Richard Cobden, *England, Ireland and America* (1835), in *The Political Writings of Richard Cobden* (London, 1903), I, p. 34

[41] J. Morley, *The Life of Richard Cobden* (London, 1896), I, p. 134

[42] Richard Cobden, 'Incorporate Your Borough', in W.E.A. Axon, *Cobden as a Citizen* (Manchester, 1907), p. 31

[43] *ibid.*, p. 39

[44] Quoted in Gary S. Messinger, *Manchester in the Victorian Age* (Manchester, 1985), p. 76

[45] A.J.P. Taylor, 'Manchester', *Encounter* (1957), 8, 3, p. 9

[46] Edward Baines, *History of the Cotton Manufacture in Great Britain* (1835) (New York, 1966), p. 6

[47] *ibid.*, p. 456

[48] Baines, *State of the Manufacturing Districts* (1843), p. 55

[49] George Head, *A Home Tour through the Manufacturing Districts of England in the Summer of 1835* (London, 1836), p. 187

[50] Vaughan, *Great Cities* (1843), p. 230

[51] *ibid.*, p. 238

[52] E.R. Jones (ed.), *The Life and Speeches of Joseph Cowen MP* (London, 1885), p. 406

[53] *ibid.*, p. 429
[54] James, *History and Topography of Bradford* (1841), p. 186
[55] *Leeds Mercury*, 11 October 1851
[56] De Tocqueville, *Journeys* (1958), p. 107
[57] *The Builder*, 294, 23 September 1848
[58] Love, *Manchester* (1842), p. 49
[59] Edward Collinson, *The History of the Worsted Trade, and Historic Sketch of Bradford* (London, 1854), p. 198
[60] P.A. Whittle, *Blackburn As It Is* (Fishergate, 1852), p. viii
[61] Quoted in Wohl, *Endangered Lives* (1983), p. 216
[62] Roscoe, *Life of William Roscoe* (1833), p. 445
[63] Haakonssen (ed.), *Enlightenment and Religion* (1996)
[64] See Robert Putnam, *Bowling Alone* (New York, 2000)
[65] John Glyde, *The Moral, Social and Religious Condition of Ipswich in the Middle of the 19th Century* (London, 1971), p. 168
[66] J. Wolff and J. Seed (eds), *The Culture of Capital: Art, Power and the Nineteenth Century Middle Class* (Manchester, 1987)
[67] Taine, *Notes on England* (1957), p. 236
[68] See Eleanor Gordon and Gwyneth Nair, *Public Lives. Women, Family and Society in Victorian Britain* (London, 2003)
[69] *Quarterly Review*, XXXIV (1826), p. 173
[70] Arnold Thackray, 'Natural Knowledge in Cultural Context: The Manchester Model', *American Historical Review* LXXIX, 3, (1974), pp. 672–709
[71] T. Wemyss Reid (ed.), *A Memoir of Dr Heaton of Leeds* (London, 1883), p. 99
[72] See R. J. Morris, *Class, Sect, and Party. The Making of the British Middle Class, Leeds 1820–1850* (Manchester, 1990), p. 243
[73] Faucher, *Manchester in 1844* (1844), p. 52
[74] *Morning Chronicle*, 10 March 1851
[75] Quoted in Robert Colls and Richard Rodgers (eds.), *Cities of Ideas* (Aldershot, 2004), p. 299
[76] Quoted in Jonathan Rose, *The Intellectual Life of the British Working Classes* (London, 2001), p. 64
[77] See W.H. Fraser, 'The Working Class', in W.H. Fraser and I. Maver (eds), *Glasgow*, vol. II (Manchester, 1996)
[78] Mabel Tylecote, *The Mechanics' Institutes of Lancashire and Yorkshire before 1851* (Manchester 1957)
[79] *Manchester Guardian*, 20 November 1847
[80] Alexis de Tocqueville, *Democracy in America* (1835), (London, 1994), II, p. 324
[81] *ibid.*, I, p. 328
[82] Alderman John Baynes, *The Cotton Trade – Two Lectures* (London, 1857), p. 66
[83] Vaughan, *Great Cities* (1843), p. 152

[84] J.A. Picton, 'Self-Government in Towns', *Contemporary Review*, XXXIV (1879), p. 679

[85] Baines, *State of the Manufacturing Districts* (1843), p. 58

[86] Vaughan, *Great Cities* (1843), p. 277

[87] Seed, 'Theologies of power: Unitarianism and the social relations of religious discourse, 1800–50', in Morris (ed.), *Class, Power and Social Structure in British Nineteenth-Century Towns* (1986), pp. 110–11

[88] Quoted in Bradshaw (ed.), *Visitors to Manchester* (1987), p. 51

[89] Shaw, *Travels in England* (1985), p. 216

[90] H.L. Jones, *A Plan for a University for the Town of Manchester* (Manchester, 1836), pp. 7–8

[91] Taine, *Notes on England* (1957), p. 229

[92] 'The Diary of Benjamin Barker of Bramley, near Leeds', Thoresby Society, MSS XI, Box 2 and 3

[93] W.L. Guttsman (ed.), *A Plea for Democracy* (Bristol, 1967), p. 155

[94] *ibid.*, pp. 103–4

[95] James E. Thorold Rogers (ed.), *The Speeches of John Bright, MP* (London, 1868), II, pp. 213–27; 227–43; 255–75

[96] *Birmingham Daily Post*, 3 January 1865

[97] Vaughan, *Great Cities* (1843), p. 296

[98] G.R. Porter, *The Progress of the Nation* (London, 1851), p. 37

[99] David Owen, *English Philanthropy 1660–1960* (London, 1965)

[100] Edward Baines, *History, Directory and Gazetteer, of the County Palatine of Lancashire* (Devon, 1968)

[101] 'Manchester, by a Manchester Man', *Fraser's Magazine*, XLVII (1853), p. 626

[102] Love, *Manchester* (1842), p. 87

[103] Taine, *Notes on England* (1957), p. 236

[104] See R.H. Trainor, 'The Elite', in Fraser and Maver (eds), *Glasgow*, Vol. II (1996)

[105] *Biographical Sketches of the Lord Provosts of Glasgow* (Glasgow, 1883), p. 89

[106] Hugh Gawthrop, *Fraser's Guide to Liverpool* (Liverpool, 1855), pp. 187–9

[107] Kay, 'A Letter to the People of Lancashire' (1831), p. 19

[108] H. Martineau, *History of England During the Thirty Years' Peace* (London, 1850), II, p. 236

[109] George Eliot, *Middlemarch* (1871) (London, 1961), p. 896

[110] Hutton, *Birmingham* (1835), p. vii

[111] Wemyss Reid (ed.), *Memoir of Dr Heaton* (1883), pp. 83–4

[112] Henry Smithers, *Liverpool, Its Commerce, Statistics and Institutions* (Liverpool, 1825), 'Biography'

[113] James, *History and Topography of Bradford* (1841), p. 379

[114] James Wheeler, *Manchester: Its Political, Social and Commercial History, Ancient and Modern* (Manchester, 1836), part VII

[115] William Howie Wylie, *Old and New Nottingham* (Nottingham, 1853), p. 47
[116] Baines, *The Life of Edward Baines* (1859), p. ix
[117] *ibid.*, pp. 22–3
[118] Samuel Smiles, *Self-Help* (1859) (London, 1986), p. 23
[119] Quoted in Rose, *Intellectual Life* (2001), p. 68
[120] *ibid.*, p. 16

5: MAMMON AND THE NEW MEDICI [pp 189–226]

[1] *The Times*, 6 May 1857
[2] 'The Diary of Benjamin Barker of Bramley, near Leeds', Thoresby Society, MSS XI, Box 2 and 3
[3] J.A.V. Chapple and A. Pollard (eds), *The Letters of Mrs Gaskell* (Manchester, 1966), p. 452
[4] Karl Marx and Friedrich Engels, *Collected Works* (London, 1975–), XL, p. 131
[5] *Manchester Guardian*, 6 May 1857
[6] Taylor, *Notes of a Tour* (1968), p. 9
[7] Wilmot Henry Jones (Geoffrey Gimcrack), *Gimcrackiana, or Fugitive Pieces on Manchester Men and Manners* (Manchester, 1833), pp. 156–7
[8] Quoted in Bradshaw (ed.), *Visitors to Manchester* (1987), p. 28
[9] Engels, *The Condition of the Working Class in England* (1987), p. 275
[10] *Leeds Mercury*, 13 August 1853
[11] Taylor, *Notes of a Tour* (1968), p. 276
[12] Matthew Arnold, *Culture and Anarchy* (1867–9) (Cambridge, 1995), 'Introduction', p. xviii
[13] *ibid.*, p. 147
[14] *ibid.*, p. 105
[15] Quoted in J.R. Hale (ed.), *The Italian Journal of Samuel Rogers* (1822) (London, 1963), p. 57
[16] Quoted in J. Mordaunt Crook, *The Greek Revival: Neo-classical Attitudes in British Architecture, 1760–1870* (London, 1995), p. 42
[17] See Helen Angelomatis-Tsougarakis, *The Eve of the Greek Revival* (London, 1990)
[18] R.J. Morris, 'Middle-class culture, 1700–1914', in Derek Fraser (ed.), *A History of Modern Leeds* (Manchester, 1980)
[19] *Quarterly Review*, XXVI (1822), p. 255
[20] See F.M. Turner, *The Greek Heritage in Victorian Britain* (London, 1981); R. Jenkyns, *Victorians and Ancient Greece* (Oxford, 1980)
[21] Crook, *The Greek Revival* (1995), p. 42
[22] *Transactions*, Leeds Literary and Philosophical Society (London, 1837)

[23] Asa Briggs, 'The Sense of Place', in *The Collected Essays of Asa Briggs* (Brighton, 1985), I, p. 94

[24] *The Builder*, 62, 13 April 1844

[25] Robert Blake, *Benjamin Disraeli* (London, 1969), pp. 60–7

[26] Disraeli, *Coningsby* (1963), p. 127. There is an interesting echo of this sentiment in A.J.P. Taylor's 1957 essay on Manchester, when he describes the city as being 'as distinctive in its way as Athens or Peking'. See A.J.P. Taylor, 'Manchester', *Encounter* (1957), 8, 3, p. 3.

[27] 'The Value of Literature to Men of Business', in T.E. Kebbel (ed.), *Selected Speeches of the late Rt Hon the Earl of Beaconsfield* (London, 1882), pp. 626–7

[28] *Manchester Guardian*, 20 November 1847

[29] *ibid.*, 18 November 1848

[30] Vaughan, *Great Cities* (1843), p. 133

[31] *ibid.*, p. 136

[32] *ibid.*, p. 28

[33] Smithers, *Liverpool* (1825), pp. 331–2

[34] *Athenaeum Gazette*, 20 January 1852

[35] Roscoe, *Life of William Roscoe* (1833), p. 32. De Quincey savaged his literature for displaying 'the feebleness of a mere *belle-lettrist*'. See *Tait's Edinburgh Magazine* (February and May 1837), p. 70.

[36] Roscoe, *Life of William Roscoe* (1833), p. 139

[37] Robert Southey, not widely regarded as a fan of the mercantile classes, paid great tribute to the work of Roscoe in his account of Liverpool. 'Literature also flourishes as fairly as commerce. A history of Lorenzo de' Medici appeared here about eight years ago, which even the Italians have thought worthy of translation. This work of Mr Roscoe's has diffused a general taste for the literature of Italy ... The people of Liverpool are proud of their townsman: whether they have read his book or not, they are sensible it has reflected honour upon their town in the eyes of England and of Europe, and they have a love and jealousy of its honour, which has seldom been found anywhere except in those cities where that love was nationality, because the city and the state were the same.' Southey, *Letters from England* (1808), II, p. 121.

[38] *ibid.*, p. 274

[39] Quoted in J. Ramsay Muir, *A History of Liverpool* (London, 1907), p. 293

[40] Quoted in Roscoe, *Life of William Roscoe* (1833), II, p. 159

[41] *ibid.*, p. 477

[42] *Manchester Guardian*, 20 November 1847. Emphasis added.

[43] *ibid.*

[44] Hale (ed.), *The Italian Journal* (1963), p. 60

[45] Quoted in M. Liversidge and C. Edwards (eds), *Imagining Rome* (London, 1996), p. 42

[46] *ibid.*, p. 61

[47] See John Pemble, *The Mediterranean Passion* (Oxford, 1987)

[48] Sir Francis Palgrave, *Handbook for Travellers in Northern Italy* (London, 1847), p. v

[49] Taine, *Notes on England* (1957), p. 288

[50] Charles Dickens, *Little Dorrit* (1857) (Oxford, 1953), pp. 192–3

[51] Hale (ed.), *The Italian Journal* (1963), p. 188

[52] Mariana Starke, *Travels on the Continent* (London, 1820), p. 515

[53] *Manchester Guardian*, 19 February 1845

[54] *The Times*, 14 January 1860

[55] E.A. Freeman, *Historical Essays* (London, 1871), p. 7

[56] J.C.L. Sismondi, *The History of the Italian Republics* (London, 1832), p. 108

[57] *ibid.*, p. 197

[58] *ibid.*, p. 23

[59] William Roscoe, *The Life of Lorenzo de' Medici* (London, 1846), p. 333

[60] *ibid.*, p. 194

[61] *ibid.*, p. 3

[62] *ibid.*, p. 83

[63] *Leeds Mercury*, 16 January 1858

[64] *The Builder*, 596, 8 July 1854

[65] Henry Edward Napier, *Florentine History*, I, (London, 1846), p. 3

[66] *ibid.*, pp. 588; 567; 583

[67] Sismondi, *Italian Republics* (1832), p. 222

[68] Napier, *Florentine History*, I, (1846), p. 589

[69] *ibid.*, IV, p. 6

[70] James, *History of the Worsted Manufacture* (1857)

[71] *Manchester Guardian*, 24 October 1846

[72] *Birmingham Daily Post*, 3 January 1865

[73] *Manchester Guardian*, 7 October 1843

[74] *ibid.*, 24 October 1846

[75] *Architect*, XV (1876), pp. 9–10

[76] *Athenaeum Gazette*, 20 January 1852

[77] Quoted in Morris, 'Middle class culture, 1700–1914', in Fraser (ed.), *A History of Modern Leeds* (1980), p. 210

[78] *Manchester Guardian*, 5 May 1857

[79] *ibid.*, 21 April 1856

[80] See Dianne Macleod, *Art and the Victorian Middle Class* (Cambridge, 1996)

[81] *Leeds Mercury*, 15 July 1856

[82] *Illustrated London News*, 9 May 1857

[83] *Art Treasures Examiner* (1857), p. i

[84] John Ruskin, *A Joy for Ever: Lectures on the Political Economy of Art Delivered at Manchester Art Treasures Exhibition 1857* (London, 1880), p. 15

[85] Cook and Wedderburn (eds), *Collected Works of John Ruskin* (London, 1903), X, p. 196
[86] Cook and Wedderburn (eds), *Collected Works of John Ruskin*, XIX p. 24
[87] Ruskin, *A Joy for Ever* (1880), Preface
[88] *ibid.*, p. 19
[89] Cook and Wedderburn (eds), *Collected Works of John Ruskin*, XVI, p. 39
[90] Ruskin, *A Joy for Ever* (1880), Preface

6: MERCHANT PRINCES AND MUNICIPAL PALACES [pp 227–258]

[1] *Bradford Observer*, 28 April 1864
[2] John Ruskin, 'Traffic', in J.D. Rosenberg (ed.), *The Genius of John Ruskin* (London, 1964), pp. 273–95
[3] Cook and Wedderburn (eds), *Collected Works of John Ruskin*, XIX, p. 24
[4] See *Bradford Observer*, 9 June, 16 June, 23 June 1864
[5] J.A. Picton, *Liverpool Improvements and How to Accomplish Them* (Liverpool, 1853), p. 24
[6] *The Builder*, 131, 9 August 1845
[7] *ibid.*, 705, 9 August 1856
[8] *Birmingham Daily Press*, 9 August 1856
[9] *Leeds Mercury*, 3 August 1850
[10] *ibid.*, 13 August 1853
[11] G.M. Trevelyan, *English Social History* (London, 1945), pp. 578–9
[12] Hall, *Cities in Civilization* (1999), p. 705
[13] G.G. Scott, *Personal and Professional Recollections* (London, 1879), p. 204
[14] *The Builder*, 587, 6 May 1854
[15] William Wilkins, *Athiensa, or remarks on the topography and buildings of Athens* (London, 1816), p. 32
[16] Vaughan, *Great Cities* (1843), p. 26
[17] Theodore Buckley, *The Great Cities of the Ancient World* (London, 1852), p. 299
[18] W.E.A. Axon, *An Architectural and General Description of the Town Hall, Manchester* (Manchester, 1878), p. 49
[19] For a broader discussion of these themes see D.J. Olsen, *The City as a Work of Art* (London, 1986)
[20] See Quentin Hughes, *Liverpool, City of Architecture* (Liverpool, 1999)
[21] Picton, *Memorials of Liverpool* (1873), p. 567
[22] *The Builder*, 635, 7 April 1855
[23] *Tait's Edinburgh Magazine*, XVI (1849), p. 213
[24] Fraser and Maver (eds), *Glasgow*, II, (1996), p. 492

25 Wylie, *Nottingham* (1853), p. 343
26 E. MacKenzie, *A Descriptive and Historical Account of the Town and County of Newcastle Upon Tyne* (Newcastle, 1827), p. 228
27 Sismondi, *Italian Republics* (1832), p. 23
28 See Alan Kidd, *Manchester* (Keele, 1996)
29 Scott, *Remarks on Secular and Domestic Architecture* (1857), p. 208
30 A sense of this disparity was apparent in the 2003 BBC series *Restoration*, in which decaying buildings were nominated for regeneration. The national winner was the Victoria Baths in Victoria Park, Manchester, an Edwardian 'water palace' which had been allowed to fall into shocking disrepair since its closure in 1993 – even as the surrounding area grew ever more in need of recreational and exercise facilities.
31 *The Builder*, 27 September 1862
32 Wylie, *Nottingham* (1853), p. 332
33 *The Builder*, 1047, 28 February 1863
34 Jones, *A Plan for a University* (1836), p. 10
35 *Building News* (1861), p. 263
36 *The Builder*, 145, 15 November 1845
37 *ibid.*, 248, 6 November 1847
38 Quoted in Colin Cunningham, *Victorian and Edwardian Town Halls* (London, 1981), p. 89
39 Quoted in Charles Dellheim, *The Face of the Past* (Cambridge, 1982), p. 145
40 Samuel Barnett, *The Ideal City* (1894) (Leicester, 1979), p. 57
41 Axon, *An Architectural and General Description* (1878), pp. 54–5
42 Wemyss Reid (ed.), *Memoir of Dr Heaton* (1883), p. 142
43 For an excellent account of the building of Leeds Town Hall see Briggs, *Victorian Cities* (1990), pp. 138–83
44 *Leeds Intelligencer*, 20 August 1853
45 Wemyss Reid (ed.), *Memoir of Dr Heaton* (1883), p. 148
46 *Leeds Mercury*, 17 September 1853
47 *ibid.*, 1 March 1856
48 'The Diary of Benjamin Barker of Bramley, near Leeds', Thoresby Society, MSS XI, Box 2 and 3
49 Quoted in Briggs, *Victorian Cities* (1990), p. 174
50 Scott, *Personal and Professional Recollections* (1879), p. 185
51 *ibid.*, pp. 191; 197
52 *ibid.*, p. 199
53 Hansard, 3rd series, vol. 164 (1861), cols 520; 536; 537
54 *Northampton Mercury*, 11 February 1860
55 *ibid.*, 2 March 1861
56 *ibid.*, 13 April 1861

[57] *ibid.*, 20 April 1861
[58] See Michael W. Brooks, *John Ruskin and Victorian Architecture* (New Brunswick, 1987), chapter IX
[59] *Northampton Mercury*, 7 May 1864
[60] *ibid.*, 26 October 1861
[61] *Bradford Observer*, 26 May 1864
[62] Thomas Baines, *History of the Commerce and Town of Liverpool* (Liverpool, 1852), p. 676

7: SEWAGE, SAXONS AND SELF-GOVERNMENT [pp 259–312]

[1] *Glasgow Daily Herald*, 15 October 1850. See also Fraser and Maver, 'Tackling the Problems', in Fraser and Maver (eds), *Glasgow*, II (1996). The creation of the Loch Katrine water supply was later commemorated in Kelvingrove Park with a water fountain – modelled, inevitably, on Walter Scott's 'Lady of the Lake'.
[2] *City Press*, 19 June 1858
[3] Owen, *Government of Victorian London* (1982)
[4] It was perhaps no surprise that in a 2002 poll for the BBC series *Great Britons*, Brunel was voted the third greatest Briton ever.
[5] See Václav Havel, *Living in Truth* (London, 1989), pp. 159, 177
[6] Hugh Trevor-Roper, *The Romantic Movement and the Study of History* (London, 1969), p. 2; see also David Simpson, *Romanticism, Nationalism, and the Revolt against Theory* (Chicago, 1993); Olivia Smith, *The Politics of Language, 1791–1819* (Oxford, 1986); H. Ben-Israel, *English Historians on the French Revolution* (Cambridge, 1968)
[7] Burke, *Reflections on the Revolution* (London, 1986), pp. 170; 148
[8] Madame de Staël, *Germany* (London, 1813), I, pp. 221–4
[9] Clare Simmons, *Reversing the Conquest* (New Brunswick, 1990); see also Philippa Levine, *The Amateur and the Professional* (Cambridge, 1986)
[10] *Leeds Mercury*, 28 March 1849; 14 April 1849
[11] *Manchester Guardian*, 13 November 1847; 18 October 1848; 10 November 1852; 12 February 1853
[12] *Archaeologia Aeliana*, I (Newcastle-upon-Tyne, 1832)
[13] William Stubbs, *The Constitutional History of England* (London, 1891), p. 2
[14] Edward Gibbon, *Decline and Fall of the Roman Empire* (1776–88) (London, 1994), IV, p. 110
[15] David Hume, *The History of England* (1754–62) (Indianapolis, 1983), I, p. 185
[16] Thomas Carlyle, *Frederick the Great*, I, (London, 1858), p. 415
[17] Elizabeth Gaskell, *North and South* (1855), (London, 1995), p. 326
[18] *Birmingham Daily Press*, 25 February 1856

19 E.S. Creasy, *The Rise and Progress of the English Constitution* (London, 1858), p. 16
20 For a fuller discussion of these ideas see Simon Schama, *Landscape and Memory* (London, 1996), pp. 75–120
21 F. Palgrave, *The Rise and Progress of the English Commonwealth* (1832), p. 552. See also Thomas Wright, 'On the Existence of Municipal Privileges under the Anglo-Saxons', *Archaeologia*, XXXII (1847); J. Kenrick, 'On the probable origin of municipal corporations', *Transactions*, Manchester Literary and Philosophical Society (Manchester, 1835)
22 *Transactions*, National Association for the Promotion of Social Science (London, 1859), p. 127
23 Kemble, *Saxons* (1849), I, p. 70
24 *Fraser's Magazine*, vol. XXIII (1841), p. 388
25 *The Times*, 15 November 1855
26 H. Hallam, *View of the State of Europe during the Middle Ages* (London, 1819), II, p. 374
27 *Westminster Review*, NS III (1853), p. 497
28 Hallam, *Europe during the Middle Ages* (1819), III, p. 35
29 W. Scott, *Ivanhoe* (1819) (London, 1986), p. 207
30 Joshua Toulmin-Smith, *Local Self-Government and Centralization* (London, 1851), p. 214n
31 'Mr George Dawson's Lecture on Alfred the Great', *Manchester Guardian*, 13 March 1850
32 H.A. Merewether and A.J. Stephens, *The History of the Boroughs and Municipal Corporations of the UK* (1835) (Brighton, 1972), p. v
33 *Westminster Review*, XXII (1835), p. 408
34 *Birmingham Daily Press*, 12 February 1856
35 J.R. Green, *A Short History of the English People* (London, 1892), I, p. 7
36 Quoted in A.D. Culler, *The Victorian Mirror of History* (New Haven, 1985), p. 27
37 Scott, *Ivanhoe* (1986), p. 26
38 *ibid.*, p. 242
39 *ibid.*, p. 286
40 E. Bulwer-Lytton, *Harold, the Last of the Saxon Kings* (London, 1848), p. xiv
41 A. Thierry, *History of the Conquest of England by the Normans* (London, 1847), p. 239
42 Disraeli, *Sybil* (1988), pp. 168–9
43 O'Farrell, *Things Can Only Get Better* (1998), p. 153
44 Lingard, *History of England*, I, (London, 1819) pp. 419–20
45 *Transactions*, NAPSS (1859), p. 130
46 T.B. Macaulay, *The History of England* (1849–55), (London, 1860), I, p. 12

47 Homersham Cox, *The British Commonwealth* (London, 1854), p. 457

48 Creasy, *English Constitution* (1858), p. 104

49 *Transactions*, NAPSS (1859), p. 131

50 *Westminster Review*, XXII (1835), p. 419

51 Thomas Wright, *Remarks on the Municipal Privileges* (1845), p. 27

52 Elizabeth Penrose (Mrs Markham), *History of England* (London, 1823), I, pp. 69–70

53 Charles Dickens, *Our Mutual Friend* (1864–5) (Oxford, 1991), p. 140

54 Alexis de Tocqueville, *The Ancien Régime and the French Revolution* (1856) (Manchester, 1966), p. 78

55 *Edinburgh Review*, CIV (1856), p. 537

56 De Tocqueville, *The Ancien Régime* (1966), p. 102

57 *The Economist*, 1 April 1848

58 E.A. Freeman, *Historical Essays* (London, 1871), I, p. 250

59 Theodore Buckley, *The Great Cities of the Middle Ages* (London, 1853), p. 243

60 *The Economist*, 1 April 1848

61 Thomas Beames, *The Rookeries of London* (1850) (London, 1970), p. 7

62 *Birmingham Daily Press*, 15 October 1857

63 *The Builder*, 189, 19 September 1846

64 De Tocqueville, *Democracy in America* (1994), I, p. 61

65 *The Economist*, 1 April 1848

66 Baynes, *The Cotton Trade* (1857), p. 68

67 *The Economist*, 22 April 1848

68 *ibid.*, 15 July 1848

69 *ibid.*, 29 April 1848

70 See R. Floud et al., *Height, Health and History: Nutritional Status in the UK, 1750–1980* (Cambridge, 1990)

71 See Paul Richards, 'R.A. Slaney, the Industrial Town, and early Victorian Social Policy', *Social History*, IV (1979)

72 W.H. Duncan, 'On the Physical Causes of the High Rates of Mortality in Liverpool', Appendix, *The Report of the Commissioners for Enquiring into the State of Large Towns and Populous Districts*, Parliamentary Papers (1844), p. 12

73 Health of Towns Association (London, 1847), p. 10

74 Hector Gavin, *Sanitary Ramblings* (London, 1848), pp. 8–10

75 Hector Gavin, 'Report of the Health of London Association on the Sanitary Condition of the Metropolis' (Health of Towns Association, 1847), p. 18

76 Viscount Ebrington, *Unhealthiness of Towns, Its Causes and Remedies* (Health of Towns Association, 1846), p. 2

77 Hector Gavin, *Unhealthiness of Towns and the Necessity of Remedial Measures* (Health of Towns Association, 1847), p. 66

[78] Charles Kingsley, *Sanitary and Social Lectures* (London, 1892), p. 205

[79] Hansard, 3rd series, LXXXVII (1846), cols 104–5

[80] *Transactions*, NAPSS (1859), p. 594

[81] See Derek Fraser, *Power and Authority in the Victorian City* (Oxford, 1979)

[82] *The Report of the Commissioners for Enquiring into the State of Large Towns and Populous Districts*, Parliamentary Papers (1844), III, p. ix

[83] See E.P. Hennock, 'Finance and Politics in Urban Local Government in England, 1835–1900', *Historical Journal*, VI, 2 (1963)

[84] Charles Dickens, 'Our Last Parochial War', *Household Words* (1853), p. 265

[85] See Francis Sheppard, *London 1808–1870: The Infernal Wen* (London, 1971)

[86] George Godwin, *London Shadows: A Glance at the 'Homes' of the Thousands* (London, 1854), p. 21

[87] Quoted in Hansard, 3rd series, LXXXV (1846), cols 579–80

[88] *Birmingham Daily Post*, 3 May 1867

[89] Toulmin-Smith, *Local Self-Government* (1851), pp. 17, 31, 60, 181

[90] For a discussion of how Joshua Toulmin-Smith's arguments played out within a more radical, working-class context see Chris A. Williams, 'The Sheffield Democrats' critique of criminal justice in the 1850s' in Colls and Rodgers (eds), *Cities of Ideas* (Aldershot, 2004)

[91] Ebrington, *Unhealthiness of Towns* (1846), p. 35

[92] Health of Towns Association, *The Sanitary Condition of London* (London, 1848), p. 20

[93] *Quarterly Review*, LXXXVIII (1851), p. 437

[94] G.K. Chesterton, *The Napoleon of Notting Hill* (1904) (London, 1982), pp. 39–40

[95] Quoted in Anthony Brundage, *England's 'Prussian Minister'* (Pennsylvania, 1988), p. 61

[96] See Jonathan Parry, *The Rise and Fall of Liberal Government in Victorian Britain* (London, 1993); R.A. Lewis, *Edwin Chadwick and the Public Health Movement* (London, 1952)

[97] *Leeds Mercury*, 12 February; 26 February; 4 March; 8 April 1848

[98] *Manchester Guardian*, 4 March 1848

[99] *The Economist*, 20 May; 13 May; 20 May; 15 July 1848

[100] Quoted in P.J. Waller, *Town, City and Nation* (Oxford, 1991), pp. 244–5

[101] Hansard, 3rd series, XCVIII (1848), cols 771; 712–26

[102] Toulmin-Smith, *Local Self-Government* (1851), pp. 207; 338

[103] Hansard, 3rd series, CXXXV, cc. 999–1000

[104] *The Economist*, 5 August 1854

[105] See Olive Anderson, *A Liberal State at War* (London, 1967)

[106] W.H. Duncan, 'Appendix', *The Report of the Commissioners for Enquiring into the State of Large Towns and Populous Districts*, Parliamentary Papers (1844), p. 32

[107] J. Chapman and B. Chapman, *The Life and Times of Baron Haussmann* (London, 1957), p. 237

[108] Quoted in Rebecca Solnit, *Wanderlust – a History* (New York, 2000), p. 205

[109] Nassau William Senior, *Conversations With Distinguished Persons during the 2nd Empire* (London, 1878), II, p. 192

[110] Quoted in Solnit, *Wanderlust* (2000), p. 199

[111] *The Builder*, 8 December 1866

[112] *The Times*, 25 February, 1861

8: JOSEPH CHAMBERLAIN AND THE MUNICIPAL GOSPEL
[pp 313–380]

[1] J.H. Muirhead, *Nine Famous Birmingham Men* (Birmingham, 1909), p. 76; Dawson quoted in W.W. Wilson, *The Life of George Dawson* (Birmingham, 1905), p. 123

[2] Anon., *Notes of Personal Observations and Inquiries ... on the city improvements in Paris*, quoted in Peter Reed (ed.), *Glasgow: The Forming of the City* (Edinburgh, 1999), p. 88

[3] Quoted in Denis Judd, *Radical Joe: A Life of Joseph Chamberlain* (Cardiff, 1993), p. 5. See also Peter Marsh, *Joseph Chamberlain* (London, 1994); J.L. Garvin, *The Life of Joseph Chamberlain* (London, 1932), I.

[4] See David Cannadine, 'Locality: The "Chamberlain Tradition" and Birmingham', in *In Churchill's Shadow* (London, 2002)

[5] *The Times*, 7 July 1914

[6] John Morley, *The Life of Richard Cobden* (London, 1896) II, p. 199

[7] For still the most insightful analysis of mid-Victorian Birmingham see E.P. Hennock, *Fit and Proper Persons* (London, 1973)

[8] Thomas Anderton, *A Tale of One City* (Birmingham, 1900), pp. 6–7

[9] *Town Crier*, November 1861

[10] J.T. Bunce, *History of the Corporation of Birmingham*, II (Birmingham, 1885), p. xxvi

[11] See Wilson, *Dawson* (1905); see also, Hennock, *Fit and Proper Persons* (1973)

[12] *Spectator*, 2 December 1876

[13] 'George Dawson' in Muirhead, *Nine Famous Birmingham Men* (1909), p. 90

[14] R.W. Dale, 'George Dawson', *The Nineteenth Century* (1877), II, p. 49

[15] Muirhead, *Famous Birmingham Men* (1909), p. 100

16 Quoted in Hennock, *Fit and Proper Persons* (1973), p. 75
17 The notion of the Council as the new Church was an idea later taken up by the Whitechapel canon, Samuel Barnett. In his *Practicable Socialism*, he contended: 'The Town Councils are, indeed, the modern representative of the Church and of other societies through which in older times individuals expressed their hope and work, and to these bodies falls the duty of effacing that social reform which will help the poor to grow to the stature of the life of men.' See Samuel Barnett, *Practicable Socialism* (London, 1894), p. 103
18 R.W. Dale, 'Liberalism: An Address to the Birmingham Junior Liberal Association' (Birmingham, 1878)
19 In *Victorian Cities*, Asa Briggs has written of this intellectual current as a 'civic gospel'. I think 'municipal gospel' is a more apposite term as a way of denoting a distinct shift from the mid-Victorian voluntarist model of city life. See Briggs, *Victorian Cities* (1990), pp. 184–241
20 R.W. Dale, 'The Public Duties of Christian Men', extracted from *The Laws of Christ for Common Life* (1884), p. 4
21 Quoted in A.W.W. Dale, *The Life of R.W. Dale* (London, 1898), p. 250
22 Quoted in Wilson, *Dawson* (1905), p. 151
23 R.A. Armstrong, *Henry William Crosskey* (Birmingham, 1895), p. 250
24 Muirhead, *Famous Birmingham Men* (1909), pp. 105–6
25 Wilson, *Dawson* (1905), p. 152
26 C.W. Boyd (ed.), *Mr Chamberlain's Speeches* (London, 1914) I, pp. 164–5
27 *ibid.*, p. 49
28 *ibid.*, p. 73
29 Hennock, *Fit and Proper Persons* (1973), p. 34
30 *The Times*, 7 July 1914
31 Quoted in Armstrong, *Crosskey* (1895), pp. 248–9
32 Garvin, *Chamberlain*, I (1932) p. 188
33 For a useful discussion see S. Szreter, 'The Politics of Public Health in Nineteenth Century Britain', *Population and Development Review* (1997), 23, 4
34 Frederick Dolman, *Municipalities at Work* (London, 1895), p. 1
35 Asa Briggs, *History of Birmingham* (Cambridge, 1952)
36 Bunce, *Birmingham*, II (1885), p. 347
37 *ibid.*
38 See N.M. Marris, *Joseph Chamberlain: the Man and the Statesman* (London, 1900), p. 113; also Hennock, *Fit and Proper Persons* (1973), p. 120
39 Bunce, *Birmingham*, II (1885), p. 407
40 Quoted in Judd, *Chamberlain* (1993), p. 61

[41] *ibid.*, p. 67

[42] *Town Crier*, March 1864

[43] Linda Jones, 'Public pursuit or private profit? Liberal businessmen and municipal politics in Birmingham, 1865–1900', *Business History*, 25 (1983)

[44] Quoted in Briggs, *Birmingham* (1952), p. 70

[45] J. Chamberlain, 'Municipal Institutions in America and England', *The Forum*, November 1892, p. 270

[46] A. Shaw, *Municipal Government in Great Britain* (London, 1895), p. 193

[47] Quoted in C.M. Allan, 'The Genesis of British Urban Redevelopment with Special Reference to Glasgow', *Economic History Review*, 2nd series, XVIII, 3 (1965), pp. 602–3. See also Brian Edwards, 'Glasgow Improvements', in Reed (ed.), *Glasgow* (1999)

[48] See Fraser and Maver (eds), *Glasgow*, vol. II (1996); Gibb, *Glasgow* (1983)

[49] James Bell, *Glasgow: Its Municipal Organization and Administration* (Glasgow, 1896), p. 232

[50] Octavia Hill, 'The Homes of the London Poor', *Macmillan's Magazine*, XXX (1874), p. 135

[51] Bell, *Glasgow* (1896), p. xxii

[52] Hansard, 3rd series, CCXXII (1875), cols. 110–11

[53] Bunce, *Birmingham*, II (1885), pp. 458; 461–3

[54] Boyd (ed.), *Chamberlain's Speeches* (1914) I, p. 63

[55] Bunce, *Birmingham*, II (1885), pp. 464–5

[56] *ibid.*, pp. 456–7

[57] Joseph Chamberlain, 'Labourers' and Artisans' Dwellings', *Fortnightly Review*, December 1883, p. 138

[58] See Jones, 'Public pursuit or private profit?', *Business History*, 25 (1983)

[59] Bunce, *Birmingham*, II, (1885), p. xxiv

[60] Anderton, *A Tale of One City* (1900), p. 20

[61] Quoted in Judd, *Chamberlain* (1993), p. 67

[62] Muirhead, *Famous Birmingham Men* (1909), p. 101

[63] See David Cannadine, 'The Brief Flowering of a Civic Religion', *The Listener*, 26 July 1984

[64] See Simon Gunn, 'Ritual and civic culture in the English industrial city, c. 1835–1914', in R.J. Morris and R.H. Trainor (eds), *Urban Governance: Britain and beyond since 1750* (Aldershot, 2000)

[65] Boyd (ed.), *Chamberlain's Speeches* (1914) I, pp. 41–2

[66] Bunce, *Birmingham*, II, (1885), p. 420

[67] J. Chamberlain, *The Forum*, 1892, p. 269

[68] Bunce, *Birmingham*, II, (1885), pp. xli–xliv

[69] Shaw, *Municipal Government* (1895), p. 120

[70] Dolman, *Municipalities* (1895), p. 67

[71] *Glasgow Daily Herald*, 8 October 1883

[72] William Young, *The Municipal Buildings of Glasgow* (Glasgow, 1890), p. 11

[73] *Art Journal* quoted in P. Kinchin and J. Kinchin, *Glasgow's Great Exhibitions* (Glasgow, 1988), pp. 48–9

[74] Bell, *Glasgow* (1896), pp. 349–50

[75] James Hamilton Muir, *Glasgow in 1901* (Glasgow, 1901), p. 46

[76] Alan Bennett, 'A Cure for Arthritis and Other Tales', *London Review of Books*, 2 November 2000, p. 10

[77] Allan, 'The Genesis of British Urban Redevelopment', *Economic History Review* (1965), p. 610

[78] Beatrice Webb, *My Apprenticeship* (1926) (London, 1979), chs III, VII

[79] *The Times*, 19 August 1902

[80] *ibid.*

[81] Quoted in Waller, *Town, City and Nation* (1991), p. 311

[82] Quoted in Susan D. Pennybacker, *A Vision for London 1889–1914* (London, 1995), p. 3

[83] Quoted in John Davis, 'The Progressive Council', in Andrew Saint (ed.), *Politics and the People of London* (London, 1980), p. 35

[84] See Pennybacker, *A Vision for London* (1995)

[85] Henry Hyndman, *A Commune for London* (London, 1887), p. 1

[86] Sidney Webb, *The London Programme* (London, 1891), pp. v–vi

[87] John Burns, 'The London County Council: Towards a Commune', *The Nineteenth Century*, XXXI (1892), p. 496

[88] This notion of municipal 'patriotism' is a curious echo of George Dawson's original formulation of the municipal gospel, which was inspired by the very real patriotism of Austrian and Italian nationalists. More recently, the idea of municipal or civic patriotism has been employed by the Chancellor of the Exchequer, the Rt Hon. Gordon Brown, MP. See his speech to the National Council of Voluntary Organisations Annual Conference, 9 February 2000.

[89] Sidney and Beatrice Webb, *A Constitution for the Socialist Commonwealth of Great Britain* (1920) (London, 1975), pp. 205; 238

[90] Shaw, *Municipal Government* (1895), p. 8

[91] *The Times*, 19 August 1902

[92] M. Falkus, 'The Development of Municipal Trading in the Nineteenth Century', *Business History*, 19, 2 (1977)

[93] Shaw, *Common Sense of Municipal Trading* (1904), p. 1

[94] S. Webb, *Socialism in England* (London, 1889), pp. 116–17

[95] *The Times*, 19 August, 23 August, 22 September 1902

[96] See John Davis, 'Central Government and the Towns', in *The Cambridge Urban History of Britain, vol. III: 1840–1950* (Cambridge, 2000), pp. 261–87

[97] Lord Avebury, 'Municipal Trading', *Contemporary Review*, 78 (1900), p. 29

[98] *The Times*, 30 September 1902
[99] *ibid.*, 22 September 1902
[100] *ibid.*, 18 September 1902
[101] Fabian Society, 'Tract 94' (1900), p. 4
[102] *The Municipal Reformer and Local Government News*, II, 1 (1899)
[103] *Clarion*, 8 June 1901, p. 181

9: LONDON: THE WHITED SEPULCHRE OF EMPIRE [pp 383–415]

[1] Henry Morton Stanley, *How I Found Livingstone* (London, 1872), pp. 409–12
[2] George Sims, *How the Poor Live, and Horrible London* (London, 1889), p. 1
[3] James Greenwood, *The Wilds of London* (London, 1874), p. 1
[4] William Booth, *In Darkest England and the Way Out* (London, 1890), pp. 11–15
[5] Webb, *London Programme* (1891), p. 2
[6] For an interesting discussion of London during the nineteenth century see Francis Sheppard, 'London and the Nation in the Nineteenth Century', *Transactions of the Royal Historical Society*, 35 (1985)
[7] Quoted in Gareth Stedman Jones, *Outcast London* (Cambridge, 1971), p. 160. Thirty years on, this work still remains one of the finest accounts of late-Victorian London.
[8] Jonathan Schneer, *London 1900* (London, 1999), p. 10
[9] See John M. Mackenzie, ' "The Second City of the Empire": Glasgow – imperial municipality' in Felix Driver and David Gilbert (eds), *Imperial Cities: Landscape, Display and Identity* (Manchester, 1999)
[10] J.A. Ingham, *City Slums* (London, 1889), p. 70
[11] See Catherine Edwards, 'Translating Empire? Macaulay's Rome' in Catherine Edwards (ed.), *Roman Presences: Receptions of Rome in European Culture, 1789–1945* (Cambridge, 1999)
[12] 'Three Letters to *The Times* from Sir Charles Trevelyan on London Pauperism' (London, 1870)
[13] Beames, *Rookeries of London* (1970), p. 2
[14] *Pall Mall Gazette*, 16 October 1883
[15] Sims, *How the Poor Live* (1889), p. 70
[16] Beames, *Rookeries of London* (1970), pp. 28; 35. See also George Godwin, *Town Swamps and Social Bridges* (London, 1859)
[17] Mayhew, *London Labour* (1985), p. 211
[18] *Pall Mall Gazette*, 16 October 1883
[19] Booth, *Darkest England* (1890), p. 16
[20] Beames, *Rookeries of London* (1970), pp. 67–8
[21] Sims, *How the Poor Live* (1889), p. 44

[22] Andrew Mearns, *The Bitter Cry of Outcast London* (1883) (Leicester, 1970), p. 55

[23] *ibid.*, pp. 58–61

[24] Dickens, *Dombey and Son* (1982), p. 184

[25] Quoted in H.J. Dyos, 'Railways and Housing in Victorian London', *Journal of Transport History*, II (1955–6), p. 15. See also J.R. Kellett, *The Impact of Railways on Victorian Cities* (London, 1969)

[26] Stedman Jones, *Outcast London* (1971), p. 169

[27] *The Times*, 2 March 1861

[28] Friedrich Engels, *The Housing Question* (1872) (London, 1942), p. 71

[29] Lord Salisbury, 'Labourers' and Artisans' Dwellings', *National Review* (1883), quoted in Mearns, *The Bitter Cry* (1970), p. 117

[30] *The Times*, 2 March 1861

[31] Lord Brabazon, *Social Arrows* (London, 1886), pp. 13–14; 17

[32] Quoted in Stedman Jones, *Outcast London* (1971), p. 128. For a more general discussion see Daniel Pick, *Faces of Degeneration* (Cambridge, 1989)

[33] J.P. Williams-Freeman, *The Effects of Town Life on the General Health* (London, 1890), pp. 34–5; 8

[34] David Feldman, 'Migration', in Daunton (ed.), *The Cambridge Urban History of Britain*, III (2000)

[35] Brabazon, *Social Arrows* (1886), p. 191

[36] Thomas Hardy, *Tess of the D'Urbervilles* (1891) (London, 1985) p. 436

[37] C.F.G. Masterman (ed.), *Heart of the Empire* (1901), p. 25

[38] See David Feldman, 'The Importance of Being English', in Feldman and Stedman Jones (eds), *Metropolis* (London, 1989)

[39] Elliott Mills, *The Decline and Fall of the British Empire* (London, 1905), p. 7. This was partly the context for the emergence of the British boy scout movement. As General Baden-Powell put it in *Scouting for Boys*, 'Don't be disgraced like the young Romans, who lost the Empire of their forefathers by being wishy-washy slackers without any go or patriotism in them. Play up! Each nab in his place, and play the game!'

[40] Webb, *London Programme* (1891), p. 6

[41] T.C. Horsfall, *The Improvement of the Dwellings and Surroundings of the People* (Manchester, 1904), p. 161

[42] See A. Wohl, 'Introduction', in Mearns, *The Bitter Cry* (1970)

[43] See Stedman Jones, *Outcast London* (1971)

[44] Samuel Barnett, *Practicable Socialism* (London, 1894), p. 241

[45] Clement Attlee, *As It Happened* (London, 1954), p. 27

[46] Webb, *My Apprenticeship*, (1979), p. 180

[47] Albert Fried and Richard Elman (eds), 'Introduction', *Charles Booth's London* (London, 1969)

[48] *ibid.*, p. 11

[49] A. White, *Problems of a Great City* (London, 1886), p. 31
[50] Alfred Marshall, 'The Housing of the London Poor', *Contemporary Review*, XLV (1884), p. 228
[51] Booth, *Darkest England* (1890), pp. 92, 93; 211
[52] George and Weedon Grossmith, *The Diary of a Nobody* (1892) (Oxford, 1998), pp. 3; 18–19
[53] Sidney Low, 'The Rise of the Suburbs', *Contemporary Review*, LX (1891), pp. 548, 550
[54] See Donald J. Olsen, *The Growth of Victorian London* (London, 1979)
[55] See Walter Besant, *South London* (London, 1912), p. 301
[56] Quoted in Olsen, *Victorian London* (1979), p. 200
[57] *The Times*, 25 June 1904
[58] See H.J. Dyos, *Victorian Suburb* (Leicester, 1961); Olsen, *Victorian London* (1979); Stedman Jones, *Outcast London* (1971); Sheppard, *London 1808–1870* (London, 1971)
[59] *The Times*, 25 June 1904
[60] H.G. Wells, *The New Machiavelli* (1911) (London, 1946), pp. 34, 37
[61] Besant, *South London* (1912), p. 307
[62] T.W.H. Crosland, *The Suburbans* (London, 1905), p. 17
[63] Robert Fishman, *Bourgeois Utopias: The Rise and Fall of Suburbia* (New York, 1989) p. x
[64] Grossmith, *Diary* (1998), p. 98
[65] Wells, *Machiavelli* (1946), p. 38
[66] C.F.G. Masterman, *The Condition of England* (1909) (London, 1960), pp. 57–8; 64–5
[67] Olsen, *Victorian London* (1979), p. 211
[68] Besant, *South London* (1912), p. 320
[69] Masterman, *Condition of England* (1960), pp. 65–6

10: GARDEN CITIES AND THE TRIUMPH OF SUBURBIA [pp 416–453]

[1] F.J. Osborn, 'Preface', in Ebenezer Howard, *Garden Cities of Tomorrow* (London, 1965), p. 22
[2] See Robert Beevers, *The Garden City Utopia* (London, 1988)
[3] F.J. Osborn, 'Sir Ebenezer Howard. The Evolution of his Ideas', *Town Planning Review*, 21, 3 (1950), p. 225
[4] Quoted in Beevers, *Garden City Utopia* (1988), p. 11
[5] *ibid.*, p. 27
[6] *Commonweal*, 22 June 1889, p. 194
[7] John Ruskin, *Lectures on Art* (1870) (London, 1910), p. 143
[8] William Morris, *News from Nowhere* (1891) (Cambridge, 1995), p. 109
[9] *ibid.*, p. 10
[10] Barnett, *The Ideal City* (1979), p. 59

[11] Webb, *London Programme* (1891), p. 212

[12] See Judy Hillman, *The Bournville Hallmark* (Bournville Village Trust, 1994)

[13] *The Municipal Reformer and Local Government News*, III, 37 (1901)

[14] *The Story of Port Sunlight* (Lever Brothers, 1953), p. 69

[15] *The Municipal Reformer and Local Government News*, III, 39 (1901)

[16] Dugald Macfadyen, *Sir Ebenezer Howard and the Town Planning Movement* (Manchester, 1933), p. 29

[17] *ibid.*, pp. 42–3

[18] See Benjamin Ward Richardson, *Hygeia – A City of Health* (London, 1876)

[19] Howard, *Garden Cities of Tomorrow* (1965), pp. 45–8

[20] *ibid.*, pp. 51–4

[21] *ibid.*, p. 126

[22] *ibid.*, p. 123

[23] *ibid.*, p. 146

[24] *ibid.*, p. 77

[25] *The Municipal Reformer and Local Government News*, III, 34 (1901)

[26] *The Times*, 19 October 1898

[27] Osborn, 'Sir Ebenezer Howard,' *Town Planning Review* (1950), p. 228

[28] *The Times*, 21 September 1901

[29] Quoted in Mervyn Miller, *Letchworth: The First Garden City* (Sussex, 1989), p. 44

[30] Raymond Unwin, 'The Art of Building a Home' (1901), reprinted in Walter Creese (ed.), *The Legacy of Raymond Unwin* (Cambridge, MA, 1976), p. 51

[31] Quoted in Miller, *Letchworth* (1989), p. 47

[32] See Beevers, *Garden City Utopia* (1988)

[33] See Miller, *Letchworth* (1989)

[34] Macfadyen, *Ebenezer Howard* (1933), p. 78

[35] John Betjeman, *The Best of Betjeman* (London, 2000), p. 37

[36] Macfadyen, *Ebenezer Howard* (1933), p. 78

[37] See W.H.G. Armytage, *Heavens Below* (London, 1961)

[38] George Orwell, *The Road to Wigan Pier*, in Peter Davison (ed.), *Orwell's England* (London, 2001), pp. 175–6; 209–10

[39] *New Statesman*, 6 May 2002, p. 57

[40] Evelyn Waugh, *Vile Bodies* (1930) (London, 1951), pp. 199–200

[41] Webb, *My Apprenticeship* (1926), p. 211

[42] See Mervyn Miller and Stuart Grey, *Hampstead Garden Suburb* (Sussex, 1992)

[43] Henrietta Barnett, 'A Garden Suburb at Hampstead', *Contemporary Review*, LXXXVII (1905), pp. 232; 235

[44] For an interesting discussion of Hampstead Garden Suburb and the Labour Party see Donald Macintyre, *Mandelson: The Biography* (London, 1999), pp. 1–15

[45] Quoted in Beevers, *Garden City Utopia* (1988), p. 134

[46] J.B. Priestley, *English Journey* (London, 1934), p. 400

[47] Macfadyen, *Ebenezer Howard* (1933), p. 29

[48] See P. Oliver, I. Davis and I Bentley, *Dunroamin'* (London, 1994); Dennis Hardy, *From Garden Cities to New Towns* (London, 1991)

[49] Charles Kingsley, *Great Cities* (Bristol, 1857), pp. 215–16

[50] Quoted in Thomas Sharp, *Town Planning* (London, 1940), pp. 43–4

[51] Clough Williams-Ellis, *England and the Octopus* (London, 1928), p. 21

[52] D.H. Lawrence, 'Nottingham and the Mining Country', in D. Trilling (ed.), *The Portable Lawrence* (London, 1980), p. 621

[53] Priestley, *English Journey* (1934), p. 401

[54] George Orwell, *Coming up for Air* (1939), (London, 2000), pp. 24; 10

[55] Stanley Baldwin, *On England, and Other Addresses* (London, 1926)

[56] Priestley, *English Journey* (1934), pp. 37–8

[57] Orwell, 'The English People', in Davison (ed.), *Orwell's England* (2001), p. 328

[58] Betjeman, 'Middlesex' and 'Slough', in *The Best of Betjeman* (2000), pp. 87; 24

EPILOGUE: STILL WAITING FOR THE ROVER? [pp 457–495]

[1] *Manchester Guardian*, 10 September 2002

[2] *Daily Mirror*, 11 October 1982

[3] *Tatler*, March 2003

[4] *Observer*, 16 May 2004

[5] Quoted in Michael Shelden, *Orwell* (London, 1992), p. 244

[6] George Orwell, *The Road to Wigan Pier*, in Davison (ed.), *Orwell's England* (2001), p. 113

[7] *ibid.*, p. 107

[8] See Eric Hobsbawm, *Industry and Empire* (London, 1990), ch. 11

[9] Priestley, *English Journey* (1934), pp. 398–9

[10] See B.W.E. Alford, *British Economic Performance 1945–75* (Cambridge, 1995), p. 7

[11] Peter Clarke, *Hope and Glory* (London, 1997), p. 372

[12] *The State of English Cities*, Office of the Deputy Prime Minister (HMSO, 2001), p. 14

[13] Quoted in the *Guardian*, 13 September 2000

[14] *The State of English Cities*, (2001), p. 12

[15] 'Competitive European Cities: Where do the Core Cities Stand?' *Urban Research Summary* 13, Office of the Deputy Prime Minister (HMSO, 2004) p. 10

[16] All of which points to improved growth in the future. New research has confirmed the vital importance of human capital to urban growth. Skilled cities are wealthy cities. See Edward L. Glaeser and Albert

Saiz, 'The Rise of the Skilled City', Harvard Institute of Economic Research, discussion paper No. 2025.

[17] Richard Florida, *The Rise of the Creative Class* (New York, 2004)

[18] See Paul Barker, 'Tired of London', *Prospect*, December 2002

[19] Downing Street Strategy Unit report, 'The London Project' (2003), www.strategy.gov.uk

[20] See Barker, 'Tired of London', *Prospect*, December 2002

[21] See the *Guardian*, 5 July 2004

[22] Orwell, 'The English People', in Davison (ed.), *Orwell's England* (2001), p. 326

[23] *London Review of Books*, 16 November 2000

[24] See John Baxendale, 'J.B. Priestley, Englishness and the People', *History Workshop Journal* (51), Spring 2001, p. 103

[25] A.J.P. Taylor, 'Manchester', *Encounter* (1957), 8, 3, p. 9

[26] Priestley, *English Journey* (1933), p. 107

[27] George Orwell, 'The Lion and the Unicorn', in Davison (ed.) *Orwell's England* (2001), p. 272

[28] Quoted in Simon Gunn, *The Public Culture of the Victorian middle class* (Manchester, 2000), p. 193.

[29] George Orwell, 'The English People', in *Orwell's England* (2001), p. 326

[30] Taylor, 'Manchester', *Encounter* (1957), 8, 3, pp. 3; 13

[31] Priestley, *English Journey* (1934), p. 196

[32] Gunn, *Public Culture of the Victorian middle class* (2000), p. 197

[33] For a discussion of these ideas see F. Biachini and M. Parkinson (eds), *Cultural Policy as Urban Regeneration* (Manchester, 1993)

[34] Tony Lane, *Liverpool: Gateway of Empire* (London, 1987), pp. 162–3

[35] *Guardian*, 2 June 2003

[36] *ibid.*, 29 March 2003

[37] Quoted in Jane Jacobs, *The Death and Life of Great American Cities* (1961) (London, 1994), p. 31

[38] Sharp, *Town Planning* (1940), p. 23

[39] See the *Guardian*, 21 July 2003

[40] Briggs, *Victorian Cities* (1990), p. 18

[41] Peter Hall and Colin Ward, *Sociable Cities* (Chichester, 1998), p. 106

[42] *ibid.*, p. 105

[43] 'Living in Urban England', Office of the Deputy Prime Minister (HMSO, 2001), p. 3

[44] See Chris Turner, 'Town Cramming', *London Review of Books* (2001), 23, 17, pp. 24–6

[45] Final Report of the Urban Task Force, *Towards an Urban Renaissance* (HMSO, 1999), p. 49

[46] *ibid.*, p. 26

[47] *ibid.*, p. 159

[48] 'Loitering with intent', *New Statesman*, 4 September 2002

[49] See speech by the deputy Prime Minister, John Prescott, to the Core Cities summit, 6 June 2003

[50] Michael Foot, *Aneurin Bevan. A Biography. Vol. One: 1879–1945* (London, 1966), pp. 71–2

[51] Quoted in Roy Jenkins, *Churchill* (London, 2001) p. 124

[52] Quoted in John Davis, 'Central Government and the Towns', in Daunton (ed.), *The Cambridge Urban History of Britain, vol. III* p. 273

[53] *ibid.*, p. 286

[54] See Tony Travers, 'The Threat to the Autonomy of Elected Local Government', in C. Crouch and D. Marquand (eds), *The New Centralism* (Oxford, 1989)

[55] Simon Jenkins, *Accountable to None* (London, 1996), pp. 156–7

[56] See Simon Szreter, 'A central role for local government? The example of late Victorian Britain' in *History and Policy* (2002), I

[57] *Strong Local Leadership – Quality Public Services*, Department for Transport, Local Government and the Regions (HMSO, 2001), p. 70

[58] Quoted in Matthew Taylor with Paul Wheeler, *In Defence of Councillors*, Improvement and Development Agency (London, 2001), p. 10

[59] Jenkins, *Accountable to None* (1996)

[60] *Strong Local Leadership* (2001), p. 33

[61] I am grateful to Professor Tony Travers of the London School of Economics for this comparison.

[62] See Anna Randle, *Mayors Mid-Term* (New Local Government Network, 2004)

[63] *Strong Local Leadership* (2001), pp. 9; 40

[64] 'Competitive European Cities: Where do the Core Cities Stand?', *Urban Research Summary* 13, Office of the Deputy Prime Minister (HMSO, 2004) p. 25

[65] Speech to the National Council of Voluntary Organisations Annual Conference, 9 February 2000. For further evidence of the popularity of Victorian thinking on the left see David Marquand, *Decline of the Public* (Cambridge, 2004) and its call for a revival of the 'Victorian public domain'.

[66] 'Living in Urban England', Office of the Deputy Prime Minister (HMSO, 2001), p. 3

[67] See Simon Jenkins, *Big Bang Localism* (Policy Exchange, 2004)

[68] Some might contend that the Rt Hon. David Blunkett, MP, did the same in the 1990s. However, his power-base was really the Labour Party's National Executive Committee rather than any kind of Sheffield machine. See Andy McSmith, *Faces of Labour* (London, 1997), pp. 144–89.

BIBLIOGRAPHY

PRIMARY SOURCES

Alison, A., *Principles of Population and Their Connection with Human Happiness* (2 vols, London, 1840)

Anderton, T., *A Tale of One City* (Birmingham, 1900)

An Observer, *Reasons Against Government Interference in Education* (London, 1843)

Armstrong, R.A., *Henry William Crosskey* (Birmingham, 1895)

Arnold, M., *Culture and Anarchy* (1867–9) (Cambridge, 1995)

Aston, J., *A Picture of Manchester* (Manchester, 1969)

Attlee, C., *As It Happened* (London, 1954)

Axon, W.E.A., *An Architectural and General Description of the Town Hall, Manchester* (Manchester, 1878)

Axon, W.E.A., *Cobden as a Citizen* (Manchester, 1907)

Baines, E., *History of the Cotton Manufacture in Great Britain* (1835) (New York, 1966)

Baines, E., *History, Directory and Gazetteer, of the County Palatine of Lancashire* (2 vols, Devon, 1968)

Baines, E., *The Life of Edward Baines* (London, 1859)

Baines, E., *The Social, Educational, and Religious State of the Manufacturing Districts* (1835) (London, 1843)

Baines, T., *History of the Commerce and Town of Liverpool, and of the Rise of Manufacturing Industry in the Adjoining Counties* (Liverpool, 1852)

Baldwin, S., *On England and Other Addresses* (London, 1926)

Barnett, H., *Canon Barnett. His Life, Work and Friends* (London, 1921)

Barnett, S., *The Ideal City* (1894) (Leicester, 1979)

Barnett, S., *Practicable Socialism* (1888) (London, 1894)

Bartholomew, A., *Essay on the Decline of Excellence in the Structure of Modern English Building* (London, 1840)

Baynes, J., *The Cotton Trade – Two Lectures* (London, 1857)

Beames, T., *The Rookeries of London* (1850) (London, 1970)

Bell, G., *Day and Night in the Wynds of Edinburgh* (1849) (Leicester, 1973)

Bell, J., *Glasgow: Its Municipal Organization and Administration* (Glasgow, 1896)

Bellamy, E., *Looking Backward: 2000–1887* (London, 1888)

Beresford Hope, A.J.B., *The English Cathedral in the Nineteenth Century* (London, 1861)

Besant, W., *East London* (London, 1901)

Besant, W., *South London* (1898) (London, 1912)

Betjeman, J., *The Best of Betjeman* (London, 2000)

Binfield, C., *So Down to Prayers* (London, 1977)

Biographical Sketches of the Lord Provosts of Glasgow (Glasgow, 1883)

Boone, J.S., *The Need of Christianity to Cities* (London, 1844)

Booth, C., *The Life and Labour of the People in London* (17 vols, London, 1891–1902)

Booth, W., *In Darkest England and the Way Out* (London, 1890)

Boyd, C.W. (ed.), *Mr Chamberlain's Speeches* (2 vols, London, 1914)

Brabazon, Lord, *Social Arrows* (London, 1886)

Braudel, F., *Capitalism and Material Life* (London, 1973)

Buckley, T.A.W., *The Great Cities of the Ancient World* (London, 1852)

Buckley, T.A.W., *The Great Cities of the Middle Ages* (London, 1853)

Bulwer-Lytton, E., *Harold, the Last of the Saxon Kings* (London, 1848)

Bunce, J.T., *History of the Corporation of Birmingham* (6 vols, Birmingham, 1878–85)

Burke, E., *Reflections on the Revolution in France* (1790) (London, 1986)

Byng, J., *Rides Round Britain* (1782–93) (London, 1996)

Carlyle, T., *The Collected Letters of Thomas Carlyle and Jane Welsh* (North Carolina, 1970–)

Carlyle, T., *Correspondence of Carlyle and Ruskin* (California, 1982)

Carlyle, T., *History of Friedrich II of Prussia, called Frederick the Great* (6 vols, London, 1858–65)

Carlyle, T., *Past and Present* (1843) (New York, 1965)

Carlyle, T., *Sartor Resartus* (1833–4) (Oxford, 1987)

Carlyle, T., 'Signs of the Times' and 'Chartism', *Selected Writings* (London, 1986)

Chadwick, E., *Report on the Sanitary Condition of the Labouring Population of Great Britain* (1842) (Edinburgh, 1965)

Chalmers, T., *The Christian and Civic Economy of Large Towns* (Glasgow, 1821)

Chamberlain, J., *The Radical Programme* (1885)

Chapman, H.S., *The Act for the Regulation of Municipal Corporations* (London, 1835)

Chapple, J.A.V. and Pollard, A., (eds), *The Letters of Mrs Gaskell* (Manchester, 1966)

Cobbett, W., *A History of the Protestant Reformation* (1829) (London, 1994)

Cobbett, W., *Rural Rides* (1830), ed. G.D.H. Cole and M. Cole (London, 1930)

Cobbett, W., *Rural Rides* (1830) (London, 1985)

Cobden, R., *The Political Writings of Richard Cobden* (2 vols, London, 1903)

Cockburn, A.E., *The Corporations of England and Wales – The whole collected and abridged from the Report of the Commissioners for inquiring into municipal corporations* (London, 1835)

Collinson, E., *The History of the Worsted Trade, and Historic Sketch of Bradford* (London, 1854)

Cox, H., *The British Commonwealth* (London, 1854)

Creasy, E.S., *The Rise and Progress of the English Constitution* (London, 1858)

Crosland, T.W.H., *The Suburbans* (London, 1905)

Cruden, R.P., *Observations upon the Municipal Bodies in Cities and Towns Incorporated by Royal Charters* (London, 1826)

Dale, A.W.W., *The Life of R.W. Dale* (London, 1898)

Dale, R.W., *The Laws of Christ for Common Life* (London, 1884)

Dale, R.W., *The Politics of the Future* (London, 1867)

Defoe, D., *A Tour Through the Whole Island of Great Britain* (1724–6) (London, 1971)

Dickens, C., *Bleak House* (1853) (London, 1985)

Dickens, C., *Dombey and Son* (1848) (Oxford, 1982)

Dickens, C., *Hard Times* (1854) (London, 1987)

Dickens, C., *Oliver Twist* (1838) (Oxford, 1982)

Dickens, C., 'Our Last Parochial War', *Household Words* (1853)

Dickens, C., *Our Mutual Friend* (1864–5) (Oxford, 1991)

Digby, K.H., *The Broad Stone of Honour: or The True Sense and Practice of Chivalry* (2 vols, London, 1829)

Disraeli, B., *Coningsby, or The New Generation* (1844) (London, 1963)

Disraeli, B., *Endymion* (Leipzig, 1880)

Disraeli, B., *Sybil, or The Two Nations* (1845) (Oxford, 1988)

Dolman, F., *Municipalities at Work* (London, 1895)

Eastlake, C., *The Gothic Revival* (1872) (Leicester, 1970)

Eliot, G., *Felix Holt: The Radical* (1866) (London, 1995)

Eliot, G., *Middlemarch* (1871) (London, 1961)

Elmes, J., *Metropolitan Improvements* (London, 1828)

Engels, F., *The Condition of the Working Class in England* (1845) (London, 1987)

Engels, F., *The Housing Question* (1872) (London, 1872)

Espinasse, F., *Lancashire Worthies* (London, 1874)

Fabian Municipal Tracts

Fairweather, E.R. (ed.), *The Oxford Movement* (New York, 1964)

Faucher, L., *Manchester in 1844* (Manchester, 1844)

Fielding, K. (ed.), *Speeches of Charles Dickens* (Brighton, 1994)

Forster, J., *The Life of Charles Dickens* (1872–4) (2 vols, London 1969)

Freeman, E.A., *Historical Essays* (London, 1871)

Freeman, E.A., *A History of the Norman Conquest of England* (London, 1867)

Gaskell, E., *Mary Barton* (1848) (London, 1996)

Gaskell, E., *North and South* (1855) (London, 1995)

Gaskell, P., *Artisans and Machinery* (1836) (London, 1968)

Gavin, H., *Sanitary Ramblings* (London, 1848)

Gavin, J.L., *The Life of Joseph Chamberlain* (4 vols, London, 1932–4)

Gawthrop, H., *Fraser's Guide to Liverpool* (Liverpool, 1855)

Gibbon, E., *The History of the Decline and Fall of the Roman Empire* (1776–88) (7 vols, London, 1994)

Glover, W., *A Practical Treatise on the Law of Municipal Corporation* (London, 1837)

Glover, G., *London Shadows: A Glance at the 'Homes' of the Thousands* (London, 1854)

Godwin, G., *Town Swamps and Social Bridges* (London, 1859)

Godwin, H., *Fraser's Guide to Liverpool* (Liverpool, 1855)

Gomme, L., *The Literature of Local Institutions* (London, 1886)

Green, J.R., *A Short History of the English People* (London, 1892)

Greenwood, J., *The Wilds of London* (London, 1874)

Grierson, H.J.C. (ed.), *The Letters of Sir Walter Scott* (London, 1932–7)

Grossmith, G. and W., *The Diary of a Nobody* (1892) (Oxford, 1998)

Guizot, F., *The History of Civilization in Europe* (1828) (London, 1997)

Guttsman, W.L. (ed.), *A Plea for Democracy* (Bristol, 1967)

Hallam, H., *View of the State of Europe during the Middle Ages* (3 vols, London, 1819)

Hardwick, C., *History of the Borough of Preston* (London, 1857)

Harland, J., *Mamecestre: being chapters from the early record of Manchester* (Manchester, 1861)

Harris, G., *The Life and Labours of the late Rev. William Turner* (Manchester, 1859)

D'Haussez, Baron, *Great Britain in 1833* (London, 1833)

Hawkes, H.W., *History and Antiquities of the City of Coventry* (Coventry, 1842)

Head, G., *A Home Tour through the Manufacturing Districts of England in the Summer of 1835* (London, 1836)

Heywood, Sir B., *Addresses delivered at the Manchester Mechanics' Institute* (London, 1840)

Hibbert-Ware, S., *The Ancient Parish Church of Manchester* (Manchester, 1848)

Hole, J., *An Essay on the History and Management of Literary, Scientific, and Mechanics' Institutes* (London, 1853)

Hope, T., *An Historical Essay on Architecture* (London, 1840)

Horsfall, T.C., *The Improvement of the Dwellings and Surroundings of the People* (Manchester, 1904)

Howard, E., *Garden Cities of Tomorrow* (1902) (London, 1965)

Hudson, J.W., *The History of Adult Education* (London, 1851)

Hume, D., *The History of England* (1754–62) (6 vols, Indianapolis, 1983)

Hutton, W., *The History of Birmingham* (Birmingham, 1835)

Hyndman, H., *A Commune for London* (London, 1887)

Ingham, J.A., *City Slums* (London, 1889)

James, J., *History and Topography of Bradford* (London, 1841)

James, J., *History of Worsted Manufacture in England* (Bradford, 1857)

Jones, E. R. (ed.), *The Life and Speeches of Joseph Cowen MP* (London, 1885)

Jones, H.L., *A Plan for a University for the Town of Manchester* (Manchester, 1836)

Jones, W.H. (Geoffrey Gimcrack), *Gimcrackiana, or Fugitive Pieces on Manchester Men and Manners* (Manchester, 1833)

Joseph, K., *The Development of Higher Education into the 1990s.* HMSO (London, 1985)

Kay, J.P., 'A Letter to the People of Lancashire, concerning the Future Representation of the Commercial Interest, By the Return of Members for its New Boroughs to the Reformed Parliament' (London, 1831)

Kay, J.P., *The Moral and Physical Condition of the Working Classes Employed in the Cotton Manufacture in Manchester* (1832) (Manchester, 1969)

Kebbel, T.E. (ed.), *Selected Speeches of the late Rt Hon the Earl of Beaconsfield* (London, 1882)

Kemble, J., *The Saxons in England* (2 vols, London, 1849)

Kingsley, C., *Great Cities* (Bristol, 1857)

Kingsley, C., *Sanitary and Social Lectures* (London, 1892)

Kingsley , C., *The Teuton and the Roman* (Leamington Spa, 1957)

Knight, C., *The Popular History of England* (London, 1856)

Langford, J.A., *A Century of Birmingham Life* (Birmingham, 1867)

Langford, J.A., *English Democracy: Its History and Principles* (London, 1853)

Langford, J.A., *Modern Birmingham and Its Institutions* (Birmingham, 1873)

Lappenberg, J.M., *A History of England under the Anglo-Saxon Kings* (London, 1845)

Lawrence, D.H., ed. D. Trilling, *The Portable Lawrence* (London, 1980)

Lieber, F., *On Civil Liberty and Self-Government* (London, 1853)

Lingard, J., *A History of England from the First Invasion by the Romans* (8 vols, London, 1819–30)

Love, B., *The Handbook of Manchester* (Manchester, 1842)

Macaulay, T.B., *The History of England* (1849–55) (3 vols, London 1860)

Macfadyen, D., *Sir Ebenezer Howard and the Town Planning Movement* (Manchester, 1933)

MacKenzie, E., *A Descriptive and Historical Account of the Town and County of Newcastle Upon Tyne* (2 vols, Newcastle, 1827)

Marris, N.M., *Joseph Chamberlain: the Man and the Statesman* (London, 1900)

Martineau, H., *History of England During the Thirty Years' Peace* (2 vols, London, 1850)

Marx, K., & Engels, F., *Collected Works* (50 vols, London, 1975–)

Marx, K. & Engels, F., ed. G. Stedman Jones, *The Communist Manifesto* (1848) (London, 2002)

Masterman, C.F.G., *The Condition of England* (1909) (London, 1960)

Masterman, C.F.G., *Heart of the Empire* (London, 1901)

Mayhew, H., *London Labour and the London Poor* (1861–2) (London, 1985)

Mearns, A., ed. and with an introduction by A.S. Wohl, *The Bitter Cry of Outcast London* (1883) (Leicester, 1970)

Mellon, S. (ed.), *François Guizot: Historical Essays and Lectures* (Chicago, 1973)

Memoirs and Portraits of 100 Glasgow Men who have Died During the Last Thirty Years, and in Their Lives did much to make the City what it is Now (Glasgow, 1886)

Merewether, H.A. and Stephens, A.J., *The History of the Boroughs and Municipal Corporations of the UK* (1835) (Brighton, 1972)

Mill, J.S. and Bentham, J., *Utilitarianism and Other Essays* (1838) (London, 1987)

Mill, J.S., ed. J.M. Robson, *The Collected Works of John Stuart Mill* (33 vols, Toronto, 1972)

Miller, H., *First Impressions of England and its People* (London, 1847)

Milner, J., *The History of Winchester* (2 vols, London, 1798)

Montagu Harris, C., *The Garden City Movement* (London, 1906)

Morley, J., *The Life of Richard Cobden* (2 vols, London, 1896)

Morris, W., *News from Nowhere* (1891) (Cambridge, 1995)

Mudie, R., *London and the Londoners: Or a Second Judgement of Babylon the Great* (2 vols, London, 1829)

Muir, J.H., *Glasgow in 1901* (Glasgow, 1901)

Muir, J.R. *A History of Liverpool* (London, 1907)

Muirhead, J.H., *Birmingham Institutions* (Birmingham, 1911)

Muirhead, J.H., *Nine Famous Birmingham Men* (Birmingham, 1909)

Napier, H.E., *Florentine History* (6 vols, London 1846–7)

Newman, J.H., *Apologia Pro Vita Sua* (1865) (London, 1994)

Newman, J.H., *Parochial and Plain Sermons* (Oxford, 1873)

O'Farrell, J., *Things Can Only Get Better* (London, 1998)

Orwell, G., *Coming up for Air* (1939) (London, 2001)

Orwell, G., Davison, P. (ed.), *Orwell's England* (London, 2001)

Palgrave, F., *Conciliatory Reform* (London, 1831)

Palgrave, F., *Handbook for Travellers in Northern Italy* (London, 1847)

Palgrave, F., *Reform of Ancient Corporations* (London, 1832)

Palgrave, R.H. (ed.), *The Collected Historical Works of Sir Francis Palgrave* (10 vols, Cambridge, 1919–22)

Parkinson, R., *On the Present Condition of the Labouring Poor in Manchester* (Manchester, 1841)

Peacock, T.L. *Crotchet Castle* (1831) (London, 1986)

Penrose, E. (Mrs Markham), *History of England* (London, 1823)

Picton, J.A., *Ancient Liverpool, In Its Architecture and Buildings* (London, 1849)

Picton, J.A., *Liverpool Improvements and How to Accomplish Them* (Liverpool, 1853)

Picton, J.A., *Memorials of Liverpool, Historical and Topographical* (London, 1873)

Pinney, T., (ed.), *Essays of George Eliot* (London, 1963)

Poole, G.A., *The History of Ecclesiastical Architecture in England* (London, 1848)

Porter, G.R., *The Progress of the Nation* (London, 1851)

Priestley, J.B., *English Journey* (London 1934)

Pugin, A.W., *An Apology for the Revival of Christian Architecture in England* (1843) (Oxford, 1969)

Pugin, A.W., *Contrasts: or, a Parallel between the Noble Edifices of the Middle Ages and Corresponding Buildings of the Present Day; shewing the Present Decay of Taste* (1840) (Leicester, 1969)

Pugin, A.W., *A Reply to Observations which appeared in* Fraser's Magazine *for March 1837, on a work entitled 'Contrasts'* (London, 1837)

Pugin, A.W., *The True Principles of Pointed or Christian Architecture* (1841) (London, 1973)

De Quincey, T., *Confessions of an Opium-Eater* (London, 1823)

De Quincey, T., *The Nation of London* (London, 1834)

Redlich, J., *Local Government in England* (2 vols, London 1903)

Reed, P. (ed.), *Glasgow: The Forming of the City* (Edinburgh, 1999)

Richardson, B.W., *Hygeia, or the City of Health* (London, 1876)

Robinson, S., *Two Addresses* (Manchester, 1838)

Rogers, J.E. Thorold (ed.), *The Speeches of John Bright, M.P.* (2 vols, London, 1868)

Rogers, S., ed. J.R. Hale, *The Italian Journal of Samuel Rogers* (1822)

Roscoe, H., *The Life of William Roscoe* (2 vols, Edinburgh, 1833)

Roscoe, W., *The Life of Lorenzo de' Medici, Called the Magnificent* (1796) (London, 1846)

Roscoe, W., *The Life and Pontificate of Leo X* (London, 1805)

Rose, J., *The Intellectual Life of the British Working Classes* (London, 2001)

Rosenberg, J.D. (ed.), *The Genius of John Ruskin* (London, 1964)

Ruskin, J., ed. E.T. Cook and A. Wedderburn, *The Collected Works of John Ruskin* (39 vols, London 1903–12)

Ruskin, J. *A Joy for Ever: Lectures on the Political Economy of Art Delivered at Manchester Art Treasures Exhibition 1857* (London, 1880)

Ruskin, J., *Lectures on Art* (1870) (London, 1910)

Saint, A. (ed.), *Politics and the People of London* (1980)

Scott G.G., *Personal and Professional Recollections* (London, 1879)

Scott, G.G., *Remarks on Secular and Domestic Architecture* (London, 1857)

Scott, W., *Familiar Letters* (2 vols, Edinburgh, 1894)

Scott, W., *Ivanhoe* (1819) (London, 1986)

Senior, N.W., *Conversations With Distinguished Persons during the 2nd Empire* (2 vols, London, 1878)

Sharp, T., *Town Planning* (London, 1940)

Shaw, A., *Municipal Government in Great Britain* (London, 1895)

Shaw, G.B., *The Common Sense of Municipal Trading* (London, 1904)

Shaw, J., *Travels in England* (1861) (London, 1985)

Sims, G.R., *How the Poor Live, and Horrible London* (London, 1889)

Sismondi, J.C.L., *The History of the Italian Republics*, Lardner Cyclopaedia (London, 1832)

Smiles, S., *Self-Help* (1859) (London, 1986)

Smithers, H., *Liverpool, Its Commerce, Statistics, and Institutions* (Liverpool, 1825)

Southey, R., *Essays Moral and Political* (London, 1832)

Southey, R., *Letters from England: by Don Manuel Alvarez Espriella* (2 vols, London 1808)

Southey, R., *Sir Thomas More: or, Colloquies on the Progress and Prospects of Society*, (2 vols, London, 1829)

De Staël, Madame, *Germany* (London, 1813)

Stanley, H.M., *How I Found Livingstone* (London, 1872)

Starke M., *Travels on the Continent* (London, 1820)

Stephens, A.J., *The Rise and Progress of the English Constitution* (London, 1838)

The Story of Port Sunlight (Lever Brothers, 1953)

Strange, W., *Address to the Middle and Working Classes on the Causes and Preventions of the Excessive Sickness and Mortality Prevalent in Large Towns* (London, 1845)

Stubbs, W., *The Constitutional History of England* (3 vols, London, 1891)

Taine, H., *Notes on England* (1872) (London, 1957)

Taylor, W.C., *Notes of a Tour in the Manufacturing Districts of Lancashire* (1841) (London, 1968)

Thackrah, C.T., *The Effects of the Principal Arts, Trades and Pro-*

fessions, and of Civic States and Habits of Living, on Health and Longevity (1832) (London, 1959)

Thierry, A., *History of the Conquest of England by the Normans* (London, 1847)

Thompson, V., *An Essay in English Municipal History* (London, 1867)

Thompson, J., *The History of Leicester* (London, 1849)

De Tocqueville, A., *The Ancien Régime and the French Revolution* (1856) (Manchester, 1966)

De Tocqueville, A., *Democracy in America* (1835) (2 vols, London, 1994)

De Tocqueville, A., *Journeys to England and Ireland* (1835) (London, 1958)

Toulmin-Smith, J., *Government By Commissions Illegal and Pernicious* (London, 1849)

Toulmin-Smith, J., *Local Self-Government and Centralization* (London, 1851)

Toynbee, A., *Toynbee's Industrial Revolution* (1884) (Newton Abbot, 1969)

Trevelyan, Charles, *Three Letters to The Times* (London, 1870)

Tucker, R., *The Marx–Engels Reader* (New York, 1978)

Turner, S., *The History of the Anglo-Saxons* (1795–1801) (3 vols, London, 1823)

Turner, S., *The History of England* (3 vols, London, 1814–23)

Tweed, J., *Biographical Sketches of the Honourable Lord Provosts of Glasgow* (Glasgow, 1883)

Unwin, R., *Nothing Gained by Overcrowding* (London, 1918)

Urquhart, D., *Turkey and Its Resources* (London, 1833)

Vaughan, R.D.D., *The Age of Great Cities* (London, 1843)

Von Raumer, F., *England in 1835* (London, 1836)

Wardell, J., *The Antiquities of the Borough of Leeds* (Leeds, 1853)

Waugh, E., *Vile Bodies* (1930) (London, 1951)

Webb, B., *My Apprenticeship* (1926) (London, 1979)

Webb, S., *The London Programme* (London, 1891)

Webb, S., *Socialism in England* (London, 1889)

Webb, S. and B., *A Constitution for the Socialist Commonwealth of Great Britain* (1920) (London, 1975)

Webb, S. and B., *English Local Government, vols II & III: The Manor and the Borough* (1908) (2 vols, London, 1963)

Webb, S. and B., *English Local Government, vol IV: Statutory Authorities for Special Purposes* (1922) (London, 1963)

Wells, H.G., *The New Machiavelli* (1911) (London, 1946)

Wemyss Reid, T. (ed.), *Memoir of Dr Heaton of Leeds* (London, 1883)

Wheeler, J., *Manchester: Its Political, Social and Commercial History, Ancient and Modern* (Manchester, 1836)

Whibley, C., *Lord John Manners and his Friends* (2 vols, London, 1925)

White, A., *Problems of a Great City* (London, 1886)

Whittle, P., *Blackburn As It Is* (Fishergate, 1852)

Whittle, P., *The History of the Borough of Preston* (Preston, 1837)

Wilkins, W., *Athiensa, or remarks on the topography and buildings of Athens* (London, 1816)

Williams-Ellis, C., *England and the Octopus* (London, 1928)

Williams-Freeman, J.P., *The Effects of Town Life on the General Health* (London, 1890)

Willis, R., *Remarks on the Architecture of the Middle Ages* (London, 1835)

Wilson, W., *The Life of George Dawson* (Birmingham, 1905)

Woolf, V., 'The Death of the Moth and other essays' (New York, 1942)

Wright, T., *Remarks on the Municipal Privileges* (London, 1845)

Young, W., *The Municipal Buildings of Glasgow* (Glasgow, 1890)

OFFICIAL PAPERS

Hansard

Parliamentary Papers 1836

Parliamentary Papers 1840

Parliamentary Papers 1843

Parliamentary Papers 1844

1846 Public Baths and Washhouses Bill

1858 Local Government Act

1855 Public Libraries and Museums Bill

1867 Representation of the People Bill

1866 Sanitary Act

1875 Artizans' Dwellings Act

Towards an Urban Renaissance, Department of Environment, Transport and the Regions (HMSO, 1999)

Strong Local Leadership – Quality Public Services, Department for Transport, Local Government and the Regions (HMSO, 2001)

The State of English Cities, Office of the Deputy Prime Minister (HMSO, 2001)

PRIVATE PAPERS

'The Diary of Benjamin Barker of Bramley, near Leeds', Thoresby Society, MSS XI

JOURNALS AND NEWSPAPERS

Archaeoligia Aeliana

Architect

Art Treasures Examiner

The Athenaeum
Athenaeum Gazette
Bentley's Miscellany
Birmingham Daily Post
Birmingham Daily Press
Bradford Observer
British Critic
The Builder
Building News
City Press
Clarion
Commonweal
Contemporary Review
The Ecclesiologist
Eclectic Review
The Economist
Edinburgh Review
Encounter
The Forum
Fortnightly Review
Fraser's Magazine
The Garden City
Glasgow Daily Herald
History and Policy (www.historyandpolicy.org)
*Journal of Public Health and Monthly Record of Sanitary
   Improvement*
Leeds Mercury
Macmillan's Magazine
Manchester Guardian
Morning Chronicle
The Municipal Reformer and Local Government News
National Review
The Nineteenth Century
Northampton Mercury
Oxford and Cambridge Review
Pall Mall Gazette
Quarterly Review
Tait's Edinburgh Magazine
The Times
Town Crier; or Jacob's Belles Lettres
Transactions, British Archaeological Association
Transactions, Leeds Literary and Philosophical Society
Transactions, Liverpool Literary and Philosophical Society
Transactions, Manchester Literary and Philosophical Society
Transactions, Manchester Statistical Society

Transactions, National Association for the Promotion of Social Science
(NAPSS)
Westminster Review

SECONDARY SOURCES

Ackroyd, P., *Blake* (London, 1996)
Ackroyd, P., *Dickens* (London, 1990)
Alford, B.W.E., *British Economic Performance 1945–75* (Cambridge, 1995)
Anderson, B., *Imagined Communities* (London, 1983)
Anderson, O., *A Liberal State at War* (London, 1967)
Angelomatis-Tsougarakis, H., *The Eve of the Greek Revival* (London, 1990)
Anstruther, I., *The Knight and the Umbrella* (Gloucester, 1986)
Archer, J. (ed.), *Art and Architecture in Victorian Manchester* (Manchester, 1985)
Armytage, W.H.G., *Heavens Below* (London, 1961)
Arnold, D., *Re-presenting the Metropolis* (Aldershot, 2000)
Ashton, R., *Thomas and Jane Carlyle: Portrait of a Marriage* (London, 2002)
Ashworth, W., *The Genesis of Town Planning* (London, 1954)
Atterbury, P., and Wainwright, C. (eds), *Pugin: A Gothic Passion* (London,1994)
Beevers, R., *The Garden City Utopia* (London, 1988)
Beier, A.L., Cannadine, D., and Rosenheim, J.M. (eds), *The First Modern Society* (Cambridge, 1989)
Bell, Q., *Ruskin* (London, 1978)
Bellamy, R., *Victorian Liberalism* (London, 1990)
Ben-Israel, H., *English Historians on the French Revolution* (Cambridge, 1968)
Berlin, I., *Against the Current* (London 1979)
Biachini, F., and Parkinson, M. (eds), *Cultural Policy as Urban Regeneration* (Manchester, 1993)
Blake, R., *Benjamin Disraeli* (London, 1969)
Boos, F.S., *History and Community: Essays in Victorian Medievalism* (New York, 1992)
Bradley, I., *Themes and Personalities in Victorian Liberalism* (London, 1980)
Bradshaw, L.D. (ed.), *Visitors to Manchester: A Selection of British and Foreign Visitors' Descriptions of Manchester from c.1538 to 1865* (Manchester, 1987)
Briggs, A., *The Collected Essays of Asa Briggs* (3 vols, Brighton 1985–91)
Briggs, A., *History of Birmingham: Borough and City 1865–1938* (Cambridge, 1952)

Briggs, A., *Victorian Cities* (1963) (London, 1990)

Bright, M., *Cities Built to Music: Aesthetic Theories of the Victorian Gothic Revival* (Columbus, 1984)

Brockliss, L., and Eastwood, D. (eds), *Union of Multiple Identities* (Manchester, 1997)

Brooks, C., and Saint, A., *The Victorian Church* (Manchester, 1995)

Brooks, M.W., *John Ruskin and Victorian Architecture* (New Brunswick, 1987)

Brown, C., *Northampton 1835–1935. Shoe Town, New Town* (Sussex, 1990)

Brundage, A., *England's 'Prussian Minister'* (Pennsylvania, 1988)

Bryman, A., *Religion in the Birmingham Area* (Birmingham, 1978)

Burrow, J.W., *A Liberal Descent: Victorian Historians and the English Past* (Cambridge, 1981)

Calhoun, C., (ed.), *Habermas and the Public Sphere* (Cambridge, MA, 1997)

Cannadine, D., *In Churchill's Shadow* (London, 2002)

Cannadine, D., (ed.), *Lords and Landlords: Aristocracy and the Towns, 1774–1967* (Leicester, 1980)

Cannadine, D., (ed.), *Patricians, Power and Politics in Nineteenth Century Towns* (Leicester, 1982)

Cannadine, D., and Reeder, D. (eds), *Exploring the Urban Past* (Cambridge, 1982)

Carey, J., *Intelligentsia and the Masses* (London, 1992)

Cazamian, L., *The Social Novel in England 1830–50* (London, 1973)

Chadwick, O., *The Spirit of the Oxford Movement* (Cambridge, 1990)

Chandler, A., *A Dream of Order* (London, 1971)

Chandler, G., *William Roscoe of Liverpool* (London, 1953)

Chapman, J., and Chapman, B., *The Life and Times of Baron Haussmann* (London, 1957)

Chapman, R., *The Sense of the Past in Victorian Literature* (London, 1986)

Charlton, D.G., *The French Romantics* (Cambridge, 1984)

Church, R.W., *The Oxford Movement* (Chicago, 1970)

Clark, K., *The Gothic Revival*, (London 1995)

Clark, P., (ed.), *The Cambridge Urban History of Britain, vol. II: 1540–1840* (Cambridge, 2000)

Clarke, B., *Church Builders of the Nineteenth Century*, (Newton Abbot, 1969)

Clarke, G.W., (ed.), *Rediscovering Hellenism: the Hellenic Inheritance and the English Imagination* (Cambridge, 1989)

Clarke, P., *Hope and Glory* (London, 1997)

Cobban, A., *Edmund Burke and the Revolt against the Eighteenth Century* (London, 1960)

Coleman, B.I., (ed.), *The Idea of the City in Nineteenth Century Britain* (London, 1973)

Coleman, D.C., *Myth, History and the Industrial Revolution* (London, 1992)

Colley, L., *Britons: Forging the Nation* (London, 1996)

Collins, B., and Robbins, K. (eds), *British Culture and Economic Decline* (London, 1990)

Colls, R. and Rodgers, R. (eds), *Cities of Ideas* (Aldershot, 2004)

Creese, W., (ed.) *The Legacy of Raymond Unwin* (Cambridge, MA, 1976)

Crook, J.M., *The Greek Revival: Neo–classical Attitudes in British Architecture, 1760–1870* (London, 1995)

Crouch, C., and Marquand, D. (eds), *The New Centralism* (Oxford, 1989)

Cullen, M., *The Statistical Movement in Early Victorian Britain* (New York, 1985)

Culler A.D., *The Victorian Mirror of History* (New Haven, 1985)

Cunningham, C., *Victorian and Edwardian Town Halls* (London, 1981)

Darcy, C., *The Encouragement of Fine Arts in Lancashire* (Manchester, 1976)

Daunton, M. (ed.), *The Cambridge Urban History of Britain, vol. III: 1840–1950* (Cambridge, 2000)

Davison, P. (ed.), *Orwell's England* (London, 2001)

Dellheim, C., *The Face of the Past* (Cambridge, 1982)

Dennis, R., *English Industrial Cities of the Nineteenth Century* (Cambridge, 1984)

Donajgrodzki, A.P. (ed.), *Social Control in Nineteenth Century Britain* (London, 1977)

Dyos, H.J., *Urbanity and Suburbanity* (Leicester, 1973)

Dyos, H.J., *Victorian Suburb* (Leicester, 1961)

Dyos, H.J. (ed.), *The Study of Urban History* (London, 1966)

Dyos, H.J. and Wolff, M. (eds), *The Victorian City: Images and Realities* (London, 1999)

Fawcett, J. (ed.), *Seven Victorian Architects* (London, 1976)

Feldman, D. and Stedman Jones, G. (eds), *Metropolis* (London, 1989)

Ferguson, P., *Paris as Revolution* (Berkeley, 1994)

Finlayson, G., *Citizen, State and Social Welfare in Britain: 1830–1990* (Oxford, 1994)

Finn, M., *After Chartism: Class and Nation in English Radical Politics, 1848–1874* (Cambridge, 1993)

Fisher, T., *Prostitution and the Victorians* (Stroud, 1997)

Flinn, M. and Smout, T. (eds), *Essays in Social History* (London, 1974)

Florida, R., *The Rise of the Creative Class* (New York, 2004)

Floud, R., Wachter, K, and Gregory, A., *Height, Health and History: Nutritional Status in the UK, 1750–1980* (Cambridge, 1990)

Foot, M., *Aneurin Bevan. A Biography, vol. One: 1879–1945* (London, 1966)

Forbes, D., *The Liberal Anglican Idea of History* (Cambridge, 1952)

Foucault, M., *Discipline and Punish* (London, 1991)

Fraser, D., *Power and Authority in the Victorian city* (Oxford, 1979)

Fraser, D., *Urban Politics in Victorian England* (London, 1979)

Fraser, D. (ed.), *Cities, Class and Communication* (London, 1990)

Fraser, D. (ed.), *A History of Modern Leeds* (Manchester, 1980)

Fraser, D. (ed.), *Municipal Reform and the Industrial City* (Leicester, 1982)

Fraser, D. and Sutcliffe, A. (eds), *The Pursuit of Urban History* (London, 1983)

Fraser, W.H. and Maver, I. (eds), *Glasgow, vol.11: 1830 to 1912* (Manchester, 1996)

Garrard, J., *Leadership and Power in the Victorian Industrial Town 1830–1880* (Manchester, 1983)

Gibb, A., *Glasgow: The Making of a City* (London, 1983)

Gilbert, A.D., *Religion and Society in Industrial England* (London, 1976)

Gill, C., *History of Birmingham: Manor and Borough to 1865* (Oxford, 1952)

Gilley, S. and Swift, R. (eds), *The Irish in the Victorian City* (Chatham, 1985)

Girouard, M., *Alfred Waterhouse and the Natural History Museum* (London, 1999)

Girouard, M., *Cities and People* (New Haven, 1985)

Girouard, M., *The Return to Camelot* (New Haven, 1981)

Glyde, J., *The Moral, Social and Religious Condition of Ipswich in the Middle of the 19th Century* (London, 1971)

Gordon, E. and Nair, G., *Public Lines. Women, Family and Society in Victorian Britain* (London, 2003)

Gunn, S., *The Public Culture of the Victorian middle class* (Manchester, 2000)

Gunn S., & Bell, R. , *The Rise and Sprawl of the Middle Class* (London, 2001)

Haakonssen, K. (ed.), *Enlightenment and Religion* (Cambridge, 1996)

Hall, P., *Cities in Civilization* (London, 1999)

Hall, P. and Ward, C., *Sociable Cities: The Legacy of Ebenezer Howard* (Chichester, 1998)

Hamlin, C., *Public Health and Social Justice in the Age of Chadwick* (Cambridge, 1998)

Hardman, M., *Ruskin and Bradford* (Manchester, 1986)

Hardy D., *From Garden Cities to New Towns* (London, 1991)

Havel, V., *Living in Truth* (London, 1989)

Hawkins, P. (ed.) *Civitas: Religious Interpretations of the City* (Atlanta, 1986)

Hennock, E.P., *Fit and Proper Persons* (London, 1973)

Hewitt, M., *The Emergence of Stability* (Aldershot, 1996)

Hillman, J., *The Bournville Hallmark* (Bournville, 1994)

Hobsbawm, E., *Industry and Empire* (London, 1990)

Hobsbawm, E. and Ranger, T. (eds), *The Invention of Tradition* (Cambridge, 1983)

Holland, F.M (ed.), *The Ruskin Polygon* (1982)

Howe, A., *The Cotton Masters* (Oxford, 1984)

Hughes, Q., *Liverpool, City of Architecture* (Liverpool, 1999)

Jacobs, J., *The Death and Life of Great American Cities* (London, 1994)

Jenkins, R., *Churchill* (London, 2001)

Jenkins, S., *Accountable to None* (London, 1996)

Jenkins, S., *Big Bang Localism* (Policy Exchange, 2004)

Jenkyns, R., *Victorians and Ancient Greece* (Oxford, 1980)

Jenkyns, R. (ed.), *The Legacy of Rome* (Oxford, 1992)

Jones, R. and Wirth, J. (eds), *Manchester and São Paulo: Problems of Rapid Urban Growth* (Stanford, 1978)

Joyce, P., *Democratic Subjects: the Self and the Social in Nineteenth-Century England* (Cambridge, 1994)

Judd, D., *Radical Joe: A Life of Joseph Chamberlain* (Cardiff, 1993)

Kaplan, F., *Thomas Carlyle* (Cambridge, 1983)

Kargon, R., *Science in Victorian Manchester* (Manchester, 1977)

Kellett, J.R., *The Impact of Railways on Victorian Cities* (London, 1969)

Kidd, A., *Manchester* (Keele, 1996)

Kidd, A. and Nicholls, D. (eds), *Gender, Civic Culture and Consumerism: Middle-Class Identity in Britain* (Manchester, 1999)

Kidd, A. and Nicholls, D. (eds), *The Making of the Middle Class?* (Stroud, 1998)

Kinchin, P. and Kinchin, J., *Glasgow's Great Exhibitions* (Glasgow, 1988)

Koditschek, T., *Class Formation and Industrial Society. Bradford, 1750–1850* (Cambridge, 1990)

Lambert, R., *Sir John Simon and English Social Administration* (London, 1963)

Landow, G., *Ruskin* (Oxford, 1985)

Lane, T., *Liverpool. Gateway of Empire* (London, 1987)

Lees, A., *Cities Perceived* (New York, 1985)

Lerner, L. (ed.), *The Victorians* (London, 1978)

Levine, P., *The Amateur and the Professional* (Cambridge 1986)

Lewis, R.A., *Edwin Chadwick and the Public Health Movement* (London, 1952)

Liversidge, M and Edwards, C. (eds), *Imagining Rome* (London, 1996)

Lubenow, W.C., *The Politics of Government Growth* (Newton Abbot, 1971)

Lutyens, M., *Effie in Venice* (London, 1965)

Lutyens, M., *Millais and the Ruskins* (London, 1968)

MacDonagh, O., *Early Victorian Government* (London 1977)

Macintyre, D., *Mandelson: The Biography* (London, 1999)

Macleod, D.S., *Art and the Victorian Middle Class* (Cambridge, 1996)

McSmith, A., *Faces of Labour* (London, 1997)

Mancoff, D.N. & Tela, D.J. (eds), *Victorian Urban Settings* (London, 1996)

Mandler, P., *The Fall and Rise of the Stately Home* (Yale, 1997)

Marquand, D., *Decline of the Public* (Cambridge, 2004)

Marquand, D. (ed.), *The New Centralism* (Oxford, 1989)

Marsh P., *Joseph Chamberlain* (London, 1994)

Messinger, G.S., *Manchester in the Victorian Age*, (Manchester, 1985)

Miller, M., *Letchworth: The First Garden City* (Sussex, 1989)

Miller, M. and Grey, S., *Hampstead Garden Suburb* (Sussex, 1992)

Miller, P., *Defining the Common Good* (Cambridge, 1994)

Morrell, J., *Metropolis and Province* (London, 1983)

Morris, K., *The Image of the Middle Ages in Romantic and Victorian Literature* (London,1984)

Morris, R.J. and Trainor, R.H. (eds), *Urban Governance: Britain and beyond since 1750* (Aldershot, 2004)

Morris, R.J., *Class, Sect, and Party. The Making of the British Middle Class, Leeds 1820–1850* (Manchester, 1990)

Morris, R.J. (ed.), *Class, Power, and Social Structure in British Nineteenth-Century Towns* (Leicester, 1986)

Mumford, L., *The City in History* (London, 1961)

Nead, L., *Victorian Babylon* (London, 2000)

Norwich, J.J., *Paradise of Cities* (London, 2003)

Offer, A., *Property and Politics 1870–1914* (Cambridge, 1981)

Oliver, P., Davis, I., and Bentley, I., *Dunroamin'* (London, 1994)

Olsen, D.J., *The City as a Work of Art* (London 1986)

Olsen, D.J., *The Growth of Victorian London* (London, 1979)

Owen, D., *English Philanthropy 1660–1960* (London, 1965)

Owen, D., *The Government of Victorian London* (London, 1982)

Parry, J., *The Rise and Fall of the Liberal Government in Victorian Britain* (London, 1993)

Pemble, J., *The Mediterranean Passion* (Oxford, 1987)

Pennybacker, S.D., *A Vision for London, 1889–1914* (London, 1995)

Pevsner, N., *Pioneers of Modern Design* (London, 1986)

Philp, M. (ed.), *The French Revolution and British Popular Politics* (Cambridge, 1971)

Pick, D., *Faces of Degeneration* (Cambridge, 1989)

Port, M., *Six Hundred New Churches* (London, 1961)

Porter, R. and Teich, M. (eds), *Romanticism in National Context* (Cambridge, 1988)

Prest, J., *Liberty and Locality* (Oxford, 1990)

Putnam, R., *Bowling Alone* (New York, Simon & Schuster, 2000)

Read, D., *The Age of Urban Democracy. England, 1868–1914* (London, 1994)

Rowell, G., *The Vision Glorious* (Oxford, 1983)

Samuel, R., *Theatres of Memory. Island Stories: Unravelling Britain.* II (London, 1998)

Samuel, R. (ed.), *Patriotism: The Making and Unmaking of British National Identity* (3 vols, London, 1989)

Schama, S., *Landscape and Memory* (London, 1996)

Schneer, J., *London 1900* (London, 1999)

Schwarzbach, F.S., *Dickens and the City* (London, 1979)

Selleck, R.J.W., *James Kay-Shuttleworth* (Ilford, 1994)

Shaw, C. and Chase, M. (eds), *The Imagined Past: History and Nostalgia* (Manchester, 1989)

Shelden, M., *Orwell* (London, 1992)

Sheppard, F., *London 1808–1870: The Infernal Wen* (London, 1971)

Simmons C., *Reversing the Conquest* (New Brunswick, 1990)

Simon, B., *Studies in the History of Education* (London, 1960)

Simpson, D., *Romanticism, Nationalism, and the Revolt against Theory* (Chicago, 1993)

Skinner, Q., *Ambrogio Lorenzetti – The Artist as Political Philosopher* (London 1985)

Skinner, S.A., *Tractarians and the 'condition of England': the social and political thought of the Oxford Movement* (Oxford, 2004)

Smith, F., *The Life and Work of Sir James Kay-Shuttleworth* (London, 1974)

Smith, O., *The Politics of Language, 1791–1819* (Oxford, 1986)

Smith, R.J., *The Gothic Bequest* (Cambridge, 1987)

Soja, E., *Postmodern Geographies: The Reassertion of Space in a Critical Social Theory* (Oxford, 1989)

Solnit, R., *Wanderlust – a History* (New York, 2000)

Spence, P., *The Birth of Romantic Radicalism* (Aldershot, 1996)

Stamp, G. and Amery, C., *Victorian Buildings of London* (London,1980)

Stedman Jones, G., 'Civilizing the People'. Unpublished paper.

Stedman Jones, G., 'The First Industrial City? Engels' Account of Manchester in 1844'. Unpublished paper.

Stedman Jones, G., *Languages of Class* (Cambridge, 1983)

Stedman Jones, G., *Outcast London* (Cambridge, 1971)

Stedman Jones, G., 'The Rise and Fall of "Class Struggle": England and France, 1789–1850'. Unpublished paper.

Summerson, J., *Concerning Architecture* (London, 1968)

Summerson, J., *Georgian London* (London, 1978)

Sutcliffe, A. (ed.), *British Town Planning* (Leicester, 1981)

Tanner, T., *Venice Desired* (Oxford, 1992)

Taylor, M., with Wheeler, P., *In Defence of Councillors* (London, 2001)

Thompson, F.M.L. (ed.), *The Rise of Suburbia* (Leicester, 1982)

Trappes-Lomax, M., *Pugin* (London, 1932)

Trevelyan, G.M., *English Social History* (London, 1945)

Trevelyan, G.O., *The Life and Letters of Lord Macaulay* (London, 1959)

Trevor-Roper, H., *The Romantic Movement and the Study of History* (London, 1969)

Tsigakou, F-M., *The Rediscovery of Greece* (London, 1981)

Turner, F.M., *The Greek Heritage in Victorian Britain* (London, 1981)

Turner, M.J., *Reform and Respectability* (Manchester, 1995)

Tylecote, M., *The Mechanics' Institutes of Lancashire and Yorkshire before 1851* (Manchester, 1957)

Wahrman, D., *Imagining the Middle Class* (Cambridge, 1995)

Waller, P.J., *Town, City and Nation: England 1850–1914* (Oxford, 1991)

Waterhouse, R., *The Birmingham and Midland Institute* (Birmingham, 1954)

Webster, C., *The Rebuilding of Leeds Parish Church 1837–41* (London, 1994)

White, J.F., *The Cambridge Movement* (Cambridge, 1962)

Wiener, M., *English Culture and the Decline of the Industrial Spirit 1850–1980* (Cambridge, 1981)

Williams, R., *The Country and the City* (London, 1973)

Williams, R., *Culture and Society* (London, 1958)

Williams, R., *The Long Revolution* (London, 1992)

Wohl, A., *Endangered Lives: Public Health In Victorian Britain* (London, 1983)

Wolff, J. and Seed, J. (eds), *The Culture of Capital: Art, Power and the Nineteenth Century Middle Class* (Manchester, 1987)

Worden, B., *Roundhead Reputations* (London, 2001)

Worsdall, F., *Victorian City* (Glasgow, 1982)

ARTICLES

Allan, C.M., 'The Genesis of British Urban Redevelopment with Special Reference to Glasgow', *Economic History Review*, 2nd series, XVIII, 3 (1965), 598–614

Anderson, O., 'The Political Uses of History in mid-Nineteenth Century England', *Past and Present*, 36 (1967), 87–106

Baer, M., 'The Memory of the Middle Ages: From History of Culture to Cultural History', *Studies in Medievalism*, IV (1992), 290–309

Barry, J., 'The Making of the Middle Class?', *Past and Present*, 145 (1994), 194–208

Baxendale, J., 'J.B. Priestley, Englishness and the People', *History Workshop Journal* (51), Spring 2001

Brabazon, 'The Decay of Bodily Strength in Towns', *The Nineteenth Century*, XXI (1887)

Cain, P.J. and Hopkins, A.G., 'Gentlemanly Capitalism and British Expansion Overseas. I. The Old Colonial System, 1688–1850', *Economic History Review*, 2nd series, XXXIX 4 (1986), 501–25

Cannadine, D., 'The brief flowering of a civic religion', *The Listener*, 26 July 1984

Cannadine, D., 'Victorian cities: how different?', *Social History*, II (1977), 457–82

Claeys, G., 'French Revolution and Political Thought', *History of Political Thought*, XI, 1 (1990), 59–81

Conner, P., 'Pugin and Ruskin', *Warburg and Courtauld*, 41 (1978), 344–50

Daunton, M.J., '"Gentlemanly Capitalism" and British Industry 1820–1914', *Past and Present*, 122 (1989), 119–59

Dellheim, C., 'Imagining England: Victorian Views of the North', *Northern History*, 22 (1986), 216–31

Dyos, H.J., 'Railways and Housing in Victorian London', *Journal of Transport History*, II (1955–6); III (1957)

Dyos, H.J., 'Urban Transformation – A Note on the Objects of Street Improvement in Regency and Early Victorian London', *International Review of Social History*, II (1957), 259–66

Eastwood, D., 'Robert Southey and the Intellectual Origins of Romantic Conservatism', *English Historical Review*, CIV, 411 (1989), 308–32

Eden, W.A., 'Studies in Urban Theory II, Ebenezer Howard and the Garden City Movement', *Town Planning Review*, XIX, 3, 4 (1947)

Edsall, N.C., 'Varieties of Radicalism: Attwood, Cobden and the Local Politics of Municipal Incorporation', *Historical Journal*, XVI, 1 (1973), 93–109

Falkus, M., 'The Development of Municipal Trading in the Nineteenth Century', *Business History*, 19, 2 (1977)

Finlayson, G.B., 'The Municipal Corporation Commission', *Bulletin Institute Historical Research*, XXXVI, 93 (1963), 36–53

Finlayson, G.B., 'The Politics of Municipal Reform', *English Historical Review*, 81, 321 (1966), 673–93

Foley, M.W. and Edwards, B., 'Beyond Tocqueville: Civil Society and Social Capital in Comparative Perspective', *American Behavioral Scientist*, 42, 1 (1998), 5–21

Garnside, P.D., 'Scott, the Romantic Past, and the Nineteenth Century', *Review of English Studies*, XXIII, 90 (1972), 147–62

Glaeser, E.L. and Saiz, A., 'The Rise of the Skilled City', Harvard Institute of Economic Research, discussion paper No. 2025

Goldman, L., 'The Social Science Association 1857–1886: a Context for mid-Victorian Liberalism', *English Historical Review*, CII, 398 (1986), 95–135

Goldman, L., 'Statistics and the Science of Society in Early Victorian Britain', *Social History of Medicine*, IV, 3 (1991), 415–35

Greenleaf, W.H., 'Toulmin-Smith and the British Political Tradition', *Public Administration*, LIII (1975)

Gunn, S., 'Class, Identity and the Urban: the Middle Class in England, c. 1790–1950', *Urban History*, 31, 1 (2004)

Gutchen, R.M., 'Local Improvements and Centralization in Nineteenth Century England', *Historical Journal* IV, 1 (1961), 85–97

Hampshner-Monk, I., 'Civic Humanism and Parliamentary Reform: the Case of the Society of the Friends of the People', *Journal of British Studies*, XVIII, 2 (1979), 70–90

Hapgood, L., 'The Literature of the Suburbs', *Journal of Victorian Culture*, 5.2 (2000)

Hartnell, 'Art and Civic Culture in Birmingham in the Late 19th Century', *Urban History*, XXII (1995)

Hennock, E.P., 'Finance and Politics in Urban Local Government in England 1835–1900', *Historical Journal*, VI, 2 (1963), 212–26

Hyde, F.E., 'Utilitarian Town Planning, 1825–45', *Town Planning Review*, 19 (1943–7), 153–60

Jann, R., 'The Condition of England Past and Present: Thomas Carlyle and the Middle Ages', *Studies in Medievalism* I, 1, (1979), 15–33

Jann, R., 'Democratic Myths in Victorian Medievalism', *Browning Institute Studies*, 8 (1980), 129–151

Jones, L., 'Public pursuit or private profit? Liberal businessmen and municipal politics in Birmingham, 1865–1900', *Business History*, 25 (1983), 240–59

Keynes, S., 'The cult of King Alfred the Great', *Anglo-Saxon England*, 28 (1999), 225–356

Lambert, R., 'Central and Local Relations in Mid-Victorian England', *Victorian Studies*, VI, 2 (1962–3), 121–51

MacDonagh, O., 'The Nineteenth Century Revolution in Government: A Reappraisal', *Historical Journal*, I, 1 (1958), 52–67

MacReid, D.S., 'Irish immigration and the "condition of England" question: the roots of an historiographical tradition', *Immigrants and Minorities*, 14 (1985), 67–85

Melman, B., 'Claiming the Nation's Past: The Invention of an Anglo-Saxon Tradition', *Journal of Contemporary History*, XXVI, 3–4 (1991), 575–97

Morris, E., 'The formation of the Gallery of Art in the Liverpool Royal Institution, 1816–1819', *Transactions of the Historic Society of Lancashire and Cheshire*, 142 (1993), 87–98

Morris, R.J., 'Civil Society and the Nature of Urbanism: Britain, 1750–1850', *Urban History*, XXV, 3 (1998), 289–302

Morris, R.J., 'Leeds and the Crystal Palace', *Victorian Studies*, XIII, 3 (1970), 283–301

Morris, R.J., 'Voluntary Societies and British Urban Elites, 1780–1880', *Historical Journal*, XXVI, 1 (1983), 95–119

Nenadic, S., 'Businessmen, the Urban Middle Class and the "Dominance" of Manufacturers in Nineteenth-Century Britain', *Economic History Review*, 2nd series, XLIV (1991), 66–85

Nord., D.E., 'The city as theatre', *Victorian Studies*, 31, 2 (1988)

Osborn, F.J., 'Sir Ebenezer Howard. The Evolution of his Ideas', *Town Planning Review*, 21, 3 (October 1950)

Parris, H.W., 'The Nineteenth Century Revolution in Government: A Reappraisal Reappraised', *Historical Journal*, III, 3 (1960), 17–37

Reeder, D., 'H.J. Dyos: an Appreciation', *Urban History Yearbook* (1979), 4–11

Richards, P., 'R.A. Slaney, the Industrial Town, and early Victorian Social Policy', *Social History*, IV, 1 (1979), 85–103

Roberts, D., 'The Social Conscience of Tory Periodicals', *Victorian Periodicals Newsletter*, X, 3 (1977), 154–70

Rubinstein, W.D., 'The Victorian Middle Classes: Wealth, Occupation, and Geography', *Economic History Review*, XXX, 4 (1977)

Rubinstein, W.D., 'Wealth, Elites, and the Class Structure of Modern Britain', *Past and Present*, 76 (1977), 99–127

Schofield, T.P., 'Conservative Political Thought in Britain in Response to the French Revolution', *Historical Journal*, XXIX, 3 (1986), 601–23

Seed, J., 'Gentlemen Dissenters: The Social and Political Meanings of Rational Dissent in the 1770s and 1780s', *Historical Journal*, 28, 2 (1985), 299–325

Seed, J., 'Unitarianism, Political Economy and the Antinomies of Liberal Culture in Manchester, 1830–1850', *Social History*, VII, 1 (1982), 1–27

Sheppard, F., 'London and the Nation in the Nineteenth Century', *Transactions of the Royal Historical Society*, 35 (1985)

Skinner, S., 'Liberalism and Mammon: Tractarian Reaction in the Age of Reform', *Journal of Victorian Culture*, IV, 2 (1999),197–228

Szreter, S., 'The General Register Office and the Public Health Movement in Britain, 1837–1914', *Social History of Medicine*, IV, 3 (1991), 435–65

Szreter, S., 'Politics of Public Health', *Population & Development Review* (1997)

Szreter, S. and Mooney, 'Urbanization, Mortality, and the Standard of Living Debate: new estimates of the expectation of life at birth in nineteenth-century British cities', *Economic History Review*, LI, 1 (1998), 84–112

Thackray, A., 'Natural Knowledge in Cultural Context: The Manchester Model', *American Historical Review*, LXIX, 3 (1974), 672–710

Tholfsen, T., 'The Artizan and the Culture of early Victorian Birmingham', *University of Birmingham Historical Journal*, IV (1953–4), 146–67

Tholfsen, T., 'Intellectual Origins of Mid-Victorian Stability', *Political Science Quarterly*, LXXXVI, 1, (1971), 57–92

Tholfsen, T., 'The Transition to Democracy in Victorian England', *International Review of Social History*, VI (1961), 226–49

Turner, F.M., 'British Politics and the Roman Republic', *Historical Journal*, XXIX, 3 (1986), 577–601

Wach, H.M., 'Civil Society, Moral Identity and the Liberal Public Sphere: Manchester and Boston, 1810–40', *Social History*, XXI, 3 (1996), 281–304

Wach, H.M., 'Culture and the Middle Classes', *Journal of British Studies*, XXVII, 4 (1988), 375–405

Wahrman, D., 'National Society, Communal Culture', *Social History*, XVII, 1 (1992), 42–73

Webb, I., 'The Bradford Wool Exchange: Industrial Capitalism and the Popularity of Gothic', *Victorian Studies*, XX, 1 (1976), 45–69

ACKNOWLEDGEMENTS

I would like to thank, first of all, the supervisor of my original thesis on Victorian civic thought, Gareth Stedman Jones. It was his commitment to the history of ideas, together with his vast knowledge of the nineteenth century's intellectual currents, which provided a continual source of inspiration and guidance through the long gestation of this book. I am greatly obliged to Thomas Dixon, Boyd Hilton, Simon Skinner, Simon Szreter, Matthew Taylor and Chris Turner for commenting on various drafts. I would also like to thank Andrew Adonis, Virginia Davis, Peter Hennessy, Jemima Hunt, Terry Morris, Rebecca Nicolson, Jonathan Parry, Emma Rothschild, Miri Rubin, David Runciman, David Sainsbury, Benjamin Wegg-Prosser, Andrew Wilson and Bee Wilson for their help over the years.

Work on this project has taken me through numerous institutions and I am indebted to the Master and Fellows of Trinity College, Cambridge; the University of Chicago; the Centre for History and Economics, King's College, Cambridge; the Institute for Public Policy Research; and the Faculty of Arts, Queen Mary, University of London. I am very grateful to the legion of curators, security guards, guides and custodians who allowed me to wander through their civic institutions. I would also like to thank Stephen Price of Bristol Museums and Art Gallery; staff at the Rare Books Room, Cambridge University Library; the 'Humanities Two' reading room at the British Library; and the Thoresby Society, Leeds, who were all generous with their time. My thanks to the John Betjeman Estate and his publisher, John Murray, for permission to quote from his works.

Ion Trewin has been an enormously supportive and wise editor at Weidenfeld & Nicolson. I am also grateful to Victoria Webb and Emma Finnigan, to Tom Graves for his superb pictorial eye, and to Linden Lawson for her excellent work in correcting my more grievous mistakes. Those remaining are mine alone. My agent Georgina Capel has provided unfailing encouragement and advice. I would also like to thank Anthony Cheetham for the original commissioning of this book. Against the sometimes lonely business of writing, I have received tremendous help from my friends and family. Juliet Thornback has lived with Victorian civic pride for longer than Joseph Chamberlain's mayoralty and I am supremely grateful for her forbearing, irreverent affection towards the historian's moody travails. This book is dedicated to my parents, Marylla and Julian Hunt. In their personal passion for urban design and municipal politics they have unconsciously crafted this history. And their love and generous support have ensured this literary Jerusalem was finally built.

ILLUSTRATION ACKNOWLEDGEMENTS

Manchester Town Hall, designed by Alfred Waterhouse, c. 1890.
(Mary Evans Picture Library)
Manchester Town Hall, mosaic, detail (photograph Mike Pilkington).
(Manchester City Council)
Manchester Town Hall, interior (photograph Mike Pilkington).
(Manchester City Council)
Joseph Chamberlain. (Bridgeman Art Library)
Chamberlain Square, Birmingham, 1897. (National Monuments
Record)
From *Garden Cities of Tomorrow*, by Ebenezer Howard, 1902 edition.
(Private Collection)
Letchworth Garden City, 1938. (©Aerofilms)
Manningham Mills, Bradford, c. 1920. (Bradford Heritage Library)
Post-war Leeds (photograph C.H. Wood). (National Monuments
Board)
Selfridges Building, Birmingham (photograph Rowan Isaac).

OTHER ILLUSTRATIONS

Preface: *Allegory of Good and Bad Government*, fresco detail, by
Ambrogio. (Bridgeman Art Library)
Part One: Glasgow, c. 1880.(Mary Evans Picture Library)
Part Two: A page from *The Builder*, 1857. (Private Collection)
Part Three: From *Dore's London*.(Private Collection
Epilogue: Birmingham, 2004 (photograph Rowan Isaac).

INDEX

ABOUT THE AUTHOR

Born in 1974, Tristram Hunt was educated at Cambridge, where he earned a PhD in history, and at the University of Chicago. He writes regularly on political and cultural issues in the British and American press, including the *Guardian*, the *Los Angeles Times*, and *Time* magazine. One of Britain's leading history broadcasters, Hunt has authored and presented numerous radio and television series for the BBC and Channel 4. He currently teaches modern British history at Queen Mary, University of London.